"The former *Sports Illustrated* columnist . . . comb... ...
storytelling. It's just great writing. . . . If you are a Lakers fan, a fan of the NBA, and just a fan of good sports stories, you will want to read this. It's an insightful look at one of the NBA's most influential teams. It is filled with just great story after great story."　　　　　　　　　　　　　　—Kurt Helin, NBC Sports

"The Showtime Lakers are the dynasty that forever changed the NBA, transform-ing a game into an entertainment spectacle. Through his relentless reporting and buoyant writing, Jeff Pearlman has delivered the story in full, from rare insight into Kareem and Magic to what *really* went on after-hours in the Forum Club. Once you start *Showtime*, you won't be able to put it down."
　　　　　　　　　　—Adrian Wojnarowski, Yahoo Sports NBA columnist
　　　　　　　　　　　　　　　　and author of *The Miracle of St. Anthony*

" A rollicking ride full of great characters, killer anecdotes, and surprising details. Pearlman is an indefatigable reporter, and here he provides an all-access pass to one of the game's greatest dynasties, with tales of Kareem, Magic, Riley, and Jerry Buss in their heyday. It's a book any NBA fan—any sports fan—will devour, likely in one or two sittings."　　　　—Chris Ballard, senior writer, *Sports Illustrated*

"Pearlman ably demonstrates how deeply flawed human beings can nonetheless create a near-flawless beauty on the court."　　　　　　　—*Kirkus Reviews*

"The book offers fantastic stories, great memories, and a behind-the-scenes look into the people who made up one of the most dominant runs the NBA has ever seen."　　　　　　　　　　　　　　　—*Forum Blue & Gold,* ESPN

"A must-read for not just all Lakers fans but NBA fans and every human being—everyone should be reading this book."　　　　　　　　　—SportsNet

"I cannot put this book down. *Showtime* is both like an excavation of a long-lost era as well as a pulsing, utterly relevant road map into our twenty-first-century sports celebrity culture. It is a fascinating window on the last time when fame not only opened doors but also then closed them behind you. It reminds me of what it once felt like to feel the presence of magic."　　　　—Dave Zirin, *The Nation*

"*Showtime* is full of good stories. That's partly because the Los Angeles Lakers of Magic Johnson, Kareem Abdul-Jabbar, and Pat Riley were exciting, successful, and rife with melodrama. It's also because Jeff Pearlman is an energetic storyteller who doesn't seem to care whom he irritates. And some of the former Lakers will certainly be irritated if they read *Showtime*."　　　—Bill Littlefield, *Only a Game*

"An era that redefined the game has found a storyteller more than up to the task. By any measure, *Showtime* is magic."

—Mark Frost, author of *The Greatest Game Ever Played*

"The names (Magic, Kareem, Worthy, Riley, Buss) and the games (four championships) have long been studied by basketball's anthropologists. But so much of the story of the Showtime Lakers, *the* Team of the '80s, took place behind closed doors. Jeff Pearlman, as is his wont, pries them open and finds . . . a whole lot of L.A. living."

—Jack McCallum, author of *New York Times* bestseller *Dream Team*

"Once again, Jeff Pearlman has produced an exhaustively researched, elegantly written book that re-creates one of the most colorful and memorable teams of the modern era. *Showtime* is a great show indeed, full of colorful (and complicated) characters as well as a trove of details that even the most passionate fans will be amazed to learn. No basketball fan's bookshelf will be complete without it."

—Seth Davis, author of *Wooden: A Coach's Life*

"Pearlman immerses readers in a golden era. There doesn't seem to be a call he didn't make, a clip he didn't read, or a game he didn't rewatch . . . and at its best, reading *Showtime* feels like rediscovering a true classic."

—Julian Benbow, *The Boston Globe*

© Leah Guggenheimer

Jeff Pearlman is the author of six books, including the *New York Times* bestsellers *Sweetness; Boys Will Be Boys,* a biography of the 1990s Dallas Cowboys; and *The Bad Guys Won!,* a biography of the 1986 New York Mets. He lives in New York with his wife and two children and blogs regularly at www.jeffpearlman.com.

SHOWTIME

MAGIC, KAREEM, RILEY,
AND THE LOS ANGELES LAKERS
DYNASTY OF THE 1980s

JEFF PEARLMAN

AVERY

AVERY

an imprint of Penguin Random House
penguinrandomhouse.com

Previously published as a Gotham Books hardcover

First trade paperback printing, October 2014

6th Printing

Copyright © 2013 by Jeff Pearlman

Part opener photographs on pages 147 and 363 are by Lipofsky Basketballphoto.com

The Library of Congress has catalogued the hardcover edition of this book as follows:
Pearlman, Jeff.
    Showtime : Magic, Kareem, Riley, and the Los Angeles Lakers dynasty of the 1980s / Jeff Pearlman.
      pages cm
    Includes bibliographical references and index.
    ISBN 978-1-59240-755-2 (hardback) 978-1-59240-887-0 (paperback)
    1. Los Angeles Lakers (Basketball team)—History. I. Title.
    GV885.52.L67P43   2014
    796.323'640979494—dc23   2013026263

Printed in the United States of America
Set in Bembo Std • Designed by Elke Sigal

CONTENTS

Prologue   ix

PART ONE

DEVELOPMENT OF A DREAM

Chapter 1   Jack Kent Kook   3

Chapter 2   Of Sand Dabs and the Marlboro Man   11

Chapter 3   The Unlikely Head Coach   26

Chapter 4   Center of Complications   50

Chapter 5   Crash   73

Chapter 6   West Fall   102

Chapter 7   Picture Imperfect   123

PART TWO

DOMINANCE

Chapter 8   Riled Up   149

Chapter 9   Clark Kent   171

Chapter 10   Clubbing   194

Chapter 11   The Departed   217

Chapter 12   Earl   243

Chapter 13   Virginal   266

Chapter 14   Worthy of Superstardom   284

Chapter 15   Bring It   306

Chapter 16   Shattered Glass   316

Chapter 17   Motown   333

Chapter 18   Good-bye, Cap   346

PART THREE

DEMISE OF A DYNASTY

Chapter 19   Undone   365

Chapter 20   Bates   373

Chapter 21   Refreshment   390

Chapter 22   Shock   411

Afterword   419

Acknowledgments   425

Notes   429

Bibliography   467

Index   470

To Catherine, Casey, and Emmett—my three diamonds.
And then a gatorsaur ate them.
The end.

PROLOGUE

S pencer Haywood?"

The name hangs there, awkwardly suspended in midair as if attached to the string of a balloon. I am looking at Jack McKinney. Jack McKinney is looking at me. It is a warm February day in Naples, Florida. We are on an enclosed patio. Small glasses of ice water have been served. A couple of birds chirp. The wind whistles gently in the background.

I am the journalist, here to interview the greatest NBA coach 999 of 1,000 basketball fans have never heard of. Jack McKinney is here to answer my questions. And yet, he can't. Well, he can—sort of. The replies start, then stutter, then stop, then start again. The thoughts seem on point, turn left, hit a traffic circle and wind up somewhere in Bethesda. There are, he insists, wonderful basketball memories circulating throughout his seventy-seven-year-old brain; joyful tales of his eight years as the head coach at Saint Joseph's College; serving as an assistant with the world champion Portland Trail Blazers in 1977; tender moments with Kareem Abdul-Jabbar and Bill Walton and Jamaal Wilkes and Jack Ramsay. "There was this one game . . ." he says—then stops. Just stops.

"What's your name again?" McKinney suddenly says, his eyes gazing downward.

"Jeff," I say. "Jeff Pearlman."

"That's right. I wrote your name down five different times before you came here. It's embarrassing, the way my memory . . ."

From the next room, his wife, Claire, speaks up. "No sob stories, Jack!" she says. "That's not the way we look at life."

With that, Jack McKinney refocuses. He glances at me; rubs his chin, looks down, then back up. "What were we talking about?" he asks.

"Spencer Haywood," I say. "You coached him . . ."

"I coached Spencer Haywood? Are you certain?"

On the table, I have placed a manila folder. It is labeled JACK MCKINNEY in brown marker. Inside are photocopies of thirty or so articles, chronicling the rise and fall of a man who, in the summer of 1979, was hired by the Los Angeles Lakers to coach a team that featured Abdul-Jabbar, the five-time NBA MVP; Haywood, a four-time NBA All-Star; as well as a rookie point guard from Michigan State named Earvin (Magic) Johnson. The clippings tell the story of a forty-four-year-old basketball lifer finally getting his shot, of a humble and decent person brought in to revive a franchise in need of a spark. At his introductory press conference on July 30, a beaming McKinney admitted to the assembled Los Angeles media that his was a relatively simple basketball philosophy. "I'd like to run very much more than we have here, a constant running game," he said, standing behind a podium inside the Forum. "I'd like a moving offense, rather than having everyone standing around watching Kareem all the time and putting pressure on him."

McKinney was immediately embraced by his players. He ignored those who said Johnson, a 6-foot-9 ball wizard, was better suited to play power forward than point guard. He spoke regularly with the mercurial Haywood, a thirty-year-old journeyman forward with unlimited talent but a penchant for moody self-confinement. He would stop practices to confront and advise Abdul-Jabbar—"And nobody, and I mean nobody, ever spoke to Kareem like that," said Michael Cooper, the Laker guard. In short, McKinney was the perfect coach at the perfect time for the perfect team. "He created Showtime," said Norm Nixon, Los Angeles' All-Star guard. "That should never be forgotten. You can talk about me and Kareem and Earvin and Pat Riley all you want. But Jack McKinney created Showtime."

Yet now, as we sit here on a patio, sipping iced water to dull the awkwardness, the man who created Showtime barely remembers creating Showtime. The Lakers jumped out to a 9-4 start that season, prompting *Sports Illustrated*'s Bruce Newman to write a glowing piece titled "Doing It All for LA." Though McKinney was personally as glitzy as a truck stop, fans loved the way his team played. Under Jerry West, the legendary Laker guard who was the head coach for the three previous seasons, Los Angeles was reduced to being a one-trick pony: See Kareem, wait for Kareem, pass to Kareem, watch Kareem shoot and hope the ball goes in. "Not very imaginative," said Nixon. "Stilted."

Suddenly, however, the Lakers were neon lights along the Sunset Strip: *pow!* and *boom!* and *wow!* Johnson and Nixon formed the NBA's fastest backcourt. Wilkes, the smooth small forward, was gliding toward the rim. Haywood seemed revived and Abdul-Jabbar, the stoic, standoffish icon, was smiling and laughing and having the time of his life. The Forum, once the land where enthusiasm came to die, was alive. "The word is *fun*," said Haywood. "We were really fun."

Back in the day, when the NBA was still relatively bare-boned, teams employed one head coach and one assistant. McKinney's sidekick was Paul Westhead, another young Philadelphia guy who played for his boss at Saint Joseph's before coaching at La Salle College for nine years. Like McKinney, Westhead enjoyed run-and-gun basketball, lengthy intellectual discussions about the sport's intricacies and, when time allowed, friendly games of tennis.

On the morning of November 8, 1979, the phone in McKinney's Palos Verdes home rang. This was the Lakers' first off day of the young season, and Westhead was itching for some time on the nearby clay court. The call stirred McKinney from his sleep.

"Want to play some tennis?" Westhead asked.

McKinney grunted—*sure*.

"I've got the court for two hours," Westhead said. "We can play singles at ten, maybe some doubles with the girls at eleven."

"What time is it now?" McKinney asked.

"Nine thirty."

"OK," he said. "Give me a chance to get some coffee. I can be there in a half hour."

McKinney showered and drank his morning joe. When he entered the garage, he found that Claire had taken their one car to a nearby church meeting with, of all people, Cassie Westhead, her close friend and Paul's wife. Leaning against the wall, however, was a red-and-white Schwinn Le Tour II. The bicycle had been a present for his son John, purchased in a Lake Oswego, Oregon, cycling shop two years earlier but ignored since the boy's recent acquisition of a driver's license.

Sure, it'd been a while since Jack McKinney had ridden a bike. But he certainly knew how.

"Of course I did," he says. "Of course . . ."

■ ■ ■

"Spencer Haywood."

The name is stated again, only this time with more confidence. "I coached him in Milwaukee, right?"

"No," I say. "With the Lakers."

McKinney glances at me, initially puzzled, then dejected. He knows I am here in my quest to tell the story of the Showtime-era Los Angeles Lakers, a story that, were it not for a day off and a tennis game and a vacant garage and a wobbly bicycle and awful luck, would feature Jack McKinney as a star, not merely a smallish name halfway through the credits. That's what haunts everyone who knows and loves the man. Not the bike ride, per se, but what could have been had the bike ride never occurred. If—on the morning of November 8, 1979—Jack McKinney decides to ignore the phone, or opts to sleep in, or jogs the one and a half miles, is Paul Westhead known as one of the godfathers of fast-break basketball and the famed guru who ran Hank Gathers and Bo Kimble to 160-point games at Loyola Marymount? Is Pat Riley an eight-time NBA champion and multimillionaire pitchman and motivational speaker? Do the Lakers ever trade Nixon to the Clippers for some kid named Byron Scott? Do they draft Dominique Wilkins instead of James Worthy? Do they keep Abdul-Jabbar around for an extra season? Does Johnson have an even more gilded career? Does Los Angeles win five NBA titles, as it did throughout the 1980s? Or six? Seven?

Is Jack McKinney universally acknowledged as one of the greatest coaches in the history of the National Basketball Association?

"I have no doubt that he would be," said Nixon. "No doubt whatsoever."

As we sit here, still talking, still sipping water, McKinney glances through the folder, searching for faded memories and long-lost sparks. He would coach again, hired by the Indiana Pacers at the behest of a guilt-ravaged Jerry Buss, the Lakers' owner. Yet despite being named the league's Coach of the Year in 1980–81, he was never the same. Members of the Pacers took the unprecedented step of writing their names in black marker along the front of their shorts so their coach wouldn't get confused. Later, in a game during his final coaching stint, with Kansas City, several Kings players told the media that, during a time-out, McKinney characterized a play as one "just like we did against St. John's"—a reference to the New York City school he coached against while at Saint Joseph's a decade earlier.

Ultimately, McKinney left the NBA altogether, devoting the remainder of his working days to selling sporting goods. He watched the NBA from time to time, but the pain of what could (and should) have been far outweighed any morsels of momentary joy that came from sitting on the couch for Lakers-Celtics. McKinney is not a bitter man, but he is human. "Life isn't always fair," he says. "I'm OK with how everything has turned out. I'm loved. But, well, it's not always fair. . . ."

In his apartment, there is only a single hint that he ever coached the Lakers—a crystal wine carafe with LAKERS etched along the side. Occasionally, Riley, now the president of the Miami Heat, will leave McKinney tickets for a game. "He always says, 'This is the guy who made my career possible,'" McKinney says. "'This is the guy.'"

There is a pause. A long, lengthy, painful, awkward, ugly pause. I want to ask Jack McKinney more about the Lakers dynasty, about Westhead and Riley and Magic and Kareem. I want to know if he ever feels as if he's been left behind, as if there were an enormous party, and he was turned away at the door.

I want to ask him so many things, but come the end of our interview, I simply shake his hand and thank him for the time.

Jack McKinney is the man most responsible for the birth of the Showtime era of professional basketball.

If only he could remember it.

PART ONE

DEVELOPMENT OF A DREAM

Dr. Jerry Buss, attending Michael Cooper's birthday party
with one of the hundreds upon hundreds of young,
beautiful women who would sit by his side

CHAPTER 1

JACK KENT KOOK

The dressing-down of Claire Rothman would begin thusly:

First, Jack Kent Cooke made certain there was always a man in the room. It could be a high-rolling executive from another NBA franchise. It could be Jimmy, the Forum's plumber. Hell, it could be one of Cooke's boyhood pals from back in Toronto, visiting the home of the Los Angeles Lakers.

Second, Cooke would demand—in the loudest of voices—that Rothman, the Forum's vice president of booking, see him immediately. "Mrs. Rothman, I want you in my office," he would hiss angrily. "Now!"

Third, once Rothman entered, the screaming commenced. It would be loud and ugly and, 99 percent of the time, uncalled for. They were out of staples. The steak at the Forum Club was undercooked. Where were the new lightbulbs? Rothman was a sports visionary when it came to utilizing an arena's full potential. Yet to the owner of the Lakers, she was often little more than a broad in a skirt, an object to be belittled as he, the 5-foot-8½, 160-pound Napoleon of Hollywood, showed off his manliness.

"Now, before you leave," Cooke would shout, nodding knowingly toward any other men in the room, "repeat after me. 'I. Will. Not. Make. This. Mistake. Again.'"

Without fail, Rothman did as she was instructed, then slunk out, humiliated.

"I'm going to be honest—Jack Kent Cooke was a real sicko," Rothman said. "He once had a heart attack, and there was supposedly some loss of ox-

3

ygen to the brain. I think that worked him a little bit. Because he was psychologically sick."

This, in the early days of 1979, was the man behind one of the NBA's marquee franchises.

This was the owner of the Los Angeles Lakers.

Not that most people were aware of Cooke's craziness. Though behind closed doors he was a snarling bully, to the business world—where the Lakers had been deemed a model of success—Jack Kent Cooke was a dignified financial genius.

Born in Hamilton, Ontario, on October 25, 1912, Cooke rose from suffocating poverty (his father, Ralph, was a struggling picture frame salesman; his mother, Nancy, a stay-at-home housewife) to earn a small fortune by purchasing struggling radio stations and magazines, turning them around and selling them for large profits. He made his first $1 million by age thirty-two, and used $200,000 of his earnings to purchase 80 percent of the Toronto Maple Leafs baseball team of the International League. His specialty was salesmanship. On preannounced nights, the Maple Leafs would distribute orchids and dollar bills to fans. He held 3-for-the-price-of-1 nights, and pregnant women were granted free admission if accompanied by a spouse. On Friday the 13th, those attending with black cats needed no ticket. The team employed its own flagpole sitter and once invited Fidel Castro, the embattled Cuban president, to Maple Leaf Stadium to throw out the first pitch.

In 1960, he sold most of his Canadian holdings, bolted for Beverly Hills and set his sights on American sports. He paid $350,000 to purchase a 25 percent share of the NFL's Washington Redskins, then buttressed his fortunes in 1964 by creating American CableVision, a company that specialized in bringing high-level screen quality to areas with poor reception.

Finally, after the 1964–65 NBA season, he bought the Los Angeles Lakers.

At the time, the franchise was owned by Bob Short, a trucking magnate and former U.S. attorney who, in 1960, had relocated the Lakers from his hometown of Minneapolis.

Short had expressed little interest in selling his team. The Lakers made a $500,000 profit over the previous season, a staggering total in a league still struggling to find its way. But when Cooke—who had never before heard of the Lakers—asked about the franchise's availability, Short named a price that he was certain would send Cooke running: $5.175 million.

"I asked to see a profit and loss statement and told him I'd think about it," Cooke said. "The P&L Short gave me was just thrown together. I couldn't make any sense of it." Cooke's basketball IQ was -17. His business IQ, however, was off all charts. Though he was reluctant to admit it, his motivation in buying the Lakers was the assumption that it would help in his efforts to bring an NHL franchise to California. "That was the only reason he acquired the Lakers," said Alan Rothenberg, formerly an attorney with the Lakers. "Jack Kent Cooke was a hockey guy."

In 1966, the Lakers played in the Los Angeles Sports Arena, a seven-year-old facility located a stone's throw from the University of Southern California's downtown campus. The only other professional organization to regularly use the building was the Los Angeles Blades, a minor league hockey team. When the NHL announced its plan to move west, Cooke met with the Coliseum Commission, the city's governing athletics body, and promised to build a stadium with his own money.

Nobody believed Cooke. Another arena in L.A.? Yeah, right—why not construct another Dodger Stadium, too? "If you look at the newspapers back then, everybody thought he was bluffing," Rothenberg said. "The commission conditionally gave him a team, knowing it was never going to happen."

It happened. The $16 million Forum was, in the sarcastic words of *The Washington Post*'s Bill Brubaker, "a modest little place with 57-foot-high columns and 17,000 upholstered seats." Though it was, technically, located 16 miles away in the decrepit city of Inglewood, the Forum was all about Hollywood glitz and glamour. Cooke called it "the finest arena built since the original Roman Colosseum," adding, "Perhaps 200 years from now, or even 2,000, people will say the Forum was one of the fine buildings erected in the 20th century."

In 1967, the Los Angeles Kings—*Jack Kent Cooke's Los Angeles Kings*—made their NHL debut, sharing the Forum with the Lakers. Before long, Cooke developed a reputation as a basketball kingpin, acquiring Wilt Chamberlain to play center in 1968, winning an NBA championship in 1972, then, in 1975, making a trade with Milwaukee for another dominant, in-his-prime center, Kareem Abdul-Jabbar. In fourteen seasons with Cooke as the owner, the Lakers went 673-472, reached six championship series and endured only three losing years. "Mr. Cooke was a genius in many ways," said Joan McLaughlin, a director of human resources with the Lakers for more than thirty years. "He was quick on his feet, very smart when it came to running a business."

And yet . . .

"He also could be quite the SOB."

On March 8, 1973, Cooke suffered a massive coronary thrombosis, returned to work after a couple of months and seemed determined to crush the collective esteem of his employees. He would call workers just to see if they'd answer the phone within three rings. If not, they were fired. He regularly berated Bill Sharman, the team's general manager, after Laker losses, and called down to the Kings' bench during games to lambaste coaches and players. He promised Rothman a substantial bonus should she book in excess of 185 annual events for the Forum. Upon reaching the goal, she asked Cooke for the money and was kicked out of his office. He would tell female employees to twirl in his presence, all the while standing to the side and critiquing their wardrobes and physical condition. "He liked to perform for people," said McLaughlin. "He thought it impressed everyone." According to a former Kings player, Cooke once demanded an employee remove his jacket—then placed the garment atop his beloved dog, Coco. In 1976, at a time when his estimated worth was $100 million, Cooke was paying his full-time houseman $8,400 annually. Chick Hearn, the longtime Lakers announcer, liked telling the story of how he suggested that the new building—dubbed simply the Forum—be called the Fabulous Forum. Cooke was so pleased, he told Hearn, "There will be a little something extra in your paycheck this week." Indeed, there was—a wallet-size photograph of Jack Kent Cooke. "He was," said Rod Hundley, the former Lakers player and broadcaster, "the number one asshole that ever lived."

Despite his limited popularity, by the mid- to late 1970s, Cooke was, arguably, the most powerful man in professional sports. He also, secretly, wanted out.

On October 28, 1977, the *City News Service* published a piece that, for Lakers fans who assumed everything was hunky-dory, shocked the senses:

> Sports entrepreneur Jack Kent Cooke may be forced to sell some of his interests in three professional teams to meet a community property challenge by his recently divorced wife, it was disclosed today.
>
> Jeannie Cooke is seeking half of an estimated $100 million fortune now tied up partly in the ownership of the Los Angeles Kings, Lakers and the Washington Redskins, her attorney Douglas Bagby said.

... Mrs. Cooke's attorneys estimate that the 64-year-old Cooke's holdings, which in addition to the Kings, Lakers and Redskins, include the Forum and two million shares of Teleprompter stock, are worth about $100 million.

Before long, Cooke had relocated from his plush Bel Air estate to Las Vegas. Though presented to the public as a chance to live somewhere fun and new, Cooke turned to the land of fuzzy dice strictly as a tax-related shelter. Thanks to Nevada state laws, Jeannie Cooke would reportedly be unable to touch her husband's holdings—as long as he resided there. If his soon-to-be-ex-wife wanted his money, she'd have to chase him to Nevada to get it. The result was a divorce that, over a two-and-a-half-year span, involved forty-one lawyers and 12,000 pages of documents. "He wasn't one to give in," said Rothenberg. "He assumed if he went to Las Vegas, he'd be protected. But, to be honest, my personal feeling is he also wanted to leave town and change his life."

Midway through all the craziness, Cooke let it be known that, were someone to come along and show a sincere interest in purchasing the Lakers, the Kings and the Forum (as a package), he would listen.

■ ■ ■

"Why do you play in that shit hole?"

The question, asked by Claire Rothman, caught Jerry Buss beneath the chin. *Shit hole!* The Los Angeles Memorial Sports Arena wasn't a shit hole . . . was it? Sure, the seats were kinda dirty, and the lighting quality was awful, and the neighborhood left one ripe for a mugging. But shit hole?

Truth be told, Buss, the forty-one-year-old owner of the Los Angeles Strings of the upstart World Team Tennis, had thought little about it. He had never owned a professional sports franchise before purchasing the Strings in 1974, and chose to have his team based out of the Sports Arena because, simply, it was available.

Then, in the winter of 1975, he received the call from Rothman. "I didn't have a plan . . . just contacted him out of the blue, because I knew he owned the Strings and I knew we had open dates at the Forum," Rothman said. "I remember telling him his team should be at the Forum, and his response was, 'I can't possibly afford that.' "

"Well," Rothman replied, "I'll make you an offer you can't refuse."

That same day, Buss came to the Forum, met with Rothman and bought a $12,500 box in the arena. Before he left, Rothman suggested that she introduce him to Jack Kent Cooke. The men lunched in the Forum's Trophy Room. Though they shared but two obvious similarities (a love of sports and a bundle of money), the connection was strong. Buss liked Cooke's bluntness, as well as the way he'd taken nothing and turned it into something. Cooke, meanwhile, heard Buss's rags-to-riches narrative and felt a genuine kinship. They were two wealthy out-of-towners (Cooke from Toronto, Buss from Kemmerer, Wyoming) who'd emerged from impoverished childhoods and made something of themselves. Buss, a University of Wyoming graduate with a masters and PhD in physical chemistry from the University of Southern California, was a full-blown real estate baron. He had purchased his first property, a fourteen-unit apartment house in west Los Angeles, in 1959, and twenty years later boasted more than seven hundred pieces of real estate, ranging from hotels to apartment buildings to valuable vacant pieces of land. He was the type of thinker Cooke identified with.

Plus, Buss agreed to relocate the Strings to the Forum. "That," said Rothman, "certainly didn't hurt."

The men began speaking semiregularly—mostly Buss listening and Cooke blathering on about this success and that victory. He could be an insufferable braggart, Buss admitted to friends, but one with a sterling track record. They were an odd couple to behold. Buss wore denim jeans ("disgustingly shabby Levis," *Sports Illustrated*'s William Oscar Johnson wrote) with a rumpled western shirt unbuttoned from the chest up. He once turned down an offer to play the Marlboro Man in a cigarette ad. Buss wasn't verbally brash and, unlike Cooke, wasn't afraid to mingle with the employees. While trying to sign Jimmy Connors to play for the Strings, Buss learned the tennis legend liked showing off his new jet-black Porsche to friends. The next time he was scheduled to meet Connors, Buss pulled up in his just-off-the-lot Maserati. He jumped out and dangled the keys before Connors. "You want it?" he said. "All you have to do is sign." (A floored Connors ultimately declined.)

In the early months of 1978, Cooke reached a decision: He would sell his Los Angeles holdings (known officially as California Sports, Inc.) and focus on the Washington Redskins. Though he took bids from seven different entities, Buss always held the inside edge. As Cooke knew well, his wasn't merely a passing interest in sports. In 1970, Buss considered purchasing the

Los Angeles Stars of the ABA. Once, he tried trading half of a resort he owned, the Ocotillo Lodge, for a percentage of the San Diego Conquistadors, also of the ABA. More recently, he had put out feelers about purchasing the Oakland Athletics and Chicago White Sox. Each time, Buss came up empty.

Although the men were close, negotiations wouldn't be easy. Cooke threw in oddball conditions—"He insisted Jerry buy a house in Las Vegas for the lady he was seeing," said Charline Kenney, Buss's assistant. "Weird things like that." Here is how *Sports Illustrated* surmised what still goes down as the most complex transaction in the history of American team sports:

> The deal is this: Buss and his partners will pay $43.5 million for the Forum and the Raljon Ranch near Bakersfield. Buss, on his own, will pay $24 million for the Lakers and the Kings and will own the teams personally. He and his partners will assume an approximate $10 million mortgage on the Forum. Cooke has a choice of taking the remaining $37.5 million in cash or $20 million in cash and $37.5 million in real estate, choosing properties from a list drawn by Buss's corporation, Mariani-Buss Associates. Cooke has a month or more to decide what form of payment to accept, but Buss says, "I would imagine he'll opt for a tax-free exchange and take the real estate. If he takes only cash, it could cost him an extra $9 million or so in taxes."

What the article failed to mention was that one of the small pieces of real estate the two traded was the Chrysler Building, the seventy-seven-story New York City landmark, which went from Buss to Cooke. "It was staggering—all of it," said Rothenberg. "These were bigger-than-life holdings being swapped like chips. It was amazing to be a part of."

The transaction was formally announced on May 27, 1979, with a bold front-page *New York Times* headline: 2 LOS ANGELES TEAMS, ARENA ARE SAID TO BE SOLD.

"It was so cool," said Jeanie Buss, Jerry's daughter. "I mean, it was neat Dad owned the Lakers, but to have the Forum at eighteen was amazing. I was like, 'You mean when Rod Stewart comes to town, I get front-row seats?'"

A couple of hours after he formally shook hands with Cooke on the exchange, Buss bought a bottle of Jack Daniel's, entered the Forum, turned on a single light from the scoreboard, sat on the hardwood floor and got drunk. "I own this!" he screamed, lying at center court. "I fucking own this!"

Before everything was finalized, however, a few details needed to be taken care of.

Jack Kent Cooke wasn't one to go out quietly.

CHAPTER 2

OF SAND DABS
AND THE MARLBORO MAN

Earvin Johnson wanted a hamburger.

He was a nineteen-year-old kid, fond of burgers and pizza and French fries and any other cuisine guaranteed to block the arteries. Sure, he happened to be sitting in the presence of Jack Kent Cooke, perhaps the world's least likely man to *ever* order a burger of any sort. But, hey, Johnson was hungry.

Scratch that. *Starving.*

It was a warm May afternoon in Los Angeles, and the most dynamic player to grace college basketball since Louisiana State's Pete Maravich a decade earlier was in town to figure out whether he should return to Michigan State University for his junior season or jump to a professional sports league that had been crippled by poor TV ratings, player indifference and a dwindling fan base. On the one hand, in East Lansing, Michigan, Johnson—a local kid out of Everett High School—was a king. He had been nicknamed Magic as a fifteen-year-old high school freshman and now, having just led the Spartans to their first NCAA men's basketball title, he could not walk the streets without being mobbed. "He really was beyond reproach," said George Fox, his high school coach. "Earvin could do no wrong."

There was, however, the siren call of the NBA and specifically the siren call of Jack Kent Cooke's thick wallet. On April 19, 1979, the Lakers and

Chicago Bulls had engaged in a coin flip to determine which team would be gifted with the number one pick in the upcoming draft. Coming off of a 47–35 season, Los Angeles was in such a position because, three years earlier, the New Orleans Jazz committed one of the worst free-agent acquisitions in league history. The team signed thirty-three-year-old Gail Goodrich, a long-ago star on his last legs. At the time, league rules mandated that the Jazz had to compensate Los Angeles with players, draft picks or money. After much haggling between the Lakers and Jazz general manager Barry Mendelson, New Orleans agreed to part with its first-round picks in 1977 and 1979, as well as a second-rounder in 1980. "Gail was great," said Bill Bertka, the Jazz vice president of basketball operations. "But he was older, and he came to us and immediately tore his Achilles. That didn't make us look so smart. Especially when we lost almost every stinkin' game in 1978–79." (The Jazz went a league-worst 26-56.)

When Larry O'Brien, the NBA's commissioner, prepared to flip the coin inside the league's New York City headquarters, the Bulls and Lakers felt their futures momentarily hovering in midair. Executives from both teams listened to the toss via speakerphone from their respective offices.

"Chicago, do you want to make the call?" O'Brien asked.

"We'd love to," replied Rod Thorn, the Bulls' general manager, who was sitting inside the team's offices on the thirteenth floor of a Michigan Avenue building.

"Is that OK with you, Los Angeles?" O'Brien said.

"Fine," said Chick Hearn, the announcer, who also worked as an assistant general manager with the team.

"We call heads," said Thorn.

A pause.

"OK, gentlemen, here we go," boomed the deep voice of O'Brien. "The coin's in the air. . . ."

Another pause.

Another pause.

Another pause.

"Tails it is!" O'Brien said.

Hearn let out a triumphant whoop.

"I was playing basketball at Venice Beach," said Pat O'Brien, at the time a reporter for KNXT-TV in Los Angeles. "The news came over a transistor radio, and people started screaming. 'Yes! Yes! We're getting Magic! We're getting Magic!'"

Johnson was equally euphoric. The last place he wanted to go was Chicago, what with its awful winters (he was never one for the snow) and perennially dreadful basketball teams. The Bulls played in dumpy Chicago Stadium, and put forth an uninspired roster highlighted by the likes of Andre Wakefield and Wilbur Holland. Los Angeles, meanwhile, was but a dream to Johnson, who rightly envisioned a paradise of palm trees and 80-degree days and gorgeous women in wallet-size bikinis. Had the coin landed heads, Johnson would have returned to Michigan State for his junior season.

So here now, a mere few weeks later, the kid was itching for a hamburger, befuddled by what was placed before him. Sitting at a table inside the Forum's Trophy Room, Johnson was in town for lunch, sure, but really to feel out Cooke and the Lakers. The draft was still two months away, and both sides wanted to know whether a partnership could be reached.

Accompanying Cooke and Johnson were Hearn and Earvin Johnson Sr. Two of the player's representatives, George Andrews and Dr. Charles Tucker, also attended. "Gentlemen," Cooke bellowed, "I'm going to order lunch for you! We're going to have some marvelous fish!"

Moments later, the plates arrived. The first thing Johnson noticed was the awful smell. He looked down and saw something bland and crusty.

Cooke observed Johnson's bewildered expression.

"They're sand dabs!" he said. "Sand dabs!"

Johnson glanced at his father, leaned close and whispered, "I don't know what a sand dab is."

Cooke was nonplussed. "Young man, do you know how much a sand dab costs?"

Johnson shook his head.

"Well, they're very expensive," Cooke said. "It's a very fine fish. Now eat."

Johnson stabbed the listless sand dab with his fork. Nudged it around a bit. Pushed it left. Pushed it right. "I can't eat this," he said.

Cooke, a man who knew a high-quality sand dab when he saw it, was outraged. "What are you talking about?" he said. "Do you know how much that fish costs?"

"If it's OK with you, Mr. Cooke, I think I'd rather have a hamburger and some French fries," Johnson said softly. "Would that be OK?"

This was not the way to make a good impression. Cooke was a formal man with formal tastes. If he wanted sand dabs, dammit, everyone was eating sand dabs. In this particular case, however, Hearn—one of the few men who had the owner's ear—intervened. "The guy's only nineteen," he said. "The only thing he knows is hamburger and pizza." A resigned Cooke sighed, then yelled toward the kitchen, "Can we have a hamburger?"

Nothing.

"A hamburger!" he screamed. "Get the man one!"

Within minutes, Earvin Johnson was gripping a burger. The accompanying smile was that of an eight-year-old securing a Happy Meal. "You know," Jerry West later said to Johnson, "nobody has ever done what you just did to Jack Kent Cooke."

Beginning with that very moment, staring at a peppy teenager biting some meat, Hearn knew something about Johnson sparkled. As impressive as he was on tape, soaring past defenders, connecting on impossible no-look passes, spinning left, driving right, he was significantly more dazzling in person. At 6-foot-9 and 215 pounds, Johnson was a mountain of a man, the biggest, most powerful point guard anyone had ever seen. Yet it was his charisma, especially at his precocious age, that floored people. At the time, the face of the Lakers was Kareem Abdul-Jabbar, a moody soul who brooded a hundred times for every forced smile. If the center was best known for his unblockable skyhook, he was equally famous for blowing off autograph seekers of all ages, creeds and ilk. Johnson, on the other hand, was a ray of sunshine. He looked people in the eye, shook hands, talked about basketball as if he were describing a beautiful woman. Oh, and that smile—that blinding, all-glowing smile. "He was just a magnet," said Claire Rothman. "You wanted to be around him. You wanted to see him smile. You wanted to have lunch with him. Earvin Johnson was perfectly nicknamed. He had . . . it."

Cooke, however, wasn't one to be swayed easily. Though he and Buss had already agreed in principle to the sale, Cooke insisted—without much argument from the soon-to-be owner—that the first pick in the 1979 draft be his call.

As he watched Johnson munch on his burger, Cooke asked what the kid was seeking as compensation. Aware that Abdul-Jabbar, arguably the NBA's best player, was making $650,000 annually, Johnson confidently uttered,

"Somewhere around $600,000 would be ideal—plus, I need an education allowance so I can finish at Michigan State."

Cooke was not amused. "Let's get one thing straight right off," he said. "I'm not paying for your education. I put myself through school, and if I could do it, you certainly can. Now, we can offer you $400,000. It's not what you're asking for, but it's a hell of a lot of money. And let me remind you that the Lakers have made the playoffs seventeen times in the last nineteen years. We'd love to have you, Earvin, and I hope you'll play here. But the team has done just fine without you."

The one thing Johnson didn't know at the time (and wouldn't know until more than two decades later) was that, in Cooke's mind, he was merely another good college player in an ocean of good college players. Why, immediately after the draft, Cooke told those within his small circle of confidants that the team could have gone with Sidney Moncrief, the high-scoring guard from the University of Arkansas. That was the advice presented to him by Jerry West, the outgoing coach, who wasn't fully convinced a 6-foot-9 point guard would function in the fast-paced NBA. Of all the ex-basketball players working for the Lakers, West was the one Cooke trusted most. "West wanted Moncrief, and he made it very clear to Jack Kent Cooke," said Rich Levin, who covered the team for the *Los Angeles Herald-Examiner*. "There was a strong belief, for a brief time at least, that Moncrief, not Magic, would wind up a Laker."

Cooke, though, was far from a dummy. Even if he weren't the smartest basketball man around, he understood that sports were as much about salesmanship as on-court success. Despite winning 47 games and reaching the playoffs in 1978–79, the Lakers sold out only once, and averaged 11,771 fans in an arena that seated 17,505. The kid sitting before him was a 100,000-foot-high neon sign screaming SEE THE LAKERS! His roster, on the other hand, was composed of standout players who seemed either indifferent (point guard Norm Nixon), shy (forward Jamaal Wilkes) or downright offensive (Abdul-Jabbar). Cooke had waited a long time for Abdul-Jabbar to turn on the charm. He now seemed to realize it would never happen. "Jack believed in star power," said Rothman. "He deserves credit for that."

So, when Johnson met Cooke's rebuff with an even stronger one—"I guess I'll be going back to school"—the owner cracked. He invited Johnson and his entourage to stay the night in Los Angeles and return to the Trophy Room the following morning. On the drive to the hotel that evening, Earvin Sr. lit into his son. He was a man who'd spent years working multiple blue-collar jobs, struggling alongside his wife, Christine, a school cafeteria worker, to feed their ten children. Now his nineteen-year-old son was insulting sand dabs? "I've worked in a factory my whole life for what he's offering you for one year!" Earvin Sr. said. "And for something you love doing! Don't be greedy, son."

The next day, Cooke and Johnson negotiated back and forth until, finally, a deal was reached. The $500,000 contract made Johnson the highest-paid rookie in league history.* With smiles all around, Cooke let his new superstar choose lunch.

"Pizza!" Johnson said. "Let's order pizza."

Cooke agreed, and before long, one of America's richest men was munching on his first-ever slice of pepperoni. "This stuff," he said, "is pretty good."

■ ■ ■

In the weeks that followed, Cooke and Buss communicated regularly. They chatted via the phone several times per day, lunched frequently, discussed personnel and facilities and the right way to move a franchise forward.

For all his shortcomings, this was one of the beauties of Jack Kent Cooke. Yes, he wanted to sell the Los Angeles Lakers. But he wanted to do so the right way. In his mind, this meant helping Buss as much as possible.

This also meant taking part in the search for the team's next coach.

Over the previous three years, the man working the sidelines for the Lakers had been Jerry West, a Hall of Fame guard so revered that the NBA's logo, designed in 1968, was his silhouette. West was, by all accounts, one of the smartest men to ever step on the court. He was perceptive, instinctive and forward thinking.

He also loathed coaching.

"Oh, it was awful," said West. "Coaching wasn't something I was really capable of doing. As a coach I was a screamer and a yeller, which I hated. When Jerry Buss came in, I knew it was my time to stop coaching once and for all. It would have been unfair to myself to keep doing a job I hated, and it would have been unfair for Jerry to have a coach who wasn't that good at his job."

---

* This would last one month, until the Boston Celtics signed Larry Bird to a $600,000 deal.

Two years earlier, Cooke had offered Jerry Tarkanian, the coach at the University of Nevada, Las Vegas, the chance to take over for West. At the time, Tarkanian had just led the Runnin' Rebels to the Final Four, and was one of the nation's hottest basketball names. After strong consideration, Tarkanian rejected Cooke's overtures. The salary ($70,000 per year, with a $2,500 raise every year) barely exceeded what he had made in Nevada. "It wasn't worth it," Tarkanian says. "Not for me or my family."

By 1979, the timing had changed.

■ ■ ■

The car was parked on the second level of a garage alongside the Sheraton Universal Hotel in North Hollywood. Because this was La-La Land, where celebrities and big spenders came to peacock, there was little unusual about this particular make of car in this particular location. Oh, the maroon-and-white 1977 Rolls-Royce Silver Shadow II was a dandy, what with its innovative high-pressure hydraulic system and its Turbo-Hydramatic 400 transmission. But considering the roll call of Mercedes and BMWs and Jaguars situated nearby, really, what was the big deal? The Rolls was merely another fancy car belonging, no doubt, to merely another high roller.

With one difference.

There was something inside the trunk.

Hidden.

Locked.

Stashed away.

The Sheraton parking lot attendant took notice early on the morning of June 17, 1979. He was doing his rounds, the same mindless stroll he'd taken hundreds of times before, when the two-tone paint job—a rich maroon on the top, blinding white on the bottom—caught his eye. Hadn't authorities been looking for a Rolls-Royce Silver Shadow II? A maroon-and-white one with a gold interior?

Before long, several members of the Los Angeles Police force arrived. Leroy Orozco, a veteran LAPD detective, matched the license plate with the missing vehicle. He proceeded to check the paint for fingerprints, pop the lock and open the trunk.

The smell shot up into the air, like a ghost set free from its crypt. There's nothing quite like that stench—rotting flesh, confined in a small space.

The decaying corpse was that of a white man, only the remaining skin, decomposed beyond recognition, had turned a shade of blackish purple. The body, wrapped in a yellow blanket, was trussed neck to waist to feet with its hands tied behind its back. A bullet hole shattered the rear of the skull, and another one penetrated the right temple. When an officer reached into the body's pants pockets, neither a wallet nor a driver's license was found. A security television monitor directly above the space where the Rolls was parked had been tampered with.

Still, no confirmation was needed.

This was Victor Weiss.

A mere three days earlier, on the evening of June 14, Weiss had seemed to be the happiest man on the planet. A fifty-one-year-old sports promoter who served as Jerry Tarkanian's representative, he had bounded out the front entrance of the Beverly-Comstock Hotel, euphoric in the knowledge that his client was about to be named the new coach of the Los Angeles Lakers. Those were the words Cooke and Buss had just used during their meeting— "We're excited to have Jerry *as the new coach of the Lakers.*"

When, two months earlier, Los Angeles had again contacted Tarkanian about jumping to the NBA, the coach seemed less than enthused. He now viewed himself as strictly a college guy, wrapped up in the oomph and rah-rah of the amateur level. Was Tark, as most people called him, a pillar of moral fortitude? Hardly. At the time, he was in the midst of fighting the NCAA over alleged recruiting violations. Was he a Dean Smith–esque master of Xs and Os? No. But few white men were better at understanding and empathizing with the young African-American basketball player. Tarkanian possessed a gift, and it was walking into the projects of Detroit or Gary, Indiana, or Newark, New Jersey, and leaving two hours later with the commitment of a 6-foot-5 kid who could jump from here to Pluto.

Tarkanian had no interest in leaving a position he cherished for one where he would be forced to serve as a glorified babysitter for a bunch of halfhearted, coked-out millionaires in a league that'd been damned by mediocre ratings, poor attendance and drug addiction. "I loved Las Vegas, my family loved Las Vegas," Tarkanian said. "When the Lakers reached out, I immediately said to my wife, 'I can't take the job, right? I just can't.'"

Still, to be polite, Tarkanian returned Cooke's call, explaining that, even if he were interested in moving to California, it'd have to be for, *ohhhhh* . . . a helluva lot more than the $70,000 offered last time.

"Like what?" Cooke said.

"Well," said Tarkanian. "It'd have to be double the $350,000 I make right now."

"That's fine," Cooke said.

"What?" said Tarkanian.

"That's fine," Cooke repeated. "We can do that."

So here was Vic Weiss, moments after concluding with Cooke and Buss, briefcase in hand, approaching the valet parking station at the Comstock, happy as could be. Not only were the Lakers willing to make Tarkanian the NBA's all-time highest-paid coach, they also ceded to his demands: a pair of season tickets for every home game, three luxury automobiles—one for Jerry, one for his wife, Lois, one for Pamela, their oldest daughter. "Everything was set," Tarkanian said. "I was the new coach of the Los Angeles Lakers."

Around the same time Weiss was wrapping things up, Jerry and Lois drove north from San Diego, where they had been vacationing, to the Balboa Bay Resort in Newport Beach. In the coming days, Tarkanian presumed he would sit down with Cooke and Buss, sign the five-year contract and be introduced to the Los Angeles media as the Lakers' tenth head coach.

"I'll meet you and Lois tomorrow morning at the resort," Weiss told Tarkanian. "This is a really exciting time for you."

■ ■ ■

The phone inside the Balboa Bay Resort rang, and Jerry Tarkanian answered. It was one o'clock in the morning of June 15. On the other end of the line was Rose Weiss, Vic's wife of nearly twenty years. She was calling from her home in nearby Encino. "Have you seen my husband?" she asked. "We were supposed to have dinner last night. He never came."

Tarkanian hadn't.

One day turned into two days. Two days turned into three. A sense of confusion morphed into a sense of dread. Finally, when police were able to match the fingerprints from the decayed body with those of Vic Weiss, the phone inside the Tarkanians' hotel room rang again. "It was devastating news," Lois said. "This was not just someone Jerry was friends with for a long time. It was someone he loved. I can't tell you how badly that hurt us."

Many of those who knew Weiss acknowledged a slipperiness to the man. Weiss's business holdings were hardly of the up-and-up genre. He apparently owned three car dealerships (Rolls-Royce, Ford and Fiat) and managed a handful of so-so boxers. Weiss always carried around a thick wad of cash (he had $38,000 in his pocket for the meeting with Buss and Cooke), and rarely left home minus his ostentatious solid gold wristwatch and matching diamond ring (purchased from Anthony Starr, a Canadian jewel thief who routinely sold Weiss hot goods). It was far from unusual to see Weiss standing ringside, talking shop with known mobsters.

What detectives later learned was that Weiss, the ultimate showman, had little to show. Though he told people he possessed the three car dealerships, he actually was merely a paid consultant. His Encino home was owned by an associate, and his car—the maroon-and-white Rolls-Royce—was leased. Weiss had run up more than $60,000 in gambling debts and—at the time of his death—was flying back and forth from Los Angeles to Las Vegas to deliver bundles of laundered cash. According to one of his colleagues, Weiss skimmed money off the top of the transactions. He had been warned repeatedly to stop and, police suspected, was killed when he didn't.

■ ■ ■

Despite it all—the murder and the suspicions and the lingering questions—Jerry Tarkanian was still the next head coach of the Los Angeles Lakers. He would be designing plays for Kareem down low, would be figuring out how to blend the talents of Norm Nixon, the incumbent All-Star point guard, with Johnson, the rookie point guard. He would have to incorporate Jamaal Wilkes, the smooth small forward, into the offensive mix, and find an answer to the long-standing void at power forward. "He was so excited to coach Magic," Lois said. "He had all these ideas about how to use him."

A week after Weiss was murdered, Jerry and Lois flew to Las Vegas, where they dined with Buss. "I know this whole tragedy has been very hard on you," Buss said. "Take as much time as you need. The offer is on the table, and it's not going anywhere. You're our coach."

Vic Weiss's murder, though, had changed things. With the death came the news (hidden until this point) of the coaching transaction. The people of Las Vegas reached out. *Please don't leave. We need you. You need us. You are Las Vegas.* The Tarkanians had four children, none of whom wanted to depart. Maybe, just maybe, money wasn't everything. Maybe $700,000 wasn't worth giving up the job he loved most.

"I don't think Jerry ever got past Vic's death," said Lois. "He just didn't get past it."

When Tarkanian called Buss to tell him he had decided to remain in Las Vegas, the new Lakers owner held no grudge. "I understand," he said. "Some things just aren't meant to be."

■ ■ ■

In the craziest of days, when Magic Johnson agreed to leave college and become a Laker, and Jerry Tarkanian was preparing to jump to the NBA, and Vic Weiss's remains were being found in the trunk of a Rolls-Royce, it was easy to forget that, for all the "inevitable" talk about the NBA approving Jerry Buss's bid to buy the team, there was little inevitable about it.

In fact, with each passing day, as the June 22 vote among NBA owners approached, Buss's anointment seemed to become increasingly imperiled. "There were many questions about whether he would be allowed to buy the team," said Roy Johnson, who covered the NBA for *The New York Times.* "This was in the day when the NBA was sort of like a company picnic . . . just not that big of a deal. And the other owners didn't exactly hide their suspicions over Jerry Buss."

Back in the 1970s, there was an expectation among the NBA's ruling class that, to earn the status as *owner*, one had to either be a large corporation (the Knicks, for example, were owned by Gulf+Western) or an individual who fit a certain profile. Namely: male, über-rich and reputable.

To be "reputable," the owner needed to fit a certain description.* Jim Fitzgerald, owner of the Milwaukee Bucks, was a straitlaced businessman who made a fortune in real estate development and cable television. Harry T. Manguarian Jr., owner of the Boston Celtics, was a straitlaced businessman who made a fortune in retail furniture and, later, as the owner of Southeastern Jet Corporation and Drexel Investments. William Davidson, owner of the Detroit Pistons, was a straitlaced businessman who made a fortune in architectural and automotive glass. Though it went unstated to the public, NBA owners—more than those of any other league—viewed themselves as *better* than the players they employed. Not merely wealthier but less, well, black. And street. And, for lack of a better word, common.

Which made Jerry Buss quite the odd fit.

Although many of the NBA owners had, at one point or another, risen

---

* A notable exception to the rule was Franklin Mieuli, the eccentric owner of the Golden State Warriors, who had a full beard and traveled most places via bicycle.

from poverty to earn their fortunes, there was something disturbingly *new money* about Buss that rubbed folks wrong.

Or perhaps it was just that he seemed to have tons of sex.

Born on January 27, 1933, Buss was thirteen when he moved with his family from Southern California to Kemmerer, Wyoming, a town of 2,656 best known as the site where, in 1902, the J. C. Penney Company store was founded. His mother, Jessie, and father, Lydus, both accountants, had divorced when he was a baby, and Jerry's boyhood was one of waywardness and financial hardship. He lived with his mother; stepfather, Cecil Brown; half brother, Mickey; half sister, Susan; and stepbrother, Jim, in a small six-room home. "I can remember standing in a WPA line with a gunny sack," Buss recalled, "and I remember having to buy chocolate milk instead of white because it was one cent cheaper." To help with the bills, Jerry worked odd jobs, shining shoes and carrying bags at the Kemmerer Hotel and setting pins at the Kemmerer Bowling Alley. He and his close friend, Jim Dover, would rig the slot machine at the hotel, then use the money to buy banana cream pies. "Jerry was very industrious," said Raymond Barp, a classmate. "If there was a job he could do and make a buck, he was there."

Buss's early career ambition wasn't to be an entrepreneur but a gambler. He was a hustler at poker, and once took his high school teacher for ten straight games of $50-a-round pool. He briefly dropped out of school to work at Union Pacific, laying and maintaining railroad tracks. It was an awful way to make a living. "There'd be two, three fights a day," he said. "It was pretty exciting for a sixteen-year-old kid. You never knew what those guys would do. I kept my mouth shut most of the time."

After four months, Buss spotted an advertisement for civil service chemists. The pay was a significant upgrade from his railroad check. He was inspired to return to high school for his senior year, and—because of a falling-out with his stepfather—moved in with his science teacher, Walter Garrett, whom Buss later called "my inspiration." Garrett saw true genius in his student, and signed him up to take a national science test sponsored by Bausch & Lomb. That earned Buss a scholarship to the University of Wyoming. "[Garrett] is the one who turned everything around for me," Buss said. "I was not academically inclined—school was easy for me, I didn't have bad grades—but he encouraged me and I was able to get a scholarship."

On the Laramie, Wyoming, campus, Buss wasn't merely another student. He petitioned to take algebra, trigonometry and analytical geometry concurrently, and earned a degree in chemistry in just two and a half years. "He never turned in a paper with an error on it, whether it was a daily quiz or a final exam," said Kenneth Doi, a classmate and friend. "That's really an accomplishment. Everything was 100 percent." Buss's 4.0 GPA resulted in graduate school scholarship offers from, among others, Harvard, Michigan, Caltech and the University of Southern California. Because of his love of college football and beautiful weather, he picked USC.

Upon completing both his masters and PhD in 1957, Buss moved to Boston to work for Arthur D. Little, a management consultancy firm. He arrived at the office at 9 A.M., took the requisite one-hour lunch break, returned to his desk—and dreaded every moment. "I couldn't stand wearing a pinstripe suit and carrying a briefcase," Buss said. He returned to California to take a job at McDonnell Douglas, and was employed briefly at a space laboratory. Once again, the uniformity irked him. "All I could see were 500 desks, 500 white shirts and 500 different colored neckties," he said. "We were a herd of very educated cattle."

In 1958, Buss asked Frank Mariani, a friend and aerospace engineer, whether he'd consider pooling some money to invest in a small apartment house in West Los Angeles. Mariani agreed, and each man put aside $83.33 a month until (along with the help of a handful of friends) there was enough to secure a bank loan to buy a fourteen-unit building. Before long, one property became two; two properties became four; four properties became, by 1962, hundreds. The two men—now officially Mariani-Buss Associates— flourished by purchasing repossessed buildings from banks and turning them around. The kid who once lived in a pool hall became the man worth millions; the men who began with a single unit owned more than seven hundred separate pieces of property in California, Arizona and Nevada.

That alone would have made Buss an appropriate NBA owner. But a person who lived and died with USC sports (Buss not only attended every Trojan football game, but nearly every Trojan track-and-field meet) wasn't content to kick back and watch his wealth accumulate. No, Buss liked the action. "Life," his daughter, Jeanie, once said, "gives him adrenaline." While buying and building up the Strings of World Team Tennis (well, he tried to build them up. The sport wound up losing Buss nearly $5 million), he became known as Los Angeles' most eligible bachelor.

Though married to his second wife, Veronica, since 1972—his first marriage, to the former JoAnn Mueller, ended in divorce; the couple had four children—Buss never tried to hide his infatuation with young, sexy women. He could often be found at the city's hottest clubs, a big-breasted blond stunner on his left arm, a big-breasted brunette stunner on the other. Inside his bedroom, he kept piles of photo albums, loaded with pictures of the women he dated. In an inexplicable way, there was honor to it. Buss never sought to exploit or embarrass. "He had this routine, where he would take a girl out to buy her a dress and a pair of shoes," said Linda Rambis, a future team employee (and the wife of Kurt Rambis, a Laker forward). "Then she would wear the outfit to dinner. It was very old Hollywood."

"With Jerry," said Charline Kenney, his assistant, "it was often more important to make sure he had a luncheon date than a meeting date. We'd arrange for one sweet thing to come for lunch, then another sweet thing for dinner. They couldn't overlap—but he kind of loved it when they did." In 1978, Buss had the good fortune of meeting John Rockwell, the actor best known for having played the title character in the 1961 TV series *The Adventures of Superboy*. Rockwell brought Jerry to the Playboy Mansion (where Rockwell lived for a spell) and introduced him to Hugh Hefner. "It was a match made in heaven," Rockwell said. "I knew all the women from the Playboy Mansion, so I introduced him to a bunch of the Playmates. They immediately liked Jerry, because he was never pushy with them. If a girl needed a new car, Jerry would gamble, make the money and buy them a new car. What wasn't to like?"

"Every man in America wanted to be Jerry Buss," said Pat O'Brien, the CBS reporter. "You're fifty, fucking underage girls, rich as can be."

Unlike the majority of NBA owners, who made for a frumpish group, Buss cast a dashing figure. He was forty-six but looked thirty-five, with long brown hair and a porn star's mustache. "When he entered a room," Rockwell said, "people noticed. Especially women."

The NBA held its official meetings at a hotel on Amelia Island, near Jacksonville, Florida, and many of the twenty-two owners in attendance came armed. Sure, Buss had the money. But wasn't he also a certainty to embarrass a league already facing seemingly insurmountable image problems? Cocaine was allegedly poisoning the league. The Buffalo Braves recently relocated to San Diego, and the New Orleans Jazz bolted for Salt Lake City. An experimental three-point line was dismissed by many as a cartoonish gimmick. The league's best player, Abdul-Jabbar, refused to engage the media, and its reigning MVP, Moses Malone, was barely intelligible.

And now, just because he had the financial wherewithal, they were supposed to approve a man who dated bimbos? Who, according to multiple rumors, engaged in odd sexual exploits that would cause Hefner to blush? Who had allegedly married his second wife, Veronica, while still married to his first, JoAnn? "There was genuine opposition," said Roy Johnson, the *New York Times* writer. "I was covering the meetings, and back then you would know pretty much everything going on, all the details. Literally, you could sit outside the meeting room and listen in."

Ultimately, the Buss acquisition was approved thanks to one man: Jack Kent Cooke. Hardly known for his eloquence, Cooke presented his cohorts with a graceful defense of his friend. Like the rest of them, Jerry Buss was a true sports enthusiast who would do his absolute best to make sure the league succeeded. He also happened to be a marketing genius. Though Buss lost millions in World Team Tennis, he put his own money where his mouth was, lavishing enormous contracts upon stars like Chris Evert, Ilie Nastase and the Amritraj brothers. "I can assure you, Jerry Buss will do wonders for the NBA," Cooke said. "I have no doubt about it. You shouldn't, either."

One night later, after the approval was official and the documents were being prepared for signing, Jerry Buss could be found inside a rickety one-bedroom apartment on Doheny Street in Los Angeles. He was there visiting his girlfriend, Debbie Zafrani, a gorgeous bunny at the local Playboy Club who was, not surprisingly, about half his age. "He was just hanging out with us, as he always did," said Linda Rambis, Debbie's sister. "For months he'd been telling us, 'Someday I'm going to own the Lakers. I love that team, and I'm going to be the owner.' My sister and I are from Chicago—we just thought he was eccentric. We'd watch the Lakers on TV, and he'd go on about owning them, usually while drinking his rum and Coke. Well, this one night he says, 'I bought the Lakers! I really did! Let's go out for dinner and celebrate.' I probably didn't even believe him. I mean, really, you bought the Lakers? C'mon."

CHAPTER 3

THE UNLIKELY HEAD COACH

The long-distance phone call made no sense.

Jerry Buss?

Who the hell was Jerry Buss?

Jack McKinney sure didn't recognize the name, even as Bill Sharman, the general manager of the Los Angeles Lakers, explained to him that the franchise was under new ownership, and that a coaching change had to be made, and that he—*yes, he!*—was being strongly considered.

Certainly, even with Jerry Tarkanian out of the running, there were *sexier* candidates for one of the NBA's marquee franchises to pursue. How about John Wooden, the UCLA men's basketball coach? Or Jud Heathcote, fresh off of leading Michigan State (and Magic Johnson) to the school's first-ever national championship? Hubie Brown, the Atlanta Hawks's forty-five-year-old hotshot coach, might be willing to head west for the right price. There was always Les Habegger, the top aide to head coach Lenny Wilkens with the world-champion Seattle SuperSonics. Or even the two Laker assistants from the previous season—Stan Albeck and Jack McCloskey.

And yet . . . as he sat on a couch inside his hotel room on Lake Maggiore, Italy, on the morning of July 11, 1979, McKinney realized that this was 100 percent serious, that Jerry Buss was the new owner of the Los Angeles Lakers, and that he had been told there was an obscure, understated assistant with the Portland Trail Blazers who knew the game as well as anyone in basketball.

"We love a lot about you," Sharman said. "Dr. Buss would like you to fly to Los Angeles and talk about the coaching position."

They spoke for a while, the fifty-three-year-old GM and the forty-four-year-old assistant coach, then agreed McKinney should leave Italy (and the basketball clinic he was running alongside Allessandro Gamba, the Italian national team coach) to come to Los Angeles in two days to chat face-to-face. As soon as he hung up the phone, McKinney's thoughts spun round and round. He'd always believed Kareem Abdul-Jabbar could be an improved rebounder and shot blocker. He'd always thought Jamaal Wilkes could be a lockdown defender. He knew that, with two legitimate point guards—Norm Nixon and Magic Johnson—in the backcourt, the Lakers could run opponents to near death. He knew the Lakers needed a legitimate power forward. They also needed to be tougher. Meaner. Less giving, more attacking. "It was a dream job," McKinney said. "You're talking about a roster with historic talent, maybe just requiring some tweaks."

When McKinney arrived, jet-lagged but jovial, he was warmly greeted by Buss, whose casual attire and youthful enthusiasm caught him off guard. Jack Kent Cooke had been the overlord of the Lakers for so long, people still half expected him to arrogantly emerge from his bunker. Instead, here was Buss ("Please, call me Jerry") offering a scotch, leaning back in a chair, anxious to hear not merely what Jack McKinney believed but, specifically, who he was.

One helluva story waited to be told.

■ ■ ■

When Jack McKinney was nine, his father snuck him into Babe Ruth's funeral.

It was one of those moments—rare, precious, special—that life doesn't announce ahead of time. The Bambino had died of cancer on August 16, 1948. The following evening, Paul McKinney, a detective with the Chester (Pennsylvania) Police Department, picked up his son from St. Robert Elementary School and drove him to the nearby State Theatre. A special presentation of *The Babe Ruth Story* was being shown, and father wanted son to know what sort of man the world had lost.

As they exited the theatre, Paul turned to young Jack. Tears were running down his cheeks. "We're gonna get up early tomorrow," he said, "and say good-bye to the Babe."

They made the two-and-a-half-hour drive from Chester to New York City, Paul McKinney telling his boy everything there was to know about Babe Ruth. The hardscrabble Baltimore youth. The trade from the Red Sox to the Yankees. The breathtaking 1927 season. The Called Shot. "My dad was a god to me, and he knew everything about sports," said Jack McKinney. "He would take me all over the place—to heavyweight fights, to Shibe Park to see the Phillies and Eagles play. Everywhere."

Upon arriving outside Manhattan's St. Patrick's Cathedral, the McKinneys were flabbergasted by the human tidal wave itching to witness history. There were men and women, boys and girls, blacks and whites and people of all ilks—packed in, twenty rows deep.

Paul McKinney took a tight hold of his son's hand and said, "Stick with me." They wove through the masses and approached a barricade. Paul spotted a New York City police officer, removed his badge from his belt and spoke with an invented Irish accent. "I drove my son all the way from Chester to New York City to see the Babe," he said. "Can you help me?"

The officer lifted the wood beam and motioned for the McKinneys to enter St. Patrick's. As he walked up the marble steps, then strode through the main entrance, Jack was flabbergasted. To his left stood Thomas E. Dewey, the governor of New York. To his right stood William Bendix, the actor who, a day earlier, he had seen on a large screen, starring as the title character in *The Babe Ruth Story*. "For a little kid, it was like being surrounded by royalty," he said. "It was larger than life."

Jack McKinney held on to that day. To the smells, the sounds, the profound sadness. Mostly, he held on to the buzz. Even on the occasion of a death, there was an indescribable magic stemming from the energy and outpouring of raw, powerful emotion. "Sports is one of the few things that has that effect on people," he said. "That sort of unique power."

Jack McKinney's first taste of basketball glory came as a student at St. Robert, when Sister Edward Francis, his fourth-grade teacher, announced that Sister Michael Anita and her fifth-grade class had challenged them to a game. With seconds remaining, McKinney stepped to the line for two free throws. His first shot was released underhanded. It soared over the backboard and landed on the stage behind the baseline. Snickers ensued. The second shot, also underhanded, went in, and his classmates burst into cheers. McKinney's point ended the threat of a shutout. His grade lost, 12–1. "The next day in class, Sister Edward Francis . . . was ready to canonize me for the greatest one-point performance of all time," McKinney wrote.

As a sophomore at St. James High School, he made the Bulldogs varsity. His coach was a young Xs and Os wonk named Jack Ramsay. "Jack was a good, but not great, player," said Ramsay. "He was a good defender, not a good shooter. But he could drive to the basket and he was intelligent. He also happened to be very likable. That never hurts." As a senior, McKinney was asked by his chemistry teacher, Father Wesolowski, to forgo baseball and come out for track. "I didn't really want to, but I wasn't doing very well in chemistry," he said. "Up until that point I'd never high jumped before then. Not once. Well, I won every meet I competed in, broke the school record and won the Catholic League championship."

McKinney earned a track and field scholarship to Saint Joseph's College in nearby Philadelphia. He played basketball as well, primarily filling the role of off-the-bench defensive specialist.

Before his junior year, Saint Joseph's hired (coincidentally) Ramsay to take over as varsity coach. Thus began the lifelong kinship of the hard-nosed player with a firm understanding of the game and the professorial coach with an appreciation for on-court thinkers. "I really absorbed his teaching," said McKinney. "We did an awful lot of setting up and arranging during the pre-season, so that, come important games, we were always prepared. He would always say, 'We're gonna work, because hard work brings about hard play, and hard play is what we want.' I wasn't someone gifted with tons of natural ability. So work ethic was my biggest strength."

Actually, McKinney's biggest strength was something much more profound: decency. He was a good person. Reliable. Capable. Empathetic. After graduating from college, he was hired by St. James High, his alma mater, to teach history, English and physical education, as well as coach varsity basketball. McKinney immediately fell in love with coaching: standing along the sideline, diagramming plays, positioning lineups, devising a strategy to overcome teams boasting greater talent. When, a couple of years later, Ramsay offered him a position as an assistant coach at Saint Joseph's (as well as the title of assistant athletic director), McKinney jumped at the opportunity.

Six years later, after a brief stint as the basketball coach at Philadelphia Textile, McKinney took over for Ramsay, who had developed a retinal problem that forced him to step down. Entering the 1966–67 season, the

Hawks featured a bottom-basement roster. Six of the top seven players had graduated, and the incoming freshman class was notably thin. Somehow, the team finished 16-10 and advanced to the MAC championship game. "Our teams used to be known for trapping and full-court presses," said Mike Hauer, a 6-foot-3 guard. "But Jack adjusted to his players' abilities. Also, he wasn't a coach with an ego. He'd listen to us, and if something wasn't working and we told him so, he'd often make the change. Even when I was at my worst, he never stopped listening. He was the kind of coach you'd be lucky to play for."

After eight full seasons, McKinney could brag of a 144-77 record, five Middle Atlantic Conference championships and four NCAA Tournament appearances. He was one of the nation's best collegiate coaches and a man other schools thought of when a vacancy loomed. He also happened to be happy. He, his wife, Claire, and their four children lived in a small house on a pretty street. "I had other offers," he said, "but I always rejected them."

On March 18, 1974, he was fired.

It happened on a Monday. Jack McKinney remembers that. It's not the day that stands out, so much as the utter shock. Until recently, McKinney had actually held the dual roles of coach and athletic director, just as Ramsay had before him. "It was great in a lot of ways," McKinney said. "But I went to the priest who was in charge and told him both jobs were too much for me. I had a family to worry about, and I couldn't do both any longer."

McKinney was asked to pick a position: Either stay as the basketball coach, or stay as the athletic director. The choice was an easy one—his love was hoops, not paperwork. The school hired the Rev. Michael Blee to take over as the athletic director. McKinney was pleased, even though Blee promptly kicked him out of his office, moving him across the hall to a room the size of a large tissue box. McKinney's load was lighter, and he could fully devote himself to Saint Joseph's rise to national basketball prominence. That year, 1973–74, the Hawks—saddled with a puny $50,000 recruiting budget and picked by one Philadelphia sportswriter to win three games—finished 19-11, and McKinney was named the Eastern College Coach of the Year. The team reached yet another NCAA Tournament, losing to Pittsburgh, 54–42, in the first round of the Eastern Regional. Three days later, Blee—a humorless seventy-year-old with an affinity for not smiling—told McKinney that he lacked "teaching value" and needed to pack his belongings.

As the fired coach rose to leave, Blee cleared his throat. "I don't think," he said, "that you should mention this until you get another job."

The next day, McKinney mentioned it. "There hasn't been a word said to me all year in a negative way by the athletic director," he told a handful of local print reporters as tears welled in his eyes. "I'm shocked. I just don't understand it. They told me it was in the best interests of the college that I not be rehired. This is something I find difficult to accept—I don't understand why I was fired."

One day later, approximately eight hundred students attended a campus rally to protest the dismissal. They marched toward the president's office, chanting "Bring back Jack!" while burning an effigy of Blee. The school's alumni association issued a statement calling for McKinney to regain his job, and for Blee to be canned. The statement termed the firing "immoral" and "illogical."

"It's a funeral," said Kevin Furey, a Hawks player. "Supposedly it was a matter of respect. No one, except for my father, got more respect from me than Coach McKinney."

Within a couple of days, the heat died and McKinney was simply another man without a job. He sulked around his house, cleaning up rooms, taking long walks, wondering if this was the end of his collegiate coaching career. He thought about sales. Or, perhaps, teaching. Surely, there was a high school team in need of someone with his experience. "That was probably the lowest I've ever seen Jack," said Claire McKinney. "Saint Joseph's was a special place to him. He went there, played there, learned about coaching there. To be discarded like that . . . I don't know if he's ever fully recovered."

That July, in the midst of his funk, McKinney set off to work his annual basketball camp in the Poconos. It would be, predictably, standard stuff—help a bunch of aspiring stars pick up the intricacies of the game. On the day he arrived, McKinney was walking down the steps of his hotel when he ran into Hubie Brown, an assistant coach with the Milwaukee Bucks.

"Hey, Jack, what are you up to?" Brown asked.

"I just got fired," he said glumly.

"Right—I heard about that," Brown said. "It's terrible. I'm really sorry." Pause.

"Hey," Brown said, "would you be interested in going to Milwaukee?"

Milwaukee! Land of . . . eh . . . bratwurst and beer and strip malls and, well, not much else.

"Absolutely!" McKinney said. "What do you know?"

Brown, luck had it, had recently accepted the position of head coach for the Kentucky Colonels of the ABA. The Bucks were in desperate need of an assistant for Larry Costello. "I'll call Larry today," Brown said of Milwaukee's head coach. "Hold tight."

Within forty-eight hours, McKinney found himself on a flight from Philadelphia to Milwaukee. Costello picked him up at the airport. The two stopped at a diner. A quick lunch turned into four hours of Xs and Os and offensive philosophies. "We never got any further," McKinney said. "He hired me and took me back to the airport."

McKinney had never considered the NBA as a landing spot. In his mind, it was a league overpopulated by disinterested tall people. Upon arriving in Milwaukee, however, he was immediately embraced as a contemplative, intellectual counterpart to the high-strung Costello. The player who valued him most was Milwaukee's center, a complicated superstar named Kareem Abdul-Jabbar. The majority of team officials steered clear of the All-Star, whose moodiness and unpredictability served as Plexiglas shields. McKinney, however, never flinched. He critiqued and criticized, assisted and enabled. Costello and Abdul-Jabbar would exchange, at most, fifty words in the course of a month. McKinney, meanwhile, became the star's sounding board. "Everyone respected Jack," said Jon McGlocklin, a Milwaukee guard. "He filled the role of the guy players could talk to and confide in."

Two years later, McKinney was hired by his old pal Jack Ramsay to serve as an assistant with the Portland Trail Blazers. The next three seasons were some of the happiest of McKinney's life. He was in his early forties, working alongside his mentor and close friend, helping guide one of the league's most talented young teams. The McKinneys lived in a beautiful home in Lake Oswego, a Portland suburb with hiking trails and bike paths and bountiful nature. "It was a great place for kids to grow up," said Dennis McKinney, Jack and Claire's son. "It was pretty perfect for us."

In 1976–77, his second season with Portland, McKinney was part of a team that won the NBA championship. Much was made of the two Philly guys walking the sideline, especially when the Blazers faced the 76ers in the finals. Should their team win, McKinney and Ramsay promised to sprint up the steps of the Philadelphia Art Museum, à la Rocky Balboa.

When Portland hosted Game 6, leading the series three games to two, a city sat on edge. There were no other top-tier professional sports franchises in town, and since the team's debut in 1970–71, Portland basketball fans had endured six losing seasons in seven tries. Finally, they were approaching something special and meaningful and uniting.

With less than ten minutes remaining in the game, the Blazers led comfortably by 12. Then by 10. 8. 6. 4. When the clock reached eighteen seconds, the advantage had been reduced to 2. Finally, after a bevy of wayward 76ers shots (Lloyd Free is blocked! George McGinnis's fourteen-footer falls short!), the buzzer sounded. McKinney looked at Ramsay, who looked back at his friend. They embraced. "The greatest day of my coaching career," McKinney would later say. "Nothing was a close second."

■ ■ ■

And now, on July 18, 1979, Jack McKinney was inside the Forum, alongside the strangest sports owner he'd ever encountered. Jerry Buss wasn't the first multimillionaire he'd met, but he was the first one to deliberately show off his chest hair.

For several hours, the two talked—some about basketball, much about life. McKinney and Buss couldn't have been more opposite. McKinney was straitlaced, "bland and businesslike," wrote Joe Gilmartin in the *Sporting News*. Yet Buss loved his narrative, the way he didn't let an unfair firing turn him bitter. The new Lakers owner was a fan of strength and stamina and athleticism. Above all, though, he was a fan of resiliency.

The men met one more time, and on the front sports page of the July 27, 1979, *Los Angeles Times*, the news became official: MCKINNEY, LAKERS SAID TO HAVE REACHED ACCORD. An introductory press conference was held on July 30 at the Forum, where thirty members of the Southern California media were offered pretzel sticks, cans of Coca-Cola and these opening words from a euphoric Buss: "The Lakers need a change from the style of play they had last year. . . ."

With that, the reporters met a man they had (with rare exceptions) never before heard of. Appropriately dressed in a dull brown suit with a dull brown tie, McKinney was neither charming nor effusive. He was as Hollywood as a tube sock. No slicked-back hair, no $5,000 outfit. "All he does," wrote Scott Ostler in the *Los Angeles Times*, ". . . is coach basketball well and get along with people—even players and sportswriters."

When asked to explain his coaching philosophy, McKinney didn't hesitate. "A constant running game," he said. "I'd like a moving offense, rather than having everyone else standing around watching Kareem all the time and putting pressure on him. I think we can do that. When you have someone like Magic, I think you can do that. We'll run every chance and under every possible situation."

Watching the press conference on a television from inside his room at the Plaza Hotel, Earvin Johnson was beaming from ear to ear.

The words were music.

■ ■ ■

In the aftermath of the NBA Draft, Magic Johnson had come to the Forum to officially meet the press and charm the masses. The Lakers sent a limousine to pick him up. The driver was a former Playboy bunny. "I'm sure he was thinking, 'I'm in the right place,'" said Bob Steiner, the team's publicity director. Before he was taken to the arena, however, Johnson stopped off at Jerry Buss's house to meet his new boss. When the doorbell rang, the master of the house was upstairs combing his hair. "You bring in Earvin and offer him a drink," Jerry Buss said to his seventeen-year-old daughter, Jeanie. "I'll be down in a few minutes."

When she opened the door, Jeanie Buss was greeted by a smile—"A magnificent, beautiful smile," she said. The two sat down and engaged in awkward adolescent banter. "I'm real excited I was drafted here," Johnson said. "I'm gonna play in Los Angeles for three years and then I'm gonna go finish my career with the Detroit Pistons, because that's where I grew up and that's who I want to play for."

Jeanie excused herself, dashed up the steps and charged into the bathroom. "Dad! Dad!" she said. "He says he wants to play for the Pistons!"

Jerry Buss barely flinched. "Jeanie," he said, "you have nothing to worry about. The first time he puts on a Laker uniform and walks out onto the Forum floor, he's never going to want to leave."

On the drive to the arena, Johnson gazed out the window at the orange trees and couldn't believe what he was seeing. Were they in California or heaven? Thirty minutes later, Johnson engaged in a session with the media that was beyond compare. This was California's first real exposure to Johnson's smile and charisma and optimism. Brad Holland, the team's second first-round pick, was also sitting at the table. He was a local kid who had played at UCLA—and he was invisible. "It was all Magic," said Ostler. "He wasn't just good. He was dazzling."

"Until that moment, the NBA was—for many Americans—black guys in short shorts snorting cocaine," said Pat O'Brien. "Magic was a savior."

Asked whether he could help a team that had enjoyed only one home sellout in 1978–79, the nineteen-year-old cleared his throat and smiled. "If there are some crazy basketball fans," he said, "tell 'em to come on out. The Lakers already be winnin' without me. Now we're gonna be exciting!"

When the press conference ended and the lights inside the Forum were dimmed, Johnson crossed the court, plopped down in an empty seat and dreamed. He pictured lobbing the ball to Abdul-Jabbar, whipping no-look passes to Jamaal Wilkes. He eventually walked into the Lakers' darkened locker room, where the nameplates seemed to glisten.

ABDUL-JABBAR

WILKES

NIXON

DANTLEY

What was he doing here? How did this happen?

Though he didn't fully see it in himself as a young boy, Earvin Johnson Jr. was meant to be a star. That's a clichéd sentiment, obviously, used a thousand times a day to describe the most charismatic and precocious among us. There's always some kid deemed by neighbors to be the next president, the next quarterback, the next Broadway standout. Yet from the time he was a tyke, growing up in a yellow frame house at 814 Middle Street just north of the Grand River on the west side of Lansing, Michigan, Earvin had "It."

He was the sixth of ten brothers and sisters. His father, Earvin Sr., was an assembly worker at the Fisher Body plant (he worked the awful 4:48 P.M. to 3:18 A.M. shift) who earned additional money on weekends by running his own rubbish route or pumping gas at the nearby Shell station; his mother, Christine, was a junior high cafeteria worker. The Johnsons ate dinner together every evening, and on Saturday nights, Christine would make a batch of homemade pizzas, and the family would gather around the television. Grades and effort were important; empathy was more important. "I ran into Earvin's fourth-grade teacher in a grocery store," Christine Johnson once said. "She laughed and started telling me a story about him. It was the first day of school in her first year of teaching, and the class was giving her fits. Spitballs were flying. Children were yelling. Earvin stood up and told his classmates to get in their seats, to behave, to listen to the teacher. She said everybody stopped and did just what he said to do."

Young Earvin's nickname was June Bug because he was always on the move, and his goals changed by the hour. He wanted to grow up and be a member of The Temptations; an astronaut; a movie star; the next John F. Kennedy. "I was a dreamer," he said. "And when you're a dreamer, I think, you dream about everything, almost, on the face of the earth."

There were jobs. Plenty of jobs. When he was ten, Earvin cut neighborhood lawns, and at fifteen, he was a stock boy at Quality Dairy. He also helped a family friend named Jim Dart on his Vernor's Ginger Ale route. On Friday nights, he took shifts as a janitor in a nearby building, vacuuming floors, emptying trash cans, cleaning bathrooms. With no one around, he'd kick back in a leather chair and prop his feet on a desk. "I'd start giving out orders to my staff," he said. "'Do this, do that.'" Throughout his career, Johnson often thought back to a television commercial from his boyhood for Camay soap. In the spot, a wealthy, elegant woman stepped into a bathtub. "See that bathtub," young Earvin said to his sister Pearl. "Someday I'm gonna have one just like that in my house."

His big dreams—coupled with an unrivaled work ethic—translated to sports. Johnson was rarely seen without a basketball, either tucked beneath his arm or bouncing against the pavement. Everywhere he walked, the weathered Spalding came along. "If I was going on an errand for my mother, I'd dribble on the sidewalk, making a game out of trying to miss the cracks," he once wrote. "Or I'd dribble one block right-handed and one block left-handed. Then I'd dribble home with a sack of groceries in my arm." When it was raining outside, he'd be in his room, acting out Warriors-Pistons with a rolled-up pair of socks. On Sunday afternoons, he and his father watched the *NBA Game of the Week* on TV. Every once in a while they'd go to Detroit's Cobo Arena to catch Dave Bing and the Pistons. "My father would point out the subtleties of the pick-and-roll play," Johnson wrote, "and explain the various defensive strategies." By fourth grade, Earvin played in four different leagues. He'd find action wherever he could—the nearby YMCA, a church gym, the Main Street school yard courts. On Sunday afternoons after church, he'd peel off his suit, slip into his shorts, T-shirt and red Chuck Taylor All Stars and dash out the front door, searching for a game. Any game.

Because he was named for his father, Johnson often went by Little Earvin. Only he wasn't little. When, as a seventh grader, he tried out for the team at Dwight Rich Junior High, Earvin stood high above the competition. He was six feet tall and could dribble with both hands, post up down low and run the court like a deer. As a ninth grader he reached 6-foot-5, and once scored 48 points in a game. Were he merely a big kid with athletic gifts, Johnson would have been simply noteworthy. However, the youngster was distinctive. He was caring and empathetic, bighearted and open-armed. Throughout junior high, he waited excitedly for the chance to attend Sexton High, a basketball powerhouse located five blocks from his doorstep. Then the news came that, thanks to forced busing, he would be sent for tenth grade four miles away to Everett High, a 92 percent white school on Lansing's south side.

Johnson was crushed. Two of his older brothers, Quincey and Larry, had been bused to Everett, and their lives were miserable whirlwinds of fights, awkwardness and rejection. "I was upset," he said in 1977. "All the dudes I went with went to Sexton. I went to every Sexton game. I was a Sexton man, and then they came up with this busing thing." Earvin braced himself for hostility and then, briefly, experienced it. But while Larry had been confrontational, Earvin decided to greet people warmly. When black students were offended that the only music being piped into the lunchroom was performed by white artists, Earvin asked the principal for a change. It was granted. Shortly thereafter, when no black girls were accepted for cheerleading, Earvin led an even-tempered protest of all the black basketball players. Before long, the squad was integrated. "Earvin had a goodness in his heart that you didn't see too often," said George Fox, the Everett High varsity basketball coach. "He accepted people for who they were, without looking at color or class. He was special—it was very obvious."

The Vikings' white returnees were slow to embrace Johnson. In his sixth game, however, he finished with 36 points, 18 rebounds and 16 assists against Jackson Parkside, and afterward was approached by Fred Stabley Jr., a writer for the *Lansing State Journal*.

"Great game, Earvin," he said. "I think you should have a nickname. I was thinking of calling you Dr. J, but that's taken. And so is Big E—Elvin Hayes. How about if I call you Magic?"

Johnson was fifteen years old and predictably embarrassed. Surely he would be mocked for this one. "Fine," he said, somewhat dismissively. "Whatever you like."

A phenomenon was born.

Fox had first seen Johnson play in the summer before his arrival at Everett, and he wondered why such a large kid was roaming the perimeter. Once practices began, however, he understood. Earvin Johnson was the Vikings' best rebounder, best shot-blocker—and best passer and game manager. "Coach Fox was the perfect coach for me," said Johnson. "He still allowed me to play guard on offense and then, of course, center on defense. And I don't know many coaches that would allow me to do that—because at that time, the tallest guy would go to center." Johnson understood the rhythms of basketball better than anyone Fox had ever seen. His decision-making abilities were beyond compare. "There was no one like him," Fox said. "I don't mean no one on the team. I mean no one anywhere on the planet."

Basketball junkies flocked to Everett games, and chants of "Mag-ic! Mag-ic!" often filled the small gymnasiums. He became a crossover star, as beloved by whites as by blacks. Oftentimes, he kicked off Friday and Saturday nights by hanging out with his black friends, then traveled across town to an Everett party with the whites. When a reporter from *The Detroit News* asked what, were he given the chance, he would write about himself, Johnson thought for a moment and said, "That he likes to get to know people. He's a fun person to talk to. . . . He's an outgoing person. He loves to sit down and talk, talk, talk."

As a senior, Johnson led Everett to the Michigan Class A state title by scoring 34 points in a 62–56 overtime victory over Birmingham's Brother Rice. Throughout the year, there was great debate as to whether he would attend the University of Michigan or Michigan State. Johnson actually visited three other schools (Maryland, Notre Dame and North Carolina), but knew, deep down, he wanted to stay close to home. Michigan was presumed to be the front runner. Johnson had attended the Wolverines' summer camp after his freshman year, and the program was coming off of a 26-4 record behind All-American Phil Hubbard. Michigan State, meanwhile, was a mess. The Spartans went 12-15, hadn't reached the NCAA Tournament in nearly twenty years and recently lost the head coach, Gus Ganakas, after a walkout of the black players. He was replaced by someone named Jud Heathcote, who last coached at the University of Montana.

Both schools pined for Johnson, especially following his showing at an AAU tournament in Florida. Johnson led the upstart team from Michigan into the finals against a club from Washington, DC. The twelve boys from the nation's capital were clear favorites—among their ranks were forward

Larry Spriggs, a future NBA player, as well as soon-to-be college standouts like Kenny Matthews, Earnest Graham, and Jo Jo Hunter. On the night before the big game, Spriggs and Co. knocked on the door of Johnson's hotel room. "You're the guy they call Magic, huh?" Spriggs said. "Well, you'll be seeing the DC All-Stars tomorrow. Be ready."

"Why we did that," said Spriggs, "I'll never know."

Johnson went off for 49 points, 15 assists and 13 rebounds, and Michigan destroyed Washington by 30 points. "He just put on a show," said Spriggs. "He was the best high school player I'd ever seen, by far."

Michigan badly wanted Johnson. The campus was gorgeous, the tradition was impressive, the opportunity for a national title undeniable. Yet Michigan State held three enormous advantages: Location, location and location. Johnson was a Lansing kid, and the Michigan State campus was a 10K run from his home. When, on April 17, 1977, he returned from an international basketball tournament in Germany, he was greeted at the Capital City Airport by more than four hundred people—including Heathcote. "I thought there might be a couple of reporters and my family at the airport, but nothing like this," he said, wiping away the tears. "It means a great deal to me to see that a lot of people really care about me."

When Heathcote promised Johnson a future at point guard, the deal was sealed. A couple of days later, he held a press conference from an Everett classroom. When he announced his choice, the students squealed with delight. "I always wanted to go to Michigan State since, I don't know, sixth, seventh grade," he said. "Once you get that Spartan in you, I guess it can't come out."

Johnson was everything Michigan State had hoped for, and he ended his freshman year by averaging 17 points, 7.9 rebounds and 7.4 assists for a team that went 25-5, won the Big Ten Conference title and reached the NCAA Tournament's Elite Eight before falling to Kentucky. The statistics were wonderful; the charisma was out of this world. For years, the Spartans seemed miserable. Johnson, on the other hand, was always happy. "What does Earvin mean to us?" Duane Vernon, a Spartan die-hard, told *Sports Illustrated*. "My God, what did Eisenhower mean to the soldiers?"

Johnson's sophomore year statistics (17.1 points, 7.6 rebounds, and 7.9 assists per game) were nearly identical to his first-season numbers, but this time he carried the Spartans all the way to the national championship game against undefeated and number one–ranked Indiana State in Salt Lake City.

The matchup was the most hyped college clash in thirteen years, since Texas Western's all-black starting lineup toppled all-white Kentucky, 72–65. The Sycamores were led by their own transcendent star, a quiet forward named Larry Bird from French Lick, Indiana. Unlike Johnson, Bird rarely smiled. Unlike Johnson, Bird could not have cared less about the spotlight. Unlike Johnson, Bird had zero charisma. Yet, like Johnson, he was a brilliant all-around player who, in averaging 28.6 points and 14.9 rebounds, captured the nation's attention. The two had actually been teammates the previous summer on America's entry into the World Invitational Tournament, and brooded side by side as the team's coach, Joe B. Hall, gave most of the on-court time to his players from the University of Kentucky. "I've never had a coach completely ignore me before," Johnson said. "Joe B. Hall was the first." When they played together—usually on the second unit during practices—Johnson and Bird soared. They were, simply, the two best performers on the court, and everyone (save for Hall) knew it. "When we scrimmaged at night," Johnson said, "we were blowing his guys off the floor."

Now they were, again, rivals. In the lead-up to the game, Johnson warmly approached Bird, but his greeting was rebuffed. Bird didn't come all the way to Utah to make friends. He was here to win.

So, however, was Johnson. For all the hype generated by Magic vs. Bird, the contest wasn't especially close. Approximately 35 million viewers watched Michigan State control Indiana State, 75–64, as Johnson was named the tournament's outstanding player. It was neither a back-and-forth affair nor a game that ended with a final-second heave. And yet, it proved bigger than anyone could imagine. Said Tim Brando, the renowned broadcaster: "Most of America defines 1979 as being the seminal moment in the history of the NCAA."

■ ■ ■

On the night of July 27, four months after he won the collegiate championship, Johnson was making his official professional debut. Though they had yet to name a full staff, and though their roster was far from determined, the Lakers—like all NBA teams—fielded a squad in the annual summer pro league. This was a place for free agents, long-shot rookies and fringe pros to try to state their case. Among the players representing Los Angeles were Mike Cooper, a second-year forward who had missed nearly all of the previous season with a knee injury; Victor King, the second-round pick from Louisiana

Tech; Walter Daniels, a third-round selection out of the University of Georgia; and Irv Kiffin, a free agent from Oklahoma Baptist. In other words, the dregs. "We were all there for the same thing—to get noticed and give ourselves a shot," said Kiffin. "Wasn't about anything else but that. Except for one of us."

The Lakers were scheduled to face the Detroit Pistons, a summer league matchup that would—under normal circumstances—draw no more than a couple of hundred fans to the Cal State Los Angeles gym.

Yet an hour before the seven thirty P.M. tip-off, the building was overflowing with spectators. By one count, 3,600 fans jammed a place that seated, uncomfortably, 3,000. Another 1,000 or so stood outside, hoping to catch a glimpse of the new kid in town.

Of Magic.

Only a day earlier, the team announced that Johnson would be playing. That meant, it was assumed, an extra 500 or so spectators might come out. Yet as the grandstands filled, fans shuffled in three deep behind the baskets and stuffed the stairways. According to a *Los Angeles Times* report, the lining of bodies caused the building's temperature to shoot into the 100s. Observing the madness, George Andrews, Johnson's attorney, turned to general manager Bill Sharman, grinned and said, "We want to renegotiate."

Johnson jogged onto the court a half hour before tip-off, a half-moon smile crossing his face. Those in attendance let loose with a thunderous applause. He was wearing a white jersey with the words ADIDAS SOUTHERN CALIFORNIA PRO BASKETBALL screen-printed across his chest. His number was—randomly, and for no apparent reason—11. For those accustomed to Johnson in the Michigan State green and white, it was a perplexing vision.

Cooper, the one returnee on the roster, had never seen anything like it. During warm-ups Johnson tapped him on the shoulder.

"What's your name, man?" the rookie asked.

"I'm Michael Cooper," he replied.

"OK . . . OK," Johnson said. "I'm gonna call you Coop. Is that cool?"

"Sure," Cooper replied, smiling. "And I'll call you Earvin."

"He had this big Afro, we did the black guy handshake," Cooper said. "I thought, 'OK, this brother's all right.'"

Johnson began on the bench, backing up the unheralded Daniels. When he rose to enter with seven minutes gone by in the first quarter, fans gave yet another ovation. Johnson jogged halfway onto the court, slapped Daniels on the hand and took an inbounds pass from Cooper, a lightly regarded slasher who grew up mere miles from the Forum.

Johnson was too new to know any plays, so he simply dribbled up the court, looking left, looking right. He was a dashing sight to behold—a long, sinewy 6-foot-9 point guard, hammering the ball into the hardwood, looking . . . looking . . .

Whoosh!

As he approached mid-court, Johnson was accosted by a blue-and-red blur. Roy Hamilton, the Pistons' first-round pick from UCLA, was also a rookie point guard, and more than a tad irked having to hear the crowd hail Johnson in his own backyard. "I mean, I went to college in Los Angeles," Hamilton said, laughing. "I had lots of friends at the game. And all these people came to see *him* play."

Hamilton recalled watching Johnson during the 1979 Final Four, and finding himself intrigued by his unusually high dribble. "He was so big, if he turned his back to you, there was very little chance of you taking it," Hamilton said. "But if he was directly in front of you, you could get the steal."

Hamilton measured Johnson, reached across his body with his right hand and quickly slapped the ball away. A shocked Johnson watched as Hamilton took off in the other direction, scoring on an uncontested breakaway layup. Welcome to the NBA. "For that one moment, everyone started going crazy," said Hamilton. "They started booing him and everything. I actually felt bad for him. It was a pretty amazing situation for him to be in.

"Later on we became friendly, and he told me, 'Roy, I was so scared . . . so nervous. And you really embarrassed me.'"

Before long, Johnson was a spinning, twirling, no-look-passing, on-court maestro. He played 28 of the game's 48 minutes, scoring 24 points and adding 9 assists, 4 steals and 6 turnovers.

When the game ended, fans surrounded Johnson, reaching out with pens and scraps of paper. He stopped briefly by the bench for his first postgame interview as an NBA player. "It was beautiful," he said, smiling. "These fans are really basketball fans, not like I'd heard. They really cheered—not only for us but for both teams. I'm really kind of excited everyone came out."

If only his soon-to-be teammates shared his enthusiasm.

■ ■ ■

Despite eventual talk to the contrary, the veteran members of the 1979–80 Los Angeles Lakers weren't exactly giddy over the arrival of their new point guard.

Way back in the fall of 1979, before Johnson and Larry Bird had emerged as all-time stars; before Michael Jordan was enrolled at the University of North Carolina; before LeBron James and Kevin Durant were even born, the NBA was a selfish, me-first, gotta-get-mine land of mistrust and animosity. Winning was important to some players. But, somewhere between Bill Russell's Boston Celtics heyday and the late 1970s, the well had been poisoned by greed and arrogance and a league-wide epidemic of substance abuse. "The NBA was going downhill—it was obvious," said Dennis Awtrey, a journeyman center throughout the 1970s. "There were drug things, there was a sloppiness to the game. It just wasn't good."

Wrote the *Times*'s Jim Murray in a column titled "Lakers Smile? It's Magic": "Some teams need a power forward, others need an outside shooter or someone to bring the ball up the court. The Lakers just need somebody to dispel the gloom. This is not a team, it's a wake. They go about the game as somber as a coroner's inquest."

Johnson was a happy-go-lucky kid who disregarded personal statistics and loved—*no, needed*—to win. Phrases such as "I want the ball" and "Get it to me and get out of the way" never crossed his lips. He was a pass-first, pass-second, pass-third ballplayer, and the other Lakers would have been wise to embrace him as their personal basketball savior.

Instead, as the players reported to the College of the Desert in Palm Desert, California, for training camp on September 16, Johnson was eyed warily and, in some cases, hostilely.

First, there were his blatant expressions of joy—the smiles, the laughs, the easy banter with the media. It all seemed so . . . collegiate and phony. "His personality was electric," said Kiffin, the rookie forward. "Some people don't like electricity."* NBA veterans—and, in particular, Laker veterans—didn't behave in such a manner. They were surly and offputting. The city treated them like royalty (free meals; free women; free drugs) and the Lakers walked and talked and carried themselves as such. Many of the players took their cues from Abdul-Jabbar, who would just as soon spend time

---

* In Johnson, nineteen, and Kiffin, twenty-eight, the Lakers had the league's youngest and oldest rookie training camp invitees.

chatting with fans as he would take an injection to the spine. "Once you accepted that Kareem was a prick," said Pat O'Brien, the CBS reporter, "you could get past it."

"I don't think anyone was mad at Earvin personally," said Ollie Mack, a rookie guard with the Lakers in 1979. "But he represented change, and veterans generally don't love the idea of doing things differently." Johnson made certain to greet every Laker employee by name and, on breaks, could be found lounging in front of a television with the staffers, watching *Days of Our Lives* and *General Hospital.* "He was one of the girls," said Joan McLaughlin, the director of human resources. "Gabbing about who was kissing who on TV."

There was also the issue of Norm Nixon, the third-year veteran out of Duquesne who had little interest in surrendering control of *his* team. During the 1978–79 season, he had established himself as one of the NBA's elite floor generals, averaging 17.1 points and 9 assists. Though only 6-foot-2 and 170 pounds, Nixon had legs resembling oak trees, and a first step that left opposing players grasping at air. "Boy, Norman was a tremendous player," said Robert Reid, the longtime Houston Rockets guard. "When he got hot he was like another Nate Archibald. He had a little lean-back jumper, he was sneaky. The only thing he lacked, to be honest, was charisma."

And thick skin. From the moment the Lakers drafted Johnson, most members of the team knew Nixon's days as a point guard were numbered. Sure, there were those who questioned whether a man standing 6-foot-9 could run an NBA team, whether he could survive the defensive pressure of swarming gnatlike opponents. "But then you saw Magic pass the ball, handle the ball, control an offense," said Cooper, "and there was no question where he was supposed to be. We were all looking at a man who could revolutionize a position. It was exciting." Nixon, however, didn't share the sense of wonder. Playing point guard for the Lakers seemed to be, in his mind, the equivalent of roaming center field for the New York Yankees or quarterbacking the Dallas Cowboys. He was *the* point guard, and Johnson—irksome rookie—would need to yank the position from his fingertips. "I felt like he was going to have to adjust his game to play with me," Nixon told *The New York Times.* "But I learned different."

"Jealousy is ugly," said Cooper. "And we all knew Norman was really jealous."

■ ■ ■

McKinney, the Lakers' new head coach, held his first official team meeting on a Sunday night. It took place inside a lounge on the ground floor of the Ocotillo Lodge, a Buss-owned property that served as the franchise's base of operations during training camp. Seventeen players attended, ranging from Abdul-Jabbar and Wilkes to unsung rookies like Dawan Scott and Brad Holland. Twelve would make the opening-night roster.

The room was dark, with dim lighting and maroon carpet. Alongside McKinney stood Paul Westhead, his new assistant. The players mostly sat in chairs—veterans primarily on one side, rookies and free agents on the other. As always, Abdul-Jabbar was in the front, the legs from his 7-foot-2 frame stretched out like twin giraffes. A handful of veteran post specialists (Kenny Carr, Don Ford and Dave Robisch) listened intently, knowing their careers were on the line. There were five rookies (Johnson, Kiffin, Mack, Scott and Holland, the sharpshooter out of UCLA) as well as a pair of second-year guards (Cooper and Ron Carter) thought to be fighting for a single spot. Abdul-Jabbar, Nixon and Wilkes were the mainstays.

McKinney wasted little time distancing himself from the high-stress, high-tension Jerry West. He spoke little of team rules and regulations, instead insisting that the Lakers would run the hell out of the rest of the league. The offensive system was a symphony: When the basketball came off the glass, one guard would immediately break for the foul line for the outlet, while the other guard slashed to mid-court. "His offensive ideas were genius," said Ron Carter. "Little dribbling, lots of passing, lots of speed."

The next morning, at nine o'clock, the new-look Los Angeles Lakers took the court for the first time. There was casual banter followed by casual stretching led by Jack Curran, the team's crusty forty-six-year-old trainer. Westhead lined the players up on a baseline and began the wind sprints— dash to one end of the court, touch the floor, dash back, dash again, dash back. Most of the veterans ran on cruise control. "Hard," said Cooper, "but not super hard." Then it was Johnson's turn. When Westhead blew the whistle, the rookie burst across the court, his long arms and longer legs blurring like a greyhound in motion. Though built like a World Wrestling Federation competitor, Johnson was shockingly fast. He moved as a sprinter, with an upright running motion similar to that of Houston McTear, the star American 100-meter runner. He left his peers in his wake, crossed the baseline and immediately popped back to run another. Some Lakers were impressed. Some were incredulous. Most were irked. "I could see right off that my intensity was very different from the cool, laid-back style of the NBA," Johnson later wrote. "Most professional athletes try to conserve their energy, especially before the season begins. My teammates were shocked."

Nixon, in particular, didn't know how to deal. Until Johnson's arrival, he was the fastest man on the roster. Were there a sprint, Norm Nixon was finishing first. "Raw speed," said Ron Carter, a Laker guard. "Norm was just super fast. No one could beat him or get the better of him. Until Earvin got to town."

Once practice officially began, the Magic Johnson Show kicked into high gear. Johnson dove for loose balls, soared for rebounds, boxed out bigger players and recklessly tossed elbows. When Nixon told him to cool it, the rookie talked trash right back. "Don't be intimidated by a kid," he barked. "Don't be intimidated. . . ." In particular, Nixon seemed to resent the way Johnson took the offense into his own hands. McKinney wanted the rebounder to immediately turn and pass up the court. When Johnson grabbed a ball off the boards, however, he dribbled. "Norm would flash across the middle and Magic would ignore him," said Carter. "Norm would get very agitated, and there was this undercurrent with Magic not following the rules."

Johnson's most striking attribute wasn't the effort. No, it was the passing. Nixon was a precise ball distributor. His passes were crisp and, with rare exception, on point. "We all knew Norm would get us the ball," said Wilkes, the veteran forward. "He was terrific. But when Magic came along, from day one, it was just— Wow!"

Actually, it wasn't *Wow!* It was *Pop!* Within ten minutes of the Lakers' first five-on-five scrimmage, Johnson was popping teammates upside the head with impossible-to-anticipate passes that seemed to curve and bend around the bodies of unsuspecting opponents. "The thing about a 6-foot-9 point guard is his ability to see above a defense," said Wilkes. "It was remarkable. I remember running my routes in those early practices. He threw me this pass—just spectacular—that I didn't see. I mean, I wasn't open, and nobody in his right mind would think I was open. But Earvin saw it, and the ball just thumped me right in the head. Pow!"

McKinney stopped practice and told Johnson that a pass was useless if the recipient couldn't see it coming. Johnson nodded, said he understood, agreed—"Then practice began," said Wilkes, "and the first pass he threw me was this wicked no-looker between defenders that nailed me in the head again. I got the point. 'You be ready for my passes, or else you won't get them.' Jack wanted Magic to adjust to us but, truthfully, *we* all needed to adjust to *him*."

One player in particular had little interest in any of the Magic hoopla. Ron Boone, an eleventh-year swingman fighting to make the team, had seen this sort of nonsense before, and he had no stomach for it. A one-time eleventh-round draft pick out of Idaho State, Boone had spent his entire career in the shadows of pretty boys and golden children. "Boone was a tough, crafty guy," said Michael Cooper. "He'd been around the block." During a particularly heated practice, Boone intentionally smacked Johnson in the back of his head with a forearm while fighting for a rebound. Johnson glared at Boone. "You better know," he said, "I'm going to get you back."

"Keep moving, rookie," Boone replied. "You're not going to do anything."

Johnson turned and punched Boone in the neck. Boone fell to the ground. "Don't you ever do that shit to me again!" the rookie screamed, as Boone charged toward him. McKinney ejected both men from practice, and as he walked toward the locker room, Johnson scanned the court and hollered, "I might be a rookie, but none of you guys are gonna punk me!" Boone uttered nary another word. His days with the team were numbered.

"Ron had averaged a lot of points [with Utah] in the ABA, and he thought he was something special," said Cooper. "Magic went to work on him—hard."

"Just knocked Ron Boone on his ass," said Lon Rosen, an intern with the team. "Earvin was respectful, but he did not take anything."*

Sharman, the general manager, particularly appreciated Johnson's intensity. The 47-win 1978–79 season had been a disappointing one, and the franchise was determined not to waste Johnson's arrival by pairing him with riffraff. With the league adding a three-point line for the first time, Sharman used the number fourteen pick in the draft on Holland, a 6-foot-3 dead-eye shooter who had averaged 17.5 points as a senior at UCLA. "Brad," Sharman raved, "was maybe the best outside shooter in collegiate history." In the off-season's most highly publicized trade, the Lakers and Utah Jazz swapped forwards, with twenty-three-year-old Adrian Dantley

---

* Boone was contacted for this book, and spoke at length. He was gregarious. However, when asked about the fight, he said, pointedly, "I don't wish to go there."

heading to Salt Lake City in exchange for Spencer Haywood, a thirty-year-old veteran.

Throughout the previous season, the Lakers had been burdened by teaming Abdul-Jabbar in the frontcourt with a pair of men (the 6-foot-5 Dantley and the 6-foot-6 Wilkes) both better suited for the small forward slot. At 6-foot-8 and 225 pounds, Haywood was *all* power forward. His arms were muscular, his torso was Herculean, his leaping ability off the charts. Nine years earlier, in 1970, he gained his first dose of national fame by launching an antitrust suit against the NBA in order to join the Seattle SuperSonics. Haywood, just twenty-one at the time, had jumped to ABA's Denver Rockets after his sophomore season at the University of Detroit but was banned from the NBA because of the league's eligibility rules. The case reached the U.S. Supreme Court before the NBA agreed to a settlement, and Haywood spent much of his time in Seattle being booed and heckled in opposing arenas. "It wasn't always fun," he said. "But it built character."

NBA owners detested Haywood. NBA fans detested Haywood. NBA executives detested Haywood. NBA players, however, generally loved the man. "Everyone called Spencer 'Woody,'" said Tom Nissalke, his coach with the Sonics. "He could run, he could jump, he was a good shooter. When he drove to the basket, it was like watching the parting of the Red Sea. And he mostly did it with a smile." After scoring 30 points per game as a rookie with Denver, he averaged at least 20 in five years in Seattle. Though Haywood's production gradually tailed off with the Knicks and Jazz, Los Angeles thought he would fit perfectly. Haywood played thirty-four games for the New Orleans Jazz in 1978–79, but when the franchise announced its relocation to Salt Lake City, he balked. "I just flat-out refused to report to camp," he said. "New Orleans is a great town. Just great. But back in the 1970s, no brother wanted to go to Salt Lake."

Around the same time Dantley learned of his banishment, Haywood was sitting in a dentist's chair, still woozy from anesthesia. The phone in the office rang, and Sharman was on the line. When the words *Welcome to the Los Angeles Lakers* entered his ear, Haywood assumed it was merely the gas playing tricks on his hearing.

"It's like a dream situation for me," he later said. "Here I am for the first time in my career with a bona fide, official team. I've been trying to get to L.A. for nine years.

"My role is going to be to assert some leadership and do some strong rebounding. I'll be the guy to get that second effort off the offensive boards. I'll be a garbage and muscle man, too."

Haywood reported to the Ocotillo Lodge two days later. Instead of languishing in Mormon Central, he was surrounded by familiar veterans and a spectacular rookie point guard. "Magic was just a kid, but his enthusiasm got to me from the start," Haywood said. "I don't care if others were turned off—I thought it was great. Magic made every practice a game, every workout a game, every drill a game. When you're in the league a while, and when you've become a little complacent, you need a wake-up call sometimes.

"Magic Johnson was our wake-up call."

CHAPTER 4

CENTER OF COMPLICATIONS

Not that Kareem Abdul-Jabbar wanted a wake-up call.

Or even an alarm to ring.

Now entering his eleventh NBA season, the Lakers' star greeted Magic Johnson's arrival with neither derision nor euphoria nor so much as a shrug. To Abdul-Jabbar, the rookie was merely the latest heavily hyped addition to a team that always seemed to be acquiring heavily hyped additions.

No matter whether Johnson soared or stumbled, the thirty-two-year-old knew he would, as always, be getting *his*. Abdul-Jabbar had averaged 23.8 points and 12.8 rebounds per game in 1978–79, and led the NBA with 316 blocked shots. His go-to offensive weapon, the deadly skyhook, was virtually unblockable, and rivals near and far agreed he was, along with the retired George Mikan, Bill Russell and Wilt Chamberlain, one of the four greatest forces the sport had ever seen. Abdul-Jabbar had already won five MVP awards, making him one of two men to capture that many (the other was Boston's Russell). "He was an absolute pain to play against," said Rich Kelley, a longtime center with the Phoenix Suns. "He wouldn't physically beat you down or talk a lot of trash. But at the end of every night you'd look up and see he hung 22 [points] and 12 [rebounds] on you. And he made it look easy."

"Kareem Abdul-Jabbar is the greatest basketball player I ever saw," said Dave Robisch, his backup in Los Angeles in 1977 and '78. "I saw Oscar Robertson, I saw Jerry West, I saw lots of legends. But Kareem was on his own level."

As Johnson spent his time in Palm Desert bounding around like a new puppy, Abdul-Jabbar went about his routine. Every year, Lakers veterans were allowed to "adopt" a rookie during camp, so Kareem paired with Magic. Instead of demanding he sing the Michigan State fight song or act out scenes from *What's Happening!!*, Johnson merely had to fetch Abdul-Jabbar the morning *New York Times*, as well as a glass of freshly squeezed orange juice. "I think Kareem was happy to have Earvin on the team," said Paul Westhead, the assistant coach. "But did he make a fuss about it? Certainly not."

What Abdul-Jabbar could not possibly grasp, though, was that there would be a direct correlation between Johnson's rapid rise to stardom and his own dour disposition. For all his greatness as a player, Abdul-Jabbar failed to understand that carrying a team and inspiring a fan base involved more than mere statistics.

It meant being nice to people.

Theoretically, Abdul-Jabbar could be. Behind closed doors, when the spirit struck, stories abound of his sharp sense of humor and keen satirical insights. He was the one who, during a training camp meal at Benihana in 1979, taught an undrafted rookie named Irv Kiffin how to use chopsticks, and who sent the son of teammate Ron Boone autographed goggles for his birthday. In the early 1980s, a pair of Laker reserves, Mike McGee and Larry Spriggs, arrived at the Forum in identical purple shirts. McGee, a 6-foot-5, 190-pound guard, wore an extra large. Spriggs, a 6-foot-7, 230-pound hulk, wore a XXXL. Alone in the locker room during warmups, Abdul-Jabbar snuck into the stalls of both men and swapped shirts. "I walk in after the game and Cap [all Lakers referred to Abdul-Jabbar as Cap—short for his status as the team's captain] is laughing his ass off," said Spriggs. "I'm thinking, 'What's up with this guy?' So I start putting my shirt on, and it's brand-new, and I can't figure out why it's so damn tight. And Geet's shirt [McGee's nickname was Geeter] is hanging off of him. Cap can't control himself— laughing like it's the funniest thing on earth."

Another time, Michael Cooper offered Johnson one hundred dollars to sneak up in the locker room and swat the *Los Angeles Times* sports section out of Abdul-Jabbar's hand. He did so, and the center guaranteed revenge. "I'm gonna get you, Coop," he said. "I'm gonna get you." A few weeks later, while Cooper was sleeping on a Northwest Airlines flight from Detroit, Abdul-Jabbar tiptoed up to his seat and placed a dollop of Nair atop his miniature Afro. "All of a sudden Coop wakes up, screaming from the burn," said Gary Vitti, the Lakers' trainer. "His head is burning, and he has a nickel-size hole in his hair, where he was bald. Kareem just sat there, chuckling. 'Heh, heh, heh.'"

In public, however, Abdul-Jabbar was the darkest of dark clouds, moody and aloof and, in the opinions of many, unjustifiably arrogant and dismissive. "He developed the habit of not looking at you," said Claire Rothman. "He'd talk to you but look over here. I've always thought he had the idea that if he didn't look at you, you didn't see him." Many fans are of the belief that, in exchange for excessive ticket prices and ceaseless adulation, athletes owe the public a bit of gratitude. Abdul-Jabbar did not. He was, as author Jackie Lapin once wrote, "a Gulliver in a world of Lilliputians," nearly as famous for rebuffing requests as he was for leading UCLA to three national titles. Endless were the stories of his airport antics; of hiding in bathroom stalls with a book (When he wasn't on a basketball court, Abdul-Jabbar was almost always reading); of telling young boys and elderly ladies and priests and nuns and rabbis and military veterans that, no, he wouldn't write his name on a scrap of paper.

"Some little kid would ask for an autograph and he'd say, 'Go fuck yourself,' said Linda Rambis, who worked as the vice president and general manager of Forum tennis during the early 1980s. "But Kareem was, otherwise, an incredible professional."

"I remember one time standing next to Kareem by the urinals inside an airport bathroom," said Brad Holland, a Laker guard. "I mean, literally, Kareem is peeing, and someone is standing there asking for an autograph. And he's supposed to be nice to everyone? It was hard, I'm sure."

"Sometimes he wouldn't even answer—just ignored the person," said Tony Campbell, a future teammate. "I liked Kareem, but I had a real problem with that."

"I was with Kareem in Salt Lake City once," said Josh Rosenfeld, the team's longtime media relations director. "We were walking across the street to the basketball arena, and a man stops his car and jumps out. His wife is in the passenger's seat, and they have a new baby with them. The man is thrilled, and he says, 'Kareem, this is the greatest day of my life! I just picked up my first son from the hospital and I'm taking him home, and now I meet my all-time favorite player. Would you mind signing an autograph for my son?'

"Kareem blows the guy off. Just blows him off completely. And the guy turns around and screams, 'Hey, Kareem, fuck you!' And Kareem looks at me with a smile and says, 'I'm glad I didn't sign for that particular gentleman.'"

With Johnson's arrival, it was as if Los Angeles fans were handed 3-D glasses and all of Abdul-Jabbar's flaws could be seen in vivid detail. What many failed to understand (or, perhaps, cared to understand) was that moodiness and anger aren't mere entities, created in utero.

No, they must be cultivated over time.

■ ■ ■

Kareem Abdul-Jabbar hated white people.

Read that sentence again.

And again.

And again.

Kareem Abdul-Jabbar hated white people and, quite frankly, why wouldn't he have? Born on April 16, 1947, in New York City, he was named Ferdinand Lewis Alcindor Jr. by his parents—Cora Lillian, a department store price checker, and Ferdinand Lewis Alcindor Sr., a transit police officer and jazz trombonist who graduated from the Juilliard School of music and later played with Art Blakey and Yusef Lateef. Lewis entered the world weighing twelve pounds, ten ounces and measuring twenty-two and a half inches long—signs that America had received its latest future beanstalk.

Growing up in Harlem's Dyckman housing complex, Lewis became increasingly aware that life for black Americans was painfully confounding. In his autobiography, *Giant Steps*, he recalled a boyhood trip with his mother to Associated, the neighborhood grocery store. "The store manager decided we were dangerous customers, or maybe he just felt like wielding a little power that day," he wrote. "He intercepted my mother and told her to check her bag up front. The store was full of people with all sorts of baggage, but he was going to make us the example. My mother took this for what it was, another in a lifetime of petty harassments, and told the man that if he had to satisfy himself that she was no thief, he could inspect the package when she left."

Lew Alcindor was not merely black. He was tall and black and painfully aware of the stares and the glares and the suspicious looks and the inevitable sight of store employees tracking his whereabouts. His first best friend was a white child named John. They were classmates at St. Jude's parish elementary school who bonded over model airplanes and funny jokes. By seventh grade, however, an unspoken racial tension divided the two. One day, during lunch, John and Lew wound up in the principal's office after a scuffle. As Alcindor left, he heard someone yelling at him. "Hey, nigger! Hey, jungle bunny! You big jungle nigger!"

It was John. "Fuck you, you . . . milk bottle," Alcindor responded.

"It was the only white thing I could think of," he later wrote. "It really pissed him off, but he didn't come anywhere near me. We never spoke again."

Because he appeared freakishly tall and thin, Alcindor was routinely presumed to be a dominant basketball star. Yet his athleticism required time to catch up with his stature. In other words, Alcindor's skills were laughable. "At ten or eleven my father recognized that I was going to be taller than normal," he once said, "so he refused to allow me to play football." He was a member of the St. Jude's basketball team in fifth and sixth grades, but served—in his words—as "comic relief." He could neither dribble nor shoot, and in practices, smaller, slower kids shoved him aside for rebounds. He finally began to develop in seventh grade—the year he first picked uniform number 33 in honor of his athletic hero, New York Giants fullback Mel Triplett. His first-ever dunk came a year later. "The whole place went crazy," he wrote. "I was bouncing up and down, ready to go for some more. Give me the ball!"

Based largely upon his height, high schools started recruiting Alcindor in seventh grade. He was 6-foot-5, with the wingspan of a pterodactyl.* The Alcindors were particularly impressed with Jack Donohue, the head coach at Power Memorial Academy, an all-boys Catholic high school located above midtown on 61st Street and Amsterdam Avenue. The admiration was mutual. "I first saw him in our gym at Power," Donohue recalled. "I had gone over to watch a CYO game. Somebody had touted me on some other kid. One of the brothers said there was a boy playing out there that was 6-foot-7. He was lanky and awkward and very uncoordinated. He was weak physically. But, then again, how can you compare

---

* Few people have ever grown like Alcindor. He left the seventh grade standing 6-foot-3, grew two inches by September and, by the end of eighth grade, was 6-foot-8. One year later, he was 6-foot-10½.

a 6-foot-7 kid to anyone else? You don't see too many 6-foot-7 kids in grammar school."

Alcindor graduated junior high in the summer of 1961, and found himself growing apart from white friends. "They made it extremely clear . . . that I wasn't at home in their crowd," he wrote. He arrived at Power Memorial that fall, uninspired by the heavy-handed Catholic doctrine. Inside his new school, Jesus was white and Pope John XXIII was infallible and masturbation could result in an eternity of blindness alongside the devil. There was one lecture after another, mostly warning the students that they were sinners who needed to repent.

For a young man who absorbed books (he was addicted to Greek tragedies) and questioned doctrine, it was torturous.

Until basketball started.

His first game, a matchup with Brooklyn's Erasmus Hall High, was horrible. Charlie Donovan, Erasmus's All-City guard, repeatedly drove over and around Alcindor, making him appear more fourth grader than high school freshman. Afterward, Alcindor retreated to the locker room and sobbed. The next game, a scrimmage against Lincoln High School and a seven-foot center named Dave Newmark, was equally humiliating. After it ended, Donohue approached his distraught freshman. "I hope you're learning what it's all about to really want to win," he said.

Before long, Alcindor was passable. Then decent. Then magnificent. "He was fifteen when he matured," Donohue said. "He seemed to develop overnight into a basketball player. He didn't work at it that much, either. He was active in all sports. He played a lot of handball, was a very good softball player and did a lot of swimming. He also loved to run. He'd always take an extra lap on the track."* Alcindor would study games that featured Bill Russell, the Celtics center. He paid special attention to the way he helped on defense and mastered the pinpoint outlet pass. It was also during the Power Memorial era that Alcindor tapped into what would go down as, arguably, the most indomitable shot in basketball history—the skyhook.

---

* Just how good an athlete was Alcindor? In grade school he longed for a new pair of ice skates. One of the local newspapers announced that it was sponsoring a speed-skating contest, with all semifinalists winning a new pair of skates. Having never before speed skated, young Lew practiced intensively, won his races and snagged the skates. He didn't even bother competing in the championship round.

The idea, he wrote in his autobiography, came to him during an elementary school contest years earlier:

One day I stumbled upon a strange and delightful experience, kind of like that exciting yet amazingly unexpected feeling you get when you know, quite definitely, that you've entered puberty. In the first half, I was in the game, which was already unusual, and a rebound fell my way right by the basket. I fumbled with it, trying to conquer the dribble, and it almost got away. Finally, with a guy from the other team at my back, I looked over my shoulder, saw the basket, turned into the lane, and with one hand put up my first hook shot. It missed. Hit the back rim and bounced out. But it felt right, and the next time I got the ball I tried it again. Neither of them went in, but I had found my shot. At halftime my teammates, surprised that I had showed some coordination, encouraged me to practice it, and from then on, whenever I got into play I would shoot it. Nobody showed me how, it came naturally.

Now, at Power Memorial, the skyhook evolved into far more than a funky experiment. It was unstoppable. That's neither hyperbole nor gross exaggeration. When Lew Alcindor, 6-foot-10 as a high school junior and 6-foot-11 as a high school senior, planted in the lane, accepted the feed, turned, extended his arm into the air and deftly released the basketball, no one was touching it. Certainly no one with pimples and braces. At age sixteen, Alcindor appeared on *The Ed Sullivan Show* and was featured in *Sports Illustrated*. As a junior he averaged 26 points per game. As a senior, that jumped to 33 points per game—tops in New York City. "His hand-eye coordination was just amazing," said Danny Nee, a Power Memorial teammate. "Lew would have been a good baseball player, a good swimmer. Everything looked so smooth and fluid. It was art."

With its center leading the way, Power Memorial emerged as New York City's basketball juggernaut. "We were a pretty good team without him," said Art Kenney, a teammate, "but a great team with him." In Alcindor's four varsity seasons, the Panthers lost but six games—five during his freshman year, and one, to Washington, DC's DeMatha Catholic High inside the University of Maryland's field house, when he was a senior. They went 71 straight games without a defeat, which remains a Big Apple record. In short,

Power Memorial was one of the most dominant teams in the history of the prep game.

And yet . . .

The fame and fanfare lavished upon Alcindor exacted a price. He was now, officially, a freak—a black museum exhibit to be gawked at and, often, ridiculed. "People stare," he said. "You can walk into a room and people look. They don't have to say anything. You know what they're thinking." In the 1960s, New York City oozed basketball. It was the sport to behold, and whether one was in high school or college or playing inside Madison Square Garden for the Knicks, stardom was accompanied by a blinding light. Wherever Alcindor went, and whatever he did, the masses followed. He was easily identifiable and easily annoyed. A woman once jabbed him with the tip of her umbrella, just to see if he was real. Donohue, his coach, decided the media would be allowed minimal access, a move that heightened Alcindor's suspicions and paranoia. "You want to see Lew Alcindor?" Donohue told inquisitors. "Well, you have to see me instead."

Members of the sports media—exclusively male, exclusively white—revolted. "On the surface," wrote Gerald Eskenazi in *The New York Times*, "it appears that Donohue exerts a Svengali-like influence." Who did this kid think he was? What sort of uppity behavior was this? "Had Alcindor been exposed to those 'prying' reporters we kept hearing about . . . Lew Alcindor might have learned a bit of the give-and-take of such sessions that tend to mirror life," wrote Arnold Hano in an angry *Sport* magazine profile. "He would have been considered less a freak and more a person, more a usual person. . . . But he was not permitted, and today he is ill at ease, terribly sober, and a bit pompous himself."

What men like Hano failed to grasp was that Lew Alcindor knew the admiration extended to him as a basketball player was exclusively about his skills on the court. Otherwise, he was, to many, a nigger. *Shut up, shoot the ball, mind your business.*

This was painfully apparent during his days at Power Memorial. The school employed a single black teacher, and Alcindor became used to the offhanded insults from authority figures. A white religious instructor, Brother D'Adamo, once told him in class that "black people want too much, too soon." A classmate, Joseph Traum, nicknamed him Schwartz, which Alcindor found puzzling until he realized *schwartze* (the word actually being used) was the German equivalent of *nigger*.

The cruelest cut came during Alcindor's junior year. Power Memorial was struggling at home against St. Helena's, a Bronx Catholic school with a mediocre team. Donohue, a coach prone to outbursts, was furious. As the players sat in their locker room for halftime, he looked directly at Alcindor. "And you!" he screamed. "You go out there and you don't hustle. You don't move. You don't do any of the things you're supposed to do. You're acting just like a nigger!"

The word cut through Lew Alcindor. Here was a white man he had trusted and almost loved. Alcindor came to Power Memorial because the coach seemed to be fair and open minded. Through the years, they had engaged in countless discussions on societal transformations and how they often occur at a snail's pace. Donohue worked hard to shield Alcindor from the spotlight, to protect him. "The toughest job was to treat him the same as all the other kids," Donohue said. "I couldn't treat him as if he were special. It wouldn't have been good for him."

And now, Donohue nailed Alcindor with the most disgusting of slurs.

When the game concluded with yet another Power Memorial triumph, Donohue called Alcindor into his office. The coach recognized he had crossed the uncrossable line. He knew it, his player knew it. And yet—"See, it worked!" he said. "My strategy worked. I knew that if I used that word, it'd shock you into a good second half. And it did."

Alcindor never trusted his coach again.

■ ■ ■

As hundreds upon hundreds of colleges recruited Lew Alcindor out of high school, there was a widespread belief that he would stay in New York and play for St. John's. Yet Alcindor, now 6-foot-11 and 230 pounds, had no interest in furthering his Catholic education. He also had been urged to check out Holy Cross College, where Donohue was recently named head coach. Alcindor made an obligatory trip, but merely for show. Furthermore, when he spoke with one of Holy Cross's few black students, a firm warning was issued. "This is the worst place to go to school," he was told. "You'll be isolated, like I am. Man, pick someplace else."

In the winter of 1965, Alcindor took his visit to UCLA, arriving in Los Angeles via TWA Flight 11 from John F. Kennedy Airport. This was the best high school player in the country connecting with the best college program in the country. Across the nation, the trip was reported with presidential seriousness. According to Joel E. Boxer, a California-based journalist, Alcindor enjoyed an in-flight meal of filet mignon and mashed potatoes. He watched the film *Dear Brigitte*, starring Brigitte Bardot, and had one conversation—a flight attendant named Karen Therkelsen asked a single question: "Who are you?"

At 7:13 P.M., Alcindor was greeted at the gate by Jerry Norman, an assistant coach with the Bruins who had been nervously pacing the terminal, hoping the country's greatest basketball talent was actually on the flight.

When he woke up the next morning, following a blissful night of sleep in the guest suite of UCLA's Rieber Hall, the recruit felt renewed and optimistic. He opened the front door to find a large bowl of fruit at his feet, and shortly thereafter, Mike Warren, one of the Bruins stars, offered a campus tour. Sure, to an eighteen-year-old Lew Alcindor, Los Angeles was the land of 80-degree days and movie stars. And sure, the Bruins had just won a second-straight national championship, playing before thirteen thousand screaming fans.

But, most important, Los Angeles symbolized open-mindedness. It was a place, in his eyes, where ideas were expressed freely and oppression was frowned upon. Alcindor was especially impressed by John Wooden, the Bruins' well-regarded head coach. When they met for the first time, Wooden spoke some about basketball, but more about academics. "I am impressed by your grades," he told Alcindor. "You could do very well here as a student, whether you were an athlete or not. We work very hard to have our boys get through and earn their degrees."

Alcindor was sold.

Back in 1965, first-year students could not play on the college varsity. Alcindor, therefore, was placed on UCLA's freshman team. On one of his first days, he and three fellow freshmen defeated four returning varsity players (all of whom had just won a national title) in three straight full-court games to 15 points. Shortly thereafter, on November 27, 1965, in a matchup witnessed by a packed Pauley crowd, the freshmen played the varsity in a real game—and dominated by 15. Alcindor totaled 31 points and 21 rebounds. "The varsity had no one able to guard me in close," he wrote, "so they had to sag their defense to prevent me from getting the ball. When they did not get there quickly enough, I scored."

"Everyone walked away from that game thinking, 'What are we going to do with this guy?'" said Bill Bertka, a Laker scout at the time. "He was such a force."

Basketball-wise, Alcindor's freshman year was dull. The baby Bruins won all 21 of their games and never traveled farther than San Diego. And yet, it was a period of great self-discovery and extended contemplation about race and oppression. If Alcindor arrived in Los Angeles with particular misgivings about Caucasians, they were only magnified through increased study. Wooden, as open-minded a white man as Alcindor had ever met, embraced his young future star—but with certain limitations. "There was warm, mutual respect," Abdul-Jabbar later said. "But because I was black, there was never this father-son thing. He couldn't put his arm around my waist and introduce me as his boy."

Alcindor began forgoing standard collegiate attire for caftans, dashikis and djellabas—Afrocentric garb ordered from Ashanti Fashions, located in the center of Harlem. An article with the headline FIENDISH IN THE VALLEY WITH LEW ALCINDOR AT THE LATTER'S SMALL BUNGALOW IN ENCINO appeared in *West Magazine* (a *Los Angeles Times* supplement), and portrayed him as an America-loathing racist bent on separatism. Asked to assess backup center Steve Patterson, Alcindor snapped, "A white boy from Santa Maria. That's all."

Alcindor expressed immediate regret for the piece, and teammates seemed to forgive. This was a young man struggling to understand himself.

Over the course of the next three years, Alcindor became one of the great players in the history of college basketball. The Bruins went 88-2, completing each March with yet another national championship. He was twice named the NCAA's Player of the Year and made three straight All-American teams. Following the 1967 season, when UCLA went 30-0, the NCAA banned dunking—a direct nod to the 7-foot-1¾ Alcindor's unparalleled dominance ("Frankly, this new rule doesn't affect Alcindor," John Nucatola, director of the Eastern College Athletic Conference, said with a shockingly straight face). In three years he averaged 26.4 points and 15.5 rebounds. "We tried to front him, hoping his teammates would have to lob him the ball," Dave Scholz, Illinois's star guard, said after a blowout loss to the Bruins in 1967. "But you just can't defense Lew. It's impossible."

As he dominated on the court, Alcindor turned increasingly divisive off of it. This was hardly the case of a man seeking out trouble. But with media scrutiny came exposure. With exposure came truth. With truth came scorn.

Alcindor emerged as a symbol—along with the likes of Muhammad Ali, Jim Brown, Tommie Smith and Juan Carlos—of the black athlete no longer merely willing to go along just to get along. He would play your sport and dribble your ball and accept your cheers. But he refused to be a pawn. On November 23, 1967, Alcindor was one of 120 attendees (and 65 collegiate athletes) at the Western Black Youth Conference, a meeting held inside the Second Baptist Church on the east side of Los Angeles. The matter at hand: Determine whether black athletes would compete in the upcoming Mexico City Olympic Games.

White media members tagged the gathering "radical," and they were correct. Harry Edwards, a twenty-four-year-old professor at San Jose State and the movement's leader, stood before the room and spoke his mind. "We've been put in the position of asking the whites for everything," he said to an ocean of nodding heads. "We're not asking anymore, we're demanding. We're fanatical about our rights. We've been put in the position of taking our case to the criminal. The U.S. government is the criminal."

Midway through the session, Alcindor reportedly rose. "I was born in a racist country," he said. "I laid my life on the line when I was born. I don't have anything to lose."

Alcindor boycotted, as did UCLA teammates Mike Warren and Lucius Allen. When they declined to participate in tryouts for the U.S. Olympic basketball team, J. D. Morgan, UCLA's athletic director, told *Sports Illustrated* the decision was based upon academics—a lie. The real reason was Alcindor's discontentment with the racial situation in America. "Kareem gets along OK with white guys, but you have to be a brother to get next to him," said Sidney Wicks, a UCLA teammate. "He still resents the white hypocrites more than ever—the people who say one thing to your face and quite another behind your back."

It was in August of 1968 that Alcindor made a bold shift, leaving Catholicism (which, to the dismay of his churchgoing parents, he believed to be racist in dogma) and making a confession of faith toward the orthodox Hanafi sect of Islam. He shaved all the hair from his body, took his Shahadah (a declaration of faith—*La illaha ila Allah wa Muhammadun rasoolollah*—that must be pronounced before a witness for one to be initiated as a Muslim) and, in his mind, began life anew. The move hardly surprised Alcindor's friends, who knew of his interest in the writings and philosophies of the late

Malcolm X. What did surprise them, however, was when he received a new name—Kareem Abdul-Jabbar (meaning *noble, powerful servant*).*

So yes, at this point in his life, he hated white people. *Hated them.* But with a catch—not individually. Though he rarely befriended whites, he was open to discussions. His spiritual guide, a former Malcolm X disciple named Hamaas Abdul-Khaalis, asked Abdul-Jabbar to look beyond skin color and understand that there were plenty of black sinners, too. Abdul-Khaalis referred to Malcolm X's famous pilgrimage to Mecca, when a militant, anti-white religious leader came to see that race—while important—wasn't the sole factor in understanding another human being.

"I had a very firm grasp of the concepts I didn't like—white authority, unbending rules, false-faced people—but was much less certain where to draw the line in real life," Abdul-Jabbar wrote. "I was wary, and angry, that I had to examine everybody I came in contact with—sort of an emotional frisking—because every touch could be a slap. All my reservations became conscious, each chance meeting with a stranger and every introduction by a friend became a potential source of pain. I read all gestures intensively, and terribly often found them racially hurtful, therefore personally unacceptable. People who tried too hard to be friendly were being patronizing racists; people who didn't try hard enough were blatant racists. People I didn't know weren't worth knowing; people I did know had to watch their step."

Abdul-Jabbar was still, to the world, Lew Alcindor when, on April 7, 1969, the second-year Milwaukee Bucks called his name with the first pick of the NBA Draft. For a young, socially conscious man who had spent his entire existence on the coasts, this was a blow. Milwaukee was a conservative Midwest town with little nightlife or excitement or open-mindedness. It wasn't Selma, Alabama, or Columbia, Mississippi. But the city was a long way from New York and Los Angeles.

Meanwhile, he was also drafted by the New York Nets of the third-year American Basketball Association. This presented an enticing option. "The Nets . . . were in real pursuit," he wrote, "and all things being equal, I would have been more than happy to play for them. The ABA was a new league,

---

* He did not officially change his name until the spring of 1971. "I waited until I knew this is how I wanted to be," he told *Sports Illustrated*. "And when the time came, I would just change my name and let the world know. Before it was no secret. But people just ignored the fact."

without the tradition and composure of the NBA, but I was no great fan of tradition and composure."

Abdul-Jabbar wanted to sign with the Nets. He expected to sign with the Nets. However, when the ABA offer was dwarfed by Milwaukee's, he had little choice. He agreed to a five-year, $1.4 million deal—then impressed his new employers by not flinching when George Mikan, the ABA's commissioner, upped his league's bid to an unheard-of $3.25 million. "This is not the way to do business," Abdul-Jabbar said. "I gave my word. I would not want to welsh on them."

Kareem Abdul-Jabbar and Milwaukee were an odd pairing. Milwaukee was a Christian town, with a couple of Jews sprinkled in. Abdul-Jabbar was Muslim. Abdul-Jabbar, as per the orthodoxy of his religion, didn't drink. In Milwaukee, beer capital of the universe, *all people did* was drink. Growing up in Harlem, at the knee of a musician, Abdul-Jabbar was a jazz fanatic. His record collection numbered in the hundreds, and he loved sitting in the back of a club, nodding his head to the groove. In Milwaukee, there was polka. Having just spent four years in Southern California, Abdul-Jabbar was all about short sleeves and comfort. In Milwaukee, October already felt like winter. "I wasn't," he wrote, "the happiest guy to be there."

And yet, Milwaukee embraced Abdul-Jabbar. Granted, he didn't immediately get around to telling folks about his name change. Or, for that matter, his mistrust of white people. But on his first day of rookie training camp, Abdul-Jabbar walked onto the court to a three-minute standing ovation, and the love fest lasted all season. Abdul-Jabbar was the runaway 1969–70 NBA Rookie of the Year, averaging 28.8 points and 14.5 rebounds per game while helping the Bucks finish 56-26 (the team lost to the Knicks in the Eastern Conference Finals). "He was not only great, he was as great as anyone could be," said Jon McGlocklin, an All-Star guard. "We regularly ran plays through him, and there was very little the opposing team could do about it. There are other excellent centers. But there's only one Kareem."

Throughout his six years in Milwaukee, the Bucks emerged as an elite team behind their elite center. They won the 1971 NBA title, powered by Abdul-Jabbar and the iconic Oscar Robertson, who had been acquired that off-season. Yet teammates from the era recall an uncomfortable man whose on-court electricity was coupled with off-court darkness. "It was very tough for him to adjust to the culture of the city," said McGlocklin. "He was walled off, and sometimes not especially approachable. But I think it's important to understand what a person has been through."

Abdul-Jabbar had an especially difficult time with the media. If the general assessments of his game were glowing, the assessments of his persona were brutal. Early in his rookie year, the Bucks came to Detroit, and Abdul-Jabbar was forced to conduct his fourth press conference of the week. He was tired and irritable and rightly irked by the all-white media corps harping on his height and religious leanings. He answered many questions with one or two words, and kept his hands buried in his pockets. This was apparently the equivalent of murdering young invalids to the *Sporting News*'s Joe Falls, whose column gutted the rookie:

> I met Alcindor for the first time when he came to Detroit with the Milwaukee Bucks to play a game against the Pistons. Alcindor is supposed to stand 7-1⅜ inches, but I can tell you he is much smaller than that. In fact, he is one of the smallest men I have ever met.
>
> . . . They brought the big guy into a press conference at a downtown hotel after the Bucks had arrived in town by plane. It would have been better for all concerned—including Alcindor—if he had gone straight to his room and not talked to anybody. Never have I seen such a discourteous display put on by an athlete in any sport.
>
> . . . None of us was there to go into his racial or religious beliefs. We didn't have the time or the space . . . or the inclination. We went there to see him because he is a great basketball player . . . to treat him as a great basketball player.
>
> . . . When he tells us, the media, that he isn't interested in us, he is also telling you, the public, that he isn't interested in you. Once more that's his prerogative. I just think you ought to know it, that's all.

If it took Abdul-Jabbar little time to realize Milwaukee wasn't for him, he knew, for certain, he wanted to make a change in the early days of 1973, when his life—already dizzying—was toppled upside down. On January 18, two adults and five children were murdered by the Black Muslims in a Washington, DC, house owned by Abdul-Jabbar. The home was being used as a Muslim headquarters, and the killings were tied to a feud among members of the Hanifi sect.

Abdul-Jabbar had nothing to do with the tragedy. He was in Milwaukee when it occurred, and only learned of it when he was called by a Bucks secretary. Yet that didn't stop the media from making the incident about—*and only about*—Kareem Abdul-Jabbar.

Over the following weeks and months, there was talk that Abdul-Jabbar was the next target. He was protected by armed bodyguards—the last thing he wanted. Really, what he desired was to be back home in New York, to play for the Knicks and once again have a familiar foundation surrounding him. In 1975, he officially asked the Bucks to be traded. "I'm not criticizing the people here," he said. "But Milwaukee is not what I'm all about. The things I relate to aren't in Milwaukee."

He was a three-time NBA Most Valuable Player and a six-time All-Star. He had brought the city its first NBA championship and quietly went about his work.

Milwaukee would never forgive him.

Because Abdul-Jabbar was a year removed from free agency, the team had little choice. After the Knicks refused to meet its demands, Milwaukee sent the greatest star in franchise history to the Lakers for four players—the forgettable Elmore Smith, the even more forgettable Brian Winters and two blue-chip selections from the recent draft: Junior Bridgeman and David Meyers. It was, arguably, the biggest trade in league history. "Frankly," Bridgeman said at the time, "I think the Bucks got the best of the deal."

The next five years were, for the most part, marvelous ones for Abdul-Jabbar. Though he had preferred to land in New York, there was much to love about Los Angeles. It was, of course, the place where he had become a national icon at UCLA; as well as a place where open-mindedness trumped paranoia and prejudice. The Forum was one of the finest basketball arenas in America. From Gail Goodrich and Cazzie Russell to Norm Nixon and Jamaal Wilkes, Abdul-Jabbar was perennially surrounded by some of the top players in the league.

There was only one problem: With Kareem Abdul-Jabbar as its star, Los Angeles never won. Oh, the team advanced to the 1977 Western Conference Finals. Overall, however, there always seemed to be something missing with the Lakers. Not talent, so much as, well, oomph. Spark. Attitude. Abdul-Jabbar arrived only two years after Wilt Chamberlain had retired, and the comparisons between two seven-footers were inevitable. Both were tall, both were tough, both were legends. Yet in his five seasons as a Laker, Chamberlain reached four NBA championships, winning one.

"When you're always measured up against someone like Wilt, it's not easy," said Michael Cooper. "Kareem was a great player. But he needed something in Los Angeles."

What was it?

"Kareem," Cooper said, "needed help."

■ ■ ■

Kid, what are you doing?

Those are the words that immediately entered Kareem Abdul-Jabbar's mind, and if they're not 100 percent accurate, it's only because a curse or two has been omitted in the name of good taste.

What *was* Earvin (Magic) Johnson doing on the night of October 12, 1979, sprinting across the court, leaping high into the air, wrapping his arms around the dignified center's neck and smothering him as if he were a Kleenex affixed to a nose?

"That hug," said Gene Shue, the San Diego Clippers coach. "That damn hug . . ."

It remains, more than three decades later, the lowest moment—and most lasting image—from Shue's long and distinguished NBA coaching career. Having relocated from Buffalo, New York, one year earlier, his Clippers seemed poised to continue the positive vibes of a 43-39 debut season. With 8,503 fans present at the San Diego Sports Arena for the 1979–80 opener, Johnson, the most heavily hyped player to enter the NBA in years, tripped and fell over his droopy pants during warm-ups (the stumble was greeted by cackles from both teams). After nine minutes, Jack McKinney pulled him from the court. "You need to relax and calm down," the coach told him. "This is no different than college or high school. It's basketball. Just basketball." The newcomer collected himself to score 26 points, but San Diego still maintained control. The Clippers jumped out to a fifteen-point first-quarter advantage over the stunned Lakers and held it through much of the game. "We were playing fantastically," said Shue, whose team held a 102–101 lead with less than a minute remaining in regulation. "We rebounded a miss and the ball was in the hands of Freeman Williams."

A former NCAA scoring champion at Portland State, Williams boasted a dead-eye jump shot, solid court sense—and an infant's ball-handling skills. With no Laker within five feet, he began dribbling up the right side of the court, then bounced the ball off his foot and watched it roll out of bounds. "Oh, my lord," said Shue. "Just unbelievable. Unbelievable. You're giving Magic and Kareem another life."

With eight seconds remaining, McKinney called a time-out to design a last play. The Lakers had many fine offensive options. Nixon was a lightning bolt driving toward the rim. Haywood still could soar. Wilkes's high release point made his jumper nearly unblockable. "But there was only one conceivable play in that situation," Johnson later wrote, "and everybody in the building knew exactly what it was."

Inbounding the ball from near mid-court, forward Don Ford watched as Johnson cut to the hoop, and Haywood stood frozen atop the three-point line. He held the ball for a moment before lofting it high to Abdul-Jabbar, who caught it on the left elbow of the free-throw line. With the Clippers' 6-foot-11 Swen Nater pressed up against his back, Abdul-Jabbar pivoted to his left, catapulted a skyhook high into the air and . . .

All net.

Lakers 103.

Clippers 102.

As the Clippers players walked off the court, the Lakers commenced their delirium. McKinney, owner of his first NBA win, rushed toward Abdul-Jabbar. Johnson, owner of his first NBA win, rushed toward Abdul-Jabbar. The rookie smiled widely, wrapping his long arms around the center's neck. Brent Musburger, broadcasting the game for CBS, screamed, "And Magic Johnson is out there celebrating, like they just won the NCAA championship! We've got Magic Man and Kareem Abdul-Jabbar!"

Seconds later, Hot Rod Hundley, also working the game for CBS, saddled up to Abdul-Jabbar for an interview.

Hundley: Great shot! What a skyhook, baby!
Abdul-Jabbar: What can I say?
Hundley: What a way to finish the game!
Abdul-Jabbar: Yeah.
Hundley: How about this season? It's gonna be a great one for the NBA!
Abdul-Jabbar: I hope so. There's a lot of new talent. I think the

people in the league office are looking to give a better image, a more complete image of what we're about.

Interview complete, Abdul-Jabbar walked toward the visitors' locker room—29 points on the stat sheet, a victory in the books. When he once again ran into Johnson, he pulled him aside for a brief chat.

"Listen," he said, "we have eighty-one more of these to go. Calm down."

■ ■ ■

Magic Johnson didn't calm down. He refused to, and whether Abdul-Jabbar liked it or not, the rookie was taking him along for the ride. Johnson had been repeatedly warned how boring the Lakers had been throughout the past few years, and he knew a big problem was Abdul-Jabbar's dead-fish approach.

The Lakers returned to action four days later, opening at home with a 105–96 win over the Chicago Bulls. A sellout crowd of 15,073 greeted Johnson with a standing ovation as he bounded across the court during player introductions. The game was hyped as a meeting between the draft's top two selections (Chicago had used the number two pick on UCLA forward David Greenwood) but symbolized significantly more to Jerry Buss. Ever since purchasing the franchise five months earlier, he had waited for this moment. The Lakers were Buss's toy, and he planned on doing things right. With the Forum's noise at an earsplitting level, Johnson played masterfully. He was one of five Lakers to score in double figures, and throughout the evening, he couldn't help but gaze toward Greenwood and the Bulls and think (had a coin landed on its head) what might have been. Save center Artis Gilmore, Chicago was a hapless lot, damned by a selfish, me-first scorer in Reggie Theus and a collection of here-for-the-paycheck stiffs. The Bulls would proceed to win thirty games, and even that was a surprise. "It was pretty bad," said Del Beshore, Chicago's second-year guard. "Earvin was an enthusiastic guy, but I'm not sure whether that could have held up with us. We were awful."

The Lakers, on the other hand, were spectacular. Raved the *Sporting News*: "Jerry Buss has replaced Jack Kent Cooke as owner, Jack McKinney has replaced Jerry West as coach and Earvin (Magic) Johnson has replaced apathy."

Jack Kent Cooke, the former owner, believed basketball needed to be coupled with a certain level of dignity. He had an organist play peppy tunes, wanted fans to get excited but not *too* excited.

Buss, on the other hand, was all about energy, buzz, pizzazz, spark. He ditched the organ and—at the suggestion of Roy Englebrecht, the team's director of promotions—brought in members of the USC marching band to sit in the stands and blast fight songs. He also allowed Englebrecht to follow his gut on what, at the time, was an unheard-of NBA idea. "The Dallas Cowboys were getting a lot of attention with these cheerleaders in high boots," Englebrecht said. "I went to Dr. Buss and said I would love to put a dance team together—not cheerleaders, dancers." Buss gave his blessing, and Englebrecht found four USC dancers and four UCLA dancers. "They spent about a month putting together a number," he said. "I went to a sporting goods store and bought eight pairs of matching sneakers, and I told everyone to keep it top secret.

"One night we decided, finally, they were ready. We all had walkie-talkies at the Forum, and when I yelled 'Code red!' the girls came out. The music starts, the announcer yells, 'The Laker Girls!' We had no idea how it would be received. Well, people went crazy, and an idea was born. We were no longer a basketball game. We were a show."

Under McKinney's guidance, the team ran whenever possible, often pushing the ball forward without waiting for a play to be called or a coach to shout out instructions. "It was fantastic," said Bob Steiner, the public relations director. "Jack was instant enthusiasm. He'd run out onto the court after a great play, slap someone on the butt. He was the perfect leader for a perfect team."

During the early days of training camp, Johnson had expressed concern over ordering Abdul-Jabbar around on the court. He was, after all, a mere twenty-year-old rookie. "I can't tell Kareem what to do," he said to McKinney. "Why would he listen to me?"

"Well," McKinney replied, "one of us has to do it. If you're not up for leading this team, I'll just have to. . . ."

"No, no, no," Johnson replied. "I'll do it."

"And he did," said Michael Cooper. "It was the way Magic gained respect right off the bat. He was unafraid of confronting the big man."

Around that same time, McKinney pulled Nixon into his office and sat him down. "Norman," he said, "you're terrific. One of the best in the league. But we have a lot of good players on this team, and I have to put them in the right position."

"What are you trying to say?" Nixon asked.

"Well," said McKinney, "I think Earvin would be a better point guard for us. I know that's hard for you, because you've—"

Nixon interrupted. "So you want me to play shooting guard?" he said.

"Yes," said McKinney.

"OK," he replied. "I can do that."

Nixon was far from elated, but he knew players don't tend to win battles with their coaches. Plus, he had to admit, there was something infectious about the kid. "If the first pick in the draft plays hard and practices hard," said Nixon, "what's the excuse for other guys to take it easy?"

After starting out 2-0, the Lakers lost their first game, 112–110, at Seattle on October 17, and also endured the first major scare of the season. With 1:25 remaining in the third quarter, Johnson collided with Jack Sikma, the SuperSonics center, while fighting for a rebound. He collapsed to the court, holding his right knee and withering in pain. The initial diagnosis, a partial tear of the medial collateral ligament, would result in Johnson spending six weeks in a splint, then another two to three more weeks in rehab. It was Buss's worst nightmare. Though the team's on-court centerpiece remained Abdul-Jabbar, the calling card was Johnson. He was the reason tickets to the Forum were flying out of the box office and the reason Hollywood royalty was filling the building's most expensive seats. "It was instant charisma," said Dyan Cannon, the actress who sat courtside for every home game. "Instant, magical charisma."

This was suddenly a charmed team, engaged in what was becoming a charmed season. Johnson missed a paltry three games, and returned with a clean bill of health on October 26 to face the Kansas City Kings at the Forum. In the best showing of his brief career, Johnson scored 26 points in twenty-eight minutes, while adding 7 rebounds and 6 assists. Los Angeles cruised, 116–104. "Johnson's enthusiasm was infectious, as usual," Scott Ostler wrote in the *Los Angeles Times*. "Abdul-Jabbar traded soul slaps with a teammate after one good play, and when [forward Jim] Chones tossed in a 20-foot jump shot in the second quarter, McKinney leaped off the Laker bench and onto the court to trade slaps with Chones."

The perennially dull Lakers were suddenly the talk of Hollywood—and the league. Every move GM Bill Sharman made seemed to pay dividends. Johnson was terrific, Haywood revived, Nixon the best two guard in the west. Worried about a lack of toughness under the boards, Sharman acquired Chones, a power forward, from Cleveland for Dave Robisch, an ineffective forward and a third-round pick. Before long, he was starting alongside Abdul-Jabbar, with Haywood coming off the bench. "I wasn't happy in Cleveland," Chones said. "Walt Frazier was my roommate, and the phone rings. It's Stan Albeck, the coach. He tells me about the deal, and I'm smiling. Walt says, 'What happened?' I told him about Los Angeles, and his face just dropped. 'Goddamn,' he said, 'that's where I wanted to go.'

"I was thrilled, because I had seen Magic Johnson play and I knew he was special. In fact, I was watching Magic play Bird in the NCAA Finals, and a friend asked, 'What do you think of that Johnson guy?' I swear to God, I told him, 'If I ever get to play with him, we'll win a championship.' That's exactly what I said."

The Lakers followed up the triumph over the Kings with four wins in their next five games. Perhaps the most memorable showing came on November 6 at the Forum, when the Lakers held STOP LLOYD FREE NIGHT in anticipation of the Clippers' dynamic shooting guard. In the lead-up to the clash, Los Angeles announced that, should Free be held below his 30.5 points per game average, every fan in attendance would receive a free ticket to a subsequent game.

Deep into the third quarter, Free was stuck at 19 points, and the Clippers were down by 18. "Being the dummy that I am, I announced to the crowd, 'Lloyd Free only has 19 points!'" said Larry McKay, the Forum public address announcer. "Free looked over toward the scorer's bench and glared right at me." He wound up scoring 29, and as the buzzer sounded on Los Angeles's 127–112 triumph, the crowd of 12,817 let out an appreciative roar. It didn't hurt that the Lakers were, once again, brilliant, with seven players scoring in double figures. "The talent on our team was phenomenal," said Holland, the rookie guard. "But it all started with Magic. He just didn't care about scoring a point. Did. Not. Care. It was all about winning for him. And because he felt that way, we all felt that way."

Los Angeles suffered one of its worst defeats of the year a night later, falling 126–109 to the Golden State Warriors in Oakland. The setback was ugly, but McKinney didn't fret. His players were tired, and their legs were sagging. Still, at 9-4, the Lakers were in the thick of the Pacific Division race, just one and a half games back of Portland. *Sports Illustrated*'s upcoming issue would feature Johnson on the cover, beneath the word *MAGIC*. The *Sporting News* praised the Lakers as the "prototype of a well-run team."

"We had it all going on," said Nixon. "You wanted to watch fun, exciting, all-out basketball at its absolute best? That was our team under Jack McKinney. We were taking the world by storm."

After the Golden State game, the Lakers flew home, arriving at Los Angeles International Airport well after midnight. Looking forward to his first day off of the young season, McKinney planned on sleeping in and being lazy. Then, at nine thirty the following morning, the phone rang.

Paul Westhead was on the line.

He wanted to play tennis.

CHAPTER 5

CRASH

Paul Westhead waited.

And waited.

And waited.

And waited.

He waited some more. And some more. And some more.

Then, a little more.

Jack McKinney was supposed to have arrived at the tennis court adjacent to his Palos Verdes condominium at ten o'clock that morning. "It was another beautiful sunny day in Southern California," said Westhead, the team's assistant coach. "It was only a fifty-yard walk from my place. I wasn't overly worried." But ten turned into ten thirty, and ten thirty turned into eleven.

"I still wasn't all that concerned," Westhead said. "I assumed he went into the office for some business. That wouldn't have been unusual for an NBA coach in the thick of a season."

Eleven thirty. Nothing.

Noon. Nothing.

Twelve thirty. Nothing.

At one P.M., the phone rang. It was Claire McKinney. "Paul," she asked, "have you seen my husband?"

Now he was worried.

Claire had returned from the nearby church meeting to an empty house.

Jack wasn't in the kitchen. Or the bathroom. "He wasn't on the bottom of the pool," she said. "Believe me, I looked." Claire reached out to the local police precinct, but nothing involving a Jack McKinney had been reported. She was told to contact the local hospitals. "We were new to L.A.," she said. "I didn't know any hospitals."

Claire opened the telephone book and came upon Little Company of Mary Hospital in nearby Torrance. She called, and spoke with a receptionist who asked that she describe her husband.

There was a deafening silence.

"You should come in right now," the woman said. "And please drive carefully, dear."

Upon arriving, Claire was ushered into a private office by a nun. "Would you like a cup of coffee?" she was asked.

"No, thank you," Claire said. "I'd like to know what you have to tell me."

A John Doe had been brought in that morning. There was a bad accident, and . . .

"Can I see him?" Claire asked.

The nun led her into a room. There was a man in the bed, unconscious, forehead swollen, the skin surrounding his eyes painted black and blue. "That," Claire said, "is my husband."

A few hours later, Bob Steiner, the team's public relations director, was about to leave for a round of golf with Bill Sharman, the general manager, when his phone rang. It was Buss. "Jack McKinney's in the hospital. . . ."

"Bill and I went in to see him," Steiner said, "and we couldn't believe what we were looking at."

Westhead arrived at his friend's bedside shortly thereafter. When he first heard the words *bicycle accident*, Westhead pictured bent spokes, a scraped knee, perhaps a broken elbow or leg. The reality was one million times worse.

While riding to the tennis courts, McKinney approached the intersection of Whitley Collins Drive and Stonecrest Road. He tapped the brakes to slow down on a slight incline. Yet, for a reason forever unknown, the gears locked, the tires froze and the bike jerked to a halt. McKinney soared over the silver handlebars and crashed, headfirst, into the concrete—"his body skidding along the street like a tossed stone along the surface of a pond," *Sports Illustrated*'s Richard O'Connor wrote.

There was but a single witness, a man named Robert N. S. Clark, who offered this recollection to police:

> I drew up to the stop sign on the corner. A man came down the hill [toward the intersection] on his bicycle. He was not speeding, as I remember. He seemed to be going at a moderate speed, then he slowed down even more and looked at the corner.
>
> My impression was that he put his brakes on and something happened then . . . his bicycle went out from under him, and all of a sudden he fell forward . . . and slid on his belly for about 15 to 18 feet.
>
> [McKinney] was practically unconscious—he could move but he seemed to be out. He had a loud, raucous breathing, like when someone's snoring. Then blood started coming out of his mouth slowly.

The first ambulance attendant to reach the accident site glanced at the unconscious man, turned toward a coworker and said, glumly, "No way. There's just no way this guy's going to make it."

Westhead will never forget the scene at the hospital. McKinney suffered a severe concussion and a fractured cheekbone along with a fractured elbow and countless bruises. "Jack has a broken arm or shoulder, so he's in a sling," he recalled. "His face is really chopped up, because he hit the street really hard. He has contusions all over his face, bandages everywhere. And he's not saying anything. It wasn't like, 'Hey, tomorrow he'll be fine.' It was very serious." (When her husband woke from his three-day coma, Claire leaned over his bed, kissed him on the forehead and handed him an article from the *Los Angeles Times*. "Is this me they are talking about?" he asked. "Is this really me?")

The last thing Westhead cared about was the basketball. Here was his dear friend, the man who had brought him along to the NBA, listless and lifeless. And yet, he had no choice *but* to think about basketball. The Lakers employed one assistant coach, and a matchup against the Denver Nuggets was scheduled at the Forum in roughly twenty-four hours. The next morning, Westhead arrived at the gymnasium on the campus of Loyola Marymount University, where the team held its game-day shootarounds. He wasn't sure what to say or, for that matter, what to do. Many players first learned of the accident when they entered the gym. Those who read the *Los Angeles Times* that morning found but a four-paragraph mention of the accident. It failed to make the front page of the main or sports sections:

LAKERS COACH M'KINNEY HURT IN CYCLE FALL

Laker coach Jack McKinney suffered a serious head injury Thursday when he took a spill while riding a bicycle near his home. McKinney, 44, was taken to the Little Company of Mary Hospital in Torrance where his condition was described as "guarded but stable."

A hospital spokesman said, "He suffered a severe head injury. He is in guarded but stable condition. He is responsive but not totally conscious. He also suffered a fractured elbow."

No other vehicle was involved in the accident which took place while McKinney was riding the bike for exercise near his home on the Palos Verdes peninsula.

Deputy Martin Weirich of the Lomita Sheriff's station said a witness told authorities that the bicycle McKinney was riding appeared to break and McKinney fell off, sliding down the street.

"I was the accidental head coach," said Westhead. "The substitute teacher. I entered the gym and I was, literally, the only person there at first. Then people start to arrive, and it's me, the trainer and the players. There was never anyone saying, 'Here's what we want you to do.' I was lucky that this was just a shootaround. I didn't have to coach just yet."

When practice ended, Westhead ran into Sharman. The general manager offered an empathetic pat on the back, and these words: "You're doing it. Because it's either you or the janitor. Take your pick."

That night, with Jack McKinney in a medically induced coma, the television in room 203 of Little Company of Mary Hospital was turned to the Nuggets-Lakers on Channel 9. For an inexperienced professional coach leading a shaken group of players, Denver was an ideal opponent. The Nuggets were not only playing their third game in three nights, but they were awful, having lost their first seven contests by such margins as 29 (to the

Bucks), 16 (Trail Blazers), 28 (the Bucks again) and 23 (Kings). "I just don't think we were ready to play when the season opened," Donnie Walsh, the Nuggets head coach, explained.

That night, the Nuggets were ready. They led the vastly superior Lakers throughout, and were up 107–105 with two seconds remaining in the fourth when Johnson spotted a wide-open Jamaal Wilkes. He shot a twenty-foot jumper that caught all net, forcing overtime. Johnson's two free throws with less than ten seconds left in the extra period iced an emotional 126–122 triumph.

Afterward, Westhead and his players took ten minutes to meet in the locker room. They talked about marching forward; about being strong; about the upcoming schedule and the following day's practice. Mostly, they talked about McKinney, and playing on his behalf.

"It should be very clear that this is Jack McKinney's team," Westhead later said, "and I am just running out the string until he returns. I have no intention of changing anything. There will be variations, but they will be variations, not changes. I will accentuate what we've been building on, which is the running game, but it's not new.

"Even if we go 71-0 the rest of the season, it's still Jack McKinney's team."

■ ■ ■

Paul Westhead was right. The Lakers were Jack McKinney's team. They utilized his up-tempo style of offense, his aggressive brand of defense. Los Angeles was fun to watch and difficult to play, and as the wins mounted and the show drew rave reviews, the NBA had itself an official marquee franchise.

Granted, across the land, riveting story lines were everywhere. In Boston, Larry Bird, Johnson's rookie rival, was reviving the Celtics while scoring 21.3 points per game and putting a nail in the "white guys can't really play" narrative. In Philadelphia, Julius Erving was soaring through midair, carrying the 76ers toward a deep playoff run. The Seattle SuperSonics, defending NBA champions, were riding Gus Williams, Dennis Johnson and Jack Sikma in another impressive championship quest.

The Lakers, though, were *the* story. Initially, the articles centered around an organization trying to overcome the loss of a coach. Gradually, however, McKinney's name began to fade away; updates on his condition appeared in full articles, then short briefs, then nowhere at all. The team won five of its first six under Westhead, and all anyone wanted to talk about was Magic . . . Magic . . . Magic. Wrote Bruce Newman in *Sports Illustrated*: "If [Johnson] is as good as his first month in the league seems to promise, at the ripe old age of 20 he just might be capable of helping the Lakers win the 1980 NBA title . . . Anyone who has seen Johnson play can tell you that despite all his raw skills, it is the sheer force of his personality that accounts for his particular genius."

After first begging Jerry West to return to the sidelines ("There was no fucking way in hell," West said), Buss named Westhead the coach for the remainder of the season. The forty-year-old former college professor handled things beautifully. He maintained a steady rotation, communicated openly with players, repeatedly credited McKinney and insisted the job was his to hold, not keep. "I think he has done a great job, considering the way this was dropped on him," Abdul-Jabbar said. "Jack was a little bit more of a disciplinarian than Paul, but they both understand people pretty well, and that's very important."

On November 16, more than a week after McKinney's accident, Buss finally allowed Westhead to hire his assistant of choice. The owner had been pushing for Elgin Baylor, the former Laker All-Star who lived locally. Westhead, however, wanted a recently retired journeyman named Pat Riley.

Buss hemmed and hawed when Westhead initially pushed forth the idea. The former Laker player, who had averaged 7.4 points over a ten-year career, was performing quite capably in his third season as Chick Hearn's on-air broadcasting sidekick. Furthermore, as far as coaching material went, Riley impressed no one. "He really had the potential to have a long, great career in the booth," said Keith Erickson, who replaced Riley when he shifted to the bench. "Chick could be very difficult to work with. He was a wonderful man, but demanding. Pat had the right temperament."

Since handing in his sneakers after the 1976 season, Riley had done very little of note. He grew his hair long, wandered the beaches of Southern California, played volleyball, contemplated life and death and his place in the world. Once, in a particularly depressing moment, Riley showed up for a Laker game at the Forum and, despite flashing his 1972 championship ring, was denied entrance to the press lounge. "Sorry," the doorman told him. "No ex-players."

Riley finally landed the radio and TV gig when Lynn Shackelford left and Hearn required a number two. He was unexpectedly good—quick with keen insight, willing to stay quiet when the egomaniacal Hearn went on a tangent, sympathetic to players but willing to criticize. Westhead and Riley were relative strangers, but their offices were across from each other inside the Forum, and casual banter morphed into mutual respect.

Riley checked with Hearn, who offered his blessing. He then took a week to ponder the career shift. "After seven or eight days of not sleeping," he said, "I'm committed to it. It's something I've always had in the back of my mind, that I would like to try it."

On November 27, Riley debuted as Westhead's sidekick. The Lakers beat the Jazz, 122–118, then won 11 of their next 16 to welcome in the new decade with a 27-13 mark. From afar, everything appeared to be running smoothly in La-La Land. The Lakers were winning, the Forum was selling out and athletic glory had returned to a fan base longing for it.

■ ■ ■

"Eighty percent."

Spencer Haywood is sitting by a swimming pool in the rear of his Las Vegas home, sipping from a glass of chilled water. The year is 2012, and he has been retired from the NBA for three decades. He no longer has anything to prove or anything to play for. There is no need for political correctness or distracting banter. A contract offer does not await. Neither does a call from a coach or GM.

He is sixty-three years old, and free to utter whatever he wants.

"Eighty percent," he says, once again. "I have no doubt about it."

The number is the answer to a question posed by a reporter: *What percentage of NBA players were using cocaine during the 1979–80 season?*

Haywood's reply is delivered with nary a flinch. Later, he directs one in the direction of his old drug dealer, who concurs with the assessment. "Oh, yeah," the man says. "It was everywhere."

Because he was young and new and a wee bit naïve, Westhead genuinely believed his men were playing with clear heads and drug-free bodies. He heard the whispers that cocaine was an issue in the NBA, and that other teams were struggling to contain the problem. But not here, not Los Angeles, not when the Lakers were performing so ably. "I was clueless," said Westhead. "Marijuana? Dope? I can honestly say I had no idea."

At the same time the Lakers were rolling along, putting forth some of the best basketball in recent memory, at least half the members of the roster were using cocaine—many recreationally, a couple dangerously. "Cocaine was the perfect Los Angeles drug," said Jeanie Buss, Jerry Buss's daughter. "People could party all night and they honestly didn't think it did them any harm. There was a belief that you could do coke and it wasn't addictive. I never tried cocaine, but one night I was at a club and this guy was hitting on me. I was nineteen, he was probably thirty. And he goes, 'Do you like snow?' I said, 'I hate skiing. It's just too cold.' Then I realized . . ."

"In our town," said Linda Rambis, "nothing said, 'I'm rich!' like a pile of coke."

Haywood recalled a party during which he got high with eight Los Angeles teammates. "It was the drug of the league," said Mark Landsberger, a backup forward who joined the team midway through the season. "With so many games it gave you energy when your body was feeling down. A lot of guys depended on it to get us up for games. If you did it once in a while, using your judgment, you were OK. If you didn't . . ."

On December 18, 1979, readers of the *Los Angeles Times* were greeted by the headline LAKERS HAVE A FAMILY PROBLEM. The piece concerned Haywood, who by now had forgotten the initial buzz of coming to the Lakers. After injuring his hip in the third game of the season, Haywood was benched in favor of Jim Chones, a more rugged bruiser who better protected Abdul-Jabbar under the boards. McKinney pulled Haywood aside at the time, assured him he was still a key contributor and played him, on average, twenty-seven minutes per game.

When Westhead took over, however, his spot on the bench stayed warm. Haywood insisted McKinney had guaranteed him a certain amount of playing time. "Well," said Westhead, "I can't do that." From an Xs and Os standpoint, it was the right call. Upon arriving in the NBA in 1970, Haywood was introduced with a *Sporting News* article titled, A NEW RUSSELL? IT'S HAYWOOD'S GOAL. He established himself as one of the league's most dynamic performers. He could shoot from the outside, score on the inside, rebound, block shots—"Everything," said George McGinnis, a longtime opposing forward. "Back in the day, power forwards were just big brutes. But Spencer was a monster. He had every tool in the case." With the Lakers, though, Haywood was becoming an embarrassment. He dropped easy passes, got lost on defense, ran at half speed. In a November 25 game against Kansas City, he botched several plays and was buried on the depth chart behind the dreadful Don Ford. (Quipped Peter Vecsey in the *New York Post*: "Ford is so disliked as a player . . . management is thinking of holding a Boo Don Ford Night.") One week later, after playing just four minutes against the Bucks, he went into an anti-Westhead tirade to teammates. "He hates me!" he screamed. "Paul Westhead fucking hates me!"

On the morning of December 14, Haywood arrived at the team's shootaround, but told Westhead he had to leave early for a doctor's appointment. That night, in a game against the Pistons, the coach motioned for Haywood to replace Chones.

"Coach, I can't see," Haywood said.

"What do you mean?" replied Westhead.

"I can't see," Haywood said. "But I'll be OK. I'll be OK."

At halftime, Haywood informed Jack Curran, the Lakers' trainer, that he was having an allergic reaction and was unable to function. The morning after the 138–122 victory, Haywood showed up on time for practice but insisted he couldn't participate. As a result, Westhead benched him for the next game, a Sunday afternoon clash with the San Antonio Spurs at the Forum. During time-outs, Haywood circled the perimeter of the huddle, making a show of not paying attention. In the second half, fans began to chant his name—"Hay-*wood*! Hay-*wood*! Hay-*wood*!" The player swirled his towel in the air and raised his fist. After the game, he referred to Westhead as a liar. "The fans," Haywood said, "know what's going on."*

Only they didn't.

Spencer Haywood was a cocaine addict.

In some ways his struggles with substance abuse were predetermined. Haywood grew up in the cotton-picking Delta town of Silver City, Mississippi, one of ten children born into addiction. Haywood's grandfather was an alcoholic, as were multiple siblings. "My sister Lina was a functioning alcoholic," he said. "My brother Joe was a functioning alcoholic. My brother Andrew died of alcoholism." Haywood started smoking marijuana during his year at Trinidad State Junior College in Trinidad, Colorado, and discovered cocaine in 1978, while playing with the New York Knicks. "I liked pot because it was organic, but coke wasn't organic at all," he said. "It was manufactured, and instead of making me mellow and relaxed, it did the opposite. I would use coke and see bugs, spiders, the most demonic things that ever existed."

---

* He was suspended three games for this statement.

Haywood, though, was hooked. When he reported to the Lakers, he convinced himself he could change. He and his wife, Iman (at the time one of the world's most famous fashion models), were parents to a one-and-a-half-year-old daughter, Zulekha, and he sought to be a good father and sound role model. In between the team's two-a-day training camp workouts, Haywood often hit the tennis court for an hour of serve-and-volley in 100-degree heat. "I didn't want to waste the opportunity," he said. "I wanted a championship."

Once the Lakers returned to Los Angeles for pre-season games, though, Haywood committed a tragic mistake. A friend in Beverly Hills told him about a new, non-nasal method for enjoying cocaine. It was called freebasing. Haywood watched several people take hits. He was intrigued. "A man can't know the world unless he's willing to be adventurous," he once wrote. "My main gripe with cocaine had been the crap they cut it with, and the damage to the nose, and this process eliminated both those problems."

Haywood asked his friend to cook the cocaine. He took a hit from the pipe.

"Harder!" his friend screamed.

Haywood inhaled deeply.

"No, harder!" he yelled.

Haywood took another powerful suck.

"Good," the friend said. "Now hold it in."

Haywood's eyes opened widely, his legs jolted with electricity. "It was like having sex and winning the lottery and scoring fifty points all at once," he said. "I couldn't stop grinning."

Haywood spent the remainder of the season craving that high. With Iman often on the road—Milan this week, Paris the next week—Haywood found himself with unlimited free time and pockets stuffed with NBA dollars. He was being paid $500,000 by Los Angeles—and spent $300 per week on drugs. "But you have to remember," he said, "I got most of my coke for free. There were plenty of folks hanging around who were more than happy to supply me with the stuff in return for being my buddy and getting closer to my glamorous world."

"Spencer," said Landsberger, "was the first crackhead I knew."

In order to bring himself down as a preface to the cocaine rise, Haywood took to warming up with two pints of Bacardi 151 rum. Then, after concluding with the pipe, he popped Quaaludes—"to get me low again," he said. On one particular night, Haywood overdosed on Quaaludes and fell asleep on his bathroom floor. He woke up five hours later to find his friend smoking his crack.

The Lakers once hosted a four-team pre-season tournament at the Forum. Afterward, a dozen players from the different clubs congregated at Haywood's home for an all-night crack session. While cooking the rock, the pipe exploded, sending shards of glass into the faces and arms of some of the NBA's elite players. "We were so shaken up that we waited a long time before proceeding with the party," Haywood wrote. "About ten minutes."

Inside the Lakers locker room, players spoke to the media as if cocaine were a foreign entity, unwelcome in a place where hard work reigned. The sentiment was nonsense. Landsberger, who admits to "letting the Hollywood lifestyle get to me," openly acknowledges having used drugs alongside Haywood, as does Ron Carter, the guard ("Spence got me to do it once, and it made me really paranoid," Carter said. "I remember leaving his place, saying, 'God, if you let me come down, I'll never do this again.'") and Michael Cooper, the second-year swingman. "I did coke with Wood a little bit," he said. "I dabbled. But when it got to the extremes—where I started getting real extreme—I was like, 'Spencer, I have to play basketball.'

"Spencer's biggest issue, I think, was loneliness. Iman was always gone with the baby, and he'd just be there in his apartment, looking for something to do, filled up with empty time. I tried to tell him, 'Wood, get out of this house. Come on over. Get away from this stuff.' I mean, we lived right down the street from each other, and my wife, Wanda, was a great cook. But he'd always say, 'No, no, no, I'm OK. I've gotta call my wife.' That was his line—'I gotta call my wife . . . I'm OK.' But he wasn't OK. A lot of us knew that."

"He just wasn't around," said Ollie Mack, a rookie guard. "That team was very tight, especially on the road. Movies, dinners. But Spencer was never seen."

Two players who didn't use were Johnson and Abdul-Jabbar. Both men viewed Haywood less as a teammate and more as a barrier between the Lakers and the NBA championship. "Boy, Kareem *did not* like Spencer," Landsberger said. "There was real bad blood."

Well aware of his stand-in status (on March 13, it was announced that

McKinney, itching to return but struggling in his recovery, would miss the entire season), Westhead treaded lightly. He let Johnson and Nixon handle the ball, tried to keep Abdul-Jabbar engaged, left Wilkes and Chones to themselves. Yet when it came to Haywood, he sought to marginalize a player who, in his mind, was a dysfunctional has-been. Haywood's playing time dwindled, and as the Lakers wrapped up a magical 60-22 season, the forward felt like an outcast. He was mad and hurt, and in denial about his substance abuse. After Los Angeles clinched the Pacific Division with a 101–96 home victory over the Jazz, bottles of champagne were distributed throughout the clubhouse. Toasts were made, booze was splashed. "This is it, baby!" Nixon shouted. "The first step."

By his locker, surrounded by reporters, Haywood surveyed the scene, smiled and raged. When asked whether his jump shot was returning (he scored 10 against Utah), Haywood smirked. "It's been there," he said. "I just need PT and confidence. The jumper has been sitting there in the cooler, like good wine."

When he was relayed the quote, Westhead grunted and walked off. To him, Spencer Haywood barely existed. He was an unwanted nuisance. "I had the greatest opportunity of my career right there in front of me," Haywood said years later. "And I blew it. I fucking blew it."

■ ■ ■

Entering the playoffs, Los Angeles appeared unbeatable. They kicked the post-season off by decimating the overmatched Suns, four games to one. "I've been in the league seven years, and I've never seen Kareem play better than he is right now," John MacLeod, the Sun coach, said after the final game, in which Abdul-Jabbar scored 35 points with 16 rebounds.

By defeating Phoenix, Los Angeles was guaranteed a meeting with Seattle, the defending NBA champions.

Though the Lakers weren't exactly a team to carry a grudge, there was something about the Sonics that rubbed them wrong. The two teams battled for Pacific Division supremacy, with Seattle finishing 56-26 and four games back. If the Lakers were sleek and smooth, the Sonics were a slab of concrete. Sikma, the team's young center, was a 6-foot-11 bruiser who had no problem using elbows and knees to keep Abdul-Jabbar uncomfortable. Shooting guard Dennis Johnson knew every trick (many of them dirty) in the book. The Sonics were trash-talk specialists, prompting Chones to throw some back before a late-February meeting. "I think we're the better team," he said. "Everybody is hung up on what they did last year. We're better."

The series opened at the Forum on April 22, and—for the Lakers—it began horribly. Coming off of a hard-fought seven-game brawl against Milwaukee, the Sonics were supposed to be leg-heavy and worn down. Instead, Fred (Downtown) Brown, the team's third guard, went off for 34 points and Sikma hit a free throw with two seconds remaining for a 108–107 stunner. "We weren't intimidated at all," said Sikma. "Were the Lakers more talented? Probably. But they didn't scare us. I think we all believed we'd win that series and repeat."

The Lakers battled back to win the second game, 108–99, and a weirdness accompanied the series as it shifted to the Pacific Northwest. Seattle played its games inside the Kingdome, also home to the NFL's Seahawks and Major League Baseball's Mariners. It was an enormous building that seated forty thousand fans, and helped the Sonics lead the NBA in attendance. However, Game 3 was scheduled for April 25, and the Mariners already booked the building for their series against the California Angels. The Center Coliseum, generally the second option, was also unavailable—thanks to the Ice Capades.

Hence, the Lakers and Sonics would play the most important game of the season inside Clarence S. (Hec) Edmundson Pavilion, a gymnasium on the University of Washington's campus that seated 8,524 fans. It was, to all involved, utterly ridiculous. Westhead took one look at the gym and deemed it "the difference between the Forum and Inglewood High School." Which was too kind. The Hec was fine for a college intramural battle between Edna's Edibles and the Tools, but little more. The floor was plagued by dead spots, the seating plan was archaic. The building was constructed in 1927, and featured brick arches, ivy-coated outside walls and photographs of Husky sports legends like Bruno Boin. On the morning of the Sonics' pregame workout, forward Wally Walker strolled beneath the bleachers and asked (with a smile), "Anybody know where the varsity locker room is?"

When Game 3 began, the Sonics seemed to hold the advantage. Hec was a dump, but it was a loud, intimate, poorly ventilated dump that favored the home team. The Lakers, however, countered with their own X factor—a 7-foot-2 center with a skyhook. Abdul-Jabbar scored 33 points, including 13 in the final quarter, as the Lakers captured a 104–100 win. Two nights later, Los Angeles again broke Seattle, coming back from a 21-point third-quarter deficit to win 98–93. Los Angeles' 24-2 surge was sparked by Abdul-Jabbar, whose 25 points led all scorers. Afterward the Sonics sat in their dilapidated locker room in pained silence. "It was embarrassing, what occurred today," said forward Johnny Johnson. "Just embarrassing."

Though it went largely unspoken, the series was over. In an uncharacteristically brazen moment, Abdul-Jabbar cracked: "They claim they like to play with their backs against the wall. At this point they're about to go over the wall." On April 30, Abdul-Jabbar scored 38 and the Lakers, back inside the Forum, terminated the Sonics, 111–105. This time, as the final buzzer went off, the center didn't browbeat Johnson for wrapping his arms around his neck. The Los Angeles Lakers would be appearing in the NBA Championships for the first time in seven years.

The hug made perfect sense.

■ ■ ■

Generally speaking, professional athletes approach the biggest series of their lives with uncompromised intensity.

The TV is turned off.

The phone is unplugged.

The wife deals with the children, the accountant handles the bills, the gardener mows the lawn.

The athlete focuses solely upon the task at hand.

For the active members of the Los Angeles Lakers, this meant setting their sights upon the Philadelphia 76ers, winners of 59 games and the newly minted Eastern Conference champions.

Philadelphia was the Lakers' polar opposite. Tough. Physical. Menacing. Though the team's best player, Julius Erving, was an ethereal sky walker who averaged 26.9 points per game, he was surrounded by a workmanlike crew of blue-collar bangers and dogged defenders. The 76ers were forward Bobby Jones diving for a loose ball; center Darryl Dawkins shattering the backboard after an earth-splitting slam; Maurice Cheeks hounding the opposing point guard. Even though the Lakers had the better record, eleven of eighteen polled NBA head coaches predicted a Philadelphia triumph. "We were anything but wimps," said Steve Mix, a scrappy reserve forward. "We would fight you, we would hound you. We were tougher than Los Angeles."

Unlike the Lakers, whose fan base had its fair share of Hollywood pretty boys and large-breasted aspiring models, the 76ers filled the Spectrum with a raw, edgy, blue-collar core. The *Los Angeles Times* rightly called the showdown "the best championship series matchup in years." Why, Game 1 would even be carried on live TV—*not* tape delay, as had been the case the previous season.

"We knew what we were in for," said Michael Cooper, the Los Angeles swingman. "Philly was no joke. They were the best team we'd play all season. We had to have our A games to have a shot at winning."

With this understanding, the Lakers went into the series with laserlike focus. Well, eleven of the twelve Lakers did. The clash was scheduled to open on a Sunday at the Forum, so Westhead called for all-out Thursday and Friday practices before a light Saturday refresher. Haywood, who played some key minutes against the Sonics (and who averaged 9.7 points and 4.6 rebounds in 76 regular-season games), told himself that he would, if nothing else, lay off the drugs until after the NBA Finals. "I'd waited eleven years to get to that point," he said. "So the idea of blowing a chance at a championship ring was ridiculous. I would never, ever be so dumb."

As Haywood departed Loyola Marymount following Thursday's workout, one of his "party pals" approached. "I came by to see if you wanted to stop by Mike's place for a while," he said, referring to a mutual user.

Haywood's brain said no. His heart said no. Every instinct in his body said *run away . . . go elsewhere.*

Instead, he smoked crack. By three A.M. he had yet to sleep, and his arms and legs were squirming and twitching beyond control. With practice only five hours away, he decided to take two Quaaludes to calm his nerves. Haywood slept for a brief spell, left Mike's house and started his car. Though his body was numb, Haywood capably backed out of the driveway. Amazingly, everything seemed fine. He was awake. He was in control. Dammit, he could do this.

Then, Haywood stopped at a red light and fell asleep.

The horns began blaring, and Haywood jolted awake. Twice more he dozed off before finally arriving at the gymnasium. Upon entering the building, Haywood did all he could to act normally. He greeted teammates, changed into his gear, strolled into the meeting room, where Westhead turned off the lights to begin showing film. *Zzzzzz.* "It's dark, and Spencer's next to me," said Norm Nixon. "He falls fast asleep. I elbowed him to wake up." The Lakers congregated on the court to stretch. Again, Haywood closed his eyes and dozed off. "We were on our backs, and that cold hardwood floor felt like a feather bed," he wrote. "Everything became blurry, including the other players. I felt myself floating over the court, like they say you do when you die. I could hear a buzz like an airplane sounds and then—boom, the big curtain."

The Laker players knew exactly what was going on. Many had used cocaine before, and some had used *with* Haywood. But there was a difference between using cocaine and handing oneself over to cocaine. Somewhere along the way, Haywood surrendered to the drug. "It had me," he said. "It just had me."

Cooper tried to stir Haywood from his repose, shaking him gently with his hand, but to no avail. When Haywood finally came to, Westhead ordered him to go home. "I tried to be as understanding as possible," Westhead said. "I wasn't trying to pick on Spencer, or make him feel like an outcast. But what is a coach supposed to do when you have this sort of behavior? What choice did I have?"

Haywood was not in an empathetic mood. "Fuck you," he muttered as he left the gym. "And fuck this team."

■ ■ ■

At 12:31 P.M. on Sunday, May 4, Abdul-Jabbar and Caldwell Jones took a jump ball at center court to begin what would go down as a classic series. The Lakers wore their home golds. The Sixers were dressed in red.

With 17,505 fans packed inside a sold-out Forum, Jerry Buss sat back and watched, a smile stretching from ear to ear. This was bliss, and as Abdul-Jabbar put up 33 points, 14 rebounds, 5 assists and 6 blocks in a dominant 109–102 Laker win, all *seemed* beautiful in the land of the beautiful.

Still buried in a drug-induced haze, however, Haywood sat on the bench and sulked. On one of the most triumphant nights in recent Laker history—as his team held Erving to 20 points with a suffocating double team; as Dawkins was rendered useless—Haywood could think only of himself, and how he should have been contributing key minutes (he played just three). In his mind, this was Westhead's doing. If Jack McKinney had never fallen off his bicycle, Haywood was sure he'd still be starting. Instead, he had to answer to some amateur coach on a power trip.

Three nights later, the 76ers evened the series with a 107–104 victory. Haywood saw two minutes of court time, and afterward entered the locker room with dark smoke oozing from his ears. His stall was situated alongside that of Brad Holland, the little-used rookie guard whose pale complexion and golly-gee demeanor won him the nickname Potsie Weber—a nerdy character in the popular TV show *Happy Days*—from teammates

As the two sat side by side in the quiet room, Haywood glared toward his left. "Gimme your tape cutters," he snarled.

Holland was a local kid. He'd played his prep ball at nearby Crescenta Valley High, and went down as one of the top two-sport athletes the state had ever seen. (Holland was heavily recruited by Notre Dame and USC, among others, to play quarterback.) Although his rookie production (2.8 points per game over 38 games) paled in comparison to his four seasons at UCLA, Holland was no shrinking violet. He developed a close friendship with, shockingly, Abdul-Jabbar, who would save the rookie a seat on bus rides in order to talk politics, literature and religion. In practices, he could be feisty and hot tempered. "I'd always dreamed of playing for the Lakers," he said. "I grew up watching the team, listening to Chick Hearn on my porch. So, certainly, I wanted to take advantage of the opportunity."

Holland would have given all the world's riches to have a sliver of Spencer Haywood's natural talent. To see it all wasted . . .

"If you say please," he responded curtly.

"If I have to say please, I don't wanna use 'em!" Haywood barked.

"Fine," said Holland. "Then don't use them."

By now, both men were screaming. Haywood stood up. Holland stood up. "You know what, Spencer, we're trying to win games here!" Holland yelled. "What is your problem?"

"What the fuck are you gonna do about it, Potsie?" Haywood replied.

The veteran expected his teammates to come to his aid and put the newcomer in his place.

"You crazy, Wood?" said Chones. "Man, you're letting us down."

What?

"Cut the crap," said Nixon. "You're being stupid."

Moments later, Buss, Westhead and Haywood met in private. The man brought in to play power forward was suspended for the remainder of the season. His days as a Laker were over. In the ultimate indignity, he would later be voted but a quarter share of playoff money.*

---

* In the early 2000s, Haywood spoke with *Slam Magazine*'s Alan Paul. He told the writer: "Years later, I sat down with Magic, Kareem, Jamaal Wilkes and Norm Nixon and they said, 'You were doing so much that we thought you might die if you had the money and live if we delayed it.' And there's something to be said for that, because I was very sick."

"It's more," Abdul-Jabbar said, "than he deserved."

With his hope crushed and his dreams dead, Haywood consumed himself in a tidal wave of drugs and pity and terrifying plots. Only one teammate, Jamaal Wilkes, had called to check on him after the dismissal. Otherwise, they were all enemies. Abdul-Jabbar for being cold. Holland for screaming. Chones for not having his back. Johnson for being so damn happy. And, most of all, Westhead, the coach who ruined everything. "I left the Forum and drove off in my Rolls thinking only that Westhead must die," Haywood said. He called a friend—Gregory, from Detroit—who dabbled in organized crime, and hatched a plan. They would sneak into Westhead's driveway at night and disable the brakes on his car. The next time the coach tried driving down the long, winding road from his Palos Verdes home, Haywood and his pals would run his vehicle off a cliff.

"Spencer supposedly flew two guys in to do it," said Westhead. "It was a very real idea."

"They were going to do the job for free," Haywood said. "For the sake of friendship and for the prestige of having done a favor for old Spencer." During a phone conversation shortly before the scheduled murder, Haywood's mother detected a sinister tone to her son's voice. "You're up to something no good, aren't you?" she said. Eunice Haywood threatened to contact the police if he acted on any urges. "I will turn you in myself," she said. "I didn't raise no fool." The killing was called off.

"Here's the amazing thing," said Westhead. "Eight years later I'm coaching college at Loyola Marymount, and Spencer Haywood enters the gym. He was in recovery, and he came to ask for my forgiveness."

"Spencer, of course I forgive you," Westhead had said. "Hell, it's great to see you. Because, if it had worked, I wouldn't be seeing you."

■ ■ ■

The Lakers flew to Philadelphia on the morning after the Game 2 setback, and for Westhead the trip symbolized a glorious journey back in time. Although his casual gait and floppy hair could suggest a laid-back West Coast demeanor, Westhead was as Philadelphia as a Pat's cheese steak.

He attended West Catholic High School, and any suggestions that Paul Westhead would one day sit upon the cusp of an NBA title would have been greeted with uncontained laughter from his classmates. As a 4-foot-11 freshman, he tried out for the basketball team—and was cut. As a 5-foot-2 sophomore, he tried out again—and was cut. As a 5-foot-4 junior, he tried out again—and was cut.

"It was awful," he said. "But I have one brother, Pete, and I would lay in the bed and he would pull my legs. And I would hang on the doors for ten, twenty minutes at a time to stretch my arms. Well, between my junior and senior year I went from 5-foot-4 to 6-foot-2. Finally, I'm ready to play varsity basketball for West Catholic. I'm ready!"

Westhead tried out and was, once again, cut.

Cy Westhead, Paul's father, worked as a soap salesman. His mother, Jane, was a telephone operator. They had little money but took out a loan to send their younger son to Malvern Prep, a college preparatory school located twenty-seven miles outside of the city. Although it was his first time playing organized basketball, Westhead led the Inter-Academic League in scoring with 23.7 points per game, and caught the eye of Saint Joseph's coach Jack Ramsay, who offered him a scholarship. (Ramsay's top assistant was a young up-and-comer named Jack McKinney.) In four years at the school, Westhead was a so-so player with lots of guts. During his senior season, the Hawks were playing at Madison Square Garden when Westhead took a hard charge, dislodging his right shoe from his foot. "I had broken my wrist earlier in the season, so I couldn't get the shoe back on," he said. "Who comes running on the court to tie my shoe for me? Our assistant coach, Jack McKinney."

Westhead lacked a reliable jumper and top-level quickness. He was, however, an excellent student. "You know, you're a really good teacher," Ramsay told him. "I don't know if you'll ever be a coach, but in the classroom, explaining things, you'd be great." Westhead went on to secure his masters in English Literature from Villanova, where he wrote his thesis on *Titus Andronicus*, one of William Shakespeare's more obscure works.

After graduating, he accepted a job as an English instructor at the University of Dayton. He told the administration that, if possible, he'd like to be involved in basketball, but no positions were available. Then, one month later, Tom Blackburn, the varsity coach, was diagnosed with terminal lung cancer. He was replaced by Don Donaher, the freshman coach, which resulted in an opening on the lowest rung. "I jumped at the chance," Westhead said. "That was my first coaching job—freshman basketball. And I loved it."

Westhead proceeded to coach five years at Cheltenham High School in Wyncote, Pennsylvania, where he inherited a 2-18 team and went 26-0 before losing in the state championship game. It was the happiest time of his life. "I was young, my first daughter was born, I'm teaching literature, which I love to do, to high school juniors, a class I love. It was great. But, maybe, I thought, there was even more for me." He went on to work alongside Mc-Kinney as a Saint Joseph's assistant for two years, then, in 1970, was hired as head coach of the La Salle College Explorers. He spent nine years at the school, always maintaining a close friendship with McKinney, who worked across town. The two compared notes, swapped stories, vacationed—even coached summers in Puerto Rico's professional leagues together.

"When Jack was hired by the Lakers and he called me about being his assistant, there was no debate," Westhead said. "You don't get many calls from people saying, 'I've been hired as the head coach of the Los Angeles Lakers. Come be my assistant.'"

Hence, as the Lakers prepared to play the 76ers at the Spectrum in Game 3 of the NBA Finals, Westhead was more than a wee bit nostalgic. How many big games had he watched here? Coached here? The walls told the story of his own basketball journey. "I can't tell you how exciting it was for me," he said. "I was coming home."

Though the Laker players liked their young coach, they shared no such nostalgia. Philadelphia was an awful place, what with the city's hardened fans and the 76ers' notorious physicality. "We weren't a team that you'd push around," said Dawkins. "If you brought it to us, we brought it right back—hard."

Maybe so. But the Lakers did, in fact, bring it. Liberated from Haywood's destructiveness, Los Angeles battered Philadelphia, 111–101, with Abdul-Jabbar's 33 points and 14 rebounds leading the way. While the season had, in large part, belonged to Johnson, the playoffs were entirely about Los Angeles's center. At 6-foot-11 and 251 pounds, Dawkins—just twenty-three at the time—was a strong, physical player who fared well against the NBA's other elite big men. Yet Abdul-Jabbar was, simply, *different*. "Kareem came up to me after one of the games and said, 'You make it hard on me every night,'" said Dawkins. "Which was a major compliment—because if I made it hard on him, guess what he did to me? I mean, I threw my weight at him, tried to push him around. But he could hit that hook from anywhere. And he was deceptively strong. That's the one part that was always overlooked. Kareem was far from a weak man."

The Sixers were so concerned about Abdul-Jabbar's impact that they took the unusual (at the time) step of charting his offensive efficiency. In the series' first two games, the Lakers scored on approximately 60 percent of the possessions where Abdul-Jabbar touched the ball. In Game 3, that figure skyrocketed to 71 percent. "I was good," said Dawkins, "but I couldn't handle Kareem all alone. I needed help."

He would receive it.

■ ■ ■

But first, there was business to take care of.

On the night of May 13, two days after the Sixers battled back with a 105–102 Game 4 win to tie the series, Jerry Buss announced that Jack McKinney would not return for the 1980–81 season. "I don't believe we have any positions available that would absorb his total capabilities," Buss told the press. "I would not hesitate, however, to recommend Jack to my dearest friends regarding a front-office or head-coaching job in the NBA."

Although, when asked, Westhead expressed his disappointment for McKinney, it was widely (and rightly) presumed that, come season's end, Buss would officially appoint Westhead to replace his old friend.

Which would have all been sort of digestible—had someone remembered to tell McKinney.

Around the same time Los Angeles's major media markets were breaking the news of the dismissal, John McKinney, Jack and Claire's third-oldest child, received a call from Frank Brady of *The Philadelphia Inquirer.*

"Is your father home?" Brady asked.

"No," said John. "Can I take a message?"

Brady identified himself, then uttered words John would never forget. "Tell him Frank Brady from the *Inquirer* called, and I wanted to get a reaction to the Jerry Buss press conference."

"What press conference?" he replied.

Jack and Claire McKinney were returning home to Los Angeles from Portland. They were, as usual, chatting away, listening to the radio, enjoying time together, when they decided to stop at a hotel in Santa Rosa to spend the night. Jack picked up the phone and called home to check in. John answered. It had been his bike that his father rode on the fateful day.

"Dad, have you heard the news?" he asked.

"What news?" McKinney replied.

"Dad," John said, "you've been fired."

Had Jack McKinney again slammed into the pavement, the pain

wouldn't have been as bad. The hurt, he said, was like a wound constantly being reopened. Fired? Just because his name ceased appearing in the *Los Angeles Times* didn't mean McKinney's fight for survival wasn't remarkable. He had been in a coma for three days and a semicomatose state for three weeks. More than 40 percent of head-injury victims never return to normal, and 60 percent can't return to work within the first year. Between the time of the accident and his phantom dismissal, McKinney had been through months of excruciating physical and cognitive therapy. "I had so many things [affected] by the fall," McKinney said. "My mouth, my lips, plastic surgery, a broken bone in my ear that controls your equilibrium. I lost all the power on one side of my body. If I leaned over to pick something up, I would fall over." Dennis McKinney, Jack and Claire's youngest child, remembers his father offering to drive him to high school one day. "He thought he was doing better than he really was," Dennis said. "The ride was terrifying. To the right, to the left, to the right. Just swerving all over. My dad's balance was really off." Come December, doctors thought McKinney could attend a Laker game as a spectator. He was warmly approached by Buss, who asked how his rehab was going. McKinney remained silent. Not out of rudeness—he didn't recognize the man.

"But my dad was such a positive guy," said Susan McKinney-DeOrtega, his oldest child. "Even when he was at his lowest, in so much pain, struggling just to remember, he told us he was going to beat it. And he believed it." Ever since he had been hired by the Lakers, eleven months earlier, McKinney thought of Buss as a kind and *loyal* person. Throughout his long, oft-arduous rehabilitation, McKinney felt the team's owner was pulling for his recovery, and that his return to the sidelines was inevitable. He was even asked to do some advance playoff scouting, and eagerly shared his observations with Westhead and Riley.

And now, after all that, he was learning of being fired—*from his son*?

"I still think of that as the moment," said Dennis, "when I first realized how shitty people can be."

And yet, even though the McKinney family was handed the worst news in the cruelest of ways, Buss was correct in his assessment. Jack McKinney had initially asked to rejoin the Lakers in mid-March, citing a handful of physicians who deemed him ready. Buss didn't see it that way. "That was surely one of the hardest things my dad ever had to deal with," said Jeanie Buss, his daughter. "My dad is a very honorable person. He wants to do the right thing, even when that's hard to determine. I'm sure he felt he had no other choice."

"I couldn't admit it at the time," McKinney said, "but Dr. Buss wasn't wrong. I wasn't ready."

And now, like that, he was gone.

■ ■ ■

Though he went largely unloved (and often unliked), Kareem Abdul-Jabbar possessed a toughness most NBA players envied. With a physique more giraffe than elephant, he was routinely the target of every conceivable form of physical thuggery. To see Abdul-Jabbar in the locker room after a game was to see a man covered in a rainbow of bruises. "The way you had to play him was with as much strength as possible," said Dennis Awtrey, a journeyman center who engaged Abdul-Jabbar in multiple battles through the years. "Kareem was a beautiful, graceful player. I mean, he was perfection on the court. So if you were guarding him, you had to mess that up."

Much like Dawkins and Detroit's Bob Lanier and Boston's Dave Cowens and the majority of other NBA centers, Awtrey went after Abdul-Jabbar with a tool box filled with elbows, forearms and scratches. Once, while Awtrey was a member of the 76ers in the early 1970s, Abdul-Jabbar jabbed him in the Adam's apple with an elbow, then slapped him across the face with his hand. "I chased him down, grabbed him and popped him below the left eye," said Awtrey. "That was our relationship."*

Yet, like some sort of futuristic cyborg, Abdul-Jabbar kept coming back. He would lose his temper from time to time (he famously cold-cocked Milwaukee's Kent Benson in the 1977–78 opener) but, more often than not, simply absorbed the abuse while collecting his 30 points and 14 rebounds. "There are guys who you know will cry and cry all throughout a game," said Cooper. "Kareem was the opposite."

After two off days, the Lakers and Sixers reunited at the Forum for Game 5. With four and a half minutes remaining in the third quarter and the score tied at 65, Abdul-Jabbar went up for a finger roll, watched the ball fall through the net, came down awkwardly and landed on the side of his left

---

* Wrote Abdul-Jabbar in his autobiography, *Giant Steps*: "The only truly dirty player I've run into, a man who took real pleasure in his viciousness, was Dennis Awtrey. . . . He was great with the blindsider, never saw him go face to face. He was a mediocre player, and that one shot kept him in the league for several extra years."

ankle, which turned over his white low-top Adidas. A shock ran up his leg, but Abdul-Jabbar limped through the ensuing couple of possessions. Eventually, Robert Kerlan, the team's physician, determined the injury was severe. He asked Abdul-Jabbar whether he wanted to depart for the hospital immediately or first watch the remainder of the game from the bench.

"Can I hurt it any more?" Abdul-Jabbar asked, wincing.

"If we tape it up, you won't be able to injure it further," Kerlan said. "But it's going to hurt a lot."

"I'll try it," Abdul-Jabbar said. "I want to play."

The men returned to the locker room, where Kerlan wrapped the throbbing ankle in white medical tape. As Abdul-Jabbar stood, winced and limped back into the arena and onto the court for the fourth quarter, the 17,505 attendees shook the building with a thunderous ovation. It was the most courageous moment of his glorious career, and all Abdul-Jabbar could focus on was the pain.

Although he couldn't jump off his left foot, Abdul-Jabbar finished with 40 points, 15 rebounds and 4 blocks (including 14 points and 6 rebounds in the fourth quarter). He completed a key three-point play with thirty-three seconds remaining that broke a 103–103 tie. "I felt just sick inside [watching him]," said Kerlan. "I have a lot of empathy because I could tell he was hurt badly. The 76ers really put their bodies on him when he came back in. I told him that in the fourth quarter it was as if he had auto-hypnotized himself to mentally block out the pain. He said, 'Yeah, I guess I did.'"

As his teammates celebrated the 3-games-to-2 lead in the locker room, Abdul-Jabbar—along with Kerlan and Steve Lombardo, another team physician—walked, via crutches, down the street to the emergency room of Centinela Hospital Medical Center. Kerlan had initially assumed Abdul-Jabbar suffered a broken fibula, but X-rays confirmed an awful sprain. The ankle was injected with a mixture of hydrocortisone and Xylocaine, and Abdul-Jabbar returned to his Bel Air home.

The next morning, he was unable to walk.

■ ■ ■

"Bullshit."

That was Darryl Dawkins's immediate reaction when told that Abdul-Jabbar wouldn't be making the trip back east for Game 6 of the NBA Finals.

"Didn't believe it," he said.

"Me neither," said Mix, the backup forward. "Kareem would be there. Obviously, he'd be there. . . ."

Sports and gamesmanship had long gone hand in hand. There was a full day off between Game 5 and Game 6, certainly enough time for a man who had just hung 40 points to kick back on an airplane, close his eyes, ice his left ankle, gobble up some Wheaties and give it the ol' UCLA college try.

"Everyone in the city of Philadelphia thought we were faking the severity of Kareem's injury," said Westhead. "Believe me, I wished we were."

On the morning of May 15, the undermanned Lakers gathered in the American Airlines terminal at Los Angeles International Airport. To his teammates' chagrin, Abdul-Jabbar—averaging 33.4 points through the first five games—was home. Haywood, who Buss briefly considered bringing back to fill the spot ("No way," Westhead said. "Absolutely no way."), was also home. Nixon, meanwhile, had torn up his left index finger in a Game 5 collision with the ball and was cocooning the hand in thick gauze. (More than thirty years later, Nixon's finger still jetted out at a disgustingly unnatural angle.) "I pretty much had one useful hand," Nixon said. "There was a big gap where my finger was supposed to be."

Because NBA teams still flew commercial, the Laker players huddled in a corner, protected from the rest of society by little more than size and status and purple-and-gold luggage tags. As he waited for the flight to board, Westhead went man to man, explaining that, with Abdul-Jabbar absent, it was time to step up. Even with his mangled paw, Nixon knew he'd have to manage much of the point. Even with his tired legs, Wilkes—who'd played 214 minutes thus far—had to take up the scoring slack. Landsberger, the bruiser acquired from Chicago, needed to beat people up down low. Holland, the twelfth man who spent most of the playoffs glued to the bench, would be asked to contribute major minutes. "Coach," Holland said, "I'll be ready." Chones, the backup center who began the season as a lowly Cleveland Cavalier and now sat on the brink of a title, assumed he would fill the void left in the post. "Not that it was possible to replace Kareem," he said. "He was so good that in scrimmages during practice, he wouldn't play with us. Because all the guard had to do was dribble down the floor and dump the ball into Kareem ten times. Game over. I wasn't that caliber."

When it was time to board, the Lakers ambled onto the airplane and took their standard seats. Buss insisted his players travel in style* and therefore had Mary Lou Liebich, the basketball secretary, buy out first class whenever possible. Those players assigned to coach were almost always placed alongside an empty chair (also purchased by the club). Seating was based upon a loose combination of seniority, status and playing time. Therefore, Abdul-Jabbar was always in the first row of first class, positioned in the aisle so that his storklike legs could extend into the walkway. This time, as Chones found his spot and Wilkes found his spot and Holland found his spot, passengers could hear the increasingly loud sound of someone belting out "Golden Time of Day," the soulful hit from Maze featuring Frankie Beverly.

> *People let me tell you*
> *There's a time in your life when you find out who you are*
> *That's the golden time of day. . . .*

It was Magic Johnson. As he turned from the jetway onto the plane, the rookie smiled widely. He usually sat in the second row of first class, alongside Cooper. This time, however, he stopped at Abdul-Jabbar's vacant seat.

"Have no fear!" he yelped. "Motherfucking Magic Johnson is here!"

He plopped down and continued crooning.

"Right then I knew we were going to win," said Cooper. "I just knew it."

"The guy was exceptional," said Chones. "Magic had creative will, and the manifestations of creative will are things like desire, attraction, cohesion. He was a rookie, but you had to believe in him."

Once the plane was in midair, Westhead and Johnson met in the bulkhead. The coach had this preposterous idea, one the rookie would surely cringe at. "I'm thinking of starting you at center," he said. "I know it's crazy, and you're best at point guard, but hear me out. I just think that—"

"I love it!" Johnson said, beaming.

"You do?" Westhead replied.

"Love it!" Johnson said. "Let's do it."

Three years earlier, Johnson had dabbled at center at Everett High

---

* Said Butch Lee, who was acquired from Cleveland before the season: "The Lakers were all about class. With Cleveland they gave us soda in the locker room after games. With the Lakers it was juices and fruit and all sorts of stuff. It was a whole different mentality. A winner's mentality."

School. There was a beautiful full-circle quality to the idea, a return to the basics of the game. The following morning, during a quick walk-through at the Spectrum, Westhead explained his plan to the other Lakers. "I wasn't sure what Westhead's intent was," Wilkes said. "I guess he was saying, 'We just lost our best player, but we have this young, charismatic phenom who is going to make it all right.'"

At the same time Westhead and Johnson were hatching a plan, the city of Philadelphia was on heightened paranoia alert. Kareem Abdul-Jabbar sightings were reported left and right. A taxi driver called into a local radio station, insisting he had just dropped the center off at the Spectrum. "I'll believe he's not coming when the game ends and I haven't seen him," Billy Cunningham, Philadelphia's coach, said. "They could fly him in at any time by private jet or something."

Immediately before the start time, Westhead reiterated the strategy to his players. "Everybody expects us to be courageous tonight," he said. "We're not here to be courageous. We're here to win." Cooper, usually the sixth man, would start alongside Nixon in the backcourt. Wilkes, generally able to freelance along the perimeter, would have to crash the boards in Abdul-Jabbar's absence. Johnson, officially listed as the starting center, would do . . . everything. "That was his job," said Westhead. "To do whatever the team needed, whenever it needed it. He was our center that night, but really the position he played was 'undefined.'" Before exiting the locker room, Johnson grabbed Abdul-Jabbar's number 33 jersey, which dangled from a hanger in an empty locker, and tossed it in a gym bag. "Thirty-three ain't here," he yelled, "but thirty-two is! Now let's go out there and kill these motherfuckers!"

Some three thousand miles away, Abdul-Jabbar sat in bed alongside his live-in girlfriend, Cheryl Pistono.* Meanwhile, inside the Spectrum, Johnson met with Westhead along the sideline before breaking for the court. "I'm gonna jump center, Coach," he said. It wasn't a request, it wasn't an order. It simply was. Westhead smiled and nodded. "That fucked Philly up," said Cooper. "They were looking around like something wasn't right. And Caldwell Jones was looking at Magic like, 'What the fuck are you doing here?'"

---

* Though the game was being televised live in California, CBS aired it on tape delay in most other parts of the country so as not to preempt two of its highest-rated shows, *The Dukes of Hazzard* and *Dallas* (both of which were already in reruns). The NBA had come a long way in Johnson's first season—but also had a long way to go.

Because sports and mythology often intertwine, the Game 6 narrative has often been one that evokes the best of a cheesy feel-good Hollywood production. Not only did Johnson take the jump ball, he won it, dribbled down the court, did a 360-degree midair flip and dunked over Julius Erving—blindfolded while eating a slice of cheesecake.

Not quite.

Jones, the 76ers long-armed 7-foot-1 center, stepped toward referee Jack Madden, and Johnson acknowledged he had no chance. "I just decided to jump up and down real quick," Johnson said, "then work on the rest of my game."

"It didn't matter whether he won or lost the jump," said Westhead. "It was a statement, establishing that he had replaced Kareem. He needed to do that. It was never like, 'I'm the center—throw me the ball down low like you do Kareem.' It was, 'I'm here, and we're going to win.' "

Over the next four quarters, Johnson played a game like none before, or since. The Lakers bolted out to a 7–0 lead, and extended it to 11–4 before Cunningham received a single point from one of his frontcourt players. The Sixers were befuddled—by the fast pace, by the sight of Johnson in the post, by Cooper's lockdown defense. Philadelphia, though, battled back, tying the score at 60. In the locker room at halftime, Westhead let Johnson have it, imploring him to play stronger interior defense. After the coach finished, Johnson gathered his teammates around. "We're about to win this game," he said. "You've got to believe that. We're about to be champions."

In his bed, Abdul-Jabbar could barely watch. "It was a real nervous time," he said. "I was sweating badly. Not your classic fan reaction. I had to turn the sound off."

Los Angeles scored the first 14 points of the third quarter but—once again—Cunningham demanded his big men work the ball inside on the undersize, overworked Laker forwards. With 5:12 remaining in regulation and the Lakers leading 103–101, Westhead called a time-out, looked Johnson in the eyes and demanded something extra. "This is your opportunity," he said. "*Your* opportunity."

Though but twenty years old, Johnson was exhausted. Dawkins and Jones had mauled him. He'd played all five positions, guarded multiple Sixers, fought for every rebound and loose ball within reach. "The greatest single-game effort ever," said Westhead. "Ever." Upon returning to the

court, Johnson tapped in a missed layup, then watched with glee as Wilkes—
who scored the quietest 37 points of all time—drove the lane, hit a layup,
was fouled and sank the free throw. Like that, in less than one and a half
minutes, the Lakers upped their lead to 7.

"After Jamaal's three-point play, I ran out into my yard and screamed,"
Abdul-Jabbar said. "Then I came back and chewed on a pillow."

With Johnson scoring nine points over the final 2:22, the Lakers turned
a close game on its head. The 123–107 margin told the story of a blowout
that wasn't. The Lakers won, but exerted every ounce of energy in doing so.
When the final buzzer sounded and the season was complete, Johnson and
his teammates retreated to the locker room, which was uncharacteristically
subdued. Erving, Philadelphia's nine-time All-Star, entered unannounced
and went Laker to Laker, offering a handshake and congratulatory words.
"So classy," said Holland. "He even knew who I was." In their hearts, most
of the players had expected to play Game 7 in Los Angeles. The Lakers didn't
even pack champagne—it was provided by the Spectrum's caterers. Butch
Lee, the seldom-used guard, popped the first bottle, and others quickly followed. "Magic was born to play and born to win," said Holland, who scored
eight key points. "It's hard to picture Magic Johnson losing."

Rick Barry, working the game for CBS, asked Johnson why, post-
triumph, the locker room was so quiet. The rookie had just compiled 42
points, 15 rebounds and 7 assists to be named the *Sport* Magazine Most Valuable Player of the series.

"Because," Johnson said, grinning, "it's unbelievable."

CHAPTER 6

WEST FALL

Generally speaking, it takes time to develop into a genius.

Sure, there are notable exceptions. Wolfgang Amadeus Mozart was six when he first performed publicly in Munich's court of Bavaria. Jonas Salk began working on a flu vaccine while still an undergraduate in college. Stephen Hawking built a computer out of clock parts, an old telephone switchboard and other recycled components when he was sixteen.

Yet, more often than not, genius is something that is crafted and constructed and nurtured. Well before Albert Einstein became known as the greatest thinker of the twentieth century, he was a subpar elementary school student with a learning disability.

In the aftermath of the Los Angeles Lakers' magnificent championship run, Paul Westhead—former obscure head coach of the La Salle College Explorers of the East Coast Conference—was proclaimed a genius. OK, the word itself wasn't literally used all that often. But when the stories on Magic Johnson's rookie greatness and Kareem Abdul-Jabbar's sixth MVP trophy and Spencer Haywood's implosion ran dry, the media turned its affections toward a professorial forty-one-year-old man who fell into a dream job and was wise enough to stick with his predecessor's philosophy.

Yet now that Jack McKinney was officially gone, hired by Indiana to coach the Pacers, Paul Westhead felt liberated to implement his own ideas and philosophies.

"When Paul became a genius," said Jamaal Wilkes, "trouble started."

The world champions reported to Palm Desert for training camp on September 12, and, from the look of things, not much had changed. Save for the departure of Haywood, who would spend the next two years trying to clean up and reestablish himself in Italy, the Lakers' eight core members were all back. It was an exciting time to be a basketball player in Los Angeles, what with the multiple endorsement opportunities, the increase in season ticket sales, the deafening buzz of a metropolis that, ever so gradually, was shifting from a Dodger town to a Laker town.

Then, to kick off the first official practice inside the College of the Desert's gymnasium, Westhead made what must be considered one of the great blunders of his coaching career. He introduced (egad) "The System."

"This is a new year and a new team," he said, "and we're going to do things differently. We're going to put in a new offense, and you'll need to trust me. Because I know what I'm doing."

Throughout the 1979–80 season, the Lakers were, in many regards, a strategic ode to McKinney's basketball intellect. They inbounded the ball quickly, pushed the pace, filled the lanes and excelled via organized chaos. "We ran past you, ran over you," said Nixon. "Just ran and ran and ran you to death. It was great."

Now that he was in charge, and empowered with a brand-new four-year, $1.1 million contract, Westhead wanted to incorporate his own ideas. No longer, he explained to the speechless players, would there be the same freelance, go-with-your-gut offensive opportunities. The Lakers would continue to run, but always with a certain level of controlled stagnation. Thought replaced instinct. Programmed evaluation trumped rapid-fire response. More than twenty newly diagrammed plays were added, most designed to get the ball to Abdul-Jabbar in the post. Nixon, the shooting guard under McKinney's vision, would handle the ball more often, moving Johnson to a nebulous point-forward-power position.

World champion Los Angeles Lakers—meet La Salle College.

"It's highly structured," Westhead explained at the time. "Every player has an exact assignment and there can be no deviation from position. What's unique is that it's highly systematic and extremely demanding."

As the players listened to their coach in those opening days, they nodded and smiled and grinned. Westhead was a genuinely nice man. He had scored big locker room points for the way he took command of the Haywood situation, and nobody could have done a better job in the aftermath of McKinney's accident.

The players even appreciated the goofy sincerity of his nonstop Shakespearean references. Once, toward the end of a close game in the 1979–80 season, Westhead looked at Johnson in the huddle and, quoting from *Macbeth*, uttered, "If it were done when 'tis done, then 'twere well it were done quickly."

Johnson listened, said nothing, paused, then smiled and asked, "You want me to get it into the big fella?"

"Right on," said Westhead.

During the playoff series against Seattle, Westhead was asked by the press what Johnson had told him during a time-out. "What did he say?" Westhead said. "'A horse! A horse! My kingdom for a horse!'"

"You had to like Paul the person," said Michael Cooper. "There wasn't a jerk bone in his body."

And yet . . .

"Something," said Nixon, "wasn't right."

If there was one man (besides Abdul-Jabbar) who stood to gain from Westhead's changes, it was probably Nixon, who fancied himself a team-leading, game-changing ball handler, not a shooting guard waiting for a pass. Though he had certainly enjoyed winning a championship in 1980, Nixon never fully accepted his role as Johnson's caddy. He still bristled over an occurrence from the previous year, when the Lakers were boarding the bus for a shootaround in Philadelphia. At 10:55 A.M., every member of the team was ready to go, save Nixon, who was often a minute or two late. "Let's drive away! Let's drive away!" Johnson shouted. "Why are we always waiting for Norm?" When Nixon finally climbed the steps, a teammate howled, "Rookie's trying to get you fired."

"Well," said Nixon, "he's young and dumb and don't know any better."

Now, a season removed, Westhead seemed willing to break up the point guard duties and let Nixon receive more plum assignments.

"Maybe that's true," Nixon said. "But it was very clear that Paul's system wasn't going to work for us. It was too restrictive. You ran to the spots and that was it. He immediately started to have problems with all of us because we all knew how to play. We weren't guys willing to just run to a spot and stand there and watch someone else play. We were all used to being involved.

"For example, Paul wanted me to run down the right-hand side of the court every time. That's just not realistic. 'Run to this exact spot and stand there' might—*might*—work in college, but not in the NBA. It was very frustrating."

Added another member of the team, who requested anonymity: "Paul went from doing a great job of coaching that first year to a lousy job the second. From that first meeting, when he explained the change, everyone just went, 'Huh? What are you talking about? What are you doing? We just won a championship.' We were disjointed from day one. It was like, as soon as they took the interim tag off, something happened to Paul where the power went to his head. I mean, he tried to run a shared point guard system with Magic and Norm, and it was destined to be a disaster. I love Norm, but it wasn't even close—Magic was the best point guard on the planet. And now, because Paul wanted to exercise his power, we have this point guard battle that became really, really, *really* awkward."

The Lakers opened the 1980–81 season by fighting back from a 19-point deficit to pull out a thrilling 99–98 road win over Seattle, then returned home and thumped the Houston Rockets, 114–103. On that night, two noteworthy occurrences took place: First, Abdul-Jabbar was accidentally poked in the right eye by Houston's Rudy Tomjanovich, resulting in a corneal abrasion that would lead to two missed games and a permanent return to the signature goggles he had last worn two years earlier. Second, Larry O'Brien, the NBA's commissioner, presented the players with their championship rings—a reminder of what was and what, the returnees felt, could not possibly be again under the current system.

Even with Abdul-Jabbar's injury, Los Angeles won its first five games. But they were . . . *off.* The Kansas City Kings took the Lakers to overtime before falling, 112–107,* and the Phoenix Suns—featuring an unspectacular roster—led in the fourth quarter, then folded, 116–109. To most of the media and fans, all appeared to be business as usual. Wins were wins, right? "But it wasn't that way," said Alan Hardy, a rookie forward. "There were real problems that needed to be addressed."

Through mid-November, the Lakers settled into a pattern. They would win two or three, then lose one. There'd be splendid moments (Johnson scored 33 points in thirty-two minutes against Utah on October 25; three days later, the Lakers pummeled the Clippers by 30) and head-scratching lulls (San Antonio's immortally ordinary Dave Corzine shone with 16 points in a 108–102 Spurs triumph on October 26).

---

* The game against the Kings included arguably the greatest pass of Johnson's career—a no-look bullet through three defenders and into the waiting arms of Jamaal Wilkes beneath the basket. It is still discussed by players who were on the floor that day.

The first outward sign of a problem came on the night of November 12, when the Lakers traveled to Houston, played three strong, up-tempo quarters against the Rockets—then started listening to Westhead's instructions. Los Angeles led by a whopping 19 points when the coach told his guards to walk the ball up the court, use as much time as possible and, with eight seconds remaining on the shot clock, dump it into Abdul-Jabbar. It was the basketball equivalent of a prevent defense, and the results were awful. Houston was a thin team. The one thing Coach Del Harris had going for him was Moses Malone, the 6-foot-10, 215-pound center who doubled as Abdul-Jabbar's personal slab of Kryptonite. Malone was stronger, more rugged and a harder defensive worker than Abdul-Jabbar. "Nobody had a chance against Moses down inside," said Major Jones, a Houston forward. "The Lakers were much more talented than we were, so to neutralize that, Moses decided he had to put his will on Kareem." In the final four and a half minutes of the game, Abdul-Jabbar repeatedly received the ball inside. With Malone's stomach and fists glued to his jersey, the Laker star missed his last four shots, including a skyhook in the lane with fourteen seconds remaining. Houston won, 107–104. "Painfully predictable," said Jim Chones. "So painful. We did the same thing all the time."

When the game ended, the Lakers players retreated to the Summit's visiting locker room, where they launched a kick-off to an inevitable mutiny. Unless you were a rookie who knew no better or the content-to-be-the-centerpiece Abdul-Jabbar, you weren't happy. "We just stopping moving," said Johnson, a glum look crossing his face. "We ran a lot of plays that didn't involve a lot of movement."

Johnson assumed the Houston defeat was his team's bottoming out. He was wrong. Six days later, in the second quarter of a game against the visiting Kings, Johnson made a cut against Kansas City's Hawkeye Whitney, heard a loud pop and crumpled. As soon as he reached the court, Kerlan, the team doctor, knew this was bad. Johnson suffered a cartilage tear in his left knee.

Prognosis: Out for at least three weeks.

Reality: He would miss 101 days.[*]

"I don't think you can understand how bad that was," said Butch Carter, a rookie guard. "Magic wasn't just a great player who did everything on the

---

[*] The injury actually initially occurred on November 11, when Atlanta's Tom Burleson fell across the back of Johnson's knee. It wasn't discovered, however, until after the Kings catastrophe.

court. He was our glue. Before we went to camp, he took all the rookies out for dinner. As rookies, every day he fed me and Alan Hardy. Every single day, he had a woman come over and cook dinner, and he'd always call us over to his apartment.

"Magic was special. During training camp, we had to run a mile on the second day of practice. I was a second-round draft pick with a non-guaranteed contract, he was the Finals MVP—and I could not catch his ass. There was no reason he had to finish first in that run, but he needed to. That's not just leadership, that's greatness."

When Paul Westhead realized his team would be without its leader for an extended period of time, he dreaded the idea of returning full power to Norm Nixon. Suddenly, without warning or preparation, the keys to the Lakers would be in the hands of a player who was neither trusted nor particularly liked by the organization's higher-ups. "Norm was difficult," said Westhead. "Talented, quick, fast—but feisty and stubborn."

Those are actually kind words, compared to the sentiment floating through the Forum's executive offices. Although fans and journalists often grouped Los Angeles with monolithic, multimillion-dollar franchises like the New York Yankees and the Dallas Cowboys, the comparison was wrongheaded. Along with Buss, the key decision makers were Lou Baumeister, the president of California Sports (the company that owned and operated the Lakers, Kings and Forum); Frank Mariani, Buss's longtime business partner; Bill Sharman, the general manager; Jerry West, the ex-coach-turned-special-consultant; and Chick Hearn, the beloved broadcaster who also served as the assistant GM. Inside the Forum, the men mixed and mingled with a dozen (or so) other employees, ranging from Mary Lou Liebich, the basketball secretary, to Claire Rothman, the vice president of booking, to Bruce Jolesch, the public relations director. "It really was like a family," said Rothman. "We did everything together. I can't imagine a closer at-work relationship."

Though disagreements arose, the majority of decision makers were united in both their love for Johnson and their misgivings for Nixon. "Norm had an agenda," said Steve Springer, who covered the team for the *Orange County Register*. "I enjoyed Norm, but there always seemed to be something brewing."

Like Abdul-Jabbar, Nixon spent much of life battling against the glacier-size chip resting atop his shoulder. He grew up in the projects of Macon,

Georgia, raised with his two older brothers by a divorced mother. Although he excelled in football and basketball at Southwest Macon High, Nixon was overshadowed by Joe Everett, a talented guard who, many assumed, would be the one to go on to NBA fame. (Everett played at nearby Mercer College, then faded away.) "Norm was really good," said Walter Daniels, a prep teammate who, in 1979, was the Lakers' third-round draft pick out of Georgia. "But he sorta flew below the radar with Joe around."

Don Richardson, Southwest's coach, excelled in development. During practices he implemented weighted jackets, palm gloves and blinders. The team perfected a suffocating 2-1-2 full-court trap, and ran opposing schools to exhaustion. "Most coaches give a team thirty seconds to run one suicide," Nixon said. "Don Richardson made us do two in fifty-five. The basketball work ethic and IQ on my team was incredible."

Nixon aspired to play collegiately in the Southeastern Conference, but in 1973 the participating colleges were still wary of bringing in too many black athletes. Instead, he accepted a scholarship to Duquesne. "It was Pittsburgh, which was a strange thing for me," he said. "But they seemed to really want me."

On March 4, 1975, Duquesne faced Cincinnati in a chance to qualify for the NCAA Tournament. With no time remaining, and the Dukes down by one, Nixon walked to the free-throw line for two shots. He looked over at John Cinicola, the head coach, and winked. "It was as if to say, 'Relax, Coach, it's in the bag,'" said Cinicola. "Then he missed, and we went home. But two years later, against Villanova in the Eastern 8 final, Norm winks again, makes both shots, we go on to play VMI in Raleigh." After four varsity seasons, Nixon left with the single season and career records for most field goals and assists.

Playing for a perennially subpar school, Nixon was overlooked for national honors. He wasn't invited to audition for the Pan Am Games or 1976 Olympic team, and was often referred to as a "sleeper" who *could* surprise people. Even when the Lakers selected him with their third first-round pick in 1977, Nixon was dissatisfied. Why had he slipped until the twenty-second and final slot of the round? And why had the Lakers taken two other players—North Carolina State forward Kenny Carr and Maryland guard Brad Davis—before him? "I got drafted by the pros and they called me the no-name guard," he said. "People wanted to know who this guy from Duquesne was."

Nixon arrived for his first training camp seduced by the warm weather but frustrated (and driven) by the perceived lack of respect. The Lakers had gone 53-29 the previous season, and Coach Jerry West showed little regard for the small kid (6-foot-2, 170 pounds) from the small school. Davis, an inch taller and the product of a major collegiate program, was the early favorite to slide into the vacant point guard spot. That lasted for four days. "Norm was so much better than Brad, it was laughable," said Adrian Dantley, a forward on the team. "Jerry never got on Brad. Not once. Instead he made Norm his whipping boy, always getting on him about how to use the pick and roll to score, how to find the open man. It was ridiculous."

Nixon started 81 games, averaging 13.7 points and 6.8 assists, but the experience was awful. West didn't so much ride Nixon as he mentally tortured him. Compliments never came. Insults soared. Nixon was a wimp. Nixon was inept. Nixon couldn't handle the spotlight. Nixon—dashingly handsome, with a wardrobe straight off the pages of GQ—was a pretty boy. Nixon wasn't committed to the game. Nixon was a whiner. A maligner. "Their relationship was very antagonistic," said Ron Carter, a Laker guard. "We all had nicknames, and Norm's was Big—it was sarcastic, because he was the smallest guy on the team, but it was serious in that he had a huge ego and he was our leader. As a coach, Jerry wanted to be the leader, and he and Norm bumped heads daily. Norm would say smart things to Jerry to get under his skin. And Jerry Buss eventually gave Norm a guaranteed contract. The moment he signed that, Jerry West lost all leverage, because Norm was making his money and he didn't care where he played.

"It wasn't unusual for Jerry to call a time-out, call a play and have Norm change it as we're walking onto the court. Norm lived to contradict him."

West was the sort of coach who wasn't afraid to put on shorts and a T-shirt during practice, and he and Nixon teed off in a series of physical matchups. "Best moments I saw Norm play," said Lou Hudson, a Laker guard, "were against Jerry."

In a January 20, 1978, game against the Bullets, Nixon tossed a wicked behind-the-back pass that soared past Dantley and into the stands. West flew into a fit. He jumped off the bench, sent Hudson into the game and berated Nixon. "Next time you try something like that," he screamed, "you fucking better be fucking sure you fucking complete it!"

During another contest, this one against the Nuggets, Nixon was trapped with seven seconds remaining, and passed the ball to Abdul-Jabbar.

The center shot up a brick, and Denver gathered the rebound and scored. West somehow missed the play and assumed his point guard was at fault. Afterward, West stormed into the locker room, glared at Nixon and screamed, "Damn it! Damn it! Who in the hell took that shot?"

"I did," said Abdul-Jabbar.

West paused. "Norm," he screamed, "how could you pass him the ball with seven seconds left?"

"Norm probably never realized this, but he was one of my favorite guys," said West. "He was very talented and very competitive. But he was wild, and he made some stupid mistakes. I was harder on him than anyone else because I knew what was there. Even to this day, I'm not so sure Norm Nixon doesn't think of me as the anti-Christ."

The Lakers cut Davis early in his second year, thereby making it clear the ball belonged to Nixon. He averaged 17.1 points and 9 assists in 1978–79, and were there a better NBA point guard, nobody on the Los Angeles roster could think of one.

By the time Johnson came along, Nixon considered himself to be a full-fledged NBA star. Yet as the rookie burst onto the scene, the incumbent faded into the background. He played excellently in 1979–80, averaging a career-high 17.6 points while shooting 52 percent from the field. Los Angeles, though, was all about *Magic! Magic! Magic! Magic!* This didn't sit well with the team's exiled shooting guard. "It was bullshit on Norm's part," said Michael Cooper. "Just bullshit. Yeah, it had been his team for a number of years, and he'd run the show really well. But you have a guy telling you, 'Listen, I want to get you twenty-five to thirty shots per night. That's what I want to do for you.' Shit, yeah! I mean, who wouldn't want that? But Norm didn't want to give up the ball. Shit, let Magic do his thing. Magic's coming down, kicking it to you. But Norm, he wanted the basketball.

"That's the good and the bad part of the NBA. The good part is the competitiveness of the players. But you can also be a competitive player in a nonconfrontational way on your team. Magic wasn't competing with Norm for anything. But Norm didn't see it that way."

Now, as Johnson healed, his adversary stepped in. With Nixon at the helm, the team dropped five of its next eight, including a pathetic 122–108 home setback to the woeful Bulls. "These are rough times," Westhead said. "It is a learning process in losing a few." Before long, Nixon was the daily subject of trade banter. There was talk of sending him to Chicago for Reggie

Theus; to Seattle for Gus Williams; to Cleveland for Mike Bratz. Los Angeles denied the rumors, but the gossip was legitimate. Westhead didn't like Nixon's attitude, and West didn't seem to like Nixon—period. He had to go.

"I knew what was up," Nixon said. "And I knew what I was up against."

As soon as the city's columnists started to pen Norm Nixon's basketball obituary, though, the team came to life. Having initially gone 11-11 without Johnson, the Lakers segued into a torrid hot streak, capturing 17 of their next 23. Part of it was a good squad coming together. Abdul-Jabbar and Wilkes had some terrific nights and Sharman, the general manager, stole a steady reserve point guard named Eddie Jordan from the Nets for a future draft pick.

On December 19, Scott Ostler of the *Los Angeles Times* wrote a piece titled LAKERS ARE FINDING OUT WHY NBA CHAMPS DON'T REPEAT. The story was a brutal state-of-the-Lakers overview. According to Ostler, players were becoming increasingly angered by Abdul-Jabbar (who was an offensive black hole) and increasingly pessimistic about Westhead. They specifically cited the coach's recent decision to bench Chones and Cooper and replace them with Jim Brewer, a so-so veteran, and Butch Carter, the rookie out of Indiana. Westhead's stated reasoning—"We need to create a better balance of energy."

Wrote Ostler: "Enough bad vibes have been vibrating to arouse speculation that the Lakers have contracted Titleitis, the dreaded disease which could prevent them from repeating."

Sharman, West and Westhead could accept criticism from the press. They could accept criticism from the fans. What irked the three, though, were the ever-increasing anonymous quotes emanating from inside the locker room. While the writers protected their sources, everyone knew the identity of the team's most loose-lipped, most negative-minded player. "If [Norm Nixon] doesn't stop talking," one Laker official said at the time, "he'll talk himself right out of L.A."

"You could approach Norm and come away with some valuable information," said Springer. "He wouldn't put his neck out there on the record, but off the record he was tremendous."

■ ■ ■

Shortly after Magic Johnson injured his knee, he told Malcolm Moran of *The New York Times* that perhaps it was an act of God. "I thought [my career] was always going to be good things," he said. "Maybe it was a blessing in disguise, to let me know it can end as fast as it started. Wham. It made me keep it in the right frame of mind. It kept me from getting a big head, and thinking that things would always be like this."

Johnson spent his time away from the court buried in a cocoon of misery. His life became an ode to mind-numbing routine—at two P.M., he'd turn on the television to watch *Ironside*. One hour later, *Wild, Wild World of Animals* began. Then *Barnaby Jones*, *M*A*S*H*, *Scooby-Doo!* (yes, *Scooby-Doo!*), *All in the Family*, the local news and, lastly, a follow-up episode of *M*A*S*H*. Sometimes, a teammate stopped by with a bag of McDonald's. Sometimes, he spent the entire day alone.

If Johnson needed some reinforcement that things wouldn't always be "like this" (championships, bubbly, endorsement deals, nonstop love), it came on the morning of February 27, when he was scheduled to return to the Lakers' active roster. In Southern California, Johnson's triumphant rebirth was celebrated with the pomp and circumstance of a general back from war. MAGIC'S BACK! pins were the rage outside the Forum, and his whereabouts and condition became pressing fodder for the region's news agencies. Upon opening the *Los Angeles Times*'s sports section over breakfast (as he always did), Johnson was greeted with a story headlined TONIGHT, THE LAKERS PUT A LITTLE MAGIC BACK IN THEIR LIVES. Written by Alan Greenberg, the piece mainly highlighted the excitement felt by Laker management and coaches. One quotation, however, jumped off the page. When asked how he felt about no longer being the primary ball handler, Nixon didn't hold back. "It's not my preference," he said. "But I don't want to be negative about it. Magic is a wiser player (than the previous season). He realizes that we sometimes can have two point guards handling the ball. The guy is a great talent. Even if there was resentment within myself, the guy plays as hard as he can, so he can do anything he wants to do."

Anyone who knew Nixon understood the words were mild compared to the sentiment. Yes, he liked the kid—in the same way all of the Lakers liked the kid. Beneath the peaceful exterior, however, was mounting resentment from players over the way people regularly spoke of the franchise as "Johnson's"—as if he were not merely a participant but the CEO and moral compass. Though the good vibes of a championship season concealed the cracks, they had been there from the start. As soon as Johnson arrived in

Los Angeles to sign with the Lakers, he was embraced by Jerry Buss in a way few owners had ever embraced a player. Buss viewed his new twenty-year-old star as both a terrific basketball standout and a magnet. The smile. The walk. The conversational skills. He was someone people wanted to be around, someone women *really* wanted to be around.

Buss—one of Southern California's great partiers—made Johnson a semiregular nightlife sidekick. Maybe he couldn't teach him how to break the full-court press. But he was sure happy to show him how to survive on three and a half hours of sleep and woo the Southern California babes. "My dad had the energy of a twenty-year-old," said Jeanie Buss, Jerry's daughter. "That was the thing about him. Most people evolve as they get older, and settle into certain life patterns. Well, he didn't. He wanted to be out until four o'clock in the morning. I used to go out with him until I was twenty-five. Then I was like, 'I can't do this any longer.' I didn't have the energy." When, in 1980, a *Los Angeles Times* story quoted Johnson as saying, "You've got to lay back a little. There's no way to have a social life like I would like to have playing as many games as we do. I do the things I like to do, but I keep it at a minimum," teammates fell to the floor laughing. Thanks to Buss, Johnson was ubiquitous. The Lakers phenom was on the dance floor of Club Soda. At the bar of The Odyssey. Listening to music at The Palace and Xenon West and a dozen other nightclubs and hot spots. "Jerry Buss was a Hugh Hefner clone," said John Papanek, a basketball writer for *Sports Illustrated*. "He was always walking around with five or six hotties hanging off his appendages." In fact, Buss was more than merely a clone. He and Hefner were close friends, and the Lakers owner could often be found at the Playboy Mansion—land of swimming pools, caviar and one hundred pairs of delectably large breasts.

Just how big a player was Jerry Buss? "My second year with the Lakers, Norm Nixon and I decided to sneak out of training camp one night," said Ron Carter, a guard. "There was a party at a club, and Stevie Nicks was holding it. So we sneak out, have a great night, and as we're leaving the club at eleven forty-five P.M. who walks in but Jerry Buss. We run into the men's bathroom to hide, and Dr. Buss sends one of his guys in to get us and have a drink with him. That man was like no other. He's the only owner I've ever heard of who'd come into the locker room and ask two important questions— 'Where are you guys going tonight?' and 'Can I come along?'"

Buss brought Johnson to the mansion, and watched proudly as he emerged as one of the most revered eligible bachelors in Los Angeles. Early in his career, teammates nicknamed Johnson Buck, and the story has long gone that it stemmed from his playing like a "young buck"—aka with great passion. "But that's complete bullshit," said Ron Carter. "It's not what people think. We called his ass Buck because during the days of slavery, the plantation owners would always use the strongest buck to impregnate all the women. And Earvin was such a whore, we called him Buck. The media never got that story right."

"Magic was ridiculous back then," said Mark Landsberger, the reserve forward. "I went out with Wilt Chamberlain one night to the opening of a club, and he must have had fifteen to twenty white girls come up to him. I was amazed. Well, Magic topped that."

Johnson was the rarest of Hollywood breeds—an overnight star. He wasn't the struggling actor waiting tables in hopes of a shot. No, he was instant Cary Grant, placed in the spotlight and handed an all-access VIP pass. Before long, Johnson's endorsement opportunities dwarfed those of Abdul-Jabbar, formerly the Lakers' top pitchman. He could be seen in advertisements for 7-Up and Spalding, a copy machine company and an outfit that designed men's pants. He even had his own chocolate chip cookie.

Nixon, on the other hand, was just Nixon. Buss took him out, but not all that often. He appeared in a movie, *The Fish That Saved Pittsburgh*, but had only a couple of endorsement opportunities. He was more handsome than Johnson but lacked the charisma and 1,000-watt smile. According to Springer, the *Orange County Register* beat writer, Nixon owns "the greatest streak in sports history—two straight years of road trips without ever being minus the company of a woman for a night."

"I knew Norm," said Springer. "I was close with him. We were in Richfield, Ohio, in the middle of nowhere on a Monday night, because we got there the day before the game. We're staying at the Holidome, which was a Holiday Inn that was basically a minimum-security prison—there was nowhere to go. There was a Dairy Queen across the street and a blizzard outside. It was probably three degrees below zero. And we're the only ones staying in this hotel. There's nobody else. Norm and I are playing Ping-Pong and I say, 'Well, Norm, it looks like your streak is going to end tonight.' He goes, 'We'll see.' At nine o'clock a Jaguar pulls up, this woman gets out in a full-length fur coat. She comes over and Norm goes, 'Go upstairs—I'm playing Ping-Pong. I'll be there in twenty minutes.' Unbelievable. Just unbelievable."

But not surprising. "The truth is, the friction between Earvin and Norm went way beyond basketball," said Cooper, who was close with both guards. "That situation went to the party life. They were fucking the same girls. That was a problem. Dr. Buss was best friends with Hugh Hefner, and that door was open to Magic. And Norm being known, until then, as the number one available bachelor in Los Angeles, as the swinging guy who liked everything, it was awkward.

"This was his team before, but he hadn't won anything until Magic came along. So they're bumping heads with girls, they're fucking the same girls. They didn't argue about it, but you could hear them talking about it— 'Well, man, you need to stay away from Peggy,' and such and such. They were friends. Good friends. But then it became competitive with them over basketball and women. We used to call ourselves the Three Musketeers, because we did everything together, and now it was as if I was torn between two lovers."

Added Ron Carter: "Norm was my friend, but he was cocky as all hell. He has zero lack of confidence, ever. On or off the court. He saw everything Magic did as a competition. For the ball. For playing time. For women. Who's the coolest? Who's the smartest? Me and Coop would sit back and just watch. They certainly respected each other. But there was this weird tension."

Predictably, Johnson's first game back was greeted in Los Angeles as a celebration of the human spirit. Two hours before tip-off, a gaggle of reporters and photographers lingered in the team's locker room, recording every step, itch and scratch. When Johnson entered the trainer's room to have tape applied to his ankles, media folks followed. Wrote the *Los Angeles Times*: "U.S. Senators receive less coverage." Added *The New York Times*: "The press coverage was like that for a departing astronaut."

When asked to explain why so much was being made of a point guard getting back onto the basketball court, Westhead thought long and hard. "I had seriously wondered if Magic was human," he said. "I doubted that he was. The day before his surgery, I thought, 'Gee, this guy's going to have surgery just like the rest of us.' The operation was at eight A.M. on a Monday and I wanted to visit him. I didn't want to go too early because he would still be doped up. I figured I'd go around six o'clock and find out what this guy was really like. So I went to the room and the door was closed and I thought, 'Aha! A sign! He's crying and moaning.' I pushed the door open and peeked in and there was Magic propped up in the bed with a Dodger cap on backward, a piece of apple pie shoved up under his face, watching a football game, yelling at his father and a bunch of friends playing cards to keep the noise down. I couldn't believe it. I walked away that night thinking, 'What does this guy have that no one I've ever known has?' I guess he's human, but it's only a guess."

A sellout crowd of 17,505 stood on its feet for forty-five seconds as Johnson was introduced by Larry McKay, the public address announcer. He smiled, nodded and spread his arms, palms up, as if to say—in the words of *Sports Illustrated*—"Why are you people treating me this way? I'm just a basketball player and this is just another game. Against the New Jersey Nets, yet." He lingered at the foul line as the army of photographers and cameramen shot away. "It's a thing I'll always remember," he said.

Before the game, Westhead pulled Johnson aside and told him, "There's a Spanish word for what I want you to be tonight. Suave, suave. Easy, easy. Take it easy tonight, OK?" Though Johnson played sloppily (12 points, 11 rebounds, 4 assists) in an ugly 107–103 win, there was a comfort having him back in uniform. With ten seconds left and Los Angeles ahead by a basket, Johnson rebounded Cooper's errant jumper, dribbled off much of the time, then passed to Abdul-Jabbar, who was fouled and made two free throws. The crowd cheered wildly.

Afterward, as his teammates wandered away and the ocean of media members parted, a single reporter remained. He was from *The State News*, Michigan State University's student newspaper, and he wanted to know if Johnson had anything to say to the folks at his alma mater.

"Just tell 'em I'm back," he said. "The Magic is back."

Only it wasn't. Not really. Under Johnson's leadership, Los Angeles did play somewhat improved basketball, completing the season by winning 11 of 17 games to go 54-28 and place second behind Phoenix in the Pacific Division. Yet the team was neither crisp nor motivated, and Nixon's pouting gained momentum as the playoffs approached. "Norm's biggest thing was always that he wanted to be bigger than Magic," said Clay Johnson, who joined the team the following season. "He had that little man's syndrome. You're little, but you wanna be big. Well, you're not going to be bigger than Magic. It's impossible."

The awkwardness between Nixon and Johnson was palpable. In the locker room, silent factions formed—those who loved Magic vs. those who liked Magic but believed a slick phoniness gift-wrapped the inside ingredients. "I liked both guys," said Eddie Jordan. "I really did. They were different, but both had their strong points."

"When Magic came back, it was treated like a Hollywood premiere," said Mike Thibault, an assistant coach. "You could sense the strong jealousies in the locker room. The other players resented how he was being treated as a savior. It was ugly."

Los Angeles concluded the regular season with a 148–146 final-day loss to Denver. The setback was deemed irrelevant—Abdul-Jabbar and Wilkes skipped most of the action. Yet when the media entered the locker room afterward, and talk turned to the Houston Rockets, the team's first-round playoff opponent, the Lakers' cavalier outlook was troubling. "We're not as good as we were against Philadelphia [in the 1980 Finals]," said Wilkes. "But it's a progressive thing. We have to beat Houston, then we have tough matchups with San Antonio and Phoenix."

Most of Los Angeles's players assumed nothing would get in the way of an easy stroll over the 40–42 Rockets, a team with a dominant center (Moses Malone), an aged point guard (thirty-two-year-old Calvin Murphy) and an unimpressive supporting cast. "There's no way we were supposed to lose to the Houston Rockets," said Jim Brewer, a reserve forward. "We were better than the Rockets."

On the morning of March 31, readers of the *Los Angeles Times* opened the sports section to find an above-the-fold article with the headline THE LAKERS' OTHER GUARD. It was penned by Mike Littwin, a young writer in his second year on the beat. At first glance, it appeared to be little more than a boilerplate playoff-eve profile of Nixon, filled with platitudes over the guard's speed, quickness and leadership. "I set out to write a story sympathetic to Norm," said Littwin. "Here was a guy who was a really good player, but who had the misfortune of being next to a guy who was all-world. Magic Johnson was an all-time player who'd be remembered for the next thousand years, and Nixon was just a very good, All-Star-caliber guy. I felt for him."

For the opening few paragraphs, the article covered standard terrain about the veteran's value. The meat of the piece, however, included some Nixon quotations. Among the dandies:

- **On Johnson arriving as a rookie:** "I thought Magic would have to come in and adjust to our game. But we had to adjust to him. The first thing they said in training camp that year was that Kareem and I had been handling the ball too much."
- **On playing alongside Johnson:** "I'm a point guard, a ball handler. Playing with Magic, I'm the number two guard. I'm not a number two guard. It's not what I do best. This is not the best situation for me personally. If I can play point guard, I can be an All-Pro. I could be that on a lot of teams."
- **On his status with the Lakers:** "I'm not one of the chosen people."

When Johnson read the piece, his heart sunk. It wasn't just that they were teammates. It was, well, Nixon and Johnson—tensions be damned—shared a certain kinship. They were the Lakers' starting guards, the men who had guided the team to a championship together. "Me and Norm on road trips," Johnson said. "I don't care where it was, we were out. Norm liked to party and, at the time, I was a young buck and I liked to, too, so we was out. It was fun."

On the day the story appeared, Nixon made certain to cross the locker room and reassure Johnson that the words were taken out of context. "Listen, listen—I hope you don't let this article go and affect your game," he said. "Because you should know me better than that. You know what I would say and what I wouldn't say."

Littwin, in fact, had interviewed Nixon more than a month before the article ran—a common journalistic practice, but one that infuriated the Lakers. Buss, generally loathe to criticize the media, offered a blistering critique of the *Times*, insisting the paper had set out to cause controversy just in time for the playoffs.* Nixon concurred. "[Littwin] took everything I said and twisted it around," he said. "He talked to me while Magic was out, and asked me about the difference in playing without him. I told him the truth—I was handling the ball more, which was probably what I did best. But it wasn't a slight against Earvin at all. I went to Magic and told him

---

* *Times* readers shared Buss's anger. Anti-Littwin letters poured into the newspaper's offices—including one, from Kelvin D. Filer of Compton, that read: "The reason the Lakers lost to Houston? One Mike Littwin."

that, but he was younger than I was, and I don't know if he handled it the right way, mentally. I think it bothered him, and then the perception was there that Nixon can't play with Johnson. And once a perception exists, it's awfully hard to change that. It turns into fact. Unfair and unfortunate, but true."

For the first time in his professional career, Johnson turned standoffish. He resented Nixon, and resented Cooper for trying to broker an understanding between the two. Johnson loved Chones, and was shocked, too, to read what he perceived to be the veteran rebounder's anti-Magic take in the Littwin story.

"The whole thing was a mess," said Nixon. "Not a good way to start the playoffs."

The best-of-three series opened in Los Angeles on April 1, and the Lakers were humiliated. Johnson and Nixon started together and performed admirably, teaming up for 48 points. Yet if the players had been agitated by Westhead's offense through the regular season, they were now—in the playoffs—infuriated. Houston's game plan was basic: Methodically bring the ball up the court and, when the time was right, dump it down low to Malone. "It was smart," said Landsberger. "Because Kareem couldn't handle Moses. He was just too physical for him . . . a monster on the boards." Malone ended the game with 38 points and 23 rebounds, and left Westhead looking for anyone other than an exhausted Abdul-Jabbar to defend. Landsberger? Chones? Brewer? "They didn't know how to guard him," said Billy Paultz, who scored 15 for Houston. "And if you couldn't figure out a way to at least neutralize Moses, you weren't going to beat us."

What enraged the Lakers was Westhead's decision to counter Houston's offensive approach by mimicking it. Johnson and Nixon were itching to attack the Rockets' mediocre backcourt, yet their coach demanded a patient, calm, milk-the-clock-and-ultimately-get-the-ball-to-Kareem methodology. This could work against so-so centers like Kansas City's Sam Lacey and Denver's Kim Hughes. But Malone was George Foreman to Abdul-Jabbar's Ted Gullick. He beat up and pounded him. By the second half, Abdul-Jabbar was spent. Which led to, in the minds of Houston's players, the singular turning point of the series.

With the Rockets leading 102–91 midway through the fourth quarter, Abdul-Jabbar received the ball on the block and turned to shoot. As the

Laker extended his arm and reached over Malone, the ball left his hand . . . floating . . . floating . . . floating . . .

Swat!

From seemingly nowhere, Bill Willoughby, a reserve forward, came off his man, floated high into the air and rejected the attempt. Superman had bled. "You could have heard a pin drop," said Robert Reid, a Rockets guard. "And the body language from those guys—just deflated. Nobody touched Kareem's shot—ever. But Bill didn't just jump. He leapt."

In twelve years in the NBA, Abdul-Jabbar had rarely been blocked. "I wasn't even guarding him," said Willoughby, a journeyman forward best known for going directly from Dwight Morrow High School (NJ) to the NBA. "I came from the corner, and I didn't actually run and jump—I went up on two feet and swatted it.

"I begged my coach [Del Harris] to let me guard him the whole series. I was 6-foot-9, and he was 7-foot-3. But I'm telling you, I could have gotten to his hook shot every time. Because I knew exactly what he was going to do. When the hook was coming, all you had to do was leave your man and jump really high. Because if you were guarding him, he held you down with his strong left hand. If you weren't on top of him, you were free to go after it."

The Lakers made a final run, but the momentum of Willoughby's unforgettable play was too much. (The following night at practice, Johnson advised Abdul-Jabbar to "break" Willoughby's arm the next time he went for a block.) A stunned Forum crowd watched as the Rockets won, 111–107, leaving the Lakers a game away from elimination. "We didn't play as hard as they did," said Johnson afterward. "It was a surprise to me—a surprise and a disappointment. We can't be distracted by a lot of other things now. We have to go out and play." That night, a despondent Johnson stayed up until five o'clock in the morning. "I try to give everybody the ball, keep everyone happy, but I guess it's never enough," he said. "I never heard of this kind of situation on a winning team. Everybody can't get the pub."

"Pettiness killed us," said Brewer. "We didn't think Houston could stay with us, and we got petty with each other. That's the kiss of death."

One night later, the Lakers traveled to Houston and beat the Rockets, 111–106, but the victory was uninspired. Los Angeles blew an early 18–5 lead, allowed Murphy to freely drive through the lane for 29 points and seemed indecisive and awkward on offense. Was this Johnson's team or Nixon's team or Abdul-Jabbar's team? Should they listen to Westhead and crawl the ball up the court, or ignore him and run, à la Jack McKinney. Before the game, Johnson admitted the franchise was a mess. He had tried reassuring his teammates on the bus ride to the arena that his concerns were solely about winning ("I'm not trying to come in here and do all this with the publicity and stuff," he said. "It's just something that happened"), yet the words were met with cold stares. "Things are *different*," he said an hour before the game. "I can't say it's jealousy because I might be wrong. I just feel kind of upset, kind of down. This is the first time I've been involved in something like this." In an awkward moment for all involved, Westhead called Johnson and Nixon in front of the entire team and begged them to work things out. "This is a bad time for all this," he said. "We're trying to win."

On April 5, a strange season came to a pathetic end. The Rockets returned to Los Angeles and beat the detached Lakers, 89–86. With ten seconds remaining and Houston up only one, Johnson drove the lane, pulled up and released a jumper from eight feet away that traveled four feet before nestling gently in Malone's outstretched arms. When the Rocket center hit two free throws, the fates of both teams were sealed. The Lakers walked off the court to stunned silence, then spent the next twenty minutes trying to explain their epic failure. The Rockets, meanwhile, would advance to the NBA Finals before losing to Boston.

"There's no way," said Chones, "it should have happened."

Afterward, Johnson sat by his locker and stared blankly into space. The most difficult and hurtful year of his life had ended in the most difficult and hurtful of ways. His team had lost, and he was the one—come crunch time—who failed. Johnson compiled 9 assists and 12 rebounds, but shot a dreadful 2 for 14 from the field.

"I blew it," he said, shaking his head. "I just blew it."

Two days later, when the locker room was cleared and the press turned its attention back to the Dodgers and the Angels, Buss and Johnson met in Palm Springs for a six-hour lunch. The owner was disconsolate—"The best way to put it," he said, "is that it was like my whole being just shifted into neutral and stayed there. There were no ups or downs. . . . I was kind of like a drone, like a hum on the radio that just goes on and on." Over sandwiches and drinks, the two discussed everything from Nixon's comments to Abdul-Jabbar's shot selection; from Cooper's feisty defense to changes that needed to be made. Buss had estimated that, by falling in the first round, his team dropped $3 million in revenue. He wasn't happy.

"One thing I'd think about," Johnson said, "is coaching."

"How so?" Buss asked.

"I like Paul," the star replied. "But something here isn't working."

CHAPTER 7

PICTURE IMPERFECT

In the first week of October 1981, before members of the Lakers had yet to report to training camp, Larry Keith, the *Sports Illustrated* basketball editor, contacted Bruce Jolesch, Los Angeles's public relations director, about arranging a photo shoot of some players for the magazine's upcoming NBA Preview issue.

"That shouldn't be a problem," Jolesch said.

A couple of days later, Lane Stewart, a thirty-seven-year-old Manhattanite, reached out. Although he had shot a noteworthy *SI* cover portrait of Indiana State's Larry Bird three years earlier, Stewart's sports knowledge extended little beyond Babe Ruth and that really tall Wilt guy. He rarely watched basketball, certainly never picked up a newspaper to check on the latest transactions. "I was sort of notorious at the magazine," he said. "They knew I didn't give a damn about sports and I made no bones about it. But I loved working with athletes, because it was a joy to be around successful, fortunate people."

Stewart had been filled in on the Lakers, and was told the picture—potentially a cover—had to convey the idea of basketball becoming an increasingly complex game, what with more sophisticated offensive and defensive schemes. He was also tipped off to Paul Westhead's background as a Shakespearean scholar with a love for teaching. "My concept was a classroom, and the coach is the teacher and the players are the students," Stewart said. "I told that to whoever was in charge, and there was never an objection or a problem with it."

As the Laker players reported to the College of the Desert for the start of camp, they were more united than ever in their disdain for Westhead. Johnson and Nixon worked to patch things up during the summer and, for the most part, they had—even traveling with Buss to Las Vegas for a weekend of women, whiskey and high-stakes poker (all funded by the boss). When it came to their coach, both players knew this couldn't end well. "There was something ironic in his system supposedly being really complex and intricate," said Nixon. "Because, if we're being honest, it was painfully simple. You run to spots. That's it. You run to spots. This wasn't personal—I think we all liked Paul as a person. But, basketball-wise, it was very flawed."

Yet the Lakers were nothing if not outwardly professional. Over a six-day span, Stewart came to the Ocotillo Lodge and, inside one of the hotel's ballrooms, created his own classroom. He bought lumber to construct a floor, rented worn desks and chairs from a Hollywood props outfit, sprayed walls with off-white paint, threw in a blackboard and some chalk. "I remember Westhead being real congenial about it," said Stewart. "But not just him. Everyone really got into it."

On the morning of the shoot, six Lakers—Nixon, Johnson, Cooper, Abdul-Jabbar, Wilkes and Mitch Kupchak, the newly acquired forward—joined Westhead for a twenty-five-minute session. "Kareem came in wearing these bright red shoes, and his feet were so big we couldn't run out and find him white or blue ones in a size 18," said Andrew Bernstein, a photographer who assisted on the assignment. "Lane was mad, but he just shot the picture. He didn't complain."

Neither did the players, even though three of the men (Nixon, Johnson and Cooper) longed for Westhead to find a new job with the Siberia Snowhawks, Wilkes thought the coach had probably lost his way, Abdul-Jabbar expressed no real opinion on the matter and Kupchak was just happy to be out of Washington, DC, and away from the floundering Bullets. Though they refused to openly gripe on the scene, Nixon and Johnson detested the picture (which wound up appearing inside the magazine—not on the cover), in that it made Westhead (dressed as a schoolmaster) look smarter and more competent than he actually was. He had been described as a Shakespearean scholar at least a hundred times since taking over the team—and it became *really* annoying. "That photograph was an awful idea," said one Laker official who requested anonymity. "It reinforced the negative feelings about Paul, and made some guys even angrier than they had been. It was a huge—and I mean huge—error in judgment."

In the aftermath of the Houston playoff debacle, the organization devoted its off-season to committing one uncharacteristic misstep after another. First, in the weeks leading up to the June 8 NBA Draft, Mike Thibault, an assistant coach who also headed much of the team's scouting, submitted his recommendations to Bill Sharman and Jerry West. The Lakers possessed the nineteenth pick, which meant the elite of the elite (DePaul's Mark Aguirre, Indiana's Isiah Thomas, Maryland's Buck Williams and North Carolina State's Al Wood) would be long gone. Thibault, however, was enamored with an overlooked Clemson University forward named Larry Nance. A 6-foot-10, 205-pound pogo stick, Nance featured the type of strength-explosiveness that brought to mind a young David Thompson. Yet he was raw and—hailing from the small town of Anderson, South Carolina—shy and deferential. He had averaged only 11.5 points and 6.7 rebounds per game in four collegiate seasons. "I thought Larry Nance could become the new prototype for forwards in basketball," said Thibault. "Here was a guy who was long and athletic and could maybe be a guy who plays against wing players even though he was mainly a four. He could run all day, and he was just a fabulous athlete. He was someone who could affect a game not just with height, but length." West, who had gradually assumed many of Sharman's duties, was in agreement. He, too, imagined Nance flying down the court, receiving one alley-oop after another from Johnson and Nixon. The Lakers flew him out to Los Angeles for a workout and dinner. He was a perfect fit. "Damn, I loved Larry Nance," said West. "He was a special player."

Under Buss, however, the head coach was given final say on player personnel. And while Westhead could appreciate the scouting reports on Nance, he had been assured by Buss that the team was set to acquire Kupchak, a 6-foot-9, 230-pound bruiser. "Dr. Buss wasn't one to get overly involved, but he came to me the week before the draft and said, 'What are we looking at here?' " said Westhead. "The draft was a very casual arrangement then. It wasn't like they had a staff with rooms and videos and meetings. I told him there were two ways we could go—forward or guard. He insisted Kupchak was a definite. So . . ."

Despite the protestations of Sharman, West and Thibault, after the New

Jersey Nets plucked Indiana forward Ray Tolbert in the eighteenth slot, the Lakers announced the selection of Mike (Geeter) McGee, a 6-foot-5, 190-pound shooting guard out of the University of Michigan "That was not a very happy night for me," said West. "Not happy at all."

Westhead loved McGee, the first player in history to lead the Wolverines in scoring for four consecutive seasons. He envisioned him charging off the Lakers' bench to substitute for Cooper or Nixon and igniting instant offense. "McGee was just too good to pass up," Westhead said at the time. "He's probably the most exciting player to come out of the draft this year. He'll have people standing on their seats to see if he'll ever stop running."

One problem: Mike McGee—nice kid, great physical skills—was one of the most one-dimensional players the Lakers had ever drafted. He could shoot and shoot and shoot. But he rarely passed, rarely rebounded and played a unique brand of nonexistent defense. "I liked Mike," said Alan Hardy, a Michigan teammate. "But he could become very individualistic on the floor. There were times when he'd forget there were four other guys."

"I dreamed about playing at Michigan since I was a little boy," said Tim McCormick, a freshman center during McGee's senior year. "Before my first game I ran out onto court for warm-ups—the band is playing, my family is in the stands. Mike came up to me said, 'I'm a senior, I'm going for all-time Big Ten scoring record. If you get the ball, don't dare shoot.'"

After McGee's selection, the Phoenix Suns, Los Angeles's Pacific Division rival, jumped on Nance. He went on to appear in three All-Star Games, make the NBA's All-Defensive team three times and, just for kicks, win the league's inaugural Slam Dunk Contest in 1984. McGee, meanwhile, lasted four and a half undistinguished seasons in Los Angeles. "That one makes me moan," said West. "Still."

One and a half weeks after the McGee blunder, the Lakers officially offered Kupchak a seven-year contract worth an outlandish $800,000 annually. Because Kupchak was a restricted free agent, the Bullets could either match the deal or negotiate a trade. Westhead had been a fan dating back to Kupchak's days at the University of North Carolina, where he was a two-time second-team All-American, as well as a member of the gold medal–winning 1976 U.S. men's Olympic basketball team. Kupchak was, at first inspection, a prototypical 1970s NBA bruiser—big, white, goonish. Yet he merged those characteristics with a deft touch around the rim. "He was just a winner," said Bob Ferry, the Bullets general manager. "Mitch took the game very seriously. He'd dive for every loose ball, guard whoever you needed him to. He was athletic and active and lively. I had a lot of players in Washington, but Mitch was probably my favorite." Like Westhead, Kupchak was known as something of an eccentric. He ate the majority of his meals at Denny's and IHOP, swore by the culinary masterpiece that was 7-Eleven's frozen burrito and insisted the telephone answering machine was the greatest invention known to man. After the Bullets beat the SuperSonics to take the 1978 NBA title, the players and coaches were invited to the White House to meet President Jimmy Carter. A memo went out, reminding all guests to wear jackets and ties. Kupchak arrived in jeans and sneakers—sans socks.

Sharman and West loved the idea of adding Kupchak, but not for $800,000 a year. Not only was the contract too big for a role player (Kupchak had averaged 12.5 points and 7 rebounds coming off the bench the previous season), but it would inevitably result in a handful of Lakers suddenly feeling underpaid and underappreciated. Westhead, however, was convinced he would serve as the ideal sidekick to Abdul-Jabbar, and urged Buss to make the move. Los Angeles promptly sent Jim Chones, Brad Holland ("Great guy," said Butch Carter, "but couldn't play a single lick") and two future draft picks to Washington—then endured a tidal wave of justified criticism. On August 6, 1981, the *Los Angeles Times* ran a top-of-the-sports-section piece headlined LAKERS GET KUPCHAK; WERE THEY SNOOKERED?—and the answer from most NBA gurus was an unambiguous "Yes."

Could an argument be made that Kupchak was worth the dough?

"No," said Jerry Colangelo, the Phoenix general manager.

"No," said Carl Scheer, Denver's president.

"I don't think eight hundred thousand dollars for a second-stringer is good judgment," said Donald Sterling, owner of the San Diego Clippers (and when Donald Sterling was questioning one's decision-making ability, you knew you had problems).

"Am I missing something?" asked Pat Williams, the 76ers general manager. "This kind of thing frightens me. You just can't operate with that kind of economic insanity. Boy, oh, boy."

Had Kupchak been, simply, a basketball player with sound credentials, the contract would have been panned. However, Kupchak wasn't, simply, a basketball player with sound credentials. He was a brittle man who underwent an operation for a herniated disc while in college, then two back surgeries in five NBA years—yet continued to compete in a manner that all but guaranteed future spans on the deactivated list. Once, while playing for Washington, Kupchak dived on the floor for *fourteen* loose balls in a game against the Kings. Abdul-Jabbar, by comparison, probably hadn't dived for fourteen loose balls the entire season. "Mitch was relentless," said Ferry. "He didn't think about saving his body or holding back."

Now he was a highly paid Laker, though far from alone in that designation. Stirred awake by the loss to Houston, Buss felt a need not merely to spend but to spend lavishly and irrationally. He made efforts to acquire two big-salaried stars (Milwaukee's Marques Johnson and Denver's Kiki Vandeweghe) via trades, and though both fell through, the league took notice. The Lakers would do whatever it took. "Is Westhead a real genius?" Buss asked a reporter. "We'll find out. He asked me to get the talent. He wanted it this way. Now we'll find out what he can do."

Although the additions of McGee and Kupchak were important, the earth-shattering move wasn't an addition but a refortification. Shortly after the trade with Washington, Buss renegotiated Johnson's contract, tearing up his old deal in favor of an unprecedented twenty-five-year, $25 million agreement that would run well into the player's retirement. Both men agreed to keep quiet about the numbers, but word leaked out of the league office. "I don't know how Magic can be totally loved by his teammates now," said Wilt Chamberlain, the former Lakers center. "He's getting all that money, and all the publicity."

Abdul-Jabbar, the longest-tenured member of the team, greeted the news of Johnson's windfall with uncharacteristic emotion. The morning after it was announced, he asked the *Los Angeles Times*, "What is [Johnson], player or management? We don't know." He was right to question whether the point guard's relationship with Buss went too far. During his rookie year, Johnson had dinner with Buss after nearly every home game. The two would play pool together, go house hunting together, talk for hours about food and women and sports. Abdul-Jabbar was not alone in finding this troubling. He derisively referred to Johnson as Buss's "favorite child," and said the team's morale was on the brink of ruination. "They were giving him all this money and saying, 'Here's the ball, go entertain everybody,'" he said. "They would never have said it, but the unstated thing was not to win, but to entertain." After the setback against Houston, Abdul-Jabbar noted, Buss suggested he would love to acquire Moses Malone, the Rockets center. Abdul-Jabbar openly wondered whether he was wanted in Los Angeles, and hinted at demanding a trade to his hometown New York Knicks. "In many ways, a basketball team is like a family," he said. "If you pick one person out and put him in front of everyone else and say, 'This is my favorite child,' other people in the family are definitely going to be affected by it. No one knew exactly what was going on. Some members of the team wondered if their value lay in competing for the affection of the owner, rather than in what they do on the court.

"I've always felt the people in New York appreciate quality basketball and I could provide that." (Buss, of course, had no intention of trading a six-time MVP.)

Nixon, jealous of Johnson even without the $25 million deal, was irate. He had tried his best to convince himself that the two were equals as star guards, star ladies' men, big-time performers. Then . . . this? Nixon ran into Johnson in a hallway at the Ocotillo Lodge. A pained expression crossed his face. "Buck, what's going on?" he said. "The guys are talking. They say you are hanging out all the time with Buss. That's a no-no in this business."

"I didn't know that," Johnson countered. "Dr. Buss is my friend."

In Nixon's mind, players and owners were Democrats vs. Republicans, pitchers vs. hitters. No, they didn't have to fight one another. But they sure as hell weren't supposed to be routinely hitting Studio 54 arm in arm.

"Players and management don't hang out together," Nixon said.

"Hey, I'm hanging out with Dr. Buss," Johnson replied. "That boat has already sailed."

"Well, I'm telling you, we don't know how to take you," Nixon said. "If something is said in the locker room, we don't know if you are going to take it back."

"What are you talking about, Norm?" Johnson shouted. "I've already been in your locker room for two years. Has anything we've said gotten back to Dr. Buss?"

Nixon shrugged and walked off in silence.

■ ■ ■

By the time the Lakers once again reported to Palm Desert for training camp, everything was a mess. Westhead greeted his men by quoting from the memoir of Viktor Frankl, a Nazi concentration camp survivor, who wrote, "Anything that does not kill me makes me stronger."

The players didn't care. About the words. About the coach. About each other.

The star guards could barely look at one another. Johnson, still recovering from the knee injury, was, in Westhead's words, "having trouble beating fourth- and fifth-round draft choices." Every time West watched McGee huck up some off-balance, one-handed twenty-five-footer, he cursed Westhead under his breath. Kupchak was an unimpressive lug with limited moves, a creaky back and a sign dangling from his neck that read I AM OVERPAID, AND EVERYONE HERE KNOWS IT. Wilkes, approaching his twenty-ninth birthday, looked a step slow. Two rookies who intrigued Westhead—forwards Kurt Rambis from Santa Clara and Kevin McKenna of Creighton—were dismissed by most of the other players as merely the latest great white hypes (in a sport that regularly produced them). Abdul-Jabbar, unusually agitated even for a man who was *always* agitated, wondered whether he should have followed through on his demand to become a Knick. His play in camp was so poor that one day, in an intrasquad scrimmage, a journeyman center named Bob Elliott (who averaged 7.5 points in 73 games for the Nets the previous season) scorched him for 40 points. "It was something incredible," said Rambis, a free agent. "Bob just lit Kareem up. Then they cut him."

The Lakers were known as Hollywood and high-flying and running and gunning and fun, fun, fun, fun. Yet there had never been a more miserable time to be a part of the club.

Thank goodness for Michael Cooper.

Throughout the history of American sport, all successful teams boast at least one player who can cross chasms of class, status and production. Back when Babe Ruth and Lou Gehrig struggled to relate with the New York Yankees, pitcher Lefty Gomez was the go-between. When the Chicago Bears struggled with a racially divided locker room in the late 1970s, Walter Payton bridged myriad gaps.

Based solely off of reading the newspapers and watching the games on TV, Cooper would have been defined as an emerging complementary player with unrivaled defensive tenacity but little offensive talent. He was, however, much more than merely a role player.

"Michael Cooper," said McKenna, "was the glue."

Unlike the majority of the Lakers, Cooper wasn't really supposed to be there. Raised within shouting distance of the Forum in Pasadena, young Michael was an infant when his parents, Marshall and Jean, divorced. He and his brother, Mickey, were brought up by a grandmother, Ardessie Butler, in a seven-bedroom house stuffed with a forever-changing rotation of cousins, aunts and uncles (Ardessie was the mother of ten children). His love of competition came via one of his uncles, Tom Butler, a former Negro League ballplayer who encouraged his nephew to engage in every possible sport. "Michael always had a mental toughness about him," Tom Butler said. "He seemed to have a jump on the other kids because he'd already have thought out the smartest way to achieve his goal."

Yet while Cooper was always one of the area's better athletes, he was damned by a physique that crossed Shelley Duvall and a light pole. No matter what he ate—ice cream and cake, mashed potatoes coated in gravy, deep-fried bacon—Cooper could not gain weight. Not that he was particularly deterred. Because his hero was Paul Warfield, the outstanding Cleveland Browns wide receiver, Cooper fancied himself one day running fly patterns in the NFL. Then, in a pickup game at Madison Park when he was eight years old, a boy named Herman Bluefur knocked young Michael unconscious with a hit to the cranium. "That was it for football," Cooper said. He gave baseball a shot, but took a particularly hard fastball to the leg in a Little League game—"and baseball was off my list, too.

"Truth is, I was best at basketball, but mainly because I could run up and down the floor without getting tired," he said. "I could outrun people for long stretches, I could defend people because I moved my feet well. I never really knew the fundamentals, but I had some talent."

Cooper's hoops awakening took place when he was fourteen and won a scholarship from the local YMCA to attend Jerry West's Camp Clutch at nearby Occidental College. Still an active player with the Lakers, West was addressing the children on the virtue of free-throw shooting when he called Cooper out of the audience to demonstrate his form. He rose, nervously approached the line and connected on all four attempts. "That was when I first said to myself, 'OK, I really want to learn how to ball,'" he said. "I caught the bug."

Cooper played junior varsity basketball his first two seasons at Pasadena High School—practicing well, working doggedly and attracting the attention of no one. Then, during varsity tryouts early in his junior year, a coach named George Terzian took notice. The kid had very few moves, a mediocre handle and was embarrassingly weak under the boards. But, man, was he long. And quick. And hardened. "Coop," he told him, "your best bet at going somewhere via basketball is learning to play defense. You need to play defense with your feet. Stop reaching with your arms, start sliding." Whenever Cooper reached with his hands during practices, he'd be forced to run five laps around the gymnasium. Terzian attached a ball to the top of a long stick, and used it to teach Cooper how to block shots with two hands. "He'd hold the stick up at different angles and different heights," Cooper said, "and I'd have to run up and block the shots. I learned it wasn't about hitting it hard so it goes out of bounds, but blocking the basketball to teammates."

Long before *stopper* was a common basketball term, Cooper was Terzian's stopper. He'd lock him up with the opposing team's best player, and watch as a star who averaged 25 points per game finished the night with 6. "We had fourteen defensive principles that we'd teach the kids," said Terzian. "And Michael mastered all fourteen. He was taking charges as a teenager, and he never flinched doing so."

"I fell in love," Cooper said, "with defending."

Such was an untraditional approach to getting noticed by college recruiters, most of whom seek out the 6-foot-10 giant or the dead-eye shooter. Cooper, however, was intriguing. Pacific University stopped by, as did Seattle Pacific and Occidental College. Marv Harshman, the University of Washington's head basketball coach, came multiple times. "Marv liked his game, liked his approach," said Terzian. "The only issue was his grades."

Because he was a low-C student, Cooper wound up attending Pasadena City Community College. He averaged 19 points as a freshman for the Lancers, and returned as a sophomore thinking his time in the spotlight had arrived. Five games into the season, however, his biology professor alerted Joe Barnes, the head coach, that Cooper (averaging 30 points per game at the time) was skipping classes and wouldn't receive a grade for the semester. He was immediately suspended. That day, Barnes called Cooper into his office and changed his life. "Michael," he said, "you can go one of two ways right now. You can't play basketball for us, but you can come to practice and work out. There's a lot of quality basketball being played down at [adjacent-to-campus] Victory Park, which will keep you sharp. But what you need to do—more than anything—is buckle down and get your grades together. I'll help you as much as I can, but it's important that you do most of it yourself. This isn't just about playing basketball. It's shaping the foundation of who you are, of how much you want to expand yourself and become something and someone of substance."

A devilish voice in Cooper's brain whispered, "To hell with it—just go get a job and play ball on the side." However, Barnes's words were louder and more powerful. Though miserable and lonely, Cooper worked his grades up to a B average, and when John Whisenant, an assistant coach at the University of New Mexico, called, Barnes raved about a young man who had found his way. What Cooper didn't know at the time was that the school was in the midst of a full-blown basketball apocalypse. The previous season, six black players quit the Lobos, accusing head coach Norman Ellenberger of racism. "The pitch Norm made to me was 'Look, I've got all these open spots I have to fill,'" Cooper said. "I'm getting all these junior college all-stars, and you have an immediate chance to start."

Though mildly concerned ("You don't want to play for a racist if you can avoid it," he joked), Cooper couldn't ignore the opportunity. He arrived in Albuquerque half expecting to find the grand wizard of the KKK but, instead, meeting another coach who would change his life. If Terzian and Barnes gave Cooper a BA in Defensive Tenacity, Ellenberger offered a combined masters/PhD program. The Lobos went a surprising 19-11 Cooper's first season, and Ellenberger set his new stopper loose. "Coach Terzian taught me about containment—push them, contain them, guide them toward your team," Cooper said. "Ellenberger was like, 'Fuck that, Coop. You're our defensive player. I don't want them to score at all.'

"Man, did I love that," said Cooper. "Absolutely fucking loved it."

As a senior in 1977–78, Cooper averaged 16.1 points per game as the Lobos—briefly ranked fourth in the country—finished 24-4 and led the nation in scoring. Though Cooper's thin frame and iffy offensive repertoire kept him off most NBA radars ("I honestly never thought of him as an NBA player," said Mark Felix, a Lobos teammate. "He was sort of a frail kid with a big heart"), he was lucky enough to play for a man (Ellenberger) who was golfing buddies with Jerry West. The Laker coach attended five Lobo games Cooper's senior year and convinced the organization to tab him with the sixtieth pick of the draft.

"I was out at the gym, because I knew I wasn't going to get drafted," Cooper said. "I'm playing basketball, and my cousin Brad comes running onto the court, screaming, 'You gotta come home! You gotta come home! You've been drafted, man! Jerry West already called the house! You've been drafted by Los Angeles!'"

Shortly thereafter, Cooper reported to the Lakers' summer league team at Loyola Marymount. Years later, he recalled walking into the gymnasium and staring at Kareem Abdul-Jabbar, Norm Nixon, Jamaal Wilkes, Ron

Boone, Lou Hudson. He was shaken from his awestruck daze by Jack Curran, the team's trainer.

"You Cooper?" he asked.

"Yup."

"OK," Curran said, "put your stuff down and get your ass over to the table so I can tape you."

The veterans disappeared at day's end, and Cooper was just another young scrub, desperate to impress West enough to earn an invite to training camp. Everything went smoothly until the third game against Phoenix, when the Suns' Andrew Wakefield tripped and toppled into Cooper's left knee. "It swelled up three times its normal size," he said. "What'd I think to myself? Easy—'Fuck!'"

As he was carried from the court, Cooper spotted a friend, Morris Davis, sitting near the baseline. "I'll be back," he whispered, "and I'm going to be a star." He had suffered a torn MCL, the sort of injury that, at the time, meant at least eight months of inaction. That night, Cooper cried himself to sleep, wondering what in the world he'd done to anger the basketball gods.

By week's end, though, he realized this was the best-possible career move. Had Cooper remained healthy, the Lakers—overloaded with veterans—almost certainly would have cut him loose. Because he was hurt, however, the team could place him on the injured reserve list with minimal contractual obligations. "Mike," West said, "what I want you to do is rehab, get your knee strong." Six months later, Cooper was given a clean bill of health. On December 22, 1978, with two minutes remaining in a blowout win over the visiting Washington Bullets, an obscure forward named Michael Cooper entered the game, replacing Ron Boone. There was no standing ovation, no excitement over the debut. He was just a skinny kid out of New Mexico. "To me, it meant everything," he said. "It meant I made it. Finally. Man, I played those last two minutes like they were the first two minutes. Game wasn't even close, but I didn't care. I'd arrived."

Cooper appeared in two more games that season, averaging a basket and one-third of an assist. Yet the Lakers saw enough to bring him back the following year. He beat out Boone for the final roster spot and established himself as not merely a valuable contributor (Cooper averaged 8.8 points in 82 games—including 23 starts) but a positive locker room influence. Cooper became tight with both Johnson and Nixon, in part because he was fun-loving and charismatic, in part because he was a threat to neither man on or off the court. "I really got to know Magic well during training camp his rookie year," Cooper said. "He'd always knock on my door to wake me up for breakfast, knowing full well I wasn't a breakfast person. That became our routine—walking over to Denny's to grab breakfast together. I would have the newspaper and he'd always say, 'Coop, gimme the sports!' We had a real bond that comes from togetherness. Same with me and Norm. A bond—like a brotherhood."

Unlike the two stars, Cooper wasn't fighting for ball-handling duties. Also, unlike the two stars, Cooper had recently married his college sweetheart, Wanda Juzang, and wasn't having sex with every other female in Los Angeles. "Michael was actually very shy back then," said Wanda. "He was quiet and quite sweet. You had to like him."

■ ■ ■

Now beginning his fourth season, Cooper's good-natured demeanor was needed more than ever. Johnson couldn't look at Nixon. Nixon couldn't look at Johnson. Kupchak was underwhelming and Abdul-Jabbar was, as usual, standoffish. Though the team went 6-1 in the exhibition season, no one was happy with Westhead's increasingly dogmatic stances. "I didn't like Paul Westhead as the coach, and I'm pretty sure I wasn't alone," said Clay Johnson, a Lakers guard. "His whole style . . . his whole setup . . . none of it worked or made much sense. He wasn't an NBA-caliber coach."

The Lakers opened the regular season with an October 30 clash against the Houston Rockets at the Forum, and while players talked a good game about cohesiveness and teamwork and finding ways to win, the sentiment was hogwash. In the days leading up, Westhead reminded his men that the offense was changing (ever so slightly) yet again. He referred to it as an "option" system—meaning the players would have multiple options to choose from. "Westhead equipped the team with about 50 possible options on offense," wrote Scott Ostler in the Los Angeles Times, "which is more than you get with Baskin-Robbins and less than you get with Heinz. But maybe more than you need on the basketball court."

Added Randy Harvey, also in the Times: "There will be more movement from everyone and less of Magic Johnson dribbling out front while waiting for the offense to set up. Norm Nixon calls himself a small forward in this offense. While that is not entirely accurate, he will be roaming the baseline more than in the past. The players admit they are confused by the offense and will be for the first few games; but they will continue to depend much of the time on the NBA's simplest play. A fist in the air means pass the ball to Abdul-Jabbar."

So how, in hindsight, would Laker players describe Westhead's approach?

Nixon: "Awful."

Cooper: "Confusing."

Kupchak: "Well, it was . . . different."

Mark Landsberger: "I still don't really understand it."

Jamaal Wilkes: "Looking back, it could have been better."

Eddie Jordan: "Paul thought half-court basketball controlled the game. And it did for most teams, but not for those Showtime Lakers."

Johnson: "Once we got down the court, it was four guys around the perimeter and Kareem following the ball. That meant Jamaal is standing now, Norm is standing, I'm standing. No throwing. No making the defense move. We were predictable. Once [Kareem] got it, he would kick it out with five seconds left on the clock. It was throwing everybody off."

Even Pat Riley, Westhead's assistant and a man of genuine loyalty, was scratching his head over the shifts. Although he never said so publicly, behind closed doors he expressed confusion over a system that deemphasized the Lakers' greatest strength—a pair of point guards who could think on the fly. Johnson found a sympathetic ear in Westhead's right-hand man, whining to him about the blessed Jack McKinney offense that won the team a title, then was promptly dismantled.

Los Angeles was a significantly more talented team than the Rockets, who now featured a Methuselahan Elvin Hayes at power forward and perhaps the weakest bench in the Western Conference. Yet with the Lakers operating a system that called for slow and steady over speedy and blurring, Houston controlled the tempo, once again repeatedly dumping the ball into Moses Malone, who scored 36 points in a 113–112 double overtime win.

Watching from his skybox, Buss was apoplectic. "What's going on?" he asked. "I just don't like this."

When the game concluded, he ventured into the locker room and was greeted by spiritless silence. He cornered Nixon, who scored but 12 points.

"Why are you playing that way?" Buss asked. "When you get down the court, why don't you [drive to the basket] like you used to? What's happening?"

"Well," Nixon said, "this is the new offense." He proceeded to sketch a diagram for Buss, further frustrating the owner. To the wealthy real estate developer, this didn't look like a high-functioning scoring machine. It looked like something from a junior high chalkboard. "Theoretically, we were going into a more pure fast break, but nobody was fast-breaking," Buss later said. "And as I talked to people, it was coming out more and more and more that this was just an entirely new offense. . . . People had criticized Paul—he felt—so severely because he had used McKinney's offense in the world championship. And then, by winning that championship, he had been made the coach.

"So he went to a different offense which would be clearly recognized as his own. I felt that he was therefore proving his point with my team. I felt he was on a crusade. . . . I felt like he was saying, 'I'm going to use this team to prove my point,' and he had done this without consulting me. I just didn't go along with it. I had specifically hired McKinney to begin with because that's the way I wanted my team to play."

Los Angeles followed with a 102–100 defeat to the inferior Portland Trail Blazers. Before the game, Westhead sidled up to Johnson and demanded more aggressiveness on the glass. "Yeah, I hear. I know," the guard replied. "You got me playing thirty feet from the basket. I got to stop the [other team's] break." Westhead wasn't having it. He insisted, again, on more boards. "Coach Westhead," Johnson said, "I can't run thirty feet in to try to get an offensive rebound, then try and be back on defense at the same time."

"Well," said Westhead, "I don't want to hear this."

That night, in the lobby of the Portland Marriott, Chick Hearn, the veteran announcer and knower of all things Lakers, approached a handful of reporters. "In a few weeks," he said, "you guys might have a really big story to write."

"We all knew," said Steve Springer, one of the team's beat writers, "that this thing with Paul couldn't last. There was just no way."

The Lakers won two of their next three games, but it mattered not. The chemistry between coach and players was becoming increasingly strained and awkward. Especially the chemistry between coach and one particular player.

"Magic really came to hate Paul," said Cooper. "I mean, he really hated him. Magic's the type of guy, when he gets on the bus he says hello to everybody—'Hey, what's up? How you doing? What's going down?' Now he would get on the bus, walk straight to his seat and just sit there. He wouldn't even look at Westhead—not even for a second. Magic would walk right past him, like he wasn't even there.

"In practice, usually Magic would be on the top of the key, asking for the ball, and he'd be bobbing back and forth, all energy. Now he would just stand straight and still. And I said, 'This shit is not looking good.' And Westhead would talk, giving instructions like coaches do, and Magic wouldn't look at him. Westhead would tell him what he wants, and Magic would say, cold as ice, 'So you want me to go over there and do that?' And he did exactly as he was told. But usually Magic would dribble and bounce and respond with energy. But with Westhead . . . you had a coach trying to get his star's attention, and his star basically saying, 'Fuck you. I don't believe in a thing you're doing.'"

On the night of November 10, 1981, the Lakers fell to 2-4 with a humbling 128–102 destruction at the hands of San Antonio. Playing without George Gervin, one of the league's elite scorers, the Spurs still had their way with Los Angeles. The Lakers appeared to have three options: (a) fast-break off a miss, (b) dump the ball into Abdul-Jabbar, (c) stand around and stare at one another. As the Spurs took a 30-point fourth-quarter lead, fans inside the HemisFair began singing the Queen hit "Another One Bites the Dust." It was humiliating, and afterward several players responded to questions by shrugging and saying, "Ask the coach."

Reporters asked the coach. "I have no answers," Westhead said. "If I had, I would have thought of them before the game."

Johnson, who scored 24 points, was despondent. He glared at the stat sheet and crumpled it into a ball. "Tonight I had to get mine on the break and tip-ins," he said. "Everybody thought I was playing bad in the first four games because I was only scoring 12 or 14 points. Everybody said, 'What's wrong?' Nothing was wrong. I only took seven shots against Phoenix [in a 101–99 loss four days earlier] because those were the only shots I had. But that's [Westhead's] system. That's what he believes in. I can't go out on my own."

Did he believe in the system?

"I'm only here just playing," Johnson said. "I just do what I'm supposed to do."

■ ■ ■

As soon as the game against the Spurs ended, the Lakers equipment team packed up all the gear, loaded the buses and departed to the airport for a quick flight to Houston. The trip that night was quieter than usual. The players were better than this. They *knew* they were better than this.

But Paul Westhead and his offense . . .

Upon arriving at Houston Intercontinental Airport early on the morning of Wednesday, November 11, the players ambled down to the baggage claim area, then headed to the bus. Without saying a word, Johnson—large headphones covering his ears, singing Earth, Wind & Fire aloud—walked to the median in the middle of the road and turned the music up. "Sometimes," he told the media, "I just have to sit in the sunshine and think."

Only it wasn't sunny. It was cloudy.

"I got on the bus, had some food in my hand," said Cooper. "I looked out the window and there was Magic, and he's sitting out there against a pole with his feet up."

Cooper approached his friend from behind and tapped him on the shoulder.

"E, what's wrong?" he asked.

"Coop, man, I ain't having fun," Johnson said.

"What are you talking about?" Cooper said. "We've just hit a little rough patch. That's all."

"No, Coop, it's not gonna get any better," Johnson said. "I'm telling you, it's not getting any better."

Cooper knew Johnson was prone to emotional highs and lows, knew the same man now brooding might be cracking a joke twenty-five seconds down the line. "E, let's get on the bus," he said. "Come on. . . ."

"No, Coop, this shit ain't fun," Johnson said. "I'm calling Dr. Buss today."

"What's that supposed to do?" Cooper asked, naïvely.

"Doc listens to me," Johnson said. "Doc listens to me."

Indeed.

"That was the moment," Cooper said years later, "when I found out

Magic had more power than anybody on the team. OK, maybe not more power, but the ability to make things happen with Dr. Buss. He called that night, and everything in the history of the Los Angeles Lakers changed.

"All it took was one call."

■ ■ ■

Here's the weird thing—the Lakers proceeded to win. And win. And win. And win. As soon as Johnson complained to Buss, Los Angeles went on its best run of the season, beating three sound teams (Houston, Portland, Phoenix), as well as the inept Pacers (coached by Jack McKinney). Nixon, Los Angeles's unofficial off-the-record marksman, anonymously told a reporter that "the only bad thing about winning is we're keeping [Westhead] alive." None of his teammates would argue the point.

In the midst of the streak, Buss called Bill Sharman, the general manager, and Jerry West, the assistant, into his office for a lengthy talk. Though the two men considered themselves the franchise's sole basketball decision makers, Buss's ear now belonged to Magic Johnson. Ever since the playoff loss to Houston, Buss increasingly shared the point guard's position that Westhead was either impossibly stubborn, in over his head or incapable of change. Now, with Johnson again directly requesting Westhead's dismissal, the owner felt compelled to act.

"Let me start off the meeting by saying that I've reached a decision that I would like to fire Paul Westhead," he told the two men. "However, there's three of us here and if the two of you want to talk me out of it, I'll let you talk me out of it. . . ."

Sharman and West had both coached the Lakers and knew the job was far from easy. Few towns came with greater media pressure and public scrutiny. They also knew what it was to cope with an agitated superstar. Sharman had the mercurial Wilt Chamberlain for two seasons, and West rarely grasped what was going through Abdul-Jabbar's mind during their three years together. In other words, while they acknowledged Westhead was far from perfect, they thought he deserved the benefit of extended time. "Paul warrants at least another week to see if things can straighten out," West told Buss.

Sharman nodded. "Jerry's right," he said. "Nobody should forget what Paul did for us in 1980."

Buss listened and seemed to agree. Maybe things would work themselves out.

■ ■ ■

The nonsense *needed* to stop.

Paul Westhead had thought this for quite some time. He believed Johnson—to the public a smiling, hugging, laughing Laker golden child—was behaving not as a leader but as a chemistry killer. Though coaches are generally insulated from intricacies of locker room banter, they also usually know what's being thought and, to a certain degree, said. No, Westhead wasn't present for Johnson's talks with Buss and Nixon and Cooper. He was, however, intelligent enough to understand the warm vibes of a championship had been lost, and that the NBA's most powerful player no longer wanted him around.

"There was friction," Westhead said. "It was obvious."

Had Westhead been coaching during a different era, with a staff of five or six assistants, perhaps Johnson and Nixon and the gang could have been reached; perhaps someone would have spoken up on his behalf, would have (rightly) noted that Westhead's career coaching record—110-50—was one of the best in NBA history.

Yet, save Riley, an undistinguished colleague who primarily kept quiet and went about his job, Westhead was alone.

On the night of Wednesday, November 18, the Lakers and Utah Jazz squared off at the Salt Palace. The game appeared to be a mismatch. The Jazz was an awkwardly constructed team, dependent on two one-dimensional scorers (the undersize power forward Adrian Dantley and the young shooting guard Darrell Griffith). Yet with Westhead's offense once again befuddling all involved, Utah stayed close. As the game neared halftime, the Lakers called a time-out. Westhead laid out a play and looked toward Johnson, who was in the process of asking Jack Curran, the trainer, for a cup of water. "Earvin!" Westhead said. "Shut up! Get your ass in this huddle and pay attention!"

"I am paying attention," he replied.

"Well," said Westhead, "you should be looking at me."

An hour later, it happened again. The Lakers led 113–110 with four seconds remaining. Jazz coach Tom Nissalke pulled his players aside to diagram a final strategy. The Lakers surrounded Westhead, and he explained that Griffith would probably come off a screen, but keep an eye on Rickey Green in the—

"Magic!"

Johnson was sitting on the end of the bench, sulking. He was purposely looking elsewhere, hoping Westhead might notice.

"Damn it," Westhead said. "How about getting in the huddle here?"

"I am in," Johnson replied with a quick bark. "I'm here."

"Forget it," Westhead said. "You're clearly not paying attention."

The coach would have been right to substitute Eddie Jordan into the game; to pull Johnson with 10,802 fans watching; to embarrass him as many a coach had done to many a player in the past. "You couldn't have blamed Paul," said Cooper. "Earvin was being disrespectful in full view."

Instead, Westhead reinserted Johnson, watched the Lakers hold on for the three-point triumph, then debated what to do next. "I couldn't wait until the next practice to speak to him," Westhead said. "It was pressing. And I wanted this to work out for both of us. I certainly didn't want to alienate him."

After the players entered the small visitors' locker room, Westhead requested a moment of Johnson's time. They walked into the nearby equipment room. Johnson leaned against a table. Westhead stood. "I'm tired of your horseshit attitude," the coach said. "And I'm not going to put up with it anymore. Either you start listening to me, or you don't have to play."

Johnson first participated in organized basketball as an elementary school student. Through the years, he had never—not once—disrespected a coach. He was a man raised to defer to authority. Yet Westhead struck him as less authority figure, more clueless bully.

"You might as well sit me down, because I ain't being used anyway," Johnson said. "Just sit me down."

"I don't want to hear that," Westhead replied.

"Are you done?" asked Johnson.

"Yes," said Westhead.

Johnson exited the room. He returned to his locker and considered all the NBA teams that needed his services. *The Knicks would love Magic Johnson. So would the hometown Detroit Pistons. The New Jersey Nets. The Golden State Warriors. The Washington Bullets. The . . . the . . .*

He turned to Jordan at the adjacent locker. "I've got to leave," he said. "It's been great and all, but I'm asking Dr. Buss to trade me. . . ."

Huh?

"I want out," he said. "I'm gone."

As is the case after all NBA games, members of the media wait outside the locker room for a fifteen-minute cooling-down period. As the Lakers writers lingered before the large white door, they were told by a ball boy that Johnson and Westhead had met in the equipment room.

When they entered the locker room, the reporters were struck by the normalcy. The scene was no different from usual. Some Laker players sat by their stalls. Others entered the showers. There was banter and joking and general happiness over a hard-fought triumph. When a scribe asked Westhead about the meeting with Johnson, he simply noted, "The almond tree bears its fruit in silence."

This was not Shakespeare. It was a Paul Westhead original.

The first reporter to reach Johnson was Dave Blackwell, a writer for the Salt Lake *Deseret News*. Because he had not been around the Lakers, he knew nothing of the mounting tension. He asked a couple of routine post-game questions, then moved on to talk with Wilkes about his 26 points.

With Blackwell out of the way, Rich Levin, a beat writer for the *Los Angeles Herald-Examiner*, planted himself before Johnson. Until this moment, Levin's claim to fame had been twofold: He played forward at UCLA under John Wooden, and Abdul-Jabbar begrudged his perceived editorial slights. Now he would forever be known as the man who opened up the floodgates.

"Magic," Levin said, "I have to ask about you and Westhead. . . ."

The other Los Angeles writers gathered around. There was an awkward moment of nothingness, the literal calm before an unprecedented storm. "I can't play here anymore," Johnson said. "I want to leave. I want to be traded. I can't deal with it no more. I've got to go in and ask [Buss] to trade me."

"Are you serious?" Levin asked.

"Definitely," said Johnson. "I haven't been happy all season. I've got to go. Things haven't been . . . I don't know. . . . I've seen certain things happening. I've sat back and haven't said anything, but I've got to go. It's nothing toward the guys. I love them and everybody. But I'm not happy. I'm just showing up. I play. I play as hard as I can. But I'm not happy. I'm not having any fun. I just want to go."

"Is this because of Paul?" asked Randy Harvey of the *Times*.

"Yeah," Johnson said. "Yeah."

Another pause.

"I'm going to go in and talk to [Buss], hopefully tomorrow, and see if a trade will happen."

Jordan was Johnson's roommate on the road. He couldn't believe what he was hearing, and made a beeline for Nixon. "Norm," he said, "I think you and I are gonna be the starting backcourt."

"Nah, nah, nah," Nixon replied. "Earvin's kidding. I'm sure he's just kidding."

"There was this chain reaction, where Earvin's words traveled around the locker room," said Kurt Rambis, the rookie forward. "I just started watching it go. It was weird—people stopped what they were doing. It turned into a firestorm."

The following morning, the beat writers met up at the airport to catch their flight back to Los Angeles. Mitch Chortkoff of the *Herald-Examiner* approached the group, a serious expression across his face.

"Guys," he said, "the airline just made a horrible mistake."

"What's that?" someone asked.

"They gave Westhead a boarding pass that says 'Coach.'"

That day's *Los Angeles Times* featured the front-page headline: MAGIC'S BOMBSHELL: HE WANTS TO BE TRADED. On the one hand, it was correct. Johnson's words were bombshell-worthy. They were also, however, ludicrous. Johnson didn't want to be traded and, despite his insistence, didn't expect to be traded. Though still a lad of twenty-one, he was no amateur. An owner doesn't sign a player to a twenty-five-year contract, then promptly ship him off to Cleveland for Kevin Restani, Paul Mokeski and two draft picks. "Look, Magic knew there was no way the team was trading him," said Mark Landsberger, the reserve big man. "He was a spoiled kid back then. We'd be on the bus and he'd be telling us, 'I'm either going to Chicago or New York. Fuck this guy!' He and Buss were so close, there was no chance he was going anywhere. He handled it like crap. He wanted to get the coach fired—period."

Although Johnson wasn't shaken by the media response, he was stung by the lack of teammate support. Abdul-Jabbar insisted such disputes be handled internally, then told *The New York Times*, "There are ways to do things which would sit better with everybody." Wilkes, the quiet veteran, noted—correctly—that "Magic is a very talented guy, but he has a problem with human relations." Cooper remained silent. And Nixon—the one Laker who disliked Westhead most of all—did nothing. As soon as Johnson finished speaking in the Salt Palace locker room, reporters scurried toward his back-court mate, assuming he would go to bat for a teammate who dared speak the truth.

"Norm, what do you think about Magic's demand?"

Nixon shook his head.

"Norm, do you think this will get Paul fired?"

Nixon shook his head.

"Norm, do you believe the team needs a new coach?"

Nixon shook his head.

"He was the biggest off-the-record agitator toward Westhead," said Randy Harvey, the *Times* beat writer. "Norm would talk all the time about Westhead. He was obsessed with him. But he wouldn't let his thoughts go public."

"Norm was always raising hell about Westhead, but Magic got the blame," said Butch Carter. "Westhead was over his head; he didn't understand how the NBA functioned at a championship level. So Magic said something—rightly. But he didn't deserve all the heat he caught."

Springer, an *Orange County Register* writer, couldn't believe what he was witnessing. Nixon routinely ripped Westhead. Now, with Johnson isolated and vulnerable, he had nothing to add? "Norm, he's out there all alone," Springer said. "He's gonna get all this shit on him. Why don't you back him up?"

Nixon wasn't having it. "He's Magic," he said. "If he says it, he gets away with it. If I say it, I get traded."

The sentiment was coldhearted and 100 percent correct. West seemed to hate Nixon when he coached him, and—as a key decision maker—he seemed to hate him equally now. "There was no advantage to me saying something," Nixon said. "For anyone."

Though Westhead held out hope that his job could be saved, he was alone. On the night of Johnson's outburst, he spoke via phone with Buss, and the two agreed to meet the following afternoon at the Forum. "I guess I was thinking maybe it could be salvaged," Westhead said. "If we just . . ."

No.

Buss greeted Westhead warmly, thanked him for two and a half years of loyal service and told him his days with the Lakers were done. He said the decision had nothing to do with Johnson's comments, that the guard was merely a player, and players don't make the decisions. "I do," Buss said. "This is my call. The offense just doesn't seem to be working. I know you disagree, but we don't see things the same way here."

Westhead refused to appear bitter. He thanked Buss for the once-in-a-lifetime opportunity, shook his hand and left, devastated. "It's a good thing I have a close family," he said. "Because it was one of the lowest moments of my career. I'm probably the only coach let go during a five-game winning streak."

Paul Westhead wouldn't say it then, and he won't say it now. The truth, however, is undeniable.

He was fired by Magic Johnson.

PART TWO

DOMINANCE

James Worthy, Earvin (Magic) Johnson, Bob McAdoo,
Mitch Kupchak, and Michael Cooper—key components of the Showtime

CHAPTER 8

RILED UP

In the world of professional sports management, there is a general rule that, with little exception, is always followed. Namely, if you're going to dismiss your coach, have a plan in place.

Though a uniquely successful businessman, Jerry Buss had never been especially good at firing people. He wasn't the cutthroat type, and avoided at all costs the awkwardness of the *"I'm sorry, but . . ."* chat. Whereas Jack Kent Cooke, his predecessor, took a certain demonic delight in watching heads roll, Buss was the opposite. He openly rooted for people to succeed, and only made changes when he believed they were indisputably necessary.

Because Magic Johnson had forced his hand with the Utah ultimatum, Buss found himself at a loss when it came to filling the team's open coaching position. That's why, when the media gathered at the Forum press lounge on the afternoon of Thursday, November 19, for an announcement, they were treated to one of the strangest fifty minutes in the modern history of organized sports.

Initially, things went relatively smoothly. Buss thanked Westhead (who wasn't present) for his service, and acknowledged this wasn't an easy decision. He insisted Johnson wasn't to blame, and committed himself to bringing a championship back to Los Angeles in the very near future.

Then things got a bit bizarre.

Earlier that afternoon, following his one thirty P.M. meeting with Westhead, Buss had summoned Jerry West and Bill Sharman to his home, the

Pickfair mansion, to figure out what to do next. In the course of the conversation, he asked West to return to his old job, as coach. To which the basketball legend responded with a cluster of words that, depending on who is asked, translated to one of the following:

- "I'll do it for a game or two."
- "Sure, that'd be great."
- "*Helllllllllll* no."

"Considering how much Jerry hated being a coach, I can't imagine he wanted that job," said Norm Nixon. "I mean, it just wasn't something he liked to do."

Somehow, Buss came to the conclusion that West not only accepted the position, but did so enthusiastically. He shook hands with the two men, then asked them to meet with Riley and explain to him the situation.

At approximately three P.M., Riley arrived at West's Bel Air house and was told—in no ambiguous terms—that *he* was the new head coach of the Los Angeles Lakers. "I'll help you out as an assistant for as long as you need, but hopefully not too long," said West, who had played alongside Riley for four seasons and considered him a close friend. "I know you're going to do great things."

As was the case for Westhead when he had replaced McKinney, Riley found himself feeling conflicted—giddy at the opportunity but somewhat disloyal to a coach he had respected. On the night Johnson demanded to be traded, Riley returned from the arena to the Salt Lake Hilton Inn, ordered a beer at the lobby bar and lamented the modern athlete. "Things have really changed," he told reporters. "In the old days a player just worried about playing, and never tried to get involved in coaching decisions. At least not publicly."

Riley initially assumed that, with Westhead's dismissal, he would be deposed, too. Instead, he was about to become the head coach. It was weird and disappointing and exciting, all in one.

As Buss stood before the media, he transitioned from bidding Westhead adieu to explaining what would happen next. Riley felt his heartbeat liven. He imagined all his boyhood friends back in Schenectady, New York, watching the transition take place, saying, "Hey, that's Pat up there! That's Pat Riley. . . ." He was thirty-six years old and at the height of professional basketball.

Pat Riley was proud.

Pat Riley was strong.

Pat Riley was . . . *confused.*

Buss announced that West would serve as offensive coach, Riley as defensive coach. Or captain. Or something sorta kinda like that.

> BUSS *(stepping to the podium):* We have appointed Jerry West as offensive captain for the Lakers. His duties will begin immediately. Pat Riley will stay with the Lakers as coach.
>
> QUESTION: Doctor, offensive coach—does that mean he's the head coach?

Buss paused to take a long drag from his cigarette. One could have forgiven those in attendance for forgetting whether they were listening to the owner of the Los Angeles Lakers or the Los Angeles Rams. Buss was a well-known USC football die-hard. Offensive coach? Defensive coach? Who did Buss want to coach the special teams?

"It was the weirdest event I'd ever covered," said Mitch Chortkoff of the *Herald-Examiner.* "Usually you know what you're going to announce *before* holding the press conference."

"We put on a clinic," said Bruce Jolesch, the team's public relations director, "on how *not* to conduct a press conference."

The session could have doubled as a *Saturday Night Live* skit. . . .

> BUSS: I did not specifically make someone head coach and someone else assistant coach. That was not accidental. I did it the way I announced on purpose. I feel that Pat is very capable of running the Laker team. However, I feel that we need a new offensive coach. I asked Jerry if he'd take that job and, fortunately, because of his relationship with Pat, I feel the two of them will coach this team together, with Jerry being in charge of the offense in particular.
>
> QUESTION: Jerry, there'll be a game tomorrow night. The game will end. Will two coaches come out to talk to us? Or will they choose which one it's going to be from game to game?
>
> BUSS: We discussed that. In reality I'm really making this change to change the offense, and since Jerry West will be in charge of

the offense, he will be the one who you will question. You can, however, talk to Pat whenever you want, as well.

QUESTION: Jerry, who picks the starting lineup?

BUSS: Who picks the starting lineup? In basketball, that's typically the coach.

QUESTION: Which one of these two?

BUSS: Oh, which one of these two? (*glances over his shoulder toward West and Riley*) Uh, I think there are some things along the line, not only the starting lineups but other considerations as well—uh, potential trades, etcetera, etcetera—that Pat and Jerry are going to have to sit down and work out what their relative responsibilities are. Fortunately, we're dealing with a situation of two men who have worked together on and off for years and therefore I have decided to leave that up to them . . . the division of their duties.

QUESTION: What will Jerry do as far as actually changing the offense?

Buss began answering, but was interrupted by Springer, who requested a response from West. The team's new "offensive captain" appeared uncomfortable and desperate to be anywhere but here. Ten minutes earlier, he thought . . . well, he didn't know what to think. He'd help Riley, toss in some ideas—not much else. And now he was a captain? How did this happen?

WEST: First of all, I'd like to clear up one thing. I'm going to be working *for* Pat Riley.

QUESTION: With or for, Jerry?

WEST: With and for. And I think my responsibility is to him because I feel in my heart that he is the head coach. And hopefully my position here won't be a long-range position.

QUESTION: Pat, will you take questions?

RILEY: Sure.

QUESTION: Pat, what are your reactions?

RILEY: Well, I haven't had a whole lot of time to give it much thought and I'm reacting rather emotionally to this thing because it's not a very fun day for me, nor is it for Paul. So until we can sit down, Jerry and myself, and discuss some of the

things we can do to improve the incentive of the team, then I
don't think I can really discuss that philosophy right now.

QUESTION: Have you talked about any assistants?

RILEY (laughing): Have I talked about any assistants? I just want
lunch.

As if the afternoon couldn't become more cartoonish, a reporter asked
Buss whether he had yet to speak with Johnson. "Well, actually, I did, yes,"
he said. "But it was in a different context. I was checking with him about a
birthday party I'm giving. I wanted to make sure he and Norm Nixon would
be on time."

The reporter promptly wished Buss a happy and healthy birthday.

"No," he said, "it's not my birthday."

When the press conference from hell finally concluded, West—not one
to avoid the occasional vulgarity—pulled Riley aside. "You're the head
coach of this team," he said. "You're the only fucking head coach."

■ ■ ■

The only fucking head coach had an idea. Two ideas, to be exact.

First, he was scrapping Westhead's paint-by-number offense and revert-
ing to a knockoff of Jack McKinney's old system.

Second, he was listening to Magic Johnson.

If that sounds particularly simplistic, well, it isn't. As soon as Westhead's
firing was announced, Johnson plummeted from the crown prince of Los
Angeles to the lowest rung of the city's dog-urine-coated parking meters. At
a time when fans and reporters were already complaining about the egos and
salaries of star athletes, Johnson would have beaten out Pat Haden, the Rams'
mediocre quarterback, and Jerry Brown, the unpopular California governor,
in a Most Hated Man in Town balloting.

In the days following the messy press conference, the mailboxes inside
the *Los Angeles Times* office were stuffed with notes from basketball die-hards
damning the Laker point guard as the second coming of Satan. Johnson tried
his best to deflect the criticism, issuing a statement that read, in part, "I'm
just happy to be here in L.A. I wasn't happy. Some of the other guys weren't
happy. But I didn't make the changes. That was up to the head man, Dr.
Buss." Nobody bought it. The newspaper printed as many letters as possible,
and the sentiment was near universal: The pampered infant was no longer

worthy of wearing the purple and gold. Jim Murray, the *Times*'s star sports columnist, went even further. "The man they thought belonged on a shelf as a stuffed toy alongside Yogi Bear and Bambi turned out to be a guy who would bait a trap for Mickey Mouse," he wrote. "Now we know why they call him Magic. He made the boss disappear."

Throughout the league, opponents thrashed Johnson as manipulative and immature. Larry Brown, coach of the New Jersey Nets, insisted he would never add the guard to his team—even though *his* awful guard rotation included Darwin Cook, Phil Ford and Foots Walker. "They can have him," Brown said. "I've seen what's happened to that team." Bob Mazza, a Beverly Hills–based public relations executive who handled Johnson's affairs, told the *Los Angeles Times* his client wouldn't be hurt. "My feeling is this is going to blow over," he said—then watched as multiple companies rushed to drop Johnson as an endorser.

Truth is, Johnson was both hero and goat, and neither hero nor goat. Westhead was losing the team, and Johnson was but one of many players overcome by unhappiness. It took courage to speak out, courage teammates like Nixon and Cooper lacked. But it was also a selfish act that resulted in a decent man losing his job. Randy Harvey, the *Los Angeles Times* beat writer, stated it perfectly: "If the perception around the country today is that he is a spoiled brat and a prima donna, that is no closer to the truth than the perception of him before as every mother's son. Realistically, he has never been as wonderful as he appears on the 7-Up commercials, and he is not as disruptive a force today as his critics would have you believe."

Riley met with Johnson the day after being hired, and told him that things were about to change. The Lakers would run again. Abdul-Jabbar would remain a focus on offense—but not *the only* focus. He wanted Johnson to return to being the free-flowing, instinctive point guard who once led the Lakers to the championship. In short, he wanted to bring back Showtime.

Ah, Showtime. That was the term a select few had used to describe McKinney's offense—an exciting brand of run-and-gun that brought spectators to their feet. Long before he actually purchased the Lakers, Buss enjoyed frequenting a club on Wilshire Boulevard in Santa Monica called The Horn. It was a small, smoky joint known for good music and stiff drinks and long-legged hostesses. The Horn was where such talents as Jim Nabors and Guy Hovis had been discovered, and where Dick Curtis once cut a record, *Live at The Horn*. In the moment before featured acts took the stage, the lights dimmed and a performer, covertly placed at one of the club's small round tables, stood and crooned, "It's shoooowwwtttttttime!" Other singers would join in, harmonizing along—"Shoooooowwwwwttttttimmmmme . . ." Buss never forgot how one electric phrase could excite an entire crowd. He came to love the idea of "It's Showtime!" and wanted his basketball team to pair with the verbiage.

When Riley took over, Buss once again talked up "Showtime" as if it were a literal basketball philosophy. He told anyone who would listen that his team was about to return to Showtime, that the Forum would be a place where Showtime reigned. To Buss, Showtime was both a basketball philosophy and an arena-filling approach. Showtime was short-skirted Laker Girls. Showtime was Jack Nicholson sitting alongside Dyan Cannon atop the court. Showtime was loud music, big breasts, screaming adoration, fans dressed in their absolute best. "My dad would always explain it like this," said Jeanie Buss. "If you have a friend coming to town to visit Los Angeles, he's going to say, 'I want to go to Disneyland, I want to go to the beach and I want to see a celebrity.' Well, where would you take him where he's guaranteed to see a celebrity? A Laker game. He made the Forum a draw in and of itself."

Said Pat O'Brien, the CBS broadcaster: "The Forum was the first place I ever saw people bring binoculars to a basketball game, because there were a million things to look at."

Buss mostly kept his distance. He wanted the Forum to be cool and hip, and he trusted his employees to deliver. Against his better judgment, he even paid a fan named Barry Richards thirty-five dollars a game to stand along the sideline in a white tuxedo and perform as "Dancing Barry"—a goofy shuffler who grooved during time-outs.

There are only two notable moments when Buss put his foot down. The first came when Lon Rosen, working in the promotions department, sent the Laker Girls onto the floor accompanied by a male baton twirler. "If you ever have something like that on again," Buss said, "it's going to be your last day." The second involved Jeanie Buss and Linda Rambis coming up with a plan for "Slam Duck," the Lakers' first-ever mascot. "He was an edgy duck with a Mohawk and a piercing," said Rambis. "We hired a cartoonist to draw him up, and we thought we could send him to schools instead of the players. Dr. Buss looked at it and said, 'No way. No possible way.' In hindsight, he was right. But the duck was cute."

For his part, Riley shrugged, smiled and said whatever needed to be said. He conducted his first practice on the afternoon of Friday, November 20, with West glued to a chair along the sideline and Buss—still somewhat confused over who was running his team—perched in the stands. Riley was thirty-six years old, as much a peer to his players as a leader. Yet as he gathered his team around for a quick pep talk, the room went silent. "I'm tired of excuses," he said. "We're too good for such nonsense. . . ."

For the first time in weeks, Earvin Johnson was Magic again. He enthusiastically dribbled the ball up and down, yapping toward teammates, hanging on all of Riley's words. His passes were crisp, his attention crisper. If some players had begun to view him suspiciously, those thoughts faded into a blur of spinning twirls down the lane; of no-look, behind-the-back dishes; of a point guard reborn and stirred to life. "Earvin needed the change," said Cooper. "He couldn't have gone on the way things were."

The new Lakers made their debut that Friday night, facing a Spurs team that had embarrassed them by 26 points just ten days earlier. Led by the unparalleled George Gervin, San Antonio came to the Forum sporting a league-best 9-1 record. "Los Angeles had a lot of scorers," said Paul Griffin, a Spurs forward. "But we felt we could play with them and eventually wear them down."

A sellout crowd packed the building, many there to make Johnson aware that he was now persona non grata. The opening introductions were awkward. Johnson was usually the first Laker introduced and the king of the palace. The enunciated syllables of his name were always drowned out by applause and squeals. This time, as Lawrence Tanter, the public address announcer, started into *"Earv . . ."* the Forum erupted in boos. This was the sort of Forum razzing reserved for Gervin and Moses Malone and Bernard King—rivals who had scorched the home team. As Johnson walked onto the court, he bit his lip and pretended not to notice the scorn. "What you must do is ride it out and not break concentration," Riley told him. "Just play your game and you'll turn the crowd around."

The general assumption was that Johnson would have to re-prove himself to the Laker faithful. This could take a few games, a few weeks, maybe even a few months.

Instead, it took approximately twenty minutes. As Riley said (and did) very little, Johnson ran Los Angeles to perfection, totaling 20 points, 16 assists, 10 rebounds and 3 steals in a 136–116 rout. By midway through the second quarter, the Forum was once again Johnson's. He dribbled down the left sideline, crossed the half-court line and tossed an alley-oop to a streaking Cooper. Less than thirty seconds later, Johnson hit a miniature jump hook. Then he connected with Abdul-Jabbar. Then he burst past Johnny Moore, the Spurs point guard, for a layup. He pumped his fist and flashed his smile and reverted to the Magic of old. "I'm just here trying to have fun and win some games," he said. With the Lakers up by 6, Johnson either scored or assisted on 18 of the next 21 points. Abdul-Jabbar contributed 30, Wilkes added 18 and Cooper and Nixon both had 12. Afterward, *Sports Illustrated*'s Anthony Cotton asked Johnson whether he was, at long last, happy. "Yeah, I'm happy—and so are him and him and him," he said, pointing to his teammates' vacated lockers. "This is the way it was two years ago, with easy buckets. You see the way we were moving tonight? Pow-pow-pow."

"That's the kind of basketball I like to watch," added Buss. "I think everyone was high emotionally, but let's give it ten or twelve games before we draw any conclusions."

Predictably, Riley was quickly hailed as the savior of Los Angeles. The Lakers won 11 of their first 13 games under their new coach, playing loose and fast and up to their talent level. The idea—backed by the press—was that Riley had brought something new to the table, that here was an offensive genius coach perfectly matched with an offensive genius point guard. Even when Riley tried pooh-poohing the praise ("Nothing changed," he said. "Nothing. Paul was a great coach. I've done nothing"), few were willing to acknowledge the truth—that Johnson was the orchestrator.

No, in Pat Riley, they had found their dashing leader.

They had found their matinee idol.

■ ■ ■

Pat Riley didn't merely hate the word. He recoiled from it.

Coach.

In his first days . . . weeks . . . months leading the Lakers, he simply wanted to be known as Pat, the guy with the glasses and the long brown hair who, if a few things broke his way, could possibly help right the ship. To Riley, *Coach* wasn't merely a word or title. It was an honor, bestowed upon those who had paid their dues and earned their glory and risen above mere mortal status.

Riley had spent his college days at the University of Kentucky, playing for the revered Adolph Rupp. *He* was Coach. He had been a rookie with the

San Diego Rockets under Pete Newell, a revered guru. *He* was Coach. With the Lakers, he'd played for Bill Sharman, a four-time NBA champion with the Boston Celtics and eight-time NBA All-Star. *He* was Coach.

"Dignity, respect, pride," Riley said. "Those are what coaches are to me."

Most notably, as a boy, growing up in Schenectady, New York, Pat had learned sports at the feet of his father, Leon Francis Riley, a longtime minor league outfielder and first baseman. In 1944, Lee Riley was called up by the Philadelphia Phillies and had one hit—a double—in twelve at-bats over four games. He was, in his son's mind, the ultimate coach. "In twenty-two years he gets a cup of coffee and a promise that they'd give him the next coaching job that opened up in the big leagues," Riley said. "He gets passed over, and he just says, 'That's it.' He went home and burned everything that had to do with his baseball career."

Patrick Riley was born on March 20, 1945, eleven months after his dad's debut with the Phillies. The youngest of Lee and Mary Riley's six children never really had a choice whether or not to play sports. He spent much of his early years in the back of a wood-sided station wagon, hopping from town to town as his father managed across the minor leagues. "We were always in hotels," Pat once recalled. "My early memories are of playing hide-and-seek in dark ballrooms, with rain against the windows."

One would think the son of an athlete would bask in the glow of a sportsman father, yet Pat was painfully familiar with the profession's dark side. Though his dad was an accomplished hitter who once paced the Can-Am League in home runs and, in 1937 and 1938, led the Nebraska State League with batting averages of .372 and .365, respectively, he retired as an active player feeling not merely unfulfilled, but rejected. Those 12 at-bats with the Phillies were a drop of chocolate syrup to the tongue, a tantalizing taste of what could have been, but never truly was. As a result, upon quitting the game as a manager, Lee devoted much of his attention to alcohol, drinking away his sorrow and anger, as well as the bitterness of multiple failed business ventures. He ran a small restaurant-bar that didn't last, then opened his own convenience store, Riley's Variety. That closed quickly, too. A dashingly handsome man, Lee walked with the grace of a runway model. He was 6-foot-1 and 180 pounds, and liked to dress in suits and ties. On the outside, he was the image of confidence. Inside he was a wreck. On more than one occasion he showed up intoxicated to his children's sporting events. He was, those who knew the Rileys said, prone to violence.

"I could sense his disappointment for years after [his managerial career ended]," Riley said. "Not being able to fulfill his lifelong dream. He never said, 'Hey, this is what they did to me or this is what happened.' I mean, even Mother rarely talked about it. But it ended very bitterly and he carried that with him for a long time."

Lee was excessively tough on his children, and viewed nurturing as something women did. "Back in those days, you didn't coddle kids, I guess, like you do today," said Dennis Riley, Pat's older brother. "He was the all-time disciplinarian. He might give you a pop if you got out of line."

Lee Riley's kids would be strong and powerful and tough—whether they were actually strong and powerful and tough or not. The family had settled in Schenectady when Lee briefly managed the local Blue Jays, a Philadelphia affiliate. It was a blue-collar town of fifty thousand residents, a place identified with the black smoke oozing from the top of railroad engines. "A great town for us to grow up," said Mike Meola, Pat's childhood friend. "There was very little violence, and enough to do to keep you occupied. Lots of playgrounds, a drive-in movie theatre, a speedway. I loved it. We all did."

When Pat was nine, his father found him sitting in the garage, weeping after some bullies had administered a pummeling. Lee demanded Pat return to the nearby park to confront the boys. Pat promptly took another beating. "A guy chased me home with a butcher's knife one time," Riley said. "I got my ass kicked."

The results: Lots of bloody noses and lots of grit. Pat Riley became a kid you didn't mess with. Not quite a thug, but certainly a ruffian. When he wasn't attending classes at St. Joseph's Academy, he could often be found hanging out on a street corner, a pack of cigarettes rolled into the sleeve of his T-shirt. He found trouble more than once—stupid little things like shoplifting and vandalism. While in sixth grade, he and some friends broke into a local school and stole ice cream from the cafeteria. They were caught by the police. "My dad came down," he said. "That was it for me. I had to change my ways."

Coincidentally, that same day the St. Joseph's sixth graders were scheduled to play a game of basketball against the ninth-grade team. It was a mere recreational exercise; get some of the younger kids on the court and have them see how the older boys worked together as a team to succeed.

Riley scored 19 points, and the sixth graders somehow won. It made no sense. "People were staring at me from the stands, wondering, 'Who is this kid?'" Riley said. "I walked into class the next day and it was the first time I ever got any recognition. The teacher [Sister Mary Samuel] talked about me, and I could see the kids looking at me with a little different look in their eyes. And I said to myself, 'That's all I gotta do?' My life changed. I could feel it."

From that day forward, Pat Riley thought of himself as an athlete. He went on to Linton High School, where he emerged as a strong-armed catcher in baseball, a starting quarterback in football and a dominant forward in basketball. Riley loved the sounds and rhythms of the gymnasium, the squeaking of sneakers against wood, the magic of a ball swishing through a net. His coach, Walt Przybylo, viewed the sport not merely as athletic competition, but as a chance to instill general lessons. Each day, before practice began, he sat his players down on the bleachers for discussions. "One day he'd go off on attitude," Riley said. "And another, on the injustice he'd suffered getting his car serviced. One night he gave our manager, Howie Lorch, and me a ride home from practice. On the way he stopped at Flavorland to get a six-pack. It was snowing and there were big banks of snow piled up. You couldn't see, and Howie said, 'Let's hide the car.' He got behind the wheel and drove the car into a fire hydrant and got it stuck there. The next day, Walt Przybylo lectured the team about what these two idiots did to him the night before."

"Only now," Riley said years later, "do I appreciate that. They slip into your subconscious, those voices. They stay in there, waiting."

Riley averaged 28 points per game as a senior, good enough for 70 to 75 schools to recruit his services. He was actually more coveted for football, and took trips to Penn State, Michigan, Michigan State, Syracuse and Alabama. "I could throw the hell out of the ball," he said. Ultimately, though, Riley was swept off his feet when Rupp, the University of Kentucky's larger-than-life basketball coach, came calling with a scholarship offer.

"When Adolph flew in," he said, "that sealed it. He came up and talked to my mother. He didn't even talk to me. But that sewed things up.

"I used to have a hard time with coaches who were loud and demonstrative. I found it distracting. I operated best in a sea of tranquility. The environment created by Rupp, his blinding emphasis on basketball, was work—but quiet, undistracted work."

Riley was a weird fit in Lexington, Kentucky, land of southern drawls and racial divides and, to a kid from a relatively multicultural background, startling close-mindedness. He was mocked by teammates for the speed of his sentences and the precision of his words. Louie Dampier, a fellow freshman, was assigned to be Riley's roommate. His first impression of the New Yorker was a memorable one—sunglasses, turtleneck sweater, pleated blazer, tight powder-blue slacks and pointy-toed loafers. "Look what we have here," Dampier muttered to himself.

Though he wasn't quite as edgy as he'd been in his youth, Riley still came across as a guy you didn't mess with. He drank hard and stayed out late enough to violate numerous Rupp curfews. He could hustle pool with the best of them. "He got down from New York, and it took me six weeks to figure out what he was saying," said Larry Conley, his Kentucky teammate. "He had this unmistakable New York swagger, and people didn't quite know what to make of it. There were times he'd say things and I'd just laugh at him. He'd look at me like I lost my mind. I'd say, 'Pat, you're so full of shit. Do you think people really buy into your shit?' And he'd smile and say, 'Well, some of them do.' "

Riley played three varsity seasons for the Wildcats, averaging 18.3 points and 8.4 rebounds. From a distance, he and the stern Rupp formed an odd tandem. Kentucky's coach was an arrogant taskmaster who didn't have much interest in hearing his players speak. He looked at the members of the Wildcats not as human beings, but as spare parts to be plugged in here and there. He was famously bigoted, once complaining that the university's president was pressuring him to "get some niggers in here."

Riley and his teammates didn't like Rupp. Players spoke only when spoken to. When Rupp cracked a joke, nobody was permitted to laugh. However, they also acknowledged his genius. "He was [General Norman] Schwarzkopf," Riley said. "He was a great, great presence. I take basically a lot of my philosophy from his coaching. I had four years of a drill-type mentality."

Riley joined the varsity as a sophomore in 1964 and the season was, by Kentucky standards, an unmitigated disaster. The Wildcats finished 15-10, and the following year was expected to be little better. Before opening the season against Hardin-Simmons, Rupp demanded an intrasquad contest between the starting five and the substitutes. The game ended with the starters winning by two, and Rupp was apoplectic. For all his skill as a recruiter, Rupp had somehow overlooked height. No starter was taller than 6-foot-5, and Riley—a junior who, in platform shoes, stood 6-foot-3½—jumped center most games. "He surprised bigger guys, because he could really leap," said Conley. "Nobody expected that sort of athleticism from a little guy like Pat. But he got up there."

Behind a breakthrough season from Riley, who averaged 22 points and 8.9 rebounds per game and was named third-team All-American, the Wildcats pieced together an undefeated year. Like their star forward, they were hard-edged and scrappy and nearly impossible to topple. They rolled through the NCAA Tournament and wound up in the championship game against number three seed Texas Western, the first team with an all-black starting lineup to play for a title. Across the nation, the all-white vs. all-black story line captivated more than just sports fans. This was old vs. new, segregation vs. diversity. "Truthfully," said Conley, "we wanted to win a basketball game. I don't think any of us thought about race in that game. Just winning."

Most members of the media assumed Kentucky's fast-breaking offense would overwhelm the bulkier Miners. Instead, Texas Western forced the Wildcats into a bevy of uncharacteristically awful shots. It hardly hurt that, over a thirty-seven-minute stretch, the Miners hit 26 of 27 free-throw attempts. "You could feel the intensity on the court," Riley said. "Trash talking started there . . . there wasn't much dunking, but [Texas Southern's David Lattin] dunked over me, ripped the net down and he said something that let me know he was serious about this game. They were committed. Very talented and committed." When the buzzer sounded and a 72–65 upset was sealed, Riley returned to the locker room and bawled. He scored a team-high 19 points, and only years later could admit Kentucky fell to the better team.

"It was," he said, "the greatest heartbreak of my life."

Riley's senior year was, from beginning to end, a disappointment. Having slipped a disc in his back in a waterskiing mishap over the summer, he never regained his old form. His scoring average fell to 17 points per game, his shooting percentage from 52 percent to 44 percent. Leading up to a January 16 game at archrival Georgia, Rupp told *Sports Illustrated*'s Larry Boeck that he was considering asking Riley to leave the team. "If Pat can't do well tonight, that's it—it's over," he said. "I just might take up his uniform."

Riley performed admirably enough in a 49–40 loss to the Bulldogs to stay (he scored 10 points, with 6 rebounds), but an ugly season never improved. The Wildcats finished 13-13.

Even though his back was a mess, and even though he was undersize, and even though his senior season had been horrific, Riley was selected seventh overall in the 1967 NBA Draft. The expansion San Diego Rockets liked his tenacity and intensity, and figured a Rupp-trained player could transition smoothly from college to the pros. They signed him to a lucrative four-year, $100,000 contract. "[Rockets coach] Jack McMahon drafted me first because he had the same operation I did," Riley said. "He said, 'If he can play with a slipped disc, he's good enough for me.'"

Riley drove from Lexington to San Diego in a yellow 1967 Corvette convertible. He made most of the trip with the top down and the music blasting. The kid was unlike anything veteran Rocket players had seen. Riley dressed like a movie star, and looked like one, too.

Having also been drafted by the Dallas Cowboys with an eleventh-round pick, Riley flew to Texas and met with Tom Landry, the team's coach. There was no chance he would play in the NFL, but the ego surge was electrifying. Riley came to California cocky and carefree—and eminently likable. "He had swagger," said Jon McGlocklin, a Rocket guard. "Not in a bad way. He knew he was good, and showed it." Yet Riley's NBA transition was a difficult one. The smallish players he dominated in college were now working as pharmacists and bookkeepers and office managers. McMahon took one look at Riley—who seemed smaller in person than on television—and switched him to guard. "I'll never forget my first day in training camp," Riley said. "After about five minutes, Jack McMahon pulled me over to the sideline and said, 'I drafted you and my job is depending on you, and that is the worst five minutes of basketball I've ever seen.'"

"Jack," Riley replied. "I've never played guard before."

"You better learn," McMahon said. "You better learn fast."

The Rockets were, predictably, dreadful, finishing 15-67 and last in the Western Division. Riley averaged 7.9 points per game and never lived up to his billing. He was the classic tweener—too slow to cover opposing guards, too small to challenge opposing forwards. His ball-handling skills were mediocre, his marksmanship awful (Riley shot 38 percent from the field). "In college, he was this white leaper," McGlocklin said. "In the NBA, that wasn't the strength of his game."

Riley spent three undistinguished years in San Diego, was claimed by Portland in the 1970 expansion draft and, five months later, was sold to Los Angeles. Chick Hearn, the distinguished Laker announcer, had suggested to team brass that Riley would bring grit to a soft roster. He was correct. Over the next six years, Riley always arrived at training camp in tiptop shape. As teammates spent their time away from the court playing golf and eating hamburgers, Riley thought of himself as a soldier in basic training. "I was always afraid of losing my position," he said. "I'd do whatever I had to do to stay on the team. But the Lakers with Wilt Chamberlain and Jerry West were a hell of a team on which to be a role player."

As a disposable part on some of the greatest clubs in NBA history, Riley had a very specific job description: Sit on the bench, play scrappy defense and, during practice, make Jerry West's life a living hell. "His number one task was to beat the shit out of me," West said. "He wasn't supposed to kill me, but he sure tried his best."

In 1971, when Bill Sharman replaced Joe Mullaney as the Los Angeles coach, he pulled Riley aside.

"You want a job?" he said.

"Hell, yes," Riley said.

"Well," said Sharman, "keep West in shape."

With Riley averaging 6.7 points in 13.8 minutes per game, the 1971–72 Lakers won a league-record 33-straight games en route to the NBA championship. Though the title failed to make up for the loss to Texas Western, Riley felt as if his career now had meaning. He knew what it had been like to be a star on a team that fell short, and now he was a scrub for the kings of basketball. "When I finally realized that I couldn't be a front-line player, I also came to the conclusion that I wanted a career in the game," he said. "I wanted to stay in the NBA."

Riley averaged a career-high 11 points per game three seasons later, but failed to ever again reach such heights. Suffering from a bad knee and limited production, on November 3, 1975, Riley was shipped to Phoenix in exchange for journeyman guard John Roche and a draft pick. He played sixty unremarkable games for the Suns. "I used to take Novocain and cortisone shots for quadriceps tendonitis," he said. "It was dumb. Once when I was with Phoenix, blood was running down my leg after two injections, one on either side of my knee. I couldn't feel anything below my thigh. That was the mentality—whatever it took."

When Phoenix placed Riley on waivers, he was thirty-one and lost. He retreated, tail between his legs, to Los Angeles, and constructed an eight-foot fence around his home. "It was a year of mourning," he said. "I'd spent my whole life with the game as my main force. When it was gone, there was a terrible, aching hollow."

Riley wrote a four-hundred-page basketball book that he showed no one. He hung out by the beach. He attended a Laker game—the one when the security guard wouldn't grant him access to the press lounge.

Then, one morning, Hearn called about the announcing gig. . . .

And—like that—he was now the head coach of the team he'd loved. Just a couple of years removed from being denied access, he *was* access. If the Lakers under Westhead had been an unimaginative lump of coal, the Lakers under Riley were a neon rainbow. The proof came on November 29, when the Rockets returned to the Forum and endured one of the worst beatings in recent franchise history. No longer was Los Angeles willing to repeatedly lob the ball into Abdul-Jabbar, then watch Moses Malone administer assault and battery. No, this time Johnson and Nixon exploded up and down the court, running circles around (and through) Houston's shoddy defense. When Malone closed in to offer defensive help, Johnson and Nixon would dish off to Wilkes (18 points) in the corner or Cooper (14 points) slashing through the lane. Los Angeles ran 48 fast breaks that resulted in 52 points—numbers that nearly doubled the highest output under Westhead.

Final score: 122–104.

"It sounds so simple," wrote Randy Harvey in the *Los Angeles Times*, "it makes you wonder why the Lakers haven't been able to do that to Houston before."

Although Buss had insisted West would handle the offense, such was not the case. He primarily sat on the bench, whispered occasional suggestions and sipped from a plastic cup of water. Not that Riley was an offensive innovator. He engineered few actual changes from McKinney's system, save for allowing Johnson to determine the course of action. "If you have a Magic Johnson, you give him all the leeway he needs," said Jim Brewer, a veteran Laker forward. "You can still have some base plays, and we did. But there are certain players who need to be allowed to run free and operate independently. That was Magic, and Pat was smart enough to see it."

Throughout college and professional sports, far too many coaches feel pressured into implementing a preferred system, even if it is a poor fit for the personnel. Not Riley. "Pat was intelligent," said Nixon. "He inherited a championship team. So you just saddle that up and ride it. He learned on the fly that championship teams police themselves. You don't have to ask a championship team to play hard, you don't have to ask them to get their rest. Pat didn't have to tell us how to practice hard, or what to expect in games.

Really, in the beginning, he just needed to keep things organized and let us play. That's not rocket science, but it's also not as easy as one might think."

On the morning of December 2, Sharman announced that the "interim" tag would be removed from Riley's title, and a couple of days later West returned to the front office. Bill Bertka, a former Laker scout who had recently worked as Tom Nissalke's top assistant with the Utah Jazz, was hired to be Riley's right-hand man on the bench. "Best situation a person could have walked into," said Bertka, who left Salt Lake City in the midst of a 25-57 season. "You had a young coach willing to learn and listen, a deep roster, a great organization. What wasn't to like?"

For the first time in months, the Lakers seemed happy. They were outscoring opponents by an average of 10.5 point per game, scoring 10 more points per game than they did under Westhead. The winning proved to be a cure-all. Johnson and Nixon stopped bickering. Cooper was turning into one of the game's most explosive slashers. Wilkes was as smooth as ever and a healthy Kupchak was good for 12 points and 11 rebounds most nights. Even Abdul-Jabbar, now touching the ball less frequently, had reason to smile: He was averaging 23.9 points and 8.7 rebounds while starring in Pioneer Fish 'N Chips' new advertising campaign—"A Big Meal at a Small Price!"—that broke his teammates up in laughter. Johnson praised the center as, among other things, "the key," "the centerpiece" and "the focus."

"Earvin was brilliant leading a team," said Bertka. "He knew running things on the court and running things off the court were both important jobs. He went out of his way to credit Kareem, to let him know how important and necessary he was. Were they the best of friends? No, probably not. But Earvin made sure there was always respect and professionalism."

The relationship between Abdul-Jabbar and Johnson was equally simple and complex. On the one hand, the Lakers boasted two of the greatest players to ever step onto an NBA court, and their unique talents (Johnson as a distributor, Abdul-Jabbar as a scorer) meshed seamlessly. There was no fighting for the last shot, no arguing over who took the ball out of bounds, who called the final play, who posted up down low. Because the Lakers ran so often—with plays generally developing, progressing and culminating within a seven-second span—it was easy to overlook the beauty and ease with which the two men excelled as one.

And yet, egos are egos, and NBA superstars rarely lack them. Abdul-Jabbar resented Johnson's contract, Johnson's buddy-buddy relationship with

Buss, Johnson's stardom. He wasn't Nixon, a flamboyant man who felt robbed of the spotlight. No, Abdul-Jabbar—awkward, standoffish, emotionally stunted—didn't quite know how to react. He wanted praise, he shunned fame. He wanted attention, he loathed attention. Why didn't more fans approach him? Why should he have to sign autographs? He craved the love of teammates. He didn't bother to talk with teammates. Whether one liked Abdul-Jabbar or loathed Abdul-Jabbar, people could agree he was the most cuckoo of cuckoo birds.

When Johnson first arrived in Los Angeles, he sought Abdul-Jabbar's approval. He imagined the two as stars in some sort of buddy movie, the aged gunslinger taking the rookie sheriff under his wing, showing him the ropes over burgers and Coca-Colas. Alas, it was not to be. Abdul-Jabbar expressed neither like nor dislike toward Johnson. They coexisted, as colleagues coexist. Few jokes, no dinners. "Not pals," said Cooper. "But friendly enough."

It mattered not. Abdul-Jabbar recognized Johnson's command of the offense, and also realized that—despite his admiration for Westhead (Abdul-Jabbar was the only player to call the coach after he was fired)—the change had been beneficial. This wasn't merely the best Laker team Abdul-Jabbar had played on. It was, he was beginning to believe, the best team he had *ever* played on—including the 1971 Milwaukee Bucks, who won 66 games and the NBA title. "We were building something special," said Kupchak. "I'd never been on a team with that much talent. Never even close."

Everything was going swimmingly until the night of December 19, when the Lakers traveled one and a half hours south to San Diego to face the Clippers. Coached by Paul Silas, San Diego reigned as the joke of the NBA. The team was 6-16, played in the dumpy San Diego Sports Arena and, rightly, ranked last in the league in attendance. "We were," said Swen Nater, the club's center, "brutal."

For the Lakers, a trip to San Diego was akin to a mini vacation. The travel was easy, the opponent dreadful. Even without Abdul-Jabbar, sitting out with a sore right ankle, Los Angeles was far superior. Riley started Kupchak—who was averaging 14.3 points and 8.3 rebounds—at center, and Los Angeles ended the first quarter with a 28–27 lead. "It was great," Kupchak said. "My parents were in the stands visiting from New York. My aunt and uncle lived in San Diego, so they were there. I was starting, which was rare."

Early in the second quarter, Kupchak was filling the lane on a break when Johnson, standing to his right, shoveled a pass his way. The Clippers' Joe Bryant* slid forward to stop the play, and Kupchak planted his left knee, hoping to avoid a collision. "It immediately gave out on me," Kupchak said. "I fell to the ground in incredible pain." With teammates gathered around, Kupchak held his knee tight and howled. The injury was diagnosed as severe yet treatable—a broken bone that would take at least eight weeks to heal. A few days later, however, a more detailed look showed that Kupchak's ligaments were torn and that he suffered major cartilage damage. "Devastating," he said. "The most devastating injury I'd ever had."

The Lakers held on for a 106–100 triumph, but news of the win was dampened by news of the loss: With Kupchak gone for the season, the Lakers needed another big man.

Sharman worked the phones, talking with Houston about the so-so Billy Paultz. He called the Clippers about Nater, Cleveland about Bill Laimbeer, Atlanta about Steve Hawes, Utah about Danny Schayes—all mediocre fill-ins with limited upsides.†

Finally, with desperation setting in (Riley even started using an un-athletic rookie named Kurt Rambis), Sharman reached out to the New Jersey Nets about a faded former superstar named Bob McAdoo. Once upon a time, in the early 1970s, McAdoo had been on the short list for the league's best player. Between 1973 and '76, he led the NBA in scoring three straight times, averaging 30.6, 34.5 and 31.1 points per game, respectively, for the Buffalo Braves. He won the league's Most Valuable Player award in 1975. "Bob was deadly, man, just deadly," said George McGinnis, the longtime Indiana Pacers star. "From seventeen feet on in, he was automatic. The best-shooting big man I've ever seen." Yet as time seemed to erode his skills and the callousness of NBA life corroded his enthusiasm, the glow faded. The Braves traded him to the Knicks in 1976, beginning a five-year, four-team odyssey from New York to Boston to Detroit to New Jersey. Were McAdoo's talents the same with the Celtics as they had been with Buffalo? Perhaps not. But back in the 1970s, the black athlete who

---

* Yes, Joe (Jellybean) Bryant—Kobe Bryant's father.
† Although, in the case of Bill Laimbeer, the upside exceeded what the Lakers envisioned. They would meet him later, when he starred for Detroit's back-to-back Eastern Conference championship teams.

dared complain about contract figures or playing time was labeled a problem child and banished to the netherworld of journeyman-ism. Even as he
continued to tally 20 points and 8 rebounds on a nightly basis, McAdoo
could not repair his reputation. Buffalo's management accused him of "ma-
lingering." The Pistons refused to return him to the lineup after he re-
habbed from an injury, and a heckler—Leon the Barber—would arrive
nightly simply to mock McAdoo with the refrain "McAdoo, McAdon't,
McAwill, McAwon't!" Multiple newspaper headline writers in multiple
cities offered up MCADOO ABOUT NOTHING to describe his brief stays in
town. "So much bullshit," McAdoo said. "So damn much."

McAdoo played just ten games with the Nets in 1980–81, and he was
now a free agent whose rights were held by New Jersey because he had failed
to present the team with an offer sheet under the league's complex right-of-
first-refusal policy. "There was this idea that we didn't like Bob in New Jersey," said Charlie Theokas, the team's general manager. "That's not true. He
just happened to be winding down, and wasn't really in our plans." Sharman
wanted McAdoo—but didn't entirely trust him. In a move that violated
multiple league rules, the Lakers quietly sent Mike Thibault, an assistant
with the organization, to New Jersey to spend three days with McAdoo. The
two bonded, talked, ate, shot baskets. "I loved Bob—just a nice man," said
Thibault. "And he was begging me to come to L.A. He said he'd do whatever it took to contribute and that he wanted to be validated as a winner. I
came back and told Jerry West he was worth the risk."

McAdoo was there for the taking—a 6-foot-9, 210-pound accomplished forward with a distinguished resume. Yet with McAdoo came . . .
issues. He was moody and, on occasion, indifferent. He seemed to take
nights off. Also, he was a scorer who would be joining a team with four
men (Abdul-Jabbar, Wilkes, Nixon, Johnson) who could pour in 20 on any
given night. "Scoring is glamorous," said Rambis. "But what we needed
was someone to defend, someone to rebound, someone to outlet the ball
and someone to run the floor. You had enough shots going around with all
the other guys. The key for that position was for the starting guy to fit in
with everybody else."

On December 24, 1981, the Nets sent McAdoo to Los Angeles in exchange
for a future second-round draft pick and cash. It was one of the happiest days of
McAdoo's life. He would, at long last, be joining a championship-caliber team.

"It was only a matter of getting there, getting adjusted and moving into the starting lineup," he said. "I couldn't wait."

What McAdoo didn't know—couldn't have known—was that, with his arrival, Pat Riley was about to make the smartest personnel move of his short coaching career.

A move no one saw coming.

CHAPTER 9

─────────

CLARK KENT

During the early years of Showtime, when glory came easy and life was but a dream, a majority of the Lakers lived in a beige three-story Fox Hills apartment building on Green Valley Circle owned by Jerry Buss. The setup was perfect. Because he valued his players, Buss offered—for the discounted monthly price of $550—luxurious one-bedroom units complete with modernized kitchens, full baths, spectacular views of the city and a quick commute to the Forum.

Before long, being a Laker felt as much like joining a fraternity as it did playing for a basketball team. Magic Johnson, Michael Cooper, Mike McGee, Eddie Jordan, Mark Landsberger, Ron Carter, Alan Hardy, Jim Brewer—all Lakers, all Fox Hills residents. Come nights after games, most members of the squad could be found inside someone's pad, listening to music, drinking wine, gorging on Fatburger (burgers topped with fried eggs were the sensation at the time), talking hoops, meeting long-legged beauties, planning a trip out to a club or bar or strip joint. "It was pretty great," said Larry Spriggs, a forward who would join the organization in 1983. "We were all together."

Well, almost.

As his teammates lived The Life, Kurt Rambis—rookie forward and all-world ragamuffin—lived, uh, life. Or, to be more precise, when he was done at the Forum after a long night of work (aka: sitting on the end of the bench, pining for a couple of minutes of garbage time), Rambis would drive off in neither Mercedes nor Bentley, BMW nor Jaguar. Hell, not even a '65 Opel Kadett. "Kurt didn't own a car—I took him everywhere," said Rich Brown. "He'd call if he needed a lift. Sometimes I'd loan him my car [a white Toyota Corolla]. Not often, but sometimes. And he slept on a mattress on the floor in my dining room."

Brown, Rambis's close friend and classmate from Santa Clara University, was not kidding. This wasn't a joke, a gag, a prank, an effort to embarrass an old chum. No, in 1982 Kurt Rambis of the Los Angeles Lakers made his everyday home in Huntington Beach, on an old mattress plopped down upon the wood floor inside the suburban dining room belonging to Rich and Carlee Brown (and their two children).

The setup was, Rambis admits, a weird one—but not nearly as weird as the man himself. Ever since he scratched and clawed and rebounded his way onto the Lakers roster out of training camp, Rambis—a free-agent nobody who had spent the previous year playing in Greece—had emerged as one of the great NBA eccentrics. "What Magic was to basketball," said Michael Cooper, "Kurt was to goofiness."

This, again, is not insult. Simply fact. Rambis refused to move out of the Browns' house because, hey, the dining room floor had served him well, and what was the benefit of a bed? Rambis owned one suit (it was a fecal shade of brown, and he wore it for his high school graduation) and only two collared shirts, because collared shirts were ugly and uncomfortable. "He would have had zero collared shirts," said Brown, "except that his mother, Becky, once bought Kurt and his brother, Randy, identical blue collared shirts. Randy's didn't fit, so Kurt took it."

When most players departed the Forum after games, they carried a gym bag, usually lightly packed with some socks, a T-shirt, maybe a pair of shorts. "But not Kurt," said Brown. "Oh, no." Rambis's tote, weighing somewhere between thirty and forty pounds, would be stuffed with any and all items from the team pantry. Cans of sodas. Bottles of beer. Bars of soap. Q-tips. Shoelaces. Hubcaps. Hall & Oates records . . .

"Kurt was weird as shit—just batshit cuckoo," said Frank Brickowski, a future Laker teammate. "A six-pack of soda is—what—two-fifty? He showed me a closet in his house, loaded with all the soda he collected for free. Fuck, I'm guessing Kurt didn't even drink soda."

For the first half of the season, this was Kurt Rambis's lot in Laker life.

He was a geeky white guy with the bad haircut, the awful wardrobe, the horn-rimmed glasses, the weighted-down bag and the weakest on-court repertoire this side of Garry Witts. In the early 1980s, every franchise made certain to have one—if not two—white players glued to their benches. It was a common (if not somewhat despicable) way to keep the white paying customers content when the game looked too black. This was far from a secret. Black players knew the deal, and hated it. White players knew the deal and, quite often, thanked God for it.

Kurt Rambis, however, *didn't* know the deal. Upon being drafted by the Knicks in the third round in 1980, he had reported to training camp with a long-shot chance of sticking, then proceeded to outwork the team's veteran frontcourt players. To the returnees, the act grew old quick. Diving for loose balls, clawing for rebounds, running extra laps after practice—who the hell did this white boy think he was? When Coach Red Holzman cut Rambis loose ("Big heart," Holzman said, "but needs work"), nary a tear was shed. "I was used to structured ball," Rambis said. "And everyone was trying to show up, make an impression. It was hard for me."

The ensuing year in Greece—living two hundred yards from the Mediterranean Sea, sharing an apartment with two young female waitresses, starring for the AEK team in Athens—was blissful. Rambis's club won the Greek title, and the young American blossomed as a minor celebrity. "There were little restaurants, and everyone knew you," he said. "Instead of handing you a menu, they'd bring you to the back and let you try everything. I can't overstate how wonderful it was." Rambis's plan was to play in Greece long enough to be able to pay his way through medical school. Then he would become one of the world's tallest doctors.

And yet, as much as he loved olive trees and chaniotiko boureki, Rambis felt the tug of an unfulfilled dream. He looked back at the Knicks experience not as a cherished sliver in time but as a dreaded *What If.* "I put a lot more emphasis on making the club than I should have," he said. "I wanted to show them I could do everything: handle the ball, pass, shoot, make steals. And, as a result, all phases of my game suffered."

After returning from Greece, Rambis was participating in a summer league in San Francisco when he was spotted by Mike Thibault, a Laker assistant who had coached against him in high school. "His greatest strength at the time was finishing around the basket," Thibault said. "He had a natural knack for finishing things off." The Lakers extended Rambis an invitation to camp, but he declined. "They were loaded," Rambis said. "What chance did I have?"

Paul Westhead, however, was undeterred. The forward reminded him of some of the bruisers he had once relied upon at La Salle. He convinced Rambis that, ever since Spencer Haywood's drug-induced implosion, the team was on the lookout for muscle and edginess. "I can't promise you a job," he said. "But you'll be given a fair chance. You don't let people push you around. I like that." Technically speaking, the last thing the team needed was another punisher. Mitch Kupchak had just joined the roster, Mark Landsberger was as big and goony as they came, veteran Jim Brewer knew every beneath-the-basket trick in the book. Yet Rambis was different. "I never met a white guy before who wasn't afraid of the black guy," said Ron Carter, a Laker guard. "But Kurt didn't care. Kenny Carr was a beast, Jim Chones was a beast, Jim Brewer was tough. Kurt fought them all." For those who subscribed to at-first-glance basketball cliché, Rambis's talent seemed marginal. But, upon closer inspection, his exterior masked an impressive skill set. He had soft hands, quick feet and a nose for the basket. Rambis averaged 19.6 points per game as a senior at Santa Clara. "He was a bruiser in college," said Ron Cornelius, who played against Rambis for the University of the Pacific. "But he was a bruiser who'd score seventeen points." Was he graceful? Hardly. Smooth? No. Did he give in? Give up? Back down? Never. "One day I looked around and I said, 'Who's this guy in the glasses that's blockin' all my shots?'" Magic Johnson said. "Then I saw he was pushin' and shovin'. He even riled up [Abdul-Jabbar] a couple of times. I said, 'Hmmmm, this boy can play.'"

"That training camp was brutal," said Rambis. "It was an all-out brawl every single day. We were diving for balls, trying to get loose balls that had already bounced twice out of bounds. We were still diving. I went into camp with the mind-set that, if they're bringing me in as a guy with a chance of making the team, I'm gonna prove that I should make it. And if they're just bringing me in as a practice player, I'm going to beat the crap out of them. I'm not going to be a punching bag for these guys. I'll be the one doing the hitting. Any time some guard came in and tried to lay the ball up, I put him down. I hit him."

Westhead was on the fence when it came to keeping Rambis. Would he hold up against the best of the best? Could he contribute? Then, during a practice, the coach was approached by Jerry West, who looked toward Rambis and snapped, "Who invited the guy with the long hair? What's he even doing here?"

Westhead was furious. How dare someone question his ability to piece together a team. At that moment, Rambis's roster spot was secured. "Years later, Paul told me that Jerry's words saved me," Rambis said. "I had no idea."

He was, however, stuck on the bench, a glorified cheerleader in glasses and short shorts. When Riley took over, he began paying the rookie more mind. Bill Bertka, the new assistant coach, liked the way the kid hustled. Riley tried both Brewer and Landsberger as the starting power forwards but found neither up to speed. Brewer was past his prime, and Landsberger lacked the basketball IQ to follow basic instructions. Bob McAdoo made his debut against the Jazz on December 29 but was rusty and slow. "The first couple of weeks he was with us, Bob couldn't make a shot," said Thibault. "He was out of shape, sort of fat, awful. People said to me, 'What the hell were you thinking, suggesting we get this guy?' "

In a game against Indiana on January 15, Rambis received his most extensive action to date, scoring just two points but collecting 14 rebounds in twenty-five productive minutes. "Herb Williams was killing us," said Rambis of the Pacers' star forward. "Riley pointed at me and sent me into the game. To be honest, I was the warm body, and he wanted anyone but Landsberger in there. But I ended up doing really well against Herb, and we won."

Two days later, six hours before tip-off against the Kansas City Kings at Kemper Arena, Riley pulled Rambis aside to tell him he'd be in the starting lineup. "OK, Coach," he said. "I'll be ready."

"It was a dream come true—an absolute dream," Rambis said years later. "But I couldn't show too much emotion. I was a professional. At least I was trying to be a professional."

That night Johnny Dolan, the Kings' public address announcer, introduced the Lakers' starting lineup. To the 9,879 fans in attendance, the names were all familiar (Wilkes, Abdul-Jabbar, Nixon, Johnson)—save one. As Rambis ambled out for the opening tip, he looked like the fortunate schlub who lucked into winning the "Be a Laker for a Day" raffle. *This* was the Lakers' power forward? Yet as Los Angeles won, 109–97, behind Johnson's 29 points, Rambis sparkled. Sure, he scored only four points and grabbed 9 rebounds. But as Riley and Bertka watched the new starting unit, they were struck by a singularly unique skill that Rambis—*and only Rambis*—seemed to possess.

Whenever the Kings scored a basket, Rambis somehow teleported from wherever he was on the court to directly under the basket. The movement was as fluid as a dolphin slicing through a wave, and could be easily missed. Rambis—*snap!*—went from there to here, reached his arms beneath the net and, in a singular motion—grabbed the ball, stepped onto the baseline and passed it to Johnson or Nixon as they darted up the court. "Kurt became the best outlet passer and inbounder in the history of the game," said Thibault. "Little skills often get overlooked in the NBA, because we value certain statistics. But what Kurt was able to do with the ball was astounding."

Before long, Rambis turned into a Forum cult hero. Fans arrived wearing fake mustaches, number 31 jerseys and replicas of Rambis's ubiquitous horn-rimmed glasses. ("They weren't actually horn-rims," Rambis later said. "They were special glasses with a rubber frame, so they couldn't break.") He appeared in a couple of commercials, and symbolized a certain genre of geek chic. He even managed to meet his future wife, a team employee named Linda Zafrani. ("Our first date didn't go so well," said Linda. "He thought I was weird because I liked video games. Kurt thinking anyone was weird was strange.")

Most important, the Lakers won seven of Rambis's first eleven starts and—after an uncharacteristic three-game losing streak in mid-February—went on a seven-game unbeaten run. The Lakers were often considered to be suspiciously soft and wimpy. Give Abdul-Jabbar or Nixon a few jabs to the midsection, they crumbled. Well, Rambis was anything but soft. His elbows were scabbed; his fingers—jammed from one-too-many misfired basketballs—jetted out at impossible angles. He wouldn't score 25 points, but he'd score six while putting an opponent on his back. "Rambis has the least physical ability of anyone who had the job," Jim Chones, the former Laker forward, said at the time. "Everyone else could do more. But they just want you to do the shit. You're asked to limit your scoring, do the garbage stuff. You're paid well and you get to be with a winner. They sell you that shit, but you're the only guy banging, getting gashes upside the head. Nobody mentions that. Over eighty-two games, you are abused. It's a hell of a spot to play, but they got it down to a science here in L.A." Throughout the season, there were multiple voices calling for McAdoo—effectively coming off the bench—to join the lineup. He was an accomplished star with a history of big shots, and 99 of 100 coaches would have given in. Inside the locker room, McAdoo's confidence was overflowing. Johnson used to get a kick out of challenging his manhood via proposed athletic matchups. "Bob was a very proud man," said Gary Vitti, the Lakers trainer. "Magic would look at him and say, 'Hey, Doo—I'll bet you can't beat so-and-so in a forty-yard dash.' Bob would say, 'Shit, I'll beat his ass in a forty-yard dash. He might get off a little bit quicker, but I'll catch him and pass him. I'll beat anybody in the one hundred, tennis, Ping-Pong, billiards.' We're in a stretching circle, and McAdoo says, 'I don't bowl.' Magic says, 'Doo don't bowl?' Bob looks at him and says—in 100 percent seriousness—'Give me two weeks to practice and I'll bowl a three hundred.' Everyone howled. Typical Bob McAdoo. Thought he could do everything." (Said McAdoo, laughing: "I never was able to hit three hundred. But I probably could have with practice.")

Riley tuned out the pro-McAdoo chorus. He was, after leading tentatively in his first few weeks, becoming a man in charge. Following an embarrassing March 12 home loss to the laughingstock Chicago Bulls, Riley entered the locker room, locked the door, picked up the stat sheet (with BULLS 111 LAKERS 105 printed atop) and issued his first-ever browbeating. He could deal with Reggie Theus scoring 13. He could deal with Artis Gilmore scoring 25. "How the hell does Ronnie Lester—Ronnie fucking Lester!?—shoot seven-for-twelve on us?" he screamed. "What kind of defense is that?" The moment was more important than Riley likely realized. The coach who rolls the ball onto the court and watches isn't a coach for very long. "That's my job," he said. "They were waiting for me to put my foot down." The Rambis decision further proved who was the boss. Riley's ideal rotation mixed finesse and toughness, speed and muscle. If players didn't fit into his plans (Mike McGee, Jim Brewer), they never sniffed the rotation. If players were confused about their roles (Nixon), he talked to them. When he sensed McAdoo's disappointment, he sat him down for a chat. "Pat was direct and professional," said McAdoo. "That's all you could ask for."

"We all saw Pat develop that season," said Rambis. "It was really impressive."

During the team's next practice, Riley had all the players line up against the wall. In front of everyone, in blunt language, Riley went man to man and teed off. "It was a come-to-Jesus meeting," said Thibault. "He told people what he was happy about, what he was unhappy about, what their roles were. It was no holds barred and sort of painful, and from that moment, everyone knew who was in charge. Some of those guys only thought of him as the radio guy who worked as Paul's assistant. Now he was coach."

The Lakers appreciated Riley's perspective. Having spent nine years as an NBA player, he knew whereof he spoke. Riley grasped the exhaustion that accompanied a third game in four nights. He understood what it felt like to be booed at home; to miss a crucial free throw; to be called out by the press. When reporters asked whether he considered himself to be a good coach, Riley shook his head. He was neither good nor awful—just learning. "I call him a philosopher because he can talk about things beyond the game that affect you," said Wilkes. "He understands the travel and the rigors of the schedule and personal problems. All those things are not supposed to affect you, but they do. He is in touch with us." Early on, Riley suggested Abdul-Jabbar focus more on defense and rebounding, less on scoring. The center spent the next six games sulking. The coach admitted it was a bad idea and scrapped the plan. In a late-season loss at Golden State, Riley called an unnecessary time-out, then lacked one when it was later needed. Afterward, when asked by reporters about the miscue, he pounded his fist into his chest. "The players get hammered when they make mistakes," he said. "Sometimes I'm to blame for losses, too."

By the time the regular season came to an end, the Lakers found themselves with a Western Conference–best 57-25 record. Their 114.6 points per game ranked second in the league, and their 2,356 assists ranked first. "When you played Los Angeles," said Danny Schayes, the Utah forward, "you knew you were going to have to work your ass off."

Paul Westhead? Who the hell was Paul Westhead? "Riley's not getting near the credit he deserves after all this," said Stan Albeck, the Spurs coach. "That situation was chaotic when he took over, a real zoo. Pat knows he's got talented guys, and he's letting them play the way they want to play."

For Buss, the man who took immense heat for siding with a player over a coach, it was sweet vindication. The Forum was the place to be in Los Angeles. Celebrities of all ilk walked through the turnstiles, ranging from Joe Namath and Jane Fonda to Michael Douglas and Don Rickles. Every night was sold out, every game an event. Riley, a sharp dresser with thousand-dollar Giorgio Armani suits and custom-tailored shirts (players jokingly nicknamed him GQ), treated the sideline like a red carpet. "God, he was dreamy," said Joan McLaughlin, the organization's director of human resources. "He was always the one the girls were looking at." Led by a visionary choreographer named Paula Abdul, the sexy Laker Girls danced and kicked away. The word *Showtime* was a definitive statement. A declaration. The Lakers *were* Showtime. Fast. Intense. Unyielding.

Having closed the season with three straight wins, *Sports Illustrated* celebrated Los Angeles's dominance with a cover piece titled THEY'RE NOT JUST GOOD, THEY'RE PERFECT. Yet even though the Lakers emerged as heavy favorites to return to the finals, many around the league questioned their strength. Riley, after all, was a rookie coach. Abdul-Jabbar was old, the bench—even with McAdoo—somewhat thin. Though Rambis had exceeded all of Riley's expectations, his statistical line (4.6 points, 5.4 rebounds, 1.2 blocks) was laughable. Mitch Kupchak, deemed the perfect Laker power forward, was wearing a thick cast on his leg while taking business classes at UCLA. "L.A. can't win with a Kurt Rambis . . . at Mitch Kupchak's forward spot," said Cotton Fitzsimmons, the Kings' coach. "All you do is leave them alone on defense and cheat over into the middle on Abdul-Jabbar. Then you can beat them in a half-court game, which is what you usually get in the playoffs, where teams really work hard to curtail the fast break."

Fitzsimmons's reasoning made sense. Playoff basketball *is* a departure from regular-season basketball. Running is curtailed. Defensive indifference vanishes. Weak links and soft spots—hidden over eighty-two games—are exposed like cold sores. And yet the Lakers had something going for themselves, something both clichéd and powerful. Unity. Heading into the 1981 first-round series against the Rockets, the majority of players had ignored their head coach and questioned their young point guard. There were jealousy issues, insecurities, bitterness. Now cohesiveness reigned.

On the night of April 23, four days before they were scheduled to open at home against the Phoenix Suns, the Lakers invited fans to observe a workout at the Forum. It was a fun, loose affair, with players tiptoeing toward the stands for autographs and light banter. A year earlier, many Lakers would have bristled at the very idea. But times had changed. Leading into the Suns opener, Riley held a meeting with his men to specifically discuss the previous season's pratfall. The bruises remained. The impact hadn't faded. "The players really remember how it felt last April 5," Riley said. "It was a painful, painful experience. If they are sincere about turning that into a positive experience, and I think they are, it's a hell of a strong force on our side."

John MacLeod, the Suns' veteran coach, had guided his team to a surprising 46-36 record. Though Phoenix lacked the Lakers' overall skill, their roster boasted enough players to make things interesting. Guard Dennis Johnson was among the league's best, as was Truck Robinson, the burly center who averaged 19.1 points and 9.7 rebounds. "The Lakers had much more in the tank than we did," said Craig Dykema, the Suns forward. "We would have to come up with something special to have a chance."

MacLeod's "something special" was something disastrous. He made the decision that Alvan Adams, his All-Star forward, would cheat in and help center Rich Kelley whenever Abdul-Jabbar received the ball down low. "We're not going to let Kareem beat us," said MacLeod. "He's beaten too many others."

On the bright side, the Suns held Abdul-Jabbar to 11 points in Game 1. On the down side, the Lakers won, 115–96.

Los Angeles rolled to a four-game sweep, then advanced to the Western Conference Finals to face San Antonio, a 48-34 team with the dynamic one-two scoring punch of George Gervin (32.3 points per game) and Mike Mitchell (21 points per game).

The Spurs, though, were not the Lakers' sole concern. At the same time Riley and his players were preparing for a tough battle, Buss and his executives were preparing to complete a transaction that would change both the dynamic of the team and the scope of the NBA.

"Let's just say," said Cooper, "that if it happens, history is rewritten. History is totally rewritten."

■ ■ ■

More than two years earlier, on February 15, 1980, Los Angeles and Cleveland had completed a trade that interested absolutely no one.

With their backcourt a tad thin and Westhead seeking another player who could help pressure opposing guards, the Lakers acquired Butch Lee, a 6-foot, 180-pound former Marquette star who had accomplished little since being selected tenth overall in the 1978 Draft. In return, Bill Sharman, the Lakers general manager, agreed to part with Don Ford, a workmanlike forward fancied by Ron Hrovat, the Cavs' general manager. Ford enjoyed a solid four and a half years in Los Angeles but was no longer a part of the rotation. "The trade made sense," said Lee. "Sometimes we all need new places to play."

In order to surrender Ford, Sharman demanded a swapping of future picks. The Lakers would give up their first-round selection in the upcoming draft, but only if Cleveland agreed to part with their first pick in either 1981 or '82. Hrovat wasn't thrilled by the demand, but with a roster featuring two up-and-coming stars (Kenny Carr and Mike Mitchell), he presumed the selection would be a relatively late one. Without much arguing, he handed Sharman the '82 pick. "Those things happen all the time," said Lee. "As a player, just trying to survive, you barely think about what future choices will become."

Now, however, the Lakers found themselves holding Willy Wonka's golden ticket. The pick they sent away (twenty-second overall in the 1980 Draft) netted Cleveland Chad Kinch, a UNC Charlotte forward who averaged 2.9 points in forty-one career NBA games. Meanwhile, the Carr-and-Mitchell-led Cavs plummeted. Cleveland completed the 1982 season with a 15-67 mark, which, pending an upcoming coin flip, would hand the Lakers either the first or second overall selection in the draft. "The way Los Angeles wound up with all those studs is amazing," said Frank Layden, the Utah coach. "I used to scratch my head, because it didn't seem fair. They get Magic Johnson when they're already great, then another top pick? Ridiculous. But you had to give credit where credit was due. Name another organization that worked the system any better."

As the Lakers and Spurs readied for action, Buss had one eye on the series, the other on Ralph Sampson, the University of Virginia's 7-foot-4 All-American center. Sampson had just completed a junior season during which he averaged 15.8 points and 11.4 rebounds per game, and experts were predicting his future as a towering NBA legend.

Sampson had until May 15 to declare himself eligible for the upcoming draft, and while he remained publicly mum, those close to him suggested a guaranteed future in Los Angeles might be enough to entice a jump. That's why, on the evening of May 12, Buss invited Donald Sterling, owner of the San Diego Clippers, to his mansion for dinner.

The sad-sack Clips had recently compiled a 17-65 record, which meant San Diego and Los Angeles were the two contenders for the top pick. While they, too, wanted Sampson, the Clippers were a long way (basketball-wise) from Los Angeles. They played in an awful arena, dressed in awful uniforms, maintained an awful roster. Cleveland was basketball hell. San Diego was basketball hell with nice weather. "There's no way I was coming out early to be a Clipper," said Sampson. "Money wasn't the issue. I didn't want to spend my life losing game after game." Earlier that season, when the Lakers had traveled east to play the Bullets, Abdul-Jabbar invited Sampson to the Hyatt Arlington at Key Bridge for breakfast. The two spent an hour together, talking pressure and skyhooks and all things basketball and life. "He was a giant of a man," Sampson said. "People never understood him, but I felt like I did. He was gentle and warm. It would have been wonderful to have played alongside him."

Buss desperately craved Sampson, and decided to take action well before the May 20, 1982, coin flip to make certain the number one selection would—no matter what—belong to his franchise. In a scene that could take place only in Los Angeles, Buss and Sterling were joined for a private dinner by (inexplicably) Gabe Kaplan, the mustached actor who had starred as Mr. Kotter in *Welcome Back, Kotter.*

Over steak and potatoes, the Laker owner told the Clipper owner he would do nearly anything to lock up Sampson. The Clipper owner told the Laker owner he, too, wanted Sampson—or lots of money, picks and players in exchange for the guaranteed right to draft him. "But, Don," Buss said, "you know there's no fucking way he's leaving college to play for you."

Kaplan suggested they flip a coin—if Buss wins, a deal is worked out; if Sterling wins, the Lakers help convince Sampson to become a Clipper. Buss nodded; Sterling frowned and rejected the plan. Kaplan said, just for fun, he'd flip the coin.

"You call it," he said to Buss.

Buss yelled, "Heads!"

It came up tails.

"Hey, Don, you won," Buss said. "You could have had it all."

Buss offered $6 million for the guarantee of the pick. Sterling declined. Buss offered $6 million plus (should he have it) the number two pick in the upcoming draft. Sterling declined. Buss offered $6 million plus the number two pick in the upcoming draft and the team's first-round pick in 1984. Sterling declined again. Buss suggested that he could, somehow, land the Clippers Moses Malone from Houston. Sterling was moderately intrigued, but he also wanted two Laker players—Norm Nixon and Michael Cooper. Buss said he'd have to think about it.

Sharman, who was in San Antonio at the time of the dialogue, was told of some of the packages Buss had put forth. He nearly choked on his tongue. Hell, they might not even need the Clippers to score the first selection. It was lunacy.

News of the Buss-Sterling dinner reached the front sports pages of

Southern California newspapers. Here were the Lakers fighting to reach the NBA Championships, and four players suddenly had new concerns. For Cooper and Nixon, it was the idea of (*Dear God, no . . .*) becoming Clippers. For Rambis, it was the idea of Sampson taking his place at power forward. For Abdul-Jabbar, it was the idea of Sampson taking his place at center. Even though Buss outwardly spoke of the two seven-footers playing side by side, the concept was a preposterous one. Both men were tall, thin, lanky low-post scorers with similar games. Surely, Sampson's arrival would hasten Abdul-Jabbar's departure.

So how did the Lakers react to the gossip? They didn't. Not one player offered a quotation (on or off the record) to the media about Sampson. Later on in his coaching career, Riley liked to use the phrase "peripheral opponents" to group the ceaseless distractions faced by professional athletes. Travel, wives, kids, parents, in-laws, groupies, speaking engagements, the press—all peripheral opponents. What the best of the best did, he said, was gather all the peripheral opponents, place them in a small cardboard box and slide it beneath the bed until the season ended. "We're twelve-plus-two-plus-one," Riley would say in reference to the twelve players, two bench coaches and one trainer. "That's all who matters."

One year earlier, the Lakers damned themselves to an early exit by focusing more on Westhead's shortcomings and Johnson's ego than the task at hand. This time, the team was hyper-focused. Sampson? Big whoop. There was a championship to win.

Though the Spurs were a potent team, Los Angeles played at a higher level. The Lakers opened at home with a 128–117 win, powered by Johnson's 13-point, 14-assist, 16-rebound How to Do Absolutely Everything clinic. They won again two days later, 110–101, then traveled to San Antonio and dismantled the Spurs for a third-straight time, 118–108.

A couple of hours before the Game 3 tip-off, Sampson—turned off by all the drama and uncertainty—issued a recorded statement to the media, declaring his decision to return to Virginia for his senior season. Buss expressed his disappointment, and also took a stab at damage control. "The minute [Sterling] mentioned a player, I said I wanted to stop this conversation," he said. "I love my players."

The words were garbage—but well-intended garbage.

Did Sampson's decision have an impact on the Los Angeles players? Hard to say. Abdul-Jabbar put forth his best effort of the series, scoring a team-high 26 points while blanketing Spurs center George Johnson beneath a cloak of invisibility (0 points, 0 rebounds). Nixon added 22, repeatedly blowing past Johnny Moore, the opposing point guard. More than anything, the game spoke to the difference between a good team with one dominant star and a great team with several. Because Abdul-Jabbar clogged the middle, the Spurs offense was reduced to Gervin hucking off-balance shots from awkward angles. His 39 points looked wonderful on the stat sheet, but felt empty. "He came out with the attitude that he was going to win it or lose it," Wilkes said.

He lost it.

Less than twenty-four hours later, Los Angeles finished off the Spurs, 128–123. It was the Lakers' eleventh-straight victory, and twenty-third win in twenty-seven tries. The day belonged to Nixon, who scored 30 points in front of a silent HemisFair Arena crowd, and afterward his teammates lathered his head in the cheapest of dime-store champagnes—twist-off caps and all. Buss, smiling from ear to ear, promised Dom Perignon after the NBA championship was sealed. "That's four more games," he said.

In the corner of the room, sitting silently by his locker, one Laker was overcome by emotion. Such happiness—such incredible, overwhelming, all-encompassing happiness—coupled by such deep sorrow . . .

■ ■ ■

When one loses a child, it never leaves. It lingers and hangs there and looms like an awful dream. A person can momentarily forget, can be distracted by a quick joke or an engrossing movie. Yet, ultimately, it remains.

Jamaal Wilkes knows this all too well. In the fall of 1981, shortly before the start of training camp, his infant daughter, Arainni Julise Wilkes, died of complications. It was the second baby Jamaal Wilkes had lost (his first, with ex-wife Joycelyn, died of a heart ailment in 1977), and the pain was unlike any he had ever endured. Though he spoke little of the tragedy at the time, for the Wilkes family, it was more horrific than even the little he let on. In 1952, before Jamaal was born, his mother, Thelma Wilkes, had lost her first son, Leonard Bruce Wilkes, at thirteen months. "He was a picture of health," Thelma Wilkes said. "He passed in his sleep; they called it crib death. I was four months' pregnant with Jamaal. I prayed for another boy."

On the basketball court, Wilkes was a 6-foot-6, 190-pound small forward whose nickname, Silk, perfectly described one of the game's smoothest operators. Wilkes could hit any shot from any distance, and look good doing so. "People forget, but Jamaal was a tremendous player," said Nixon. "There wasn't much he couldn't do with a basketball in his hands." Yet despite his quiet outward demeanor and ubiquitous warm smile, Wilkes's 1981–82 season had been a trying one. Like most Lakers, he didn't understand Westhead's offense. Early on he had been rumored to be headed to Milwaukee in exchange for Marques Johnson, and three weeks into the season he was shooting 39 percent—almost 10 percent lower than his career average. After scoring just two points in a November 10 loss to the Spurs, he suggested he might take a temporary leave of absence to clear his head. "I was looking forward to the year, especially after being eliminated so early in the playoffs last year," he said. "But [the death of his daughter] happened so late in the summer, it disrupted my life going into training camp. I can't describe how something like that . . . you know. I just reacted to it."

Teammates convinced Wilkes that the comfort of the basketball court would prove more soothing than sitting on the couch at home. "His life was depressing," said Riley. "The team was depressing. When he said, 'I need time off,' I could understand that. He's very aware and in tune. He's more in touch with his feelings than most players. He listens to his feelings and emotions. He does what his heart tells him to do."

Wilkes's heart told him to play—a decision that, as he sat in the corner of the locker room in San Antonio, seemed wise. This was, after all, the reason Jamaal Wilkes fell in love with basketball all those years ago. The sense of teamwork. The joy of shooting. The thrill of winning. As a boy in Ventura, California, Jackson Keith Wilkes (he went by Keith until 1975, when he converted from Baptist to Islam and changed his name to Jamaal) couldn't stay away from the town's multiple pickup courts. He would play in the morning, play at night, play through the weekends. One minute, Keith would be shooting hoops at Washington Elementary School. The next minute, he'd be running back and forth at West Park. Then, a few hours later, the Boys Club. "I was six feet tall when I was eleven, so I was always one of the taller boys," he said. "I was real fast, and I was clearly one of the better players for my age. I started playing against bigger kids, and it got hard. They kept blocking my shots, pushing me around, beating me up. I really had to adjust."

Wilkes did, by making a singular alteration that transformed him from a nice local player into a future NBA All-Star. "I redid my shot," he said. "Changed it completely."

From that point on, when Keith Wilkes released, he did so from atop his head, as if pulling back a medicine ball and slinging it with all his might. The result was a thing of crooked beauty—a shot that looked simultaneously awful (upon release) and gorgeous (upon swooshing through the twine). "To me," Westhead once said, "his shot is like snow falling softly off a bamboo leaf."

Though Keith felt pulled toward the playgrounds, he was never overtaken by them. The trash talk, the selfishness, the arrogance—not his style. That's primarily because his parents, Leander (a former Oakland Naval base employee who turned to the ministry after losing his son) and Thelma (a bookkeeper at the University of California, Santa Barbara), refused to step back. Sure, sports were important. But not nearly as important as integrity and discipline. Other kids collected baseball cards—Keith Wilkes collected candles. Other kids listened to the Rolling Stones—he listened to John Coltrane.

"Jamaal was raised and supported in a home environment where we strove to be more reasonable and rational than others," Leander once told *Sports Illustrated*. "There was sometimes a different set of values on the playgrounds, but Jamaal was always secure. That shows. Players who aren't secure will show a weakness of character in times of stress, be it anger or loss of control. That doesn't happen with Jamaal."

Keith was the kid who, among other things, set picks and properly rolled to the basket and took pride in defense. He began playing in organized leagues at age eight and endured only one losing season through college—that being with a team in third grade. As Ventura High's starting center, Wilkes was both an All-CIF first teamer and the student class president. However, when his father was relocated to the Second Baptist Church in Santa Barbara, the family moved. "I planned to stay in Ventura for my senior year," Wilkes said, "but as the fall approached, I missed my mother's cooking." The move was, basketball-wise, a difficult one. When Wilkes came out for practice, the team's coach, Jack Trigueiro, took one look at his shooting form and stopped everything. "He had Jamaal square his shoulders up and hold the ball in front," said Bob Thompson, a guard. "During practice, it was the weirdest experience. He was shooting air balls. He was no good at all. After practice, there was a two-on-two game with the coaches, and Jamaal went back to what was natural. Trigueiro said, 'I'll guard him.' Jamaal just lit him up. Trigueiro said, 'What the hell, Keith, from now on you shoot the ball whatever way you want.'"

As a senior at Santa Barbara High in 1969–70, Wilkes guided the Dons to 26 straight wins and the playoff semifinals. He was every Division I coach's daydream. Wilkes could play inside and outside, pass and rebound, shoot free throws and drain rainbows from far away. He was a straight-A student with a model home life. "We always had dinner together at six o'clock," said Thelma. "Everybody expressed themselves at the table. We listened and tried not to be judgmental. We wanted the best for them but did not want them to think that everything was mine, mine, mine." His older sister, Lucy, skipped two grades and entered Stanford University at sixteen. Keith, too, skipped a grade. He was quiet, though not a mumbler. When Wilkes spoke, his words carried meaning. "A long time ago I saw what winning meant," he said of his high school experience. "I decided to dedicate myself to that phase of the game, even to the point of never being flashy. It's possible to do things differently from others and still get the desired results."

Keith decided to attend UCLA because John Wooden, the coach, relied on neither nonsense promises nor used car salesman–esque fast talk. "He was straightforward," Wilkes said. "A lot of people I talked to left me in a haze. He didn't tell me I'd be first string. I appreciated that."

In four years at Westwood, Wilkes emerged as one of the nation's elite players. He was a two-time All-American, as well as a two-time national champion. To the delight of Bruin teammates, coaches and fans, he was also the nicest person they'd ever met. Following the conclusion of a game against USC during his senior year, for example, Wilkes changed into his street clothes, left the Pauley Pavilion dressing room and walked through the stands as the city high school playoffs were about to begin. It was, Dwight Chapin of the *Los Angeles Times* wrote, "Like Dylan strolling in to start a concert."

"There he is!" a girl shouted.

"Hey, Keith!" someone else yelled. "How's it going?"

"Right on, baby!" said another.

"Is there anybody you don't know?" Chapin asked.

Wilkes quietly averaged 15 points and 7.4 rebounds in his UCLA career, doing whatever tasks Wooden requested. "If Keith Wilkes could have his way," Cliff Gewecke wrote in *The Christian Science Monitor*, "he'd be as anonymous as a store detective." His biggest spotlight moment came as a senior, when Leonard Lamensdorf, a young movie producer, cast Wilkes as Nathaniel Cornbread Hamilton, the lead character in the feature film *Cornbread, Earl and Me*, about a quiet basketball star wrongly shot and killed by police officers. "Keith was fantastic," Lamensdorf said of a performance that was hailed by the *Los Angeles Times*. "He can do anything he wants to do, be anything he wants—doctor, lawyer, actor, anything."

Wilkes was selected eleventh overall in the 1974 Draft by the Golden State Warriors, and—playing second fiddle to superstar Rick Barry—won an NBA title as a rookie. Teammates made fun of his youth (he was twenty-one when he debuted) and his form (Barry: "It's about the worst looking shot I've seen. I can't stand to watch Keith shoot. He does everything wrong."), and he took it all with a smile. "The only thing he wanted to do was come to work and blend in," said Al Attles, the Golden State coach. "Every coach should have one team like that one, and one player like Jamaal."

A testament to Wilkes's reputation came after the season, when—to little fanfare and protestation—he announced the changing of his name to Jamaal Abul-Lateef Wilkes. He had first dabbled in Islam during his freshman year of college, and the focus upon meditation and inner peace appealed to him. He officially converted as a senior, to the heartbreak of his devout Baptist parents. At the time, many misunderstood *Islam* to be a synonym for *violent* and *angry*. "Does this mean you hate white people?" his mother asked.

Jamaal laughed. "No," he said. "Not at all."

Shortly after signing with the Warriors, Wilkes told Dick Vertlieb, the team's general manager, that: (a) He had converted to Islam; (b) he would be taking a new name in the coming weeks. *Jamaal Abul-Lateef?* How the hell was the franchise supposed to spin that one? "Absolutely not," Vertlieb replied. "We signed you as Keith Wilkes, you'll play as Keith Wilkes."

He did, and when—after the championship—the name change was again broached, no one within the organization dared challenge him. Here was a man who played hurt, who played hard and who played well. If Keith Wilkes wanted to be known as Benji Bear or Paulie Olkowski III, so be it. "He was that good," said Attles. "Just a perfect part of a team."

Wilkes enjoyed three seasons with the Warriors. Toward the end of his time there, however, the mood began to sour. Franklin Mieuli, the team's owner, had promised Wilkes a new contract should he have a productive second year. The forward averaged 17.8 points and 8.8 rebounds, asked about the raise and was given the silent treatment. He was also going through a divorce with Joycelyn. "As it all played out, I started thinking I might need a fresh start somewhere else," he said. "The idea of being back near UCLA, back near my parents was appealing. And, of course, the Lakers were the Lakers. They were a model franchise."

Wilkes signed a four-year, $800,000 free-agent deal, then discovered no situation was without problems. Sports fans are suckers for homecomings, but Wilkes's was awful. Hampered by a broken finger and a handful of other maladies, he appeared in just fifty-one games, averaging a career-low 12.9 points. The Los Angeles media proved unsympathetic, referring to Wilkes as both a disappointment and a bust. There were excuses to be made and scapegoats to be exposed. Wilkes said nothing. "Jamaal just wasn't a guy who'd point fingers," said Nixon. "He was better than that."

With improved health (both physical and mental), Wilkes rebounded in 1978–79, averaging a career-high 18.6 points per game. When, the following year, Johnson arrived, he found an on-court soul mate. And vice versa. It was the perfect pairing of the league's best passer and the league's softest hands. Wilkes may well have been the only Laker not to take repeated Johnson passes upside the head, or in the buttocks, or on the shoulder blade. "You had to be ready," he said. "And you had to always keep your head up and one eye on Earvin."

On the night Wilkes scored 37 points in Philadelphia to help the Lakers beat the 76ers in Game 6 of the 1980 NBA Finals, the people of Santa Barbara celebrated like never before. Leander and Thelma cried and hugged, their joy a testament to two proud parents and a wonderful son. To them, Johnson's turn at center was a side story, as was Westhead's rookie success and Abdul-Jabbar's injury.

This was Jamaal Wilkes's moment, and they loved every second of it.

■ ■ ■

Two years later, the Lakers would again be facing the Philadelphia 76ers in the NBA championship series. Once more, Wilkes would be needed not only as an offensive force but as an able body to lock down Julius Erving, one of the league's superstars.

For NBA executives, television bigwigs and countless fans, the pairing was a basketball downer. Throughout the regular season the league's best team had been the Boston Celtics, who won 63 games to dominate the Atlantic Division. As the Lakers and Celtics worked their way through the playoffs, a buzz mounted over the likelihood of a finals pairing Johnson and Larry Bird, his collegiate rival and the Celtics' best player. The Johnson-Bird connection dated back to the 1979 NCAA championship matchup, when Michigan State beat Indiana State in what was, at the time, the most watched basketball game in history.

When Philadelphia pulled an upset in Game 7 at Boston Garden, a nation of basketball junkies sighed with resignation. Perhaps no one was more dejected than McAdoo, the Laker sixth man who had spent a miserable twenty games with the Celtics three seasons earlier. McAdoo looked at Boston, what with their predominantly Caucasian roster and their arrogant coach (Bill Fitch, who, after the Game 7 loss bellowed, "Let me just say this. If we had played the Lakers we would have beaten them") and their racist loyalists, and he didn't merely want justice. He wanted revenge. "I sought to destroy them," he said. "We all did. It was in our blood."

The Sixers, on the other hand, were (yawn) the Sixers. Erving and shooting guard Andrew Toney, their two best all-around players, were classy and subdued. Billy Cunningham, the head coach, was a blue-collar Brooklyn kid who outworked everyone in the gym. Center Darryl Dawkins was flawed but loquaciously lovable, and Maurice Cheeks, the point guard, knew his role and played vigorously. It was a team that won through physicality and blunt force. "Look, it wasn't the same as playing Boston," said Cooper. "We didn't hate Philly, or even dislike Philly. They were nice guys, good players. The NBA Finals are always intense. But . . ."

But this wasn't Boston-Los Angeles. "It just wasn't," Cooper said.

The series opened at Philadelphia on May 27, following a twelve-day layoff for the Lakers. Though Riley lacked Westhead's Philly-boy-comes-home story line, there was intrigue over how he would hold up his first time coaching on the big stage. With their star-studded lineup and awe-inspiring 8-0 playoff roll, the Lakers were heavy favorites to not merely wipe out Philadelphia but go down as a transcendent team. To many, the only one who could screw things up was Riley. Two days before Game 1, Scott Ostler of the *Los Angeles Times* penned a column titled A STAR IS BORN that broached the rookie coach's emergence. At the start of the season, Riley had been as noteworthy as a doorknob. Now, he was being stopped everywhere—complimented, insulted, advised, hounded for autographs. "Two years ago he couldn't have made the down payment," Ostler wrote. "He's like the passenger who lands the jumbo jet after the pilot and co-pilot crap out in midflight. Except that nobody had to tell Riley when to lower the flaps or how to read the radar."

As the Lakers trotted onto the Spectrum floor for pre-game shooting, they were greeted by the familiar Philly sound of hostile howling. The noise continued throughout the first half, as the hometown Sixers built a comfortable 61–50 lead. For Los Angeles, the game was a disaster. Riley warned his players about Philadelphia's physical tempo, but to no avail. Dawkins was tossing Abdul-Jabbar aside beneath the boards, and Erving—driving through the lane at will—had burned Wilkes for 14 points and 5 assists. "Wilkes looked as if he needed more than just an oilcan to get unhinged," Mike Littwin wrote in the *Times*. "He needed Kuwait."

Not one for hype chats or rah-rah speeches, Wilkes retreated to the locker room for halftime and, as usual, retreated into himself. He had let Erving take him away from his strengths—pulling up for jumpers on offense, denying the baseline on defense—and now the Lakers were in a deep hole. When the third quarter began, Wilkes woke up. He scored 16 of his 24 points over the twelve minutes that followed, powering a 40–9 spurt that flipped the game. With Johnson and Nixon pushing the ball at every opportunity, Wilkes was nearly unstoppable, slicing to the rim, pulling up and hitting jumpers over Erving and Bobby Jones. By the time the game ended, the Lakers cruised to a 124–117 triumph. "Jamaal did so much, and he did it quietly so he was often overlooked," said Cooper. "But sometimes you looked at him and realized, 'This man is as good as anyone in the league.'"

Afterward, to Riley's delight, Laker players broached the idea of sweeping the Sixers and the entire playoffs. "It's something we think about just among ourselves," Johnson said. "It's kind of something we laugh about right now. But we think about it."

That stopped quickly. Philadelphia rebounded to take Game 2, 110–94, and afterward, Erving—rarely prone to mental gaffes—committed one. When asked by Dave Anderson of *The New York Times* to explain the night's meaning, the beloved Doctor didn't mince words. "In our practices the last few days, we taught ourselves how to beat the Lakers," he said. "How to beat their trap, we exposed it as a zone in the first half. How to make 'em pay for gambling. How to get offensive rebounds and make the second shot. Now it's up to them to adjust to us instead of us guessing how to play them."

Though Riley was still new to the craft of mentally manipulating his players, here was a softball tossed his way. *Taught ourselves how to beat the Lakers? Now it's up to them to adjust to us?* Philadelphia hadn't "figured out" the Lakers. No, Los Angeles merely played an underwhelming game. When Riley next met with his men, he made sure Erving's words were presented. "Philadelphia thinks they've got you figured out," he said. "They think they're going to win this thing. What do you have to say about that? How will you respond?"

When the series returned to Los Angeles, the Lakers took control. Riley was now employing a seven-man rotation of Nixon, Johnson, Abdul-Jabbar, Wilkes, Rambis, McAdoo and Cooper (the *Los Angeles Times* took to calling them The Magnificent Seven) and the cohesiveness was magical. Cunningham was using almost every available player, which meant the Sixers were (bright side) rested, but (downside) relying on subpar NBA talent. Erving and Cheeks scared people. Steve Mix and Earl Cureton did not.

In Game 3, Nixon and Johnson attacked Philadelphia's porous defense. Because he was talkative and funny and big, Dawkins—nicknamed Chocolate Thunder—emerged as a media darling. Yet, as a defensive low post presence, he was vastly overrated: CHOCOLATE THUNDER, OR CHOCOLATE SOUFFLE? a *Los Angeles Times* headline asked. If one wasn't blowing past Dawkins, he was almost certainly getting fouled by him. Nixon, in particular, took advantage, scoring a game-high 29 points in an easy 129–108 win. Though Cooper contributed only 12 points, he spent much of the game spewing trash toward the opposing players. He liked Erving and respected Erving. He did not, however, fear Erving. "You think we're fucking adjusting our game?" he said. "You think you figured us out? Take a look at the scoreboard, motherfucker."

In the victory's aftermath, Riley praised Bill Bertka, his assistant coach and a renowned defensive guru. Years earlier Bertka had received a letter from Clair Bee, the esteemed college basketball coach who first implemented the 1-3-1 zone defense. "Bee swore by it," said Bertka. "I always thought of him. When we beat Philly, we sprung the 1-3-1 half-court trap on them, and they didn't have a clue. That was all Clair Bee."

Two nights later the Lakers won again, 111–101, and the drama of a close series was gone. Though Erving spent the post-game assuring writers his team was not a corpse, his team was a corpse. "Even we knew we had to play our absolute best," said Dawkins. "The Lakers were better than us. I hate to say it, but they were. They were a deep, deep team."

The Sixers pulled together to win Game 5, but on the night of June 8, a sold-out Forum watched the Lakers capture their second NBA title in three years, 114–104. Though the chatter was of Riley and Johnson (who was named MVP by averaging 16.2 points, 8 assists and 10.8 rebounds), Wilkes made the difference. He scored a team-high 27 in the finale, hitting one clutch shot after another.

When the game came to an end, Wilkes entered the locker room, grabbed a bottle of champagne and poured it atop his head. The cool liquid streamed over his eyes and onto his lips. As Buss had promised, this wasn't the cheap stuff. It was Dom Perignon—ninety dollars per bottle and well worth the price.

What had started off as the worst season of Wilkes's life had ended sweetly.

"All I wanted to do," he said, "was soak it all in."

CHAPTER 10

CLUBBING

There have always been genuine debates concerning the hierarchy of the 1980s Los Angeles Lakers.

Was the most important star Magic Johnson or Kareem Abdul-Jabbar?

Was Michael Cooper a better all-around player than Jamaal Wilkes?

Would Bob McAdoo have been a more suitable starter than Kurt Rambis?

One thing, however, is universally agreed upon: Of the sixty-nine men to wear the purple and gold between 1979 and 1991, no one matched the pure stupidity of Mark Landsberger.

By "stupid," we're not referring to court smarts (or lack thereof) or worldliness (or lack thereof) or even the ability to break a one-dollar bill into four quarters (or lack thereof).

No, Mark Landsberger was stupid in the way of a granite slab. He had a brain and all the proper neurons and dendrites other human beings are gifted with. And yet Laker players and employees seemed to take universal delight in arguing whether Landsberger's IQ was closer to 10 or zero or, if this is even possible, -14.

"Mark Landsberger was a nice kid," said Claire Rothman, the team's longtime vice president of booking. "But he was dumb like a post. I'm guessing he literally could not walk and chew gum simultaneously."

"Good lord, Mark was the dumbest person I've ever met," said Michael Cooper. "Friendly—but historically dumb."

Landsberger arrived in Los Angeles via trade from Chicago in February 1980 and impressed with his rebounding ability and immense size. He was 6-foot-8, 230 pounds and built like a large pile of sand. He once collected 29 rebounds in a game against Denver. When he crashed the boards, Landsberger was almost certainly the one coming up with the ball. "It's amazing, because he had no hops whatsoever," said Ron Carter, a Laker guard. "Mark would always have two or three of his shots blocked every game. But he really rebounded."

Yet of all the (small) things Landsberger brought to two Los Angeles title runs, his greatest contribution was unintentional laughter. Simply put, Mark Landsberger—cursed and blessed with a staggering lack of self-awareness—made teammates crack up. Within the first few days of joining the Lakers, Landsberger met with Riley to review the playbook. Over the course of two hours, the then-assistant coach went through the team's assignments and packages. Landsberger had played collegiately at Minnesota and Arizona State, then for two and a half years in the NBA with the Bulls. He was a well-established veteran and Riley presumed most of this stuff was self-explanatory. Hence, he was shocked when Landsberger asked, with 100 percent seriousness, "Do you guys have any rebounding plays?"

"That's a true story," said Steve Springer, the veteran Laker beat writer. "But it's just the tip of the iceberg."

"I once asked Mark's wife how the off-season was," said Lon Rosen, a Laker employee. "She said it was great—'Mark's now using knives and forks when he eats.'"

Landsberger stories come in all shapes and sizes. There was the time, for example, when the Lakers promotional department sent Landsberger to a local supermarket to meet the fans. A boy approached with a team poster. "Can you sign your name and number?" he asked.

"Why do you want my number?" Landsberger asked.

"I'd just like to have it," he replied.

"OK," said Landsberger, sighing. He proceeded to scribble *M-A-R-K L-A-N-D-S-B-E-R-G-E-R* in script, then added *3-1-0-7-5-0-6-7-2-8.*

"Dumb," said Josh Rosenfeld, the team's media relations director. "Just really dumb."

"Mark spoke at my summer basketball camp," said Mike Thibault, an assistant coach. "He was there to give an hour-long clinic on rebounding. He took seven minutes and ran out of words."

The Lakers played an exhibition game against the Clippers in Palm Springs. Several hours before tip-off, Landsberger sat in the hotel lobby, inexplicably wearing his gold number 54 jersey while drinking a large chocolate milkshake he had purchased at McDonald's. Jack Curran, the team's trainer, suggested Landsberger either change his shirt or drape a napkin over his chest.

"I'm fine," Landsberger said. "Don't wor—" *SPLASH!* The shake spilled out of the cup and splattered across his torso. Landsberger jumped up and cursed as those around him broke out in laughter. "Fucking Landsberger," Curran said. "That's the only jersey we brought with us."

That night, Landsberger checked into the game with what appeared to be a Frisbee-size splotch of dog feces across his jersey. "It was hilarious," said Rosen. "But that sort of stuff doesn't help you stick around for long."

Had Landsberger been a hard worker, he might have contributed. However, his stupidity was coupled with a love of the nightlife and, occasionally, cocaine. Though players always dismissed any suggestion of drug use on the team, white powder was as much a part of the Lakers as it was any other big-city, easy-access 1980s sports franchise. According to one person who traveled with Los Angeles, flights often involved numerous trips to the bathroom for snorts of flake cocaine. "If anyone says the Lakers didn't have guys who did blow, it's laughable," he said. "There was never a shortage of cocaine." Cooper, who also used the drug, said his most vivid memory of Landsberger is "Mark walking around with a bag of coke in his hand."

Teammates loved telling Mark Landsberger stories and, specifically, "Mark Landsberger with Unattractive Black Women" stories. They nicknamed him Jig, short for Jigaboo, and guffawed many nights away sitting at a table inside a black club in Detroit or Oakland or Chicago and watching the world's goofiest white man maneuver his way with the 300-pound sisters. "Mark just loved black women, probably even more than we black guys loved black women," laughed Cooper. "He also loved the strip clubs. It'd always be, 'C'mon, Coop, let's go to the strip clubs! Let's go!'"

Was Mark Landsberger the biggest partier on the Lakers? Maybe, maybe not. He certainly didn't have the access to gorgeous women that came to Johnson and Nixon, certainly never used as much cocaine as Spencer Haywood. And yet, there was one thing about the man that separated him from not only every teammate but (in all probability) every other NBA player—his marriage.

To the bafflement of everyone on the roster, Mark and Marianne Landsberger told each other almost everything. Under their unique family guidelines, what happened on the road didn't have to remain a secret. "It was strange," said Cooper. "The Landsbergers weren't what you'd call a conventional couple."

This had all been well and fine until the early weeks of the 1982–83 season, when Landsberger—already out of favor with Riley for sloppy, dumb, uninspired play—committed the most unspeakable of professional NBA sins. At the time, the Lakers were on top of the basketball world. They were not only the defending champions but the *improved* defending champions.

After Ralph Sampson decided to return to the University of Virginia, Los Angeles won the coin toss for the number one pick in the NBA Draft and selected James Worthy, the All-American forward out of the University of North Carolina. Worthy was a 6-foot-9, 225-pound bundle of talent, one who—over time—would prove to be a significantly better NBA player than Sampson.

Furthermore, any remaining morsels of trepidation had vanished from Riley, who was now fully in charge and implementing a McKinney-esque run-and-gun offensive philosophy that thrilled his players, exhausted opposing teams and delighted the fan base. After losing the opener to Golden State, Los Angeles took seven straight wins, and 12 of 14. They were fun, exciting, unique, flashy. And *really* horny.

At least that's what Mark Landsberger told his wife, in the type of vivid detail Chick Hearn tried to bring to every Laker telecast. According to Mark, this guy was doing this, that guy was doing that, these two guys were doing this with her and her and her.

He hardly lacked material. When professional athletes come to Los Angeles, they're promised a bevy of easy sexual conquests. When professional athletes come to Los Angeles and win, they're *handed* them. Life for the world-champion Lakers was akin to some sort of aphrodisiac circus. Decked out in short skirts or tight leather pants, groupies lined the hotel lobbies by the dozens. "I'll always remember pulling into Houston one year in the middle of the night, and there were five drop-dead gorgeous women in the lobby of the hotel," said Rosenfeld. "And as the guys went to their rooms, you saw the women one by one go to the pay phones." Perfume-scented notes always awaited the players—one or two for someone like Landsberger or Mike McGee, thirty or forty for stars the magnitude of Johnson or Nixon.

Pick a hotel—any hotel—and regular faces and names and glares awaited. The Hyatt Regency in Atlanta. The Camelback Sahara in Phoenix. The Crown Center in Kansas City. The Holiday Inn-Coliseum in Cleveland. "It was as if they were in a rock band," said Linda Rambis, Kurt Rambis's wife and a sales and marketing associate with the team. "They'd go to a town, and the groupies were everywhere."

"It was crazy," said Ron Carter, the guard who later worked as Buss's assistant. "They were a team of whores, and Magic was the biggest whore. Not just on the team—the biggest whore I'd ever seen. He loved women— two, three at a time. One day we were on the road and I asked him, 'When the hell do you sleep? Do you ever sleep?' We'd show up at a hotel in a new city, and there'd be two or three women specifically waiting for him. He'd sleep with them, then kick them out. At shootaround later in the day, there'd be two or three more girls. He'd sleep with them. Then, after the game, there'd be two or three more girls. He'd sleep with them. Earvin didn't drink and Earvin didn't smoke and Earvin didn't touch drugs. His vice was women."

"I went out with Magic, and he must have had thirty to forty girls clinging to him," said Landsberger. "There's just so much temptation—you go to a club and a dozen girls are hitting on you. What are you supposed to do? Say no?"

Johnson, at least, was young, single and free to live life as he felt fit. So, for that matter, was Nixon, his near equal as a lothario (Nixon's nickname was Savoir Faire— defined by Merriam-Webster as the ability to say or do the right or graceful thing). If the pickings were particularly slim, four . . . five . . . six . . . seven . . . eight players would catch a taxi to the hottest strip club in town. Once there, lap dances (and more) were generally on the house. To have a Magic or Coop or Norm or Worthy in your establishment was worth its weight in advertising gold, and the Laker stars knew it.

The problem, however, was that Landsberger knew it, too. He was there. In the hotels. In the strip clubs. Buying shots, snorting lines, dancing with scantily clad women. The world was the Lakers' oyster, and Mark Landsberger had to share the excitement with the one person he loved most—his wife.

"I was walking through the press lounge at the Forum one night in 1982," said Carter. "I was working for Dr. Buss. There were about seven Laker spouses and girlfriends sitting at a table. I was trying to get through the room as fast as possible, and as soon as I saw them, and the way they were looking at me, I thought, 'Um, this is not good. This just is not good.'"

The first to speak up was Wanda Cooper, Michael's wife of four years. The unofficial leader of the Laker Wives, Wanda was a quick-witted woman who carried herself with the confidence of a saber-toothed tiger. Mark Landsberger had confided in Marianne that Michael Cooper was fooling around on the road. "Wanda found out via my wife," Landsberger said. "She tricked my wife. I told my wife to keep it confidential. So Wanda told my wife that I was cheating on her, and then Marianne told her what I'd said. It got pretty ugly."

On the Lakers, errant passes were forgiven and botched layups were forgotten. Johnson regularly made amends with Nixon, and Nixon regularly made amends with Johnson. The one thing none of the players were willing to overlook, however, was disloyalty. By letting his wife in on their secrets, Landsberger had violated the unspoken code of the professional athlete: What happens behind the scenes stays behind the scenes. "That's the angriest I've ever seen Kareem," said Butch Carter. "Mark was so fucking stupid. He got Kareem in trouble, Coop in trouble . . . just so fucking stupid."

On the evening of November 15, the Lakers arrived at the Camelback Sahara, the hotel they regularly stayed in when traveling to Phoenix. Riley arranged for the players, coaches, staff and traveling media members to meet in a private banquet hall at noon the following afternoon for an early Thanksgiving feast. "All the players were at one table," said Randy Harvey, who covered the Lakers for the *Los Angeles Times*. "The writers were at another table. And Mark Landsberger was at a table by himself—exiled. That was Mark's suspension for sharing stories. He was all alone."

Despite some initial anger, most of the wives were fully aware of their husband's extracurricular activities. At the time of the Landsberger exile, Harvey spoke with one off the record, asking whether she was concerned that her spouse was fooling around on the road. "Nah, it's OK with me," the woman told him. "It's just one less night I have to suck his dick."

No one within the organization tried especially hard to keep the wild behavior covert. Everything started at the top, where Buss—fifty years old, but with the libido of a rabbit—paraded around town with women barely of age to drive. "Jerry loved the excitement of it," said Rothman. "And the little nymphettes thought he could get them movie careers." It was, to the uninformed, a disconcerting sight. Though Buss was certainly a handsome enough man, he looked downright grandfatherly alongside many of his women. Buss seemed to date a different person every week, and—before moving on to the next bubbly beauty—would snap a photograph and place the image in one of his dozens of scrapbooks. Every so often, upon request, he would break out an album and talk about the experiences. Many names he remembered. Many, he forgot. "Jerry once told me something I've often thought of," said Lance Davis, Buss's longtime friend. "He said, 'Lance, people try and give me shit over the women I go out with. Why would I want to go out with an older woman when I can go out with one with a fresher, hotter body? Why wouldn't I go out with a twenty-six-year-old Playmate with a hot body?' Jerry said it kept him young and alive—and it clearly did. He was the king, and the Forum was his palace."

When Jack Kent Cooke initially built the arena, he insisted there be a place where he could play host to the inevitable line of dignitaries and financial bigwigs who would come calling. The resulting space, the Forum Club, was—under Cooke—a nice yet uninspired room with a kitchen, a bar, a dining facility and a meeting area. Cooke could be found there during games, but few people actually went looking for him. One celebrity, a comedian from *Rowan & Martin's Laugh-In* named Arte Johnson, attended somewhat frequently. "We had to wear a suit and a tie in there at all times," said Harold Zoubul, the Forum's general manager for food and beverage. "There was a piano player, and the room was fairly quiet. It was nice, but not all that fun. Mr. Cooke never invited more than eight, ten people. I think he felt as if he was above inviting people. He really was quite the asshole."

When Buss assumed control of the organization, he took one look at the Forum Club and saw endless possibilities. The same man who fired the organist and replaced him with USC's marching band; who initiated the Laker Girls and approved their skimpy outfits; who stuffed the building with as many celebrities as possible—well, he wanted a spot where the action happened.

Rothman was put in charge of taking a space with all the pizzazz of a library and creating something that, a decade later, Detroit Pistons forward John Salley would call "the sexiest place in the league." She began by special-ordering an enormous red canopy that announced THE FORUM CLUB in large letters. On a recent trip to Las Vegas, Rothman had visited a shopping mall where the concrete floor was treated with an acidic glaze that brought out a rainbow hue. "So we did that outside the Forum Club, too," she said. "We put down new carpet, made a finish out of walnut shells . . . just spared few expenses to make it amazing."

Before long, the Forum Club wasn't merely a bar inside an arena. It was one of the hottest spots in Los Angeles. In the hours leading up to almost every game, as 250 or so people ate fancy sit-down meals, Buss hosted a dinner for friends and celebrities at his personal table. Employees anxiously wondered who would show up on any given night—Rob Lowe? Charlie Sheen? Tony Danza? John Candy? Dyan Cannon? Jack Nicholson? Ali Mc-Graw? Luther Vandross? John Travolta? With a cigarette perpetually stashed between his fingers and a Playmate of the Year candidate by his side, Buss reveled in the beauty of his success. This was *his* room inside *his* building, and everyone was there to watch *his* team. When the game began, Buss sat far off the court, in a section near the top of the building. He didn't need to be near the players to feel the action. He had the Forum Club. "Dad was so happy," said Jeanie Buss. "He knew how fortunate he was."

If the Forum Club seemed lively before games, it was wild and exotic and enrapturing afterward. Being a Laker in the 1980s came with multiple perks—none greater than regular access to a world thought to be written about only in *Penthouse* essays. As soon as the fourth quarter wrapped up and the average fans headed toward the parking lot, the Forum Club exploded into bright color and neon light. "We'd rush to the locker room, change and rush into the Forum Club," said Clay Johnson, a backup guard. "We reserves had to get up there before Magic and Norm arrived. Because once they were there, we had no chance. We wanted first dibs on the women." Select high-end season ticket holders could purchase Forum Club passes for the relatively inexpensive price of three hundred dollars. Once inside, they mingled with athletes, actors, dancers and singers.

"In a way, visiting teams probably enjoyed the Forum Club more than our guys did," said Linda Rambis. "It was an escape for them. A vacation from Milwaukee or Detroit or wherever they played. It'd be, 'OK, you kicked our asses—now where's the Forum Club?'"

Behind the bar, Donna Grinnel mixed screwdrivers and bloody Marys and martinis while people reached into their wallets to pull out hundred-dollar tips. "Jerry West taught me how to drink at the Forum Club," said Ron Carter, the guard. "I was standing at the bar and he said, 'Hey, kid, you don't just come into a place like this and lean against the bar doing shots. Order a few shots now, then order straight orange juice. Everyone watching all night will be impressed that you're drinking straight orange juice—when truth is you've already had three shots of tequila.'"

Toshio Funaki, the executive chef, served twenty-two-dollar seafood medley salads and sixty-dollar steaks. "I went there every night I could," said Pat O'Brien, the CBS sports personality. "The Forum Club was Studio 54, but maybe better. Think of everything you'd want in a scene, it had it."

O'Brien speaks the truth:

- **Scantily clad women:** "Oh my God," said Larry Spriggs, a Laker forward from 1983 through 1986. "It was as if you were a shark and you had a room filled with tuna. You had your pick of the litter at the Forum Club."

  Buss boasted a quirky entourage of friends the local media referred to as the Seven Dwarves. They followed him everywhere, and included John Rockwell, a character actor, and the Wilder brothers, Dave and Ron. The most charismatic of the group was Miguel Núñez, a nineteen-year-old Hollywood wannabe who had appeared in a handful of low-budget horror movies. During games, one of Núñez's jobs was to scour the stands, look for the most breathtaking females and hand them post-game passes to the club. Women would attend the games hoping to get noticed and, ultimately, selected. "Then they'd all show up and fill the room," said Cooper. "Gorgeous women all over. Usually in life, guys go to clubs to meet the girls. At the Forum Club, girls came to meet guys."

  Members of the Laker Girls were paid thirty dollars per game. The perks were a free meal, a morsel of fame, forty-one exciting nights during the regular season . . . and Forum Club access. When the games ended, many of the women (all young, all gorgeous) changed from their purple-and-gold outfits into equally revealing ensembles. "If you were a part of it, you could go there," said Aurorah Allain, a longtime Laker Girl. "Well, we were a part of it."

  "The Forum Club? Unbelievable, unbelievable, unbelievable," said Wes Matthews, who visited as a journeyman guard, then joined the Lakers in the late 1980s. "Magic had his own section in the back where he had twenty-five to thirty women waiting for him. Why wouldn't you go there? It was the pickup spot. You go in there, you're gonna come up, as they say in the hood. You're coming up with something. A lot of the players will tell you they couldn't even concentrate, they wanted the game to end ASAP so they could go upstairs. Everyone and their mama was trying to get in, trying to get with the Laker Girls. They could have opened that place alone, just as a club."

"If you couldn't get laid at the Forum Club," said Jeanie Buss, "you couldn't get laid."

• **Drugs:** According to one Forum Club regular, many of the waiters doubled as either cocaine dealers or the middlemen for cocaine dealers. "Pretty much everybody had their coke hookup there," he said. "It was a great place to get drugs, because nobody really cared. It wasn't like security was going to bust you."

Technically speaking, drugs weren't allowed in the Forum Club. Also, technically speaking, the sinks inside the Forum Club bathrooms didn't serve as coke stations. "You remember that scene from *Scarface* with the big pile of cocaine?" said Zoubul. "Well, I had something like that inside the Forum Club. Someone put a big pile of coke on the table, and I took my hand and slapped it all onto the floor. There was this one guy, a known dealer, and he really wanted to have access. He tried bribing me to get in. I told him, 'I know what you do. . . . I know what you want.' But, really, it didn't matter. These were the 1980s. I couldn't stop cocaine from the Forum Club. It was impossible."

• **Restricted Access:** For Laker players, the best thing about the Forum Club wasn't who could get in—but who couldn't. Namely, wives were rarely permitted. On nights when the family attended the game, Laker players would skip the Forum Club and head home. On nights when the wife and kids were out of town, the Forum Club was ideal. "I actually didn't know we weren't supposed to be in there," said Wanda Cooper. "I rarely went, and maybe that's why. There were a lot of hoochie mamas in there. But there was something to walking in the midst of the hoochie mamas and knowing who you are. 'I'm Mrs. Michael Cooper—you're a wannabe. I have his children, his ring, his word. This is *my* man.' So when I walked into an environment like that, I wasn't coming for combat or even to see. I was coming to grab a glass of wine—and you better back off my man.'"

Said Michael Cooper: "The Forum Club was the best fucking place in the world, but, man, Wanda hated it. Hated it. My wife wanted it shut down. It was worse than Las Vegas. It was sin city. If I told my wife I was going to the Forum Club, it was 'Why? Why are you going up there? What for? You want a beer? We'll stop on the way home for one.' Wanda was understanding of the NBA lifestyle, but if I ever went up there, I had to go up with her."

Kareem Abdul-Jabbar, the stoic center, rarely ran wild with his teammates. He was a father of four and had a steady live-in girlfriend named Cheryl Pistono. Yet the Forum Club was somehow protected by a magical invisible force field, where nothing got in and nothing got out. "He had a set of twins he was often with at the Club," said Zoubul.

"Kareem was with one of the Laker Girls for years," said Suzy Hardy, a Laker Girl for four seasons. "It wasn't cool to go with players, because we all knew those guys weren't going to be exclusive. But, hey, it happened. Especially at the Forum Club."

A favorite Forum Club story of the era comes at the expense of Nixon, who used to date Diane Day, the former Las Vegas showgirl and a member of Motion, a dance troupe on the popular television show *Dance Fever*. One night, Carter and Nixon entered the Forum Club after a particularly hard-fought game. They approached the bar to order drinks and heard, from a corner, the harmonic voice of Jeffrey Osborne, the soul singer who had performed that night's National Anthem. Osborne was sitting backward on a chair, his chest peeking out from a halfway-unbuttoned shirt, and he was crooning his hit, "Love Ballad," to a swooning Day.

"Norman's face went blank," said Carter, laughing. "Me

and Cooper just cracked up until we cried, it was too funny. But that was the Forum Club. You never knew what was gonna happen. It was the place where anything was possible."

If basketball die-hards thought the 1981–82 champion Lakers personified basketball perfection, the following season left them breathless. First, the Lakers now had a full season of McAdoo, who often spelled Rambis midway through the first quarter. Second, though Rambis averaged only 7.5 points per game, he was playing with a barbaric physicality many of the soft western teams lacked. Newspaper columnists referred to Rambis as the Lakers' weak link— two words that turned a normally mild-mannered ballplayer into a bull. "Kurt would kill you if it meant getting the ball," said Mitch Kupchak. "Without reservations."

The biggest change, though, was the addition of Worthy.

When he was selected first overall by Los Angeles, rival executives moaned about the unfairness of the league's best team adding one of college basketball's best players. Yet, for all the hype and accomplishments, he arrived for training camp and underwhelmed. Worthy hailed from Gastonia, North Carolina, a town of just under 50,000 residents, and felt out of place in Hollywood. Kupchak once described Worthy as someone who "looks like he'd make a good undertaker"—meaning his emotions stayed within and his expression rarely changed. At the University of North Carolina, Worthy— blessed with unusually lengthy arms and a rapid-fire first step—dominated the ACC as a power forward. The consensus thinking was that he would come to the Lakers, humiliate the un-athletic Rambis and the aged McAdoo, and become an immediate starter. "I thought that, too," Worthy said. "I knew I was quicker than Kurt, so I thought I'd kick his butt and steal his position. Then Kurt embarrassed me. He was fundamentally sound and much more skilled than anyone—myself included—gave him credit for. He knew all the angles, all the tricks. It was no contest."

Riley couldn't hide his disappointment. Before the opening game of the season, he took the rookie aside and asked him to focus on core fundamentals. Worthy was a so-so rebounder and a poor defender. His outside shooting was inconsistent. He worked hard, but most of the Lakers worked even harder. "You could see the natural talent in James," said Rambis. "He needed to learn to play in the NBA. It's a different universe." Over the season's first few weeks, Worthy was used selectively. Not wanting to take away minutes from Jamaal Wilkes, Riley initially tried him at power forward, and the results were merely so-so. Then, gradually, Riley began inserting him for Wilkes. A few minutes here, a few minutes there. No fuss, no mess. While the draft's number two selection, forward Terry Cummings from DePaul, was being asked to carry the Clippers, Worthy simply blended in. "Worthy is lucky," said Dick Motta, Dallas's coach. "Being picked number one, you usually live in a glass house where everything you do is magnified. You have very little leeway to grow up properly."

Over time, Worthy discovered confidence, and Riley discovered faith. The coach began offering more minutes (he averaged twenty-seven per game through January), and the results were eye-opening. On December 29, in a game against Golden State, Worthy shot perfectly—6-for-6 from the field, 5-for-5 from the line—and exploded past forward Larry Smith with a twisting, spinning, twirling move that an impressed Johnson nicknamed the Dipsy-Do-360-Clutch-Skin-and-In spectacular. For all his shortcomings, Worthy possessed a burst that even Nixon—perhaps the league's fastest player—couldn't keep up with. "His speed was remarkable," said Cooper. "Guys that big aren't supposed to move like that."

By January 30, the Lakers appeared to be running away with the Pacific Division. At 34-10, they boasted the conference's best record. They had just demolished the Atlanta Hawks, 109–85, to win their seventh straight game, and arrived in Boston for a matchup with the Celtics feeling unbeatable. In a meeting with his players, Riley implored them to not merely outlast Boston but drub them. "Make this a statement game," he said. "You want them to remember taking a beating."

In the lowest moment of the season, the Celtics dismantled the Lakers, 110–95. Larry Bird scored 21 and Cedric Maxwell 16, but the star was center Robert Parish, who walked past, around and over Abdul-Jabbar for 24 points and 18 rebounds. With increased frequency, centers were playing Abdul-Jabbar not as an object to handle with care but one to clobber. Moses Malone had written the manual, and Parish—not as skilled as Malone, but plenty strong—followed carefully. Abdul-Jabbar shot 8 of 15 from the field in the first half, but was held to 7 points in the second. "They weren't doing anything different," Wilkes said. "They were just doing it more aggressively."

If the game itself were a disaster (and it *was*, unambiguously, a disaster), the aftermath was a thousand times worse. That night, Abdul-Jabbar's palatial $1.7 million Bel Air mansion was destroyed in an extensive electrical blaze. His girlfriend, Cheryl, and their son, Amir, woke up surrounded by flames, but were able to escape. "The AP called me, and I got there at four in the morning," said Josh Rosenfeld, the team's media relations director. "It was an awful scene. Just heartbreaking." The center could deal with the loss of the structure itself. What crushed him, however, was the incineration of his three prized collections—oriental rugs, irreplaceable Middle Ages Qur'ans and more than three thousand jazz albums. "My record collection," he said, "was probably the single most important thing that was destroyed.

"The beautiful pieces of glass and art that I had bought and gathered over the years were gone, as were my basketball trophies, my childhood pictures, all my clothes."

Abdul-Jabbar left to return to Los Angeles, and the Lakers began their worst stretch of the year. They were shamed in a 21-point loss to the Spurs at home, then three days later fell to the meek Kansas City Kings. The Celtics traveled to Los Angeles for a February 23 rematch, and won again, this time 113–104. "The Lakers aren't in a slump," Mike Littwin wrote in the *Los Angeles Times*. "The economy is in a slump. The Lakers are in a depression."

Watching from nearby was Jerry West, the team's recently promoted general manager. As a coach, the former Laker star struggled with the ups and downs of an NBA season. He was volatile and high-strung and an awful fit for the job. Now, as the GM, his angst level—heightened by a lack of control—was even worse. During games, West often either sat in his office or drove around the Forum, listening to Chick Hearn on the radio. He didn't have the stomach to watch in person. "The Lakers were my life, and I took it, probably, too seriously," said West. "I loved it, loved the game and the job, but I didn't get the joy out of it that I should. It's a classic example of putting too much pressure on yourself."

West closely examined the Lakers' struggles, and he developed a handful of conclusions. First, with Kupchak out for the year and Landsberger a mediocre sloth, the team required a backup center (after talk of adding Houston's Caldwell Jones or Cleveland's James Edwards, the Lakers underwhelmed by sending a future second-round draft pick to Chicago for Dwight Jones, a ten-year veteran with faded skills). Second, Mike McGee, the seldom-used shooting guard, was a waste of space and needed to be moved elsewhere (West found no takers).

Third, Norm Nixon was a problem.

This, of course, was nothing new to West, who had coached Nixon through the guard's first two seasons. To the general manager, Nixon had always been the sort of player a team could do without: gifted, yes, but high maintenance and egotistical beyond compare. When he was playing well and helping the franchise win, the negatives could be tolerated. Now, however, Nixon was in the midst of his worst season. He was averaging 15.1 points per game while shooting a career-low 47.5 percent. His assists and steals were both down, as was—it seemed—his confidence. Nixon fought knee problems throughout the year, and insisted pain was the cause of his trouble.

West, however, had other ideas. Over the course of Nixon's time in Los Angeles, rumors circulated that he was a hard-core user of cocaine. The notion wasn't without reason. Nixon was one of the NBA's great partiers, a man whose late-night exploits and sexual conquests were Grade A locker room fodder. West was well aware of the reputation, as well as of Nixon's profound love for the Forum Club. "Once the perception of being a drug user is out there, it's very hard to erase," said Nixon. "There were articles that talked about me buying Quaaludes and cocaine—totally untrue. Look, I love L.A., and I was friends with some of the actors and celebrities. I owned a clothing store at one time, so I dressed in nice clothes, but always bought it at cost. All these things led to the perception of what I was. But was it real? I'd argue no."

West could tolerate much. A serial philanderer during his playing days, he knew Lakers drank, Lakers smoked, Lakers had sex with groupies. Such was life in the NBA. Cocaine, however, wasn't merely a drug. It was an energy sapper; a focus snuffer; a career killer. Therefore, the general manager of basketball's marquee franchise took a step that would forever contaminate the already toxic relationship he had with his veteran point guard.

Combining pragmatism and paranoia, West hired a private investigation agency to follow Nixon and file a detailed report on his behavior. It was straight out of *Mannix*—weird, creepy, unprecedented in the history of the franchise. Throughout the second half of the season, Nixon unknowingly had people trailing his car, watching his house, keeping tabs on his every move. "I had no idea," he said. "When I found out, it really shook me."

One day, while at his house in Beverly Hills, Nixon was approached by a neighborhood kid. "Hey, Norm," he said, "somebody is going to get robbed."

"What do you mean?" Nixon asked.

"There've been cars parked at both ends of our street with telescopes," the child replied. "Guys looking into houses. People are setting somebody up."

Several days later, Nixon pulled into his driveway at the end of a late night out. He was walking toward the steps when someone emerged from the bushes. "Hey, man," the stranger said, "I need to talk to you."

"Whoa," replied Nixon, who assumed he was being robbed. "What the hell is going on?"

According to Nixon, the man spent the next twenty minutes explaining how the Lakers hired him to work as an investigator. "I've been following you for the last two weeks," he said. Nixon didn't believe it. *Followed? By his employer?* No way. Then, however, the details of the past two weeks of Nixon's life were laid out. He had gone to the bank, then the supermarket, then the drugstore, then a restaurant, then . . .

"If you still don't believe me," the man said, "I'll tell you where we are parking. We are at either end of the block. I've got a job to do, but I like you and I felt an obligation to tell you. Now I've got to get back to work."

The following morning, Nixon backed his Mercedes-Benz into the street, checked his rearview mirror and spotted one of the black cars following him.

Enough was enough. He had given his all for the Lakers. He played hard, played tough, won two NBA championships. When Johnson came along, he swallowed his pride and moved to shooting guard. This was his reward?

On the next afternoon, Nixon confronted West in his office. "You have people following me?" he said. "Are you kidding me?"

West was unrepentant. "You've been hanging out with some drug dealers," he replied. "And we know that you do a lot of drugs."

"Jerry, I'm not going to admit that to you," Nixon replied. "I don't care where you say you saw me, or what you say you saw me doing. I'm not going to simply tell you for your satisfaction that I do drugs."

"That's the first thing drug users do is deny, deny, deny," West said. "That's the first thing they do."

Nixon was incredulous. He told friends and teammates about the stand-off, and watched their faces drop. Many assumed the spying wasn't related to drugs but to rumors that Nixon was having an affair with the married daughter of an NBA owner. Whatever the case, were West willing to follow Nixon, who was to say he wouldn't follow them, too? Why, Cooper (also rumored to have issues with drugs) later learned private investigators had been employed by the team to trail him as well. Ron Carter, the Laker guard and Nixon's friend since childhood, was particularly incensed. "I was with Norm regularly, and I can tell you, drugs weren't happening," he said. "Was there cocaine around? Absolutely. It was L.A. in the 1970s and '80s. It was everywhere. Everywhere. But you can't play at a high level and do coke. It ruined Spencer Haywood. But Norm taught me how to be around that stuff and not become a part of it." Carter recalled a particular incident involving Nixon and Phyllis Hyman, a well-known R&B singer. "We were out at a club," Carter said, "and Hyman pulled out a vial of cocaine and snorted coke on the table right in front of us. The moment she did that, Norm tapped me on the leg under the table, said, 'Get up,' and we walked away. He told me, 'Ron, we can't be seen in public with someone who does stuff like that.' I'll never forget that. I'd never even seen cocaine before."

Drug user or not, Norm Nixon's time with the Lakers seemed to be coming to an end.

■ ■ ■

The Lakers recovered.

Under Pat Riley, the Lakers would almost always recover. This was one of his greatest strengths as a coach. Resiliency. Riley rarely panicked, and if he did panic, he was excellent at hiding the accompanying emotions. Even with Landsberger spewing secrets. Even with Nixon being followed. Even when, on April 10, an awful turn of events damaged the team's title hopes.

With ten seconds remaining in the third quarter of a game against Phoenix, Worthy jumped up to tip in a missed shot, landed awkwardly on his left leg and collided with Maurice Lucas, a Suns forward. Worthy fell to the floor, holding his left knee. He was carried off the court and rushed to Centinela Hospital for X-rays. The prognosis was crushing—Worthy suffered a fracture of the lateral tibial plateau of his left knee, and would miss the remainder of the year.

Of late, Worthy had emerged as one of the most important Lakers. McAdoo had been out nursing a dislocated toe, and in his place the rookie was shooting 57 percent from the field while scoring in double figures in 17 of his last 19 games.

"I'm just numb," Riley said.

Publicly, West and Riley said all the right things. *The Lakers would be fine. McAdoo was coming back ASAP. Obstacles had been overcome before. The measure of a man's heart comes in times of strife.*

In reality, a title favorite morphed, overnight, into something of a long shot. The Lakers moved quickly to fill Worthy's spot, signing a journeyman by the name of Billy Ray Bates. A former star at Kentucky State, Bates had battled substance abuse issues throughout his career and was about to join a club in the Philippines, when the phone rang. Jack Ramsay, the longtime Blazers coach, once described Bates as "like Mount St. Helens—it's bubbling and agitating under the skin, waiting to erupt"—and he was right. Bates arrived, practiced, sat on the bench and confused the other Lakers with his oddball banter and gestures. "Guys didn't like playing with Billy," said Lon Rosen, a team employee, "because he had a really moist Jheri curl, and the ball would get all slippery." When he stepped into the court, he was dreadful. Bates shot 2 for 16 from the field. Four of the attempts were air balls. "Billy did crazy stuff every single day," said Joe Cooper, a Laker backup center for a brief spell. "Crazy, crazy stuff."

Rarely had a defending champion entered the playoffs on less of a roll. The team released Bates (who later was sentenced to seven years in jail after attempting to rob a gas station), activated McAdoo and signed Steve Mix, a veteran forward of little regard but, unlike Bates, of full sanity. He initially hedged ("I was in my thirteenth season, and sort of done," he said) then was promised a doubled playoff check—the organization would take his postseason earnings and multiply them by two. "I didn't have to be asked twice," he said.

Despite finishing with the Western Conference's best record, the Lakers limped into the playoffs. The club lost five of its final ten games, including twice to the Trail Blazers, its first-round opponent. Randy Harvey, the *Los Angeles Times* basketball writer, had spent his year chronicling the highs and lows of a difficult season. In the April 19 newspaper, he angered readers by picking the San Antonio Spurs to reach the NBA Finals. "San Antonio," he wrote, "is too physical for the Lakers."

Words are often disposable. Harvey's were not. Riley clipped the article out of the *Times* and hung it in the team's locker room. He realized, technically, Harvey had a point; the Spurs had acquired center Artis Gilmore from Chicago before the season, and he was the type of physical force Abdul-Jabbar struggled with.

That said, Los Angeles still featured two of the game's top five players

(Johnson and Abdul-Jabbar) as well as, in Nixon, Wilkes and McAdoo, three men who could carry a team. Were they particularly deep? No? Explosive? Not like past years. But the Lakers were still the Lakers.

On April 23, a day before they were to open at home against Portland, Riley read his team a three-page motivational rallying cry he had written the night before. It was titled "Winning Time II."

"Don't ever forget what it looked like and felt like on June 8," he began. "Remember . . ."

Of all the Lakers, Abdul-Jabbar took the words most to heart. He was thirty-six and playing the worst basketball of his adulthood. Abdul-Jabbar's scoring (21.7), rebounding (7.5) and block (2.2) averages were career lows. "But Kareem had pride," said Cooper. "More pride than anyone I've ever played with."

He also seemed to possess newfound warmth in his heart. For years, Abdul-Jabbar looked at fans wearily. He trusted few, and with good reason. "Life as a museum piece isn't fun," Mark Eaton, the Utah Jazz's 7-foot-4 center, once said. In the aftermath of Abdul-Jabbar's house fire, however, people across America responded. At first, the packages trickled in to the Laker offices—one jazz record here, another two or three there. Before long, Abdul-Jabbar was besieged with dozens upon dozens of albums. The team checked into hotels on the road and front-desk attendants greeted him with "Mr. Jabbar, there's a package here for you. . . ."

"I remember somewhere in the Midwest . . . it might have been Dallas," said Rosenfeld, the media relations director. "And there was a rural Southern couple—white, with a kid. And as Kareem was walking out to the bus, the kid hands him three old, old jazz albums. And Kareem stops and looks at each one and I could tell . . . he didn't just blow by them. He thanked them. You could see those things touched him."

Against the overmatched Blazers, Abdul-Jabbar looked twenty-three again. OK—not physically. His miniature Afro was long gone, replaced by a closely cropped receding hairline and small wrinkles stretching from the corners of his eyes. He did, though, *play* as if twenty-three again. Guarded by Wayne Cooper, Portland's wobbly center, he enjoyed one of the great playoff series of his life, scorching the Blazers for 30.8 points in a dizzying five-game romp. Portland tried every conceivable trick. During Game 3, a microphone caught Jim Lynam, a Blazer assistant, imploring forward Kenny Carr to take his arm and "whack him good one time."

"Knock him into the basket support," added Jim Paxson, a guard. "Who gives a shit?"

Los Angeles advanced to the Western Conference Finals where, predictably, the Spurs awaited. Ever since taking over as San Antonio's head coach in 1980, Stan Albeck had worked to construct a team capable of toppling Riley's bunch. The former Laker assistant called it "The Blueprint"—a player-by-player, step-by-step design to knocking off the NBA's elite franchise. That's why, before the season, the team had sent Dave Corzine, Mark Olberding and a bag of cash to Chicago for Gilmore, a 7-foot-2, 240-pound All-Star. "The way to beat them—if there is a way—is to be physical," Albeck said. "And we have the physical team that can cause them problems." In five head-to-head matchups during the regular season, Gilmore averaged 21.6 points and 12.2 rebounds against Abdul-Jabbar.

The series opened before a crowd of 15,063 at the Forum on May 8, and Albeck's big plans fell flat. Abdul-Jabbar outscored Gilmore 30 to 7, fading away from the basket with a bevy of skyhooks and short-range jumpers. Gilmore, meanwhile, went from trying to punish the Laker to trying to avoid him. By early in the third quarter, he had already picked up a fourth foul. Los Angeles won with ease, 119–107. "We're going to have to reevaluate our plans," Gilmore said afterward. "I've got to neutralize Kareem a little bit more, try to do some things to slow him down."

Though San Antonio managed to win two games, Albeck's dreams were again crushed. He noted early in the series that Abdul-Jabbar would have to work to guard Gilmore, and that the exhaustion would impact his all-around game. That's not what happened. The talk of Gilmore's inevitable domination didn't merely irk Abdul-Jabbar—it motivated him. Furthermore, there were the Baseline Bums, a group of tasteless Spurs fans who waved warped record albums as Abdul-Jabbar shot free throws. "Kareem," Riley said, "has brought a different mentality to the playoffs." Abdul-Jabbar roasted the Spurs for 25 points in a 113–110 Game 3 win, then added another 26 as Los Angeles took Game 4, 129–121. By the time the series ended with a thrilling 101–100 triumph at San Antonio in Game 6, Gilmore was reduced to a pile of rubble. Abdul-Jabbar scored a game-high 28, and the Lakers advanced to yet another NBA championship series. Over the six games, he averaged 26.5 points—almost 7 more than Gilmore.

Once again, the Philadelphia 76ers were waiting.

■ ■ ■

Much like the Spurs, the Sixers—two-time finals losers to the Lakers—had a plan.

An exceptional, remarkable plan.

San Antonio added Gilmore, thinking—if things went well—he could potentially neutralize Abdul-Jabbar.

The 76ers, however, one-upped everyone. On September 2, 1982, the team announced the free-agent acquisition of center Moses Malone, the reigning league MVP who was coming off a season in which he averaged 31.1 points and a league-best 14.7 rebounds for the Rockets. During his six seasons in Houston, Malone led the league in rebounding three times and improved his scoring every year. Malone wasn't merely good or great. He was dominant—the type of player who could single-handedly control a game. He signed a record six-year, $13.2 million contract, and was probably underpaid.

As an added perk, Malone particularly disliked the Lakers.

That feeling dated back to January 31, 1982, when he was a member of the Western Conference's All-Star team. Through three quarters at New Jersey's Brendan Byrne Arena, Malone had been spectacular, compiling 12 points and a team-high 11 rebounds in just twenty minutes. Then, without explanation, Riley benched him and let Abdul-Jabbar play down the stretch. The East won, 120–118, and Malone stewed. "That," said Robert Reid, a Houston teammate, "made the big fella mad."

An angry Malone was a frightening Malone. As a thirteen-year-old boy growing up in Petersburg, Virginia, he once accompanied his parents on a family vacation to New York City. "There was this playground tournament up about 165th Street and Amsterdam Avenue," Malone recalled. "There were these three fancy city dudes, and they were using their flashy behind-the-back and between-leg stuff to beat everybody. My cousin looked at them and said, 'Hey, I know a guy who can beat you all.' They said, 'Who?' and he pointed at me." The city kids guffawed—Malone was 6-foot-6, but gawky and frail. The laughter set him off. "I found two guys who couldn't even play," Malone said. "We played to 32, and my team won, 32–20. I got 30."

In 1974, Malone seamlessly jumped straight from high school to the pros. He combined Hulk-like power with an unmatched work ethic. With Darryl Dawkins and Caldwell Jones at center, Philadelphia had been an excellent team with some interior weaknesses. With Malone, everything changed. The 1982–83 Sixers established themselves as one of basketball's all-time dominant franchises. Their 65-17 record paced the league, and Malone was again named NBA MVP, averaging 24.5 points and 15.3 rebounds. When asked to describe his game, he said—simply if not eloquently—"I goes to the rack." With Malone situated down low, the Sixers' perimeter stars—Julius Erving, Andrew Toney, Maurice Cheeks and Bobby Jones—were free to slash and cut and bomb away. "He took them to a level no one had ever seen before," said Otis Birdsong, a Nets guard. "All bets are off if someone like Moses comes to town." When asked how he thought the 76ers would fare in the playoffs, Malone—deep voice, pronounced Southern twang—bellowed, "fo', fo', fo'." Translation: All three series would be four-game rolls.

They opened with an easy sweep of the New York Knicks, then won the first three games of the Eastern Conference Finals against the Bucks before dropping Game 4 in Milwaukee. Philadelphia recovered to take Game 5 and earn a rematch against the Lakers. "If I owned a farm, I'd bet on Philly," Milwaukee coach Don Nelson said afterward. "This is the best team I've seen in ten years. They are the next world championship team."

Though loathe to admit it, Riley knew Los Angeles faced an uphill battle. Philadelphia was the stronger, deeper club. For as well as Abdul-Jabbar played against Gilmore, Riley understood there was no possible way he could handle Malone one-on-one. The plan, therefore, was a desperate one: Throw Rambis at Malone. Throw Landsberger at Malone. Throw McAdoo at Malone. Throw Abdul-Jabbar at Malone. Throw two guys . . . three guys . . . anyone who might have a prayer at Malone, and hope for the best.

It didn't work.

In what *Sports Illustrated* called "an astounding display of muscle and will—qualities the 76ers had always seemed to lack," the Lakers were swept from a series that was never close to being close. Malone averaged 25.8 points and 18 rebounds, and was named MVP. In his wake were the battered remains of Los Angeles's interior players—"None of us could handle him," said Rambis. "And suggesting we could was a joke."

It hardly helped that Nixon suffered a separated left shoulder in the opening minutes of the first game—the result of a violent collision with Toney. (As he walked off the floor, Nixon was asked by Riley whether he needed a rest. "No," he replied, "a casket.") The Lakers tried concealing the severity of the injury, fearful the Sixers would take advantage. Then, between games three and four, Buss absentmindedly blurted to a reporter, "What do you expect of us? Nixon's had a separated shoulder the whole time."

It mattered not. The better team won handily. "We toyed with people, just toyed with them," Billy Cunningham, the 76ers coach, said after the 115–108 Game 4 victory at the Forum. "It was really something."

In the aftermath of the series, Buss, West and Riley met multiple times to plan the next stage. There was a fine line in the NBA, one that divided perennial contenders from flukes and wannabes. Unless Los Angeles made some changes, there was no reason to believe the team wouldn't drift off into mediocrity. Such was the power of aging and the status quo.

"The good teams adjust with the times," said Cooper. "The bad teams hope a good year carries over, without doing anything to improve.

"We were the Los Angeles Lakers. We always adjusted."

CHAPTER 11

THE DEPARTED

One of the worst spans of Norm Nixon's life began with a newspaper headline. It appeared in the June 16, 1983, *Los Angeles Times*—seven simple words no professional athlete ever wants to see.

LAKERS' NIXON PLANS APPEAL IN PATERNITY SUIT

Despite a blood test that showed a 98.95 percent chance that Nixon had fathered a child with an Oakland woman named Elizabeth M. Fuller, and despite detailed testimony about the two meeting in Los Angeles when he was a basketball star and she a flight attendant, Nixon remained steadfast. "This is something that has almost become inevitable for the single, professional athlete," he told United Press International. "You can expect two things—a paternity suit and to be traded."

For those reading the article in the Lakers' executive offices, it was almost as if the words jumped off the page and lingered in midair. . . .

. . . *to be traded.*

. . . *to be traded.*

. . . *to be traded.*

Nixon had never been traded. Not once. Oh, Jerry West often fantasized of a world without his whining and moaning and insistence that he was the greatest player in the history of basketball. But, when push came to shove, Nixon gave the Lakers the best chance to win. If Magic Johnson was the NBA's top guard, Nixon was not especially far behind.

In the aftermath of the Philadelphia bloodbath, however, a seismic philosophical shift had overtaken the Forum. For the first time since Paul Westhead's dismissal, panic trumped certainty. Had the Lakers dropped a close seven-game series, perhaps the team could remain largely unchanged. The finals, though, were embarrassing, and served to reveal Riley's club as flawed and a bit old. "We needed to reassess," West said. "That's what it came down to."

The Lakers weren't going to rid themselves of Abdul-Jabbar (he was a free agent, but re-signed for $3 million over two years), Johnson or Worthy. At age thirty, Jamaal Wilkes's game was slipping, as was his market value. Kurt Rambis interested no one. "It made sense to look into dealing Norman," said West. "He was a terrific player. I've never said he wasn't. But we were lacking balance, and we needed someone in the backcourt who didn't need the ball all the time, someone who was a better defender and a better shooter."

Put differently: Nixon was a pain in the rear, approaching his twenty-eighth birthday, struggling with tendinitis in his knees and not quite as explosive as he had once been. Plus, Johnson was tired of him.

The Lakers reported to Palm Desert for training camp on the final day of September, and when the talk wasn't of Worthy's rehabilitated limb ("Worthy has enough hardware in his left leg to make a salvage operation thinkable," wrote the Los Angeles Times's Richard Hoffer), it concerned Nixon's future. The guard wasted little time irking West and Co. by arriving a day late—sans excuse or explanation. He pulled up on a Friday night, casually exiting his white Mercedes-Benz. "What's going on?" he asked reporters in the hotel lobby, strolling past.

The following morning, Nixon sat down with the team's beat writers and listened to the rumored trades. He was going to Golden State for Joe Barry Carroll. To Boston for Kevin McHale. To New Jersey for Albert King. West had offered Nixon and Eddie Jordan to Indiana in exchange for the draft's number two pick, Missouri center Steve Stipanovich. The guard shrugged. "It's inevitable," he said. "How many players play with just one team their whole career? I'm not saying I want to go—it would be great to spend my whole career in L.A. But it's inevitable. Everyone gets traded."

That night, however, Nixon's mood darkened. He was sitting in his room at the Ocotillo Lodge, stewing over the gossip, when he called Lon Rosen, who worked as the director of promotions. "We've gotta talk," Nixon said. "You tell the man I want out of here."

"What do you mean?" Rosen asked.

"I'm done," Nixon said. "I don't want to be here."

Rosen immediately contacted West and relayed Nixon's desire. "OK," West said. "We're going to make a deal."

One day later, West asked Josh Rosenfeld, the team's media relations director, for a favor. "I need you to do something," he said. "The Clippers are scrimmaging in San Diego, and I want you to go down there and get a video of it." Rosenfeld was excited. A covert assignment! He had planned on dining that night with several of the team's beat writers, but called to cancel. "Well, I never canceled anything," Rosenfeld said. "That was a red flash for Mitch Chortkoff [of the *Herald-Examiner*]. He knew something was going on, and eventually learned that I'd gone to San Diego."

In the meantime, Nixon called Rosen again. He had been optimistic about a trade to Houston, where he could join Ralph Sampson, the draft's first overall pick. Now he was hearing San Diego—the place where good ballplayers went to rot. "You didn't tell Jerry what I said, did you?" he asked.

"I did," said Rosen.

"You know, I was just frustrated," Nixon said. "I want to stay."

It was too late.

On October 10, the Lakers and Clippers completed one of the biggest trades in the history of either franchise. Los Angeles sent Nixon, Jordan and a second-round pick 120 miles south in exchange for center Swen Nater and the rights to shooting guard Byron Scott, San Diego's recent first-round draft choice out of Arizona State. Save Donald Sterling, the Clippers' eccentric owner, nobody in the franchise's front office was happy with the transaction. When General Manager Paul Phipps landed Scott with the fourth overall selection, he thought he had acquired a building block to place alongside star forward Terry Cummings. The Clippers finished 25-57 in 1982–83, 33 games behind the Lakers. They needed youth. "Byron would have been great, but Don refused to pay him," said Phipps of Scott's request for a four-year, $1.75 million deal. "It wasn't like Byron was making crazy or unreasonable demands. Don just didn't want to pay money. I don't even know how to explain it."

"I do," added Pete Babcock, the team's director of player personnel.

"Some people said we'd drafted Byron too early and questioned the pick. Don never told us who we should take, but he asked a lot of people their opinions—whether it was a busboy or someone at a dinner party. And, after getting enough opinions, I don't think he was enamored by the pick." Sterling and Buss were friends, and the Clipper owner knew his colleague was shopping Nixon. San Diego suffered from Laker envy—Sterling wanted to have his own genre of Showtime, only without having to spend money. He called Buss without consulting Phipps or Babcock and finalized the transaction. "Don, we don't want to do this," Babcock told him. "Norm's at the end of his career, and Byron's going to be a very good player. We've done the research—Byron Scott is a good kid, great character, outstanding potential. With him we have the pieces to be a good young franchise. But not with Norm Nixon."

Sterling paid Babcock no mind. The trade was completed, and at the same time Clipper employees were letting out deep sighs of resignation ("Our hands were tied," said Phipps), the Laker gatekeepers were euphoric. In many ways, the addition of Scott paled in immediate scope to the glee brought forth by Nixon's departure and Swen Nater's arrival.

Yes, Swen Nater.

For far too many years, West had bemoaned the Lakers' lack of front-court depth. The line of centers employed as Abdul-Jabbar's backup was long and undistinguished, ranging from Jim McDaniels and Cornell Warner to Dave Robisch and Mark Landsberger. Ever since joining the ABA's Virginia Squires out of UCLA in 1973, Nater had been one of professional basketball's elite rebounders, averaging 12.6 per game. He even appeared on the January 25, 1975, cover of the *Sporting News* alongside the headline, MR. RE-BOUNDER.

There was also a remarkable story to be told, one that explained the determination that helped a clumsy 6-foot-11, 240-pound Dutchman go from never having started a college game to being named a two-time ABA All-Star. Born and raised in Den Helder, Netherlands, Nater was three when his parents divorced, and shortly thereafter, his mother and stepfather left for the United States without him. At age seven, Swen and his sister, Rene, were abandoned by their father and placed in a Dutch orphanage. Of the sixty children at the orphanage, Swen and Rene were the only ones whose parents were still living. "Well, before the orphanage, first we were in three foster homes," he said. "During that time my stepfather and my little brother said they were going to go to America, make money and send for us. That never happened."

When Nater was nine, a strange, life-changing event took place. The producer of the American television game show *It Could Be You* learned of his family's plight, and flew Swen and Rene to California to appear as guests. "It was like *This Is Your Life*," he said. "My mom and stepdad were invited to watch the show, just thinking they were there as part of the audience. Then my sister and I came out of a windmill and surprised them. They were shocked." The on-air euphoria expressed by his parents was but a performance. That night, driving home from the studio, Swen's stepfather, Charles, glanced toward the backseat and said, in clear Dutch, "Now we have two more mouths to feed."

"He was a bad man," said Nater. "He beat us, he whipped us, I never went to the dentist until I was in college. I was so excited to come to America. I had ice cream for the first time on the plane ride over. Then we got here, and it was awful."

Nater knew nothing of basketball before arriving in the United States, and played only occasionally, on the pickup courts of Long Beach, through high school. He attended Cypress College, a small junior college, and was eating lunch one day when he was approached by Tim Tynum, a member of the basketball team. "He asked if I was planning on coming out," Nater said. "I was six-foot-nine and one hundred eighty pounds, and I couldn't jump, couldn't touch the rim twice in a row. But I was tall." Nater joined the Chargers, appeared sparingly as a freshman, but spent his free time shooting 600–800 hook shots per day with Tom Lubin, a Cypress chemistry teacher and assistant coach. As a sophomore, armed with a deadly hook and a nose for the ball, he was named a first-team Juco All-American. His 39 rebounds in a game against Antelope Valley remains a junior college record. "I discovered myself," he said. "I paid attention, watched the nuances, kind of figured it out."

Nater enjoyed the uncomplicated beauty of the game. After years of being told by his stepfather why he was good for nothing, it turned out he was good for something—rebounding. Nater was recruited by 150 Division I programs, and picked UCLA because of the school's winning tradition. Once there, however, he found himself stuck to the bench behind Bill Walton, one of the sport's all-time greats. In two seasons in Westwood, he never started, averaged a mere 4.9 points and loved every minute of it. "Who can blame John for going with Walton?" he said. "He's just great. But the coach never forgot about me. And thanks to him, I learned the ins and outs of playing center."

Professional scouts drawn to campus to watch Walton were also impressed by the lad with the weird name assigned to guard him. Wooden told all comers that Swen Nater could have starred at most other colleges. The sentiment was proven during a ten-year, six-team career that included, until now, five wonderful seasons as a Clipper (backing up, coincidentally, Walton). "Yes, I loved being a Clipper," he said. "I loved San Diego, my family loved San Diego, and I wanted to bring the city and fans a championship. When I found out about the trade, I was unhappy. I had to be convinced this was a good thing. Eventually, I figured out that this was a chance to win an NBA title. I couldn't really complain about that."

Nor, for that matter, could Scott. At the time, belonging to the Clippers was the NBA equivalent of a solitary confinement sentence. As soon as he heard that he had been selected by San Diego, Scott wished he could go to Milwaukee. Or Cleveland. Or Kuwait. Then, suddenly, his rights belonged to a team that had appeared in three of the last four NBA Finals series, a team that played twelve blocks from his childhood home in Inglewood. "Comparing the Lakers to the Clippers," said Bob McDonald, his agent, "is like night and day."

It was a dream come true—as well as a nightmare. Shortly after the draft, Scott was asked by a television reporter to assess his game. He reply would haunt him. "I think I've got the ability of a smaller Magic [Johnson]," he said. "I'm quicker and I can shoot better than Magic. I'm a crowd-pleaser. I'm a great outside shooter and I'm flashy."

After the trade, Jim Dunlap, the Clippers' media relations director, called Rosenfeld and insisted there was context behind the quote. "He said the writers asked Byron two or three times, and he refused to compare himself to anyone," Rosenfeld said. "He finally made the Magic comparison, but as a joke. Well, no one on our team knew that."

Despite Nixon's faults, many of the Lakers were heartbroken by the trade—none more so than Michael Cooper. As soon as Cooper heard the news, he called Nixon and offered a tearful farewell. Riley pieced together a Norm Nixon highlight video and showed it to the team on a locker room television. "It was almost like a funeral for Norm," said Ron Carter. That night, Nixon celebrated his twenty-eighth birthday with a heavyhearted dinner at Mr. Chow's, the trendy dining hot spot. Five Lakers—Johnson and Cooper included—attended (as did Jack Nicholson, Lou Adler, Burt Bacharach and Carole Bayer Sager). Toasts were offered, tears were shed. Then, after being told of Scott's comments, Cooper fumed. "He's not going to be given that job," he said. "I was always content with my role as sixth man as long as the two starting guards were there. Now, one of them is traded. The starting job is not something I'm going to let slip away."

Scott agreed to a four-year contract on Saturday, October 15, and reported to training camp two days later. He was a quiet kid, with a low Afro and a steely gaze. Teammates greeted him warily, and Scott responded in kind. Though he had likened himself to Johnson, they were night and day. There was nothing seemingly bubbly or lovable about Scott. He had been raised by a single mother in a gang-infested neighborhood, where the Crips and the Families ran things and the color of your shirt could determine whether you lived or died. "They admired athletes," Scott once said. "You never heard about an athlete getting shot over just nothing. There was never any pressure on me to join a gang, although if I went up to the leaders of the gangs—and I knew them all in the neighborhood—they definitely would have invited me to join." Scott's brother, Jeff, was doing time in a Utah prison for burglary. One of his childhood friends, a boy known as Little G, was stabbed to death in a gang fight. Another boyhood pal wound up strung out on crack. One day he asked Scott for money to pay off a dealer. Scott declined—and the man was later shot and killed. "Byron was street smart and knew how to handle himself," said Jay Humphries, his childhood friend and a future NBA guard. "When you grew up in Inglewood, it wasn't always fun and games."

If the veteran Lakers wanted to treat Scott like a ball of garbage, so be it. He wasn't the one who decided to trade Nixon. And he certainly hadn't intended to belittle Johnson. An interviewer asked a question—he answered it. Period. On that first day, Scott was given the silent treatment. He introduced himself to people, and was met with the sound of air. During a break in action, he poured himself a cup of water from a cooler. "You want some?" he said to Abdul-Jabbar. The center refused to look his way.

Throughout the first week, Scott was a bruise waiting to be punched. Every time he drove to the rim, someone—Cooper, Rambis, Wilkes, Johnson—hacked him. "It was like there was a fraternity," said Riley, "the Laker Alpha Mega, and they made things a little rough. It's not as if they strapped him to a tree and left him there in the dark, but he did have to pay his dues." Yet Scott never complained. Not once. "We tried to break him," said Bob McAdoo. "But he wouldn't give. He didn't come in all wide-eyed, nervous about being with the Los Angeles Lakers of Kareem and Magic. Nope. He just played."

"I always thought of myself, Norm and Magic as the Three Musketeers, and Byron broke that up," said Cooper. "So fuck him. We didn't talk to him, we hit him, we did everything to fuck him up. I saw Byron play a little bit in college, but he wasn't so impressive to me. So when he came, he had to pay his dues. Well, he did. He took it all like a man."

Johnson was the first to break what Scott termed "the sound barrier." He treated the rookie to lunch and talked to him about expectations and NBA life and surviving a long run. About to begin his fifth NBA season, Johnson was the undisputed leader and kingpin of the Lakers. Shortly after the big trade, Riley had Ron Carter—the former Laker now back in camp with the team—playing point against Johnson during drills. In the midst of a particularly physical exchange, Johnson slapped Carter across the face. Carter, a graduate of the Virginia Military Academy, screamed, "What the hell are you doing?" and pushed back. Johnson threw a punch, and Carter pinned him to the ground—"It took me five seconds," Carter said. The players were separated, and as he rose, Johnson waved toward Carter, smiled and said, "Bye-bye."

"I got a call three hours later from the front office, telling me I was cut," said Carter. "That was Magic's decision. He wanted me gone—I was gone. He wanted Norm gone—he was gone, too."

There was no point guard controversy, no debate over who would handle the ball. Abdul-Jabbar surrendered any power long ago. Most important, Johnson was—as always—the team's most dogged worker. He reported to training camp in fabulous shape, then ran harder, longer, faster than the other Lakers. Although teammates were troubled by Scott's cockiness, Johnson couldn't care less. He was one to feel neither threatened nor angry. As long as the kid could play, he'd fit in just fine.

■ ■ ■

There was just one problem—the kid couldn't play.

OK, maybe that's an exaggeration. Scott immediately impressed his teammates with the most extensive long-distance range the club had seen since Jerry West's heyday. Scott's shooting touch was awe-inspiring, from release to arc to the inevitable soft swish through the twine.

Shooting, however, was only one element of NBA success. His footwork was dreadful, and he was barely capable of going left with the ball. Any expectations of Scott sliding into the starting lineup were quickly put to rest. For now, he was a bench player.

When Los Angeles opened at home against the Kansas City Kings on October 28, it was almost like watching a bunch of actors performing a Lakers tribute skit. Johnson and Abdul-Jabbar looked the same, but . . . was that—wait—Mike McGee starting at the off-guard? Is Swen Nater playing the post? And who the hell are Calvin Garrett and Larry Spriggs (answer, respectively: a free-agent pickup from Houston, and a rookie forward out of Howard University). Los Angeles won, 117–107 behind 25 points apiece from Abdul-Jabbar and Wilkes, then took a 120–115 decision at Utah to start 2-0.

Generally speaking, teams like the Lakers have very few "big" games early in the season. A PR department might generate hype; players might talk smack; a coach might break out clichés about "tonight being a statement on dignity and pride." But when a franchise reaches three of four championship series, November contests rarely matter.

On the morning of November 2, the Lakers woke up for a game that mattered. Players and coaches boarded a bus for the two-hour ride to San Diego, where the Clippers—and Norm Nixon—awaited.

For the most part, games against the Clippers were as predictably scripted as a *Rocky* sequel. The first quarter might be close, then—by midway through the second—Los Angeles would pull away and win by 15–20 points. When the clashes were held in Los Angeles, 30 percent of the attendees vanished by the fourth quarter. When the clashes were held in San Diego, Laker fans outnumbered Clipper fans by a significant margin.

For the first time in, oh, ever, there was genuine intrigue. Having recovered from their initial sadness over Nixon's departure, many of the Lakers were now merely angry. Even though they had lost in the 1983 Finals, Los Angeles seemed to be a dynasty in the making, a team that could regularly represent the West for a decade. "I thought Norm blew it for us with his selfishness," said Cooper. "I really did. I felt bad for Norm, because nobody in their fucking mind wanted to be a Clipper. But I also thought he was really stupid. It's the classic curse of getting what you ask for. He'd complained a lot when he was with us. Well, congratulations. You're a fucking San Diego Clipper."

A sellout crowd of 11,629 packed the San Diego Sports Arena, and Nixon needed no extra motivation. Ever since the trade, he had been living in Room 239 of the Sports Arena Travel Lodge—a far cry from his Beverly Hills abode. Where were the Laker Girls? Dancing Barry? The courtside celebrities?

As players from both teams mingled during shootaround, McAdoo pulled out a crumpled-up piece of paper and handed it to Nixon. It was a copy of a *Los Angeles Times* story that explained how the Lakers would be better sans their old point guard. Translation: To hell with you.

"We wanted to beat his ass," said McAdoo. "Once the whistle blows, it's on."

Cooper and Johnson hugged Nixon before the game, then spent the rest of the night trying to catch him. In thirty-eight minutes of play, Nixon was a white, red and blue blur. San Diego took a 32–18 lead in the first quarter, with Nixon scoring 15 of the points. "He came out with both barrels loaded," Cooper said. "And he let us have it with both of them."

When the game ended, the scoreboard read CLIPPERS 110, LAKERS 106. Nixon scored a game-high 25 points, coupled with 12 assists. (Scott, meanwhile, had 8 quiet points off the bench.) He was giddy. "Tonight, I can think about winning my first game against my old team," he said. "But you can savor nothing in this league. There just isn't enough time." He was mobbed by teammates, all of who seemed to sense a new era in San Diego Clippers basketball. Coupled with forward Terry Cummings and center Bill Walton, Nixon expected to help his organization challenge for the Pacific Division. "Anything is possible," Walton said. "With Norm, anything is possible."

The Clippers would go on to finish 30-52.

■ ■ ■

The Lakers, meanwhile, continued their sustained excellence. Even though Johnson missed fifteen games with a dislocated finger, and even though McGee never fully emerged as Nixon's replacement at two guard (he started 45 games, averaged 9.8 points and infuriated teammates with his dreadful shot selection), and even though Mitch Kupchak's long-awaited return from his knee injury was anticlimatic (he averaged 3.1 points in 29 games), and even though Nater joined the ranks of forgettable Abdul-Jabbar caddies (he averaged 4.5 points and

3.8 rebounds in 69 games and retired at season's end), and even though Scott dazzled no one with his 10.6 points per game, and even though Lakers players led the NBA with 103 total missed games due to illness or injury (Wilkes faced the worst of it, contracting an intestinal infection in February), there was a mounting sense that something big was about to happen.

For the first time in fifteen years, the Lakers and Boston Celtics were truly destined to play for the NBA championship.

Once again, Los Angeles was the class of the West, running away with the Pacific Division and posting the conference's best record (54-28). In the East, meanwhile, Boston had pieced together one of the great campaigns in modern NBA history. Much like the 76ers a season earlier, the Celtics (62-20) often seemed downright invincible. They featured six players who averaged double figures in scoring, arguably the second-best point guard in the NBA (Dennis Johnson, acquired from Phoenix before the season began) and, in Robert Parish and Kevin McHale, a pair of long, rangy frontcourt stars who could pester Abdul-Jabbar.

There was also some kid from Indiana. Went by the name of Bird.

"Fucking Larry Bird," said Cooper.

That is how most Laker players viewed Boston's all-everything forward. He wasn't merely Larry Bird. He was *fucking* Larry Bird or, quite often, *motherfucking* Larry Bird. Ever since arriving in the league along with Johnson in 1979, Bird had confused, befuddled and antagonized opposing forwards, all of whom—at one time or another—judged the gawky, white non-jumper to be vastly overrated. There was a pattern to those who guarded Bird. First, a player would assume his athleticism and talent would overwhelm the Celtic star. Second, Bird would get the ball early in a game, juke once or twice, then—swish. Two points. Then swish again. And again. And again. And again. Third, Bird would talk to you. About your sorry-ass defense. About the ten shots you missed. About your team being down by 15. Fourth, Bird would slap the ball away from you. Or force you into taking an unbalanced leaner. Fifth, you'd glance at the post-game stat sheet and read:

BIRD: 32 points

YOU: 8 points

"He did everything it took to beat you," said Rambis. "That was the only important thing to Larry—beating you. And if he made you look pathetic, all the better."

"Larry attacked you from so many different angles," said Johnson. "And with Larry, you had to guard him five and ten feet past the (three-point) line. Five feet past the line was nothing for Larry. One time, I was hurt. I was on the bench. Larry comes by during warm-ups and says, 'Don't worry, Earvin. I'm gonna put on a show for you.' I think he scored forty that night and I think he only missed two shots. He'd get that walk goin' and that blond hair floppin' and you knew you were gonna be in for a long, long night."

Rambis detested Bird. Cooper loathed him. Worthy abhorred him. Were you an opposing player, there was nothing to like about Larry Bird. Not his game, not his socks (frumpy and white), not his choice of beer (Budweiser), not his slow Indiana drawl. Absolutely nothing. Of all the Lakers, though, the one who had the most hostile feelings was Johnson. He and Bird had famously paralleled each other, first languishing as disgruntled teammates (but not friends) on a U.S. amateur team that played in the World Invitational Tournament in the summer of 1978,* then—of course—serving as the key figures in the historic 1979 Michigan State-Indiana State NCAA title game. That matchup served to forever link the two as blood rivals, not unlike Joe Frazier and Muhammad Ali or Chris Evert and Martina Navratilova. Because he was quiet and standoffish, Bird usually responded to Magic questions with a shrug and a quick word. "My thing was when you compete, you're really not friends," Bird said. "You wanna keep an edge. Earvin is an outgoing guy. He loves everybody, he wants to high-five. And he's got that big smile. My goal was to try and take three of them teeth home with me." Bird was neither complimentary nor critical. Simply matter-of-fact. "I don't go out to dinner with him," he once said, in a rare expressive moment. "I just know him on the basketball floor, and that's it. If he thinks he's going to drive the lane and I'm going to lay down, he's crazy. I've got a job to do." Johnson, on the other hand, couldn't say enough kind things about his rival. Bird was the best, Bird was amazing, Bird was awesome, Bird was the king of the game. Inside, though, he maintained a jealousy for Bird that existed with no other. While they played on opposite coasts, Johnson tracked Bird. He read every detail of his line in the daily newspaper box score, had teammates hush up when his name or image ap-

---

* Kentucky's Joe B. Hall was the coach. The starting lineup for the American team included Rick Robey, Kyle Macy and Jack Givens—all Wildcats—while future stars like Joe Barry Carroll, Darrell Griffith, Sidney Moncrief, Bird and Johnson sat on the bench. "That's the first time probably in both our lives that we sat on the bench," Johnson told David Letterman in 2012. "And I don't think neither one of us liked that at all."

peared on the latest sportscast. When Bird soundly beat him out for the 1979–80 Rookie of the Year award, Johnson was shocked. When the Celtics won the 1981 title over Houston, he couldn't speak. Bird, a forward, and Johnson, a guard, rarely guarded each other on the court, but to the public they were Cain and Abel (who was who depended on one's rooting interest). "Put fifty basketball minds in a room and ask them to pick a player to start their team," said David Stern, the NBA's commissioner. "Twenty-five will pick Magic, twenty-five will pick Larry."

"They'll say it's not a one-on-one game, and they'll point out that they're not even guarding each other, and you can't blame them for doing that," said Pete Newell, a basketball legend who worked as a consultant for the Golden State Warriors. "But if you were Raquel Welch and you lived across the street from Marilyn Monroe, you'd make damn sure you looked good every time you went out the front door."

Johnson desperately wanted to directly steal a championship from Bird—to make his case as the game's best, to jab a stake in his rival's heart. Bird desperately wanted to directly steal a championship from Magic—to earn a payback from Michigan State-Indiana State, to jab a stake in his rival's heart. "They're simply two of the all-time greats," said K. C. Jones, Boston's coach. "They're so alike, but they're so different. Earvin's black, so that those who want can identify with him, and Bird's white for those who want to identify with him. Earvin's a great passer, rebounder and scorer. Larry's all that and he can shoot better than any big man I've ever seen. Magic's strength is pushing the ball up the floor. When he's in control, there's nobody like him. They've got such creative imagination on the court. People sit there and marvel at what they can do."

The Celtics strode through the playoffs, struggling against the Knicks in a seven-game semifinal series, but making quick work of Washington in the first round and Milwaukee in the Eastern Conference Finals. The Lakers, meanwhile, downed the Kings, Mavericks and Suns to reach their fourth championship series in Johnson's five years.

When Los Angeles ousted Phoenix with a 99–97 Game 6 win, the sense of accomplishment in the locker room was, collectively, less than usual. In the past, taking the West was a huge deal. This time, however, a blood rivalry loomed. The conference crown would mean nothing without destroying Boston. For younger fans, the thought was primarily about Johnson one-upping Bird. But for Laker loyalists who had been around since the team's arrival from Minneapolis in 1960, the series carried unique significance.

At the time, the rafters inside the Boston Garden dangled fourteen NBA championship banners—seven of which were earned against the Lakers. The first triumph came in 1959, when the Celtics swept Minneapolis in a humiliating four games. The remaining six all occurred when the Lakers were a California team, with star-packed rosters and dreamy expectations. The disdain for Boston grew with each setback—from mild to strong to intense to fierce to unrivaled. In 1962, there was Laker guard Frank Selvy missing an open fifteen-footer with seconds remaining in Game 7. In 1966, there was an eight-and-a-half-minute span in Game 7 during which Los Angeles failed to score a single point—and lost by two. In 1969, the last time the teams clashed for the crown, Jack Kent Cooke was so certain of a Lakers' Game 7 victory that he had balloons hanging from the Forum rafters, waiting to drop. He hired the USC marching band to play "Happy Days Are Here Again" during the inevitable post-game celebration. "I suppose you're going to ask me about those damn balloons," Cooke said years later. "I sent them all to a children's hospital where the kids had a great time with them. Certainly a better time than I did."

"I'm a nostalgia buff," Riley said. "The ghosts of Sam Jones, Jerry West, Bill Russell, Elgin Baylor and all the rest from the past will be hanging from the rafters, looking over a new generation."

The Lakers entered the finals rightly worried about Bird, but believing Cooper, the league's finest perimeter defender, could handle him. A greater concern was the Celtic mystique or, as Cooper said, "all that bullshit Red Auerbach did." A revered NBA figure who had coached Boston for sixteen years before becoming the team's general manager in 1966, Auerbach took sadistic pleasure in making sure Boston Garden served as a hell trap for visiting teams. First opened in 1928, the building was now drafty and poorly maintained, with brownish water often oozing from the taps and shower knobs that were rusted and decayed. When the Lakers came to Boston during the summer, the visiting locker room always felt as if it were 120 degrees. On cold winter days, it'd drop to 20. "All the things you heard about Red Auerbach—most of them were true," said Lon Rosen, the Lakers director of promotions. "The locker room smelled, it was dirty, disgusting. He'd have people call the players' hotel rooms in the middle of the night so they didn't sleep well before games. He was an incredible basketball mind, but very childish."

"Actually, not everything you heard was right," said M. L. Carr, the longtime Celtic guard. "I don't think he turned the heat on when it was really hot out. He just turned the cold water off."

Though Riley tried to sound indifferent toward Auerbach, he viewed the man as one would a cockroach. There was a right way to do things and a wrong way to do things, and Riley believed the Celtics were in the wrong. When the Lakers had traveled to Boston earlier in the season, Riley spotted a container of water on a courtside table during shootaround. "The Celtics left it there for us," said Dave Wohl, a Lakers assistant. "To drink." Riley ordered that the container be emptied, scrubbed out, and refilled. "Who knows," he said, "what the Celtics might have put in there to make us sick."

Because the Celtics finished with the NBA's best record, Los Angeles traveled to Boston for the first two games. Having just wrapped up the Suns series, the Lakers flew directly from Phoenix. Upon landing at Logan Airport on May 26, the players groggily walked off the plane. The Western Conference Finals had been bruising, with the scratch marks and black-and-blue welts to show. "It's hard to regain your energy in the NBA," said Wohl. "Takes time."

So how did the Lakers spend their first hour in Boston? By standing alongside the luggage conveyer belt, waiting for forty-five minutes. When the purple-and-gold bags finally emerged, half were unzipped. "The message was clear," Johnson said. "It was just Boston's way of letting us know we shouldn't get comfortable here."

The airport was overrun by Celtic fans decked out in green-and-white apparel. As Johnson picked up his bag, he was approached by a teenager in a green shirt. The Laker guard expected an autograph request. "Hey, Magic," the kid said, "Larry is going to make you disappear!"

"This little old man comes up to me, all kinda hunched over, and he gets right up in me and says—hissing—'Larry is going to *kill* you,'" Johnson said. "So now we get our bags and get on the bus and our bus driver is wearing a Celtics cap. And I'm thinking, 'Are we going to make it to the hotel all right?' Then we go to check into the hotel and everyone at the hotel— everyone!—is wearing Larry's jersey and Celtic jerseys and mean-muggin' us. Just being real nasty. And the lady behind the counter goes—hissing— 'Here's your key!' Just staring at me."

The Lakers smiled and laughed it all off. Players knew, however, what this was, in no small part, about. Every single fan who approached in the airport and the hotel lobby was white. Not 95 percent, not 99 percent—100 percent. McAdoo, the only Laker to have played for the Celtics, devoted considerable time to relaying to his mates stories about the awful way the city and organization treated minorities. "When I arrived in Boston, it was well known as a place that destroyed black careers," he said. "That organization wasn't disliked only by me. It was a graveyard for blacks."

■ ■ ■

The Lakers spent the night before Game 1 inside the Copley Marriott, a beautiful facility with twenty-four-hour room service, a crystal blue swimming pool and king-size beds in every room. Riley insisted his players register under faux names, so that Auerbach and Co. couldn't engage in the usual hijinks.

On the bright side, it worked beautifully—no one called.

On the dark side, the *Boston Globe* had listed the team's whereabouts inside its sports section. The hotel's fire alarm system went off—*three times*.

"You kind of get used to it," said Josh Rosenfeld, the team's media relations director. "But it sucks."

To eleven of the Laker players, the disturbances were an irksome nuisance. The men had to rise out of bed, find slippers or shoes and trudge down nine flights of stairs while mingling beneath the dark sky with Jim the accountant from Cleveland and Nancy the housewife from Urbana.

To Abdul-Jabbar, the thirty-seven-year-old center, it was torture.

Twenty-three years earlier, while visiting a relative in North Carolina, he first experienced the sensation of a vice clamping down upon his brain. "The pain was intense, and I felt nausea and a great sensitivity to light," Andul-Jabbar said. "All I could think about was when it would stop. I sat in a dark room for an hour and it passed." This was his introduction to the migraine.

At UCLA, Abdul-Jabbar spent days in bed, paralyzed by pain. While visiting Germany in 1975, he suffered a migraine that lasted, uninterrupted, for two weeks. He tried everything—acupuncture, yoga, electrodes attached to his scalp—to ease a feeling he likened to, "an alien in your head trying to come out your eyeballs." Finally, in the early 1980s, he made an appointment with Dr. David Bresler, a former director of the UCLA pain-control unit. Bresler concluded that Abdul-Jabbar's condition was food-related, and that a change of diet (MSG and shellfish—bad; carrots and tomatoes—good) could have an enormous impact. "And it did," said Bresler. "When a reporter in the *Los Angeles Times* asked him why he stopped missing games, he mentioned us. All of a sudden, we had fifteen thousand people applying to come to the pain clinic."

Though Abdul-Jabbar suffered fewer migranes, occasional flare-ups continued. As he stood outside in the cool night, fireworks exploding within his head, he wondered whether playing Game 1 was possible. The following morning, he missed a team meeting and breakfast in the hotel lobby, then missed the team bus to the Garden. Light flashed before his eyes. The *thump!-thump!-thump!*ing inside his skull was unbearable. Could the Lakers actually kick off the NBA Finals with Swen Nater starting at center?

With an hour until game time, Abdul-Jabbar exited a taxi and entered the visiting locker room, head in hands. The room was sweltering ("I had a tan suit on," said Bertka, "and I could have taken off my pants and wrung them out"), but he didn't notice. He approached Jack Curran, the longtime trainer and master of a thousand trades. Curran had solved many problems in seven years with the Lakers, from uniform issues to equipment malfunction. He told Abdul-Jabbar to lie down on a table, grabbed his neck with his meaty hands and—POP! POP!—adjusted the vertebrae. Never one to smile, Abdul-Jabbar smiled. The pain vanished.

That afternoon, the Laker center reminded a national viewing audience that, even at age thirty-seven, he was still *the* Kareem Abdul-Jabbar. Throughout the league, talk of elite centers had often turned away from Abdul-Jabbar and toward Parish, Moses Malone and Ralph Sampson. It angered him. "As I get older, it's assumed that there is a situation of diminishing returns," he said curtly. "I've been able to beat those odds."

Boston, which had won nine-straight playoff games at home, was overwhelmed. After Bird opened the game with a layup for a 2–0 Celtic lead, Abdul-Jabbar sprinted down the court, UCLA style, took a long pass from Johnson, stepped toward the hoop and fired a mini-hook over Parish while being fouled on the arm. "He tried to outrun that headache!" said Tommy Heinsohn, who was calling the game for CBS. "That's pretty good for an old fella like Kareem!"

The lead mushroomed, as the Celtics seemed surprisingly disinterested. "Maybe we were so happy to be here," said K. C. Jones, the Boston coach, "that we came out here awfully flat." Abdul-Jabbar, meanwhile, hit his first seven shots from the field, and wound up with 32 points, 8 rebounds and 5 assists. By midway through the third quarter, Los Angeles was up 81–62, and the Boston Garden—holding 14,890 spectators—felt like a crypt. Parish fouled out with 12 points.

When the game ended with a 115–109 Laker win, visions of an easy series danced through the minds of many Los Angeles fans. Riley had instructed Cooper to stick to Bird like masking tape, and he did so, holding the star to 24 points on 7-of-17 shooting. He lined up Worthy, the 6-foot-9 forward, on Dennis Johnson, and the Celtic point guard struggled to get to the lane. "We were the better team," said Cooper. "That's what I thought—we were simply better."

Four days later, Los Angeles set out to prove it. On a rainy night in Boston, the Lakers fought to take what would be an insurmountable 2-games-to-0 lead. Before tip-off, Riley explained to his men what a victory would mean. "You'd be cutting their hearts out," he said. "They didn't expect to lose once at home. To lose twice, and have to come to our building—devastating. So let's devastate them."

Immediately before the start, as both teams were finishing warm-ups, Johnson stood along the sideline next to CBS's Pat O'Brien. Decked out in the team's snazzy purple-and-gold warm-up jacket, Johnson exuded the serenity of a Buddhist monk. His expression was laid-back and cool. His arms dangled casually to the side. To him, this wasn't pressure, and the Celtics weren't to be feared. The point guard was twenty-four years old, living the dream.

> *O'Brien:* You're not gonna hear too many people here cheering for Magic Johnson. How does that affect you and the team? Does that get you going more?
>
> *Johnson:* Oh, yeah. It gets you up and gets you ready to play.
>
> *O'Brien:* Any place you'd rather be?
>
> *Johnson:* Well, I'd like to be in L.A., and I'd like to be in Lansing . . . say hello to my mom and dad.
>
> *O'Brien:* There you go. The Magic man.

Over the forty-eight minutes that followed, Johnson put forth his best playoff performance since the 42-point masterpiece in Game 6 of the 1980

NBA Finals. He scored 27 points, collected 10 rebounds, added 9 assists and 5 steals. Abdul-Jabbar shot only 9 for 22 from the field, Cooper missed 9 of his 13 shots and Scott was repeatedly roasted by guard Danny Ainge, who hit a string of jumpers. Johnson, though, kept the Lakers in the game. Boston led only 61–59 at the half, and 90–87 after three quarters. They held a slim advantage throughout most of the fourth, but Johnson's two free throws with thirty-five seconds remaining put the Lakers up, 113–111. Kevin McHale missed two free throws, and, with eighteen seconds left, the Lakers looked to be a lock. They had the lead, the ball, the game.

Or so it seemed.

Riley had instructed Johnson to call a time-out only in the case of McHale sinking both shots. Somehow, Johnson botched the command and, following the second miss, signaled for a TO. Riley fumed—now Boston could set up its defense. Coming out of the time-out, Worthy stepped to the sideline toward the left of his team's basket and took the ball from Jake O'Donnell, the referee. On the floor for the Lakers were Johnson, Abdul-Jabbar, Scott and McAdoo. In past years, no NBA team handled this sort of situation better. The Lakers had been the only organization with two superstar point guards in the starting lineup, and both Johnson and Norm Nixon were pinpoint passers and wicked ball handlers.

With McHale standing before him, arms waving, Worthy held the ball above his head and passed it to Johnson at the top of the key. Bird shifted over, and Johnson immediately tossed it back to Worthy, who lingered inches from the baseline. Instead of dribbling, Worthy looked across the court, where he spotted Scott, seemingly alone. He looped a high floater to his teammate—more rainbow than pass. As soon as the ball left his hands, Worthy knew he had committed an unforgivable blunder. Gerald Henderson, Boston's quick guard, sprinted toward the baseline, cut in front of the pass, caught it, drove toward the hoop and laid the ball in over an outstretched Worthy. The Boston Garden came alive. Screamed Heinsohn, a Celtic legend—"The leprechaun at work here at Boston Garden!"

"You make mistakes throughout a game—some big, some small," said Worthy. "But that one will always stay with me. I've never been able to flush it out."

Ironically, Worthy knew well the impact of one misguided throw. As a junior at North Carolina in 1982, he sealed the Tar Heels' championship game victory by stealing an errant pass from Georgetown guard Freddie

Brown with eight seconds remaining and his team up by one. The play became an immortalized college basketball moment. Now, Worthy—who had scored 29 points for the Lakers in his best-ever playoff showing—felt Brown's pain. "I was the goat," he said. "It was awful."

Thirteen seconds still remained in regulation, with the score tied at 113. Riley called a time-out, during which the crowd chanted, "Beat L.A.! Beat L.A.!," as the words flashed from the scoreboard. When action resumed, Worthy walked to mid-court to, again, deliver the inbounds pass. He threw (successfully) to Scott, who tossed the ball to Johnson.

Eleven seconds remained on the clock.

Ten . . .

Johnson dribbled against Boston's Cedric Maxwell.

Nine . . .

Eight . . .

Seven . . .

Johnson dribbled some more against Maxwell.

Six . . .

Five . . .

Four . . .

And some more.

Three . . .

And some more.

Two . . .

One . . .

With but a second left and the players and coaches on the Los Angeles bench screaming, Johnson passed to McAdoo, whose attempt was released too late. At the time, NBA shot clocks were placed on the floor, near the base of the basket. With the swarm of press photographers lined along the baseline, the digital red digits were obstructed. Johnson had no view.

"The Lakers don't get a shot off!" said broadcaster Dick Stockton, his voice combining excitement and bewilderment. "That was a thirteen-second play that went fifteen."

"I'll never forget the look on Magic's face," said Boston's Quinn Buckner. "It was one of absolute disbelief. He never messed up."

Twice, Los Angeles had Boston right where it wanted. Twice, the moment was blown. The Celtics held on for a 124–121 overtime win, and afterward the overheated visiting locker room was silent. Worthy was near tears.

Johnson spent twenty minutes alone in the shower, trying to figure out what, in God's name, he had been thinking.

"We snatched defeat from victory," the ever-wise Abdul-Jabbar said. "I guess that's kinda inside out, though."

■ ■ ■

The teams had two days off before resuming on a Sunday afternoon in Los Angeles, which was enough time for the enormity of Game 2 to settle in.

Had Worthy's pass not drifted gently through the air, the Celtics were done and the Lakers were cruising toward exorcising all the ghosts of Boston-Los Angeles Past. Instead, momentum was now with the visitors. The Celtics faced Johnson and Co. at their best, and they survived. "L.A. is a beatable team out here," Henderson said the afternoon before Game 3. "I sincerely believe that. We have a good chance to win one, maybe even steal two."

Performing as if the miscues never occurred, Los Angeles destroyed Boston, 137–104. Riley urged his team to stop playing into the Celtics' hands by slowing the pace. Johnson listened. His 21 assists set a finals record, and he initiated the majority of his team's 51 fast-break opportunities. "We tried to get them to run themselves to death," Maxwell, the Celtic forward, cracked. "That was our strategy."

Afterward, as members of the media milled outside the Los Angeles locker room, Scott Ostler of the *Los Angeles Times* asked why the long holdup.

"They're handing out rings," someone said.

Wrote Ostler in the following day's newspaper: "This series isn't over. The Celtics might bounce back. The Lakers might slow down. It might snow tomorrow in Laguna Beach."

Never had Boston's players been so humiliated. Having spent the past eight months eating up their Eastern Conference foes, the Celtics had developed a false sense of their own greatness. There was a belief, among some of the players, that the championship series was a mere formality, that they were ready to be crowned back in February. Then the Lakers ran them out of the building. "Maybe that woke them up," said Larry Spriggs, a reserve forward. "Maybe the way we sprinted past them stirred them. Because all of a sudden they started letting us know that the finesse stuff wasn't going to be working any longer."

At their core, the Celtics were basketball bullies. They played hard, they played slow, they tossed around lots of elbows. The way they were treated by the Lakers through the first three games wasn't merely upsetting. It was offensive. "You guys have already written us off," an agitated Dennis Johnson said to the media. "Why even bother going on with this series? What's the point?"

Even before it began, Game 4 felt . . . *different*. Although it was being played in Los Angeles, before a crowd featuring sunglass-wearing stars and starlets, the mood was very Boston-esque. Harsh. Gritty. Bird had referred to his teammates as sissies—a rallying cry to get serious. One day earlier, Jerry West told a reporter that, were the series to end after three games, he would have selected James Worthy (who, despite the mess-up, was averaging 20.7 points thus far) as MVP. When the Celtics heard this, they exploded. MVP? After three games? "It took me six games to win an MVP award," Maxwell said of receiving the honor in 1981. "And they're giving it to Worthy after three?"

Throughout the first two and a half quarters of Game 4, the Lakers were the Lakers. They ran and ran and ran, turning rebounds from Abdul-Jabbar and Rambis into repeated fast-break opportunities. Were a basketball newcomer watching his first game, he'd assume Los Angeles was far superior in both talent and operation.

Then, everything changed.

With six minutes, fifty-three seconds remaining in the third quarter, Dennis Johnson shot an eighteen-footer that clanked off the front of the rim. Abdul-Jabbar collected the rebound and fired off a one-handed baseball pitch to Worthy, who was streaking down the left side of the court. As soon as he caught the ball, Worthy—guarded by Henderson—zipped a perfect chest pass to Rambis, charging along the right side toward the basket. It was, in the moment, Showtime basketball at its most beautiful—one lightning-quick outlet pass, four gold-and-purple uniforms bolting at full speed.

As he went in for the layup, however, Rambis was clotheslined by McHale, who extended his left arm and jerked the Laker forward to the floor. Rambis immediately bounced to his feet, spun, and charged McHale. Worthy, a peaceful sort, stepped between the two men and accidentally pushed his teammate backward over a cameraman and onto the hardwood. Both benches cleared, with Cooper flying into the middle of the gold-and-green sea, anxious to hit anyone wearing Celtic colors. "You knew this was going to happen," Stockton said. "You could see it coming."

Amazingly, no one was ejected. A flagrant foul was called on McHale, and Rambis sank one of two free throws. Yet, in that singular moment, the mood shifted. Not just in the game, but in the series. One day earlier, while talking with Ainge, McHale said, "We've got to foul someone hard." Ainge had dismissed the words as jest—his friend was the last Celtic to get nasty. Now McHale was in the heat of it all. "Pat pulled the team aside and said, 'No layups! Absolutely no layups! If they go in for one, hit 'em hard!'" said Spriggs. "Pat was a New York guy. He was hardened. A football player. He told us that if they were going in for a layup, put them on the free-throw line. 'If they're gonna throw our guy down, we'll do the same thing to them.'"

The Lakers, however, weren't particularly tough. They liked to think of themselves as rugged. But, truth be told, there is a softening element to playing in Los Angeles, living in the warm sun, having Jack Nicholson and Penny Marshall sitting courtside. The Lakers were faster than the Celtics, more talented than the Celtics, better-coached than the Celtics. But once the series went from flash to fists, the momentum changed.

The Celtics spent the rest of regulation manhandling the Lakers. Criticized through three games for soft play, Parish had his way with Abdul-Jabbar, scoring 25 points and adding 12 rebounds. Bird, meanwhile, was transcendent, with 29 points and 21 rebounds. With sixteen seconds left, he calmly hit two free throws to tie the game at 113. Riley called his team's final time-out and designed a play for Johnson to locate Worthy for the last shot. Just as he had done two games earlier, Johnson dribbled the time away. The crowd began to make noise when the clock hit ten seconds, and with each tick the apprehension grew. Inexplicably, Johnson dribbled. Then dribbled some more. He moved nowhere—just dribbled.

Finally, with three seconds remaining, he sent the ball to Worthy, who was posting up Parish. The pass was both lazy and awful, and Boston's center stepped in for the steal. The game was heading for overtime.

"They weren't going to win," said Carr. "I really believed that. Once you don't put away a team in regulation, as they should have, it's awfully hard to do it in overtime."

By most standards, Carr was a bit player in the Celtic-Laker rivalry. One of only four Guilford College products to ever reach the NBA, Carr had enjoyed modest success early in his career, averaging a career-high 18.7 points for the Detroit Pistons in the 1978–79 season. Yet now, at age thirty-three, he was a glorified towel waver, cheering on teammates, riling up the fans and talking huge heapings of trash from the bench.

Most of the Laker players either never thought of Carr or hated him. In a league of jabberers, he was the worst offender. Jog past Boston's bench, you were guaranteed to be socked with every name in the book. Throughout the series, he repeatedly taunted Johnson with cries of "Cheese-o"—in honor of his ubiquitous smile.* Yet for Worthy, Carr maintained a certain soft spot. Upon entering the NBA, the Laker was signed to a shoe endorsement deal by New Balance—at Carr's urging. "I was a New Balance guy, and I told them Worthy was the real deal and worth going after," Carr said. "So whatever James thinks of me—and I consider him a friend—he can thank me for an eight-year contract that paid him $1.2 million."

The two teams spent the five-minute overtime period going back and forth. With thirty-five seconds left and the score deadlocked at 123, Magic Johnson stepped to the line for two. Scott and McGee, glued to the bench, covered their eyes in fear. Johnson, an 81 percent free-throw shooter, stared longingly at the rim before each shot—and missed both. Moments later, Bird sank a turnaround jumper over Johnson with sixteen seconds to go, and Boston led, 125–123.

The Lakers had one final opportunity. Cooper inbounded the ball, and Worthy was fouled by McHale as he missed an attempted layup. There were ten seconds remaining, and as he stepped to the free-throw line, Worthy was passed by Carr, who had been in the game for defensive purposes. The Boston benchwarmer offered a handshake, looked at his friend and said, "Don't choke."

At the moment, Worthy was the best player on the floor. He had hit twelve of his last thirteen shots, and scored nine of Los Angeles's 10 overtime points. "There was no one better to be in that position," said Rambis. "There's a reason he's known as 'Big Game' James. He's clutch."

Worthy took five dribbles, bent his knees, squared to the basket, released . . . and the ball hit off the front of the rim. Maxwell raised his arms in victory, crossed the lane and offered Worthy the international choke sign—hands around the neck. Worthy sank the second, but it wasn't enough. The Celtics persevered for the 129–125 win.

---

* Before the start of Game 7, Carr jogged onto the court in goggles, a direct mocking of Abdul-Jabbar. Boston fans loved it.

Series: Altered.

"I don't think any of us thought Worthy was a choker, any more than any other player is," said Carr. "I would have said the same thing to Kareem, to Coop, to Magic. I mean, I had to say something. If he makes those two free throws, we're in trouble."

Afterward, Riley came unglued. He accused the Celtics of everything short of setting fire to the village. They were crooks. Criminals. Batterers. Assholes. "What Boston did was the equivalent of two gang warlords meeting the night before a rumble and deciding the weapons," he said. "They both say bare fists, and one of them shows up with zip guns." Riley specifically targeted McHale, a normally lovable sort. Unlike the stoic Bird, McHale was always laughing, joking, kidding. Less than a minute after hammering Rambis, he tried to apologize. The gesture was met with an indifferent shrug.

"We're not going to lower ourselves to the level of a Kevin McHale and his tactics," Riley said. "But I'll tell you what we're going to do. We'll be ready for anything. What they did is they came into our territory, a neutral zone, and decided to use zip guns. Weapons that we didn't plan on using, because this is a game of basketball. We understand the physical part.

"We want to win. They want to win. It takes something like what McHale did to change the whole mood of physical play. Now it's Katie-bar-the-door, that's all. McHale's play changed the whole mood of the thing. That's the mood it's gonna be for the next three games. Now it's an ugly situation."

Riley was thirty-nine years old, a youngish man still figuring his way. Beginning that night, in a hallway in the bowels of the Forum, the Laker coach learned something he would never forget: Don't give your opponent what it most desires.

When the Celtic players read Riley's words, they figured the series was theirs. "We got in their heads," said Carr. "That's exactly what you want to do."

"Before, the Lakers were just running across the street whenever they wanted," said Maxwell. "Now they stop at the corner, push the button, wait for the light and look both ways."

Six days later, the Lakers' magical run came to an end. After splitting games 5 and 6, they dropped the decisive Game 7, 111–102, in familiar fashion. Boston out-rebounded Los Angeles, 52–33, and out-hustled them, too. "[The Celtics] muscled and fought and hammered their way to an NBA championship," wrote Mike Littwin in the *Los Angeles Times*. Afterward, Boston's fans stormed the Garden floor, knocking down baskets, grabbing jerseys, stealing Abdul-Jabbar's trademark goggles off his forehead. "I can't tell you how awful that was," said Spriggs. "The lowest of lows."

In a private moment, Riley admitted something to Nater. "I had a dream last night that we lost this game," he told the backup center. "And my dreams almost always come true. I never felt good about this one."

Because the game ended late, the team had to fly out the following morning. That night, while their bus drove from the Garden to the hotel, the Lakers were accosted by a hundred or so fans. They rocked the vehicle back and forth, hurled beer cans and rocks at the windows. "It was frightening," Johnson said. "Our nerves were shot to begin with . . . and now everyone is freaking out because we were surrounded and we couldn't go anywhere."

The police broke up the mob, and the Lakers spent the night wallowing in disbelief. Johnson, more than anyone, took the loss to heart. He blamed himself for dribbling out the clock, for poor passes, for not doing more. All he had wanted was to send Bird to another defeat, to see the look on his rival's face as he walked off the court a loser.

Instead, Johnson sat on his bed and cried.

CHAPTER 12

■■■■■■■■

EARL

W hen an organization falls one game short in a championship series, it's often more inclined to make drastic off-season changes than had it gone, say, 22-60. There's something tauntingly painful about coming so close, then having to start all over again. Executives tend to believe if they simply add one more big piece, glory will ensue.

In the aftermath of the Boston heartbreak, Jerry West, the Lakers savvy general manager, refused to panic. On the one hand, the Celtics had exposed his team as somewhat soft and, to a certain degree, unable to play slow-down basketball for prolonged stretches. On the other hand, they had come *t-h-i-s* close to winning a third title in five years, and the roster remained loaded.

Therefore, instead of trying to package some players in a deal, West looked toward June 19, 1984, when all twenty-three teams would gather inside Madison Square Garden for the NBA Draft.

One of the league's keen talent evaluators, West prepared for the event like few others. He was obsessive about getting it right, and insisted he and his crew of scouts and assistants go through every possible player once . . . twice . . . ten times. A couple of days before the draft, he would hand Josh Rosenfeld, the media relations director, a list with four or five player names. "If you know any of the local sportswriters or sports information directors, give them a call," West would say. "Find out what you can about these guys." Were there a one-armed point guard averaging 22 points per game for the University of Delaware, West wanted to know about him. Were there a

7-foot-10 sheepherder working on a farm in Djibouti, there damn well better be a scouting report. "Jerry treated all Laker employees wonderfully," said Gene Tormohlen, a longtime scout with the organization. "But he rightly had high expectations. He was all about the team winning."

Because the Lakers reached the finals, they owned the twenty-third spot in the draft, a place where no Akeem Olajuwons (the University of Houston center—picked first by the Rockets) or Michael Jordans (North Carolina guard—drafted third by Chicago) were generally found. There was, however, one name among the second-rate rubble that carried some weight inside the Forum offices, one name that leapt off of a page otherwise filled with uninspiring second-rate nobodies like Cory Blackwell, Tony Costner and Steve Burtt.

"Earl Jones," said West, years later. "Earl fucking Jones."

Yes, Earl fucking Jones*—easily the nation's finest 7-foot, 190-pound senior Division II center. West had often told people, "If you're gonna make a mistake in the draft, make sure it's a big mistake," and Jones was, without fail, big. As a freshman at Mount Hope High School in Mount Hope, West Virginia, Jones stood 6-foot-4. Three years later, he was 6-foot-10 and, as a senior at Spingarn High in Washington, DC, exactly 7 feet. "I like being tall," he said. "Except when you have to duck."

During his final prep season, there was talk around the league that Jones might leave directly for the NBA. He was a two-time high school All-American who led Mount Hope to 63 wins in 72 games over three seasons and famously lit up Patrick Ewing in a summer league battle. Why, when UCLA coach Larry Brown paid him a visit, one of the first things Jones said to him was, "Jones 29, Ewing 6." It was a line he used often.

"I guess he was trying to impress me, which he didn't have to do," Brown said. "He was considered the best player in the nation." Yet Jones was painfully quiet, emotionally stunted and academically invisible. At the end of his junior year, he had compiled sixty-three unexcused absences during the spring semester and failed most of his classes. (Hence, his transfer to Spingarn High.)

He was, however, dominant on the court—America's elixir for every other shortcoming. On the morning after his spectacular debut for Spingarn against Chevrus High in Portland, Maine, the *Portland Press Herald* led

---

* Not his real middle name.

with the (long, awful—yet telling) headline EARL JONES' OVER-THE-HEAD, EXCUSE-ME-PLEASE SLAM DUNK IN THE FIRST HALF PRETTY MUCH SUMMED UP MONDAY NIGHT'S GAME. Professional scouts flocked to his engagements, watched him soar, but left with a near-unanimous take: oodles of talent, not physically or mentally ready for the NBA.

Though he was recruited by numerous Division I programs (his grades improved at Spingarn, and he reached the necessary SAT score while averaging 20.2 points, 17 rebounds and 7 blocked shots), Jones decided to attend the University of District of Columbia, a downtown commuter school lacking dorms and a centralized campus. The announcement, big enough to garner coverage in *The New York Times*, was greeted with bewilderment. *The University of the District of Columbia?* "I didn't want a big school, with all that pressure," he said. "They said if I came to UDC I could help put it on the map. Coach [Will] Jones said I could make the school better, the area better, make everything very exciting. I was into that."

Will Jones was right. With Earl Jones manning the middle, UDC emerged as one of the finest Division II programs in the country, winning the 1982 national title and losing close games to Division I programs like Western Kentucky and Wichita State. "We wanted to play Georgetown and Maryland," said Greg Carson, a Firebirds guard. "But they would have nothing to do with us."

Yet despite averaging 21.7 points over four seasons, Jones was an enigma. Bob Ferry, the Washington Bullets general manager, watched him play and raved, "We're talking about a number one draft pick here." By languishing in Division II, however, he rarely went up against top-flight centers like Ewing, Olajuwon and Ralph Sampson. His weight was an issue, as was his attitude. Jones seemed to run at half speed, quarter speed and, occasionally, no speed. Many thought that, by facing only Division II hacks, his game had regressed. He once told the *Washington Star*'s Betty Cuniberti, "All I want to be is a pro and drive an Eldorado." The quote generated a collective groan. Marty Blake, who operated the official NBA scouting service, offered this yin-and-yang evaluation: "This player could go anywhere in the draft. . . . He is the original mystery man. . . . He has not played up to his potential the past two seasons. . . . Despite his frame he can do everything . . . run. Pass, shoot, block shots, etc. . . . He handles the ball very well for a big man. . . . I do not know if he can gain weight."

Technically speaking, the Lakers didn't want Jones. There were dozens of players who rated higher—including George Singleton, a Furman forward who would fall to them in the third round. "I thought Earl Jones was a phony," said Tormohlen. "One of those guys who tells you exactly what you want to hear." Yet seven-footers didn't show up every day, and with Abdul-Jabbar, almost thirty-eight, hinting this might be his final season and Mitch Kupchak's knees (tattered) and Swen Nater's departure (the Lakers refused to offer a no-cut contract, so he left for Italy), West made up his mind. When the 76ers used the twenty-second pick to take a Lamar University guard named Tom Sewell, the Lakers grabbed Jones.

Comedy ensued.

There had been some modestly funny draft moments through the recent years. In 1980, the Lakers used their sixth-round pick on a North Alabama guard named Otis Boddie, then proceeded to spell his name O-D-I-S in all media and official material. "I guess," said Boddie, "they never bothered to double check." Two seasons later, the team's ninth-round selection was Rutgers's Tim Byrne—a guard whose name, when called, baffled the experts. "That's because I never played college ball," said Byrne. "My neighbor was friends with Jerry Buss. I was picked as a gag."

Jones, though, brought forth a new level of unintentional hilarity. For an organization licking its wounds after a nightmarish finals, his arrival was a breath of fresh air. Or nitrous oxide. He signed his $75,000 contract on August 15, and reported to the team's rookie camp at Loyola Marymount four days later. The Lakers handed him uniform number 1, a figure that perfectly matched his physique.

"The guy had a ton of physical talent," said Singleton. "But, well . . ."

"He couldn't play," said Lance Berwald, the team's fifth-round pick out of North Dakota State. "Nice guy, no doubt. But very soft."

"God, was he awful," said Richard Haenisch, the seventh-round pick out of Chaminade. "He would get dizzy every time we ran up and down the court. Whenever people asked him to compare himself to someone, he'd say Ralph Sampson. Right—if Ralph Sampson were soft and stupid."

Had the Lakers not wasted a first-round pick, Jones likely would have played a couple of summer league games before being sent home to Mount Hope to begin pursuing his career as the world's tallest used-car salesman (an endeavor that, years later, he fulfilled). However, the public embarrassment of admitting such a mistake would trump the sight of Jones bumbling through practices with Johnson, Abdul-Jabbar, Worthy and the Lakers. So he stayed.

In Earl Jones, Los Angeles found a player who combined Mark Landsberger's intellect with a desk lamp's court sense and a three-year-old's life sensibility. One day during camp, Dave Wohl, one of Riley's assistant coaches, was asked to call Jones after he failed to show up for practice.

"Where are you?" Wohl asked when Jones picked up the phone.

"I overslept," replied Jones.

"Well," said Wohl, "grab a taxi and get over here."

"A taxi?" said Jones. "That's gonna cost me fifty dollars."

"But, Earl," replied Wohl, "it's gonna cost you a one-hundred-dollar fine if you don't show up."

A lengthy pause followed—"Earl doing the math," said Wohl. He never arrived.

Jones was unlike any other Laker—ever. His teeth were yellowed and rotting, and Riley demanded Josh Rosenfeld, the media relations director, take him to the dentist. "He had something on every tooth that needed repair," Rosenfeld said. "I don't think he'd ever gone before." Because he was quiet, and spoke with a pronounced backwoods West Virginia twang, teammates thought him to be slow. Every so often, though, he would offer up a one-liner that had people rolling on the floor. Once, while sitting alongside Gary Vitti, the team's trainer, Jones watched as West burst into an expletive-filled rant. "Jerry walks away, and everything's quiet," said Vitti. "And Earl just looked at me and says, 'That Jerry West is fucking nuts.'"

Another time, the ever-eclectic Kurt Rambis entered the locker room, slipped out of his practice clothes and wrapped a towel around his waist. He picked his jockstrap off the floor, held it to his nose, glanced toward Jones and said, "This is my favorite part." He inhaled deeply.

Jones waited until Rambis was out of earshot. "That white boy," he said, shaking his head, "just ain't got no sense."

As fun and (unintentionally) funny as Jones was on a bench, he was at his absolute Dangerfield-esque best on the court. About to begin his sixth season, Johnson reported to camp in no mood to goof around with the rookie screwup. In Jones, he spotted everything he didn't want in a teammate—so-so skill, no dedication, no understanding of the game. As a result, Johnson made Jones a target.

Throughout the pre-season, not a day would go by without Johnson throwing a pass that—POP!—slammed—POP!—into—POP!—Jones's head. There were passes on the break—POP!—and passes in the post—POP!—and passes between two defenders—POP! Johnson wasn't, literally, launching basketballs at Jones's noggin. No, he simply knew the kid lacked the vision to keep up. That, alone, infuriated Johnson. "We all got hit by Earvin's passes from time to time, because they were really good and you had to be ready at all times," said Worthy. "But Earl was always tiptoeing through the daisies, and Magic embarrassed him. Earl had zero passion for the game."

Counting the number of basketball-induced welts on the side of Jones's head became a competition for the Laker players. They would hoot with laughter every time—POP!—he was nailed. "It was funny, but you'd also feel sorry for Earl," said Larry Spriggs. "He just couldn't cut it."

"No work ethic to speak of," said West. "A complete waste of talent, and the most disappointing draft pick I've ever been involved in."

Years later Jones—being Jones—disputed this assessment. Given a chance, he insisted, he could have been the next Wilt Chamberlain–Bill Russell–Jesus Christ hybrid. "When we stepped on the floor, well, put it this way—couldn't nobody guard me," he said. "Kareem couldn't guard me—I was too fast for him. If I got the ball outside, I could take anybody. I mean it—anybody."

Jones actually lasted much of the season with the Lakers (again, rare is the team that cuts its first-rounder), but spent most of the time stashed on the injured list with sesamoiditis—technically an inflammation under the big toe, but really a twelve-letter word that translated to "This kid can't play and we have to do something with him." He appeared in two games, missed his only field goal attempt and was dumped at season's end. Though he brought little joy to West, Riley and Johnson (who, during training camp, made Jones fetch him the requisite glass of freshly squeezed orange juice and *USA Today* every morning), both Rosenfeld and Lon Rosen, the team's director of promotions, considered him a gift from the Lord Almighty.

The Lakers fined Jones $150 for every skipped physical rehabilitation session. For *three straight months*, Jones failed to show up. "Because Josh and I didn't make much money, Pat would take all the fine money from the year and that'd be part of our playoff share," Rosen said. "Earl Jones got fined so many times he made us practically rich."

"God bless Earl Jones," added Rosenfeld. "God bless him."

■ ■ ■

Jones, however, was only one half of the season's second greatest *extraordinarily tall person experiment*. In Houston, Rockets coach Bill Fitch was pairing Ralph Sampson, the 7-foot-4 reigning Rookie of the Year, with Akeem Olajuwon, the 7-foot number one pick out of the University of Houston. They would be known as the Twin Towers.

In Los Angeles, something out of a warped parallel universe was unfolding.

Because Abdul-Jabbar was, in all likelihood, wrapping up his career, West turned over every stone in search of a capable replacement. That's why the team added Nater, why they drafted Jones. And why, on August 22, they signed a 7-foot-5, 217-pound extension ladder who was uniquely unskilled in all phases of the game. Los Angeles, meet Charles Goodrich Nevitt.

"Everyone," he said, "called me Chuck."

Houston's third-round draft pick in 1982, Nevitt played four seasons at North Carolina State, averaging (you are not about to misread this) 3 points, 2.4 rebounds and 0.2 assists in ninety career games. When he appeared in six games for the Rockets that season, he became the tallest player in NBA history. Over the next two years, he aimlessly bounced from team to team and camp to camp. "People always ask me if I'm a basketball player, and I say I am," he once cracked. "Then they want to know who I play for. So I say, 'This week or in general?' "

The Lakers spotted Nevitt in a Los Angeles summer league. He was long and gangly and as pale white as a quart of whole milk, with the high socks and bushy mustache only enhancing the image. Unlike Jones, Nevitt happened to be a hard worker and, as an electrical engineering major in college, quite intelligent. What he lacked in talent, he made up for in likability. "You won't find a nicer guy," said Rosenfeld. "But Chuck used to hurt people all the time, because he was 7-foot-5 with these really sharp elbows. I remember when Mitch [Kupchak] came back from tearing up his knee, and Nevitt got him with an elbow one day. He needed forty stitches over his eye. Chuck felt awful."

NBA teams either keep players or don't keep players. Nevitt, however, was a special case. Though he outplayed Jones, Nevitt was the final cut in camp. But instead of letting him walk, the Lakers hired Nevitt to assist Rosen with promotions. "Most of the time I was in the gym, working out, lifting weights, doing conditioning with a running coach from UCLA," said Nevitt. "But if there was an appearance they'd need a player to go to, they'd send me."

This, of course, resulted in an inevitable scene being repeated (in one form or another) more than once:

Step 1: Excited basketball fans arrive at supermarket opening, anxious to meet a real Laker.

Step 2: Excited basketball fans dream of Magic Johnson or Kareem Abdul-Jabbar or James Worthy or even Larry Spriggs.

Step 3: Announcement is made: "Ladies and gentlemen, we are honored to welcome Clark Mivett. . . ."

Step 4: Awkward silence.

"It was funny," said Rosen. "Chuck was a great guy, but a bad player. Jerry West wanted him to stay in basketball shape, so he asked me to bring him along to play pickup games with me and my friends. He'd show up and, can I tell you, he wasn't the best guy there. He was really tall and really sweet, but we were pretty ordinary players—and so was he."

Nevitt wound up appearing in eleven games for the Lakers in 1984–85, enough to earn a solid paycheck and to convince West that the organization absolutely needed its star center to play as long as possible.

On October 14, Abdul-Jabbar told the *Los Angeles Herald Examiner* that the odds were "50-to-1" against his return.

On October 22, he signed a contract extension through the 1986–87 season.

■ ■ ■

When he was thirty-seven years old, Wilt Chamberlain was one year into his retirement.

When he was thirty-seven years old, Bill Russell was three years into his retirement.

When he was thirty-seven years old, Willis Reed was six years into his retirement.

When Kareem Abdul-Jabbar was thirty-seven years old, he was elite.

Granted, he wasn't the Kareem of old, averaging 30 points and 16 rebounds while carrying a team on his back. But as younger, stronger, faster centers entered the league, all branded "game-changing" and "new wave," the Laker captain continued to play at a high level. Against all odds, he averaged 22 points and 7.9 rebounds in 1984–85, leading the Lakers in both categories and bettering his totals from the previous two seasons. He also became the NBA's all-time scoring leader, surpassing Chamberlain with his

31,420th point in a game at Utah on April 5, 1984. "I guarded him in practice all the time, and he was still awesome," said Nevitt. "Too often everyone wants to be the power dunker, to make these amazing moves. Great. But once your knees and legs go, what you can bring to the team falls apart. With Kareem, as old as he was, he could always shoot that damn hook shot. He just perfected different aspects of his game. And no matter how I guarded him, he was unstoppable."

Yet as their teammate aged, many Lakers found him to be exasperating. On the court, Abdul-Jabbar was a 10,000-pound fast-break anchor, slowing down Showtime and often stopping it altogether. Earl Jones was awful, but he could (when he tried) dart down the hardwood. Abdul-Jabbar, in contrast, was an old leather boot. Johnson, Worthy and Scott all longed to sprint. Abdul-Jabbar wouldn't. And couldn't. "Earvin actually told me at one time, 'Man, I can't wait for that guy to leave, because then you'll see the real Magic Show,' " said Steve Springer, the longtime beat writer. "A bunch of the players even had these matchbook covers printed up that read TRADE KAREEM. There was a lot of resentment toward Kareem. Really, he brought a lot of it upon himself."

Off the court, Abdul-Jabbar remained as detached as ever. Before big games, players pumped one another up with motivational words. Abdul-Jabbar, meanwhile, sat quietly, reading a book and dismissing the bluster as moronic bellowing. "He was a man who always saw the cup as half empty," said Springer. "He was rude to a lot of people when he didn't have to be." Following the 1983 fire that destroyed his house, there was a brief span when people raved about a kinder, gentler, happier man. That turned out to be short-lived. Abdul-Jabbar confused teammates with his eternally shifting moods and demeanors. One moment, he could crack a joke across the locker room. Other moments, he could walk past you without saying a word. He baffled teammates by waiting until everyone was done with their showers— then simultaneously turning on all twelve heads and strolling through one time before drying off.

Josh Rosenfeld, the longtime media relations director, recalls the Abdul-Jabbar who shunned one journalist after another but spent nearly an hour with two quirky reporters from a Finnish radio station. "CBS Sports got nothing from him that day," Rosenfeld said. "And the Finland guys are having a blast. Why? Because they asked him about jazz, not basketball." Abdul-Jabbar famously maintained a blood feud with Rich Levin, the veteran

Herald-Examiner beat writer who had also played basketball at UCLA. In 1978, Levin wrote a piece that criticized Abdul-Jabbar for agreeing to fulfill a charitable request only if he were paid five thousand dollars. "I'm never speaking to you again," Abdul-Jabbar said—and he kept his word. If Levin entered the elevator, Abdul-Jabbar exited. If Levin waited around the center's locker for a post-game quote, Abdul-Jabbar wouldn't talk until he left. "I don't think Kareem is a bad man," said Levin. "But he was difficult and moody. He was supposedly cerebral, but I'm not so certain. . . ."

Teammates watched Abdul-Jabbar blow off fans enough times to tire of the act. *Maybe* they could defend the way he treated the press (In his book, he described reporters as "wheedlers, little guys who derived great satisfaction from tweaking the tiger's whiskers"), even when he seemed to intentionally swivel his body midway through post-game interviews so that his bare buttocks would be in the faces of reporters. But his public persona was downright nasty. On September 29, 1984, Abdul-Jabbar was driving his black Mercedes-Benz 500 SEC down an alley from Junior's Deli to Midvale Avenue when he collided with a Motobecane ten-speed bicycle. The rider, a thirty-two-year-old *TV Guide* writer named Andy Meisler, wound up sprawled across the hood with a bruised thigh. "A big man gets out," Meisler recalled, "and he's not happy. I just reverted to the school yard and said, 'Hey, it's my fault—I'll pay, no problem.'"

Later on, when he received a five-hundred-dollar estimate, Meisler reconsidered. So Abdul-Jabbar proceeded to sue a man who made approximately one-two hundredth of his salary. He wound up winning $571.67 in small claims court, but there was no victory dance. The news was greeted by the city's denizens with rightful derision—what sort of millionaire takes a poor cyclist for $571.67? "Just because someone's riding his bike on the sidewalk doesn't mean you can run him over," said Barbara Pond, Meisler's insurance agent. "I can't believe the man is pursuing this."

Such was Abdul-Jabbar's way. Though he contributed to causes and read extensively and was, along with Nevitt, the most intelligent of Lakers, he possessed the emotional IQ of a toddler. At the same time he sued Meisler, Abdul-Jabbar and his girlfriend, Cheryl Pistono, were renting a residence in Brentwood from a woman named Barbara Bergen. They were paying $3,800 a month to stay in the home where Bergen, a divorcée, had raised her two children. "It was three thousand square feet, and with my kids grown I didn't need that space," Bergen said. "Well, they ruined it. They had friends come over and park on my lawn. They dug up the master bathroom, painted the walls, stuccoed the den." When Bergen confronted the couple, she said they were unsympathetic. So she sued for $20,000—then was shocked when Abdul-Jabbar's attorney, John Gaims, portrayed her as a money-hungry hustler. "It's a very typical and minor dispute," he said. "The landlord upgrades everything tremendously and tries to charge it all to the tenant, alleging the damages were caused by the tenant."

The two sides wound up settling, but Bergen never understood. "What sort of person ruins someone's home and takes no responsibility?" she said. "What does that tell you?"*

Again, the lawsuit made Abdul-Jabbar appear three feet tall and—from the outside looking in—wasn't worth the blow to his reputation. Yet that was how the basketball star behaved, and, behind his back, teammates bemoaned it. The Lakers were supposed to be classy and engaging and, above all, professional. Abdul-Jabbar was none of the above.

Fortunately, he could play. Though the 1984–85 Lakers weren't all that different roster-wise from the 1983–84 Lakers, there were three factors—along with Abdul-Jabbar's excellence—that led to a Western Conference–best 62-20 record (they took the Pacific by twenty games) and made them a more dangerous team come playoff time:

Byron Scott: As a rookie, Scott battled not only the typical NBA growing pains but teammates who blamed him for Norm Nixon's departure. "It was tough for him last year," West said. "People expected him to come in and be Norm Nixon right away, and you just can't do that. It was a very emotional time for all of us." By his second season, however, Scott was mature, confident and one of the NBA's top gunners. He averaged 16 points for the Lakers, and led the league by hitting 43 percent of his three-pointers. Although Abdul-Jabbar was Johnson's first passing option and Worthy his second, Scott became the point guard's trusted security blanket. When all else was clogged, he knew Scott would be open somewhere. "I think he's the best shooter in basketball," Riley said. "From fifteen to twenty-five feet, there's no more consistent shooter." Scott also worked hard defensively, al-

---

* In 1985 Abdul-Jabbar also sued the North American Bear Co. for selling a goggles-wearing teddy bear named Kareem Abdul-Jabear. The two sides settled out of court, with the company handing over its remaining bears to the basketball star. Said Barbara Isenberg, the company's owner: "It was fine. It got us some publicity and him some free toys."

lowing Johnson to take the easier backcourt assignment. "Byron's able to guard the great point guards other people have and hit his shots," said Johnson. "He's ready. He's calm. He's confident." Scott started 65 games in 1984–85, at times showing his youth (his inability to drive to his left was a problem), but often proving the difference between victory and defeat. On January 25, 1985, the Lakers—29-14 at the time—hosted the Philadelphia 76ers at the Forum. Still blessed with center Moses Malone and forward Julius Erving (as well as a butterball rookie forward named Charles Barkley), the 76ers were 34-7 and the thinking man's favorite to return to the NBA Finals. Scott proceeded to dominate, shooting 11 for 16 from the field and repeatedly embarrassing Andrew Toney, one of the league's great defensive off-guards. "That was definitely a preview of what's to come," said Johnson.

To the surprise of no one who had played with him at Arizona State, Scott wasn't solely a spot-up shooter. As a rookie, he entered his third game, at the San Diego Clippers (the team that drafted him), to jeers. Bob McAdoo turned to him and said simply, "They booed you, boy. You gotta dunk on somebody now." The first time he touched the ball, Scott bypassed an open jumper, drove the lane and slammed over Michael Brooks, San Diego's 6-foot-7, 220-pound forward. It was a scene that, come season two, was frequently repeated. "He was just a fantastic athlete," said Ronnie Lester, a reserve guard with the Lakers. "I think people missed that about Byron. He wasn't just a shooter. He was a specimen."

So how to explain the transformation from year one to year two? Acceptance. As the other Lakers came to realize that Scott was a Nixon-level player, sans selfishness and ego, they embraced him as one of their own. He never demanded the ball, never whined about playing time, never felt threatened by Mike McGee for minutes. One night, while on the road, he knocked on the door of Johnson's hotel room and thanked him for guiding him. "He didn't have to help me at all, but he did," Scott said. "Telling me little things like taking the ball to the basket strong instead of flipping it up like I could get away with in college." He also opened up. Teammates learned that Scott was a master impressionist (be it Mr. T or Eddie Murphy) with a sly sense of humor (while taking a tour of the White House, he scanned the presidential portraits and asked the guide, "Why are there only white people on the wall?"), a devoted family man (he met his wife, Anita, during the season, and married her within the year) and a dogged competitor. Most practices included $20-to-the-victor long-distance shoot-outs—three-pointers were worth three points, shots from out of bounds were worth four, and five points were granted to baskets made from behind the Forum's courtside seats. Scott was a lock to depart with cash in his pocket. "The rest of us just kind of hurl it up there," Johnson said. "Byron shoots jumpers."

Before long, Scott, Cooper and Johnson were inseparable. They went to movies together on the road, spent pre-games talking strategy, enjoyed late-night dinners in one another's hotel rooms.

"It took us a while after Norm left, but eventually Byron was beloved," said Cooper. "He was family."

James Worthy: Over the course of his first two seasons, there were those around the league who questioned whether the Lakers had mistakenly used the number one overall pick on Worthy. The man selected directly behind him, Clippers forward Terry Cummings, was a dynamic low-post player who averaged more than 20 points and 10 rebounds per game. The man selected third, Hawks forward Dominique Wilkins, was a high-flying dunking acrobat who brought electricity to a dormant franchise. Worthy, meanwhile, was merely excellent. He had long arms and quick feet but couldn't even beat out Kurt Rambis for a starting job. "There were certainly those who thought we made a mistake," said Mike Thibault, an assistant coach. "Cummings was terrific, Dominique was terrific. But, at the end of the day, it was about fitting what we were doing. For all of Dominique's talents, he needed the ball in his hands . . . needed to be the focal point. When you have Magic and Kareem, you don't want a third focal point. It took time for James to fit in, but, boy, when he did . . ."

With McAdoo now thirty-three and fading, and Wilkes, thirty-one, out for most of the season with torn ligaments in his left knee, Worthy filled the void. In 80 games (76 starts) he averaged 17.6 points, 6.4 rebounds and 2.5 assists, playing with an artistic flair that even Riley—a constant critic of his shortcomings—had to admire. Worthy gained early praise for his low-post moves, yet he bolted down the floor at breakneck speed. When Scott and Worthy played their best, Showtime clicked in a way it never had before—Rambis rebounding the ball, snapping it to Johnson, Worthy and Scott filling the lanes, Abdul-Jabbar taking up the rear. "Man, James could run like the wind," said McAdoo. "If he got a step on you, you were dead and done. Watching him play was amazing."

Pat Riley: Now in his third full season as head coach, Riley was peaking as a motivator and game strategist. Early on, if Johnson had a suggestion,

Riley felt compelled to take it. If Johnson wanted things done a certain way, Riley complied. "It was Magic's world," said Cooper. "He called the shots." But as the roster slowly turned over and fewer players thought of him as Westhead's replacement, Riley felt more comfortable being the man in charge. This was his team, and the decisions made were his alone. "Early on in his career, it was a lot of, 'So, this is what I think—what do you guys think about that?'" said Rambis. "He was almost like one of the players, fitting in with everybody. But as time passed, he discovered his philosophy. You could see the change."

"Pat was born to teach fast-break basketball," said Bertka. "He stressed and stressed and stressed lane recognition—as soon as we got possession of the ball, we're pushing up the middle of the floor, with the lanes on both sides filled. Under Pat, we rarely had to call plays one, two and three. I mean, we had a play—'Fist'—which was take the ball to the left side and throw it into Kareem. But, really, Pat believed in running with purpose and running with intelligence. When you had Magic pushing the ball, and Byron in the right lane and James in the left lane, running, and Kurt rebounding, well, it was as good as it could get. Basketball paradise."

Berkta had been around the sport for more than three decades, and he'd never seen a team practice as hard as the Lakers. Every scrimmage was a war, overloaded with testosterone and trash talk. Had they been in his shoes, many coaches would have stepped in, separated combatants and issued some empty warning about "keeping things professional." Riley never did. He wanted his players scarred and battle-tested, wanted them tougher, harsher, meaner. If they sought to brawl against one another, imagine how they'd approach the Celtics in the finals. "He made us mean," said Rambis. "That's a talent."

Riley's greatest gift was as a communicator. At the start of every season, the Laker families gathered for a large dinner at a player's home. Riley would inevitably give a speech that, though heard by all, was directed toward the wives and girlfriends. In words that sounded both passionate and soothing, he explained how, for the next eight months, they would be required to handle all off-the-court issues. "Your men need to be focused only on basketball," he'd say. "That's how we become champions." The apparent meaning behind the words: *Let your husbands sleep as long as possible. Don't expect them to change a diaper, mow a lawn, cook a meal, take you out for dinner. Don't follow us on the road, because they'll probably have sex with a groupie or two. Don't ask too many questions. Actually, don't ask any questions. Just support our plight, and you'll wind up with some big bucks and a really pretty ring. Well, your husband will get the really pretty ring. But we'll let you ride on a float in the parade. Probably.*

"I get that, in hindsight, it sounds weird, almost like a cult or something," said Wanda Cooper, Michael's wife. "And I can't say we didn't know—kind of—what went on on the road. But we knew we were needed, and we were all in it together. Pat made everyone feel important. He was very good at that."

■ ■ ■

The Lakers and Celtics were destined to meet again.

Everyone in Los Angeles knew it.

Everyone in Boston knew it.

Lakers-76ers had been done three times in recent years, and the world was over it.

Celtics-Rockets (yawn) had been done once, in 1981, and it was pedestrian stuff.

But Lakers-Celtics was everything the NBA could possibly want in a finals. The teams completed the season with the league's two best records (Boston, at 63-19, won one more game than Los Angeles), and the Magic-Bird story line was one that refused to grow old. For both teams, the playoffs had been fairly easy—Boston cruised past the Cavaliers, Pistons and 76ers; the Lakers made mincemeat of Phoenix, Portland and Denver. Now the kid stuff was over.

There were things that needed to be proved. The Celtics wanted to establish themselves as a dynasty, not merely one of the era's better clubs but as the franchise of the decade. At age twenty-eight, Bird had just won his second-straight MVP award and was becoming an iconic ballplayer.

The Lakers had their own issues. Though the 1984 Finals went seven games, the series was humiliating. It's one thing to lose. It's another to be taunted and mocked and pummeled. The lasting memory from that series wasn't Bird hitting jumpers or Parish's rebounding. It was M. L. Carr talking trash.

This time, Worthy was intent on proving that the errant passes and missed key free throws were aberrations. Scott was intent on showing that he was, like Nixon, a prime-time performer. (The *Sporting News*'s Paul Attner derisively referred to him as a fringe player.) Abdul-Jabbar was intent on staving off Father Time. Mostly, there was Johnson—intent on erasing the most crushing span of his professional career.

Immediately after the loss to Boston, a despondent Johnson escaped. He fled to the Bahamas, desperate for warm weather and blue waves and tasty coconut drinks with fancy umbrellas poking out from the glasses. All he wanted to do was forget the repeated blunders and gaffes that plagued the Lakers.

As he entered the lobby of his hotel, Johnson was at peace. "That's when I saw [Boston's] Cedric Maxwell," he said. "I came all this way to get away, and there he was, on his honeymoon."

Though he could shrug off the chance meeting, it stung. He spent the summer in a stupor, desperate for answers that never emerged. Was he really to blame? Would Nixon have made similar mistakes? Was he overrated? In over his head? More flash than substance? "I sat back when it was over," he said, "and I thought, 'Man, did we just lose one of the great playoff series of all time, or didn't we?' This was one of the greatest in history. Yet all you read was how bad I was." When McHale laughingly referred to him as Tragic Johnson, the words tore through his body. When Laker fans glumly reminded him of how close they had come to glory, the sentiment brought tears to his eyes. (Interestingly, the hostility between Johnson and Bird had lessened. After the 1984 Finals, they filmed a pair of commercials together and spent the time between takes catching up. Though far from friends, a frosty relationship had evolved to mild acceptance.) Some wondered whether he was devoting too much time to women, too little time to the sport. By now, Johnson's reputation as a hound was sealed. He was having sex nearly every day—often twice and three times a day. Teammates knew it, management knew it. "My car was in the shop one day," said Rosen. "So while it was being fixed, Earvin let me drive his Mercedes. I was driving around, doing some errands, when suddenly something under the hood exploded. I called him up and said, 'Earvin, I've got some bad news. Your car blew up.'" Johnson's response: "Were you able to save the phone number that was in the glove compartment?"

Said Rosen: "I said, 'Earvin, listen to me. Your forty-thousand-dollar car is sitting in the middle of the street. It's toast.' But he said to forget the car, that he'd have somebody pick it up later. All he kept asking me was, 'Did you save that number?'"

The local media was relentless, questioning whether Johnson even deserved to be compared to the flawless Bird. A *Los Angeles Times* headline asked, EARVIN, WHAT HAPPENED TO MAGIC? A columnist for the *Los Angeles Herald-Examiner* called him "the tarnished superstar" and "the goat of the series," while noting that "right there against his arch rival, Larry Bird, he failed."

Failed?

"Those wounds from last June stayed open all summer," Riley said. "It never leaves your mind completely. Magic is very sensitive to what people think about him, and in his own mind I think he heard those questions over and over again to the point where he began to rationalize and say, 'Maybe I do have to concentrate more.' I think the whole experience has made him grow up in a lot of ways."

Johnson enjoyed one of the best regular seasons of his career, averaging 18.3 points and 12.6 assists. Yet, for the first time, it didn't matter. He had always taken pride in looking over a score sheet and seeing his impact on a game. He had always enjoyed watching highlights of his fanciest passes, of the no-look, behind-the-back beauties he delivered to Worthy and Scott and Cooper. "*Whooooo*, boy, did you see that?" he'd howl. Now, though, every evening was merely a stepping-stone toward his dream. Stats? Who cares? Highlights? Who cares? He craved a rematch with the Celtics, and only a rematch with the Celtics. Nothing else would heal the pain.

When the Lakers decimated Denver, 153–109, in the fifth and final game of the Western Conference Finals, Johnson let loose a roar of gleeful delight. Earlier that evening, Boston eliminated Philadelphia, setting the clash in stone. "Can the Celtics slow down the Lakers, who averaged 131.2 points in compiling an 11-2 playoff record?" Sam Goldaper wrote in *The New York Times*. "Can the Lakers match up against the Celtic front line of Kevin McHale, Larry Bird and Robert Parish?"

"There were a lot of questions to be answered," said Cooper. "But as far as I was concerned, I knew one thing for certain. We were about to kick Boston's ass."

■ ■ ■

The VHS tapes rested atop a television in his office, each one labeled in black marker on crudely placed masking tape.

BOSTON VS. LAKERS GAME 5

BOSTON VS. LAKERS GAME 7

GAME 2 LAKER-CELTIC GAME

In the days leading up to Game 1 of the NBA Finals, Pat Riley watched them all. It was fun. It was awful. He felt the joy. He felt the pain. "I don't think there's any doubt that we gained strength from what happened to us last year," he said. "But, hey, that was the past. I don't think last year will have anything to do with the outcome of this one. This is the present. Let's enjoy it for what it is."

The Lakers enjoyed it—for three minutes. That was how long, more or less, they were competitive in the series opener, a 148–114 Celtics rout at the Boston Garden on May 27 that came to be known as the Memorial Day Massacre. The 34-point margin of victory was the second-greatest in championship play history, behind only the Washington Bullets' 117–82 defeat of the Seattle SuperSonics in 1978. The Celtics set multiple finals series records, including most total points, most points in a half (79), largest lead at halftime (30 points, 79–49) and field goal accuracy for a game (61 percent). "I've never seen a team—except ours at times—shoot from the perimeter like that," Riley said. "They came out on all cylinders for this first game." Scott Wedman, a forgettable reserve, made all eleven of his shots. ("Who the fuck is Scott Wedman?" Riley screamed in a film session the next day.) McHale scored 26 on 10-for-16 shooting. "In my mind, I couldn't imagine any way we'd be able to beat Boston after that," said Gary Vitti, the team's trainer. "They were *that* superior."

Following the game, the Lakers slunk back into the locker room, shocked, crushed, hurt, humiliated. Generally, this was a moment for either Riley or Johnson to stand up and talk away the wounds. Instead, it was Abdul-Jabbar, jersey drenched in sweat, goggles wrapped atop his forehead, who cleared his throat. He had just completed one of the worst performances of his career—a 12-point, 3-rebound embarrassment that was greeted with ridicule by the crowd. Though he hadn't told anyone, his head was once again pounding. "I want to apologize to all of you," he said, staring toward the floor. "I had migraines and I played like garbage. But I won't play like that anymore. We're going to win this thing.

"I promise," he said, "we are going to win this thing."

His teammates were stunned.

"It was like E. F. Hutton—no one said a word," said Spriggs. "To hear that from Cap was very powerful. When he spoke, the words had great meaning."

If Celtic fans were already fitting themselves for Back-to-Back shamrock T-shirts, members of the team were decidedly less presumptuous. Yes, it was a glorious win. But the Lakers were too good to meekly vanish into the night. "It's definitely time to back off [trash talking]," Maxwell said. "It's not like backgammon or cribbage, where if you beat someone bad enough, you get two wins."

The second game was scheduled for three days later, and as the Lakers boarded the bus to take them from the Marriott Copley Place to the Garden, players couldn't believe what they were witnessing. Abdul-Jabbar entered the vehicle followed by Ferdinand Lewis Alcindor Sr.—his father. Under Riley's strict rules, no relatives were permitted to ride with the team. Ever. Yet when the coach saw Alcindor, he greeted him with a warm handshake. "Kareem's father was a metro cop in New York," said Vitti. "He went into the tunnel, on the train tracks, chasing an armed man. Alone, he went in there. I don't know about you, but that takes balls. For the rats, I wouldn't go in there—let alone after an armed suspect. Not a word was spoken. Not one word on that. Kareem's father didn't say a word; just his presence said something."

When the Lakers arrived at the arena, Riley skipped his usual pre-game strategy session for simpler sentiment. Inspired by Abdul-Jabbar, the coach talked about his own dad, Leon Francis Riley, and how the final words he'd ever spoken to his son still resonated. It was on June 26, 1970—Pat's wedding day. As Leon was leaving the reception, he turned to his son. "He told me that, at some point, you've got to plant your feet, stand your ground and kick somebody's ass," Riley said to his players. "He was right." (Leon died less than three months later.)

"When he spoke of fathers and voices," Cooper said, "the score was already five to nothing for us before the start. That was appropriate. It was subtle. It was dramatic. It was true."

Having endured Boston Garden's 105-degree visitors' locker room the previous June, Vitti special-ordered two portable cooling units, called MovinCool, which the Los Angeles Raiders had used on the sidelines during particularly hot games. "George Anderson, the Raiders trainer, gave me the number for these guys, and it turned out they were huge Laker fans," said Vitti. "They agreed to bring their product to Boston in exchange for two tickets." With unbridled glee, Vitti plugged the MovinCools into the socket, then watched as a blown circuit took out half the building's power. "Boston-piece-of-shit-Garden," said Vitti. "Shithole probably had fuses instead of circuit breakers. The building complained that we were using too much power, and I told them to go to hell. That felt great. And, for the first time in forever, our locker room was cool and comfortable."

In one of the most striking turnarounds of the season, Abdul-Jabbar—DOA three days earlier—tallied 30 points, 17 rebounds, 8 assists and 3 blocks in a 109–102 Los Angeles win. For the first time in years, Abdul-Jabbar was the team's emotional centerpiece. He was tired of the trash talk and fed up with Parish's physicality. From the bench, Spriggs, McGee and Kupchak couldn't believe what they were witnessing. "You see him swinging the left skyhook and the right skyhook, and he kept going wider and wider with it," said Spriggs. "That's how intense he was. It wasn't just in the paint. It was truly like art. We were pointing to him on the floor and he was screaming back, saying, 'See, I told you!' He was just so excited. He was like, 'Yeah! Yeah!' Seeing all those emotions coming from Cap, it was a treat. Because Earvin was usually the spokesperson. To see that from Cap . . . He said he was gonna do it and he did it."

After the game ended, Rosenfeld brought Abdul-Jabbar back from the locker room to conduct an on-court interview. As he waited, fans taunted him with shouts of "Lew! Lew!"—his former name. "It was the one thing that pissed him off," said Rosenfeld. "He hated that." Moments earlier, Rosenfeld had been handed a wet towel by Rambis. Overcome by the moment, he threw it at the fans. "Just emotion," he said. "It wasn't at anyone in particular."

When Rosenfeld returned to the locker room, he was high-fived by Johnson, Cooper and Worthy. "Nice going!" Cooper said. "You've earned your playoff share."

"What'd I do?" Rosenfeld asked.

"When you threw the towel, you hit Robert Parish's wife in the face," Cooper said. "M. L. Carr was here, all pissed. Nice fucking job, man. Nice going."

The Celtics were incensed. So was Riley, who hated off-the-court distractions interfering with his game planning. "How are you going to manage this?" he asked.

Rosenfeld promptly wrote an apologetic letter to Parish, and planned on having it handed to the Boston center. However, when Rosenfeld found himself at the Celtics' workout before Game 3 at the Forum, he decided to take care of it himself. When Parish entered the building, Rosenfeld quietly tapped his shoulder and said, "Robert, can I talk to you for a minute?" Because TV cameras had gathered around, the two walked ten rows into the stands where they could be alone. "Look, Robert," he said, "I wrote you this letter because I want to apologize to you. I didn't know that was your wife, and it was totally out of character for me to do." For three or four minutes, Rosenfeld blathered on about how awful he felt, how he'd gladly speak directly to Nancy, how it was the lowest point of his career. His voice cracked. His hands were shaking. Parish, nicknamed Chief after the uncommunicative Native American in *One Flew Over the Cuckoo's Nest*, said nothing.

"Are you mad at me?" Rosenfeld asked.

Parish, who had yet to utter a word, smiled. "Not at all," he said. "I've been telling that bitch to keep her mouth shut for ten years, and you're the first guy to finally get her to do it."

They shook hands.

■ ■ ■

The Lakers dominated Game 3, 136–111, but the Celtics tied the series when Bird scored eight straight fourth-quarter points, then later passed to Dennis Johnson for the winning jumper in a 107–105 Game 4 squeaker. For a spell, it appeared that one of the great series in NBA history was being trumped by an even better one a year later. These were two equal teams, going back and forth like perfectly matched pugilists in the center of a ring. K. C. Jones, Boston's coach, rightly compared the organizations to middleweights Marvin Hagler and Tommy Hearns, who had recently staged one of the most memorable fights in boxing history.

This was, it seemed, anyone's series to take.

And then it wasn't.

David Stern, the NBA commissioner, warned both teams that they needed to cut back on the sharp elbows and sharper words, but only Boston seemed to comply. Riley unleashed his two goons—Rambis and Mitch Kupchak—on the Celtics, insisting they could change the series without scoring a single point. In a 120–111 Game 5 win, the two combined for 38 minutes, 11 points, 13 rebounds and 3 fouls. Kupchak was now a sad copy of his old self—bad knee, no mobility, couldn't jump over a quarter. But he was stubbornly physical. "It was about setting a tone," said Rambis. "That was our job."

"No fear, no backing down," said Kupchak. "Just hard nosed."

Wrote Thomas Bonk in the *Los Angeles Times*:

Rambis is generally viewed in Laker circles as Clark Kent, but in Celtic broadcaster Johnny Most's eyes as a bespectacled rat. Whether Rambis emerged from a phone booth or from a sewer, as Most suggested, the 6-8 Laker forward still managed to lug home nine rebounds in 27 minutes and inspire the Lakers to switch from white collars to blue.

Two days later, on the parquet court of Boston Garden, before 14,890 agitated fans, the Lakers pummeled the Celtics, 111–100, finally beating their tormenters and exorcising the ghosts of a lopsided rivalry. "That was the greatest day of my basketball life," said Bertka, the assistant coach. "I sat there and prayed to God, 'Somehow help us win this game. Somehow get us past these guys. . . .'"

Abdul-Jabbar scored 29 points to be named the unanimous series MVP, and his marvelous all-around play capped the signature series of his career in Los Angeles. The victory, however, was more a gift from the Celtics than a Lakers masterpiece. Though Boston's starters wore the familiar green-and-white uniforms, they played an undisciplined, unskilled game. Guards Dennis Johnson and Danny Ainge combined to shoot 6-for-31 from the field and Bird—damned by floating bone chips in his right elbow and a jammed right index finger—misfired on 17 of his 29 attempts, scoring a poor man's 28. Many of those shots were taken with his left hand (Bird is right-handed), and the hometown crowd often watched in bewildered resignation. "I thought I could carry this team, but today I was just out there," he said afterward. "I'm the type of guy who is supposed to bring us through. And I failed.

"When you lose, you're a failure. Your goal is to win a championship, and if you don't win it, you're a failure. Today, we played like a bunch of guys who failed." As he wrapped up the Q&A session with the media, a Celtics' aide offered to get Bird's car for him.

"I'm in a Jeep," he sighed. "That's all you can afford when you're a loser."

As Los Angeles's players stormed the locker room, champagne burst from dozens of bottles, leaving a sticky-sweet layer of foam on the concrete floor. Four members of the Lakers (Abdul-Jabbar, Cooper, Johnson, Wilkes) took part in the finals triumphs over Philadelphia, and they had been under the impression that basketball victory could be no better. Here, however, inside Boston's awful locker room, it was better. "*So* much better," said Cooper. "It's one thing to win. It's another thing to beat Boston for the first time, and to kill off a demon. That was the best. It wasn't just about us. It was about history."

Ronnie Lester, a seldom-used guard who largely kept to himself, sat on a stool and observed the celebration. He watched the expressions cross his teammates' faces, and found it interesting how the looks weren't merely ones of euphoria. Sure, they were gleeful and thankful, he noted. "But also relieved," he said. "For Earvin, Kareem, James, that was the number one feeling.

"Happy relief."

CHAPTER 13

VIRGINAL

If one were in with the Los Angeles Lakers after the 1985 championship season, he/she had an opportunity to party at two of the hottest spots in America.

The mansion belonging to Jerry Buss.

The mansion belonging to Magic Johnson.

The two abodes, located mere miles apart, came complete with swimming pools, hot tubs, bars, home theatres, expansive kitchens, enormous yards and hosts who embraced—in no particular order—women with large breasts, women with long legs, women with gymnastlike flexibility, women in their twenties and women with a proclivity for sex.

Buss resided in Pickfair, the Beverly Hills mansion Mary Pickford and Douglas Fairbanks chose as a home after the two cinematic idols married in 1920. It had been the first private property in the Los Angeles area to include a swimming pool. Throughout the 1920s, dinners at Pickfair became the stuff of Hollywood legend. Among those who attended were Amelia Earhart, Charlie Chaplin, Rudolf Valentino and George Bernard Shaw. However, when Fairbanks (who destroyed his marriage by having an affair with Lady Sylvia Ashley) and Pickford divorced in 1936, the magic vanished. Pickford remained in the home but lost herself to alcoholism and depression. She let the place fall into disrepair, and, by the time she died in 1979, Pickfair was a dump.

Buss, however, believed in the power of Hollywood Past. In September

1980, he paid $5,362,500 for the estate, and shortly thereafter brought his daughter, Jeanie, to 1143 Summit Drive in the San Ysidro Canyon for a look-see. "It wasn't good," she said. "I thought we were just visiting, so I took a picture in every room. I didn't know he was about to buy it, but my dad believed in the fantasy. He loved movie stars and entertainment, and to him, Pickfair was perfect."

Before long, Buss transformed the twenty-two-room home into a magnificent ode to classic décor meets 1980s adventurism. His dinner parties were fantastic. His guest list was magnificent. Buss thought of Pickfair as a souped-up Playboy Mansion. "Jerry was a night owl," said John Rockwell, an actor who befriended the Laker owner. "He spent a lot of time at night in Pickfair, playing poker, drinking rum and Cokes. One time I had to drag him from Pickfair to the Forum for a game. He never wanted to leave that place."

"I'm no prince of a guy, but with Jerry and Pickfair it was like, 'Really? You're fiftysomething and still dating twenty-year-olds?'" said Scott Carmichael, who worked for the Los Angeles Kings at the time. "He had Playmates coming in and out, these twenty-five-year-old bimbo girlfriends coming in and out. He was very into stars and stardom."

Buss hungered for adventure. When Charline Kenney, his longtime assistant, once called at nine A.M., he groggily replied, "Charline, calling me at nine is like calling me at three A.M." He regularly chartered jets for nights and weekends with his crew in Las Vegas. Every summer he and Lance Davis, a friend, would visit San Diego, drive across the Mexican border and hit Tijuana to watch bullfighting. "Then he'd tell me, 'Lance, they drag that bull out back and make it into tacos,'" Davis said. "So we'd eat tacos. He'd laugh at me—'Lance, you're eating the bull! You're eating the bull!'"

Thanks to Pickfair, the good times came to Buss. On a monthly basis, he allowed different charitable foundations to hold fund raisers on the Pickfair lawn. Though the philanthropic Buss was well intentioned, the events often went deep into the night, a cesspool of alcohol and sex and—on occasion—cocaine. "I went to work for Jerry after I was done playing (in 1983), so sometimes I'd go to Pickfair for parties," said Ron Carter, the former Lakers guard. "I learned quickly I couldn't go and hang with him and still make it to the office the next morning. I got married to get away from Jerry. That wasn't a life I could live."

If the goings-on at Pickfair were wild, the events hosted by Johnson were orgasmic. The star point guard had lived in one of Buss's apartment complexes until 1984, when he purchased his own nine-thousand-square-foot Bel Air mansion. Though not quite as awe-inspiring as Pickfair, Johnson's Tudor home had once belonged to the French consulate, and contained (among other things) an indoor racquetball-basketball court, a sauna, a whirlpool and a disco complete with strobe lights and thousands of records. Alongside the master bedroom was a tiny room with a sunken hot tub and a panoramic view of the canyon his home overlooked. The house also boasted something close to his heart—the greatest stereo system anyone had ever seen. With speakers the size of Cadillacs, the eighteen rooms filled with the sounds of Michael Jackson and Earth, Wind & Fire and Marvin Gaye.

While Johnson didn't host as many shindigs as Buss, the ones that took place were beyond compare. The Lakers point guard neither drank alcohol nor did drugs, but his parties were odes to excess and extravagance. Many Lakers agree the most beautiful women they ever met were encountered at Johnson's. They were models, strippers, actresses, exotic dancers. There was no hotter ticket than an invite to the mansion, but—while Laker players and opponents were almost always allowed—women had to meet certain criteria. First, they had to be gorgeous. Second, they had to be promiscuously dressed. Third, they had to be willing to do . . . things.

Johnson fancied himself not merely an entertainer, but a maestro. "If you ever die and go to heaven, you want heaven to be Magic's house parties," said Frank Brickowski, a future Lakers teammate. "He would have the finest girls in L.A. there. The absolute finest. And at midnight you had to get busy with somebody or you had to get the fuck out. So if you were a guy, at midnight you'd get as close as you could to the hottest possible woman. Magic went around in this freaky voyeuristic way. He'd check on you. He'd go throughout the house, the pool. He'd order people to start doing things. All you had to be was near a chick. There were guys who would yell, 'Magic, she's not getting busy! She's not!' He'd run over and she'd get busy. Celebrity is seductive in L.A. Girls have this desperation about them, like moths to a flame. It's sad. But when you're young and single, fame matters."

Just because one was a Laker didn't mean sexual conquests *always* came easily. Yet Johnson wasn't merely the most eligible bachelor in Los Angeles—he was the most eligible bachelor in California. He once wrote of his rendezvous: "Some were secretaries. Some were lawyers. Quite a few were actresses or models. Others were teachers, editors, accountants, or entrepreneurs. There were bimbos, too, but not that many. Most of these women were college-educated professionals. Some were black, some were white, some were Hispanic, or Asian. Some of these women were very open about what they were doing, and some were more discreet. A few would even brag about all the players they had slept with. For others, this was all a part of a very secret life.

"Most of them were in their mid-twenties. Every now and then you'd come across a teenager, but if you were smart you stayed away from her. These kids were simply too young—not only legally, but emotionally, too."

This was the Sodom and Gomorrah–esque world that greeted A. C. Green.

He was the Lakers' latest first-round pick, a twenty-one-year-old power forward out of Oregon State whose drive and hustle made him, on paper, a perfect fit for a team that specialized in all-out effort. Having wasted his previous top selection on Earl Jones, West (not one to forgive himself) was determined to make sure Los Angeles landed a contributor in the twenty-third spot. Leading up to June 18, 1985, most of the team's scouts and executives were pushing for Terry Porter, a 6-foot-3 guard out of the University of Wisconsin-Stevens Point. Porter had averaged 19.7 points and 5.2 rebounds as a senior, and Gene Tormohlen, the Lakers's top scout, insisted he was a potential star. "I just thought he had the chance to become excellent," said Tormohlen. "He would take the pressure off Earvin, sort of like Norman once did. But Jerry was sold on A.C., and when Jerry's sold on someone . . ."

West liked that Green played without an ego. When the Beavers needed him to score, he scored. When they needed him to rebound, he rebounded. There were hundreds of minutes of Oregon State game tapes inside the Forum offices, and not once did Green appear to mope, whine or talk trash. He was a power forward in the most traditional of models—hammer the boards, block shots, charge ahead, work to the point of exhaustion. "He had no airs about him," said Roger Levasa, an Oregon State football player and close friend. "A.C. wasn't cocky or arrogant or someone who thought being athletic made him special. He just wanted to do well and do the right thing."

There was just one small problem: A. C. Green was a virgin.

By "problem," one means not to imply that avoiding premarital sex is somehow wrong. No, it's just that, on the Lakers, virginity wasn't mocked or ridiculed—it was impossible. From Johnson and Abdul-Jabbar to Michael Cooper and James Worthy, Los Angeles's players came to appreciate the special carnal perk of being a member of basketball's elite team. There was sex to be had, and more sex to be had. There were strip clubs to be visited, prostitutes to call, groupie fantasies to fulfill.

Virginity? Virginity was for priests.

Even before Green reported to the team, players shared among themselves his off-the-court scouting report.

- Never curses.
- Has the world's moistest Jheri curl.
- Knows every page of the Bible by heart.
- Has probably never kissed a girl (who wasn't a relative).

In particular, they laughed over an incident that took place his sophomore year at Oregon State, when Green entered the student bookstore and was aghast to see copies of *Playboy* being sold alongside *Time* and *Sports Illustrated*. When the manager refused his request to move the magazines elsewhere, Green led a protest, encouraging students to shop at the nearby Circle K. "Then I went to the Circle K, and they sold the same pornography," he said. "So I protested them, too." Before long, Green and several other Oregon State students generated national attention, and he spoke openly about his decision to remain celibate until marriage. When the Beavers traveled to Arizona State, Green stepped to the free-throw line and was greeted by fans, situated behind the basket, waving posters of bikini-clad girls. "It was funny," Green said. "Really, that was as bad as it got."

Until he arrived in Los Angeles. Upon joining the team, all rookies were required to partake in a training camp ritual known as the Buck a Rome Show—an evening when each newcomer had to sing and perform skits for the veterans, coaches and executives. When Green was called to the front of the room, Johnson shouted out, "Sing your fight song!"

Green didn't know the words to "Hail to Old OSU."

"Well," said Johnson, "give us 'Billie Jean.'"

"Billie what?" said Green.

"'Billie Jean' by Michael Jackson," Johnson replied with disbelief.

"I don't know that one either," Green said, his voice drowned out by cackles.

Johnson ran off a series of singers: Prince. Phil Collins. Aretha Franklin. James Brown. New Edition. Chicago.

Nothing.

"Look, rookie, you're singing," Johnson said. "You have no choice."

"Well," said Green, "name a gospel song. . . ."

Silence.

More silence.

More silence.

Finally, James Worthy, the quietest Laker, piped up from the rear. "Sing 'Swing Low, Sweet Chariot!'" he said.

"Uh . . ." said Green.

"Sing it!"

"Sing it!"

"So I did," said Green. "Not well, but well enough. That broke me through and gave me my first real connection with the team. Not that they went easy on me."

In what had been one of the busier off-seasons in recent team history, West let Jamaal Wilkes and Bob McAdoo depart. Though both men were past their primes, the moves were unpopular with players, and left Green in the uncomfortable role as replacement to legends. Was it his fault? No more so than it had been Scott's when he was traded for Norm Nixon. Yet the Laker mainstays were upset that two trusted hands were gone, and the virgin was here. "They knew I wasn't the normal rookie," Green said. "So they tested me."

The team opened with a two-game Texas road swing at San Antonio and Dallas, and Johnson and Co. wasted little time. While taking the bus from the San Antonio International Airport to the hotel, the Laker star yelled toward Green, "Rook, we haven't figured you out yet, but we're going to take a bet."

"What sort of bet?" the rookie asked.

"Once you start seeing these girls around the NBA," he said, "you won't be thinking any of that Christian and God stuff."

"Really?" said Green. "You think so?"

Johnson liked the newcomer's confidence. He also laughed at it. The NBA was the land of long legs and quick bangs. Few could resist its charms. "We'll give you two months, and you'll be done," he said. "Two months." Johnson removed the baseball cap from his head and passed it around, urging his teammates to plunk down some money. By the time the hat returned to its owner, Green was staring at nearly three hundred dollars in crumpled

bills. "You don't get laid once in two months, the money's yours," said Johnson. "But there's no fucking way. . . ."

Less than a month later, the Lakers were in Portland to face the Blazers.
Green, who was reared in the city, scored 11 points in twenty seven minutes
of action ("I played lousy," he said), and afterward stood outside the locker
room, chatting away with a striking young woman. "I saw all the guys sorta
looking over, wondering what was going on," Green recalled. "Finally
someone comes over and says, 'Hey, rookie, who is this?'"

Green smiled. "Oh, meet Vanessa," he said. "My sister."

The Lakers came to appreciate Green. It took time, however. Coming
out of college, he viewed it as his job (really, his obligation) to guide wayward souls toward Jesus. The NBA was important, but eternal salvation took
precedence. A conversation with the rookie over basketball or movies or
chicken and rice inevitably involved Christ and salvation and the Holy Spirit.
It grew tiresome—not merely because most of his teammates were living
sinful lives, but because Green was a broken record. "I had to adjust—they
were right," Green said. "Some of the guys talked to me. They said they admired my faith, but didn't need to hear about it all the time. I could understand that. It was a lesson for me."

Coming off of yet another championship season, 1985 was also a lesson
for Jerry West, whose personnel genius was put to the test. Ever since Kurt
Rambis joined the team in 1981, there had been calls from fans and the media for his benching. Rambis was too slow, too unathletic, too clunky, too
mechanical. When Worthy was drafted, it was presumed Rambis would be
gone. No. When Green was drafted, he was hailed as the new starting power
forward. No. West understood Rambis's value—the rebounding, the toughness, the quick inbounds passing. But he, too, felt there *had* to be an upgrade.

Enter: The Great Maurice Lucas Blunder.

On August 19, 1985, two months before the season opened, West sent
two future second-round picks to Phoenix for Lucas, the thirty-three-year-
old power forward who boasted one of the league's best (and most appropriate) nicknames—the Enforcer. There were pretty tough guys in the NBA
and really tough guys in the NBA. But nobody's toughness matched Lucas's,
whose two primary claims to fame came from once dropping 7-foot-2 center Artis Gilmore with a two-punch combo and, in Game 2 of the 1977
NBA Finals, popping 76ers center Darryl Dawkins with a roundhouse to the
rear of his skull. If one were a teammate, he thanked the lord for Lucas, who

was as much power forward as bodyguard. However, opponents feared him. "He had to psych himself up to be that tough guy and be the enforcer," said Lionel Hollins, a Portland teammate. "He always took care of me. On the court, I never had to worry about someone hurting me or trying to hurt me. I knew Luke was behind me."

The Lakers greeted Lucas warily—because he had probably delivered a hundred blows to Abdul-Jabbar's kidneys, and because they knew he was there to supplant the beloved Rambis. "It was a bad idea from the very start," said Gary Vitti, the trainer. "We were a team with great chemistry, and we brought in very bad chemistry." The Laker players expected newcomers to tread softly and feel things out. Lucas, however, stomped around with the air of a Hall of Famer. During an early-season players-only locker room meeting, Johnson threw out a question for teammates. Abdul-Jabbar answered, then Cooper answered, then Lucas started to answer. "No, no—shut the fuck up," Johnson said. "Nobody asked you yet."

The room grew silent, and Lucas stormed out. Shortly thereafter, while waiting in an American Airlines terminal, Vitti, who doubled as the team's traveling secretary, handed Lucas his boarding pass (the team still traveled commercial). The forward stepped onto the airplane, but returned five minutes later. "You gave me the wrong seat," he said. Vitti looked at the ticket— "Uh, no. It's the right seat," he said.

"But that's a coach seat," Lucas said.

"I know," Vitti responded. "You're in coach today."

"But I've got seniority," Lucas said. "I've got seniority."

Under the contract negotiated by the players union, seating priority was designated by experience. Scott, Cooper and Johnson were all placed in first class, despite having significantly less NBA time. "Well, it depends what kind of seniority you're referring to," Vitti said. "We have Animal Farm seniority on the Lakers."

Animal Farm seniority? Lucas marched toward Riley, who was standing a couple of feet away. Though he and West were generally in agreement on personnel moves, Riley hedged on the Lucas addition. He didn't want him and didn't need him and didn't particularly like him. Now Lucas was inches from his face, demanding a first-class seat. "Are you fucking kidding me?" Riley said. "Get on the plane."

"But I've got seniority!" Lucas said. "I've got seniority!"

Soon, dozens of travelers were watching as Riley and Lucas exchanged curses and accusations. "Maurice, we have great chemistry on this team," Riley said. "Are you going to be the guy who messes it up?"

"But I have seniority," he replied.

"Maurice," Riley said. "Everybody on this team makes sacrifices. Again—are you going to be the guy who ruins it?"

"But . . . I have seniority," Lucas said.

"Pat's starting to turn red," Vitti said, "and the carotid artery is popping out of his neck. They're going at it, and it's getting really heated. They're volleying back and forth, and nobody's cracking." Finally, after five minutes, Lucas snatched his boarding pass back from Vitti and screamed, "You haven't heard the end of this!" He filed a complaint with the union, and a representative called Riley with a formal complaint.

"Yeah," the coach replied, "I'll get right on that."

Lucas was an outcast from the very start. He possessed an idealized vision of his abilities that failed to match reality. In Los Angeles, Abdul-Jabbar was the first offensive option, Worthy the second, Johnson the third, Scott the fourth. "They were running no plays for Kurt or A.C., and both those guys were accepting of it," said Vitti. "But not Maurice Lucas. He thought he should have been the second or third option. So when the ball would go to him, he was going to shoot it. This didn't make the other guys happy." Lucas had averaged 14.6 points over his career, including 20.4 for the 1978–79 Blazers. But his range was six feet in, and his limited offensive repertoire had deteriorated. In a game against Phoenix on December 12, Lucas went on a rare roll, scoring 17 points in twenty-two minutes against his former team. Midway through the third quarter, however, Johnson glared disgustedly toward the shot-happy Lucas and signaled for a twenty-second time-out. "What's going on?" Riley said to Vitti. "Is somebody hurt?" Vitti shrugged. The players approached the bench, and Johnson looked Riley in the eye. "I can't play with this motherfucker," he said, pointing at Lucas. "Get him out of the fucking game."

Lucas was pulled. "That was pretty much it for Maurice," said Vitti. "Any respect was gone."

It would be a stretch to suggest Los Angeles failed to repeat as NBA champions because of Lucas's presence. It would not, however, be altogether preposterous. Though the team finished 62-20 during the regular season, the chemistry was damaged. Rambis felt slighted by Lucas's temporary as-

Though the NBA has seen its fair share of center-guard tandems, few—if any—have matched the production and entertainment value of Kareem Abdul-Jabbar and Earvin (Magic) Johnson.

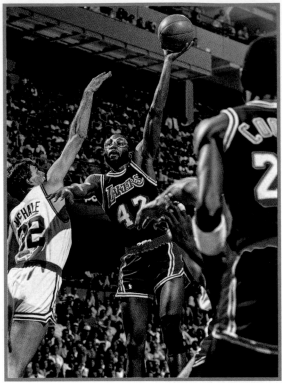

The No. 1 pick in the 1982 NBA Draft, James Worthy overcame early struggles to become a centerpiece of the Showtime dynasty. His long arms and deadly low-post moves made him nearly impossible to guard.

Lipofsky Basketballphoto.com

A largely ignored prospect out of New Mexico, Michael Cooper (here with Bill Bertka, an assistant coach) emerged as the Lakers' defensive stopper, as well as a deadly three-point shooter.

The Lakers thrived with Norm Nixon in the backcourt, but his unease with surrendering control of the team to Magic Johnson ultimately resulted in a blockbuster trade that sent him to the Clippers for Byron Scott.

A rugged kid from Inglewood (here passing to Magic Johnson against the Celts), Scott opened the floor with his long-distance shooting.

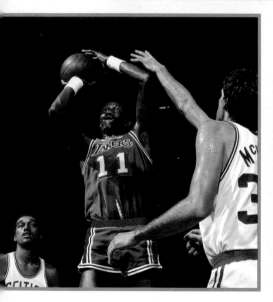

Although Magic Johnson and Kareem Abdul-Jabbar received much of the attention, the Lakers would not have owned the 1980s without the low-post contributions of Kurt Rambis (top), Bob McAdoo (above), and A. C. Green (right). Rambis reveled in taking supplies from the locker room, Green was America's most famous virgin, and McAdoo believed he could beat anyone in anything.

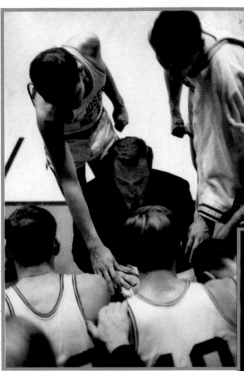

Forgotten by most Laker fans, Jack McKinney (left) designed a coaching blueprint that proved the cornerstone of Showtime. Paul Westhead (below) took over after McKinney's bike accident and led the Lakers to the 1980 title. Pat Riley (bottom left) was both a coaching genius and a fashion icon during his time at the Forum.

Wes Matthews joined the Lakers as a lightly regarded backup guard—but earned his teammates' respect with his feisty play and toughness.

Acquired by the Lakers before the 1979–80 season, Spencer Haywood was thought to be the answer to the Lakers' power forward prayers. Instead, drug abuse ruined him.

Mark Landsberger was a useful low-post player who infuriated teammates by telling his wife the details of the Lakers' away-from-home, off-the-court activities.

Life was but a dream for the Laker players, who celebrated on the Boston Garden court after downing the Celtics in game 6 of the 1985 championship series.

Life wasn't always but a dream for the Laker wives, who were asked to cook, clean, raise the children, and turn a blind eye to off-court activities. Here, from left, Angela Worthy, Christine Vitti, Anita Scott, Wanda Cooper, Linda Rambis, and Chris Riley (sitting) enjoy time together.

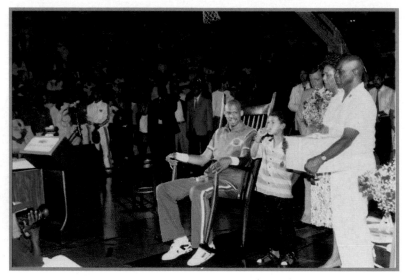

The Lakers bid farewell to Kareem Abdul-Jabbar with a rocking chair (and myriad other gifts) before the April 23, 1989, regular season finale against Seattle. Abdul-Jabbar retired as the NBA's all-time leading scorer but was a shell of his former self during the final year.

cension, and Green wasn't ready to play a prime role. McAdoo—confident, boastful, hilarious—was terribly missed. "Those years with McAdoo, that team was awfully close," said Johnson. "We were all so tough-minded. We would go on the road and just say, 'OK, how many games we got?' We'd see there were six. 'We're gonna win all six.' And then we'd go and win all six. We would push each other to make sure. Coop would be on me. I would be on Coop. Or we could get on one another. That was the respect we had for one another. That was the sign of a true championship team, that we could get on one another."

There was the additional matter of Riley. When the coach took over for Westhead, he was a humble listener who sought the team's input. However, by 1986 he was morphing into a one-man marketing machine. Riley charged ten thousand dollars per motivational speech and had clothing companies knocking down his door. He was rarely named the NBA's Coach of the Month, but not because he was unworthy. The award was sponsored by Farah pants, and Riley refused to pose in such pedestrian duds (as the recipient was asked to do). He was dashing and handsome and smooth and intelligent—and more than happy to share that information with anyone who asked.

Like Westhead before him, Riley began to start viewing himself as a genius, which was funny to those who realized 70 percent of his basketball strategy came from the pages of Jack McKinney. Whereas once he was agreeable and open, he turned suspicious and grouchy. Riley used to be a beat writer's best friend, happily sitting down over beers and wings to explain strategy, personnel, Xs and Os. Now, though, he insisted his men be wary of interview requests. He viewed all non-players and coaches as suspicious interlopers, and questioned the loyalty of many. "You were either with Pat or against Pat," said one employee. "That's how he saw it."

Riley was particularly cruel to Josh Rosenfeld, the team's nebbishy media relations director. Now in his fourth season with the franchise, Rosenfeld could often be found alone in his office at all hours of the morning and night. He was the ultimate workaholic. "My life was the Lakers," he said. "Nothing else." Yet Riley seemed to take a bully's delight in abusing the little guy. "I was a peripheral opponent," Rosenfeld said. "He told me once, 'If a bus is scheduled to leave at eleven, you had better be there at ten forty-five, because I'm never going to hold it for you. If all twelve guys are on the bus, we're leaving.' It was Pat. My feeling was, whatever Pat was doing was working. So even if I didn't see the value to it—if he thought it was important, it was important."

Riley worked Rosenfeld to the bone, even when tasks had nothing to do with the press. Generally, those in Rosenfeld's shoes attended team practices but paid little attention to the on-court details. "Pat didn't allow me to read a newspaper at practice," he said. "He'd say, 'If you're gonna be at practice, you're going to be attentive and you're going to watch.'" Occasionally, if he wasn't involved in a drill, Johnson would sit down alongside Rosenfeld to chat. "Oh, Pat would get pissed," Rosenfeld said. "But never at Magic—just at me."

On February 20, 1986, the Lakers were in New Jersey for a game against the Nets. Worthy was out with an injury, and during the morning shoot-around, Bill Bertka, the assistant coach, needed an extra body for a three-on-three drill. "Josh!" he called. "Get over here." Rosenfeld, Rambis and Kupchak proceeded to somehow thump Abdul-Jabbar, Lucas and Larry Spriggs. "Just thrilling," Rosenfeld said. "It's probably my greatest sporting accomplishment, because I actually made a couple of shots." Five days later, the team was in Dallas, and again Bertka required an extra player. "I get out there, and guys are kind of goofing around, Spriggs is trying to block my shot," Rosenfeld said. "And Riley stops the practice and screams, 'What the hell are you doing out there?' I look over at Berkta, and he has his back turned to me and is walking away. He wants no part of it. I said, 'Pat, you needed an extra guy.' He says, 'Get the hell off the court.' I get off the court and he says, 'Get off the bench.' I go two or three rows into the stands and he says, 'Get the hell out of the gym.' Now I've got to go out. All the writers are waiting there to do interviews, and I'm banished. It was embarrassing."

"At times Pat was a great guy, and at times he could be a big douchebag," said Richard Crasnick, the team's director of promotions. "One time the Lakers were practicing, and Pat had me close the curtains so the other team—the Mavericks—couldn't watch. I closed them, but not enough for him. He started screaming at me—'Why the hell are they still opened?' I had to, literally, get duct tape and tape them closed. Dick Motta was the Mavs coach at the time, and he sees the curtains and says, 'What the fuck is this?' Pat looked at me like it was my fault."

There was also the matter of Riley's wife, Chris, a psychologist who attached herself to the Laker spouses. Whenever Wanda Cooper and Linda

Rambis and Angela Worthy and the other women gathered for events, Chris would attend and, sometimes, organize. She was, by most accounts, friendly—but also a lieutenant in the Pat Riley brigade. Chris Riley insisted the best way the women could help Los Angeles win a title was by mindlessly going along with everything her husband said. Resistence was futile. "We bought into it," said Linda Rambis. "We made a pact that we, the wives, would do everything we could to help the team. So Kurt would never wake up with the kids in the middle of the night, because he needed sleep. I was OK with that—we had a cause." If that cause translated into staying away from the Forum and preparing warm meals and sitting by as their husbands fondled stewardesses, hey, so be it. The number of Laker players who didn't fool around on their wives: "Probably one—A. C. Green," joked a spouse. "And he was an unmarried virgin."

There was a Stepford-like approach to it all, a mindless adherence to rules and regulations set forth by the Rileys. "It took me a while to figure those two out," said Claire Rothman, the Lakers vice president of booking. "And then I got it. Pat would, in a way, be the pleasant one, and then Chris would say what he wanted to say. And I really disliked that. She would come into the offices and say, 'You know, if you would play different music during the game, we wouldn't lose.' And I'd say, 'Uh, Chris, I have nothing to do with the music. That's someone else.' That wasn't the right answer for her—ever. 'Well,' she'd say, 'something should be done.' Truth is, that was Pat speaking through her. They were kind of a team."

Chris Riley wound up handing Richard Krasnick, the team's promotions director, a song list that needed to be played during time-outs. Krasnick paid it no mind. Chris Riley handed him another list. Krasnick again paid it no mind. Chris Riley handed him another list. This time, Krasnick asked Jerry West what he should do. A meeting was held, ideas were tossed around. A week later, West returned with advice. "Ignore her," he said. "Just ignore her."

What saved Pat Riley was that he had emerged as one of the NBA's elite coaches. Even with Lucas's damaging presence and with Abdul-Jabbar, now thirty-eight, rebounding like a big shooting guard (6.1 per game), and with moments of desperation creeping forth (at one point, center Petur Gudmundsson, a borderline pro but the pride of Reykjavik, Iceland, received key minutes), the Lakers still won the Pacific Division by *22 games* over Portland. In an strange twist, Riley did his best work in the midst of the team's worst stretch of the season. On January 15, McAdoo—a free agent just waiting to be signed—was presented an offer sheet by the Philadelphia 76ers. He officially joined the team two weeks later. News of the transaction crushed many Lakers players who had hoped, with Lucas's poutiness and poor play, West would somehow be persuaded to bring McAdoo back into the fold. What ensued (coincidentally or not) was an awful string during which the team dropped nine of nineteen contests. The bottom seemed to fall out on the night of January 24, when the Clippers—in their second season in Los Angeles after moving up the coast—embarrassed the Lakers, 120–109, at the Sports Arena. In the team's defense, Johnson and Rambis were sidelined with minor injuries. But . . . *the Clippers?* Since the relocation, the Lakers had gone 9-0 vs. their neighbors. "We'd always get really pumped up to play the Lakers, though they probably could care less about playing us," said Kurt Nimphius, the forward who scored 19 for the Clippers that night. "On those rare nights we beat them, it felt like Christmas."

One night later, the Lakers again fell to an inferior opponent, the Denver Nuggets, and followed up with scattered setbacks to the Knicks and Warriors—awful teams with losing records.* Finally, after Los Angeles traveled to East Rutherford, New Jersey, only to endure a 121–106 beating at the hands of the so-so Nets, Riley lost his cool. Following the setback, he bypassed any sort of post-game speech or interviews and took a shower. Players and coaches boarded a bus for the two-and-a-half-hour drive to Philadelphia. Riley remained quiet the entire journey. Not one word was spoken.

His message was clear—*I'm pissed. Now stop playing like the Manhattanville College women's team.* If that were not enough, he decided to bench Scott, the Lakers' best outside marksman, for twelve games. The third-year guard was actually playing well, averaging 15.4 points on 51 percent shooting, but he infuriated Riley by marrying his girlfriend, Anita, on February 8 in Las Vegas during the All-Star break. Along with reporters and hangers-on, the coach filed such events under the "peripheral distraction" category. Instead of sending Scott some nice wineglasses or a bread maker, he punished him by inserting McGee into the lineup. "Pat was both really smart and a little

---

* Against the Warriors on February 11, Riley was ejected from a game for the first time in his career. "There's no popcorn in the locker room, no beer or anything," he said afterward. "It's lousy."

paranoid," said Anita Scott. "Actually, not paranoid—overprotective. He wanted to limit distractions."

The Scott benching marked the official kick-off of a new love-hate relationship between Riley and his players and, for the coach, it was brilliant. When he was first hired, Riley sought to foster friendships. However, he came to understand that great coaches were not great friends. Vince Lombardi wasn't doing shots with Bart Starr. Joe McCarthy and Joe DiMaggio didn't attend Broadway shows together. Riley had always recoiled at Adolph Rupp's harshness at Kentucky, but now he understood. Sometimes, one had to be cold. This was about winning, not community.

So if benching Scott for McGee was what it would take to have the Lakers focus, so be it. "Pat was very smart—very, very smart," said Spriggs. "He understood dynamics, and how people related to situations. He knew what buttons to push. There was an art to it."

Scott returned to the starting lineup in late February, and the team took off. Beginning with a 127–117 win over Golden State on March 3, the Lakers won 9 straight, and 13 of 14. "It's time to start driving for the playoffs," Riley said after the Warrior game. "There are twenty games left, five weeks. Last year we finished 36-6, a forty-two-game drive. We had a purpose. We'd gotten beat in the seventh game of the finals the year before. Our purpose was born of anger. It was born of frustration. We have to kick ourselves to get to that level again. Our purpose is to repeat. Our players can't be satiated because they won the championship the year before.

"We've only had two constructive practices in the last month, because of traveling and all that. But you have to travel and practice. That's what our job is. You can't wait for the playoffs to start. If you wait for the playoffs to come up to you, you might not be ready for the first round. Injuries have been a factor. We wouldn't have had as much trouble without our flurry of injuries the last five weeks. But we've still got to kick ourselves into high gear."

Los Angeles defeated Portland, 120–114, on April 8 for the sixtieth win, and the revival seemed legitimate. Yet even with Riley's motivational manipulations, something wasn't working. The Lakers appeared to be sedated. Or, as Blazers guard Clyde Drexler noted after the game, "They looked like they were bored stiff."

Added Rambis: "We're kind of like a horse that doesn't run until it's behind."

This was hardly an ideal way to enter the playoffs. The team closed out the season with a listless 127–104 loss to the Dallas Mavericks—in the Lakers' defense, Gudmundsson started at center against the Mavs, Cooper at point guard—and in the three days until their first-round playoff opener against San Antonio, Riley presented his men with an offer: Either play outstanding basketball, or drastic changes would ensue.

Los Angeles opened the post-season by sweeping the Spurs in three games, then rolled over Dallas, four games to two, in the Western Conference Semifinals. All along, Riley's greatest concern was the Houston Rockets, the talented, deep number two seed that loomed in the conference finals.

The two teams had met five times during the regular season, with Los Angeles losing only once. Yet Riley genuinely worried about Houston and, specifically, the threat of their two seven-footers, Akeem Olajuwon and Ralph Sampson.

Both West and Riley had been around for years, yet neither had ever seen anything quite like the Rockets' Twin Towers. Olajuwon, just twenty-three and in his second season, averaged 23.5 points, 11.5 rebounds and 3.4 blocks as the center while Sampson, twenty-five, contributed 18.9 points, 11.1 rebounds and 1.6 blocks at power forward. It was as if Bill Fitch, the team's coach, possessed matching Bill Russells. They were powerful, quick, dominant. Against the Lakers, the 7-foot-4 Sampson would guard Abdul-Jabbar, forward Rodney McCray—a defensive standout—would stick Worthy, and Olajuwon knew to roam the middle of the free-throw lane and serve as emergency help for whoever needed it. "Bill had a system that took advantage of both our skills and sort of merged us together," said Sampson. "It wasn't easy, and it was kind of unprecedented."

Throughout the season, Riley had repeatedly insisted that McAdoo's departure was far from a big deal. Now, though, with Olajuwon and Sampson looming, the coach would have surely donated his own salary to have McAdoo back in the purple and gold. He was a man with long arms and a veteran's court smarts and enough savvy to (partially, at least) exploit two young kids. Though Riley had sometimes been loathe to pair Abdul-Jabbar and McAdoo on one court, the duo would have been a suitable antidote to the Twin Tower puzzle. "Could we have used Mac?" said Cooper. "Absolutely. We missed him terribly."

For most of the decade, the Rockets had played Joe Perry to the Lakers' Steven Tyler. They were a model franchise, with high-level stars and deep rosters and sold-out games. Yet, save 1981, they could never get past Los An-geles. "They always had just a little more talent than we did," said Robert Reid, the veteran guard. "It was close—closer than people might think. But they had the edge."

Midway through the season, when Sampson was whining about his re-duced offensive role, Ray Patterson, the Houston general manager, asked the forward whether he wanted to be traded. Patterson told the press of the dis-cussion, but added, "He'll never, ever, ever play for the L.A. fucking Lakers. Ever." Patterson, along with many team executives, found it fishy how the best team in the West always wound up with high draft picks and superstar additions. Yes, the Rockets had landed Sampson and Olajuwon. Not by lop-sided trade, though, but via the draft following two awful seasons.

When the Western Conference Finals opened on May 10 at the Forum, all went as planned. The Lakers won, 119–107, with Abdul-Jabbar abusing Sampson for 31 points. Johnson played his best game of the season, scoring 26 points and making one scintillating pass after another (he compiled 18 assists). At one point, the crowd of 17,505 offered a two-minute standing ovation after he bounced a no-look fireball to a slashing Worthy. Johnson nodded sheepishly to the fans before returning to work.

Afterward, the Rockets' locker room was deathly quiet, and the media pronounced the series a dud. "Out dripped victory," wrote Chris Jenkins in the *San Diego Union-Tribune*, "and the distinct impression that Houston is not long for these playoffs."

"Truth is," said Reid, "we had them right where we wanted them." The Lakers played perfectly in the opener, the Rockets played awfully—and the margin was only 12 points. Were Houston's starting guards, McCray and Lewis Lloyd, going to shoot 6 for 17 again? Was Sampson going to turn the ball over five more times? "It could only get better," said Reid. "I mean, we couldn't play any worse."

Because Sampson was 7-foot-4 and perpetually leaning over Abdul-Jabbar, it was easy to forget that the Rockets' best player was, in fact, Olaju-won, the Nigerian-born Muslim. Save height and hype, he graded higher than Sampson in all areas. Olajuwon was a lovely man with a child's smile, and his laugh filled rooms. Yet on the court, he was downright punishing. In 1982, Abdul-Jabbar asked Lynden Rose, the Lakers' sixth-round draft pick out of the University of Houston, whether the "big African kid" was for real. "Oh, he'll be your heir apparent," said Rose. "He's that good."

The Rockets shocked the Lakers with a 112–102 victory at the Forum in Game 2, and the initial tone of the series never returned. Fitch had pleaded with his team to attack Los Angeles defensively, to stop allowing Abdul-Jabbar to post up on the blocks and to keep Scott from setting up behind the three-point line and to resist Johnson and Worthy and Cooper when they tried penetrating. Even before stepping onto the court, the Lakers were masters of intimidation. Such mojo came with four-straight appearances in the NBA Finals. "Take it back!" demanded Fitch. "Fight for what's yours!"

Led by Olajuwon, who blocked six shots, and Sampson, who blocked five, the Rockets refused to back down. They held Los Angeles to 4 points in the first four minutes. "One time, I think they dropped somebody out of the ceiling on me," said Abdul-Jabbar, who made only 9 of 26 shots and scored 21 points. "It was a tough night." Even Lucas, the Lakers' enforcer, looked like a cockapoo alongside the Twin Towers. Riley inserted him into the game to own the paint. It didn't work. "This gives us a lot of confidence going back to Houston because we can't lose there," Olajuwon said. "We'll do whatever it takes to win."

Over the course of the next three games, Olajuwon emerged from being merely one of the NBA's better young players to part of an elite force. There would be no more grouping him with Sampson as "two of the best," no more flimsy comparisons to peers like Abdul-Jabbar and New York's Patrick Ewing. No, Akeem Olajuwon was uniquely magnificent. He scored 40 and 35 points in back-to-back wins at the Houston Summit, then another 30 in the 114–112 Game 5 clincher at the Forum before a silent sold-out crowd. Though it was Sampson's desperation toss from twelve feet out that clinched the triumph (after Olajuwon had been ejected from the game for fighting with Kupchak late in the fourth quarter), the series belonged to Olajuwon. Abdul-Jabbar covered him, Rambis covered him, Lucas covered him. Even Gudmundsson covered him. The only semi-viable Laker who didn't take a shot was Cooper, the team's elite defender (though a man with the frame of a Gumby doll). "He was just too good," said Rambis. "We never knew which way he was going to turn. He had moves in both directions, up-and-under moves. He was tall, he was long, he would fade away, he would block shots. Just too good."

Not all that long ago, members of the media were talking about the Lakers as one of the great potential dynasties in NBA history. They had won more than 60 games in back-to-back years; had appeared in five of the last seven finals series—winning three of them; had boasted the deepest, most star-studded roster in the league; had featured a deified point guard and a history-making center.

Now, for the first time, Buss and West wondered whether they were headed down the wrong path.

Whether maybe, just maybe, a big change was in order.

CHAPTER 14

WORTHY OF SUPERSTARDOM

Throughout his first four years in Los Angeles, James Worthy often went out of his way to pooh-pooh a city he apparently didn't much care for.

When anyone asked, Worthy insisted he would—without question—ultimately return to North Carolina, where the grass grew tall and the air was clean and simplicity and humility reigned. "People in Los Angeles are a lot freer," he said. "They're good people, but they are different from what I'm accustomed to." James Worthy was anything but a Hollywood guy, the narrative went, and perhaps he even believed it himself. Give the man a hammock, a warm breeze and an ice-cold lemonade—he was happy.

Sort of.

Coming off of the best season of his professional career, Worthy was now a bona fide NBA elite. He had averaged 20 points and 5.2 rebounds for the Lakers, and was voted to start his first All-Star Game. A growing number of companies requested his appearance at events, endorsement opportunities were mounting and a James Worthy sighting was usually accompanied by squeals and shrieks.

Though known to be happily married to Angela Wilder, his college girlfriend and a former University of North Carolina cheerleader, Worthy was also earning a reputation within the Forum as something of a dog. "James was quiet, but—like most of us—he had a dark side, too," said Mark Landsberger, the former forward. "He liked all those women and the titty bars."

Worthy was twenty-five years old and, in Los Angeles, a superstar. Yet not an ordinary superstar. There was something mysterious in James Worthy, something different from the other Lakers. He lacked Magic Johnson's magnetism, and Abdul-Jabbar's stature. He was warm and friendly, but not *overly* warm and friendly. Bruce Newman, a scribe with *Sports Illustrated*, nailed it perfectly when he wrote that Worthy "usually looks kind of sad, and vaguely worried, like a porch-climber who has just heard a dog growl. Worthy has the kind of face you might see in an Ingmar Bergman movie, representing something fairly depressing, or pitiful, or both, with subtitles. It is the kind of face that, were you to turn around suddenly during a funeral service, you might very well find standing at the back of the mortuary, counting the house."

In short, Worthy was impossible to read. Was he happy or sad? Content or jumpy? A hero or a heel? Nobody—not even his teammates—knew for sure.

In the aftermath of the playoff fiasco, however, one thing Jerry Buss did know was that change was in order. Though far from Steinbrennian in his need to punish failure, Buss demanded excellence. And when, for one reason or another, excellence failed to materialize, he sought out reasons and scapegoats.

To the owner's credit, rare were the times he stuck his nose too far into basketball operations. The most memorable occurrence took place in 1979, when—buying into the local hype and thinking ticket sales over skill set—he strongly encouraged Jack Kent Cooke to use the club's second first-round pick (after Johnson) on Brad Holland, the undersize UCLA shooting guard. How did that work out? Holland—blessed with the maneuverability of a suitcase—averaged 2.9 points in 79 career games with Los Angeles. One spot later, the Pistons took Michigan's Phil Hubbard, who enjoyed a productive ten-year career. "Jerry is a genius," said Lon Rosen. "But he screwed up on that one."

Now, Buss appeared ready to screw up on another. Ever since the Lakers' elimination, he had listened intently as Johnson talked up the virtues of Mark Aguirre, Dallas's star forward and his longtime friend. The first overall pick in the 1981 draft, Aguirre came equipped with long arms, powerful hips and a bevy of below-the-basket moves. Like Johnson, Aguirre was a Midwest kid (from Chicago) with a hard edge masquerading behind a bright smile. When the Lakers lost at Boston in the deciding game of the 1984 Finals, it was Aguirre (and Detroit's Isiah Thomas) who consoled a sobbing Johnson in his hotel room. He and Magic weren't simply pals. They were tight.

Hence, in the days before the June 17, 1986, NBA Draft, Buss reached out to Donald Carter, the Mavericks owner, about acquiring Aguirre. The men talked at length and committed themselves to a deal that would involve Worthy relocating from California to Texas. Oddly (but not *really* oddly), Buss purposefully failed to consult with Jerry West, basketball's best general manager. Why? Because if Johnson thought Aguirre would be an upgrade, Buss thought Aguirre would be an upgrade, too. He trusted the point guard's judgment more than anyone else's—including the GM's. So what would have been the point of soliciting West, when—in this case—it mattered not? "Earvin, as the vocal leader of the team, came to me with suggestions all the time and I listened," West wrote. "But he never came to me on this one. My real disappointment, though, was with Jerry, for not talking to me about this and for dealing with Carter directly."

On the day of the draft, both Buss and Carter believed a deal was in place: Worthy to the Mavericks in exchange for Aguirre and the number seven pick, which would be used on Michigan forward Roy Tarpley. When word inevitably reached West, he went berserk. He called Buss and told him the trade was an enormous blunder and that Aguirre—while talented—was a me-first player who would destroy the Lakers' chemistry. (West had recently parted ways with Maurice Lucas for this very reason.) Worthy, he explained, could do twenty different things to help a team win. If Aguirre wasn't receiving the ball and scoring, he was useless. "Jerry and I have kind of developed a lot of rules," Buss later said. "I can speak my mind and tell him exactly who to play, how to draft, what coach we should have, what style of basketball we should have. And after I finish my speech on all of these things, he then tells me how we're really going to do it."

Buss informed West that he and Carter had already finalized the transaction. Had papers been signed? No. Had players been alerted? No. The media? No. "Then," West said, "it's not done." The general manager gave the owner an ultimatum: *If this goes through, I quit.*

Buss caved.

West called Carter and told him the trade was dead. Dallas's owner was understandably irate, but acknowledged there was no recourse. He was stuck with Aguirre and Tarpley.*

---

* Had the trade gone through, the consequences would have been, for the Lakers, cataclysmic. Aguirre was Aguirre—a skilled, selfish player. Tarpley, however, became an NBA casualty tale. He played only 280 games, his career ruined by drug addiction.

Worthy had been at a hotel in Chapel Hill, North Carolina, unable to watch the draft on television, when he began receiving calls from friends. They told him that the commentators were speaking of a Lakers–Mavericks swap that had been "approved by Magic Johnson."

"Hey," Worthy thought, "we're making a trade. . . ."

Then he heard the specifics. "I can't tell you how hurt I was," Worthy said. "I felt like I was really starting to gel with the team and become a full part of things." That same day Frank Brady, a reporter with the *Los Angeles Herald-Examiner*, called, seeking comment. There are right times for journalists to reach out to subjects, and wrong times. This was, for Brady, the *perfect* time. Worthy tended to be an awful interview subject—quiet, deferential, indifferent. "Nice guy," said John Black, the team's media relations director beginning in 1989. "But James was a real pain in the ass to work with." One time, in fact, the two were playing golf at the North Ranch Country Club in Westlake Village, California, when Black stared down a forty-five-foot putt with a ten-foot break. "If you make this," Worthy said, laughing, "I'll do every interview you ask of me for the next year."

"Really?" said Black.

"Really," said Worthy.

Black pulled back his putter, hit the ball and watched it roll closer and closer and . . . *in.* "I fall to the ground, laughing my ass off," said Black. "A couple of months later I asked James to do an interview, and he said, 'No, I'm not doing it.' "

"Putt!" said Black.

Pause.

"Dammit, that fucking putt," said Worthy. "That fucking putt."

"He kept his word and did everything I asked for a year," said Black. "But he hated every minute of it."

In the immediate aftermath of hearing about the trade, Worthy was *itching* to talk. He rambled on to Brady for ten minutes about respect and loyalty and a franchise not appreciating the contributions of a star. He would go to Dallas and make the Lakers pay. Just watch Aguirre try guarding him in the post. Just watch . . .

"I was a young kid and I was really upset," Worthy said. "Then forty-eight hours passed and I realized that's just the way it is. The Lakers didn't have to call me. They could do whatever they wanted.

"I was immature. The first thing I should have done was take a step back and call Jerry West. I didn't have the experience, and the spin caused me to react before checking it out." Plus, the more he considered Dallas, the more accepting he became. Worthy's brother, Danny, lived in the city. His college teammate and friend, Sam Perkins, was on the club, as was one of the game's best young players, shooting guard Rolando Blackman. Dallas had won forty-four games the previous season without him. "We would have been very good," he said. "But . . ."

It never happened.

Johnson spent the next several weeks focused on damage control. Five years earlier, he had insisted to Buss that Paul Westhead be fired, then denied any involvement when—*cough, cough*—Paul Westhead was fired. Now, after telling Buss that Worthy-for-Aguirre was a can't-lose proposition, he told anyone who would listen that Worthy-for-Aguirre was a *can't-win* proposition. "Earvin loved Mark Aguirre, but he loved James as a player," said Rosen. "Winning was the most important thing to him. There's no way he would have wanted that trade."

Nonsense.

Because Johnson was the face of the Lakers, criticism of his behavior from other players was, once again, muted. When the team reported to camp in October, however, he and Worthy sat down for a much-needed discussion. Johnson explained that, admittedly, he wasn't vocally against the trade—but only because Dallas would be surrendering a loaded package. "Plus, he and Mark were really close," said Worthy. "He obviously would have liked playing with his friend." Worthy, meanwhile, apologized for jumping the gun. "I felt betrayed," he said. "But that was no excuse." When pressed by the assembled media, Worthy expressed relief over still wearing a purple-and-gold singlet. But also confusion. "Wilt Chamberlain got traded," he said. "So did Kareem. Why should I be any different? I've always known, sooner or later, some trade talk would come up. But coming this early in my career, especially after I didn't have too bad a year last year, it was a shock. It wasn't even a center involved."

Though Johnson and Worthy were two of the team's three superstars, their off-the-court relationship barely existed. The men liked each other well enough. But they were different personalities with different voices who ran in opposite social circles. When Johnson held one of his famous (or infamous) shindigs, Worthy wasn't an automatic addition to the invite list. "There was tension—anyone could see it," said Frank Brickowski, a reserve forward. "Magic got all the attention, James wanted some of the attention. There was a battle, to some degree, between those two, to be the man."

"We were good teammates," said Worthy. "I was quiet, but I was also stubborn and strong-headed. I had to learn that Magic was in charge, and what he said went. That was great. I mean, he deserved that. But it took adjusting."

This was the major dilemma facing Riley as the Lakers attempted to regain their footing and recapture their championship. He was a coach whose entire philosophy was predicated upon single-minded focus. There could be no distractions. Had two marginal players been in conflict, Riley would have banished one, if not both. But with Johnson and Worthy, he had to hope professionalism would reign. Which it did. "First and foremost, it was about winning," Worthy said. "About another ring."

Although the Worthy-Aguirre swap fell through, the Lakers returned a significantly different roster for the 1986–87 team. Lucas was gone, as were two other bruising forwards—Larry Spriggs (allowed to walk as a free agent) and Mitch Kupchak (retired to the front office). Having long ago tired of his one-dimensional game, West finally jettisoned Mike McGee, sending him to Atlanta for the rights to Billy Thompson, the Louisville forward the Hawks had just selected with the draft's nineteenth pick.

The strangest pickup came on October 13, when the Lakers agreed to terms with Wes Matthews, a free-agent point guard who started forty-six games for San Antonio the previous season.

Beginning with Norm Nixon's departure, West longed for a suitable ball handler to back up Johnson. Ronnie Lester, the former University of Iowa star, had been underwhelming, as had Eddie Jordan, the Rutgers product brought back briefly in 1984.

When Laker players first heard of Matthews' arrival, there were more than a few arched eyebrows. Since being drafted by the Bullets out of Wisconsin in the first round in 1980, he bounced from one franchise to another: Washington to Atlanta to San Diego to Atlanta to Philadelphia to Chicago to San Antonio. The thinking among executives was always the same—great talent, iffy makeup. Matthews was a tough kid from Bridgeport, Connecticut, who (basketball cliché alert) was rescued from the streets by after-school programs at the North End Boys Club and Father Panik Village. Though he now traveled from one city to another in first-class accommodations, he remained the in-your-grille 6-foot-1 runt who refused to back down. Matthews talked garbage and spewed venom and worried not about the repercussions. "Whenever I'd go in to negotiate with a general manager, the first thing I'd be asked was whether Wes would keep his nose clean and be a good boy off the court," said Robert Ezor, his agent. "It wasn't like Wes was out killing people. He just lacked control."

Most of his new teammates best remembered Matthews from the previous season's first-round playoff series. The Lakers had swept past the Spurs in three games, winning by an average of 31 points. Late in the third game, with his team once again far behind, Matthews jogged past the Los Angeles bench. "You make your reservations for Club Med yet?" Johnson shouted.

"Yeah, maybe," replied Matthews, who scored 30 points on 13-for-21 shooting, "but I got mine!"

Without skipping a beat, Johnson smiled. "That was the game plan all along," he yelled. "You stupid motherfucker . . ."

All of the Lakers—players and coaches—erupted into laughter.

West, who wrestled with the Lakers' perpetual lack of toughness, liked Matthews' snarl. (Which was good, because Matthews hated West. "Motherfucker was too arrogant," he said. "I understood why—great player, legend. But arrogant as fuck.") Then the new point guard reported to camp and confused everyone. "He was insane," said Gary Vitti, the trainer. "Nowadays you'd diagnose him as ADD or ADHD. But, really, he was just crazy. I remember we would be practicing, and we'd be in a half-court set and Pat would be talking to the team. Wes couldn't concentrate that long, so—right in the middle of what Pat was saying—he'd turn around, dribble the ball all the way down, dribble back, then come back. He needed those thirty seconds to reset."

"Wes was wacky," said Josh Rosenfeld, the media relations director. "I remember, once the season started, we were playing the Knicks at Madison Square Garden and he asked me for tickets to the game. I said, 'Um, Wes, we're already in the second quarter.' He'd forgotten his mom was coming. Or something like that. It was always something."

On the road, Matthews ate all his meals at either McDonald's, Burger King or Wendy's. Teammates nicknamed him Wild Wild Wes. "He'd stay out all night," said one player, "then come straggling into practice and run, do the full practice, then go out again."

Though he was the craziest of the new Lakers, Matthews wasn't the only recent arrival with a touch of quirkiness. In his effort to create the perfect roster, West was willing to mix and match, add and subtract, risk and reward. By deporting McGee to Atlanta, he brought in Thompson, a 6-foot-7, 210-pound specimen from Camden, New Jersey. On paper, the Louisville rookie was everything one could desire: "Man, was he a great, great, great, great, great, great athlete," said Matthews. "Unlike anyone I'd ever seen.

"But," added Matthews, "Billy Thompson was *not* playing with a full deck."

There's an old adage in Los Angeles: When Wes Matthews says you're not playing with a full deck, you've got problems. During his four years at Louisville, Thompson was known for his prodigious talent as well as a reputation for dabbling in cocaine. By the time he joined the Lakers, he had sworn off all drugs and accepted Jesus Christ as his savior. On the bright side, Thompson was living a clean life. On the downside, even Jesus Christ couldn't help his organizational skills. With the possible exception of Earl Jones, no player drove Riley to drink like Billy Thompson. He was late to practices and late to games and late to workouts and late to appearances and late to the bus. During a December practice in Richfield, Ohio, he famously reached into his gym bag and pulled out two left sneakers. "Man," he said, grinning sheepishly, "can you believe this?" In April, he forgot to set his watch ahead an hour for the spring solstice and arrived forty-five minutes late to the arena. "We told everyone, 'Spring forward and fall back,'" an exasperated Riley said. "And he fell back. . . ."

"My favorite Billy moment might be one of my all-time favorite Laker moments," said Kurt Rambis. "Pat is talking to the team and Billy is looking all over, eyes in the air, not paying any attention. Suddenly he unleashes a huge sneeze and his front teeth go flying out. [Thompson's teeth had been dislodged while at Louisville, and a bridge was placed inside his mouth.]

"The whole team is cracking up. Billy's cracking up. But Riley is standing there, stern. He wasn't happy."

Another time, while the Lakers were waiting to board a plane, Thompson engaged in a lengthy conversation with a man at the airport. "They were talking God and the Bible, and they really hit it off," said John Black, an assistant to Josh Rosenfeld at the time. "So Billy offered the guy his tickets for the next night's game, and told him he'd leave them at will-call. Well, come that night, Billy—of course—forgot the guy's name. So he puts the tickets in an envelope and writes GUY AT THE AIRPORT on it."

Unlike Matthews, an adept ball handler who could ably guide the team,

Thompson immediately branded himself as useless. For all his physical talent, he never understood the NBA game. He lollygagged, was a lousy defender and struggled to grasp the pick and roll. "He could have been great," said Mike Smrek, the new backup center. "But he was living in another universe. I remember one time we were sitting on the bus, getting ready to go to a game. It's 'Where's Billy? Where's Billy?' They're calling his room—no answer. They're banging on his door—no Billy, no Billy. Finally, they get the manager to open the door, because they're worried, and there's Billy sitting on the bed. He's just sitting there going, 'Oh.' Then you'd think he'd have sprinted to the bus. Nope. He just kind of walked there slowly.

"That," said Smrek, "was Billy Thompson."

■ ■ ■

Even with an insulted Worthy and a new corps of space cadets, the Lakers were, as always, the Western Conference's top dog. The core was largely the same, though the philosophy was not. At long last, Riley decided it was time for the Lakers to radically reduce Abdul-Jabbar's role as the offensive centerpiece.

Approaching his fortieth birthday and beginning his eighteenth season, the center was now a very good—but no longer great—NBA player. He was slow and a bit frail, and on defense stood out as an increasingly painful liability. Whereas once he was abused strictly by A-listers like Moses Malone and Akeem Olajuwon, now the Jack Sikmas and Mike Gminskis were having their way, too. Riley wanted to limit Abdul-Jabbar's minutes, but the team failed to acquire a suitable backup. A deal for Chicago's Jawann Oldham fell through and Smrek, who had been released by the Bulls, was mountainous (7-foot, 250 pounds) but raw. So, against his wishes, Riley would again be forced to keep Abdul-Jabbar on the court long after the red EMPTY light started to flash on the dashboard. Magic Johnson was in command, and Abdul-Jabbar was but a fading sidekick.

"You know when I learned about Magic's power, and that he was the man much more than Kareem?" said Brickowski, new to the organization. "I signed with the team and arrived in Chicago for a practice before a preseason game against the Bulls. Everyone welcomes me, Pat introduces me, he brings us in for a huddle, everyone puts their hands in and Pat says, 'We'll do this and we'll do that, and we'll be out in two hours and fifteen minutes.' And Magic goes, 'OK, an hour and fifteen and we'll be done.' And Pat says,

'No . . . no . . . two hours and fifteen minutes.' And Magic says, 'No, no, no—I thought you said, because we played back-to-back games and we're tired, it'll just be an hour and fifteen minutes.' Well, there are three seconds of silence and Pat says, 'We're sharp—one hour and fifteen minutes.' Magic walks away, smiles at me and says, 'That's what I thought you said.'"

The Lakers opened the season by going 12-2 in November, at one point peeling off nine straight victories. Johnson was off to the best start of his career, averaging 20.5 points and 11.5 assists. Any hostilities with Worthy were placed to the side, as he and Byron Scott continued to fill the offensive void left by a decaying Abdul-Jabbar. "Those guys were like a machine," Brickowski said of Johnson, Worthy and Scott. "Fast, quick, strong and deadly. I'd never been on a team with players like it."

After years of hearing fans and media types suggest that Rambis should be replaced, Riley finally acted. Though A. C. Green remained unpolished, the coach liked his athleticism and hustle. In his first four starts, he averaged 15.7 points and 9 rebounds—numbers Rambis could not match. "A.C. is probably more effective as a starter," Riley said. "He gets into a rhythm and seems to get stronger while everyone else gets tired." Green also benefited from the presence of Thompson, whose nonstop Bible thumping served to distract players from the never-ending virgin jokes. "Billy was crazy," Matthews said. "Crazy trumps no sex."

Never one to complain publicly, Rambis took his demotion hard—as did his legion of followers. Through the years, as he progressed from fringe player to starter to championship contributor, Rambis noticed that a growing number of fans arrived at the Forum wearing black horn-rim glasses, fake mustaches and gold T-shirts with *31* (his uniform number) scribbled across the front. "I initially thought they were mocking me," Rambis said. "I mean, it wasn't like I enjoyed wearing those ugly glasses. When I wore normal glasses, they broke, so I found indestructible ones. These guys show up, and they're clearly making fun. So I arrange a meeting inside the Forum Club, in order to ask them to stop. And when I walked through the door, you would have thought I was Jesus Christ or Elvis. I mean, they were like, 'Oh, we love to watch you play! You're great!' So, I was like, uh . . . oh . . . um . . . never mind."

Though their hero was now coming off the bench, members of Rambis Youth (as the group was known) continued to begrudgingly watch the NBA's most extraordinary show. On December 12, Riley's squad traveled to

Boston to resume the rivalry. Having taken out the Houston Rockets in six games in the previous season's finals, the Celtics stood, once again, as the league's defending champions. But they were weakened. Bill Walton, the highly regarded center now in his second season in the green and white, was out with inflammation of the right ankle, and Larry Bird and Robert Parish were playing through injuries. The Celtics were in the midst of a 48-game home winning streak, but even Red Auerbach, the cigar-chomping team president, seemed to know it could be ending. "We're not one hundred percent," he noted glumly.

On the day before the game, Bird and Johnson were asked about each other. It was, by now, a Boston–Los Angeles media ritual. Neither man usually said much; Bird would grunt, Johnson would laugh it off—then they'd play.

This time, though, the mood felt slightly different. Time and experience and championships and All-Star Games and a couple of shared commercial shoots had melted much of the frost. The two still weren't making dinner plans. But Bird admitted he liked Johnson. Johnson admitted he liked Bird. A couple of years earlier, they would have barely glanced at each other on the court. "Now, it's like, with that look," Johnson said. "Never words, but a look. *Yeaahh*. I think that, before, the media separated us so much—Magic vs. Bird—and we as individuals created that inner rivalry, too. It's not that we hated each other, but there was a dislike. I didn't want him to win, and he didn't want me to win." To the shock of many (and dismay of Riley), Johnson even attended one of the Celtics–Rockets finals games . . . *and rooted for Boston*. "Honestly, I think Earvin always wanted Larry's approval," said Michael Cooper. "I don't know why, except that he's one who needs love."

So did Johnson take it easy on the Celtics? Hardly. Los Angeles returned from an eight-point fourth-quarter deficit to shock the Boston Garden with a 117–110 win. Johnson scored 31 to lead his team, but the statistic was a small part of the story. With Boston's defense focusing heavily on his motions, Johnson repeatedly drove the lane before hitting Abdul-Jabbar with an array of passes. The center scored 14 of his 26 points in the final ten minutes, while Cooper shut Bird down, blanketing him to the tune of 6 fourth-quarter points. "We were very bad in the fourth quarter," said K. C. Jones, Boston's coach. "And they were very great."

The Lakers were a juggernaut. Less than a month after their nine-game winning streak was snapped, they went eight more contests without a loss. This string included two defeats of the Rockets (sans Abdul-Jabbar, Johnson scored 38 in a 103–96 victory, then—five days later—put in another 30 for the 134–111 win), a 26-point walloping of the Philadelphia 76ers (Johnson went for 28) and a gleeful 155–118 decimation of Phoenix.

The blowout of the Suns gave Riley particular satisfaction. Not only did his team tie an NBA record with 89 first-half points, they refused to take any abuse. A hapless team limping toward 36 wins, Phoenix compensated for minimal skill with flagrant cheap shots. With four minutes, forty-one seconds remaining in the fourth quarter, Grant Gondrezick, a rookie guard from Pepperdine, hit Brickowski in the throat with an elbow. The Brick (as he was nicknamed by teammates) fired back with fists. As referees stepped in to break up the brawl, Matthews began screaming unintelligible blatherings at Al Bianchi, a Suns assistant coach. Bianchi was a fifty-four-year-old man who probably weighed 180 pounds. He was wearing a suit and a tie, and appeared as threatening as a bottle of Yoo-hoo. Yet Matthews charged forward, as did Bianchi, who took several swings at the guard. Both were ejected, and William Bedford, the Sun's 7-foot-1 center, carried Bianchi off the court. "I don't give a damn if he's 5-foot-2 or 7-foot-2, I'm not taking that shit from anybody," Bianchi said. "Particularly that helium head."

Huh?

"Yeah, airhead," Bianchi added. "You know what airheads are."

When told of the comments, Matthews scowled. "When he wants to meet in the parking lot, that's fine with me," he said. "But he's too old. I got brains and he don't. He's an old man and I'm still young."

Afterward, Riley was thrilled. Brickowski and Matthews had provided an out-of-nowhere spark. Through the years, the coach had seen many powerful teams turn complacent. It happens easily—one win becomes two, two wins become four. Your legs get tired, your concentration wanes, you see an easy game coming up and play lazily. "It's unavoidable," said Matthews. "It's a very long season. It's very hard to go all-out all the time."

Matthews' words were spoken on the evening of January 2. One month later, they rang particularly true. On the night of February 2, the Lakers fell at home to the Mavericks, 103–99. It was Los Angeles's third loss in five contests. The game wasn't particularly awful or embarrassing—Dallas outrebounded Los Angeles, 51–33, and Abdul-Jabbar looked slow and stiff, yet the Lakers still had the ball and a chance to win, with twelve seconds left. The issue was intensity. Or lack thereof. Johnson scored 18, Worthy 15 and Scott 21, but the performance was sluggish. "I was actually pretty surprised," said Riley. "There was no energy there. You would have thought we would have kicked it in, but we looked lethargic. You would have thought that we were playing our fourth game in five nights."

In the following morning's *San Diego Union-Tribune*, writer Barry Bloom suggested that the Lakers—34-11 and once again running away with the Pacific Division—were in trouble. In a piece headlined ONCE-UNSINKABLE LAKERS' SHIP NOW APPEARS TO BE FILLED WITH HOLES, he wrote:

> The Lakers . . . are a team with gaping holes. . . . They are short one big man who is desperately needed to help the club off the boards. They are a very ordinary team when taken out of their fastbreak offense. They are an even more ordinary team when Magic Johnson has an ordinary night. Last night, with the top team in the Midwest Division playing its fourth game in five nights, all three elements led to a crucial Lakers loss.

What went unwritten by Bloom and unspoken by others was that Johnson—in the midst of a season that even Bird called "worthy of the MVP trophy"—was enduring one of the lowest spans of his eight-year career. On the court, he continued to glow, continued to smile, continued to make miracle passes. Even with Abdul-Jabbar playing poorly and with a waif-thin bench, Johnson was averaging 23.3 points and carrying the ball club. But he was, internally, devastated. On January 23, his older half sister, Mary, had died from leukemia, leaving behind four children to be raised by Johnson's mother and father in Lansing, Michigan.

Lost in all the talk about Johnson the basketball player and Johnson the celebrity was that, at his core, he was a hometown kid. Though he lived full-time in Los Angeles, Johnson returned to Lansing for long stretches every summer. He would knock on the doors of old neighbors, stroll down to the nearby park for softball games with his lifelong chums, eat at local dives and stay up late into the night talking about the good ol' days. He had an unusually close relationship with his parents and nine siblings. They spoke regularly, and visited as often as possible. Johnson quoted his father's doses of wisdom on a regular basis. The most cited words usually came from a time when, as a teenager, he joined his dad, Earvin Sr., doing sanitation work. It was an icy day, and young Earvin rushed to empty a can, then jumped back into the warm truck. His father sent a glare his way. "If you do this job halfway, then you'll be a halfway basketball player, you'll be a halfway student," he told him. "You have to do things the right way."

Mary Johnson had shared this philosophy. Work hard. Give your best. Be prideful. On the night she passed, Johnson called his mom, Christine. She was handling things well, but her husband was a wreck. The Lakers were scheduled to play at Dallas the following day. "What should I do?" Johnson asked. "Come home and be with Daddy, or play the game?"

"Go ahead and stay," Mary said. "It'll give him something to do. I think he'd like that."

Against Dallas, Johnson totaled 25 points and 12 assists. The Lakers lost; his concentration was zilch—and nobody much cared. That night Johnson returned home for the funeral. He dedicated the rest of the season to Mary's memory and played with an unusually heavy heart. He could take losses, poor shooting nights, media criticism. The death of a sister, though, was too much to bear.

It also didn't help that, when he wasn't back home in Lansing, Johnson was dealing with the heartache on his own. Much is made of the glorious life of the professional athlete, yet little is uttered of the accompanying loneliness. For all the splendor of a $350 hotel suite, it is a suite that usually goes unshared. For all the palatial luxury of Johnson's eighteen-room mansion, they were eighteen rooms often lacking life.

It was well known in Los Angeles that Johnson had a longtime girlfriend, Earleatha "Cookie" Kelly. The two had met back at Michigan State in 1977, and she graduated four years later with a degree in retailing, clothing and textiles from Cornell's College of Human Ecology. When asked, Johnson spoke giddily of her beauty and poise. "In high school, I was dating all over—you know, basketball player and stuff—just going crazy," he said. "Then I met this great young lady, a super girl. She brought me down to being a one-woman man." Every so often, Kelly would be seen out and about with Johnson, and a blurb might follow in one of the Los Angeles newspapers about their long-standing romance. To the shock of thousands of Southern California–based women, during training camp in 1985, Johnson announced that he had finally popped the question.

Less than a year later, he called it off.

When asked, Johnson explained it thusly: "Well, I'm so into this— basketball and my work—that I felt it would be better if I got married after I'm done. Because I think I can be just as good a husband during that time as

I am in basketball. I'd hate to send a lady through what I go through now. It would be unfair and I realize that. Take now, for example. During the play-offs, I'm so intense. Every day I'm intense and I'm moody and I need to be by myself. . . . I know just dating that it's hard on a date because I'm just snapping. Just think—if it was my wife, I'd probably just go off, and I don't want that to happen."

The truth—as many members of the Lakers organization suspected—was that Johnson broke off the engagement not out of some moral fortitude, but because he liked sex with women not named Earleatha. So he told Kelly the wedding wouldn't be happening, and she was crushed.

On occasion, so was Johnson. The women were gorgeous and experimental, but, to Johnson, mere disposable items. They came, they went. Jerry Buss had similar relations, only he liked to take his young dates under his wing, provide them with opportunities, guide them through life, even keep in touch. Johnson, for the most part, simply relished the conquest. He spotted a hottie at a game, he had a note delivered her way, they met in a closet, they, ahem, mingled, they departed. Was it fun? Sure. Exciting? Absolutely. Fulfilling? No.

"I think, in Los Angeles at that time, with the Lakers, with stardom, maybe it was hard *not* to be that way," said Brickowski. "I remember one day walking through the office, and I go to make a phone call in one of the rooms, and Mike Tyson is in there fucking a girl on the desk. He looks at me, says, 'Hold on one minute,' and continues fucking. I'm not making fun of Mike Tyson, but that sort of thing was in the air at the Forum. It just was."

Perhaps. But when his sister died, and Johnson had no one to be with . . . no one to embrace, well, it hurt. He was the most popular man in Los Angeles, yet all alone. "I've been talking to my folks every day," Johnson told the *San Diego Union-Tribune*. "I had a woman who I was involved with for the last few years. But we're not seeing each other anymore. She wanted to get married.

"I guess I'm not ready for that yet."

■ ■ ■

Though the Lakers could be—at times—inconsistent, the highs remained incredibly high. On February 4, the pathetic Sacramento Kings, sporting a 14-31 record, came to the Forum. This was, in Hollywood speak, a giveaway game. Meaning, if one were a season ticket holder, and an irksome friend or relative was always pining for a visit to the Forum, here was the game to skip.

Or, if one enjoys watching an ant being crushed by a bulldozer, perhaps not.

The Lakers jumped out to a 29–0 lead.

They were up 40–4 at the end of the first quarter.

The Kings—who lost to the Lakers for the twenty-second-straight time—missed their first twenty-one shots.

"I've never seen anything like that," said Michael Cooper of the 128–92 flogging. "I'm just glad to be part of it."

Even with such an overwhelming victory, Jerry West knew his team was flawed. For the past few years, he had desperately attempted to acquire another skilled big body, but to no avail. Earl Jones—bust. Chuck Nevitt—useless. Petur Gudmundsson . . . Jerome Henderson . . . Mike Smrek—no, no, no. At one point he even tried landing Bill Walton from the Clippers, but when the oft-injured center failed a physical, West passed. (To the Lakers' great dismay, Walton then went to Boston and helped the Celtics win the 1986 championship.)

Beginning in late January, Los Angeles kicked off a crusade to (money and difficulty be damned) finally acquire frontcourt depth. At the time, Riley was using the six-foot-eight Rambis as Abdul-Jabbar's primary reinforcement—an idea as laughable as it was ineffective. At long last, he pulled off a deal for a legitimate backup center to assist Abdul-Jabbar. Los Angeles surrendered Gudmundsson, Brickowski, two draft picks and cash to San Antonio for Mychal Thompson.

Back in 1978, the Portland Trail Blazers had used the first pick in the draft to take Thompson, a long, athletic 6-foot-10 force from the University of Minnesota. The selection was a no-brainer—Thompson was an All-American who averaged 22 points and 10.9 rebounds as a senior Gopher. "We don't have anybody who can contain Mychal Thompson," said Lute Olson, Iowa's coach, during his senior season. "*Nobody* has someone who can contain Mychal Thompson."

Though far from a bust as a pro, Thompson never met expectations. He was a good, solid complementary player damned by the most sideways of compliments: "Mychal," said Otis Birdsong, the longtime NBA guard, "is an exceptionally nice guy. Maybe too nice."

Thompson was born in the Bahamas, and as a boy his primary sport was soccer. He never touched a basketball until age sixteen, when he began playing in a league sponsored by his church, the Central Gospel Chapel in Nassau. With his size (he was 6-foot-9 by his seventeenth birthday) and freakish athleticism, the games turned into farce. In one, he grabbed 61 rebounds. In another, he blocked 22 shots. His older brother, Colin Thompson, urged him to try playing in the United States. A couple of years earlier, Colin had been a power-hitting outfield prospect in the Los Angeles Dodgers' minor league system. Following his first spring training, though, he grew frustrated, quit and returned home. The regret would forever gnaw at him. Colin stressed to his little brother the value of taking on challenges and making the most of opportunities. "People would say I should get off the island and pursue a career," Mychal said. "I didn't know much about it, but I really loved playing." The Thompson family used to vacation in Miami, and when his son turned seventeen, Dewitt Thompson sent him to the city. Mychal was placed with a family friend named Maude Tappan. For fifty dollars per month, he was provided a bed, food and, at Jackson High School, real competition. "I was raw," he said. "I had never played in front of a crowd before in my life, and even though I was only a half-hour flight from Nassau, I felt like I was in another world. I was so nervous before my first game I almost passed out."

Behind its new center, Jackson finished 33-0 and won the state Class 4A championship. Thompson went on to Minnesota, where he teamed with forward Kevin McHale to form one of America's best frontcourt duos.

Yet throughout his high school, college and professional careers, Thompson was always something of a goofball. While at Jackson he attached tassels and bells to the laces of his sneakers. "That's how I got the nickname Bells," he said. "It became Sweet Bells after people saw some of my moves on the court." In college he changed the spelling of his name from Michael in an effort to generate media attention. He wore a necklace on the court, and explained it away as his "voodoo necklace." He told the media he was cousins with David Thompson, the high-flying Denver Nuggets star. (He wasn't.) In his bestselling book *The Breaks of the Game*, David Halberstam wrote of Thompson sneaking two women onto the team bus after a Portland loss. He was a happy, friendly, cheerful man who would greet opponents not with a scowl but with a wide smile. Jack Ramsay, his coach with the Trail Blazers, used to bemoan Thompson's lack of seriousness. "A lot of times, if I didn't show a lot of sadness or remorse after a loss, [Ramsay] would really yell at me," Thompson said. "I wouldn't be laughing and joking in the locker room after a loss, but the next day in practice the game's over with . . . so I'd forget it. Maybe I had a little problem with that as far as my attitude was concerned."

The Trail Blazers finally tired of Thompson's act, and in June 1986 dumped him on San Antonio for Steve Johnson, an unspectacular center. It was a low moment, and he wondered whether his NBA career was dwindling toward the end. On the afternoon of February 13, Thompson drove to the HemisFair Arena for a game against the visiting Clippers. The Spurs were 18-31, and Thompson was averaging 12.3 points as Artis Gilmore's backup. He entered the locker room, greeted teammate Alvin Robertson, changed into athletic garb and went to the training table. "What are you doing here?" asked John Henderson, the Spurs' trainer.

Henderson was a known kidder—Thompson never took him seriously.

"You've been traded to the Lakers," he said.

Ha.

"Really, you've been traded to the Lakers."

Yeah, right.

"Mychal, you don't play for us any longer. I'm not joking."

Thompson remained skeptical. Back in the Bahamas, when he was able to catch the NBA every so often on television, the Lakers were *his* team. "Wilt, Jerry, Goodrich—I knew the Lakers backward and forward," he said. "I dreamed of coming to Los Angeles to play."

Finally, another San Antonio employee confirmed the news. "I was a Laker!" Thompson said. "A Laker! It was like going from the spare bedroom to the master bedroom. Oh, my goodness."

Around this same time, Mitch Kupchak, now an assistant general manager, was trying to locate Brickowski. He finally reached him—at the home of actor Charlie Sheen. "Charlie and I were close friends, so I was hanging with him," Brickowski said. "The trade was a good opportunity for me to get playing time, but it was a real kick in the nuts. I was young, single and living in L.A. Now I was going to *Texas*."

Thompson flew to Los Angeles on the night of Saturday, February 14. The following afternoon, the Lakers were hosting the Celtics, who were once again dominating the Eastern Conference, with a 37-12 record (the same mark held by Los Angeles). Boston had won 10 of 11 games, and was 24-5 since losing to Los Angeles at the Boston Garden on December 12. "With them beating us in the Garden, that puts them one up," K. C. Jones, the Celtics coach, said. "Now they want to win in L.A. to establish they're the best team in the league. Yeah, it's important. It's going to be a wild-west shootout in the Forum. They'll all be pumped up, same as us."

When asked twenty-four hours before tip-off how much time he'd need to adjust to the Lakers, Thompson said, "Give me a game. I'd say after a game and a practice, I'll be comfortable."

While tying up his laces in the locker room, Thompson looked at Johnson on one side and Abdul-Jabbar on the other. He tapped A. C. Green on the shoulder and said, "I feel like I'm with Mick Jagger and Keith Richards." Green nodded, but failed to respond. This wasn't a time to joke. It was business. "Why is everyone so serious around here?" Thompson said to Scott.

"Because," he said, "we hate Boston."

In the most electric game of the season, the Lakers outlasted the Celtics, 106–103. The star, as usual, was Johnson, who scored 39 points in forty-five minutes—including a forty-six-foot, one-handed push-from-the-chest shot to close out the third quarter. Thompson's debut was equally jolting. He stepped onto the court with 1:13 left in the first quarter to a standing ovation from the sellout crowd, and even though the Forum scoreboard spelled his name Michael, there was nothing confusing about his performance. His first shot, a jump hook over center Robert Parish, swished through the hoop, and moments later he hit Worthy with a perfect bounce pass for a layup. Thompson scored 10 points in twenty-nine minutes, but the key contributions came defensively. Entering the game, the Celtics' hottest player had been McHale, who was averaging 26.7 points and 10 rebounds while shooting a league-best 61 percent. There were a fair number of Mychal Thompson detractors throughout the league, but no one questioned his ability to match up with his old college teammate. When they stood side by side, McHale and Thompson could be mistaken—body type–wise—for clones. They both had long torsos and elastic arms that dangled down toward their knees. Thompson knew McHale's game as an interrogator knows his subject, and even when an irritated Bird told the Los Angeles media, "There isn't anybody we know about in the league that they could pick up who can stop Kevin McHale," he was concealing genuine concern: Thompson was the closest thing McHale had to a human shadow.

Through much of the fourth quarter, Riley kept A. C. Green on the bench and went with Thompson. Wherever McHale went, he went—and it worked. McHale scored 16 points against Green in the first half. In the second, he was held to 7. Afterward, Bird was dumbfounded. "Why would San

Antonio do something like that?" he said. "If they wanted money, we would've been glad to keep them in business. Maybe they'll lend us Artis Gilmore for a while."

It was, he knew, wishful thinking.

■ ■ ■

In what would ultimately become a twenty-three-year career as an NBA general manager, Jerry West made some magnificent trades. Few, however, matched the impact of Thompson's arrival in Los Angeles.

It's not that the newest Laker was a dynamic scorer or even a magnificent rebounder or such an outstanding locker room presence.

No, what Thompson did was make Abdul-Jabbar's increasingly painful decline more digestible.

Although he still posted passable numbers (17.5 points, 6.7 rebounds per game), the soon-to-be-forty-year-old Laker was a liability. Were his last name Smith or Jones, and were he lacking the pedigree of a seventeen-time All-Star, Riley would have benched Abdul-Jabbar long ago. Why, even before Thompson's arrival, there were those inside the organization who believed Mike Smrek, the plodding but athletic reserve, would be a greater overall help to the team. In an off-the-record conversation that made its way into the column of *New York Post* basketball insider Peter Vecsey, West tore into Abdul-Jabbar. "For the most part," he said, "he's not hustling, showing any motivation or leadership."

When he heard about the quotation, West flipped, denying the words had been spoken. Of course, they *were* spoken—those who covered the team knew West was good for at least 12,471 off-the-cuff quotations per year, and that he would later deny uttering the very words he uttered. In this case, the anti-Kareem sentiment had been repeated by West many times. Abdul-Jabbar *was* playing lazily, and his defense *was* awful, and his attitude *was* iffy, and none of the other Laker players (with the quirky exception of Matthews, who looked at Abdul-Jabbar as one would a spiritual guru) had much to do with him. "I remember seeing him blow off a kid in an airport who wanted his autograph," said Billy Thompson. "The child said, 'Mr. Kareem, can you sign this?' and he said no. I asked Magic, 'Is that how he always is?' He said— 'Yup. Kareem assumes that, by now, everyone in the world has his autograph.'"

In his defense, Abdul-Jabbar had reason to lose focus. Widely regarded as one of the league's most intelligent players, the Lakers captain's smarts didn't translate to financial security. The previous summer he filed a $55 million lawsuit against his former agent, Tom Collins, for mismanagement. More recently, he placed his four-bedroom, three-and-a-half-bath, four-fireplace Bel Air mansion on the market for $4.3 million. Abdul-Jabbar denied the sale had anything to do with losing much of his fortune, but that was hard to believe. In his lawsuit, Abdul-Jabbar said he had been reduced to "borrowing money" from Collins to meet basic living expenses. (When writer Gordon Edes reported his difficulties in the *Los Angeles Times*, Abdul-Jabbar cut him off from future interviews.) Around this same time, Alex English, the Denver Nuggets' star forward, sued Abdul-Jabbar for $155,000 for "failure/refusal" to repay a loan. Abdul-Jabbar responded by making English a defendant in his lawsuit against Collins, who once represented both players. When the Nuggets and Lakers met at the Forum on March 10, Johnson took Abdul-Jabbar's place in the pre-game meeting of captains and referees. Los Angeles's center didn't want to shake English's hand.

Despite the drama, on March 26, the Lakers clinched their sixth-straight Pacific Division title, beating Detroit 128–111 at the Forum. The post-game celebration was muted. "They only want to drink champagne when they win it all," Riley said. "They're aware they won it and they're not taking it for granted. But our goals are a lot loftier than they've been in past years. This is just one level. The last time we popped a cork for a Pacific Division title was in 1981–82, my first year. But we were in a race that year."

Though Riley's results could not be questioned, some Laker players wondered whether this was, in fact, a healthy way to exist. Byron Scott wanted his wife, Anita, to be able to join the celebration—*no*. Worthy thought maybe it'd be OK to show some happiness—*no*. "Pat was too controlling at times," said Matthews. "You play hard, you deserve to feel good about it." Paul Westhead may not have been the greatest NBA coach, but he allowed his men to be human beings. When they won, they laughed. When they lost, they sulked. Riley, on the other hand, didn't merely have athletic expectations—he had emotional ones, too. The team wouldn't celebrate until *he* said it was time to celebrate. There was little satisfaction in day-to-day achievements, and no acknowledgment of success until the absolute end. Riley's motto for the season was YOUR PERSONAL BEST, and he repeated it ad nauseum. Only your best was acceptable. Nothing less. If the Lakers won a championship, the season was an unqualified success. If they didn't, the year was a waste.

"Riley was intense—that's the way to put it," said Rambis. "Basketball was my job, and I took it seriously. For Pat, it was more than that. It was life."

Having experienced the devastating playoff loss to Houston in 1986, Los Angeles's players saw the upcoming post-season as a chance at redemption. This had been, in the minds of many, the Lakers' greatest team. They posted the second-best record in franchise history (65-17), and took the Pacific Division by (ho-hum) 16 games. In a way, Abdul-Jabbar's decline made others better. At age twenty-seven, Johnson enjoyed the top season of his career, winning his first MVP trophy by averaging 23.9 points, 12.2 assists, 6.3 rebounds and 1.7 steals. Worthy chipped in 19.4 points, and five other players (Abdul-Jabbar, Scott, Green, Cooper and Mychal Thompson) averaged in double figures. The pressure to hurry up and wait for the big man to arrive near the basket was mostly gone. The Lakers ran like greyhounds, and if you failed to hang, you were a goner.

Somewhat predictably, the playoffs were a joke. The Lakers swept past the Nuggets in three games, routed the Warriors in five and blitzed the Seattle SuperSonics in the Western Conference Finals, winning in four straight. "It was never about those teams or those games," said Matthews. "We wanted to prove that, once again, we were the best team in the NBA.

"We wanted the Boston Celtics."

CHAPTER 15

―――――――

BRING IT

Michael Cooper remembers the first time he was ever asked to guard Larry Bird one-on-one for a prolonged stretch.

The date was January 18, 1981, and the Lakers traveled to the Boston Garden to face the hated Celtics. At the time, Cooper was feeling awfully good about himself. With Magic Johnson sidelined with an injury, he was a fixture in the starting lineup, right alongside stars like Kareem Abdul-Jabbar and Jamaal Wilkes and Norm Nixon. Cooper stood as a key cog on basketball's best team and, he says, "I was as cocky and confident as I'd ever been."

To Cooper, Larry Bird was still merely *larry bird* (lowercase intended)—an overrated Great White Hype who captured a nation's imagination more for his pigmentation than his playing ability. Cooper had seen it all before. Doug Collins. Mike Dunleavy. Tom McMillen. Mike O'Koren. White guys came, white guys went. Larry Bird? Who the hell was scared of Lar—

"I'm getting ready to wear your fucking ass out."

The words were uttered softly. Almost in a whisper. Had the white boy just spoken in such a manner to Michael Cooper? Had he really said such a thing? Barely two minutes had passed in the opening quarter and Bird was already slinging yang.

"Bring it, motherfucker," replied Cooper, hardly a linguistic wallflower. "Bring it."

Larry Bird brought it.

Celtics guard Nate Archibald dribbled the ball down the court. Cooper followed Bird toward the top of the key—"Larry's standing there talking to me, talking to me. Nonstop talking"—then shadowed him as he walked down the lane and circled around a Robert Parish pick. "About to wear your ass out," Bird said. "Wear . . . it . . . out . . ." Bird pushed off Cooper. Cooper pushed off Bird. "Bring it," the Laker said. "C'mon, fucker. . . ." Bird jumped back, caught a pass from Johnson. "I'm still here, motherfucker," Cooper said, grabbing a handful of Bird's green-and-white jersey. "I'm still here." Abdul-Jabbar, guarding Parish, stepped off his man to help. Bird jumped to shoot, and Cooper lunged toward him—certain he was about to block the shot. Then, quick as a dragonfly, Bird somehow brought the ball down and wrapped it around to a wide-open Parish. "I still have no idea how he got the ball to him," said Cooper, "because my hands are up in the air, Kareem is coming out—and the only way he could have gotten it to him was to lob it over the top. But he didn't lob it over the top. I'm still confused." Cooper spun, just in time to see Parish slam the basketball through the hoop.

He looked back toward Bird, who smirked. "Wearing your ass out, motherfucker," he said. "Wearing it out. . . ."

Those words stuck with Michael Cooper. That moment stuck with Michael Cooper. Throughout his first eight-plus NBA seasons, he had been assigned to guard players of all shapes, sizes and builds. One night he might find himself standing before Utah's Rickey Green, the league's fastest point guard. The next night, it could be Denver center Dan Issel. Or Milwaukee small forward Junior Bridgeman. Or Knicks shooting guard Michael Ray Richardson. "He was worthy of Defensive Player of the Year every year," said Greg Ballard, the Golden State forward. "He was long, fast, stronger than you'd think. Coop was made for defense."

Although the Magic Johnson–Larry Bird connection was forever discussed and hyped, it was Cooper who felt tied to the Celtics star. He obsessed over Bird's moves, over his thinking, over his patterns and tendencies. If a Celtic game was televised, Cooper watched, his eyes glued to number 33. He looked toward nights against Boston as one would a wedding. It was Michael Cooper's moment.

"Covering Larry—that meant everything to me," he said. "People said he was overrated . . . fuck, no. If anything, he was underrated. What made him so good was you didn't just have to worry about his scoring. You had to worry about this guy's defense, his passing, his ability to save balls from going out of bounds, his ability to set picks and get people open. Larry could beat you in many ways. And he was the hardest player for me to play against, because you had to guard against all those things. Most players are one- or two-dimensional. Larry was ten-dimensional."

When people praised Cooper's defensive ability, what went unspoken was that, beyond foot speed and quickness and intelligence, he was driven by the power of paranoia.

Michael Cooper was the NBA's most paranoid player.

Paranoia can lead to unjustified suspicion; to constant worries; to fear that someone bigger, stronger, better will inevitably come along and ruin a good thing. For Cooper, however, paranoia made him who he was. From the very day he joined the Lakers, Cooper was looking over his shoulder. "He was the biggest character they had, because he was totally paranoid, totally insecure and always thinking he was about to be traded," said Steve Springer, the longtime beat writer. "We were in the Midwest once on a road trip, and Coop really screwed up his ankle. Riley told him to sit out a couple of games and heal.

"Well, Coop comes up to me during a game and sits down. He's in street clothes. And he says, 'You've been good to me, so I just want to let you know I'm out of here.'"

Springer was shocked. He was usually on top of things but had heard nothing of a trade. "Coop," he said, "what are you talking about?"

"It's done—I'm gone," he replied. "I'm not fucking stupid. You don't think I know they want to get rid of me? It's already done. There's a deal. Well, fuck them. Fuck the Lakers. I will come back and kick their fucking asses. I'm sick of this shit. They've been waiting to get rid of me for a long time. Fuck them."

When the game ended, Springer approached Cooper in the locker room and kindly said, "Coop, are you sure you want me to print that?"

The Laker laughed. "Nah," he said. "You know I'm . . ." Cooper turned to Jack Curran, the trainer, who was walking past. "Jack," he said, "what's the word I'm looking for?"

"You're paranoid," Curran snarled. "Fucking paranoid."

Magic Johnson—not even remotely paranoid—occasionally played defense as if he were missing a leg. Abdul-Jabbar—not even remotely paranoid—didn't seem to mind if someone like Golden State's Joe Barry Carroll lit him up for 25 points and 10 rebounds (as he did in a December 4 Warriors win). Cooper, however, played every possession as if his career depended on it.

When someone scored a basket over him, he didn't merely get upset. No, he took it personally, and wondered whether the next stop in action would result in his inevitable benching. "I never relaxed," Cooper said. "Never. Not once. My agent once told me I was always the first name other teams brought up in trades. Well, that scared the hell out of me. I wanted to be a Laker, and only a Laker." Whenever he would run into Jerry West, Cooper made certain to irritate him.

Cooper: Jerry, just checking if I'm being traded.
West: Shut the fuck up. We're not trading you.
Cooper: But I heard . . .
West: Shut the fuck up.
Cooper: Are you su—
West: OK, we're trading you.
Cooper: Fuck. Forget I even asked.

"Coop was always one step away from food stamps," said Lon Rosen. "All through his career he thought it was over."

As the Lakers prepared for their third finals matchup with the Celtics in four years, Cooper was as paranoid as ever. He was coming off the best season of his career, one during which he had not only made a seventh-straight appearance on the NBA's all-defensive team, but sank 89 three-pointers to rank second in the league (one behind, of all people, Bird). With Abdul-Jabbar's decline, it was Cooper's assistance in widening the court that helped Scott (17 points per game) find open looks and Worthy (19.4 points per game) streak through the lane uncontested. He was a gunner to be reckoned with.

Yet his own personal fear remained. For the first time since West's playing days, Los Angeles was an overwhelming favorite to defeat Boston. "This is their year," Doug Moe, Denver's coach, said after his team was swept in the Western Conference's first round. "Everything is popping right for them. Everything is flowing their way. They've had no injuries, no problems. They've come together. It's just one of those years. A dream year." Unlike the Lakers, the Celtics—battered, increasingly geriatric—barely survived the East. They got past the Detroit Pistons in a classic seven-game series, and only after a 117–114 Game 7 triumph that included 13 ties and 22 lead changes. Though they had won fifty-nine regular-season games, K. C. Jones's club appeared to be a cheap imitation of past renditions. Fringe NBA players like Jerry Sichting, Fred Roberts, Greg Kite, Darren Daye and Conner Henry were logging major minutes. Parish, at age thirty-three the third-oldest of the Celtics, hobbled through the Pistons series, barely making it up and down the court. McHale, meanwhile, had yet to fully recover from a broken bone in his right foot. Bird's back—forever a problem—was throbbing in pain. Bill Walton, thirty-four, the team's savior a season earlier, hurt himself every other step and played only ten regular-season games because of a stress fracture in his right foot. "Physically, after all those playoff games, we were destroyed," said Henry, who grew up in Claremont, California, rooting for the Lakers. "The starters had logged a lot of minutes, and the legs were sort of dead."

Were the Lakers to prevail, Cooper was certain all credit would go to Johnson, the league's hands-down Most Valuable Player. It would go to Abdul-Jabbar, and to Worthy, and even to Scott and A. C. Green and Mychal Thompson and Wes Matthews and Billy Thompson and the towel boy. Should they fail, however, everyone in the world would look at images of Cooper being smoked by Bird and think, "His fault." He would be exiled to western Ukraine. Or, even worse, to the Clippers. "Coop drove himself crazy," said Josh Rosenfeld. "Always. There's a story we all love—one day the team was walking through the airport, and Rich Levin [a beat writer with the *Herald-Examiner*] found a screw on the ground, picked it up and told Coop, 'Mike, I found it.'"

"What did you find?" Cooper replied.

"The screw you lost," said Levin.

If 100 percent healthy, the Celtics could—on a very good day—match up with the Lakers. Injured as they were, however, they had little hope. Wrote Bob Rubin of the *Miami Herald*: "The shamrocks, leprechauns, parquet, mystique and mirrors that enabled Boston to get this far are not going to frighten a poised, veteran Laker team that has clearly been best in the league all year. The Lakers are as healthy, rested and deep as the Celts are not, and after eight days off, they are going to come out at 900 miles per hour in tonight's opener at the Forum."

Everyone seemed to know this, including Bird, who in private expressed some doubt over a repeat title. If the Celtics had any chance, they would have to play physically and angrily. They would have to abuse Los Angeles and hope to expose its soft California-tanned underbelly. "We know our turn is coming," Mychal Thompson said after watching the Celtics survive the Pistons. "I think Mike Tyson and Hulk Hogan will be the first two picks in the draft this year."

The series opened at the Forum on June 2, and the game was as lopsided as many had predicted. The Lakers jumped out to a 9–0 lead, holding Boston scoreless until McHale hit a fade-away jumper nearly three minutes in. Los Angeles enjoyed a 39–8 advantage in fast-break points and on four different occasions had streaks where they scored at least eight unanswered points. The Lakers were a blur—*pass, pass, pass, layup, steal, pass, layup*. The Celtics were an assisted living community. "If this were a championship fight," CBS's Dick Stockton said, "they'd stop it." Worthy scored a game-high 33 points (along with 10 assists and 9 rebounds), Johnson chipped in 29 points, 13 assists and 8 rebounds and Scott went for 20 points. "This was one of those scrimmages they had in Santa Barbara," K. C. Jones said afterward, referring to the Lakers' practices as they waited for the Boston-Detroit winner. "They totally blew us out. What you saw out there was totally spectacular. It took both teams some time to get started, but that was when Magic and James said: 'Enough of this. Let's get out and run, and get this thing over with.' After that, it was a romp."

One Laker, though, was less than satisfied. When he returned to the locker room after the 126–113 triumph, Cooper walked past Bruce Willis and Don Johnson (both actors were allowed in for a visit), stared at the score sheet and cursed himself out. McHale had been held to 15 points, Parish to 16 and Danny Ainge, the pesky shooting guard, to 11. Yet there, in what seemed to be bold, red letters, were Bird's statistics: THIRTY-TWO POINTS ON 14 OF 25 SHOOTING.

"I took pride in being a defensive stopper," said Cooper, who scored 10 points in twenty-three minutes. "When I didn't do my job well—even in a win—it really grated me. I had to come back strong."

If the opening game was heartache for the Celtics, the follow-up was a full-blown coronary explosion. This time, Boston actually jumped out to a 19–14 lead midway through the first quarter. Then—*whoosh!* Come the second quarter, Los Angeles took off, outscoring Boston 37–22 with a buffet of layups, jumpers and dunks. Cooper, still upset, played the game of his life, scoring 21 points and hitting 6 of 7 three-pointers. Bird, meanwhile, was stifled. His 23 points were empty calories, and came on 9 of 17 shooting. Cooper talked his regular brand of trash, and Bird—in the rarest of circumstances—had little to say. When time expired, Los Angeles owned an easy 141–122 triumph and a 2-0 series lead.

"We've got a bunch of gutsy human beings here, and we can't bail out now," Bird said. "We've got to make some major adjustments, and I think we will—especially getting back on defense and hitting the boards and pushing some bodies around. Never, ever, ever count us out."

The words sounded empty.

"They were over," said Matthews. "That wasn't their year. It was ours."

The series shifted to Boston, which always put Riley in a particularly awful mood. The team stayed at the Boston Sheraton, and that first night, at three A.M., the fire alarms were predictably set off. When the team gathered at the Boston Garden for a practice, the players and coaches were greeted by a filthy locker room, a broken video monitor, no towels, drinks or blackboards. "That's Boston Garden," Gary Vitti, the trainer, said. "No cooperation. No class."

The Celtics had won 84 of their last 86 at home, and they were able to take a Game 3 squeaker, 109–103. That night, Riley and Bill Bertka, his top assistant, stayed up until three A.M. watching the tape. When the team met the next day to practice at the Garden, Riley explained that the biggest problem wasn't poor shooting or lazy passing or simply a good Celtics team having a fine night.

No, it was . . . *the wives.*

Dating back to his "peripheral distractions" operating philosophy (anything unrelated to the game itself was an unnecessary burden that could only stand in the way of victory), Riley chewed out his players for allowing a handful of spouses to come to Boston. He was correct—among those in attendance for Game 3 were Wanda Cooper and Anita Scott, both of whom had paid their own way to fly commercially. Riley spotted the women in the crowd (in an ocean of white Bostonians, a pair of African-American females screaming for the Lakers were not especially difficult to locate), and stewed. "Last week we made a deal," he told the team. "No wives or girlfriends would come back until Monday. We all agreed that we'd get to Boston, we'd practice, and we'd try to get a third game out of the way. We were unanimous. We would go together as a team and that would be it.

"Today I found out that a number of the wives flew in on their own Friday night. You were supposed to be settling in, resting and preparing mentally for the game, without distractions. I'm not going to fine you guys. I'm not going to bench you, or send you home, or yell and scream at you. And I definitely don't want you to go back to your hotel rooms and yell at your wives for getting you in trouble.

"But I want you to think about what happened. We've created a little white lie. We lied to ourselves."

Riley was serious.

The Lakers were agape.

They'd lost to the Boston Celtics at home in a *really* close game. This was the fault of the wives? Magic Johnson could screw around on the road all he wanted, and that was fine? But heaven forbid a spouse come—on her own dime—to support her husband? That was wrong?

The Cult of Pat Riley never ceased to amaze.

Yet were there hope in Boston that this was another version of the big bad Celtics using their home-court advantage to physically abuse the soft, sensitive Lakers, well, such thinking was quickly put to rest. In a contest that lived up to past Los Angeles-Boston tussles, the Lakers and Celtics beat the snot out of one another, exchanging punches and elbows without stepping backward. It was Cooper—who gazed into the mirror and saw Andre the Giant staring back—demanding his teammates refuse to cower in the face of hostile crowds and hostile opponents. "They're gonna try and make this a war," he said beforehand. "Well, fuck them. They go after us, we go after them. Take control of the tone."

While driving for a layup in the second quarter, Worthy—the Boston beating boy dating back to M. L. Carr and Cedric Maxwell—was hammered high by Dennis Johnson and low by Greg Kite. He fell to the ground, jumped to his feet and charged Kite, fists flailing. Both men were assessed technicals. "I wasn't trying to hurt James," said Kite. "It was just really rough out there. I had nothing but respect for James Worthy." One quarter later, Cooper and McHale exchanged shoves, and after that McHale and Scott nearly came to blows. "It definitely gets a team excited if another team takes cheap shots at them," Scott said. "It always seems to get us more into the game."

The Celtics led 85–78 after three quarters and, with 1:40 to play, held a 103–97 advantage. Then, in a stretch of uncharacteristically undisciplined basketball, Boston fell apart. Parish turned the ball over to Abdul-Jabbar and watched as Cooper nailed a three-pointer to slice the lead to three points. On the Celtics' next possession, Bird—owner of a hoops IQ of 450—uncharacteristically threw away the ball. When Worthy hit a fade-away jumper with fifty-nine seconds remaining, the Celtics' lead was reduced to a single point. "We gave it away—no question about that," said Bird. "The last couple of months we've done that—lost leads we shouldn't have."

Moments later, Bird missed a gimme jumper, and the Lakers rebounded the ball and raced toward the other end, where Abdul-Jabber slammed home an alley-oop from Johnson. With twenty-nine seconds remaining, Los Angeles held a 104–103 lead. The Boston Garden, basketball's most hostile arena, was dead. The Celtics called a time-out and Bird walked to the sideline, head hanging, baffled by what had transpired. With Cooper and Worthy attached to his hip for much of the game, he had hit just 6 of 17 shots. The Celtics were finished. Over. Gone.

Wait.

On the next possession, Dennis Johnson whipped a pass to Ainge along the top of the three-point circle. He found Bird in the corner, momentarily alone. Freed from Worthy when the Laker forward mistakenly rotated toward Ainge, Bird caught the ball and, with fourteen seconds remaining, fired a three-pointer that barely eluded the tips of a leaping Thompson's left-hand fingers. The ball hung, hung, hung, hung, hung, hung, hung, hung in the air. . . .

Net.

"Heartbreaking," said Thompson. "I was that close."

The Garden shook. The Celtics were up, 106–104.

"I had the best view of it," said Magic Johnson. "I was under the basket—and knew it was going in. I just said, 'My goodness. That's Larry.' "

Riley signaled for a time-out and designed a play for Abdul-Jabbar, who took a pass from Worthy and, with eight seconds left, was hacked by Parish on a wide left hook shot. He sank the first free throw but missed the second. The basketball was batted out of bounds and Ainge, believing possession belonged to Boston, gleefully jumped up and down. However, the officials ruled it touched McHale last. With seven seconds on the clock, the Lakers received one final chance.

Riley called his last time-out. He had a plan. Positioned along the baseline, Cooper inbounded the ball to Johnson, who stood just outside the three-point line. Worthy cleared out, Abdul-Jabbar posted, then shifted away from the paint, and Johnson drove past Ainge, past McHale and into the lane. With three seconds left, he released a running jump hook over the outstretched arms of both Parish and McHale. Like Bird's shot moments earlier, Johnson's ball hung high in the air, the Garden's silent tension seeming to serve as its helium. It floated through the net, and Abdul-Jabbar leapt for joy. "A junior, junior, junior skyhook," Johnson later said, describing the shot.

Bird's final-second jumper hit the rim and bounced out, and Los Angeles escaped with a riveting 107–106 win. Afterward, when asked by CBS's James Brown whether he thought the Celtics had intentionally increased their physicality for the game, Johnson flashed his glistening smile. "Well," he said, "it was a conscious effort on our part, too."

■ ■ ■

And that was pretty much it. The Celtics managed to take another win in Boston, but it was a fleeting last gasp. Bird, who praised Johnson as the best player he'd ever seen, acknowledged his team's odds of winning two at the Forum were somewhere between none and none.

When Los Angeles finished off the series with a 106–93 Game 6 demolition, the burdened Cooper took a long breath of relief. The finals were over, as was something much deeper. The greatest rivalry the NBA had ever known had reached its conclusion. The Celtics were looking like an old Buick Electra, with hubcaps and spare parts falling off to the left and right. Bird's back was a mess. Parish's skills were diminished. Dennis Johnson had slowed significantly. The bench—once a Celtic hallmark for depth and talent—wouldn't have started for most CBA teams. One year earlier, the franchise had used the number two overall pick in the NBA Draft to select a potentially great Maryland forward named Len Bias. When, two days later, he died of a cocaine overdose, the future of Boston-Los Angeles battles seemed to die, too.

"People ask if I hate the Boston Celtics," said Kurt Rambis. "That's always been the wrong word. It was actually more like a love, born out of competition. The hatred is that you love to compete with those guys at that high of a level. If you're truly a competitive athlete, you want to beat the best team playing their best in the most hostile environment possible. That's what makes competition fun. I looked at Larry and Kevin and Robert and I thought, 'I want to do everything in my power to beat you.' That's not hatred. That's not even close to hatred.

"You know what it is? It's love."

CHAPTER 16

___

SHATTERED GLASS

For the first time since 1983, the Lakers entered the off-season without an opening-round pick in the upcoming NBA Draft.

This was Jerry West's turf.

The Los Angeles general manager was emerging as one of the greatest personnel gurus the sport had ever seen. He was also— Well, let's allow those who observed him to tell it:

- Mike Downey, *Los Angeles Times* columnist: "A pretty strange dude. There was a blind spot in his personality."
- Keith Erickson, Lakers broadcaster: "Always nervous—Jerry was *always* nervous."
- Don Greenberg, *Orange County Register* beat writer: "Wrapped up tighter than anyone on the planet."
- Randy Harvey, *Los Angeles Times* beat writer: "Jerry West was crazy. Really crazy. All the writers knew he was crazy. But we didn't quite know the depth of it. He couldn't stop himself from saying what was on his mind, and he was always pissed at you the next day because you quoted him. I never got a call from him denying that he said what he said, but he would just say things— crazy things. 'Kareem's a dog.' You quote him the next day and he says, 'Why'd you use that?' Well, you said it and you didn't say don't use it. 'I know I said it but I didn't say use it!' Just crazy."

People within the Laker organization loved West—and it had nothing to do with his status as one of the NBA's all-time superstars. West had played fourteen seasons for the team, averaging 27 points, appearing in fourteen All-Star games and helping the franchise capture the 1972 championship. "But that wasn't what was so great about Jerry," said Joan McLaughlin, who worked in the team's human resources department for more than thirty years. "You could talk to him—really talk to him. I could go in there and say, 'You know, Jerry, I'm ready to kill someone.' And he'd listen to me and talk me out of it. The other thing is, Jerry hated his celebrity. He had no interest in fame or VIP treatment. He wanted to be a guy who did a job."

"When I was an intern with the team, someone called me with a speaking request for Jerry," said Richard Crasnick, who later became the director of promotions. "I told Jerry how much it paid, and he accepted it. Well, months later I received a personal check in the mail from Jerry. It was commission for the speech. How many guys would have done that? Would have even thought to have done that? He was a special man."

Behind the Ken Doll looks and confident exterior, however, was a tortured soul. Quirkiness wasn't mere quirkiness. Irrational moments weren't simply irrationality. His personal battles were kept hidden until 2011, when he released an autobiography, subtitled *My Charmed, Tormented Life*, that delved into his lifelong battle with depression. The caricature of West had often been that of a hick from West Virginia who clawed his way out of the coal mines and into a life of NBA glory. He was nicknamed Zeke from Cabin Creek by Elgin Baylor, and, though he'd usually smile when the words were uttered, he hated it, hated *everything* about it. He was raised in Chelyan, West Virginia, by an abusive father, Howard West, who caused him to feel tormented. His older brother, David, was killed in the Korean War when Jerry was twelve, compounding his depression. As a young teen, he slept with a shotgun under his bed and was always prepared to use it on his dad in anticipation of another beating. "I would go to sleep feeling like I didn't even want to live," West said. "I've been so low sometimes and when everyone else would be so high because I didn't like myself."

It was a love for basketball that helped him rise above and, eventually, run the Lakers. But he was never fully able to shake a nightmarish past. "I think most people would agree on this: there are certain events that are important in your life and can do damage to it. Life-changing events," West wrote. "And I've had some of those, and, unfortunately, they happened to me when I was young. But they, perhaps more than anything else, formed much of the crucible of who I am, and almost certainly made me into the determined person and sick competitor that I became. A tormented, defiant figure who carries an angry, emotional chip on his shoulder and has a hole in his heart that nothing can ultimately fill."

In an effort to hide—if not heal—a lifetime of scars, West threw himself into the job. Losses destroyed him. Wins also destroyed him—a sloppy moment, a poor coaching decision, a bad pass. When the team sealed the championship against Boston, West smiled for approximately 4.1 seconds. Then he thought about all the things that went wrong. Every failing and shortcoming was taken personally. "He lived and died with our success," said McLaughlin. "I think Jerry felt like it was all on him. Like it was his fault if things went poorly."

This was never more true than the drafts. Although the organization wound up with the number one picks that landed Magic Johnson and James Worthy, the Lakers' annual championship runs resulted in multiple late-round selections. The challenge enticed West and his cohorts—the idea of holding, say, a twenty-third pick in the 1985 Draft, watching others swing and miss on the likes of Kenny Green (Washington Bullets), Alfredrick Hughes (San Antonio Spurs) and Uwe Blab (Dallas Mavericks), then scoring a future All-Star like A. C. Green. Sure, the Lakers occasionally misfired (Earl Jones would always haunt West's soul), but more often than not, they hit.

This time, however, the task was especially daunting. Having traded their first- and second-round picks, the Lakers were forced to wait until the sixty-ninth and final spot of the third round to acquire a player. It was, for a man who struggled to sit still, torturous. West knew the franchise wouldn't be drafting Navy center David Robinson or UNLV forward Armen Gilliam, the two grand prizes. But as one mediocre yet passable college standout after another fell from the board, things turned ugly. When, at picks 56 and 57, Millerville's John Fox and Alaska Anchorage's Hansi Gnad were plucked, it was official—no one even approaching Earl Jones–esque potential was left to be had.

"So," said Josh Rosenfeld, the media relations director, "we took a shot on Willie Glass."

If West couldn't draft big, he insisted upon at least drafting athletic. At 6-foot-7 and 210 pounds, Glass was the star of St. John's University highlight films. There were two-handed dunks and one-handed dunks and behind-the-back moves that left opponents dizzy. He first dunked as a seventh grader at Central Junior High in Atlantic City, New Jersey, and through the years became increasingly explosive. He averaged only 16.6 points as a senior with the Redmen. But, boy, could Glass levitate. When asked by Earl Bloom of the *Orange County Register* about the pick, West was uncharacteristically bubbly. "He can run and jump with the best," he said. "When you see him in training camp, I don't know if you'll be impressed by his basketball ability, but you'll be impressed with his athletic ability. He is spectacular."

West loved the idea of adding yet another diamond in the rough to his list of draft conquests. Then Glass reported to the Lakers' summer league team. He had been listed in the St. John's media guide as standing at 6-foot-7. The Lakers, having heard he was a smidge shorter, wrote his name in press releases alongside "6-foot-6."

"Well, he shows up, and he's small," said Rosenfeld. "Really small." Though the organization maintained 6-foot-6 in its registry, Glass measured three inches shorter. When camp opened, he was thoroughly outplayed. "Was I intimidated? Sure," he said. "When I was in college our center was Bill Wennington. Now I'm playing with Kareem Abdul-Jabbar, with Magic Johnson, with James Worthy. I thought I did OK, but it's a different level." Riley later said he'd never coached a player with less court sense than Glass. West agreed. Glass failed to understand defensive rotation and play calls. He ran fast and hard, but rarely in the right direction. Veterans like Johnson and Scott found him likable enough, but far from worthy of wearing a Laker uniform. He did, however, leave Los Angeles with one great story.

Jerry Buss always made certain to welcome the team's top draft pick to the city with a nice dinner. He ordered Rosenfeld to find a veteran, and the two of them would escort Glass. "I called Michael Cooper," Rosenfeld said. "He asked if he could pick the restaurant. I couldn't see why not." Cooper insisted upon Mr. Chow, one of Beverly Hills's trendiest eateries, and had Rosenfeld book a limousine for the occasion. "Michael did the ordering," said Rosenfeld. "We ordered five different lobster dishes, three bottles of pink champagne. The bill was in the thousands." When the evening was complete, Rosenfeld returned Glass safely to his hotel. "We just had this huge meal, we drank fantastic champagne, and we're driving back," Rosenfeld said. "And Willie has the limo stop at McDonald's—where he orders two Big Macs, two large fries, two apple pies and two milk shakes."

On October 21, the Lakers cut Willie Glass, who scored two points in one exhibition game. Before long, he was a member of the Youngstown Pride of the fledgling World Basketball League.

To participate, one had to be 6-foot-5 or shorter.

■ ■ ■

Even though Glass failed to measure up, West was thrilled by another strong possibility entering the 1987–88 season: Kareem Abdul-Jabbar was thinking about retiring.

It was, for many Lakers players and executives, a long time coming. Now forty and increasingly skeletal, Abdul-Jabbar was merely another of the league's OK starting centers. "I think Kareem is a good person," said Lon Rosen. "But there are things he did that were always different than the other guys. It was a generational thing, really. He was from a different generation, and that gap was felt."

"Thank God Kareem was my teammate, because I used to cringe at the way he treated people," Johnson said. "There was a way to say no. You could say, 'I'm busy right now' or 'Sorry, not today.' But Kareem didn't do it in a very kind way. Sometimes he'd have people in tears."

As he aged, Abdul-Jabbar turned into a hindrance during training camp and practices. From the day the players reported, Riley made it clear that his goal was to repeat—*and only to repeat*. Before the start of every season, Riley insisted every player have his body fat measured, then partake in a stress test—where one would sprint on a treadmill with electrodes attached to the body. "You felt like you were going to die," said one player. "Your lungs feel like they're going to explode, sweat everywhere. Riley wanted to see what you were made of." The Lakers were known for their intense workouts, but Riley upped it to a new level of tenacity. "I never saw anything like it," said Jeff Lamp, a fourth-year guard who beat out Glass for the final roster spot. "I went to high school in Louisville, Kentucky, where basketball is everything and all you do is play, play, play. But the Lakers—man. Pat was *so* demanding. You had to do it right, or you didn't bother doing it. And Magic set this tone of all-out intensity. Wind sprints, little drills—everything you did, you did to win. I was on the second team, and we'd always scrimmage the starters in practice. In other places I'd been, the reserves beat the starters every so often. I mean, we're all NBA players. But with the Lakers—not once. Literally, not one time did we beat them. There was a core group of guys who refused to lose. That's awfully powerful."

Abdul-Jabbar was, once upon a time, among the core. Now he couldn't keep up. He skipped scrimmages and sometimes full workouts. Mychal Thompson and Mike Smrek would fill in, and the team often played better. Many Lakers thought (actually, *knew*) Thompson should have been starting in the middle. Abdul-Jabbar was, simply, too slow to partake in Showtime. But, even for powerful men like Riley, some moves are impossible to make. The Lakers would have to win with Abdul-Jabbar and, often, in spite of him. "The scrimmages were better when Kareem wasn't playing," Johnson said. "We'd run up and down and up and down with no big man to slow us down." Johnson urged the center to get his rest—half because he genuinely wanted Abdul-Jabbar to take it easy, half because Showtime basketball alongside Thompson was bliss.

Luckily, the Lakers boasted a new deadly weapon in their arsenal. Not that Byron Scott was new, per se. Now in his fifth NBA season, the shooting guard was twenty-six years old and firmly entrenched as a part of the core. But something had snapped in Scott, something the Lakers had been waiting for since acquiring him in the controversial Norm Nixon trade. The change began during the previous season's finals, when Scott rendered himself invisible at the Boston Garden. He shot 2-for-9 in Game 3, then 3-for-10 in Game 4. After scoring a mere 7 points on 3-for-10 shooting in the fifth game, Scott experienced a miniature meltdown. On the flight back to California, he wallowed in self-pity, questioning his ability to perform in hostile environments. "The Boston mystique, the crowds, what they were writing in the papers—I let myself get to the point where I thought maybe I couldn't get the job done," he said. "I was thinking about my shots, and how I wasn't taking them. That stuff pretty much took over me. I pretty much was listening to what everybody was saying. I thought maybe they had lost confidence in me. That hurt more than anything, that my two best friends on the team—Magic and Coop—might have lost a little confidence in me."

Though Johnson and Cooper insisted it was nonsense, Scott was shaken. Johnson went so far as to ask Riley to invite Scott into his office for a one-on-one meeting. The point guard did so assuming Riley would offer up one of his famed pep talks about Scott's value and ability. Instead, the coach told Scott that, indeed, he was blowing it. "I used Kareem, James and [Magic] as examples," Riley said. "If you want to walk in their shoes, you have to learn to take the criticism and perform."

The words sunk in. Scott hated being thought of as a peashooter in the

Showtime weaponry. He had been a star in high school, a star at Arizona State. The Lakers surrendered one of their best players to acquire him, and the results were mixed. Scott averaged a career-high 17 points in 1986–87, but rarely hit a key shot in a crucial moment. "We almost never called a big play for him when it counted," Riley said.

As the Lakers spent the off-season having their attentions diverted in 1,001 different directions (Jerry Buss fought a $25 million palimony suit against a woman named Puppi; Cooper and his wife took a tropical vacation; Johnson attended a 4-H rally in Michigan, appeared at a camp in Kentucky, attended Pacer center Herb Williams's wedding in Indiana, ran clinics in Thousand Oaks and San Diego), Scott focused on basketball. He spent mornings, evenings and nights either with his wife and two children, or at the gym—lifting weights, popping jumpers, running wind sprints. "Byron is very strong in his beliefs," said Anita Scott, his wife. "When he decides he wants to do something, he does it well. He goes after it with purpose and intensity."

The Byron Scott who reported to training camp was an upgraded model. Instead of settling for long jumpers, he drove to the basket. In the past, Cooper knew Scott would go toward the right 95 percent of the time. Now he was mixing things up. On defense, meanwhile, Scott's intensity was unlike ever before. He had always admired Cooper's approach to being a shutdown player. He was suddenly one, too. "Now I know that whoever's guarding me is in for a rough night, and they'd better be ready to give me forty-eight minutes of strong, aggressive defense," he said. "Because I'm going to give them forty-eight minutes of strong, aggressive offense *and* defense. They're going to have their work cut out for them."

Featuring an improved Scott, the Lakers soared. In the immediate aftermath of the finals, Riley had irked many of the players by guaranteeing Los Angeles would become the first team to repeat as champions in nineteen years. It was the sort of pressure few wanted or needed. "Just when we thought we'd done everything we could do, Riles makes this guarantee," Scott said. "I thought he was crazy. [But] guaranteeing a championship was the best thing Pat ever did. It set the stage in our mind. Work harder, be better. That's the only way we could repeat. We came into camp with the idea we were going to win it again."

Los Angeles set a franchise record by winning the first eight games of the season, and—with the exception of the opener, during which he shot

1-for-9—Scott was brilliant. In the second game of the season, a 101–92 bettering of the Rockets, he hit five of his first six shots and led the team with 23 points. Six days later, he lit up Golden State for 27 points on 12-for-20 shooting. Scott was neither the strongest nor quickest guard around. But his catch-and-release motion was instantaneous, and his confidence was peaking. "When you play on a team of superstars, it's easy to get overlooked—and Byron probably did," said Lamp, Scott's backup. "But he really did everything well. He could go full speed, stop and hit the jumper, which is really hard to do. He also defended opposing point guards, and he did so well. He would lock guys down."

Once again, the Lakers were the talk of the league. And the league—as represented by the Seattle SuperSonics—decided to respond. On November 24, the two Pacific Division rivals met for a game at the Seattle Center Coliseum. Under the guidance of Bernie Bickerstaff, their combative third-year coach, the Sonics believed they were legitimate challengers to Los Angeles's dominance. In forward Tom Chambers and shooting guard Dale Ellis, the team featured two of the league's most explosive scorers. More important, despite their somewhat effeminate green-and-yellow uniforms, the Sonics were tough. Veteran center Alton Lister was a 7-foot, 240-pound steel vault, rookie center Olden Polynice was built like a Zeus statue—and then there was Xavier McDaniel, the 6-foor-7, 205-pound second-year forward from Wichita State. Featuring a shaved head and Manson-esque scowl, McDaniel was the NBA's answer to a hockey goon. If anyone messed with Seattle, they messed with the X Man.

Playing their third game in five days, Los Angeles came out listless. Seattle led 25–22 after one quarter, and 55–40 at the half. The Lakers had lost their first game of the season to Milwaukee two days earlier, and Riley wasn't happy. During the halftime break, he questioned his team's collective manhood and wondered aloud whether they would simply allow the Sonics to steal both a game and their air of invincibility. Many of the players tuned Riley out—they'd heard this before, blah, blah, blah, blah, blah. One man, however, received the message.

Midway through the third quarter, shortly after he was sent in to replace Johnson, Wes Matthews was the recipient of an unusually hard pick by McDaniel. On Seattle's following possession, Matthews stole the ball from point guard Nate McMillan and promptly dribbled it off his right foot. Matthews dove for the ball while intentionally kicking McDaniel in the face. Without pause, McDaniel lunged for Matthews, wrapping his meaty hands around a bony neck. "My first reaction," McDaniel said, "was I wasn't going to take any crap from him."

Cooper stepped in and separated the two, though the bad blood had only just begun. After the game, Riley praised Matthews' toughness. His team played meekly in the 103–85 defeat, but the diminutive guard heeded his words. Why, the Lakers even went on a 22–4 run in the altercation's aftermath. Asked about the skirmish, Riley snarled, "We should have done it earlier."

When reporters approached Matthews for comment, they presumed bygones were bygones. Though thought to be mildly insane, Matthews was also a warm and gregarious character who relished signing autographs and chatting with young fans. His smile was inviting, and teammates came to love him. Gordon Edes of the *Los Angeles Times* asked whether he was still upset over the fight.

"I've got nothing to say," Matthews said.

OK, then . . .

"Except," Matthews continued, "that he's a fucking faggot. And when he comes to L.A., he's mine."

Uh, Wes. He's a half foot taller than you are. He outweighs you by thirty-five pounds.

"He should have been thrown out of the game for grabbing my neck," Matthews said. "I can't wait to play him again, because his bald head is mine."

Matthews was not laughing. Matthews was not kidding. Matthews knew he would one day cave in Xavier McDaniel's skull with a brick. "He was a bum," Matthews said years later. "He was a bum then, he's a bum now. If he walked in where I was sitting right now, I'd bust him in his face. I'd just bust him."

David Stern, the NBA's commissioner, watched the tape of the altercation and issued no fines. He expected the participants to move forward and forget the whole thing. Stern didn't know Wes Matthews.

One week after the Laker game, the Sonics traveled to New York to play the Knicks. According to Matthews, two friends from Bridgeport, Connecticut, visited Madison Square Garden to "chat" with McDaniel. They met him in a tunnel beneath the arena after shootaround and, Matthews said, told him that if he played, he would receive a post-game beating either at the arena or via a visit to the team's hotel. "They called me later," Matthews said, "and told me, 'Yo, you don't have to worry about X no more.'"

"What'd you do?" Matthews said he asked.

"Don't worry," he was told. "X might not even play tonight."

Several days later, Matthews was contacted by the NBA. "I was fined ten thousand dollars for threatening another player," he said. "I said, 'What are you talking about? I'm in L.A. I didn't threaten nobody.' They didn't believe me."

Is Matthews' account truthful? Hard to say. McDaniel never spoke of the incident. A durable player, he missed but four games that season.

One was against the Knicks.

■ ■ ■

As the Lakers cruised through yet another regular season, a new threat was emerging in the East. Though nothing was officially written, the Boston Celtics were no longer the class of the region or the concern of Los Angeles fans. Larry Bird and Co. would go on to win 57 games and reach the conference finals, but an element of past dominance had vanished. A small part of this was due to the listless way they fell to the Lakers in the '87 Finals. A big part of this was due to the rise of a new breed.

The Detroit Pistons were, after years of steady improvement, on the verge of arriving. Or, in the opinion of many NBA players, on the verge of establishing the league's first thug academy. Under the guidance of Jack Mc-Closkey, the team's widely respected general manager and a former Lakers assistant, the Pistons had constructed a deep and talented roster. Detroit specialized in taking cast-offs from elsewhere and—with coach Chuck Daly's Zen-like tutelage—cobbling the pieces into a cohesive unit. The team's starting center, Bill Laimbeer (who Tony Kornheiser of *The Washington Post* once nicknamed Bill "Would It Be Terribly Inconvenient if I Jammed My Fist Into Your Kidney on This Possession" Laimbeer), had been an underwhelming goon with Cleveland before the Pistons got him for a package of players and picks. Power forward Rick Mahorn played five relatively nondescript years in Washington when the Bullets happily dealt him for Dan Roundfield. From shooting guard Vinnie Johnson (acquired from Seattle for Greg Kelser) to backup center James Edwards (nabbed from the Suns for forward Ron Moore and a pick) to Joe Dumars, a first-round pick out of McNeese

State two years earlier who had yet to distinguish himself, the Pistons roster was a Who's Who of Who's That?

With one notable exception. When Detroit used the second overall spot in the 1981 NBA Draft to select an Indiana University sophomore guard named Isiah Thomas, it wasn't merely adding a quick, instinctive court general from Chicago's rough-and-tumble West Side. No, in Thomas, the Pistons were getting their very own gnat. Were Thomas a teammate, you loved him. Were Thomas an opponent, you wanted to hurt him. Blessed with the fastest first step anyone had ever seen, Thomas's ball-handling ability was straight from the Pete Maravich playbook. Coming out of college, Thomas was compared by *Sports Illustrated*'s William F. Reed to a certain Laker, noting that, "When Isiah Thomas smiles, when his eyes light up and his teeth flash and those huge dimples appear, you can't help but think of the last sophomore guard who took a Big Ten team to the NCAA basketball championship—Earvin (Magic) Johnson."

Yet in his first six seasons, Thomas's on-court excellence (20.7 points, 10.2 assists per game) was coupled by the mounting reputation as an arrogant, me-first fraud, one who smiled for the cameras and fans but would steal your wallet or break your heart if it helped his cause. He was, in professional wrestling speak, the heel, jabbing your ribs, kicking your shins, wrapping his hand around your wrist in a fight for a rebound. In public, he played the cuddly teddy bear. On the hardwood, he was Roddy Piper.

Just as the Lakers fed off of Johnson, the Pistons absorbed Thomas's demeanor. What they lacked in the transcendent skill of a James Worthy or Byron Scott, they made up for with borderline-criminal play. It was Mahorn, a 6-foot-10, 240-pound bus, who said that a physical game for the Pistons was when every opponent was bleeding from the mouth. "The way I saw it, we would be like the old Oakland Raiders," Thomas once wrote. "They had all the characters on their team, they were a bunch of misfit guys just grouped together. That's the same portrait that had been painted of our team: a bunch of crazies all assembled on one basketball team. The implication was that none of us really belonged, that our locker room was a padded cell, and that Chuck Daly was coaching in an insane asylum."

Together, Thomas and his teammates lifted a line from *Scarface*, the beloved Al Pacino film, and adopted it as their own—"Say hello to the bad guy, because you'll never see another bad guy like me." The words served as a rallying cry for thuggery and aggressiveness. "Toughest team I've ever seen," said Chuck Nevitt, the former Laker center who spent a brief spell with the Pistons. "They wouldn't take anything from anyone."

Although Thomas was among the NBA's least-liked players, Johnson loved him. The two first met in 1979, introduced by Mark Aguirre, a mutual friend who, at the time, was starring at DePaul University. They bonded over the game they owned and the desire to play at the highest level. When Thomas declared eligible for the NBA Draft, Johnson invited him to his home in Lansing, Michigan, to train. Through the years, whenever he visited Los Angeles, Thomas stayed in Johnson's house, in quarters referred to as the Isiah Room. (When people would ask about the spare bedroom, Johnson would say, "Oh, that's Isiah's.") The stars would dine the night before a game, laughing about old times. In the off-seasons, Thomas, Johnson and Aguirre took twice-a-summer Hawaiian vacations together—one to relax with wives/girlfriends, the other to train on the sandy beaches. The three men would also annually rent a bus in Detroit and travel to Sandusky, Ohio, home of the Cedar Point amusement park. "Every time Detroit lost in the East, Isiah would come out to Los Angeles," said Gary Vitti, the Lakers trainer. "And Magic would let Isiah come into the locker room and training room and show him all the things it took to succeed. Isiah absorbed it."

Johnson had heard all the Isiah bashing through the years, and he passionately defended his friend. "You don't understand," he said on multiple occasions. "Inside, Isiah is a beautiful soul. You just don't understand. . . ."

The dynamic shifted, however, with Detroit's loss to Boston in the 1987 Eastern Conference Finals. Thomas had helped blow the series with an errant inbounds pass that was intercepted by Larry Bird at the end of Game 5. After the Celtics wrapped things up two games later, the Pistons—led by Thomas—behaved as infants. Dennis Rodman, the team's rookie power forward, suggested that Bird was vastly overrated. Then, in a moment that would forever scar his career, Thomas was asked what he thought of his teammate's assessment. "Larry Bird is a very good player," Thomas said. "An exceptional talent. But I'd have to agree with Rodman that if he were black, he'd be just another good guy."

Thomas later insisted he was speaking in jest, and begged detractors to listen to the audio tape. Indeed, his words were followed by a slight chuckle. "Anyone who knows me well," he told Brent Musburger, "knows I tease a lot." Johnson knew Thomas well. Johnson knew Thomas teased a lot. Johnson did *not* find the line funny. On the day after the comments, with the backlash mounting, John Black, who worked in the Lakers' media relations office, called Johnson. "Your boy Isiah has done it," Black said. "What do you want me to tell people?"

"Leave me out of it," Johnson replied.

Throughout their careers, Johnson and Thomas had always been there for each other. When Johnson sat inconsolable in a Boston hotel room after the 1984 Finals, Thomas arrived to comfort him. When Thomas's pass was intercepted by Bird, Johnson was immediately on the phone. Yet while the two considered themselves tight, what Johnson felt for Bird was more profound. They weren't especially close, and spoke only on occasion. Yet they were fused by brotherhood. Instead of phoning Thomas, Johnson found himself dialing Bird's number. "Isiah doesn't speak for me," he told the Celtic.

"It doesn't mean anything to me," Bird said. "Really, I could care less."

To Johnson, however, Thomas's behavior drove a wedge in their relationship. He was no longer 100 percent certain what this man stood for. It was as if, with the words "If he were black . . . ," Johnson was snapped out of a spell and forced to see the real Isiah Thomas.

On January 8, 1988, the Lakers traveled to Detroit bolstered by a 12-game winning streak and, at 23-6, the NBA's best record. The Pistons' 19-8 mark had them second in the Central Division. In the lead-up, Johnson insisted he and Thomas remained pals. No, they hadn't seen each other in four months, and no, they didn't talk quite so often, but, well, uh, eh, yeah.

Before the game, Riley reminded his players that the Pistons were similar in style to the Celtics—only dirtier. The NBA's largest crowd of the season, 40,278 spectators, packed the Pontiac Silverdome, hoping to witness the first stage in a changing of the league's power structure. "This," Mychal Thompson said afterward, "was a preview of what World War III will look like."

Thanks to Scott's 35 points and a missed jumper from Laimbeer with two seconds remaining, Los Angeles—which trailed by 11 at the half—held on for a riveting 106–104 victory. The contest featured multiple technicals and a stream of vulgar trash talk. The most interesting exchange, though, came fifteen minutes after the final buzzer. A member of the Detroit scoring crew interrupted Riley's session with the media to ask whether he harassed the referees at halftime in order to seek better calls. Not one to lose his temper before the cameras, the coach went ballistic. Just as he had suspected Red

Auerbach of playing puppet master in the Boston Garden, he had little trust for the Pistons. "I've never gone to the officials' room and fucking begged for anything in my life!" he growled. He edged closer to the inquisitor. "That is absolute bullshit," he said. "Where did you come up with something like that? That came from your fucking asshole. That's it. Period. We won this game, fair and square. It's an absolute insult to ask me a question like that." Riley stormed off and slammed the dressing room door behind him.

The outburst was, to a small degree, about the question. It also likely reflected a genuine fear manifesting within Riley. The Detroit Pistons were not only exceptionally good, but also exceptionally smart when it came to playing the Lakers. On too many occasions, the Celtics had caught themselves running up and down the court at breakneck speed, trying to match Showtime. It used to frustrate Bird, and he'd implore his teammates to calm themselves. Detroit, on the other hand, played a consistently steady pace. Their personnel were designed to bang and bruise, and the team stuck to the script.

When, five weeks later, the Pistons came to Los Angeles for a rematch, they again faced a juggernaut on a roll. The Lakers had won six straight games over eight exhausting days, including batterings of the Celtics (115–106) and Rockets (111–96) and a magnificent overtime road win against the high-flying Atlanta Hawks (126–119). "No team is this good," Scott Ostler wrote in the *Los Angeles Times*. "So many things could happen to derail the Lakers. If Pat Riley runs for president, as suggested by actress Teri Garr on a recent David Letterman show in a flash of lucid inspiration, it might interfere with Riley's concentration and adversely affect the Lakers' delicate chemistry."

As was the case in Michigan, the Pistons jumped out to an early lead, holding a 12-point advantage at halftime. Once again the game was bestial. Only a few days earlier Al Davis, owner of the Los Angeles Raiders, sent the Pistons a box filled with silver-and-black sweaters—a symbolic bonding of blood-and-bone franchises. Mark Heisler of the *Times* called Daly's squad "basketball's answer to a herd of stampeding rhinos." He was dead-on.

"Nobody has attacked us that way in a long time," a sweat-drenched Riley said after Los Angeles came back to snag a 117–110 triumph. "Nobody." A moment from the first half perfectly encapsulated the new rivalry. Abdul-Jabbar connected on a hook shot in the lane as Laimbeer swatted him below the ear with a forearm. The Lakers captain pointed and growled, "Don't hit me in the head."

"Get out of my face," Laimbeer replied, "and keep on playing."

Though Thomas tallied 42 points and 10 assists, the Lakers remained a half step ahead. Worthy scored 24, Scott 23, Abdul-Jabbar 20 and Johnson added 19 points and 13 assists. Riley also turned to the one member of the team who seemed to know what it was to perform angrily. Wes Matthews, normally a deep reserve, had often been compared to Thomas when he starred collegiately at Wisconsin—and it always irked him. "Shit, I was a better player," Matthews said. "We'd go head to head in college, and I never had problems with him. He couldn't stop me." Now, late in the game, Riley asked Matthews to guard Thomas. With thirty-eight seconds remaining and the Lakers up 112–110, Detroit's star drove to the lane, where he was met by Thompson, Johnson and Abdul-Jabbar. The ball was knocked from his hands and retrieved by Matthews. He calmly sank two free throws to finish with 14 points and finish off Detroit.

"We all knew we'd see those guys again," Matthews said. "It was a lock."

■ ■ ■

Perhaps it was the Wes Matthews influence.

Perhaps it was the Detroit Pistons influence.

Perhaps it was the influence of an increasingly popular genre of music known as gangsta rap; the influence of the Raiders; the influence of violent movies and violent television programs and a coach who could scream his head off. Whatever the case, as the Lakers pieced together one of the best seasons in franchise history, life grew increasingly violent.

It began with the Wes Matthews–Xavier McDaniel scuffle, but didn't end. There was the bench-clearing brawl at the Forum on January 22, during which Pat Cummings, the Knicks veteran forward, slapped A. C. Green across the face and, as punishment, was sucker-punched by a hard-charging Cooper. The two exchanged blows and tumbled over the courtside seats. "I knew I had to keep my head down," Cummings recalled years later. "Because in a fight with Michael, I'd be the one to get knocked out."

"The message has to be out that this stuff about 'Beat the Lakers up and you beat the Lakers' has no meaning," Cooper said. "It's bullshit and we won't stand for it."

The most eye-catching incident occurred on the afternoon of April 21, and involved Abdul-Jabbar, an Italian tourist, a Phoenix shopping mall and a ridiculously large video camera.

The season was going surprisingly well for the Lakers center, who averaged less than thirty minutes per game for the first time in his career and, as a result, felt fresh as the playoffs approached. He decided, after much debate, to put off retiring yet again, meaning Johnson, Cooper, Scott and Co. wouldn't be all-out running anytime soon. "What people forget is that, even at forty and forty-one, Kareem was better than most centers," said Bill Bertka, the assistant coach. "No, he wasn't what he was at twenty-five. But he was still good."

In town to play the Suns in the penultimate game of the regular season, Abdul-Jabbar headed to the Metrocenter, a shopping mall within walking distance of the team's hotel. While cruising from store to store, he noticed a bulky camcorder pointed in his direction. Abdul-Jabbar said he asked the man to stop taping, and—when the request was refused—pushed the device aside in order to pass. "I didn't touch him," Abdul-Jabbar said. "All I did was brush the camera out of my way. If he didn't push the camera in my way, I probably wouldn't have taken any notice of him. I was just in a hurry and didn't feel like having the guy following me with a camera."

Fernando Nicola, the forty-year-old owner of a chain of foreign language schools in Frosinone, Italy, saw things differently. In town visiting his brother, Christian, he told police he was videotaping the mall itself—"He thought it was just fabulous, and not like anything he had back home," said Stephen Leshner, his attorney. "We watched the tape, and when Kareem walks by in the distance you can hear [Nicola] say, in Italian, 'Look at that long black man.'" Nicola said Abdul-Jabbar aggressively charged forward. "He straight-armed the guy, knocked the camera into him and knocked the camera down," Leshner said decades later. "I have nothing to gain from saying this—it was a long time ago. But it was obvious that Kareem was in the wrong here."

Abdul-Jabbar and Nicola wound up settling out of court, but, for Leshner, the lasting memory had nothing to do with the amount. "I took Kareem's deposition, and he was just an incredible jerk," he said. "I used an office space in L.A., and Kareem told us no one in the building was allowed to talk to him, or even look at him. He was very specific—no eye contact allowed. Ever. By anyone."

Abdul-Jabbar skipped all but eight minutes of the final two games (both victories), and Los Angeles completed a 62–20 season that marked the franchise's fourth straight with at least 60 wins. They had survived an injury-plagued campaign during which Cooper and Johnson missed considerable time. They had endured the pressure of Riley's guarantee and the inevitability of Abdul-Jabbar's decline. When *Sports Illustrated* featured the entire Lakers roster on its April 18 cover, alongside the headline HOW GOOD?, the answer was obvious but unspoken: Really friggin' good.

The Western Conference playoffs, presumed to be child's play for the best team in basketball, were anything but. The Lakers swept the Spurs in the opening round, then struggled against Utah and Dallas, respectively, needing all seven games against both clubs. When his team finally vanquished the Mavericks, 117–102, in Game 7 at the Forum, a relieved Riley took a deep breath, stared down a bushel of microphones and displayed all the modesty of Napoleon.

"We've got a chance of being the greatest team ever," he said. "I really do believe that. Whether people want to believe me or not, whether they think I'm crazy or not, we now have a chance to be something very special."

A mere 2,283 miles away, members of the Detroit Pistons had gathered at the team's practice facility to see who they would be meeting in the NBA Finals. One day earlier, they had eliminated the Celtics in a gutsy Game 6, and their collective confidence was as high as it'd ever been.

"It is," said Thomas, "our time."

CHAPTER 17

MOTOWN

In the early months of 1988, Tony Campbell was—without much debate—the happiest professional basketball player to *not* be on an NBA roster.

For three years, he had been a guard with the Detroit Pistons, the team that selected him out of Ohio State with the twentieth overall pick in the 1984 NBA Draft. It was supposed to be a wonderful time for the kid from Teaneck, New Jersey, who was raised by a single mother and dreamed of one day becoming a prime-time baller. Yet life at the top wasn't all it was chalked up to be. Campbell entered the league having averaged 18.6 points per game as a senior with the Buckeyes, and on draft night Lou Carnesecca, the St. John's coach who was helping with USA Network's coverage, raved. "I think the Detroit team is the team of the future," he said. "Tony Campbell is an excellent scorer. He's aggressive—he can shoot well, can run well, can rebound."

Campbell, however, was never given much of a chance. Chuck Daly, the Pistons coach, found his defense to be lacking and his shot-selection to be dreadful, and Campbell was relegated to the deepest depths of the bench. When he played, he played moderately well. But the opportunities were scarce. "It was disappointing," he said. "The whole experience put a very bad taste in my mouth."

As a result, when the Pistons let him walk after the 1986–87 season, Campbell felt an odd sense of relief. He attended training camp with the Washington Bullets, played six pre-season games, broke his nose and failed to make the team, then signed with the Albany Patroons of the Continental Basketball Association. It was there, in the last spot he ever wanted to be, that Tony Campbell rediscovered his mojo. "I thought I'd be miserable," he said, "but it was just the opposite." To his great surprise, Campbell loved everything about the Albany experience. The Patroons played in the Washington Avenue Armory, and regularly filled all 3,500 seats. Though the team certainly wouldn't compete in the upper echelons of the NBA, its roster was loaded with players (Campbell, Sidney Lowe, Rick Carlisle, Tod Murphy, Scott Brooks) who would one day contribute in the league. "We were all very tight," said Murphy. "Tony was a dominant scorer in Albany, on a team that owned the CBA. He was probably the best player there. He also happened to be a great guy."

Campbell was so enamored of Albany that, as NBA teams began to call with contract offers, he turned them down. The last thing he wanted to do was surrender a good thing (Campbell earned four thousand dollars per month in Albany, was granted a free hotel suite and paid only for food) for a ten-day deal in Cleveland or Atlanta. Even when Mitch Kupchak, the Lakers assistant general manager, reached out in March, Campbell was dismissive. "We have a ten-day contract waiting for you. . . ." Kupchak said.

"No," replied Campbell. "I can't do that."

One week later, Kupchak tried again. "We're fighting for another NBA championship," he said. "You're in the CBA. We have a ten-day deal with your name. . . ."

"Sorry," Campbell said. "I can't do that."

Finally, in late March, Jerry West called—this time with an offer Campbell couldn't refuse. Billy Thompson, Los Angeles's scatterbrained forward, was placed on the injured list with a knee problem, and the team needed a replacement. Should Campbell come to the Forum, he would be handed a guaranteed contract for the remainder of the season, as well as the following year. "If Jerry West calls, you listen," Campbell said. "Jerry West called. I listened."

On March 30, Campbell officially became a Laker. When he arrived for his first day of practice, he anticipated the same standoffishness that had been a trademark of the moody Pistons. "Instead, everyone treated me as if I'd been there for ten years," he said. "It freaked me out, because that wasn't the way I'd seen things in the past." Campbell did not play a big role for the team. He appeared in thirteen regular-season games, started once and scored

28 points in a meaningless matchup with the Warriors. Mostly, he sat alongside Mike Smrek, Milt Wagner and Wes Matthews on the bench, clapping and drinking water. "My job was limited," he said. "But I was happy."

When the Lakers and Pistons were cemented as the finals matchup, Campbell rose from spare part to CIA informant. Although Johnson knew Thomas the person, Campbell knew Thomas's *game*. He'd practiced against him for three years, understood his strengths and weaknesses, how he thought while looking over a defense and what rattled him. The same went for Joe Dumars, Detroit's young shooting guard. And Adrian Dantley, the veteran forward. Campbell could write a five-hundred-page dissertation on the Pistons. "The main thing was defense," he said. "When I was there, Chuck incorporated a system that emphasized tough defense over all else. I knew it, I understood it. That doesn't mean I could make a difference between winning and losing. But I definitely had insight."

In the three days between the win against Dallas and the June 7 opener against the Pistons at the Forum, Campbell was as much coach as player. He filled Cooper's head with a man-by-man breakdown, and advised Abdul-Jabbar on all of Laimbeer's tricks and gimmicks. He warned against Mahorn and Rodman, who reveled in dirtiness. By the time the two teams dug in for the opening tip-off, the Lakers—heavily favored by nearly all prognosticators—felt as ready as they'd ever been for any finals series.

Glub.

Perhaps Riley should have seen this coming. As Jack McCallum noted in *Sports Illustrated*, the Lakers "have looked a little faded in recent weeks, often seeming to show up in pallid lavender and yellow rather than regal purple and gold." They had struggled against the Jazz, then against the Mavericks. Many of the key players (Johnson, Cooper, Worthy) were battling nagging injuries, and Johnson was fighting off early signs of the flu. He was experiencing mild fever and sweats, but kept details out of the media—no need to give the Pistons an extra incentive to forearm his ribs.

Meanwhile, Detroit entered the series on a high. It was the franchise's first appearance in the NBA Finals since relocating from Fort Wayne, Indiana, in 1957, and any expected pressure or nervousness proved nonexistent. As they sat in the Forum's visiting locker room before the opening game, Thomas and Dumars talked feelings.

"Are you even remotely nervous?" Thomas asked Dumars.

"Nope," he said. "You?"

"Not even a little," Thomas replied. "Zero."

"I said to Isiah, 'I wonder how you're supposed to feel,'" Dumars said. "Maybe it was good that we didn't know."

In an NBA Finals first, Game 1 began not merely with handshakes, but with a kiss. As Johnson and Thomas approached each other before the opening tip, they leaned in and smooched on the cheek. The display of affection was kind of weird, kind of cool, kind of confusing. Bird, watching back home on Indiana, was repulsed. He knew damn well it was for show, that the two players would kill each other for a trophy. When asked whether he, too, would have puckered up with Johnson, Dennis Rodman quipped, "Before that, we'd have to get engaged."

In practices, Riley had devoted much of his energy to shutting down Thomas and Dumars, one of the NBA's most explosive backcourts. The strategy was wise but failed to account for Dantley, the long-ago Laker small forward who averaged 20 points during the regular season. At 6-foot-4 (he was an inch smaller than his listed height) and 208 pounds, Dantley was unlike any player in the league. Though undersize and not particularly quick, he owned countless below-the-basket moves, and positioned himself with remarkable precision. Teammates nicknamed him Teach for all the tricks he'd taught them. Wilt Chamberlain once called him the greatest low-post player of all time. "His footwork was marvelous, and he was very clever," said Frank Layden, who coached Dantley for five seasons in Utah. "At the end of games, you had to get Adrian the ball, because he never felt pressure and he always hit his free throws. He was clutch."

Dantley had resented the Lakers since they traded him for Spencer Haywood in 1979, and the chance for payback was especially sweet. In Game 1, he exploited Los Angeles's perimeter-oriented defense, scoring 34 points on 14-for-16 shooting against an overmatched and confused A. C. Green. "At times I was out of position on defense, and he scored every time," Green said. "For the most part I was within our defensive game plan." During one stretch, Dantley scored 12 straight points. When Riley finally began doubling down on Dantley, the ball was flicked out to Thomas and guard Vinnie Johnson, who teamed up for 35 points.

When Dantley hit a layup with six minutes remaining in the game, giving Detroit a 92–75 advantage, thousands of spectators began filing out of the Forum. The 105–93 loss was one of the uglier playoff setbacks of the Riley era. When the coach woke up the following morning, he read multiple newspaper columns rightly slamming him for using a limited seven-man rotation that ignored Wes Matthews (the Isiah badgerer), Campbell (the knower of all things Pistons) and Kurt Rambis and Mike Smrek (physical goons unafraid to rough up opponents). He was out-coached by Daly, and out-muscled by the league's strongest team. "What I remember is that all of our guys were beat up and tired," said Smrek. "The Pistons made you work."

The teams met two nights later, and Riley again limited himself to a seven-man rotation. Within the team's locker room, the tactic was greeted with puzzled expressions—especially considering that Johnson, his body now ravaged by the flu, was struggling to stand for more than a handful of minutes. "I don't wish this on nobody," he said. "The other night I had the chills and sweated a lot and was always going to the restroom. I don't have the fever or chills anymore, but I'm still doing the restroom thing."

The point guard played one of the most courageous games of his career, totaling 23 points and 11 assists. Yet while he received the bulk of the attention, it was James Worthy who saved the Lakers from disaster. Ever since the Celtics had branded him a choker four years earlier, Worthy's ability to produce when it mattered had been mildly questioned. His nickname—Big Game James—was either dripping with pride or with irony, depending on the source. He was a spectacular low-post scorer (Adrian Dantley–esque, only with five more inches and longer arms), but some in the media questioned whether he could carry a team in tight spots.

Trailing by as many as 12 points in the second half, the Pistons went on a 17-to-5 run to tie the game at 80 with 8:17 remaining in the fourth quarter. With the Forum silent and Detroit's bench players on their feet, Riley called a time-out and immediately reinserted Worthy, who had been resting, into the lineup for Mychal Thompson. "I loved the tough, pressure moments," Worthy said. "I always felt like our practices prepared me for them, because they were so intense. Guys like Mike McGee and Larry Spriggs and Mitch Kupchak and Kurt Rambis early in my career—they'd beat me around, make life miserable. So when moments arrived in games, you were ready." Over the next three and a half minutes, Worthy led an 11–2 Los Angeles run, scoring 6 points on a bevy of electric moves. Johnson shot an air ball—Worthy was there to snatch it and lay it in. Worthy drove on John Salley, missed, got his own rebound and—in one motion—tipped the ball in with his left hand over the 6-foot-11 giant. "Who's got Worthy?" Laimbeer could be heard screaming. "Who's got Worthy?" Johnson was trapped along the sideline, spotted Worthy slashing toward the rim and hit him with a no-look, behind-the-back bounce pass for a layup (on a goaltending call). Before the Pistons knew it, they were trailing 91–82. They rallied late, but to no avail. Worthy's 26 points, 10 rebounds and 6 assists were too much to overcome. Los Angeles won, 108–96. "James was a quiet guy—very quiet," said Green. "Maybe people confused that with his on-court persona. Because, with the basketball, he could take over."

The series shifted to Detroit, and the Lakers continued their running ways, soaring past the Pistons in Game 3, 99–86. It was masterful Showtime, with Los Angeles scoring 22 third-quarter points off 13 fast-break opportunities. Johnson had lost seven pounds from the flu, and the IV marks remained visible in his right arm. He looked haggard—but played marvelously (18 points, 14 assists, 7-for-8 shooting). Afterward, he was giddy. His father, Earvin Sr., was petrified of flying, so this was the first time he had watched his son up close in the finals. The Lakers, meanwhile, ate like kings, enjoying a locker room meal of chicken, sweet potato pie and corn bread cooked by Christine Johnson, Magic's mother. Once again, everything was going their way.

"I think the flu was a blessing in disguise for Earvin," Riley said with a straight face. "He lost seven pounds of fluid. I think he was quicker." The Pistons, by comparison, appeared to be slow and cumbersome and painfully outclassed. "We kept searching for something out of our own offense," Laimbeer said afterward, "and we simply forgot to get back on defense."

"We played like high schoolers," Salley said afterward. "No poise."

■ ■ ■

"What the fuck are we doing?"

The question, asked by Bill Laimbeer in the aftermath of Game 3, was directed toward Rick Mahorn and John Salley and Dennis Rodman and Isiah Thomas and the rest of his teammates. The Lakers had streaked past the Pistons as if they were blue-and-red cardboard cutouts. This wasn't Detroit basketball. This wasn't even close to Detroit basketball. Enough with Worthy slashing to the hoop and Scott hitting open jumpers and Johnson firing off no-look passes. Someone needed to be put on his ass—and quickly. The Pistons had excelled all year as black-and-blue basketball players. "We were a physical team," said Dantley. "It was our calling card. But now . . ."

Something had changed. Though the Piston players didn't feel nervous, or look nervous, or act nervous, they were playing nervous. It was as if the Bad Boys felt the Lakers deserved more respect than other teams, and it had to stop.

The Pistons used Game 4 to remind America that they belonged in the finals, standing alongside the world's best basketball team. Not only did they dominate Los Angeles, 111–86, but they sent a very clear message. Less than an hour after they once again kicked off the game with a kiss, Thomas and Johnson engaged in two heated exchanges. First, the Pistons point guard shoved his counterpart in the chest. Then, moments later, Johnson elbowed Thomas in the kidney. Thomas rose and threw the ball at Johnson before lunging for him.

"You see what I've been getting!" Johnson screamed. "Well, now I'm giving it back!"

The two were separated. "[Magic] made the statement that if I came through the lane he would smash me," Thomas said. "I came through the lane; he smashed me."

Johnson insisted he wasn't trying to make a statement to his chum. Years later, however, he changed his story. "I *did* target Isiah," he said. "Pat Riley had questioned me in front of the guys whether I'd take him out. I needed to show them I was willing to do it."

One night later, at approximately seven o'clock, Thomas found himself at St. Joseph Mercy Hospital in Pontiac, witnessing his wife, Lynn, deliver their first child, Joshua Isiah Thomas. Because Thomas was so hopped up on painkillers, Lynn was brought to the hospital by Sondra Nevitt, Chuck's wife. The boy weighed six pounds, five and a half ounces, measured nineteen and a half inches and arrived two weeks earlier than expected.

When he entered the Silverdome for Game 5, Thomas was a walking zombie. He hadn't slept, he'd barely eaten and his stiff back had him crookedly walking to and fro like the Tin Man. He was greeted at his locker by a dozen blue-and-white congratulatory balloons, the strings tied to his stool. When a reporter asked about Joshua, Thomas shushed him away. The Lakers, he noted, wouldn't be offering handshakes and easy paths to the basket. In fact, Los Angeles's players had used the in-between off day to watch tapes from Game 4. What they saw infuriated them. Thomas, Laimbeer, Rodman— all a bunch of provocative thugs. None, however, was worse than Mahorn, who clearly went out of his way to terrorize. The Lakers thought of him as one would a dumb, oversize school yard bully. Mahorn's skills were raw and awkward—coming out of Weaver High in Hartford, Connecticut, he was better known as a potential Division I defensive lineman. He had not even participated in organized hoops until turning seventeen. "I'd messed around a little bit with basketball, but I never played in anything until my senior year of high school," he said. "I'd been a fat kid and stayed with football until I grew."

Based upon his size–power potential, Mahorn earned a scholarship to Hampton Institute, where he set eighteen school records by—in large part—being wider, tougher and more intense than the competition. When a ball came near, Mahorn went for it like a jaguar after a kill. He would either grab it or decapitate an opponent in trying.

The Washington Bullets saw enough to take him in the second round in 1980. Upon arriving in camp, he impaled as many as he impressed. Mahorn's shooting touch was below average and his footwork atrocious. No one, however, set a meaner pick. "He just has a physical style," said Gene Shue, the Bullets coach. "Of course, there are very few players who want to go against someone who is holding his ground. When you have a big body, and you're as strong as Rick is, that's how you should be playing."

Opponents came to view Mahorn as Lucifer in high-tops. His on-court scowl (narrowed eyes, a sinister smile revealing the thin gap between his front teeth) doubled as a TREAD CAUTIOUSLY sign. "You'd think from looking at Mahorn that he's an off-the-street type guy who'd knock your teeth out soon as look at you," said Tom McMillen, a former teammate. "But obviously appearances are deceiving. He's funny—he's like a playful tiger off the court. I like him."

The Lakers did not. The Game 4 tapes revealed one low blow and forearm shiver after another. For the four or five obvious infractions he committed in the course of the game, there were dozens that went unnoticed. "He can dish it out, but can he take it?" Johnson said. "He throws out all this cheap stuff, but he doesn't want you to come back at him. Well, if it happens in Game 5, I'm going to have to hit him right back."

This was what the Pistons loved to hear. The Lakers were tough to crack. Boston's M. L. Carr and Cedric Maxwell had broken through in the 1984 NBA Finals, but Riley's men generally remained controlled and calm. Yet Detroit brought out the worst in them. Before a playoff-record crowd of 41,732, Los Angeles jumped out to a 15–2 Game 5 lead, then watched helplessly as Dantley (25 points, 7 rebounds) and Co. chipped away. The Pistons out-rebounded the Lakers 53–31, and Rodman—overlooked on a team with bigger names—played the game of his life, holding Johnson to 4 of 15 shooting. Worthy spent the night in foul trouble, and was limited to 14 points and twenty-six minutes. The Pistons walked off with a 104–94 victory, a 3-games-to-2 series lead and a special place in the minds of their opponents. It had never been a real possibility (to anyone but the Pistons) that the Lakers might lose. But here they sat, one game from elimination.

"I couldn't even believe it," said Tony Campbell, who played five minutes in the setback. "It didn't register. We couldn't lose. Could we?"

■ ■ ■

They could.

The Lakers were genuinely confused, and Riley was, too. He'd tried running past the Pistons, and that stalled. He tried muscling up the Pistons, and that was a joke, too. "We read in the papers the Lakers were going to bully us," Rodman noted. "You don't do that against us." Riley's pre-game speeches rotated between angry, compassionate, motivational and pleading. Nothing stuck. Mike Downey of the *Los Angeles Times* asked a fair question— whether Detroit, long denied of glory, was hungrier. "Who wanted it more?" he wrote after Game 5. "The Pistons wanted it more. They wanted it, and they got it."

So . . . what now?

Answer: Italy.

In his meeting with reporters the day before Game 6, Riley said that—to hell with it—he was leaving for two weeks in Italy as soon as the series ended. "It's a little villa in southern Italy," he said. "While Jerry West is drafting next week, I'll be . . ."

"Drafting beer!" someone shouted.

"Guaranteed!" Riley replied.

This wasn't a hard one to decipher: The coach was so 100 percent, beyond-the-shadow-of-a-doubt certain the Lakers would win both games at the Forum that he could start dreaming of a bottle of Rosso di Montalcino alongside a plate of ravioli caprese. "I'm very confident," he said. "The table is set for us right here. We have tremendous respect for the Pistons, but the one thing that's obvious is, they had the chance to win it there and they didn't do that."

The coach's words sounded great—until the game began. Los Angeles held a seven-point halftime lead behind the marvelous play of Worthy, who scored 19 points over the first two quarters. Yet Riley's trapping defense was unable to contain the driving, swirling, slashing, popping Thomas. The Lakers were up 56–48 early in the third quarter when Detroit's point guard went to work, scoring the Pistons' next 16 points on a pair of free throws, a short jumper off an offensive rebound, four more jump shots, a bank shot and a layup. "He was just red hot," said Johnson. "Unconscious."

With three minutes remaining in the third quarter, however, Thomas passed to Dumars on a fast break, landed on Cooper's left foot and crumpled to the court. His ankle—swollen and black-and-blue—was badly sprained. "I couldn't believe this was happening to me," he later said. "Not to me. Not now. Not fifteen minutes away from an NBA championship." Blood dripped from a wound above his cheek. A finger had been dislocated. His vision was blurred from a poke to the eye. Thomas was helped off the floor, presumed to be done for the afternoon. Instead, to the audible groaning of 17,505 assembled Lakers fans, he checked himself back in thirty-five seconds later. By the time the quarter ended, Thomas had scored 25 points on 11 of 13 shooting—a record for points in one period. The Pistons were ahead, 81-79. "Detroit came in here," Riley said, "and played their hearts out."

The teams battled back and forth throughout the fourth quarter. It was the best stretch of the series—no hostility, no anger, no nonsense. Just exceptional basketball featuring three stars (Thomas, Johnson, Worthy) playing at Oscar Robertson–esque levels. With one minute remaining, the Pistons held a 102–99 lead, and it began to feel as if Riley's guarantee would come up empty. CBS, which was televising the series, insisted the NBA transport the championship trophy into Detroit's locker room so everything would be ready for the celebration. Bill Davidson, the CEO of Guardian Industries as well as the Pistons' owner, entered the room. Hats and T-shirts were placed at each locker. Cases of champagne were wheeled inside. "We were in a position to do it," Daly said. "We were in a good position."

Eight seconds later, though, Scott stationed himself in the lane, leaned in over a hobbling Thomas and hit a twelve-footer, cutting the lead to a single point. On the subsequent Detroit possession, Thomas, who would finish with a stellar 43 points, 8 assists and 6 steals, forced up a fall-away baseline jumper that clanged off the rim and into the hands of Worthy. With twenty-seven seconds remaining, the Lakers called a time-out.

Johnson brought the ball down the court. He had no open look. Neither did Worthy or Scott. The pass went down low to Abdul-Jabbar, an increasingly forgotten man. He turned to release his skyhook along the right baseline, and was hacked by Laimbeer. The ball missed, but he hit both free throws. Lakers 103, Pistons 102.

Daly diagrammed a final play—a pass to Thomas, who would take the shot. However, while running his route, he collided with Dantley. The ball went to Dumars, and his double-pump banker at the other end missed. Scott rebounded the ball and was fouled. He missed both shots, then held his breath as the Pistons failed to get off a last-second desperation heave. The Lakers survived.

"That was probably the most interesting, exciting game I've ever played in," Johnson said. "It tops the Boston experience [Game 4, a one-point L.A. win] of last year's finals. That says a lot."

When Game 6 ended, it was presumed that Thomas would be unavailable for the finale. His ankle was the size and shade of an especially large blueberry muffin. It was also widely presumed the Lakers would win. They had endured the Pistons' fiercest punch—what could possibly be left? Especially with an injured star, on the road, against an experienced and battle-tested opponent.

Detroit, though, received help from an unlikely source. Even though Al Davis, the Los Angeles Raiders' outlaw owner, was a semiregular attendee of Laker games, he felt a kinship with Detroit's attitude and approach. Civic loyalty? To hell with civic loyalty. For the next two days, he instructed his entire training staff to cater to Thomas and the Pistons. The Lakers had offered help in the form of a bucket of ice. The Raiders, on the other hand, opened their facility to Thomas. Trainers placed him in the dreaded "Boot"—an enormous plastic shoe, filled with ice and water, that acted as a cold-compression unit. If Thomas wasn't inside his room at the Airport Marriott in his boot, he was with the football staff in his boot. "I'll never forget the help they gave me," Thomas later wrote. "Their trainers tried every conceivable method to alleviate the pain and swelling."

On the night before Game 7, Thomas held a press conference at the hotel to tell seventy-five assembled reporters that his ankle was awful and terrible and ready for the blender. He arrived on crutches and answered an initial inquiry with "It's pretty fucked up, I can tell you that." There were some who, knowing Thomas's reputation as a con man, dismissed the media session as mere show. Gamesmanship had been a Thomas specialty through the years. Perhaps he wasn't as hurt as it'd seemed. Perhaps he would perform with the same explosiveness the Lakers had grown accustomed to.

Or, perhaps not. The early narrative of Game 7 belonged to Thomas, who approached the court with a determined gait but a devastated body. The pain, he later admitted, was unlike any he had ever felt. Just standing, just walking. That he somehow played twenty-eight minutes remains one of the more remarkable physical feats in NBA lore. That he limped his way toward 10 points and 7 assists is even more astonishing.

Detroit led 52–47 at halftime, but during the break, Thomas unwisely removed his right Converse Weapon, and the ankle again ballooned. The Pistons were outscored 36–21 in the third period, and the Forum shook with anticipation of yet another crown. Detroit, though, made one last charge. With Thomas watching from the bench, Dumars hit an open jumper with 1:18 remaining to slice the Laker lead to 102–100. Johnson was immediately (and unwisely) fouled by Rodman, but made only one of two free throws, increasing the Los Angeles lead to three. Detroit called a time-out with 1:14 remaining. On the ensuing possession, Laimbeer—one of the NBA's top-shooting big men—found himself wide open at the top of the three-point line. He took a pass from Vinnie Johnson and launched the shot. Up, up, up—clank. It bounced off the rim and, after a valiant chase, out of bounds. Moments later, Worthy lost the ball on a drive, but Rodman, a dreadful marksman outside of two feet, let loose a medium-range jumper that missed and was rebounded by Scott. (A nation of lip-reading viewers watched Daly mouth, "What the fuck is the matter with Rodman?") The Laker guard hit two free throws with thirty seconds left, and the victory was secured.

Los Angeles 108

Detroit 105

"It was a nightmare to the very end," Riley said afterward. "I kept saying, 'Please don't let this end in a nightmare.' We were a great team trying to hold on."

Worthy, named the series MVP, recorded the first triple-double of his career, finishing with 36 points, 16 rebounds and 10 assists. Though Campbell played but two games and fourteen minutes, he felt fulfilled. His scouting reports had been on point. He also was now the first man in basketball history to win CBA and NBA titles in the same season. "It's nice to be the only one who can say that," he said. "Gratifying."

Afterward, as the Lakers doused one another in bubbly, the drained Pistons returned to their locker room in silence. Some players cried. Others were too tired to cry. The pain was indescribable. After about ten minutes, there was a soft knock on the door. When no one answered, Abdul-Jabbar, who averaged 13.1 points, sheepishly stuck his head through the crack, then entered. He had just endured seven days of abuse courtesy of Laimbeer, Mahorn, Edwards and Rodman. Now he went man to man, shaking each hand.

It was the classiest act many of the Pistons had ever seen.

CHAPTER 18

GOOD-BYE, CAP

In the modern history of the NBA, there has never been a more socially retarded superstar than Kareem Abdul-Jabbar.

This is, admittedly, harsh. It is also, admittedly, fair. His track record for mistreating people is epic, but not as intentional as one might believe. There is an Asperger's-type quality to the longtime Laker, an inability to properly read people or situations. Such does not make Kareem Abdul-Jabbar a bad guy. It simply makes him an oft-clueless one.

However, that same lack of awareness could result in great entertainment value. On June 30, 1988, for example, the Los Angeles Lakers visited the White House to meet with President Ronald Reagan. It was old stuff for many of the veterans, who had taken this trip multiple times before and were no longer wowed by the Rose Garden or Oval Office. Abdul-Jabbar, however, was in his element. Josh Rosenfeld, the team's public relations director, had nicknamed Abdul-Jabbar Cliff Claven after the know-it-all character from the TV show *Cheers*. "But unlike Cliff Claven," Rosenfeld said, "you got the sense Kareem actually knew what he was talking about."

As the Laker players were offered a guided White House tour, Abdul-Jabbar threw out one question after another. By the fourth or fifth room, the tour guide would ask, "Anything anyone wants to know?" while looking directly at the center. At one point, several Lakers noticed Abdul-Jabbar staring intently at a painting. Byron Scott nudged a teammate and whispered, "This is gonna be good."

"Excuse me," Abdul-Jabbar said.

"Yes," the guide wearily replied.

"You said this painting was done in the nineteenth century?"

"That's right," he said.

Abdul-Jabbar returned his gaze to the piece of art.

"You're certain?" he asked.

"Uh . . . yes," the guide replied.

"I don't know," Abdul-Jabbar said. He pointed to a small detail, a certain style of footwear, perhaps—"Because *these* weren't invented until 1908."

Lakers players chuckled aloud. "I'll get back to you on that," the guide said. "Now, if we can move on . . ."

Abdul-Jabbar concluded his White House experience by shaking Reagan's hand and telling him, firmly, that he disagreed with his policies and positions. The president smiled, but was surely happy to see the 7-foot-2 liberal exit the building.

As was, for the most part, the Lakers organization.

At long last, the strange, winding Kareem Abdul-Jabbar roller-coaster ride was nearing an end. The 1988–89 season would be his finale, and to suggest members of the Lakers were ready is no overstatement. In his fourteen years with the team, Abdul-Jabbar had won five titles and three MVP awards. He was the league's all-time leading scorer, and perhaps the nation's most recognizable figure. Yet trying to understand his moods and quirks and oddities was as simple as dressing a porcupine in a T-shirt.

From the moment the Lakers reported to training camp at the University of Hawaii in Honolulu (Buss had vacationed there for years, and aspired to make it a base for the team), the number one concern—from Johnson to Riley to Rosenfeld to Jerry West and Jerry Buss—was how to make Abdul-Jabbar's farewell season productive, comfortable and seamless. This was no easy task. The man was forty-one, and uncertain what the future held. His former agent, Tom Collins, had allegedly robbed him of a large chunk of his fortune, leaving him anxious, uncomfortable and not especially well off. His relationship to his longtime girlfriend, Cheryl Pistono, recently ended. Buoyed by his enthusiastically received cameo in the 1980 film *Airplane!*, Abdul-Jabbar pondered a career in acting, seemingly unaware that his inability to emote might be a problem. There were dozens of investment opportunities (car dealerships, restaurants, etc.), but little that appealed to him. The best money around was the $3 million he would be paid by Buss for

1988–89. Once that ended . . . well, Abdul-Jabbar didn't want to talk much about that.

"He reported . . . looking creaky," wrote George Vecsey in *The New York Times*, "a step slower. The body forgetting what the mind knew." There was hope—from Buss, at least—that somehow the warm Hawaii breeze and a tropical night or two might infuse some pep into the big man. For the other Lakers, life was but a dream. When they were inside Klum Gym, the tiny sweatbox of a building in the foothills of the Koolau Range on Oahu, the work was hard. Sprints. More sprints. Scrimmages. Riley was a taskmaster, and he demanded 100 percent effort for the four hours the players were together. "I'll never forget my first practice with the Lakers," said Mark Mc-Namara, a journeyman center signed to be Abdul-Jabbar's latest backup. "There was no air conditioning—which was the way Riley surely wanted it. Practice begins, and we start with something called the Easy Run Drills, and there's nothing easy about it. You're running around the outside of the court, and Magic leads. He paces. The whole time you have your hands over your head. You run down the length of the court, then slide along the baseline with your back to the court, then you run down backward, then slide, then run. It keeps getting faster and faster. Bill Bertka stood on the baseline, and as you went by, he'd throw you a medicine ball. Magic's picking up the pace more and more. Then we did the drill—Laker Layups. They were these crazy drills where you have three lines, and you rotate, and the ball starts in the middle but moves around, and you're sprinting from corner to corner. I mean—brutal. More than brutal. It goes on and on and on and on. I had to say to myself, 'I've never quit a drill in my career and I won't now.' But I'd never poured out so much sweat, ever."

Once the session ended, however, Hawaii belonged to the Lakers. The food. The women. The weather. Players would lounge by the beach, or by the pool, then spend nights out at the hottest bars and clubs. Even here, 2,560 miles away from Los Angeles, the players were kings. "Oh, Hawaii was amazing," said Tony Campbell. "You felt like basketball royalty. We'd have team dinners, we'd tour the sites, we'd go to the beach, get on a boat or a raft. It was just another reminder that you were with the first-class organization."

Yet Abdul-Jabbar wasn't part of the crowd. When he signed his final contract shortly before the 1987–88 season, it was stipulated that he had to practice only once during two-a-day drills in training camp. Riley struggled with the idea, and insisted the center show up for the second session, even if he were to merely sit and watch. Abdul-Jabbar was not pleased. His Hawaii time was spent at practice, then eating at a Thai restaurant, then reading Hunter S. Thompson's *Generation of Swine* at the team hotel, then at practice, then more of the same. He had nearly two decades on several teammates, and struggled to relate. "All the guys who broke in with me are now gone," he wrote in a diary he kept during the season. "I can remember, very keenly, being a rookie and wondering what guys did after playing professional ball. . . ."

On the first night in Hawaii, the team congregated in a private room at the hotel for the official welcoming dinner. Though the core stars remained, three familiar faces were no longer part of the team. Billy Thompson, the absentminded former first-round pick, had been taken by the Miami Heat in the expansion draft. ("Once I left," Thompson memorably said, "it was hard for them to keep winning.") Kurt Rambis, the beloved power forward whose playing time went to A. C. Green, was now a Charlotte Hornet. And Wes Matthews, insanity personified, wasn't offered a new contract. (He would spend much of the year with the CBA's Tulsa Fast Breakers.) After everyone arrived, West stood, tapped his glass with a fork and asked for attention. "This is Cap's last year," he said, and his voice cracked. West gathered himself, and paid homage to the most remarkable career in NBA history. He described a player who changed the league; a player unafraid to stand up for righteousness; a player who altered the trajectory of the Los Angeles Lakers. It was a beautiful moment—whether the players liked Abdul-Jabbar or not, they were sitting alongside a legend. At the start of every season, Riley picked the team's theme song. This year it would be the Shirelles' "Dedicated to the One I Love"—in honor of Abdul-Jabbar.

That said, everything was now complicated. Two years earlier, when Julius Erving played his final season with the Philadelphia 76ers, the NBA and its twenty-three teams spared no expense honoring the man known as Dr. J. His arrival in rival cities was celebrated as if a reigning king were in town, and rightly so. Few players had ever been so revered.

Abdul-Jabbar, however, was not revered. He had spared no city's fans in refusing autograph requests; rarely made quality time for road reporters; never met an opposing center he hadn't hit in the larynx with an elbow. "Nobody liked him, because he's an asshole," said Danny Schayes, the Denver Nuggets center. "He did the retirement tour right on the heels of Dr. J's.

When he came to Denver, Julius couldn't have been more gracious—he talked about what a great ABA city it had been, how he would have loved to have played for us. Well, Kareem comes and no one on our team wants to do the ceremony. Not one guy. We gave him a ski trip to Vail as a present and we all hoped he would break his leg.

"Kareem instilled venom in people. Not indifference—venom. He once wrote a book, and when he came through Denver to promote it, none of the local reporters gave him the time of day. It was, 'Fuck you. You never gave us any help in fifteen years and now you want a blowjob? No fucking way.'"

This is what the Lakers had to deal with—a faded superstar with a large ego wanting to be feted, a public and league largely indifferent. Save New York (where Abdul-Jabbar had been born and raised) and Los Angeles, the nation's passion for Kareem could be surmised with a stifled yawn. Yes, he had been a transcendental player, and when he came to town, fans showed up to watch. Yet the man who once desired privacy over all else now possessed an inexplicable need for a last hurrah. He signed on as a sneaker pitchman with a second-rate apparel company named LA Gear. He agreed to a deal with Warner Books to keep a season-long diary. He told Rosenfeld that he would conduct a press conference wherever the team went. "When you think about it, anybody would be overwhelmed with the idea of arena after arena full of people honoring you," Lorin Pullman, Abdul-Jabbar's personal assistant, said at the time. "It's overwhelming for anybody. Knowing him, he's never been one to look for all that. Kareem's very touched, that's my feeling. He's very flattered. Every time I tell him about another ceremony or another honor, he's like, 'My goodness.'"

The Lakers and the NBA spent much of the pre-season making certain everyone was on board. This couldn't be a halfway effort, where some teams presented him with cars and vacation packages while other teams treated him like a bag stuffed with dead cats. New Jersey governor Thomas Kean agreed to hold a day in his honor. New York arranged for a ceremony involving old high school teammates. The Washington Bullets decided to give him a jukebox, the Milwaukee Bucks a Harley-Davidson motorcycle, the Mavericks a Verdite sculpture of an elephant and the Spurs a self-portrait and a $10,000 check to be used for two charities. It was nice and lovely and terribly uncomfortable. Read an editorial in the St. Louis Post-Dispatch: "Everyone is trying to keep up with the Joneses when it comes to saying goodbye, and there's more than a little awkwardness in the whole situation. It's as if people are embarrassed that they don't know him better after twenty years in the NBA, an unprecedented six MVP awards and more than 38,000 points. 'Your Texas hospitality has been warm and generous,' Abdul-Jabbar said at the presentation. 'You don't play around with your feelings, you let them show.' Ah, if only the same could have been said of Abdul-Jabbar throughout the years."

Far worse than the farewells was that Abdul-Jabbar wasn't faring particularly well. Were he a so-so NBA player in 1987–88, he was now nothing short of a bad one. The Lakers could see it in camp, when he either sat to the side during drills and scrimmages or had his lunch served to him by McNamara.

Once the regular season began, his fall-off was even more notable. Abdul-Jabbar's NBA-record 787-game double-figure scoring streak was snapped during the 1987–88 campaign, and now he could barely find the bucket. In one embarrassing episode, Johnson waved Abdul-Jabbar out of the post—a first in their decade together. Riley immediately called a time-out and, looking squarely at his point guard, said, "I don't *ever* want you to do that again." Yet Riley, too, was frustrated, and regularly pleaded to Rosenfeld—the on-again, off-again buffer between West and him—"Where's my big man?" Through the Lakers' first eight games, Abdul-Jabbar scored in double figures one time. Following a 106–97 road loss to the dreadful Sacramento Kings, in which he totaled 4 points and 3 rebounds in seventeen minutes, Abdul-Jabbar approached Johnson in the shower and asked, "Buck, what's wrong with me?"

"Cap," Johnson replied, "you just ain't been aggressive. You're not hungry like you used to be. You're not attacking. You don't go after the ball. You don't go after your shot. You're not yourself."

The media criticism was harsh. Bill Conlin, the *Philadelphia Daily News's* well-known columnist, called Abdul-Jabbar "worthless, totally worthless . . . a zero on defense, like a barber pole." Mike Lupica of New York's *Daily News* was only slightly less harsh. "This guy," he wrote, "has stayed too long at the dance." The public criticism was even worse. Abdul-Jabbar had often been heckled on the road. Now, however, crowds at the Forum were losing patience. There were smatterings of boos and, even worse, modest applause when he retreated to the bench. Against the Houston Rockets on January 16, Abdul-Jabbar scored on a skyhook over Akeem Olajuwon to open the game. Moments later, Olajuwon posted, received a pass and wheeled around Abdul-Jabbar for a layup. "Quit while you're even!" a courtsider screamed.

When interviewed, Riley expressed his support for the big man. In private, he was feeling the strain of having a 7-foot-2 anchor pulling his team toward the bottom of the Pacific Ocean. Though Los Angeles led the division for most of the season, nothing came easily. Through thirty-three games, the Lakers were 13-0 at home and 9-11 on the road. Riley was forced to call a meeting with his players to silence their internal griping over who should—and shouldn't—be starting at center. "I want to make it clear right now," Riley said. "This is our team. Kareem's on it. He's here. He's gonna stay here. He's still a force, and I believe in him. The guy has carried us for fourteen years. Fourteen years! We're all wearing rings because of him. The way I figure it, we've gotta back him up. We owe him that. We owe him respect." Shortly thereafter, during a shootaround before a game against the visiting Cavaliers, Riley told Abdul-Jabbar that, were he to continue to stink, he would be benched midway through the glorious farewell tour. At the time, he ranked twenty-third among NBA centers in rebounding and reached double figures in scoring just ten times in twenty-seven games.

"Give us more," Riley said.

"OK, I'll give you what I've got," Abdul-Jabbar replied.

Riley admitted to Mike Downey of the *Los Angeles Times* that Abdul-Jabbar had "gone stale." The center agreed. "This past summer, I, well, I [trained], but the fire just wasn't there," he said. "I suppose I was taking a breather from the whole ordeal of the past several years."

Because he was tall and ornery and famous, Abdul-Jabbar was the easy target. He was not, however, the only deserving one. Ever since Johnson arrived on the scene in 1979, the front office had always gone to great lengths to upgrade the roster before every training camp. The track record was phenomenal—from signing Kurt Rambis to acquiring Byron Scott and A. C. Green to trading for Mychal Thompson, Jerry West was widely regarded as a personnel magician. Now, however, the Lakers simply weren't as good as they had been. Having tired of his unpredictability (and uncomfortable with his reputation as an excessive partier), West let Matthews walk, and used the twenty-fifth pick in the draft to replace him with David Rivers, a 6-foot, 170-pound shoot-first point guard out of Notre Dame.

If talent equaled personal narrative, Rivers would have catapulted past the University of Kansas's Danny Manning to the top of the draft board. In the summer of 1986, leading into his junior year, Rivers worked at the Port-a-Pit Barbecue, a catering company in Elkhart, Indiana. One night, after wrapping up a shift, he was sitting in the passenger seat of a Chevy van driven by Kenny Barlow, a recently graduated Notre Dame star (who, coincidentally, had just been drafted by the Lakers in the first round, then traded to Atlanta). As they headed down Route 30, an oncoming car swerved into their lane. Barlow jerked the steering wheel hard to the right, and the vehicle went off the roadway, flew through the air, slammed into an embankment, rolled multiple times and came to a halt some eighty-nine feet from the road. Rivers, who had not been wearing a seat belt, was launched through the windshield and sent twenty feet in the air. By the time he landed in a nearby cornfield, his stomach was sliced fifteen inches across and oozing innards. "The body is an amazing thing," Rivers said. "Just amazing. I felt no pain at all, and when Kenny found me, I was talking to him the way I'm talking to you right now. I knew I was cut from side to side, and I knew my organs were in my hands. I was trying to keep the gash closed."

Barlow suffered only minor cuts on his legs. He covered his friend's bloodied torso in a shirt, then ran to a nearby house to call for help. Rivers sat alone for twenty minutes. "I wasn't afraid to die," he said. "The idea didn't even bother me. I was peaceful."

The incision missed his heart by two inches, and he lost three pints of blood. Somehow, Rivers survived. "I asked the doctors how many stitches I needed," Rivers said, "and they told me there were too many to count." He spent eight days in Elkhart General Hospital before beginning a horrific rehabilitation regiment. His days as an All-American were almost certainly over. Yet Rivers, known for his stubborn doggedness, returned to South Bend and averaged 15.7 points as a junior and 22 as a senior. What he lost in quickness he gained in toughness. "You had to like what he could bring," said West. "He gave us something we didn't have. But, if I'm being honest, it was not the right time for someone his size in the league. All the guards were bigger."

Rivers lit up practices—buzzing around Johnson, past Cooper, through Scott and Worthy and the gang. "Oh, he was impressive," said Mychal Thompson. "He dribbled so low to the ground, no one could stay with him." Dazzling behind-the-scenes moments, though, didn't necessarily translate into dazzling big-time moments. Rivers lacked Matthews' defensive intensity and instincts, and was dwarfed by most opposing guards. With the spotlight off, he hit one deep shot after another. Covered by a Gerald Wilkins or Michael Jordan—not so much. He appeared in forty-seven regular-season games, averaging 2.9 points. "He was a pretty good little player," said Worthy. "But—*little*."

West's other quirky addition sent small shock waves throughout the NBA. With rare exception, when the Lakers brought in veterans, they made certain the newcomers would fit in with the team's philosophy and personnel. Way before Mychal Thompson slipped into a purple-and-gold jersey, the team had asked two hundred questions to former teammates and coaches about his character and willingness to fill a role. "It was a pretty meticulous organization," said Ronnie Lester, the former Laker guard turned scout. "When something was done, it wasn't without thought."

Hence, the collective gasp when, on August 10, 1988, veteran forward Orlando Woolridge (like Rivers, a Notre Dame product) was signed to a four-year, $2.9 million contract. *Sports Illustrated* once wrote that Woolridge "earned the reputation as a selfish, one-dimensional player who, when he wasn't shooting the ball, was thinking of ways to shoot the ball . . . [his] uniform] number— 0—matched his commitment to winning." This was true. Woolridge was selfish, one-dimensional and defensively inept. The biggest issue, however, was his off-the-court behavior. Woolridge first tried cocaine as a rookie with the Bulls in 1981, and the drug soon consumed him. He played five years in Chicago before joining the New Jersey Nets as a free agent in 1986. His new coach, Dave Wohl, had been an assistant with the Lakers, and he was excited to add someone of Woolridge's gifts. Here was a 6-foot-9, 215-pound stallion. Woolridge ran like a point guard, but with the physicality of a power forward. "He had some amazing skills," said Wohl. "But there was a dark side."

The Nets held their training camp in Princeton, New Jersey, and one day Wohl received a phone call from the manager of the Scanticon Princeton Hotel, where the team stayed. "He asked me to come up to Orlando's room," said Wohl. "I walk in and it looks like World War III. There's drug paraphernalia, the room is trashed, money and credit cards are everywhere. Orlando walks in and I say, 'O, what's up with this?' He says, 'Well, I was with this girl and she . . .' I said, 'O, don't do this. Please, just don't.' He admits the whole thing. So I called the general manager [Harry Weltman] and told him Orlando had a drug problem and we needed to take action. They ended up just slapping him on the wrist with a warning and telling him not to do it again. It was embarrassing."

Woolridge lasted two seasons in New Jersey, but his dependency issues caught up with him. He played only nineteen games in 1987–88 before enrolling in a Van Nuys, California, inpatient drug rehabilitation center. He spent nearly two months there, and emerged—in his words—clean and sober. Yet Woolridge had uttered such things before. As a young Bull, he even devoted much energy to speaking to Chicago elementary school children about the dangers of addiction. Then, as soon as the sessions ended, he'd snort cocaine. "When things were going easy for Orlando, he was OK," said Wohl. "But when things got difficult, you worried."

"Orlando would battle with the best of them on the court and stand his ground, but off the court he couldn't," said Pat Jackson, his wife. "Whatever felt good and got him through the day was what he took."

Life with the Lakers was always pressure packed. There were expectations to meet and sold-out houses to please and one time demand after another. So why would West risk relative harmony on a known drug addict, when he'd witnessed Spencer Haywood's meltdown nine years earlier? "There are certain people in your locker room who you believe have enough strength to help someone prevail," West said. "You convince yourself they have a chance, with a great team and great ownership, to be great. I thought that could happen. Maybe I was naïve. Orlando was a real talent. But he was a fucking druggie. That's hard to combat."

Woolridge reported to camp in tremendous physical shape and was, his wife said, clean. Even though he was the team's seventh or eighth man, Woolridge seemed content. He produced his lowest totals in points (9.7) and minutes (20.1) since his rookie year, but felt loved and appreciated. "L.A. was the ideal fit," said Jackson. "We were in a restaurant in Santa Monica once and Michael Keaton came to our table to talk to Orlando. I'm thinking, 'You want to talk to him? I want to talk to you.' It was cool. Orlando liked how warm and friendly people were. He didn't care about starting or points—he'd been a starter before. He wanted to be a part of Showtime."

Sadly, as was the case with Rivers, Woolridge was a square peg in a round hole. "Orlando just couldn't work," said Bill Bertka. "He was a hell of an athlete, but he didn't fit into our system."

While it remained en vogue to blame Abdul-Jabbar for all shortcomings, the Lakers were flawed and, perhaps, in slow decline. In Johnson, Worthy and Scott, Riley possessed three cornerstones, all of whom would average more than 19 points per game. A. C. Green was an above-average power forward. Cooper, thirty-two, and Thompson, thirty-four, were both fading, and Tony Campbell was—at best—a player Riley preferred to use only when necessary. "Things changed," Cooper said. "Things in sports always change. You can't age and remain as dominant as you once were. It just doesn't work that way."

For the first time in the Riley reign, the Lakers had to fight for the Pacific Division title. Led by a pair of young stars in point guard Kevin Johnson and forward Armen Gilliam, the Phoenix Suns were everything the Lakers suddenly were not. On December 26, the two teams met at the Arizona Veterans Memorial Coliseum, and those in attendance could not be criticized for believing a passing of the torch was at hand. Not only did the Suns demolish Los Angeles, 111–96, but they did so with the same speed-and-pressing-defense formula the Lakers had once perfected. The low point came in the fourth quarter, when Magic Johnson refused to hand the ball back to referee Billy Oakes after a questionable call. Johnson tossed the ball, and Oakes tossed Johnson—only the second ejection of his ten-season NBA career. "I'm frustrated from losing," Johnson said. "I've never been through this before. I maybe had to get this out of me. I'm sorry it happened to the team. But when you've never gone through anything like this, you don't know how to react." With the setback, the Lakers (17-10) led Phoenix by two games, and the Suns proved stubborn all season. West and Riley tried everything to rediscover the spark of yesteryear, but their efforts were met with frustration. After the Lakers beat the Rockets on January 16 to improve their record at the Forum to 15-0, Riley boldly predicted his club would become the first in NBA history to go undefeated at home. When asked if he was being serious, Riley didn't flinch. "You asked the question," he said, "and I don't see why not." Players responded angrily. Were they five years old, needing banal motivational incentive for every little thing? Riley's words only served to irritate and, they believed, motivate other franchises. Eight nights later, when the Knicks came to Los Angeles and, behind Patrick Ewing's 25 points, ended the home streak, some Lakers were mildly relieved. Their coach needed to shut up and do his job.

This, however, seemed increasingly hard for Riley, who was largely insufferable. When he'd first arrived on the scene, Riley maintained his success was based on the play of Johnson and Abdul-Jabbar and the other stars. Now, while he occasionally uttered such sentiments, they lacked feeling. "There's an ego factor with Pat that didn't used to be there," Johnson said.

"Wanting to be recognized as a good coach. He's not overbearing about it, he just needs it."

Riley appeared on the January 1989 cover of *Gentleman's Quarterly* magazine, and the accompanying article was eye-opening. When Riley didn't talk about how great he was, he talked about how great he was or, on occasion, how great he was. He felt disrespected during pre-season contract renegotiations with Buss, and had threatened to resign. He was genuinely upset that, in seven seasons, he had never been named the league's Coach of the Year. He once approached Gary Vitti, the trainer, during a winning streak to complain that the chalk he was given to write with was "too hard." (Vitti's response: "Pat, what the fuck does that mean?") Early in training camp in Hawaii, he demanded the rims on the basket be painted bright orange, and the bolts on the backboard be replaced.

Once upon a time, the *GQ* piece would have humiliated Riley. It was self-indulgent narcissism from a coach who stressed the meaning of the word *team*. If a player had promoted himself in such a way, he would have either been mocked or disciplined (or both). But Riley, in the minds of his players, was beginning to believe he was the one who invented basketball. "Things were," said Cooper, "getting a little uncomfortable." On the night of March 28, the coach-player relationship reached a new low. The Lakers had again celebrated a trip to Phoenix by being throttled by the Suns, 127–104. Abdul-Jabbar was held to 6 points, and Johnson sleepwalked his way to 10 points. The Suns led 58–47 at the half, then outscored the Lakers 36–27 in the third quarter. Watching from the sidelines, Riley was furious. Losing, he could sort of accept. Mediocrity, he could not. Afterward, he told the media his team was "humiliated" and he demanded a change in attitude. "We came out tonight and quit," Riley said, venting before a question was even asked. "Obviously, I haven't gotten through to the players. There's something tremendously lacking, and they just think they can turn it on.

"I have failed miserably in trying to drive home how important this is. A serious inventory from an individual standpoint has to happen. What is happening now shouldn't be happening to a team trying to win a championship. We were humiliated tonight."

With the loss, the Lakers dropped to 47-21—impressive enough, but misleading. Dominance had been a staple of Showtime basketball. It now seemed to be a thing of the past. "What is particularly irksome to Riley is the Lakers' recent bout with inertia," Sam McManis wrote in the *Los Angeles*

Times. "Instead of gearing up for the playoffs, they seem to be grinding to a halt. The Lakers have won four of their last seven games, but three of the victories have come in the final seconds."

West made effort after effort to upgrade, but to no avail. He called the Indiana Pacers about a Woolridge-for-Herb-Williams swap and was rebuffed. Elgin Baylor, the Laker legend and close West friend, was now the general manager of the Los Angeles Clippers. He dangled Benoit Benjamin, the team's skilled yet boneheaded center. West inquired, but quickly learned he had no chance. Meanwhile, Abdul-Jabbar collected one gift after another (a sailboat here, a portrait there) while playing in slow motion.

On the afternoon of April 23, Abdul-Jabbar's seemingly interminable farewell tour reached its finality at the Forum. Two days earlier, the Lakers picked up their fifty-sixth victory, beating the Trail Blazers 121–114 to edge out the Suns by two games and clinch yet another Pacific Division title. Now, before the final regular-season contest, Abdul-Jabbar was brought to center court, placed in an oversize rocking chair and rocked by teammates while the song "That's What Friends Are For" blared from the PA system.

"May you enjoy your retirement for many, many years," Buss said. "But please, please, don't start it until late June."

The next forty-five minutes were an ode to Abdul-Jabbar, but also an ode to weird professional athletic excessiveness. The Lakers played in a magnificent building that was surrounded by one of the region's most downtrodden neighborhoods. More than 20 percent of Inglewood families lived below the poverty level, and less than 15 percent of adult residents had attained a college degree. It was a city of liquor stores and pawn shops and men huddled together on corners, smoking Camels and drinking Piels from brown paper bags. Inside the building, the faces filling the stands were almost all white, many with artificially fortified breasts and $100,000 smiles. Inglewood was the Lakers' home, but the relationship was one-sided.

As Abdul-Jabbar looked on, his eight-year-old son, Amir, sang the national anthem. The NBA's all-time leading scorer then received trips for his parents, Cora and Al, to Hawaii and Orlando, Florida, as well as a personal tennis court from Buss. There was a telegram from President George Bush and two standing ovations. A street outside the Forum was renamed Kareem Court. Finally, Johnson took the microphone. "Since you've been carrying us on your back for so long, here's something to carry you around," he said. "It's definitely not enough. We should give you more. When I came here as a rookie I was a snotty-nosed kid. Not only did you wipe my nose clean, but you showed me the path to become the player I wanted to be and the man I wanted to be."

Abdul-Jabbar was presented with a white 1989 Rolls-Royce. As tears streamed down his cheeks, he addressed the sellout crowd. "We've had a certain amount of success here," he said. "You can see by the [five championship] banners up there. Hopefully when the playoffs start we can see about getting another one up there."

Adbul-Jabbar's voice cracked. "I just want to say," he whispered, "I love you all."

Los Angeles won, 121–117.

Abdul-Jabbar scored 10 points. Following the game, he retreated to the locker room, where he found his designer jeans sliced to pieces and dangling from a hanger. "It was a final practical joke by his teammates," said Lon Rosen. "They saw it as a way to end things on a lighthearted note."

Abdul-Jabbar stormed out of the building without saying a word.

■ ■ ■

This was going to be ugly.

That much, people knew. The Lakers were ripe for an upset, ready to fall apart and crumble like the underwhelming team they had become. Sure, Johnson had averaged 22.5 points and 12.8 assists in winning another league MVP award. But Riley's club was as vulnerable as it'd ever been. When *The Palm Beach Post* asked Ron Rothstein, the Miami Heat coach, to size up the playoffs, he dismissed Los Angeles as a faded flavor. "They're not the defensive team they were last year—we had 13 layups against them in the game in L.A. a couple of weeks ago—and they're not as hungry defensively," he said. "Maybe they're bored, I don't know."

Rothstein *did* know. The Lakers were flat, tired, uninspired and thin. Anyone who grasped the game as Rothstein did could recognize an imperiled franchise when he saw one.

The Lakers, it was clear, were decaying. The playoffs would certainly cement their demise.

And yet . . .

The first round was a cakewalk. Los Angeles swept Portland in three relatively easy games. Ho-hum—nothing surprising there. The Blazers were a mediocre club with a losing record (39-43). They had lost all five regular-season meetings with the Lakers and featured a center, Kevin Duckworth, who battled his weight as much as he did opposing players. When the series ended, the Laker players were low-keyed and relaxed. One day earlier, the Knicks had swept the Philadelphia 76ers, then behaved as amateurs by, literally, using a broom to sweep the court. "You see some teams jumping up and down like they won the world championship after they just won the first round," Mychal Thompson said. "We've got twelve wins to go. It's no time to get excited now. I saw the Knicks pushing a broom. I thought that was low-class."

The second round was a cakewalk. The Seattle SuperSonics were a strong franchise with a 47-35 record and, in guard Dale Ellis and forward Xavier McDaniel, two All-Star-caliber players. Leading up to the opener, Bernie Bickerstaff, the team's young coach, suggested the Sonics were outclassed. "We probably don't stand a chance," he said after beating the Rockets in four games. "They're playing well; they're the best team in basketball." It was an attempt at reverse psychology. Bickerstaff knew the Lakers were yesterday's news, and believed the Sonics were about to reach the team's first Western Conference Finals since 1987. Instead, Seattle was swept. In the aftermath of Game 4, as he sat in a somber locker room, Ellis appeared to be shocked. "We wanted to win one," he said. "We came out with a lot of fire and we were hitting our shots. We tried to jump out early and we did that, but we weren't able to sustain it. They're playing good basketball and its going to be difficult for anyone to beat them. They were consistent in every game."

Riley looked over the assembled media members, many of who picked the Lakers to die off. He smiled knowingly. "It was a great win," Riley said. "There are a lot of teams who are supposed to be here, Utah, Dallas, and Portland. But we're here. The Final Four."

The Western Conference Finals were a cakewalk. Wait. How could this be? Another four-game sweep? The Phoenix Suns were supposed to supplant the Lakers. They were younger, stronger, deeper. Right! *Right?* "The Phoenix Suns had never played a Lakers playoff team. Now they know what it's all about," said Magic Johnson after totaling 20 points and 21 assists in the 122–117 Game 4 win at Phoenix. "We are not the same team we were in the regular season." Johnson, who averaged 18.5 points through the first three rounds, looked reengaged and re-inspired. Scott and Worthy, who combined for 55 points in Game 4, were running the court like young elks. Cooper had been used sparingly throughout the regular season, but he was once again a defensive stopper and long-distance gunner. "I have never seen a team play any better than the Lakers played today," said Suns forward Tom Chambers, who scored 41 in the defeat. "They were awesome. They didn't make any mistakes. Every time they needed to do something, every time they needed a basket, they got it. You think they might let us slide one time, but they came out more intense than they had all series. It was unbelievable."

The biggest surprise was Woolridge, who scored 14 points and clamped down defensively. For a once-benched drug addict with a soiled reputation, here was the sweetest redemption. While playing with the Bulls, he often gazed longingly toward the west, where the Lakers stood majestic. Now he was with them. "Orlando's body was like a missile, blocking shots, changing shots," Riley said. "We could have packed it in today because we had a three-game cushion. Instead, we played our best game of the series, like it was the seventh game of the series. More than ever, that's the mark of greatness."

With the three sweeps, the critics vanished. The Lakers were now winners of sixteen straight games, and approached the finals with the sort of momentum that usually foretold the inevitability of a championship. Wrote Mark Zeigler of the *San Diego Union-Tribune*: "Incredible, extraordinary, stupendous, awesome—no, those don't really do the Lakers justice. At this point, they are beyond adjectives."

As they celebrated their eighth trip to the finals in ten years, Lakers players assumed they could kick back and bask in the glory. Out east, the Pistons—winners of a league-best sixty-three games—were engaged in a heated conference finals series with the Chicago Bulls and their twenty-six-year-old superstar, Michael Jordan. As Detroit finished off their Central Division rivals in six games, they gave Los Angeles a full nine days to recoup. It was a wonderful gift for an aged roster, and twenty-four of twenty-five NBA coaches would have surely embraced the recovery period.

Pat Riley, however, wasn't one to follow convention.

He had an ego, after all, and it was now as large as the state in which he coached.

PART THREE

DEMISE OF A DYNASTY

*By the end of their run together, Pat Riley
and Earvin (Magic) Johnson weren't always on the
same page. Ego killed what joy built.*

CHAPTER 19

UNDONE

Pat Riley could have waited. A day. Two days, perhaps. He could have taken some time to think about his players and his team; whether they would be best served by peace and solitude and a light work load; whether a veteran point guard who had endured 2,886 minutes in the regular season and a forty-two-year-old center and a battered roster would, perhaps, benefit from some time away from the court, sitting on a beach or inside a movie theatre or at home with the wife and kids.

He could have.

He chose not to.

Following the series-clinching win over Phoenix, Riley was asked by Mark Zeigler of the *San Diego Union-Tribune* whether he would allow for a period of rest and relaxation. The coach didn't pause to consider a reply. "Our players," he said, "will wish that this series went longer. It will be a very hard week for them. The practices will be tough. Now is no time to relax."

On the morning of May 31, 1989, the Lakers traveled ninety-five miles north to Santa Barbara, where they would spend much of the subsequent three days locked inside the Westmount College gymnasium (aka: the depths of basketball hell). Three hours before the first two P.M. practice, the team bus stopped at the luxurious Biltmore in Montecito, a hotel that charged $500 per night for a room. This was Riley's little touch—a carrot in front of the wagon. Rich basketball players like fancy accommodations, and the coach surely thought his men would be wooed by the fine linens and a top-shelf room-service menu. He was, however, wrong.

The members of the Los Angeles Lakers were pissed off.

"I told Pat this was a bad idea," said Bill Bertka, the assistant coach. "Pat was on a mission to three-peat, and he wasn't thinking entirely logically. The guys needed rest. When we drove to Santa Barbara I told him, 'Pat, if you turn the screw one more time, it's going to break.' He got pissed off at me and told me the guys were at the top of their games, and we had to leave no stone unturned. I'm not so sure he was thinking straight."

Throughout his coaching career, Riley always demanded excellence. Players had to commit themselves 24/7 to the task of winning a championship. Wives had to commit themselves 24/7 to the task of helping their husbands win a championship. You were a (admittedly well-compensated) slave to the system, and what Riley said wasn't to be followed but obeyed. *Yes, Coach. Of course, Coach. Whatever you say, Coach.* This sort of unblinking adherence to one man's rule of law made many of the players uncomfortable—none more so than Abdul-Jabbar, the ultimate free and original thinker. Riley's Jedi mind tricks worked on most of the Lakers, few of whom passed for Einsteinian scholars. Yet the center often viewed his coach's procedures as gimmicky and simplistic, amateur psychology for the weak-willed. During his final season, Abdul-Jabbar traveled with a publicist, Lorin Pullman, who was friendly and well liked. One time, when the Lakers traveled to Cleveland to face the Cavaliers, she was stranded at the Sheraton in Cuyahoga Falls, Ohio. Riley refused to let her ride the team bus to the airport, even when others pleaded her case. Why? Because he could. When Abdul-Jabbar learned of this, he turned indignant. What happened to his old coach? The one who was understanding and personable? Where did he go? Many Lakers players had recently been told that Riley—without uttering so much as a word—had officially purchased the trademark rights to the phrase *three-peat*. The term had first been coined by Wes Matthews, the former backup point guard who, after the last championship, turned to Riley in the locker room and yelled, "Don't break this up—we're gonna three-peat!"

"Riley was like, 'Three-peat? I like that,'" Matthews said. "Then the bastard went and patented it. I was pissed. I was really pissed."

Abdul-Jabbar was fed up. The ego was bad enough. But the pre-finals training camp. Why? "Riley thinks he's doing the team a favor by getting us up [to Santa Barbara] and away from the distractions," Abdul-Jabbar wrote in his season-long diary. "But I don't feel there are any distractions at home; on the contrary, it's where I'm most comfortable. For me, being away from home is the distraction; it's a sacrifice to be up there."

If Riley's goal was to unite the Lakers, it worked. Only the uniting wasn't against the Detroit Pistons, the team they'd meet in Game 1 of the finals on Tuesday, June 6, in Detroit. No, it was against Riley. Whereas long ago, Riley was liked by an entire roster, he now was viewed as a wannabe dictator set in his ways, even if his ways lacked logic and common sense. Nobody—Johnson, Bertka, Cooper—could convince the coach that this mini-training camp was a dopey idea. "Our goal is to go there and work hard," Riley said. "This is an opportunity. We had huge layoffs in '82 and '87 and I think if our players use proper preparations, we can take advantage of this opportunity. We can hone and replenish."

What ensued were three days of intense, hard-core, unyielding sessions that made the workouts in Hawaii feel like a day at the spa. Pummeling two-a-days and full-court scrimmages were the norm; sweat poured by the bucket.

"Pure hell," moaned Cooper.

"The thing that upset us more than anything else was how hard we worked," said Scott. "It was like training camp all over again. We didn't feel that we really needed that."

"I thought it was too much," said Gary Vitti, the team's trainer. "It was a boot camp, but I didn't criticize him for it. Look at his track record. You had to assume he knew what he was doing. He almost always did."

Riley barked and screamed like a man possessed. He was no longer merely a basketball coach trying to win. He was a flesh-eating hoops zombie, focused on killing off the Pistons and continuing his team's world domination. He slept Pistons, ate Pistons, walked Pistons, talked Pistons. "[The Pistons] are so committed to the revenge thing," he said. "Their mission is to beat us. They are challenging us more than anyone's ever challenged us. We've got to want them more than they want you. If we go in there and say we just want to 'three-peat' and win one for Kareem, then you don't have the right competitive attitude. You've got to stimulate [the players'] minds more, bring back all the little things that were said last year, bring back some videotapes. You got to bring it all back, otherwise they forget. Then, after the first or second game, they'll realize what it was like."

The Lakers returned from Santa Barbara an exhausted, though well-prepared, team. Riley's squad arrived in Detroit on a Monday morning, checked into the Marriott, then held a closed (to the media) practice inside the Palace at Auburn Hills. Generally, teams in the Lakers' position (finals, on the road) use the day-before session to stay loose, review opposing personnel, adjust to their surroundings. "Nice and easy," said Vitti. "Nothing too tough."

Riley didn't want to hear it. As was the case in Santa Barbara, he had his players go all-out. There would be no downtime, he insisted, until a third-straight title was secured. That's why the Lakers were conducting a box-out drill, which called for the players to crash the boards and fight for rebounds. "Pat was setting the tone in practice, and I understand that," Vitti said. "But, theoretically, if you don't know how to box out or you don't have the mentality to do it the day before the first game of the finals, you're not going to develop it.

"So we're doing this box-out drill, which in retrospect doesn't seem very bright . . ."

POP!

Byron Scott dropped to the floor. Not as if he were shot. No, more like a tree being cut down by a lumberjack. The Laker shooting guard was jostling for position with David Rivers when he fell off balance, landed awkwardly and ruptured his left hamstring. It took Vitti less than two minutes to know that Scott would not be participating in *at least* the first two games of the NBA Finals. He wound up playing nary a game. "It was devastating," Vitti said. "For the team, for Byron . . . devastating."

"All we needed was to have a nice, relaxed shootaround," said Bertka. "But instead Pat wants to do some intensive work, and Byron fucking hurts himself."

By now, Scott was more than just an elite sharpshooter. He was a borderline All-Star who averaged 19.6 points during the regular season and owned Phoenix in the four-game Western Conference Finals sweep. "You can't overstate his value," said Rivers. "He did everything you'd want from your two-guard. When Magic needed an outlet, he knew to look for Byron."

Riley tried his best to hide his disappointment. Cooper, in his eleventh season, wasn't as explosive as he had once been, but he remained capable of quality play. This was, the coach insisted, an opportunity for others to step in and step up. Tony Campbell, the former Piston, would certainly receive big minutes. So, in all likelihood, would Jeff Lamp, a seldom-used shooting guard from the University of Virginia. Even Rivers, all six feet of him, could wind up getting time. "This is not the end of the world," Riley said. "We can—and will—overcome." Laker players didn't necessarily disagree. Scott was important, but not Johnson-and-Worthy important. Yet, even if his words rang true, Riley was the villain. Why had he pushed them so hard? So long? So rough? What the hell was Scott even doing down low, boxing out a teammate the day before the biggest game of the season? "It wasn't smart," said Campbell. "I loved playing for Pat. But it just wasn't."

The Pistons opened the series with a decisive 109–97 win, and Scott's absence was the difference. Los Angeles shot just 1-for-6 from three-point range, and Detroit backed far off Cooper and Campbell and dared them to try. Worthy shot 6-for-18, scoring 17 points. "It hurt," Johnson said of Scott's absence, "but we can't think about it. We didn't do what we were supposed to do. Defensively, we didn't guard anybody. When you don't guard a great team as they are, you usually lose."

Were the clubs both at full strength, it's still unlikely the Lakers would have won the series. Detroit was the better, deeper and more motivated team. The Pistons also seemed more cohesive. As the fatigued and irked Lakers regularly tuned Riley out, Coach Chuck Daly's voice carried oomph with Detroit's players. He was a warm man who encouraged input.

On the day off between action, Riley made it clear to his men that, even without Scott, Game 2 was a must. The Lakers played with a sense of desperation and, behind Johnson's 19 points and 9 assists, led at the half, 62–56. He had promised to "go crazy" on Detroit, and now was delivering. Then, with 4:48 remaining in the third quarter, the unthinkable happened—*again*. With Los Angeles holding on to a 75–73 advantage, Mychal Thompson's shot was blocked by John Salley, and Isiah Thomas pushed the Pistons on a four-on-two fast break the other way. As he whipped a pass, Thomas turned and saw Johnson pull up and grab his left hamstring. He had felt a slight twinge early in the third quarter, but paid it no mind. This time, though, it wasn't a mere twinge. It was a pull, and the pain was unbearable. A similar injury had caused him to miss five regular-season contests, as well as the All-Star Game. Riley called a time-out, and Johnson limped around on the court, trying to evict the injury from his body. "I came out onto the floor, and he described to me what had happened," Vitti said. "I immediately told him, 'You're done for today, but you might not be done for the series.'" Johnson pushed Vitti away like a crumpled napkin across a table, but was resigned to the fact that he could no longer play.

Without Johnson, the Lakers battled back, only to lose 108–105. "You've just got to get them any way you can," the Pistons' Joe Dumars said afterward. "You can say that we escaped with a win tonight; that's fine, we're still ahead 2–0."

The third game would be played at the Forum on June 11. This gave Vitti a full two days to work on Johnson's hamstring. From morning until evening, the two men tried everything. Ice. Heat. Stretches. Equipment. Prayer. Johnson told teammates he would definitely play. Then he told teammates he would definitely not play. The frustration gnawed at him. He and Thomas were still friendly, but the wedge from the previous year remained. Johnson hated the thought of Thomas and the Pistons taking the title. Especially in Los Angeles. "We were back here at the Forum on the night of the game, and we were back in the boiler room so nobody could see us," said Vitti. "I got him this heavy wrap for his hamstring, and he's cutting, trying to make these cuts in and out of the boiler poles back there. We didn't want to give Detroit knowledge of whether he could play or not.

"I actually remember telling Pat, 'Magic said he can't do it.' I remember being choked up because I felt helpless, and I felt as if I'd let Pat down. I let the team down. I let the fans down. I let Magic down."

And yet, when Lawrence Tanter, the Forum's public address announcer, introduced the starting lineups, there was Johnson jogging onto the court, the crowd standing and cheering. Maybe, just maybe, everything would be OK. Maybe, just maybe, the Lakers could return from the brink and . . . and . . .

Johnson lasted four minutes and forty-six seconds.

Watching him try to play was akin to seeing Ruffian hobble around the bend in her final race at Belmont. As he limped from the court, the silent audience of 17,505 seemed to know that hopes of the three-peat were limping off with him. Although the Lakers again kept it close, the backcourt trio of Cooper, Campbell and Rivers was, on a good day, Grade C. Dumars and Vinnie Johnson, Detroit's two top shooting guards, dominated the replacements, shooting 20-for-32 while scoring 48 points. The Pistons won, 114–110.

"I'm always optimistic," said Worthy, who scored 26 in the setback. "I always like to think there's a way, that you can always fight. But, in the back of my mind, I was thinking, 'Oh, shit, how can we possibly win this without Magic?' It was like a plane losing a few engines. You can still land, but there will be problems."

"We knew we needed a miracle," said Thompson. "Miracles happen in one game—but in seven games, against that Pistons team, we knew the odds were greatly against us. It was almost like the odds of winning the six-hundred-million-dollar lottery. It can happen. But, with Tony Campbell and David Rivers playing big minutes, it probably won't."

Because professional athletes are expected to emote a certain way, the Lakers talked the talk. *They'd come back before. Never underestimate the heart of a champion. You've gotta believe.* In Los Angeles—as in every other NBA city—one mostly stuck with the cliché and uttered the right words and phrases.

So, when asked, Campbell followed the script and talked about how sad he was for Johnson, how he wished he could return to the lineup and guide the team to another championship. It was only partially true.

"Honestly, I was happy to finally get a chance," said Campbell. "Because I felt like I could fill that role and give the team what it needed to win a championship. I mean, we needed Magic. But I felt we could have won with me, too. That's how I really felt. Here was my opportunity to shine."

Campbell scored 11 points in twenty-three Game 3 minutes, then another 6 points as the starter in Game 4, when the Pistons finished out the series with a 105–97 win. Based in large part upon his tough play in trying circumstances, Campbell was acquired by the first-year Minnesota Timberwolves at season's end. He went on to average more than 21 points per game over the next two seasons. "I'm not happy those guys got hurt, and I'd certainly have rather won," Campbell said. "But it did help my long-term career."

Cooper, too, carried himself well. An afterthought for much of the year, he started all four games, committing only two turnovers. "At the end of the series I gave Michael a jockstrap with two brass balls in it," Bertka said. "I said, 'Michael, this is for you. You've got brass balls.'"

Rivers, on the other hand, shot 1-for-5 in twelve minutes in Game 4, appearing confused and overwhelmed. The same man who owned practices learned the hard way that, with millions watching, everything changes. "It killed his career," said Mark McNamara. "I felt bad for the kid. He went from never playing to playing big minutes against a powerhouse in the finals. He couldn't win."

Rivers would appear in a total of sixty-seven more NBA games, all with the Clippers, before moving overseas and becoming one of European basketball's all-time legends. "It worked out," he said. "Everything turned out nicely."

Not for the Lakers. With nineteen seconds left in Game 4, and his team down seven, Riley begrudgingly gave in. He motioned for Orlando Woolridge to leave the bench and enter. Tanter leaned in to his microphone atop the scorer's table and bellowed, "Orlando Woolridge, in for the Captain. . . ." The crowd came alive one final time—"*Ka-reem! Ka-reem! Ka-reem! Ka-reem!*"

Afterward, in a locker room filled with heartbreak over the defeat, and anger toward a coach who'd pushed too hard, Abdul-Jabbar was asked how it felt to be done after twenty years. The NBA's all-time leading scorer, who averaged 12.5 points in the series, paused to search for the right words. This was his final press conference as a Laker, his final time wearing an NBA uniform. "It really hasn't sunk in yet, the deeper meanings of it," he said. "I'm just thankful I could last this long and walk out the door. I am very thankful."

A mere 2,845 miles away, in Bridgeport, Connecticut, the world's happiest ex-Laker sat in his home, watching Abdul-Jabbar on television. Wes Matthews had bristled when the team let him walk while keeping the inferior Rivers, and he bristled again when Riley stole *three-peat* without proper acknowledgment.

Now, however, as the Pistons celebrated and the Lakers sulked (Riley told his players, "There's nothing to learn from this series—nothing"), Matthews relished the delicious irony. Two months earlier, he had hit a last-second three-pointer to lift the Tulsa Fast Breakers to a 114–111 victory over the Rockford Lightning in the fourth and final game of the Continental Basketball Association's championship series. Matthews played brilliantly, scoring 29 points that night and connecting on seven three-pointers. "You won't believe it, but winning the CBA championship was as meaningful to me as the NBA championship," he said. "ESPN televised it, I got a beautiful ring, I played big minutes.

"Best of all," he said, "Pat stole three-peat, and I was the only one to three-peat.

"I, Wes Matthews, was the only fucking one."

CHAPTER 20

―――――

BATES

One of the strangest marriages in Lakers history began—as most marriages do—with a tropical trip.

Three and a half months following the finals sweep, Pat Riley found himself back in Hawaii, this time staying at the beautiful Sheraton Waikiki in Honolulu. He was, after a long summer of remorse and regret and self-doubt, elated to be surrounded by paradise. Here, the pineapple was sweet, the breezes were warm, the women were gorgeous, the sand was soft and inviting.

The Lakers' forty-four-year-old coach was not alone. Along with the familiar faces gathered for training camp at the University of Hawaii's Otto Klum Gymnasium, Riley was happy to see his newest squeeze—free-agent signee Quintin Dailey.

For those who worked in professional basketball, Dailey was one of the nine or ten most naturally gifted players in the game. A 6-foot-3 shooting guard from Baltimore, Dailey could do—when he tried—everything. He dribbled as well with his left hand as he did with his right. He could run a team from the point, or slide to the two-spot and torch bigger opponents for 25 points. Though not particularly tall, he deftly positioned himself below the boards. While starring at the University of San Francisco in the early 1980s, Dailey was a two-time West Coast Conference Player of the Year who, as a junior, averaged 25.2 points per game. In seven NBA seasons—first with the Bulls, then the Clippers—Dailey averaged more than 15 points per game five times. "Quintin was an incredible player," said Norm Nixon, who teamed with Dailey on the Clippers. "He had so much ability to do so many things. He could have gone down as a true great."

Unfortunately, Quintin Dailey came with baggage. In the early morning hours of December 21, 1981, while still in college, he allegedly entered the room of a twenty-one-year-old nursing student inside Phelan Hall and held her captive. According to a police report, Dailey wanted the woman to "fellate" him and forced her to masturbate him. When she reached for the telephone to call the police, Dailey allegedly wrapped his fingers around her throat. The investigation resulted in three charges (including attempted rape) that were dropped, and three years of probation. During the court proceedings, it was also revealed that Dailey had been given a $1,000-a-month job while in college that didn't require him to show up.

Shortly thereafter, under pressure from faculty and the NCAA, the University of San Francisco dropped its basketball program. Also shortly thereafter, the Chicago Bulls used the seventh overall pick in the 1982 Draft to select Dailey.

The reaction was fierce. To celebrate his home debut, an anti–domestic violence organization, Take Back the Night Coalition, picketed outside Chicago Stadium. Women's groups threatened to boycott the Bulls, and even Wallace Bryant, a former college teammate who played center for Chicago, suggested Dailey "might do it again." Fans showed up for games dressed as nurses. Dailey begged the Windy City for understanding, but received little. Wrote John Schulian of the *Chicago Sun-Times*: "If you really want to know how badly the values of sport have been distorted, examine the presence of Quintin Dailey on the NBA's doorstep. . . . I can't help believing that if Dailey weren't a basketball player, if he were just another creep off the street, he would still be learning what a chamber of horrors the halls of justice can be."

It was all downhill from there. Dailey became a poster child for NBA drug excesses, twice being suspended by the league for his addiction to cocaine and attending three in-patient rehabilitation centers. He often failed to show up for games, and his weight would balloon with comical regularity. When he played, he played hard—sometimes. Or indifferently. Or sloppily. He was the laziest man teammates had ever seen, and took quizzical pride in being labeled a dog. "I'd never been around a drugged-out player before Quintin," said Don Casey, his coach with the Clippers. "He was as good a catch-and-shoot player as I'd seen, but his attitude was awful."

In the past, Jerry West and the Lakers were reluctant to add men like Quintin Dailey to the mix. In the world of Magic Johnson, the ultimate uniter, cancers were not to be tolerated or endured. You either played hard for the Lakers, or you didn't play for the Lakers.

Riley, however, had adjusted his thinking over recent years, and came to believe that, under his magical powers, even the most dysfunctional basketball player could find his way. Look, it worked moderately well with Orlando Woolridge, another former substance abuser who became a model citizen and solid producer. So what if Quintin Dailey was a drug addict who, while playing with the Clippers in 1988–89, was suspended for weighing 225 pounds—20 above what was demanded? So what if he was as reliable as a dollar store appliance? Talent was talent.

Los Angeles signed Dailey to a guaranteed one-year, $400,000 contract and welcomed him into the fold. "It's an honor to play with a team that can win the championship," said Dailey upon agreeing to the deal. "I'm not here to take a position, just to help them win. I want to be established as a winner. I've thought of myself as that, but now maybe this will be a chance to prove it to everybody else."

The Lakers reported to Hawaii for their first team meeting—which was mandatory—on the evening of Thursday, October 6. Dailey, who had missed his flight from Los Angeles, was nowhere to be found. He arrived later that night, and showed up for Friday morning's practice looking suspiciously frail. He entered the gym, shook some hands, patted some backs—then lasted barely an hour before complaining of stomach pains and dizziness. "First practice, it's 'Where's Dailey?'" said Bertka. "Oh, he's outside throwing up." When asked to explain, Dailey said he was so excited for camp that he hadn't eaten food in two days. "The gym was a steam box, and we were doing a drill at the very beginning and Quintin couldn't complete it," said Larry Drew, a free-agent guard who had played with Dailey on the Clippers. "He ended up going outside to get air, and they sent him back to the [Sheraton Waikiki]. That set the tone. If you're going to be a Laker, you have to be in shape."

One week later, after oversleeping and failing to attend a morning practice, Dailey was gone. The Lakers ate the $400,000 and sent him off into the abyss.

"He just didn't come in mentally or physically ready to perform," said an exasperated Riley. "We've got a lot of young guys on this team, and we cannot tolerate this kind of thing. I sort of feel sorry for the guy, a little bit. He's had an opportunity to play for the Lakers—just keep playing in the league—and he does this. Look, he missed a flight, he missed a meeting, he fell out from the first practice, and then he oversleeps today. And he's begged off (working out) in a couple of other practices, too. It's unconscionable that a player would do what he's done. We don't think it's a privilege to play for the Lakers, but there are certain things we won't put up with."

One month into the season Josh Rosenfeld, the media relations director, quit after a confrontation with Bob Steiner, his boss. A day or two later, the phone in his home rang. "It was Quintin Dailey, out of the league, calling to see how I was doing," said Rosenfeld. "He said, 'I know how much that job meant to you—I just want to make sure you're OK.' I was truly touched. Talk about an enigmatic man . . .'"

Perhaps, had Dailey arrived at a different time, in a different year, he could have stuck. This, however, was the worst possible moment for someone who required soothing and guidance to become a Laker.

Pat Riley was in a foul state of mind.

For years, this had been brewing. With every success, with every magazine feature and endorsement opportunity and paid speaking engagement, those around the Lakers saw his ego grow like a well-watered fern. The Pat Riley of old could laugh at himself and tell one story after another until the bar was empty and the tables cleared. The modern version, though, lacked both perspective and a sense of humor. Defenders within the organization would say Riley was simply obsessed with winning and didn't want to let people down. Those who knew him well, and who were honest in their feelings, could express the truth. Put simply, Riley had forgotten that, come day's end, he was merely a basketball coach, and the Lakers merely a basketball team. He equated winning and losing with life and death, with Biblical tales and the fight for righteousness and . . .

"It got," said John Black, "ridiculous."

Early on in the 1989–90 season, Black took over from Rosenfeld as the team's media relations director. He was excited to work closely with one of the great coaches in NBA history. One day Riley told Black that, as part of the position, he would have to file regular detailed statistical reports on the team's players. "It would have been two hours a day of adding shit up, compiling statistics, figuring trends and percentages and bullshit," Black said. "I hate that shit. Josh was a numbers guy—he'd happily lock himself in his office and dig through stats. Not me." Black didn't offer an immediate response, and asked West whether it was something he had to do. "Absolutely not," the general manager said. "That's not your job." A few days later, Riley cornered Black once again. "So," he asked, "are we good?"

"Actually," Black said, "we're not." He was thirty years old and supposed to do (under Riley Law) whatever the coach asked. If that meant handling statistics or mopping the floor or singing Amy Grant love songs, so be it.

"What do you mean?" Riley said.

"I mean I'm not going to do it," Black replied. "It's not part of my job. I know Josh was doing it for you, but that was something Josh enjoyed doing. It's not something I like."

Riley stormed off. For the next two weeks, he refused to speak to Black—*the person responsible for handling all dealings with the enormous Lakers media contingent.* "I was getting a half-dozen interview requests for Pat every day . . . things he had to do every day after practice," said Black. "I had to work with the man, and the guy wouldn't talk to me. It was so dysfunctional. He really had become the most miserable, fucked-up bastard."

If one were to watch the team in Hawaii, he would think it was all business as usual. Though Kareem Abdul-Jabbar was, for the first time since 1975, not a Laker, he showed up to assist in camp. Magic Johnson was throwing passes, James Worthy was slashing to the lane, Byron Scott was popping jumpers. Everything was the same as it had always been, with a slight difference: People now walked on eggshells. Not just low-level staffers and men like Black. No, *everyone.* Wrote Mark Heisler in his book *The Lives of Riley*: "Laker employees grew used to seeing [Riley] in the office on the morning after a loss, unshaven, looking gaunt, a shell of the dandy they'd see the night of games. He made myriad demands of them. There were itineraries to be changed at a moment's notice and he was impatient if they couldn't get it done now."

Those who once supported Riley no longer came to his defense. Cooper, the ball-hawking stalwart, was thirty-three and about to begin his final year with the club. Long ago, when Riley demanded something, Cooper jumped to attention. No more. "Everything gets old," he said. "Old and stale." Scott behaved similarly. Riley spoke, he shrugged. Or yawned. Abdul-Jabbar, who disliked Riley so much that the two barely spoke, nicknamed him Norman Bates after the character from *Psycho*.

The most noticeable change came in Riley's relationship with West.

The two were not only former Lakers teammates, but close friends for more than two decades. Yet everything Riley was becoming, West abhorred. West was a man who shunned celebrity, who ducked crowds, who was happiest in casual attire, sitting in the rear of a room. He had played basketball for the pure love of the game, and worked in the front office because he felt he could help others achieve greatness. One of the favorite (of many) Jerry-West-is-simply-an-awesome-guy stories told by Lakers staffers occurred on a night in Hawaii, when he agreed to take ten team employees to dinner. To his great chagrin, the group settled upon Ruth's Chris Steak House. "Fuck Ruth's Chris!" West said. "That place sucks. Motherfuckers don't know how to make a steak."

West, however, was the lone dissenter. The men entered the restaurant, sat down, ordered their meals. When West's steak arrived, it was under-cooked. "This isn't right," he told the waiter. "Can you take it back and cook it some more?" The server shuffled off, and West urged the others to eat. His steak returned five minutes later, now overcooked. "Mr. West," the waiter asked, "is it OK?"

"Goddamn it," West said, "it's overcooked. The steak is overcooked."

"Oh, my," the waiter replied, "let me get you another one."

"No, no, no," West said. "I don't want another one."

"Please, Mr. West . . ."

"No, really," he said. "I don't want another one. I'm not even hungry now."

A moment later, the manager arrived at the table. "Mr. West, I'm so sorry," he said. "Please let us make you another one. We'll comp you it."

West had had enough. "I told the waiter I don't want another one," he said. "I don't want another one, and I don't want you to comp it. Keep it on the bill."

"But, Mr. West, we could never charge you for—"

"I said keep it on the bill," he said. "I want you to charge me for it."

The attendees laughed hysterically, and went around the table asking one another about their steaks. "Mine's great—how about yours?"

"Oh, fantastic! Yours?"

"Amazing! Best steak I've ever had!"

"So the meal ends, and we're brought the check," said Black. "And Jerry always picked up the tab—always. And we're standing there waiting for the car at valet parking. And he looks down at the check and he says, 'Can you believe the nerve of those motherfuckers? They charged me for the god-damned steak!' When I tell you tears were rolling down my face, it's no ex-aggeration.

"But that was Jerry. He was crass and hard, but giving and funny. He knows that he's a celebrity, but he fights not wanting to be one. He just wants to be a regular guy. People would approach him all the time for auto-graphs and he'd say, 'Really, I'm nothing special.' That wasn't false modesty—it's how he felt. Ordinary."

Immediately after the Lakers cut Jamaal Wilkes in 1985, West choked up during a televised interview and excused himself. Josh Rosenfeld found him in the men's room, crying. "I guess," West said, "you're seeing a side of me few people see. My wife works with Jamaal's, and he's going to have to go home tonight and tell her he lost his job." When Kurt Rambis left for Char-lotte in 1988, West was heartbroken. When Abdul-Jabbar finally retired, he felt as if he had retired, too. When Rosenfeld was stressed and overworked during his final summer with the team, West entered his office with an or-der. "I'm sending you to Hawaii for a week," he said. "Tell Jerry Buss you're going there to make training camp preparations. Just go over, relax, have fun, get laid. I've taken care of the arrangements."

West wanted his coach to display similar empathy, to recall what it was to be a player and take some weight off the accelerator. Yet Riley refused. Or, perhaps, simply couldn't. "Ego killed the old Pat," said Scott Carmi-chael, who ran the Lakers' speakers bureau. "The same guy who used to laugh and joke would pass you in the hallway and no longer say hello. There were many times I loathed him." Riley was obsessed with winning at all costs and, perhaps, obsessed at proving he could win without depending upon a 7-foot-2 iconic center. Before long, his yelling, berating, screaming ways had worn down the entire team. This included his final defender—Johnson. "Riles changed," Johnson said. "With that much success and what was coming to him off the court, yeah, you have to change. He changed, but so did we. He became a coach. Yeah, it happened. He became a coach and he thought his way was the way.

"He wore his losses. I'm a guy who took mine home. I'd turn off all the lights—where he wore his on his face. And you knew what was coming. Some mornings at airports, he didn't speak to anybody. I don't think he could bring himself to say anything. And we knew all hell's gonna break loose at practice."

Riley and his players were no longer on the same page. There was open hostility and decaying trust. If the team had any hope of succeeding, it needed an ice breaker; a distraction; a cuddly plush toy.

It needed Vlade Divac.

■ ■ ■

He was an uncommon draft choice and an uncommon Laker. For the first time in his seven years as a general manager, West gave the green light to spend a first-round pick on a player he had never before met or seen in person. This, of course, caused the man great discomfort. West was a creature of habit and a slave to order. Using the twenty-sixth selection in the 1989 NBA Draft—then surrendering big money—to a shadow figure from a bunch of grainy game tapes wasn't exactly comfortable. Especially when all he really hoped for was solid frontcourt depth.

The University of Missouri had set forth toward the pros a senior center, Gary Leonard, who seemed to perfectly suit the team's needs. He stood 7-foot-1, and possessed the requisite skills to ably serve as an OK yet unspectacular backup lug for the next half decade. When West asked his top scouts—Ronnie Lester and Gene Tormohlen—whether the team should go with Leonard or this Yugoslavian Divac person, both picked the safety of the known American. Mitch Kupchak, the assistant general manager, agreed. "I told Jerry I was scared," Tormohlen said. "The bottom line is, if every team knew how good Vlade Divac was, why was he still there [late in the Draft]?"

But how could West allow himself to pass on this one? The Lakers were stuck in the Land of Center Abyss—Abdul-Jabbar retired, Mychal Thompson aging, Mark McNamara not especially good. The world wasn't exactly crawling with athletic giants, especially twenty-one-year-old 7-foot-1 centers with pillow-soft hands and a ballerina's footwork (who, by the way, had just started on the silver medal–winning Yugoslav Olympic team). Sure, no one with the Lakers had actually witnessed Divac on a court. And, OK, it was a bit alarming to watch a projected Top 15 pick slip down, down, down the board, beneath such future luminaries as Jeff Sanders and Anthony Cook. And, eh, yeah, he did have that little Yugoslavian military commitment thing hanging over him.

With five minutes remaining before the Lakers had to submit their selection, West called Jerry Buss, who was vacationing in Hawaii. "Early on with the Lakers, I made a strong suggestion about a draft choice in the first round," Buss said, referring to the Brad Holland disaster. "It was the last time I stepped out of line. So when [Jerry] told me about this seven-foot Yugoslavian and said, 'What do you think?' I said, 'Go ahead. In our position, we should gamble.'"

Los Angeles gambled.

Decked out in the only suit he owned ("I came to this country wearing jeans, a T-shirt and sneakers," he said. "I went to pick up a suit, but you can't pick up a seven-foot suit just like that. So I was looking not good"), Divac sat inside Madison Square Garden, waiting for someone to call his strange name. "They told me I would go pretty high," he said. "So I was very disappointed. Then the Lakers picked me and I was like, 'Wow! It can be no better!'"

A native of Belgrade and the small Serbian town of Prijepolje, Divac left his parents when he was twelve so he could play basketball for a cadet team, KK Partizan, 114 miles away in Kraljevo. Four years later, he was 6-foot-9 and excelling at his nation's highest professional level. By seventeen, he led the Yugoslav Junior Olympic team to a gold medal at the World University Games. By twenty, he was an Olympian and the pride of a sports-infatuated people. His July 1, 1989, wedding was televised nationally.

Yet throughout his rise, Divac feared for Yugoslavia, which sat on the threshold of civil war. He didn't know who to trust and who not to trust, what was safe and what wasn't. He played basketball with national pride, but wasn't always certain what that even meant. Yugoslavia was about to be torn asunder and here he was, a Serbian, playing alongside his best friends who, as Croatians, were morphing into enemies. "It was all very confusing and difficult," he said. "And then I was handed a dream. . . ."

West arranged for Divac's military obligation to (poof!) be deferred, paid his old club (Partizan) a fee for his rights, and—like that—he was a Laker. He agreed to a three-year contract on August 7 and, along with his new wife, Snezana, was immediately enrolled in daily two-and-a-half-hour English courses to learn a language he neither spoke nor understood. Divac was presented with a home in Marina del Rey, a car and a sixty-nine-year-old interpreter named Alex Omalev (the former head basketball coach at Cal State Fullerton and the language coordinator for basketball venues during the L.A. Olympics in 1984) to tell him the difference between a haircut and a hedgehog. When he was assigned uniform number 12, reporters asked if it was a homage to Riley, who wore the number during his career. "Yes," said

Divac—and the media carried the story. "Truthfully, I had no idea," he said years later. "That was my number as a kid."

Readers of the Los Angeles newspapers were frequently reminded that the name was pronounced VLAH-day Dee-VATZ-ay, and West and the Lakers did everything they could to lower expectations. Divac, they made clear, wasn't here to replace Abdul-Jabbar or fight Thompson for a job or even contribute much. He was young and inexperienced, and—with good fortune—might one day develop into a player.

On August 8, he joined the Lakers' team in the Summer Pro League.

He was a player.

Facing real competition for the first time since June's European Championships, Divac dominated a Denver-Sacramento hybrid team with 20 points, 18 rebounds and 3 blocked shots in a 125–121 win at Loyola Marymount's gymnasium. For Riley, who watched from the stands, the sight was surreal: Divac, inexplicably donning a number 32 singlet, oftentimes ignoring his team's guards, gathering rebounds, dribbling down the court and either dishing or driving. The five hundred fans in attendance oohed collectively when he shoveled a no-look pass to Eric McLaughlin, a rookie free agent out of Akron. Afterward, Riley reached for Divac's hand and called him "Big Magic."

"His passing skills surprised me," Riley said. "The fact that he can handle the ball means we have to change some things. We have to play around his skills."

Divac met up with his new teammates in Hawaii, and he was relatively unchanged. His English remained dreadful (tucked in Riley's pocket was a list of thirty common basketball terms written in Serbo-Croatian), his concern for his homeland painfully real. Expectations were as low as they could be—in the era before the European influx, foreign players were presumed to be soft and unathletic. When the veteran Lakers saw Divac, they could barely contain their chuckles. He was gangly and pale and walked with a slight hiccup to his step. With his scratchy dark beard and arched eyebrows, he looked to be a cross between Yakov Smirnoff, the Russian comedian, and Raffi, the Egyptian-born Canadian children's singer. He chain-smoked cigarettes and chugged Coca-Colas as if they were glasses of water. In restaurants, he ordered hamburgers—a word he grasped.

"Everyone stopped laughing at him as soon as they played him," said Jim Eyen, a first-year assistant coach. "I think guys were shocked by how good he was. He's six-foot-ten and doing guard drills. He's dribbling with both hands. Some guys with that length and passing ability might be light in the ass and won't play low. Well, Vlade could guard in the post and do it big and strong. He combined physicality and mobility." Divac shot with either hand, and his funky low-post moves were a little bit James Worthy, a little bit A. C. Green. Though nobody dared say so aloud, Divac was already superior to Thompson, the twelve-year veteran.

For Los Angeles players, Divac was a Godiva gift basket. First, he became the perfect distraction. Whenever he ran the wrong way, or bungled a play, or failed to pass to a guard, Riley went berserk. If the coach was busy teeing off on the rookie, he wasn't teeing off on them. Second, he was goofiness personified. Divac mangled words and phrases and paragraphs, but never seemed deterred. He would explain the plots of movies like *Field of Dreams* or *Dead Poets Society* and have onlookers rolling on the floor. "There is this man, you see, and he has this hat. . . ."

Once, someone asked Divac to try and tell a joke in English. "Did you hear of baby in Belgrade," he said, "born with more eyes than teeth?"

Tap tap. Is this thing on?

"We had a flight during training camp," said McNamara, the backup center. "I'm sleeping and all of a sudden Bill Bertka screams, 'Wake up! Wake up!' He smelled a cigarette. It was Vlade, smoking in the bathroom. A federal offense. Everyone laughed."

"As a trainer, his smoking shocked me," said Gary Vitti. "I told him how stupid it was. We once even got a bill from a hotel for smoking in a room. I screamed at him—'Vlade, $250 for smoking in a room!' He told me it was my fault."

"How is that my fault?" Vitti asked.

"Why," replied Divac, "did you put me in a nonsmoking room?"

Because he had spent a spell playing professionally in Italy, McNamara communicated with Divac via broken Italian. They bonded, and before long Riley would turn to McNamara and ask him to explain a concept to his new teammate. "After I made the team, Riley told me, 'Don't think we didn't notice how willing you were to help a guy fighting for your job,'" McNamara said. "That meant a lot."

Conveniently, Divac always understood compliments but rarely grasped criticisms. He seemed to smile during 95 percent of a day, flashing a carefree look that irritated Johnson. The veteran guard zeroed in on Divac, making him both project and scapegoat. Divac's soft hands were inviting bull's-eyes.

Divac's casual gallop was infuriating. He showed up on time—but *just* on time. Johnson took every possible opportunity to scream at Divac, to bark at Divac, to insult and disparage Divac. "Oh, Earvin was hard on Vlade," said Vitti. "Really hard." It was the ol' Earl Jones treatment—only Divac rarely had a ball hit him in the head and never appeared rattled. Johnson yelled—Divac responded with a friendly nod. "I think Vlade's a good player but he has a tendency to be a little lazy," Johnson said during camp. "Maybe over there [in Europe] he was so talented that he could get away with coming at a different speed than what we're accustomed to. But Riley wants you to do things quick, because he wants you playing quick. So he's got to get used to that.

"[But] he can do a lot of things. He can run and he can catch the ball [well] for a big man. He can *play.*"

■ ■ ■

Coming off of the finals sweep at the hands of Detroit, and having lost Abdul-Jabbar, the Lakers were supposed to take a few more steps back toward the rest of the NBA pack.

Instead, the opposite occurred. For the first time in franchise history, Los Angeles went undefeated in eight exhibition games, then opened the regular season by winning ten of eleven. Everything was going swimmingly—Thompson and Divac were teaming to average more than 18 points and 12 rebounds per night, Johnson and Worthy were (as always) playing at All-Star levels and A. C. Green had continued his emergence as one of the league's three or four best power forwards. The bench—led by Divac, Drew and Cooper—was its deepest in years. "We were unbelievable," said Drew, Johnson's backup. "From the day I arrived, I felt a focus and determination I'd never seen before. I'll never forget when I first got there, and Magic educated me on each player—where they liked the ball, how to use them most effectively, who was the first option, who was the fourth. The whole team worked so hard in practice and off the court, when the games started, it was a breeze."

But, for too many Lakers, it was no longer fun. Save for Divac's quirky antics and scattered moments of levity, Riley and Johnson were sapping the joy from the franchise. The star point guard would win his third MVP award in four seasons, but devoted too much time to berating and screaming. Having played so long for Riley, he was now *becoming* Riley. His practice comments no longer included soothing touches. If you messed up, Johnson rode you hard. With Abdul-Jabbar's departure came a certain behavioral liberation. Johnson's inner-dictator was emerging. This was not a good thing. "He was really pushing us in practice, telling us, 'Hey, you got to do this better, you got to do that better,'" said Cooper, his closest friend on the team.

Riley was no better. "Shootarounds turned from forty minutes to one and a half hours with a lot of video," Cooper said. "It was mentally fatiguing more than anything else. Coach Riley had changed a little bit. He wasn't as open as he used to be. If you had a suggestion, he didn't take it wrong. He just didn't take it. He heard you. Then it was like, 'OK, you gave it to me, fine, but we're going to do it this way.' Where in the past, he really would listen to you and kind of compromise with you. Just the aura he started putting out that year. You felt, don't invade his space today, not now, not the time. So 'Not now, not the time' turned into the whole season. We were kind of hesitant. We were looking at each other out on the court. It was the first time I can remember players making a mistake and glancing over at the bench for a second. We never had done that before."

Unhappiness and discomfort replaced peace and tranquility. Riley behaved more like a schoolmaster than a coach. Little unimportant details now held tremendous importance. Riley didn't like how, come the fourth quarter at the Forum, the crowds paid more attention to the Laker Girls than the game. Consequently, he forced the cheering squad to sit during the period. Thanks to Buss's generosity, the Lakers traveled on the luxurious MGM Grand plane, which featured individual staterooms. Riley, for a reason no player understood, insisted everyone be relegated to the seats he assigned. "He's just like that," Johnson told Mark Heisler of the *Los Angeles Times*. "What happened, he wanted to control everything. . . . He tried to control the whole arena. He wanted to control the locker room, the band, the Laker Girls. He tried to control everything and he got away from what he was there to do."

Cooper, a faded copy of the high flyer he'd once been, averaged twenty-three minutes per game and cursed Riley out beneath his breath. Scott, a stubbornly confident man, was shooting thirteen times per game—far too low for a player of his stature. Worthy was worn down by the negative vibes. Divac endured Johnson's nonstop criticisms. In January, Cooper, Worthy and Johnson—the three captains—met with West to complain about Riley's abusiveness and some of his on-court strategizing. There was, Johnson told the general manager, a gap in communication that needed to be resolved. Shortly thereafter, West held a team meeting for everyone to clear the air. He told the press it was a "small thing." This was a lie.

Riley didn't like what was he was seeing. He believed players were done listening to him and no longer sought out his approval. "He'd always say that," said Bertka. " 'Bill, they're tired of hearing what I have to say.' " Riley also seemed to cringe at the spoils of success lavished upon the franchise. Worthy spent $2.675 million on a gated mansion in Pacific Palisades. CBS hired a producer named Renée Valente to film a (painfully awful) made-for-TV movie, *Laker Girls*, starring Tina Yothers. Johnson agreed to a $1 million pay-per-view one-on-one game against Chicago's Michael Jordan (it was canceled when the NBA refused to sanction the event). Divac drew interest from a surprising number of merchandisers. To a coach who bemoaned "peripheral distractions," everything now seemed to be a peripheral distraction. Control was gone. There was even speculation that, come season's end, NBC would make Riley an offer to jump to TV. "Guys tired of Pat," said Vitti. "His style is such that you can get burned out on it. Because he keeps tightening that bolt tighter and tighter and tighter and tighter."

Despite the turmoil, the Lakers wound up winning sixty-three games, the second most in Riley's career. With four new expansion teams (Charlotte, Miami, Minnesota, Orlando) having been added over two seasons, the NBA wasn't quite as deep as it had been. Regardless, Los Angeles compiled the league's best record, and the feeling of accomplishment after wrapping up the top seed was real. "You had to be proud," said Divac. "You reached a goal—a very hard goal."

Los Angeles faced the Houston Rockets in the first round of the playoffs, a matchup that lacked the luster of the Kareem-versus-Moses and Kareem-versus-Sampson days. Houston was a nondescript .500 team, and the series was taken by the Lakers in a benign four games.

Yet while even the most diligent of Showtime fans probably recall little of the action from a forgettable battle, John Black, the media relations head, will never forget what transpired shortly after the team checked into the Stouffer Renaissance Hotel on Monday, April 30, for the third game.

"Everybody was coming back from dinner, and the elevator door opens," Black said. "It was Earvin, Cooper, Byron, Orlando Woolridge and one other guy. . . ."

Black looked over the crowded space and suggested he'd wait for the next ride. A long arm grabbed him by the shirt and yanked him inside. "John," Johnson said, "we're gonna fill you in."

The men retreated to a suite, where the following hour was devoted to a verbal slaying of the prison guard known as Patrick James Riley. "They had a team meeting and they're motherfucking him," Black said. "Motherfucker this and motherfucker that and all these motherfuckers directed at Pat. I didn't know it was to that extent. And I was like, '*Holy* fuck.' It was all melting down."

The Lakers were scheduled to play Phoenix in the next round, and nobody (literally, not a single newspaper prognosticator) predicted a Suns triumph. Coach Cotton Fitzsimmons's team had been good enough to win fifty-four regular-season games, and the Kevin Johnson-Jeff Hornacek backcourt was one of the NBA's elite. But Phoenix—despite starting some guy named Rambis at power forward—had lost three of four to Los Angeles in the regular season. Even after they shocked the Lakers in the opener with a 104–102 win at the Forum, few were anticipating much of a run. Los Angeles fought back to take Game 2, and order was rightly restored.

Or not.

The series shifted to Arizona, and the Suns grabbed Game 3 with an uncharacteristically simple 117–103 victory. If one were attending his first NBA game, he would have left convinced that Phoenix was the far superior team. Kevin Johnson repeatedly zipped through the lane, past Magic Johnson and Scott, to score 22, and Hornacek, the deadeye shooting guard, hit 10 of 16 for 29 points. The Suns were younger, stronger and more eager. "I do have faith," Riley said afterward. "I do, because we've experienced this before."

The Lakers had been in past holes. But they'd never been this divided; this angry; this intent on telling their coach to go to hell. They wanted to win. But did they *need* to? Did it consume them? No. Riley's motivational speeches—delivered in high-pitched, desperate tones—fell upon tin ears. All the old themes (Family. Unity. Peripheral distractions) had shriveled and died. Players like Johnson, Worthy, Scott and Thompson were no longer eager kids seeking out guidance. They were hardened and jaded. The rah-rah blatherings failed to take.

On the morning after Game 3, Black received a call from the league that Riley had been named the NBA Coach of the Year. It was his first time receiving the honor, and the repeated slight had gnawed at him like a subway rat. He knew he was the best coach in basketball. And yet, he was continuously snubbed.

Black found Riley lounging by the pool at the Ritz-Carlton, shirt off, taking in the sun. "Hey, Pat, congratulations," he said, gritting his teeth. "I just found out you won Coach of the Year. We need to schedule a press conference."

Black waited for a reply. There was none. Riley, once again, was ignoring him. Just because he could. "It's so fucked up," Black said. "I'm telling him he won Coach of the Year, we need to schedule it, and he's giving me—at most—yes and no answers." Finally, Black said, curtly, "Pat, when do you want to do it?"

"Fuck it," Riley said. "I'm not doing it."

"What do you mean you're not doing it?" Black said.

"I'm not doing it," Riley replied. "Tell the league to go fuck themselves. I'm not gonna do it."

"Pat, you're not going to do a press conference?" Black said. His voice was raised. He was angry. "You just won the Coach of the Year. . . ."

"That's right," Riley said.

Black marched away.

"Of course, he did it," Black said. "But that's what it was like all year long. Every day I'd go into him with interview requests, and he was just a miserable prick. There's no way I would have stayed with the Lakers if it meant working with Pat for another year."

Riley begrudgingly accepted the Red Auerbach Trophy in a press conference on the morning of Tuesday, May 15, two days after the Lakers had wasted Johnson's 43 points in a 114–101 Game 4 setback. He said all the right things ("This is a residual award of winning and I'd like to thank the players for that. . . ."), but by now words carried zero weight. Heading into Game 4, Riley had delivered a behind-closed-door sermon to his players that was, even by Hulkamania–meets–Jerry Falwell standards, downright crazy. Excluding Johnson, Riley went around the room and blamed everyone. Scott's defense was invisible and his shots weren't falling. Thompson was playing like an old woman. Worthy, averaging 23 points in the series, was forcing the action. Woolridge was a loser who belonged on loser teams. "He singled me out the other way and that kind of killed everything," said Johnson. "'Only one guy playing good in this whole group and that's Buck!' I was saying, 'Oh, man.' It was over. We were through after that meeting . . . no way we could beat them."

Game 4 had been a mess. Scott, who demanded more shots, missed four early on, and Riley used a time-out to, specifically, humiliate him. "O.K., Buck, forget it!" Riley screamed. "If they're not going to play, I'm going to run the same play every single time!" For most of the rest of the night, Riley called play after play for Johnson. Only he and Worthy took more than ten shots. "And I changed [a play] one time and he got mad at me!" an incredulous Johnson said. "'I told you to shoot!'"

The series returned to Los Angeles for Game 5, with the Lakers on the brink of elimination. That morning, during shootaround, Johnson and Cooper—Showtime brothers for more than a decade—nearly came to blows. Cooper accused his pal of ripping the team to the press; his exact words to the *Los Angeles Times* were a seemingly inoffensive "More guys have to play better."

"You went in the paper and said guys got to play well," Cooper said. "You're pointing the finger!"

Johnson was stunned. "Michael," he said, "did I say that Michael Cooper has to play well? Did I say that Byron Scott has to play well? Did I say that Orlando Woolridge has to play well?"

That night, the most miserable 63-win season came to a merciful completion. The Suns won, 106–103, and nary a tear was shed in the locker room.

The Lakers were happy to be done with it all.

CHAPTER 21

REFRESHMENT

On the afternoon of May 17, 1990, Pat Riley held his final team meeting of the season, expressing his great disappointment to a room stuffed with basketball players who detested him.

Afterward, he congregated in a Forum tunnel with the Lakers beat writers—almost all of whom had come to detest him, too. In quiet, thoughtful tones, he explained that he wasn't certain whether he wanted to return for a tenth season as coach. "I've been with the Lakers for twenty years [as a player, broadcaster, assistant coach and head coach], and I can't honestly say what I'm going to do," he said. "That's all. I don't know. I have to sit down and think about what is in the best interests of the team. I love coaching. I know what it's all about, but I can't emphatically say right now."

The media speculated. Riley stalled. Jerry Buss jabbered. Jerry West blathered—"I can't imagine that a team can win sixty-three games and all of a sudden you want us to bomb the ship." But as soon as the Phoenix series ended, Lakers executives agreed they would fire Pat Riley.

"He wanted to return," said John Black, the media relations director, "and he would have come back were it up to him."

Black sat in meetings with West and Buss as they decided how the whole awkward affair should be handled. Though Riley had grown out of favor, no one was looking to humiliate him. He was as responsible as anyone for bringing the franchise its greatest success. Riley's 73.3 percent winning percentage was the best in league history. His 102 playoff victories were unrivaled. Plus, Jerry Buss didn't do negative. It wasn't in his catalogue. "We had this meeting," said Black. "Pat was there, me, Jerry West, Jerry Buss. It wasn't mean-spirited or even awkward. It was just, 'How are we gonna do this? What are we gonna call this?'"

On June 11, 1990, members of the media were invited to the Forum for a press conference that had an eerily familiar feel. Nearly nine years earlier, Riley had stepped to a similar podium and—amidst great confusion—was named co–head coach of the Los Angeles Lakers. Now, amidst more great confusion, he was being fired. No, not fired—replaced. Well, sorta replaced, sorta resigning, sorta stepping aside, sorta just, ahem, leaving. "Man's greatest fear is his fear of extinction, but what he fears more than that is insignificance," Riley told a packed room, his voice cracking with emotion. "There is nothing wrong with being unique. They [the Lakers] were unique—above and beyond.

"The pressure to win in this league and the desire to win is so high. We know what we're getting into when we get hired. I'm not fed up and I'm not burned out from coaching. I have as much energy as I've ever had at forty-five."

The oddness of the event cannot be overstated. First, nearly everyone affiliated with the Lakers had known Riley was being dumped. Second, most of the reporters in attendance arrived under the assumption that he was being dumped. Third, Magic Johnson, the closest thing Riley had to a basketball son, was nowhere to be found. (Johnson issued a statement that read, in part, "When I'm older and somebody talks about Showtime, the first person I'll think of is Pat Riley.")

Fourth, those assembled could surmise the Lakers had already decided upon a replacement. He was, after all, sitting alongside Riley.

Not that Mike Dunleavy felt uncomfortable. Or awkward. Or, for that matter, much of anything. At the moment, he was simply in a happy-numb state, a thirty-six-year-old basketball junkie being handed the keys to the greatest franchise in the NBA. "It was," he said, "the highlight of my career."

Though the entire event was clouded by the unspoken knowledge that a torch passer was surrendering a flame he preferred to keep, Dunleavy's glow served to obscure Riley's gloom. As soon as the new Lakers coach began to speak, it was as if Riley vanished from the stage and a warm, refreshing breeze blew through the room. Could it be the team was now led by a man who wasn't condescending? Who didn't think himself to be God's gift to coaching? Who would listen to his players and avoid demeaning them?

"I'm a lucky guy!" he yelped, explaining why he was hired. "I've been lucky all my life and this is no different."

Dunleavy barely contained his excitement, and with good reason. What was he even doing here? Just one year earlier, he was working as the Milwaukee Bucks' number two assistant, when he ran into West during the Los Angeles Summer League. "Jerry was the most respected guy in the league," Dunleavy said. "I knew him well enough to say hello, but we'd never had a conversation before." This time, Dunleavy took a deep breath and asked whether the Laker general manager could spare a moment to offer some advice. West invited him to sit down, and Dunleavy—a former journeyman shooting guard who'd played nine NBA seasons—emoted. He was working his rear off in Milwaukee but wasn't sure it was getting him anywhere. "I could move to two teams and be their top assistant," he said, "but do I need that to be considered for a head coaching position?"

"Absolutely not," West said. "As a matter of fact, if Pat Riley resigned today, you'd be one of the first people I'd call."

Dunleavy was speechless. *One of the first calls?* Hadn't his playing career been an ode to scrappy mediocrity? Hadn't he been a sixth-round draft choice out of South Carolina who survived on elbow grease and gumption? Wasn't he an 8-point-per-game scorer? Even his coaching career was largely undistinguished. Thirteen years earlier, when he found himself jobless after being cut by the Philadelphia 76ers, Dunleavy served as the twenty-three-year-old player-coach of the Carolina Lightning of the All-American Basketball Alliance. His club won seven of eight games before the enterprise folded. "Mike was OK, I guess," said Norton Barnhill, a Lightning guard. "But nothing much memorable about him."

On December 1, 1984, Dunleavy, at the time a guard with Milwaukee, was a passenger on the Bucks' flight to Baltimore when, while taxiing toward the gate, the plane jerked to a stop to avoid hitting a truck. His back went out, and never healed. His playing career was, for all intents, over. "I felt robbed," said Dunleavy, who received a large financial settlement from the airline. "I had planned on playing a lot longer." He became a Wall Street stockbroker, then, quickly, a miserable Wall Street stockbroker. "Wall Street was work," he said. "Basketball is not like working to me." He returned to the NBA before the financial crash of 1987, and never looked back.

Now he was on West's list.

"How can you rate me that highly?" Dunleavy said. "I haven't done anything."

"Well," said West, "does Don Nelson know you?"

The legendary former Bucks coach loved Dunleavy.

"And does Del Harris know you?"

Harris was Milwaukee's coach. He, too, raved about Dunleavy, and trusted him with every facet of the game.

"Well," West said, "they're very good friends of mine and they say great things about you. I've watched you coach in the summer league, and you're very good."

What Dunleavy didn't know was that, around the league, he was a hot property. Here was a savvy basketball mind with a human touch. Dunleavy possessed the rare ability to relate with all players—black, white, rookie, veteran. He was young enough to have been in their shoes a short time ago (when the Bucks needed an emergency fill-in during the 1989–90 season, Dunleavy actually played, scoring 17 points in five games), but carried enough weight to demand respect. "If you have a coach who knows what's going on—who really knows what's going on—it's a huge advantage," said Tony Smith, a rookie Lakers guard familiar with Dunleavy from pickup games at Marquette University's gym. "Mike knew what was going on."

Dunleavy returned to Milwaukee after the meeting with West and helped the Bucks compile a solid 44-38 run. When the season ended, he and his wife, Emily, traveled to Los Angeles for a vacation. He called Mitch Kupchak, an old friend, and asked if he'd like to grab some dinner. The Lakers-Suns playoff series was going on, and Kupchak—Los Angeles's assistant general manager—invited the Dunleavys to attend Game 5. The following morning, Dunleavy was eating breakfast at the Brighton Coffee Shop in Beverly Hills, casually thumbing through *The National*, a daily sports newspaper. "And at the end of this column," Dunleavy said, "it read, 'If Pat Riley loses this game tonight, look for Mike Dunleavy or Doug Collins to take this gang to Hawaii for training camp.'

"I was like, 'What the hell is this crap? How stupid.'"

Though Dunleavy and Riley weren't friends, an unspoken kinship existed based on New York upbringings (Dunleavy was born and raised in Brooklyn), hardscrabble playing careers and a passion for Xs and Os. Riley had been hardened by an unrelenting father who demanded perfection. Dunleavy had been hardened by playground basketball on the asphalt courts of Bedford-Stuyvesant. "I saw a lot at an early age," he said.

Dunleavy called Kupchak and told him it'd probably be best if he not show up at the Forum. The Lakers assistant general manager agreed. That night, Los Angeles was eliminated by the Suns, and Emily joked, "We should have just extended our trip to start looking for houses."

They returned to Milwaukee, and in the coming days Dunleavy received two head-coaching offers—one from the Bucks, one from the Pistons. West also called, though only to gauge his interest. "Jerry, I'm flattered, and I'd love to coach the Lakers," he said. "But I can't turn down two offers for the possibility of an offer." Dunleavy, in fact, had just finished dining with Herbert Kohl, the Wisconsin senator who owned the Bucks.

"Well, we want you," West said.

Dunleavy was exultant. He also, however, was a stubborn New Yorker who stuck to his guns. He agreed to a four-year, $500,000 contract, but demanded a real estate clause so that, if the Lakers were to fire him, they would be responsible for his home. West called Buss, who signed off on the deal.

Although he was told Riley was out, Dunleavy knew few of the intricacies. Fired? Resigned? What difference did it make? The two spoke briefly before the press conference, shook hands, exchanged phone numbers, then Riley took the podium. It was only hours later, when Dunleavy was resting in his hotel room, that the phone rang. "Hey, Mike, it's Pat."

Well, this was a surprise.

"Mike," Riley said, "I wanted to see if I could ask you a favor."

One of Riley's assistant coaches, Randy Pfund, had interviewed for the head position. He was crushed when he failed to land the job. "Mike, I'd like for you to hire Randy as a person on your staff," Riley said. "It would mean a great deal."

This was a test. Dunleavy could tell Riley to bug off and establish himself as his own man. He could hire Pfund and risk employing a malcontent. "I met Randy, and I liked him a lot," Dunleavy said. "But everyone in the whole world is telling me not to hire a guy who was an assistant . . . he has bonds with the players you don't . . . it can't work out." Dunleavy sat down with Pfund and made an offer: "Here's the deal," he said, "if I give you this job, and you say anything or do anything to undermine me, you're gone.

Even if I just get spooked, you're gone. I know it's unfair, but it's the way it has to be. Is that something you can agree to?"

Randy Pfund became one of Dunleavy's most trusted confidants.

■ ■ ■

It took the new coach little time to establish himself as the perfect replacement for Riley. Well before the start of the franchise's third Hawaiian training camp, Dunleavy reached out to all the returning players, promising them fair shakes and universal open-mindedness. Any past prejudices were gone. They would be treated with respect.

Though the Lakers were coming off of a 63-win run that would have satisfied other owner-executive tandems, Buss and West used the off-season to reevaluate, reassess *and remove*. The biggest change—but perhaps the least-surprising change—came with the subtraction of Michael Cooper, who had worn a Laker uniform since 1978. From ownership to players to fans, there was universal acknowledgment the defensive specialist was, at age thirty-four, a horse with one leg in the glue plant. For years, Cooper had dazzled Forum regulars by finishing off spectacular alley-oop dunks. (Passes from Johnson to a soaring Cooper came to be affectionately known as Coop-a-loops.)

Now, though, Cooper, who averaged just 6.4 points in 1989–90, needed to let go. Shortly after Dunleavy had been hired, Buss took Cooper out to dinner. "I have two options for you, Coop," he said. "We can either release or trade you, and you can try and play elsewhere. Or I've got a five-year deal for you to work in the front office. Jerry [West] will give you a title and a position, and you'll contribute to the organization. I don't want to trade you—you're a Laker. But I want you to do what's best for you. . . ."

Cooper was touched. He'd been told hundreds of times that professional basketball was strictly business, and that most organizations viewed their players as mere chips. "But here was Dr. Buss, a man who genuinely cared," Cooper said. "They didn't make them any better than him."

Still itching to play, he signed a three-year, $5-million offer from Il Messaggero Roma of the Italian League, moved his family to Europe and, for thirteen months, had the time of his life. "But basketball became a job," he said. "So I came home, called Dr. Buss and asked if the offer still existed. He told me to come right in. Dr. Buss was a great owner, a great man, a great person, a great friend. A great provider. He provided something for all of us."

Along with Cooper, the Lakers ridded themselves of Orlando Wool-ridge and Mark McNamara, elevated Divac to the starting lineup and signed free-agent forward Sam Perkins, a former Dallas Maverick who had been college teammates with James Worthy at North Carolina. West almost pulled the trigger on a bold trade that would have sent Byron Scott and A. C. Green to Cleveland for guard Craig Ehlo and forward John Williams, then thought otherwise. It was one of the shrewdest deals he never made.

Like Riley and Westhead before him, Dunleavy was smart enough to take a step back and let things unfold naturally. The new coach had been warned that Riley's greatest sin was overbearingness, and the last thing these players wanted was a leader who was always on. As training camp began at Honoulu's Otto Klum Gymnasium, Dunleavy wisely went out of his way to observe as much as instruct, to let things play out in a minimalist approach. His first priority was *not* to walk in Pat Riley's footsteps. "Mike made it fun from the get-go, and it wasn't that way the year before," said Divac. "If you were late for practice, Mike would say, 'OK, shoot three-pointers for double or nothing. Make 'em, you're forgiven. Miss, you run.' It was so much fun. With Riley, if you were late, you were in trouble.

"He would challenge you to these games of H-O-R-S-E," said Jason Matthews, a rookie guard out of Pittsburgh who was invited to training camp. "He was still a phenomenal shooter. If I lost to him, I had to do five suicides. If he lost to me, he had to shake my hand. It was funny. He was a coach you knew was in your corner. I'll never forget that when Mike cut me, he was very compassionate about it. He said, 'You can play overseas, but you don't have to. You're going to be more successful as a businessman than as a pro athlete. That's a good thing—you're intelligent.' "

Dunleavy told the players their wives were welcome to travel on the road—an enormous policy shift. He told the players their input was not only acceptable but desired—another huge change. One day, while sitting on the bench, he turned to Pfund and Bill Bertka, the longtime assistants, and said, "Don't you guys have anything to fucking add?"

Pfund fumbled for words. "What the hell?" said Dunleavy.

"Well," Pfund explained, "Pat didn't like us to talk during the games."

"What the fuck is that?" Dunleavy said. "I mean, what are you here for?"

"To coach," said Pfund.

"Well," said Dunleavy, "start fucking coaching."

"He understood the game really well, but he also understood people," said Jim Eyen, an assistant coach. "To me, he seemed like a regular guy who loved the game and would have been happier putting on a uniform and playing. Unfortunately, he was stuck in a suit. There was a running joke for us that he probably had a jersey on beneath his jacket. Just in case."

Throughout training camp, the most intriguing development was the forging of the Magic Johnson–Mike Dunleavy partnership. No matter how he felt toward Riley near the end, Johnson had become an NBA megastar under his former coach. Riley trusted Johnson and confided in Johnson, and viewed him as an on-the-court extension of himself. Ultimately, Riley behaved as if there were the Lakers players and then, on a higher perch, sat the superstar point guard.

Yet the Johnson who arrived in Hawaii for training camp wasn't the Johnson of ten (or even five) years ago. He was bigger and more powerful, but also slower and less quick. At age thirty-one, he was now the league's third-oldest starting point guard. He was relying more on guile, less on physicality. "It was never a matter of having people accept they were getting older," said Dunleavy. "It wasn't even about running less. It was more about running efficiently, and balancing it with our defense. Earvin was still a great, elite player. You just had to be aware of when to run, when not to. We talked about it. He understood."

Dunleavy had to tread lightly, and he knew it. There's no easier way to marginalize oneself than to lose your best player. So instead of barging in with a new offense, a new defense and an "I'm the coach, dammit!" swagger, he let the Lakers play their game. Throughout training camp, Johnson ran the show as he always had—with little input from the sideline. "To be honest, from the very beginning Magic was the coach of the team," said Tony Smith. "Mike might call a play, but if Magic didn't like it, he'd just wave it off. You had that going on about 50 percent of the time, but it wasn't awkward. I think, for a new coach, it made things easier. There was someone to rely on."

The Lakers were scheduled to make their pre-season debut against the Portland Trail Blazers (who also held camp in Hawaii) on October 12 at the University of Hawaii's Blaisdell Arena. Dunleavy arrived for the game wearing one of those goofy lime-green floral-print Hawaiian shirts, and the smile plastered across his face suggested a laid-back, happy man. Yet in the hours before tip-off, Dunleavy told his players that this was no ordinary exhibition, against no ordinary opponent. The Lakers had spent the past decade owning the Pacific Division, but in 1989–90 they outlasted Portland by only four games, then watched their rivals reach the NBA Finals (where they lost to the Pistons). The Blazers spent the off-season talking trash about Los Angeles, telling those who would listen that their time had arrived. Mychal Thompson, the ex-Portland standout, usually spent his summers working out with a handful of Blazer players at the Mittleman Jewish Community Center in Portland. For the first time ever, none of the team's stars—Clyde Drexler, Jerome Kersey, Terry Porter or Kevin Duckworth—reached out. "I wasn't invited," he said. "I'm not blaming them. I guess I wasn't in their plans this year."

Translation: Go to hell—you're the enemy now.

Dunleavy rolled with it. "I made a decision," he said. "It wasn't an exhibition game—it was a statement game. I would take my starters out only when [Blazers coach Rick Adelman] took his starters out. I would only stop when he stopped. I wanted to convey to my guys that, no matter how much the Trail Blazers talked, they couldn't beat you. You're better than they are, you're smarter than they are. They might be more athletic, but you've got the brain power and the know-how."

What followed was a game fueled by finals-like intensity. With Portland leading by 11 points early in the third, Johnson—who played an exhausting forty-three minutes—took over, scoring 19 second-half points and repeatedly slamming his body into Kersey and Porter. His final statistical line—28 points, 10 assists, 8 rebounds, 6 steals—told the story of a man who understood the significance of an insignificant game. Los Angeles won, 119–115, and afterward the players were drained. "There wasn't anyone from Maryland State out there," Thompson said in the locker room. "I can't remember that sort of playoff atmosphere in an exhibition before."

The Laker players quickly came to love Dunleavy. Even when the team opened by losing four of its first five games (the worst start for the franchise in twelve years), he maintained a sense of calm Riley had lacked. There were adjustments to be made and assignments to understand and new teammates getting to know one another. "I could sense a little bit of a black cloud over the locker room," Dunleavy said. "I told them to be patient, that I was 100 percent confident in their ability and that we'd get it right. We were close—we just needed a few adjustments. One or two breaks . . ."

Breaks can be good and breaks can also be bad. On the afternoon of Thursday, November 15, the team received an awful one. According to police reports, James Worthy, perceived to be the ultimate NBA family man, was arrested at three P.M. at the Stouffer Hotel in Houston on charges of solicitation of sexual services. Ralph Gonzales, a police sergeant with the city, told reporters Worthy had contacted an escort service and requested that two women meet him in his hotel room. What the five-time All-Star didn't know was that the business—shut down long ago—was being run by the police department, and the hookers sent to his room were undercover officers. Worthy was arrested after telling the women what he wanted (a blowjob) and how much he would pay ($150). He was released on $500 bail, and actually played in much of his team's 108–103 overtime win over the Rockets later that night.

The days to come were awful for Worthy, but enlightening for the wives and girlfriends of many NBA players. Less than a week after the arrest, the Associated Press reported that Worthy's name appeared on the log of a Portland-based escort service, Allstar Model and Escorts, that was linked to prostitution. Police confirmed with the local Marriott that Worthy had stayed in the room listed on the log on the night of a transaction.

Even though professional athletes could often procure the women of their choice, a large number regularly solicited prostitutes and escorts. Somehow, it was less like infidelity, more like a business transaction. Or so the thinking went.

Inside the Lakers locker room, Worthy was an enigma. He was well liked, but quiet and distant. Whereas Johnson looked at his teammates as family, Worthy looked at his teammates as coworkers. There was a sense, among many, that Worthy resided on a higher plateau, that he was blessed with a character and moral fortitude too often lacking in professional athletes. A. C. Green, the virginal power forward, felt a brotherhood with Worthy based upon their upbringings in religious households. "There was a moral similarity," Green said. "We shared that." Just seven months earlier, Worthy's wife, Angela, had given birth to the couple's first child, a daughter named Sable. The new father was ecstatic.

With Worthy's arrest, it was as if the invisible fourth wall had come crashing down. If James Worthy was sleeping with call girls, lord only knows who else was. In particular, the news came as a punch to the ribs of Angela, James's college sweetheart. Stunningly beautiful, with cocoa skin and high cheekbones, Angela endured a three-year long-distance relationship with James before—while eating at a T.G.I. Friday's in Los Angeles in 1983—he plopped down on one knee and said, "I think it's time we go shopping for a size six."

What ensued was a marriage that, on the outside, appeared storybook, but was crippled by clichéd roles and one-sided giving. Like most of her Laker wife peers, Angela followed the Pat Riley diagram and devoted herself to being the perfectly pieced-together athlete bride. When, on August 15, 1984, James handed Angela a one-page typed prenuptial agreement, she swallowed her hurt feelings and signed. She even purchased a license plate frame for her Mercedes-Benz that read, I AM WORTHY OF JAMES. As she later wrote: "For all intents and purposes my vows might as well have read, 'I, Angela, take you, James, to be my superior. I promise to support your dreams and goals. I will stand by you through good times and bad. I plan to become as inconspicuous as possible, to suppress my dreams and goals, to look the other way when I see things that I don't agree with, and to keep up the appearance of "happily ever after" until death us do part.' "

Such was the modus operandi for Laker wives throughout the 1980s. *Don't ask too many questions. Make sure dinner is hot and the diapers are changed. Come to the Forum on time, and look as pretty as possible.* Only now, a seismic shift had taken place. Mike Dunleavy was the coach, James Worthy was in jail and Magic Johnson was newly engaged to his longtime on-again, off-again girlfriend, Cookie Kelly. There were no excuses to be made for Worthy's behavior, and Chris Riley—departed self-appointed mother hen of the lemming Laker wives—would not (at Pat's urging) encourage Angela to turn the other cheek and take back her man. "I no longer love my husband in a way that makes me want to have more children with him," Angela wrote in her diary. "I . . . wanted to always be in love with James. To realize that part of our relationship is no longer alive is truly a depressing loss for me. It seems that, with the exception of . . . the material things we've acquired, the theme of our marriage is loss."

Shortly after her husband's arrest, Angela left. She made it clear to all who listened that she did not want her daughter thinking it OK to stand by an unfaithful man. "I've always admired that," said Wanda Cooper, Michael's spouse. "Angela wasn't a follower or an enabler. When James embarrassed her, she walked away and never returned. That's self-empowerment."

This was not how Dunleavy anticipated the season beginning—a shoddy record, a humiliated superstar, a fan base pining for Riley or Westhead or any sort of competent coach. After the Lakers dropped to 2-5, Dunleavy eavesdropped as his players moped about awkward new defensive rotations, necessary because of Divac's inability to stop opposing centers. "After one month I've learned one thing," Dunleavy told Mark Heisler of the *Los Angeles Times*. "Pat Riley was a defensive genius." Dunleavy spent hours at home in front of the living room television, rewinding and fast-forwarding game tapes. He urged his players to keep the faith, and in an impassioned locker room speech begged them to stay the course. "Look, if you don't think I work my ass off, if you don't think I know what I'm talking about, if you don't believe in me—you can blow me up to the press," he said. "You can push it all on me—'Hey, young coach, first year, whatever.' You can do that. And I'm telling you, if you think that, you *should* do that. But hopefully you see me standing here, and you know I know what the fuck I'm talking about. And I can see where we're going and I'm totally confident."

Moments after he was finished talking, Dunleavy was told by a ball boy that Jerry Buss needed to see him immediately. The coach was befuddled— was he about to be dismissed? "I wasn't overly concerned, because if he fired me I'd have said, 'This is a fucking mistake,'" Dunleavy said. "I knew we were heading the right way. I just knew it in my heart." Dunleavy knocked on Buss's office door, walked in and sat before his massive desk. Though far from a physically imposing figure, Buss carried himself with confidence. He wasn't intimidating, but he was powerful. "You know, Mike, when you had the first day of training camp five weeks ago, I watched practice and I thought, 'Boy, we've hired one really smart coach,'" Buss said. "We felt really good about it then. Really, really good about it.

"Well, we're struggling. And do you want to know how I feel about it right now?"

"No," Dunleavy said, "but I'm sure you're gonna tell me."

"I feel," Buss said, "like we hired one really smart coach. And I just want you to know that we believe in you. You shouldn't change anything of your philosophy because of the bad start."

Dunleavy shook Buss's hand and bounded back to the locker room. He couldn't control his players' sex lives and he couldn't help whether fans thought him to be in over his head. He could, however, skillfully coach a basketball team. The Lakers beat the Rockets on the afternoon of Worthy's arrest, lost at Dallas a day later, then won 8 in a row and 12 of 14.

Said Johnson: "When we were 2-5, I thought he made some of his best moves because he said, 'Look, we've got a good team, we're going to be all right. Nobody get down. We're not going to start pointing fingers and it's going to come for us.' He dealt with everybody on an individual basis."

This was not the vintage club of the mid-1980s, with stars lined up to dominate. The Lakers were good, but no longer great. Los Angeles had two studs (Johnson and Worthy), four above-average players (Scott, Green, Perkins, Divac) and, otherwise, a bunch of scrappers and grinders. There were multiple highs (Johnson scoring his 16,000th career point, a 16-game winning streak midway through the season, an agreement to represent the NBA in the 1991 McDonald's Open tournament in Paris), but a looming reality that Portland had passed them by. On January 2, a day before the Lakers and Blazers were to play at Portland's Memorial Coliseum, Johnson conceded the division. His team was 7½ games behind the 27-4 Blazers. "Any time you go 27-4 and do it on the road the way they have, you have to take them seriously," Johnson said. "They're for real. And I think they're going to be that way all season. . . . I think they're going to wind up with the best record in basketball."

Though Los Angeles beat the Blazers, 108–104, they concluded the season five games back with a 58-24 record. Yet anyone who viewed the record as an indictment of Dunleavy's coaching was painfully naïve. What Dunleavy decided early on was that the Lakers—the formerly running, gunning Lakers—needed to excel via defense. He demanded accountability on the other end of the ball, and would pull players for sloppy shifts and lazy approaches. As a result, Los Angeles held opponents to 99.6 points per game—second-best in the NBA. The team lacked a competent backup point guard, and Divac, who averaged 11.2 points as the starting center, was bloated and out of shape. (Johnson made a sport out of demeaning his teammate, so much so that Divac considered returning to play in Europe at season's end.) Scott had the second-lowest shooting percentage of his career (47 percent), and Worthy the lowest (49 percent). Green was benched in favor of Perkins and suffered through dreadful stretches of low confidence. Terry Teagle, acquired via trade from Golden State to provide firepower as the first guard off the bench, proved a poor man's Brad Holland. "We were not a great team anymore," said Worthy. "We were still good. But not the same."

Come playoff time, however, the Lakers found themselves reenergized. They opened with a best-of-five series against Houston, a team convinced its destiny was to upend a hobbled dynasty. The Rockets won a franchise-record 52 games, at one point taking 29 of 34. With Hakeem Olajuwon (he was no longer "Akeem") in the middle and Vernon Maxwell and Kenny Smith in the backcourt, Houstonians considered it the best club in the franchise's twenty-four-year existence. "Last year we went against the Lakers with a hope and a prayer," said Maxwell. "This year it's different."

Los Angeles and Houston engaged in a riveting opening game—one that featured back-and-forth scoring, magnificent showings from Olajuwon (22 points, 16 rebounds) and Johnson (17 points, 10 assists) and the ejection of Teagle after he slugged a Rockets forward named Dave Jamerson. With 28.8 seconds remaining in the fourth quarter, Maxwell swooped in for a fast-break layup, only to have Divac stick his hand through the net and pop the ball out. Wrote Frank Brady of the *San Diego Union-Tribune*: "This maneuver is not permissible in basketball—even in Prijepolje, Yugoslavia." The goaltending offense cut the Los Angeles lead to 91–90. Johnson worked the clock, casually dribbling up the court, taking his time, watching the seconds tick away. With six seconds left, he kicked out to Scott, who dribbled, shot and hit a three-point shot—just after the shot clock expired. No basket, Houston possession with three and a half seconds remaining.

The game's three referees, Bruce Alexander, Jack Madden and Dick Bavetta, huddled together. The Forum went silent for a minute until the three striped men emerged with a ruling—the shot was good. Don Chaney, the Rockets' coach, stood at mid-court, screaming for anyone to listen. "I thought it was ridiculous," he said later—and he was right. The call was an awful one.

The Rockets wound up losing the game, 94–92, and the series. Los Angeles swept Houston, then advanced to play the surprising Golden State Warriors. Coach Don Nelson's team featured three of the sport's top young stars (Tim Hardaway, Chris Mullin, Mitch Richmond), and often employed a five-guard lineup whose tallest player, Sarunas Marciulionis, stood 6-foot-5. "It doesn't get much stranger than that," said Dunleavy. "Nothing [Nelson] does would surprise me."

The Lakers took the series in five games, exploiting the size advantage by often using Perkins (6-foot-9), Divac (7-foot-1), Worthy (6-foot-9) and Johnson (6-foot-9) in a rotating game of Back the Midgets Down and Pound Them Inside. Dunleavy's master stroke came in the decisive Game 5, when he ordered Elden Campbell, the 6-foot-11 rookie out of Clemson, to blanket

Marciulionis. A funny kid, Campbell was tall and athletic, but often distracted. At one point during the regular season, he was spotted in the locker room, ninety minutes before a game, dining on sour cream potato chips and Hawaiian Punch with a book tucked beneath his chair, titled *The Thinking Man's Guide to Nutrition.*

"I believed in Elden," said Dunleavy. "He ran with a waddle, so people interpreted that as lazy. But he could play. Against the Warriors I said, 'Elden, you're like a fucking praying mantis. This guy's whole game is getting people up in the air and jumping into them and getting fouled and finishing. When he's out on the perimeter I want you to just stand there with your hand up. And when he starts putting the ball on the floor, I never want you to jump in the air until he has absolutely jumped in the air. Don't go for any fakes. You'll catch up to him.'"

Marciulionis shot 0 for 5. The Lakers won, 124–119.

The victory set up a matchup many had anticipated, and everyone was hoping for. The Portland Trail Blazers—universal pick as basketball's best team—advanced to the Western Conference Finals after a five-game struggle against the Utah Jazz. Though the Blazers were playing only so-so basketball (they'd lost three of four road playoff games), they were itching to meet the Lakers, who remained the barometer by which other franchises were judged. Portland had upended Los Angeles in three of five meetings during the regular season, and a computer simulation of the series, via *Basketball—The Pro Game from Lance Haffner Games,* had Portland prevailing in six. In Las Vegas they were listed as 9-to-5 favorites. "We match up well against Los Angeles, because we are deep," said Cliff Robinson, a reserve forward. "We are able to go with different lineups and still hold an advantage."

For the first time in more than a decade, the Lakers were prohibitive underdogs. The players, however, did not see it that way. Johnson promised his teammates that they were destined to reach yet another championship series, and they believed him. The teams split the opening games at Portland, then traveled to the Forum, where the Lakers walloped the Blazers in Game 3, 106–92. The difference was Divac, who spent the first two contests being barreled over by the enormous Kevin Duckworth. Within a six-minute span to start the third quarter, Los Angeles's center scored 10 points, blocked 3 shots and had a steal in an 18–7 charge. He finished with 16 points and 7 rebounds, while holding Duckworth to 5 points, 5 fouls and 5 turnovers. "How much is a duck worth?" wrote Zander Hollander. "Not much."

Johnson had spent much of the past two years riding Divac like a disobedient child. He believed the center had a chance to emerge as one of the game's best, but needed to have the blasé Euro nonsense slapped from his system. Whenever Divac resorted to pretty twinkletoe maneuvers, Johnson let him have it. "Vlade, cut that fucking shit out!" he once screamed. "Play like a motherfucking man!"

"He was just so competitive," said Divac. "He had to win at everything. I didn't mind the insults, because it was all to make me better."

Two days later, on a Sunday afternoon, the Lakers took command of a suddenly one-sided series, sprinting past Portland, 116–95, in a Showtime revival that had Jack Nicholson and Dyan Cannon dancing along the court. The Lakers shot 51 percent from the field, forced 19 turnovers and ran at every given opportunity. Johnson looked twenty again, scoring 22 points and adding 9 rebounds and 9 assists. His team led 32–23 after one quarter, and never turned back. "A lot of people say that [Showtime is dead]," he said afterward. "But it's not. It just took us this long to get to it."

Portland rebounded to win the fifth game, 95–84, but—for the Lakers— the problem wasn't the loss so much as the injury. During the first quarter of Game 5, Worthy sprained his left ankle, and though he returned for part of the third quarter, neither two retapings nor an electronic nerve stimulator helped regain his maneuverability.

Now, heading into Game 6 at the Forum, a serious question mark lingered. Without a healthy Worthy, the Lakers would have to depend more on Green (who battled inconsistency all season) and Thompson (seldom used and in rapid decline). This was the opening Portland needed. "The playoffs— that's what it's all about, challenge," said Terry Porter. "If [Worthy] can crawl, I believe he's going to be on the floor."

Though he did walk onto the court for the opening tip, Worthy was largely useless, shooting 3 for 12 in thirty-eight minutes. Appearing in his team-record 181st playoff game, however, Johnson put forth one of the greatest all-around efforts of his career. Over forty-seven minutes of play, Johnson (25 points, 8 assists, 11 rebounds) did everything everywhere every way. With 1:48 remaining in the game, he fed Divac for a layup, then hit two free throws, to put Los Angeles ahead, 89–85. Portland fought back to cut the lead to one, but Divac (having received another gorgeous feed from Johnson) hit two free throws after being fouled on a miss. The score was 91–88. Forty-three seconds were left.

The Blazers played with rightful desperation. Porter hit a jumper over a lunging Perkins, and with 12.5 seconds remaining, Divac's attempted layup was blocked. The twenty-four-second clock expired, and Portland—down 91–90—had one last chance.

Following a time-out, the Blazers inbounded the ball at half-court to Porter, who flipped it back to Drexler, the team's top scorer. Drexler dribbled toward the paint, found himself covered and passed back to Porter, who stood eighteen feet from the basket. He squared up and, with 5.8 seconds left, fired a jumper over Green's outstretched arms. The basketball hit the rim, bounced up into the air, then was grabbed by Johnson beneath the boards.

In the most intelligent play many had ever seen, the Laker guard immediately heaved the ball over his head and down the court, placing enough spin on it so—instead of quickly rolling out of bounds—it bounced . . . bounced . . . bounced . . . bounced . . . bounced to the baseline. By the time the ball was dead, there was but one-one hundredth of a second on the clock. The game was done. So were the Blazers.

"I knew they were going to foul me," Johnson said, "so I threw the ball out."

The Los Angeles Lakers were returning to the finals.

The NBA's marketing dream had come true.

■ ■ ■

Heading into the NBA's Eastern and Western Conference Finals, there were four championship series possibilities:

The Detroit Pistons could face the Portland Trail Blazers.

The Detroit Pistons could face the Los Angeles Lakers.

The Chicago Bulls could face the Portland Trail Blazers.

The Chicago Bulls could face the Los Angeles Lakers.

From a strictly marketing standpoint, none of the options particularly bothered the league. If, worst-case scenario, the Pistons and Blazers met again, there was always the redemption vs. dynasty story line to peddle, re: the two teams returning for a rematch. The Pistons and Lakers offered up Isiah vs. Magic—friends whose relationship had grown strained; and the Bulls and Blazers gave the world Michael Jordan and Clyde Drexler—the best shooting guards around.

Of all the pairings, however, none elicited public relations goose bumps quite like Chicago vs. Los Angeles.

Or, to put it more succinctly, Michael Jordan vs. Magic Johnson.

"Oh, boy. Oh, boy, oh, boy, oh, boy, oh, boy," read the staff editorial in the *St. Louis Post-Dispatch*: "Magic and Michael. Michael and Magic. The heart and soul of the Los Angeles Lakers versus the bread and butter of the Chicago Bulls. The Most Valuable Player versus the Most Unbelievable Player. The best playing at their best against the best."

At the time, Jordan was twenty-seven and, though marveled at, also increasingly dismissed as a me-me-me player who could accumulate points in droves (he averaged 31.5 points during the regular season, good for his fifth-straight scoring title) but not carry a team to a title. In his first six NBA seasons, Jordan's Bulls had never reached the finals. He was the greatest athlete pitchman who ever lived, the face and voice of Nike, McDonald's, Spalding and dozens of other products. But a winner? No one was entirely sure.

Throughout the requisite pre-series analysis, lazy prognosticators pretended basketball was a game played solely by elite superstars. Everything came down to Magic vs. Michael and Michael vs. Magic. In the three days between the completion of the Western Finals and the opening of the NBA Finals, one couldn't watch television or listen to the radio for more than six minutes without catching the two men being referenced. "Michael and Magic, Magic and Michael," wrote Mark Heisler in the *Los Angeles Times*. "You hear it so often, you wonder if Michael Jordan and Magic Johnson have been joined at the hip, or if NBC has turned them into a two-headed promotion for the NBA finals."

When the Lakers opened the series in Chicago by winning, 93–91 on a three-pointer from Perkins with fourteen seconds remaining, all the commercial prayers appeared to be answered. Johnson was splendid, totaling 19 points, 10 rebounds and 11 assists, while Jordan—with a game-high 36 points (plus 12 assists and 8 rebounds)—was his expected ungodly self. "This was the way basketball is supposed to be played," Johnson said afterward. "This was just a great game to be in."

"We won the first game," said Scott, who scored 9 points, "and we said, 'Hey, we can beat these guys.'"

Surely, we were looking at a six- or seven-game series.

Surely, Magic and Michael would put on epic performances.

Surely . . .

Pfft.

Lost in the increasingly obnoxious glow of the Michael-Magic nonsense was the disheartening fact that the Bulls, who had finished 61-21, were a far superior team.

The Lakers played brilliantly in Game 1 . . . and *still* struggled to pull out a victory. The Bulls felt like the franchise of now—Jordan was magnificent, forward Scottie Pippen was a blooming star, Bill Cartwright was a solid center and Horace Grant, B. J. Armstrong, John Paxson, Craig Hodges and Will Perdue were all useful contributors. Though coach Phil Jackson received much credit for the franchise's success, the Bulls were powered by the thinking of a little-known sixty-nine-year-old assistant named Tex Winter, who introduced something called the Triangle Offense. For the first time in memory, the Lakers weren't concerning themselves with an opponent's set plays, because the Triangle was all about spacing the floor and reacting to defenses. With a do-everything star like Jordan at the forefront, the Bulls were devastatingly efficient. "Tex Winter is a genius," said Jerry Krause, Chicago's general manager. "He's forgotten more basketball than most guys ever knew. People used to sit at his feet and study."

The Bulls rebounded three days later by routing the Lakers, 107–86, at Chicago Stadium, then pulled out Game 3 in overtime at the Forum, 104–96. Were it merely a case of Jordan being too young, too athletic, too spectacular (all of which he was), the Laker players probably could have accepted what seemed to be their fate. But what made their task all the more daunting was that Worthy never fully recovered from the left ankle sprain he suffered against Portland. Though he started the first four games against Chicago, he was damaged. "There was the thought that I would miss the series, but it was never an option for me," Worthy said. "I'd been hurt before, so I knew how to play through pain. But it was hard, because I couldn't really play the way I wanted."

"I thought we were better than the Bulls—I really did," said Irving Thomas, a reserve forward. "But when you can't match up the way you want to, and you're going against a very determined Michael Jordan, it's pretty impossible."

Because Worthy was relying on a single leg, he couldn't guard Jordan one-on-one—as was Dunleavy's plan. Consequently, the Lakers' defensive strategy crumbled. Even worse, with Worthy a reduced threat, the Bulls barely concerned themselves with him as a scorer. Jackson had his defense relentlessly hound Johnson, daring other Lakers to be the heroes. The result: Johnson—the team's leading scorer with 18.6 points per game—shot just 43 percent from the field, and only Divac (18.2 points, 8.8 rebounds) played particularly well. "James Worthy was our stopper," said Dunleavy. "James Worthy was our press breaker. I mean, Byron Scott—I love him. He's a good defender, a great shooter. But Byron couldn't take a piss with his left hand. He was all right. So once James went out, they just started playing full court on Magic, turning him all the time, throwing fresh bodies—Jordan, Pippen, whoever they wanted it to be—at him. They just wore Magic down. We had some other injuries, but the key was James not being himself. We never recovered."

As the lopsidedness came into focus, the pre-series hype faded away, and Magic-Michael turned into, solely, Michael. "You're dejected. You're frustrated. You're anticipating a great series and they dominate us like this," Johnson said. "But I can't feel bad—they're giving us a good butt kicking." The Bulls won three straight games at the Forum (Worthy re-aggravated the ankle injury in Game 4, and sat out Game 5; Scott also missed the fifth game with a bruised right shoulder), including the title-clinching 108–101 triumph that sealed Jordan's status as the NBA's new reigning elite. He scored 30 points in the finale, and was an easy choice for Finals MVP. Afterward, as Jordan hugged the trophy in the visiting locker room, he couldn't help but sob. "I don't know if I'll ever have this same feeling," he said. "I guess what you see are the emotions of hard work."

Twenty minutes later, with little fanfare, a smiling Johnson entered the Chicago locker room. He went Bull to Bull, offering handshakes and hugs to every member of the team. When he reached Jordan, he gazed upon his rival superstar with both sadness and glee. Johnson was far from a selfish man; he liked the idea of someone coming along to join the club he and Bird had started. And yet—that was *his* trophy.

"When I went to congratulate him after the game," Johnson said, "I could see tears in his eyes. . . . I know what he's going through, too. There's no better feeling. It's unbelievable, it's unreal."

Earlier in the week, Johnson had suggested that this might be his final run. It had been a trying twelfth NBA season, filled with highs and lows and massive turnover. He was a tired man who knew his prime had passed. Watching Jordan caress the trophy, however, stirred something deep within. The Lakers had reached the NBA Finals with a rookie coach and a revamped roster.

Wouldn't it be wise, he was asked, to stick around?

"I'm sure I'll be back," he said. "Any time you have a tough season like this, you want to come back and be on the other side of it. Hopefully, it'll be our turn next year."

With that, Earvin (Magic) Johnson left the Forum.

Showtime walked out with him.

CHAPTER 22

SHOCK

On July 12, 1991, Magic Johnson suffered from heat exhaustion. It happened while he was in Hawaii filming a television segment, and caused him to skip Michael Cooper's basketball camp a couple of days later.

On August 8, 1991, Magic Johnson told the Torrance *Daily Breeze* that he expected to play three more NBA seasons, one season in Europe—then retire to try to become an owner. He also said he planned on being a part of the 1992 U.S. Olympic basketball team.

On August 18, 1991, Magic Johnson visited the nation's capital to speak to two hundred youngsters inside the Washington Metropolitan Police Boys and Girls Club. "It's a lot of fun to see the looks on their faces and the opportunity not only with basketball but life," said Johnson. "You want them to know that you're a human being, too, because they see you as not being human at times. I want them to know that, 'Hey, I was here, too. I grew up the same way you did and I made it through hard work and dedication and you can, too.'"

On September 14, 1991, Magic Johnson and Earleatha "Cookie" Kelly were finally married at the Union Missionary Baptist Church in Lansing, Michigan. Magic wore a double-breasted white jacket and black pants. Cookie wore the dress she had purchased a year earlier—when they were originally supposed to have wed. His best man was Dale Beard, a longtime friend. Throughout the service, Rev. Rick Hunter was interrupted by shouts of "Amen!"

"It was like everyone was just so glad it finally happened," said Kathy Staudt, a family friend.

The reception was held at the Kellogg Center on the Michigan State campus. Later, Cookie wrote: "I felt like God was saying, 'Girl, you went through so much with this man that I'll give you a great wedding.'"

On September 20, 1991, USA Basketball announced a "dream team" comprised of Magic Johnson, Michael Jordan and eight other NBA superstars would play in the following summer's Barcelona Olympics. "In the amount of time we have to practice," Johnson said, "we'll just have to go to work."

On September 25, 1991, Magic Johnson released a statement asking for the resignation of a Lansing, Michigan, school board member who referred to Johnson as "a big, dumb black kid" during his time in high school. The man, William Carter, made the comments during a board meeting. He said he regretted them but refused to resign. "It was a dumb thing to do," he said. "A poor choice of words."

On September 30, 1991, Magic Johnson was introduced as the new spokesperson for the flagship candy bar of The Nestle Chocolate and Confection Company. "Nestle Crunch embodies the winning spirit," Johnson said, "and I'm proud to represent that message as I enter the new NBA season."

On October 13, 1991, the Los Angeles Lakers flew to Paris to take part in the four-team McDonald's Open basketball tournament. The journey also served as a honeymoon for Magic and Cookie. They took long strolls, ate romantic dinners, spent time alone as a new married couple. He could not, however, fully escape the trappings of fame. During a trip to the Eiffel Tower, Johnson—wearing his uniform for a photograph—was besieged. "It was ugly," said John Black, the team's media relations director. "I almost punched two French photographers. It was a mob scene." Johnson enjoyed his week in Paris as a basketball player (he had 21 assists in a win over Limoges), but also felt run-down. His internal clock was off, there was a lot of up and down, left and right, back and forth. The fourteen-hour plane trip back to California was hardly a relief.

"We need to get back," he said. "Get some rest."

On the afternoon of Friday, October 25, 1991, Magic Johnson was sitting inside his room in the Salt Lake Hilton. The Lakers were visiting Utah to play an exhibition game against the Jazz—one Johnson had little interest in. He was exhausted and in need of a day off. He told Gary Vitti, the trainer, how he was feeling. "He said, 'I'd really like to take these last few games off, I'm really tired,'" Vitti told ESPN. "'If you want me to be ready for the season opener, I could use these last few days off.' He was jetlagged still." The Lakers, however, insisted Johnson play. The fans had paid good money to see Magic, and he was a key part of the franchise, and . . . and . . .

The phone inside Johnson's room rang at 2:15. It was Dr. Michael Mellman, the team physician and one of Johnson's personal doctors. Johnson had been rejected for a life-insurance policy the team had taken out. "Can you come home?" Mellman said.

"OK," said a puzzled Johnson. "I'm gonna play the game and I'll be there tomorrow."

"No," said Mellman. "You have to come home right now."

Johnson caught a taxi to Salt Lake City International Airport, then a 4:28 P.M. Delta flight that would arrive at Los Angeles International Airport at 5:15. His Laker teammates assumed Johnson was simply bailing out of a meaningless contest. "I figured he was just pulling some seniority," said Worthy.

Vitti, though, couldn't keep the bad thoughts out of his head. "It just kept going around and around in my head, what it could be," he told ESPN. "During the game, I can't even concentrate, because something's up."

Johnson wasn't particularly concerned. He was thirty-two, running three to four miles every day, lifting weights for thirty to forty-five minutes. "I was actually in the best shape of my NBA career," he told Sports Illustrated. Johnson was picked up at the airport by Lon Rosen, the longtime Laker employee who now worked as his agent. They talked about high blood pressure—Johnson's father, Earvin Sr., had struggled with it for much of his life. They talked about heart problems. One year earlier, Hank Gathers, a basketball star at Loyola Marymount University, had collapsed on the court and died from a heart-muscle disorder, hypertrophic cardiomyopathy.

Upon arriving at the physician's office, Johnson entered an empty waiting room. He sat, picked up a copy of *Ebony* magazine. Michael Jordan was
on the cover, alongside his wife, Juanita. "You know," he said to Rosen, "it
would be nice if Cookie and I could be on the cover like that." After five
minutes, he was ushered into the doctor's office. The room was small and
white, and the look on Mellman's face was grim. He motioned toward an
empty chair. "Sit down," he said. No emotion. He turned around and, from
atop his desk, opened a Federal Express envelope. A couple of weeks earlier,
Johnson had undergone an extensive physical examination. "Earvin," Mellman said, "I have some news to tell you. . . ."

On the evening of Friday, October 25, 1991, Magic Johnson called his wife.
She was surprised to hear his voice. He was supposed to be on a basketball
court in Utah.

"What are you doing, calling me?" she said.

"I'll tell you when I get there," he said.

Oh, no, she thought. *Does he want a divorce?*

On the evening of November 1, 1991, the Lakers opened the regular season
with a game at Houston. For the first time since 1978, Earvin (Magic) Johnson was not the starting point guard. "It was strange," said Sedale Threatt,
who filled in and scored 7 points in a 126–121 double overtime loss. "Just
didn't seem right for Earvin not to be in there. Who was I?"

On the afternoon of November 6, 1991, Lon Rosen came over—
unannounced—to Mike Dunleavy's house. Johnson had now missed the first
three games of the regular season with what was being reported as "flu-like
symptoms." *Flu-like symptoms?* Like Johnson, Dunleavy had been a player
who needed to be minus three limbs to sit out a game. This made no sense.
"Mike," Rosen said, "Earvin wanted me to tell you about something he's
dealing with. We're trying to find the right way to handle it publicly, but . . ."

On the evening of Wednesday, November 6, 1991, John Black's phone rang.
And rang. And rang. The Laker publicist was out on a date, so he was unavailable to take Lon Rosen's call. By the time he heard the message, it was
ten P.M. "Hey John, it's Lon. Listen, you need to be at my house at eight
o'clock tonight."

Oh, well, Black thought. *I'll just deal with it tomorrow.*

When he arrived at work early the next morning, Black was told to go to the office of Lou Baumeister, the Lakers team president. He was irked—there were press releases to write, reporter phone calls to return. Who had time for this? "I walk down the hall, about a hundred feet, and I enter Lou's office. And Lou's at his desk, and I see Jerry West sitting in a chair, crying. And I think to myself, 'Why the fuck is Jerry West crying?'

"A few minutes later, walking back to my office, my knees buckled.

"They just buckled."

On the morning of Thursday, November 7, 1991, John Black—back in his office—received a phone call from Randy Kerdoon of KFWB Radio. It was approximately ten thirty. "We've just heard a story that Magic is going to retire," Kerdoon said. "Is this true?"

Silence.

"I was like, 'Holy fuck—how did this leak out?'" said Black. "'Holy, holy fuck.'"

Black asked for understanding and a couple of hours of patience. Kerdoon agreed. The Lakers were planning on holding a Thursday afternoon press conference. That would no longer do. Black called Johnson. "Earvin, the news is going to break," he said. "We can't wait until tomorrow."

"OK," Johnson said. "Let's do it today at three."

A release was immediately written and sent out to the media. MAGIC JOHNSON TO HOLD PRESS CONFERENCE AT FORUM . . .

On the morning of Thursday, November 7, 1991, Johnson and Rosen wrote up a list of everyone who needed to be called. One by one, Rosen dialed the numbers.

Michael Jordan began to cry. "No," he said. "This can't be happening. . . ."

Pat Riley, now coaching the New York Knicks, couldn't speak.

Isiah Thomas pulled off the road and called back from a pay phone. "Tell me it's not true. . . ."

Larry Bird was leaving his home in Boston. "Oh my God," he said. "This can't be true."

Arsenio Hall, the talk show host and Johnson's good friend, told Rosen he would cancel that night's program. "Earvin will kill you," Rosen said. "He needs you to carry on with your life."

Kareem Abdul-Jabbar said he would come to the press conference. Kurt Rambis, now playing for Phoenix, departed practice for the next flight to Los Angeles. "I have to leave," he told Cotton Fitzsimmons, the Suns coach. "I can't tell you why. You'll just have to trust me on this one."

On the late morning of Thursday, November 7, 1991, Mike Dunleavy cut short the Lakers' practice at Loyola University. He gathered his players in a huddle. "One o'clock, I want you at the Forum," he said. "No exceptions. If you have anything planned, cancel it."

"No one said anything," said Keith Owens, a rookie forward out of UCLA. "But people were kind of thinking the worst."

Forty minutes later, Owens went to his parents' house to take a quick shower. As he was getting dressed, his grandfather, Sidney Allen, pointed to the screen. There was a photograph of Johnson. "Do you know anything about this?" Sidney asked.

On the afternoon of Thursday, November 7, 1991, Johnson entered the Lakers locker room at the Forum. It was one thirty. All the players were sitting at their stalls in street clothing. "Guys," Dunleavy said, "Magic wants to address you. . . ."

"He came in and told us what was up," said Owens. "He went around the room, hugged everybody. Dudes were crying. Then he left to go to the press room."

The Lakers followed him out. It felt like a funeral procession.

On the afternoon of Thursday, November 7, 1991, Johnson walked toward—of all places—the Forum Club. Before entering, Rosen pulled him aside.

"Are you OK?" he asked.

"I'm fine," Johnson said.

With that, he led a parade through the rear of the room—Johnson, his new bride, Cookie, Jerry West, Abdul-Jabbar, Mellman, Rosen. The Forum Club was packed. Hundreds of photographers. Hundreds of reporters. David Stern, the NBA's commissioner, sat on the dais, directly to his left. Cookie sat directly to his right.

Johnson wore a dark blue suit, a red-and-blue tie. He reached the podium, then waited ten seconds for everyone to be seated. He looked around, pursed his lips, removed his hands from his jacket pockets. There was modest talking within the media corps. Johnson grabbed the silver microphone holder. *Thump!* The room went quiet. Johnson leaned toward the microphone. He looked calm. There was no trademark smile.

The building had been his home for twelve magnificent seasons. He knew every nook of the Forum; every corner; every closet. The ushers and vendors and custodians considered him one of their own. He wasn't just a basketball player. He was a Los Angeles Laker. An icon. Others had been on the team before him, others would come after. There was, however, only one maestro. Only one Magic. Without him, there would never have been five championships, never would have been the fast breaks and the pinpoint passes and the invaluable entertainment. He was here when Spencer Haywood imploded, when Kareem Abdul-Jabbar dominated, when Bob McAdoo saved the day and Norm Nixon forced his own departure. He had dozens of teammates, ranging from Rambis and Jamaal Wilkes and Byron Scott to Earl Jones and Ronnie Lester and Swen Nater. Through it all, Magic Johnson had been the linchpin.

He was—at its very core—Showtime.

"First of all, let me say good after . . . late afternoon," he said. "Um, because of the"—lengthy pause—"HIV virus that I have attained, I will have to retire from the Lakers today. . . ."

AFTERWORD

In the summer of 2012, Jeanie Buss and Linda Rambis returned to the Forum.

The Lakers had played their final game inside the building thirteen years earlier, thereby escaping to the new, state-of-the-art Staples Center in downtown Los Angeles. The NBA had changed drastically from the time Showtime reigned, and the Forum became an 8-track relic in an iTunes age. A league that once aired its finals games on tape delay was now a multibillion-dollar industry. Stadiums were replaced by arenas; plain ol' seats were important, but not nearly as important as (cha-ching!) luxury boxes. Hot dogs and sodas continue to be peddled, but so are sushi rolls and Tazo Chai Tea Lattes. When Jerry Buss purchased the team from Jack Kent Cooke, he dreamed of turning basketball into more than mere basketball. He desired the game to be a full-throttle entertainment experience, replete with dancers and loud music and halftime shows and balled-up T-shirts launched into the crowd. "My dad wanted it to be a happening," said Jeanie. "And he succeeded."

With that success, however, a purity was lost. In a sense, Buss was damned to receive what he wished for. The Lakers grew bigger. Flashier. Bolder. More prominent. What had once felt like a mom-and-pop operation (with Jerry Buss starring as both mom and pop) now seemed increasingly corporate. Jeanie and Linda used to walk through the Forum and know the ushers, vendors and janitors ("Every single one," Jeanie said) by name. Inside the Staples Center, that was no longer the case. Employees came, employees went. They were mere name tag holders. "I like the new building," said Jeanie. "I do. It's just not the Forum."

Now they were back, two women who grew up in the building; who discovered basketball bliss in the building; who saw Magic morph into a man and Riley morph into a head coach and Kareem snarl and Spencer Haywood snort and Norm Nixon scheme and Byron Scott and James Worthy and Michael Cooper and Kurt Rambis and dozens of others find themselves and their own senses of glory. As they walked through the hallways, and gazed upon the shadowy court, their minds flashed back to confetti raining down on five championship teams, to the best times they would ever know. "We hadn't been back in years," said Jeanie. "But there were some old pictures we needed to pick up that we never took with us. It was very emotional. . . ."

The Forum, they found, is no longer the Forum. Everything is dark and dank. Whereas once the building was a palace, it now is a crypt for bygone excellence. Outside, white-and-gray paint peels from the beams, and sentiments like ALEX + ALEXIS and crude illustrations of penises are etched into the siding. The blue plastic signs are cracked, and lettering has faded. Some green bushes remain, yet they are pocked by litter. Empty McDonald's bags. A plastic ValuSoft Napkins wrapper. While the red Forum Club awning remains, it no longer leads to a world of wonder and intrigue. Now it welcomes nonexistent visitors to an abandoned room.

Though, technically, the Lakers left the Forum at the conclusion of the 1998–99 season, an argument could be made that—with Johnson's announcement and immediate retirement—Showtime exited the building for good. With the solid-yet-forgettable Sedale Threatt taking over at point guard, the team went 43-39 in 1991–92 before losing, listlessly, in the first round of the playoffs to the Portland Trail Blazers. The ensuing years— overloaded with one too many arrogant, self-indulgent players—were bleak. Even when Johnson returned, briefly, in 1996, the buzz was short-lived. "It was never the same," said Worthy, who retired in 1994. "The guys who came in didn't share the work ethic and intensity. There wasn't as much heart or as much love. That era was so special. But once it ended, it ended hard and never came back."

■ ■ ■

Only that's not entirely true.

The Showtime Lakers exist—in video, in books, in word-of-mouth, in YouTube clips, in yellowed newspaper articles, in LeBron James and Kevin Durant and Chris Paul and modern players who aspire to recapture similar brilliance.

Most important, in the men who brought it to us.

In the immediate aftermath of Earvin (Magic) Johnson's HIV revelation, we all presumed we were about to watch one of America's iconic sportsmen shrivel up and die. That was the understood lot in life for HIV carriers— weight loss, infection, lesions, decimation, death. Ron Carter, the former Laker guard, was sitting on a bed inside the Deerfield Inn in Deerfield Beach, Florida, when he turned on the television and saw Johnson's press conference. "I called Norm Nixon, and Norm called Michael Cooper," he said. "We were talking about all the broads we screwed. We were trying to get a list of all the girls we had sex with back then in common with Magic. Because AIDS was the kiss of death. Magic was clearly going to die. We didn't want to die, too, and we were scared out of our minds."

That was twenty-two years ago.

Now fifty-four, Johnson has not merely outlived many of those who anticipated his extinction—he has emerged as one of America's most improbable success stories. The man who ran the Laker offense now runs Magic Johnson Enterprises, a company with a net worth of $700 million. He is also a part owner of the Los Angeles Dodgers, which he and his partners purchased in 2012 for a staggering $2 billion. Whereas he was once the face of the Lakers, then the face of the NBA, then the face of HIV, he is now a face seen everywhere. "He's one of the great men of all time," said Dyan Cannon, the actress and Laker fanatic. "His nature, his generosity, his down-to-earthness, his spirit, his Showtime attitude. He's our Muhammad Ali.

"Of course he's beaten HIV. He's Magic—he always finds a way."

Throughout his numerous incarnations, Johnson has always been—first and foremost—number 32, charging down the court, looking left, passing right to a streaking Worthy or a posting Abdul-Jabbar. It remains his strongest identity, the image that ties him to millions upon millions of people.

In this, he is not alone. At age sixty-nine, Pat Riley is the president of the Miami Heat. Since being fired by the Lakers after the 1989–90 season, his success has been striking. He took a perennially underachieving New York Knicks team to the 1994 NBA Finals, then coached the Heat to the franchise's first title, in 2006. Like Johnson, he is one of sport's most recognizable faces, and has accumulated a small fortune via motivational speaking and endorsements. Yet he will forever remain the coach of the Showtime Lakers. "It was the greatest period of my life," he said. "Bar none."

A similar sentiment is echoed—in one form or another—by nearly every prominent participant of the era. Abdul-Jabbar, a prolific author and historian, calls his time in Los Angeles "meaningful and defining." Byron Scott coached the New Jersey Nets to back-to-back Eastern Conference titles. "But he's a Laker," said Anita Scott, his wife. "Always." Worthy never followed through on his promised return to the peace and tranquility of North Carolina, and serves as a Los Angeles–based studio analyst for Time Warner Cable SportsNet and Time Warner Cable Deportes. "Showtime was beautiful for me," he said. "It changed my life." Bob McAdoo is an assistant coach with the Heat. His four Laker seasons were, statistically, the least productive of his career. "But they were the best," he said. "Easily the best." After his trade, Norm Nixon played four quality seasons with the Clippers. "I'm a Laker," he said. "A proud one." Kurt Rambis went on to coach the Lakers and Minnesota Timberwolves, and recently returned to the Lakers as an assistant. "I don't think, for most of us, that time period has been replaced," he said. "You move on, but that excitement was once in a lifetime." Michael Cooper coached the Los Angeles Sparks to two WNBA titles, then spent four years coaching the women's team at the University of Southern California. "Big jobs," he said. "But I'm still known as a Laker. Probably until I die."

Even for the players who lived on Showtime's fringes, the memories serve as glow sticks through life's darkest times. Wes Matthews still thinks back to his days with the Lakers as "the highlight of my existence." Earl Jones takes pride in "playing with the best of the best." Billy Thompson, a pastor at the Jesus People Proclaim International Ministries Church in Miami, loves his lord, his savior and his purple-and-gold journey. "Being a Laker," he said, "is eternal and beautiful." Those who attended training camp with the team, but failed to stick, occasionally retreat to a closet or chest where they pull out random keepsakes. Jay Triano, an eighth-round pick out of Simon Fraser in 1981, still has his practice shorts. Rick Raivio, the 1980 fifth-rounder from the University of Portland, held on to his jersey. "It's somewhere around here," he said. "A reminder of something amazing."

"On the afternoon I was cut, I went up to every player and got autographs," said Ron Vanderschaaf, a 1987 seventh-round draft choice out of

Central Washington. "I still have them. James Worthy wrote, 'It was nice knowing you,' even though he never really knew me. Magic Johnson wrote 'I hope all your dreams come true.' And, in a way, they did. I was a Laker. It was brief and fleeting, but I was a Laker."

On a cold April day in 2012, Mike Smrek sat inside a barn on his property in Port Robinson, Canada. In many respects, he had been the most unlikely of Showtime Lakers. "Growing up on a family farm, my life was work," he said. "We had cows to milk and animals to feed. In my spare time I enjoyed building dune buggies and motorcycles. I didn't even try basketball until I was sixteen." At the urging of his shop teacher, Smrek played one season for the team at Eastdale High School, and was awful. But he was awful—*and enormous*. Based upon his 7-foot, 250-pound stature and raw athleticism, Canisius College offered him a scholarship, and he went from averaging 2.5 points as a freshman to 15.8 as a senior. He graduated in 1985, and a year later found himself in Los Angeles, backing up Abdul-Jabbar.

Toward the end of his first season, Smrek and the Lakers prepared for the playoffs by training in Santa Barbara. The team was staying at Fess Parker's Red Lion Inn, and one morning Smrek made certain to be first aboard the shuttle bus parked outside the hotel. "I got there fifteen minutes before anyone else," he said, "because I wanted to show how dedicated I was to winning." Gradually, the rest of the players arrived. Scott. Worthy. Rambis. A. C. Green. When Johnson climbed the steps, he looked at Smrek and pointed toward the door. "Get off," he said. "You're on the other bus."

"Why?" said Smrek. "I've been sitting here for fifteen minutes."

"Because," Johnson replied, "you're not a Laker yet."

A humiliated Smrek rose from his seat and—eyes glued to the floor—exited. None of the other Lakers uttered a word. He had appeared in thirty-five games for the team, even started three. He practiced hard and often stayed late to work with the assistant coaches. Was that not enough? What more did Mike Smrek need to prove?

Two weeks later, on June 14, 1987, the Lakers beat the Celtics at the Forum to capture the NBA championship. Smrek had played but nine minutes in the six-game series, contributing two points, five rebounds and four personal fouls. With the champagne flowing and the music blasting, Smrek was as happy as he'd ever been. The bus incident was long forgotten, a bad moment in an amazing year.

Midway through the celebration, Smrek felt a tap on his shoulder. He turned to face Johnson, who opened his arms and wrapped the backup center in a long hug.

"Mike," he whispered, "congratulations."

Arguably the greatest point guard in NBA history was grinning from ear to ear. Arguably the most mediocre backup center in NBA history was grinning from ear to ear, too.

"Now," Johnson told him, "you're a Laker."

ACKNOWLEDGMENTS

On the afternoon of March 29, 2012, I overflowed Spencer Haywood's toilet.

It's true.

I had spent roughly one and a half hours with the former Laker in his Las Vegas home. We talked hoops and recovery (he's been clean for thirty years) and family (he's the proud father of four girls) and memories of basketball players long gone. The time flew by, and toward the end, I was euphoric over yet another fabulous interview with yet another Showtime participant.

Before I left, I asked whether I could use his bathroom. Haywood pointed me in the right direction, so I went inside, closed the door and peed. Seriously, that's . . . all . . . I . . . did. I peed. And not even a big pee. Just a normal, average, run-of-the-mill piss.

As soon as I flushed, however, the tidal wave began. Higher and higher and higher. Water rose from the porcelain depths, and even as I took every possible step to stem the tide, well, nothing worked. Before long, the floor had morphed into Lake Mahopac, and liquid started to seep beneath the door and into the adjacent bedroom's carpet.

When I mustered the courage to inform the 6-foot-8, 250-pound

Haywood that I'd ruined his lavatory ("Spencer, I overflowed your toilet! But I swear, all I did was pee!"), he glanced upon me as if I were telling him something as pedestrian as the arrival of that day's mail. "Don't worry," he said. "These things happen."

■ ■ ■

I have long maintained that writing a book is a nightmare, and, indeed, it often is. The nights are long, the hours are ceaseless, the road is lonely (though, admittedly, one can do worse than spend the winter months kicking back in Los Angeles), the search for interviews can be maddening. No words or experiences, however, can embody the process better than overflowing Spencer Haywood's toilet—and having to tell him about it. Then, and only then, is the nightmare complete.

Hence, I would like to start by thanking Spencer for his insight, for his plunger (you can't go wrong with the PlumbCraft Plastic Stow-Away Plunger II) and his candor. Though he was a Laker but for one season, Spencer's powerful road to recovery could fill twenty volumes. He is a man of strength and conviction, and it was an honor to spend time together. Along those lines, I'd like to acknowledge all of the Showtime-era Lakers who contributed to this project, with a special tip of the hat to Bill Bertka, Frank Brickowski, Tony Campbell, Michael Cooper, Mike Dunleavy, A. C. Green, Brad Holland, Earl Jones, Mitch Kupchak, Mark Landsberger, Ronnie Lester, Wes Matthews, Jack McKinney, Norm Nixon, Kurt Rambis, Lon Rosen, Mike Smrek, Larry Spriggs, Billy Thompson, Mychal Thompson, Jerry West, Paul Westhead, Jamaal Wilkes and James Worthy. Equal gratitude to the men who reported on the Lakers during the time period—namely Mitch Chortkoff, Scott Ostler, Steve Springer, Earl Bloom, Don Greenberg, Mark Heisler, Randy Harvey, Roy Johnson, Mike Littwin, Joe McDonnell, Pat O'Brien and John Papanek.

During the Showtime era, two men—Josh Rosenfeld and John Black— were charged with handling the organization's media relations efforts. Both are top-shelf individuals who represented the Lakers extraordinarily well, and both were kind enough to answer my repeated questions. Furthermore, Gary Vitti remains basketball's best trainer, as well as one of its best talkers. The words were invaluable.

During the course of researching Showtime, Jerry Buss, the Lakers' brilliant owner, passed away. Though I was unable to interview him before his death, I was fortunate to hang with Jeanie Buss, his daughter. There are OK people in sports, good people in sports, great people in sports. Jeanie—class personified—tops them all. So, for that matter, does Linda Rambis, who knows the organization as well as anyone. Linda was an encyclopedia of stories and contacts, and has guaranteed herself a lifetime of Pearlman Family Chanukah cards (be warned).

Early on in my research, I was urged by Michael Cooper to contact (of all people) his ex-wife, Wanda. "She's very honest and very real," Michael told me. "And she has a great memory." Thank goodness I listened. *Showtime* is my sixth book, and for the previous five, I always developed a deep connection with one person whom I knew I could call whenever I needed to grasp a concept or filter a theory. In this case, Wanda fit the bill. Not only was she present for 98 percent of the era, but she speaks with a uniquely authoritative perspective. Showtime isn't Showtime without her.

I've now been writing books for ten years, and although it's my name that graces the cover, I've been propped up by a literary dream team. David Black, agent to the stars, continues to stand out as the Kyle Brady of his field. Michael Lewis, my longtime friend and purveyor of the greatest wedding dessert spread in human history (an egg cream menu!), has as sharp an eye as anyone in the business, and Casey Angle is the Eddie Lee Wilkins of fact checkers (admittedly, this makes no sense; I just thought it'd be neat to compare Casey to Eddie Lee Wilkins). Paul Duer, the former associate mayor of Christiana Towers, continues to supply keen insights, and I would be lost without the handiwork of Stanley Herz, one of Palm Beach Garden's top fifty senior citizen tax advisors, and Gary Miller, owner of the world's only Josh Hamilton–themed kosher coffee mug emporium. There is no better place in the world than the *Sports Illustrated* library, and no better people than the Kid 'n' Play of research, Joy (Kid) Birdsong and Susan (Play) Szeliga. Oh, and Elizabeth Newman and B. J. Schecter—thanks for letting a bum in.

Showtime is my second collaboration with Gotham, and I'm honored to have the confidence of the great William Shinker. Charlie Conrad is the type of editor any writer would be lucky to work with, and the PR team of Lisa Johnson and Anne Kosmoski is the best in the business. Hats off to Stephen Brayda for the wonderful cover design.

It would be impossible to name everyone who assisted in this process, but mighty appreciation to Liz Monaghan, Anita Scott, Mark Kriegel, Mike Mingione, Victor Ugolyn, Franco Miele, Laura Fasbach, J. A. Adande, Beverly Oden, Angela Taylor, Elizabeth Camp, Rob Easterla, Chris Wittyngham, Andy Dallos, Matt Zimmerman, Michelle Herbert, Marlo Norma, Daniel Monaghan, Orli Moscowitz-Urbas, Jack McCallum, Jon Wertheim, MC White Owl, Steve Cannella, Jeff Bens, John LaQuatra, Marina Adese, Kopal Goonetileke, Schmoopie Monaghan, Lisa Joseph, Matthew Walker, Larry Luftig, Frank Zaccheo, Dyan Cannon and the interminable Steve English.

Growing up on the mean streets of Mahopac, New York, a kid fought to avoid a future of either slinging crack or peddling Amway products out of a cardboard box. I am forever grateful to my parents, Joan and Stan Pearlman, for guiding me down the righteous path. Every time I order another $4.25 Espresso Affogato at the Swirl Coffee and Tea Shop, I think of what could have been. An equal dose of appreciation to Dr. David Pearlman, Daniel and Naya Pearlman, Dr. Martin Pearlman, Laura and Rodney Cole, Jessica Guggenheimer, Chris (Buckeye) Berman, Richard Guggenheimer, Leah Guggenheimer, DJ Norma Shapiro and the accounting firm of Jordan and Isaiah Williams, Inc. A moment for the lovely Chantay Steptoe-Buford, whose life was one of great purpose.

Lastly, a huge nod to home base. I'm guessing there's nothing quite like being wed to a health-anxiety-consumed, self-employed writer who insists on blogging about his latest twelve trips to the bathroom. Yet Catherine Pearlman—the gem of gems, editor of editors and collector of ensuings—continues to both support and love me. I did not merely marry up—I married the queen of goodness (and a friggin' awesome proofreader).

My children, Casey and Emmett, are remarkable little creatures who—over the course of *Showtime*—introduced me to *Bop* magazine, attacking cicadas, blueberry skies, MC Hammer flute renditions, 16 Handles obsessions, Popcorn Friday, splashes of vanilla, oddball world-record facts and (as always) unyielding love. That my two miracles know all the words to Run DMC's "Christmas in Hollis" only reinforces their awesomeness.

Let's hope we all keep chillin' and coolin' just like a snowman.

NOTES

PROLOGUE

x **"I'd like to run very much more than we have here"** Scott Ostler, "Jack McKinney: Low-Key Coach with Upbeat Offense," *Los Angeles Times*, July 31, 1979.

xi **On the morning of November 8, 1979** Ian Thomsen, "The Man Who Could Have Been Pat Riley," *National Sports Daily*, April 19, 1990.

CHAPTER 1

4–5 **"I asked to see a profit and loss statement"** Roland Lazenby, *The Show*, p. 97.

6 **According to a former Kings player, Cooke once** Rick Reilly, "Larger than Life," *Sports Illustrated*, December 16, 1991.

6 **Chick Hearn, the longtime Lakers announcer** Bill Brubaker, "The Golden Rule: A Cooke's Tour of Life," *Washington Post*, July 17, 1988.

6 **"He was," said Rod Hundley, the former Lakers player** Roland Lazenby, *The Show*, p. 99.

7 **The result was a divorce that, over a two-and-a-half-year** William Oscar Johnson, "Jerry Is Never Behind the Eight Ball," *Sports Illustrated*, June 18, 1979.

8 **He once turned down an offer to play the Marlboro Man** Neil Amdur, "A New Type of Owner in Sports Establishment," *New York Times*, May 30, 1979.

8 **While trying to sign Jimmy Connors** Ted Green, "Buss Unmatched as a Big Wheel of Sports," *Sporting News*, June 23, 1979.

8 **He would sell his Los Angeles holdings** Matthew Walker, "Skyscraper Mystique," *Fortune*, October 8, 1979.

9 **The deal is this** William Oscar Johnson, "Jerry Is Never Behind the Eight Ball," *Sports Illustrated*, June 18, 1979.

CHAPTER 2

12 **At the time, league rules mandated that the Jazz had to compensate Los Angeles** Scott Ostler and Steve Springer, *Winnin' Times*, pp. 68–69.

12 **When Larry O'Brien, the NBA's commissioner, prepared to flip the coin** Scott Ostler and Steve Springer, *Winnin' Times*, pp. 70–71.

13 **"Gentlemen," Cooke bellowed, "I'm going to order lunch for you!"** Bruce Newman, "From High above the Western Sideline," *Sports Illustrated*, April 9, 1984.

13 **Cooke, a man who knew a high-quality sand dab** Chick Hearn and Steve Springer, *Chick*, p. 66.

14 **Aware that Abdul-Jabbar, arguably the NBA's best player, was making $650,000 annually** Earvin Johnson with William Novak, *My Life*, p. 100.

15 **Despite winning 47 games and reaching the playoffs** Ted Green, "Lakers Book a Magic Show into the Forum," *Los Angeles Times*, May 17, 1979.

17 **Hadn't authorities been looking for** Cy Egan, "Sports biggie is found slain in trunk of his Rolls-Royce," *New York Post*, June 19, 1979.

18 **Was Tark, as most people called him** Mike Douchant, "Sutton, Tarkanian Decline Other Offers," *Sporting News*, July 21, 1979.

20 **What detectives later learned was that Weiss** Michael Connelly, "Who Shot Vic Weiss? A Trail Gone Cold," *Los Angeles Times*, June 11, 1989.

22 **"I can remember standing in a WPA line with a gunny sack"** Lesley Visser, "It's All That Glitters," *Boston Globe*, June 2, 1987.

22 **To help with the bills, Jerry worked odd jobs** Ross Siler, "Buss Station," *Daily News of Los Angeles*, April 8, 2007.

22 **Garrett saw true genius** Ross Siler, "Buss Station," *Daily News of Los Angeles*, April 8, 2007.

23 **"I couldn't stand wearing a pinstripe suit and carrying a briefcase"** Lesley Visser, "It's All That Glitters," *Boston Globe*, June 2, 1987.

23 **The two men—now officially Mariani-Buss Associates— flourished** Neil Amdur, "A New Type of Owner in Sports Establishment," *New York Times*, May 30, 1979.

23 **Though married to his second wife, Veronica, since 1972** No byline, "Suit Seeks $100M Turnover by Basketball Tycoon," *New York Post*, April 15, 1983.

CHAPTER 3

27 **They spoke for a while, the fifty-three-year-old GM and the forty-four-year-old assistant coach** Jack McKinney and Robert Gordon, *Tales from the Saint Joseph's Hardwood,* p. 18.

28–29 **"The next day in class, Sister Edward Francis"** Jack McKinney and Robert Gordon, *Tales from the Saint Joseph's Hardwood*, pp. 10–11.

30 **"I had other offers," he said, "but I always rejected them"** Richard O'Connor, "After the Fall," *Sports Illustrated*, October 20, 1980.

30 **That year, 1973–74, the Hawks** No byline, "Jack McKinney: Low-Key Coach with Upbeat Offense," *Los Angeles Times*, July 31, 1979.

31 **"There hasn't been a word said to me all year in a negative way"** Jack Scheuer, "McKinney Fired by St. Joseph's," *Spartanburg Herald-Journal*, March 19, 1974.

31 **One day later, approximately eight hundred students attended** Jack Scheuer, "Students Protest Firing," *Gettysburg Times*, March 20, 1974.

31 **"It's a funeral," said Kevin Furey, a Hawks player** Jack Scheuer, "St. Joseph's Coach Fired Despite Top Cage Record," *Gettysburg Times*, March 19, 1974.

33 **"bland and businesslike," wrote Joe Gilmartin** Joe Gilmartin, "Sharp Coach?," *Sporting News*, November 17, 1979.

33 **"The Lakers need a change from the style of play"** Phil Elderkin, "New Navigator on the Lakers' Bridge," *Christian Science Monitor*, August 9, 1979.

33 **"All he does," wrote Scott Ostler in the *Los Angeles Times*** Scott Ostler, "Jack McKinney: Low-Key Coach with Upbeat Offense," *Los Angeles Times*, July 31, 1979.

35 **"I ran into Earvin's fourth-grade teacher"** Roland Lazenby, *The Show*, p. 189.

36 **"I was a dreamer"** Mark Heisler, "He's Still Taking Care of Business," *Los Angeles Times*, November 2, 1990.

36 **When he was ten, Earvin cut neighborhood lawns** Richard Hoffer, "Magic's Kingdom," *Sports Illustrated*, December 3, 1990.

36 **"If I was going on an errand for my mother"** Earvin Johnson and Roy S. Johnson, *Magic's Touch*, p. 27.

36 **"My father would point out the subtleties"** Earvin Johnson with William Novak, *My Life,* pp. 23–102.

38 **"Coach Fox was the perfect coach for me"** Chris Solari, "Magic Johnson, in 5,000 of His Own Words," *Lansing State Journal* online, August 3, 2012.

39 **When, on April 17, 1977, he returned from** Seth Davis, *When March Went Mad*, pp. 39–48.

39 **"What does Earvin mean to us?"** Douglas S. Looney, "And for My Next Trick, I'll . . ." *Sports Illustrated*, April 30, 1979.

41 **Only a day earlier, the team announced that Johnson** Scott Ostler, "L.A. Soaks Up Its 1st Magic Moment," *Los Angeles Times*, July 28, 1979.

43 **"Some teams need a power forward, others need an outside"** Jim Murray, "Lakers Smile? It's Magic," *Los Angeles Times*, August 9, 1979.

44 **"I felt like he was going to have to adjust his game"** Malcolm Moran, "Magic Show Has Cut Nixon's Role in Half," *New York Times*, January 23, 1980.

45–46 **"I could see right off that my intensity was very different"** Earvin Johnson with William Novak, *My Life*, p. 107.

47 **During a particularly heated practice** Larry Bird and Earvin Johnson, with Jackie MacMullan, *When the Game Was Ours*, pp. 77–78.

47 **"Brad," Sharman raved** Scott Ostler, "Lakers Sign Holland," *Los Angeles Times*, September 7, 1979.

48 **Around the same time Dantley learned of his banishment** Scott Ostler, "Did the Lakers Merely Get the World's Tallest Flutist . . . ?" *Los Angeles Times*, September 21, 1979.

CHAPTER 4

52 **He was, as author Jackie Lapin once wrote, "a Gulliver in a world of Lilliputians"** Jackie Lapin, "The Tall Men: Life Grows Complicated Away from Arenas," *New York Times*, June 8, 1976.

53 **Born on April 16, 1947, in New York City** Gene Boswell, "Lew Warms to the Spotlight," *New York Post*, May 5, 1965.

53 **"The store manager decided we were dangerous customers"** Kareem Abdul-Jabbar with Peter Knobler, *Giant Steps*, pp. 8–9.

53–54 **His first best friend was a white child** Ibid., pp. 23–24.

54 **"At ten or eleven my father recognized that I was going to be taller than normal"** Ronald B. Scott, "Remember That Famous Scowl—the New Kareem Abdul-Jabbar Is Trying to Phase It Out," *People* magazine, November 24, 1975.

54 **The Alcindors were particularly impressed** Kareem Abdul-Jabbar with Peter Knobler, *Giant Steps*, p. 27.

54 **"I had gone over to watch a CYO game"** Maury Allen, "A Reunion with 'Lewie,'" *New York Post*, December 26, 1968.

55 **"He was fifteen when he matured"** Ibid.

56 **"One day I stumbled upon a strange and delightful experience"** Kareem Abdul-Jabbar with Peter Knobler, *Giant Steps*, p. 18.

57 **"People stare," he said** William Gildea, "Little Old Ladies Frighten Alcindor," *Washington Post*, March 25, 1967.

57 **A woman once jabbed him** Arnold Hano, "The Heart of Lew Alcindor," *Sport* magazine, April 1967.

57 **"On the surface," wrote Gerald Eskenazi** Gerald Eskenazi, "Lew Alcindor in Search of College," *New York Times*, March 28, 1965.

57 **A white religious instructor, Brother D'Adamo** Kareem Abdul-Jabbar with Peter Knobler, *Giant Steps*, pp. 50–63.

58 **"And you!" he screamed. "You go out there and you don't hustle"** Ibid., pp. 66–67.

58 **"The toughest job was to treat him the same as all"** Maury Allen, "A Reunion with 'Lewie,'" *New York Post*, December 26, 1968.

58 **"This is the worst place to go to school," he was told** Kareem Abdul-Jabbar with Peter Knobler, *Giant Steps*, p. 110.

59 **Alcindor enjoyed an in-flight meal of filet mignon** Joel E. Boxer, file to *Sports Illustrated*, 1965.

59 **"The varsity had no one able to guard me in close"** Kareem Abdul-Jabbar with Peter Knobler, *Giant Steps*, p. 136.

60 **"There was warm, mutual respect"** Ronald B. Scott, "Remember That Famous Scowl—the New Kareem Abdul-Jabbar Is Trying to Phase It Out," *People* magazine, November 24, 1975.

60 **Alcindor began forgoing standard collegiate attire** George Kiseda, stringer file to *Sports Illustrated*, August 28, 1968.

60 **"A white boy from Santa Maria. That's all"** Curry Kirkpatrick, stringer file to *Sports Illustrated*, March 23, 1969.

60 **"Frankly, this new rule doesn't affect Alcindor"** Gordon S. White Jr., "Ban on Dunking May Hamper Shorter Men," *New York Times*, April 6, 1967.

60 **"We tried to front him, hoping his teammates"** Dean Fischer, file to *Sports Illustrated*, February 2, 1967.

61 **On November 23, 1967, Alcindor was one of 120 attendees** Chuck Brown, stringer file to *Sports Illustrated*, November 24, 1967.

61 **J. D. Morgan, UCLA's athletic director** Lois Dickert, stringer file to *Sports Illustrated*, February 29, 1968.

61 **"Kareem gets along OK with white guys"** Robert Landauer, stringer file to *Sports Illustrated*, March 14, 1972.

61 **It was in August of 1968 that Alcindor made a bold shift** Peter Carry, "Center in a Storm," *Sports Illustrated*, February 17, 1973.

62 **"The Nets . . . were in real pursuit"** Kareem Abdul-Jabbar with Peter Knobler, *Giant Steps*, p. 191.

63 **"This is not the way to do business"** Alex Mistress, "U.C.L.A. Star Asks Halt to Bidding," *New York Times*, March 30, 1969.

63 **"I wasn't," he wrote, "the happiest guy to be there"** Kareem Abdul-Jabbar with Peter Knobler, *Giant Steps*, p. 196.

64 **"I met Alcindor for the first time when he came to Detroit"** Joe Falls, "Farewell, Alcindorella," *Sporting News*, November 15, 1969.

65 **"I'm not criticizing the people here"** Steve Cady, "Abdul-Jabbar Traded by Bucks for Four Lakers," *New York Times*, June 17, 1975.

66 **Johnson, the most heavily hyped player to enter the NBA in years** Earvin Johnson with William Novak, *My Life*, p. 108.

68 **"Jerry Buss has replaced Jack Kent Cooke as owner"** Yvonne Parks, "Los Angeles," *Sporting News*, October 13, 1979.

70 **"Johnson's enthusiasm was infectious, as usual"** Scott Ostler, "The Magic Numbers Are Simply Dazzling," *Los Angeles Times*, October 27, 1979.

71 **Praised the Lakers as the "prototype of a well-run team"** Joe Gilmartin, "Sharp Coach? Lakers Have One," *Sporting News*, November 17, 1979.

CHAPTER 5

74 **While riding to the tennis courts, McKinney approached** Richard O'Connor, "After the Fall," *Sports Illustrated*, October 20, 1980.

75 **"I drew up to the stop sign"** Scott Ostler, "Condition of McKinney Is Serious but Improved," *Los Angeles Times,* November 10, 1979.

75 **McKinney suffered a severe** No byline, "Lakers Coach M'Kinney Hurt in Cycle Fall," *Los Angeles Times*, November 9, 1979.

75 **When her husband woke from his** Steve Springer, "The Fall Guy," *Los Angeles Times*, October 27, 2006.

76 **The Nuggets were not only playing** Scott Ostler, "Nuggets, Like Gold, on Way Up," *Los Angeles Times*, November 9, 1979.

78 **"If [Johnson] is as good as his first month** Bruce Newman, "Magic," *Sports Illustrated*, November 19, 1979.

78 **"I think he has done a great job"** Scott Ostler, "He's Just Watching the Store for McKinney," *Los Angeles Times*, November 15, 1979.

78 **Once, in a particularly depressing moment** Scott Ostler and Steve Springer, *Winnin' Times*, p. 181.

79 **"After seven or eight days of not sleeping"** Scott Ostler, "Lakers Name Pat Riley Assistant Coach," *Los Angeles Times*, November 26, 1979.

80 **On December 18, 1979, readers of the *Los Angeles Times*** Scott Ostler, "Lakers Have a Family Problem," *Los Angeles Times*, December 18, 1979.

80 **Upon arriving in the NBA in 1970** Frank Harway, "A New Russell? It's Haywood's Goal," *Sporting News*, February 28, 1970.

80–81 **"Ford is so disliked as a player"** Peter Vecsey, "Sitting on Laker Bench Makes Haywood Sick," *New York Post,* December 17, 1979.

81 **Haywood started smoking marijuana** Spencer Haywood with Scott Ostler, *The Rise, the Fall, the Recovery,* pp. 182–190.

82 **He and his wife, Iman** Sue Reilly, "Tall, Dark and Handsome: That's L.A. Laker Spencer Haywood and His Wife, the Model Iman," *People* magazine, April 21, 1980.

84 **After Los Angeles clinched the Pacific Division** Scott Ostler, "Lakers Take a Big Step in Stride," *Los Angeles Times*, March 24, 1980.

84 **"I've been in the league seven years"** Scott Ostler, "Jabbar Moves Lakers a Giant Step Closer," *Los Angeles Times*, April 16, 1980.

85 **"I think we're the better team"** Scott Ostler, "Lakers' Chones Issues a Challenge," *Los Angeles Times*, February 26, 1980.

85 **The series opened at the Forum on April 22** Scott Ostler, "L.A. Doesn't Have a Downtown, but Seattle Does," *Los Angeles Times*, April 23, 1980.

85 **Westhead took one look at the gym and deemed it** Scott Ostler, "Lakers Get Hec of a Win, 104–100," *Los Angeles Times*, April 26, 1980.

86 **Afterward the Sonics sat in their dilapidated locker room** Scott Ostler, "Lakers Have the Champions of the World on a String," *Los Angeles Times*, April 28, 1980.

86 **Even though the Lakers had the better record** Scott Ostler, "Lakers Flex Their Championship Muscles, 111–101," *Los Angeles Times*, May 11, 1980.

87 **The *Los Angeles Times* rightly called the showdown "the best championship"** Scott Ostler, "Finally, an NBA Final with Some Glamour: Lakers vs. 76ers," *Los Angeles Times*, May 4, 1980.

87 **As Haywood departed Loyola Marymount** Spencer Haywood with Scott Ostler, *The Rise, the Fall, the Recovery*, pp. 203–207.

89 **He'd played his prep ball at nearby Crescenta Valley High** Marc J. Spears, "Groomed to Coach; Holand Learned Game from the Best," *Daily News of Los Angeles*, December 2, 1997.

89 **"If you say please," he responded curtly** Scott Ostler and Steve Springer, *Winnin' Times*, pp. 120–121.

93 **On the night of May 13, two days after** Carrie Seidman, "McKinney in Dark," *New York Times*, May 15, 1980.

93 **"Dad, have you heard the news?"** Richard O'Connor, "After the Fall," *Sports Illustrated*, October 20, 1980.

94 **The hurt, he said, was like a wound constantly being re-opened** Carrie Seidman, "McKinney Makes Fresh Start after Ordeal," *New York Times*, October 13, 1980.

94 **"I had so many things [affected] by the fall"** Jay Searcy, "McKinney Feels He Has Plenty to be Thankful For," *Oregonian*, November 29, 1987.

96 **"Can I hurt it any more?" Abdul-Jabbar asked** Kareem Abdul-Jabbar with Peter Knobler, *Giant Steps*, pp. 315–316.

96 **"I felt just sick inside"** Ted Green, "Are the Lakers a Foot Away from the Championship?," *Los Angeles Times*, May 16, 1980.

99 **"I wasn't sure what Westhead's intent was"** Larry Bird and Earvin Johnson, with Jackie MacMullan, *When the Game Was Ours*, p. 61.

99 **Kareem Abdul-Jabbar sightings were reported left and right** John Papanek, "Arms and the Man," *Sports Illustrated*, May 26, 1980.

101 **"Magic was born to play and born to win"** Ted Green, "Magic Tells the Captain: Let's Dance," *Los Angeles Times*, May 17, 1980.

CHAPTER 6

103 **"It's highly structured," Westhead explained at the time**
Scott Ostler, "Wanted: Magic Formula," *Sporting News*, October 11,
1980.

104 **The players even appreciated the goofy sincerity** Scott Ostler
and Steve Springer, *Winnin' Times*, p. 142.

105 **Abdul-Jabbar was accidentally poked in the right eye** Sam
Goldaper, "Accidents Produce Odd-Looking Pair," *New York Times*,
October 14, 1980.

106 **In the final four and a half minutes of the game** Scott Ostler,
"Lakers' Tunnel Vision Sets Them Up for a Fall," *Los Angeles Times*,
November 13, 1980.

106 **Six days later, in the second quarter of a game against the
visiting Kings** Scott Ostler, "Magic's Knee Goes Down for Third
Time," *Los Angeles Times*, November 19, 1980.

108 **On March 4, 1975, Duquesne faced Cincinnati** Ellis Cannon,
"Where Are They Now? Norm Nixon," *Pittsburgh Sports Report*, November 1998.

108 **"I got drafted by the pros and they called me"** Richard Levin,
stringer file to *Sports Illustrated*, February 1, 1978.

109 **During another contest, this one against the Nuggets, Nixon
was trapped** Scott Ostler and Steve Springer, *Winnin' Times*, p.
198.

110 **"These are rough times," Westhead said** Ibid., p. 132.

111 **Westhead's stated reasoning—"We need to create a better
balance of energy"** Scott Ostler, "Westhead Tries a Shakeup," *Los
Angeles Times*, December 8, 1980.

111 **"Enough bad vibes have been vibrating to arouse"** Scott Ostler, "Lakers Are Finding Out Why NBA Champs Don't Repeat,"
Los Angeles Times, December 19, 1980.

111 **"If [Norm Nixon] doesn't stop talking"** Scott Ostler and Steve
Springer, *Winnin' Times*, p. 132.

111–112 **"I thought [my career] was always going to be good things"** Malcolm Moran, "With Johnson Out, Lakers Are Having the Tables Turned," *New York Times*, January 12, 1981.

112 **His life became an ode to mind-numbing routine** Earvin Johnson with William Novak, *My Life*, p. 147.

112 **"It's not my preference"** Alan Greenberg, "Tonight, the Lakers Put a Little Magic Back in Their Lives," *Los Angeles Times*, February 27, 1981.

115 **Two hours before tip-off, a gaggle of reporters and photographers lingered** Alan Greenberg, "Magic's Back—Lakers Glad They've Got Him," *Los Angeles Times*, February 28, 1981.

116 **A sellout crowd of 17,505 stood** Malcolm Moran, "Magic Weaves Laker Victory," *New York Times*, March 1, 1981.

116 **He smiled, nodded and spread his arms** John Papanek, "And Now for My Reappearing Act," *Sports Illustrated*, March 9, 1981.

116 **Before the game, Westhead pulled Johnson aside** Earvin Johnson with William Novak, *My Life*, p. 149.

117 **Los Angeles concluded the regular season with a 148–146** Mike Littwin, "A 294-Point Game Gets the Lakers Tuned for Rockets," *Los Angeles Times*, March 30, 1981.

118 **"I thought Magic would have to come in"** Mike Littwin, "The Lakers' Other Guard," *Los Angeles Times*, March 31, 1981.

120 **"We didn't play as hard as they did"** Mike Littwin, "Who Can Stop Malone and Start the Lakers?," *Los Angeles Times*, April 3, 1981.

121 **Before the game, Johnson admitted the franchise** Mike Littwin, "Johnson Feels Some Lakers Are Resentful," *Los Angeles Times*, April 4, 1981.

121 **"I'm not trying to come in here and do all this with the publicity"** Scott Ostler and Steve Springer, *Winnin' Times*, p. 136.

121 **"The best way to put it," he said, "is that it was like my whole being just shifted"** Bill Dwyre, "Buss Still Delighted by His Expensive and Unpredictable Toys," *Los Angeles Times*, October 31, 1981.

122 **Buss had estimated that** Thom Greer, "Kings' Grunfeld: It's Survival by Determination," *New York Daily News*, April 12, 1981.

CHAPTER 7

126 **"McGee was just too good to pass up"** Mike Littwin, "Lakers Find the Good Points," *Los Angeles Times*, June 10, 1981.

127 **He ate the majority of his meals at Denny's and IHOP** Bruce Newman, "Rich, but Not Spoiled," *Sports Illustrated*, November 23, 1981.

127 **Not only was the contract too big** Mike Littwin, "Kupchak Gets an Offer; Lakers May Be Team," *Los Angeles Times*, June 20, 1981.

127 **"No," said Jerry Colangelo** Mike Littwin, "Lakers Are Set to Bite a $5.6-Million Bullet," *Los Angeles Times*, July 28, 1981.

127 **"I don't think eight hundred thousand dollars for a second-stringer"** Bruce Newman, "Rich, but Not Spoiled," *Sports Illustrated*, November 23, 1981.

127 **"Am I missing something?"** Richard Hoffer, "The Mitch Kupchak Caper, Cont'd," *Los Angeles Times*, August 7, 1981.

128 **"Is Westhead a real genius?"** Scott Ostler and Steve Springer, *Winnin' Times*, p. 150.

128 **"I don't know how Magic can be totally loved"** Scott Ostler, "Money Talks," *Los Angeles Times*, September 9, 1981.

128 **"They were giving him all this money"** Bruce Newman, "Magic Faces the Music," *Sports Illustrated*, May 13, 1985.

129 **"In many ways, a basketball team is like a family"** Mark Heisler, "Abdul-Jabbar Decides L.A.'s Really the Place," *Los Angeles Times*, August 4, 1981.

129 **Nixon ran into Johnson in a hallway at the Ocotillo Lodge** Larry Bird and Earvin Johnson with Jackie MacMullan, *When the Game Was Ours*, p. 87.

130 **Johnson, still recovering from the knee injury** Scott Ostler and Steve Springer, *Winnin' Times*, p. 153.

131 **"Michael always had a mental toughness"** Michael Cooper with Theodore J. Lynn Jr., *No Slack*, p. 2.

133 **The previous season, six black players quit** Alfred Romo, "A Perfect Storm: The 1977–78 New Mexico Lobos," www.wolf-bytes. com/index_files/Calendar/AR00.htm.

134 **"I'll be back," he whispered** Michael J. Cooper with Theodore J. Lynn Jr., *No Slack*, p. 15.

135 **"Westhead equipped the team with about 50"** Scott Ostler, "Back to the Classroom with Paul Westhead," *Los Angeles Times*, November 16, 1981.

135 **"There will be more movement from everyone and less of Magic Johnson"** Randy Harvey, "Lakers Take Up Where They Left Off—With Rockets," *Los Angeles Times*, October 30, 1981.

136 **"Paul thought half-court basketball controlled the game"** Roland Lazenby, *The Show*, p. 211.

136 **"Once we got down the court"** Scott Ostler and Steve Springer, *Winnin' Times*, p. 151.

136 **Watching from his skybox, Buss was apoplectic** Scott Ostler and Steve Springer, *Winnin' Times*, pp. 154–155.

138 **On the night of November 10, 1981, the Lakers fell** Randy Harvey, "San Antonio's Subs Torpedo L.A., 128–102," *Los Angeles Times*, November 11, 1982.

139 **"Sometimes," he told the media, "I just have to sit in the sunshine and think"** Randy Harvey, "Magic's Bombshell: He Wants to Be Traded," *Los Angeles Times*, November 19, 1981.

141 **"Earvin!" Westhead said. "Shut up! Get your ass in this huddle"** Earvin Johnson with William Novak, *My Life*, p. 155.

143 **The first reporter to reach Johnson** "Obituary: Dave Blackwell," *Deseret News*, April 4, 2005.

144 **Wilkes, the quiet veteran** Roy S. Johnson, "Lakers Are Gearing Up to Play 'Showtime' Basketball," *New York Times*, November 22, 1981.

CHAPTER 8

150 **"Things have really changed"** Scott Ostler and Steve Springer, *Winnin' Times*, p. 167.

151 **The session could have doubled as a *Saturday Night Live* skit** Bill Dwyre, "It Was as Complicated as Westhead's Offense," *Los Angeles Times*, November 20, 1981.

153 **"I'm just happy to be here in L.A."** Randy Harvey, "Buss Makes Westhead Disappear; It's Magic," *Los Angeles Times*, November 20, 1981.

154 **"If the perception around the country today"** Randy Harvey, "In Laker Firing, Only Timing Was Wrong," *Los Angeles Times*, November 23, 1981.

156 **"What you must do is ride it out"** Roland Lazenby, *The Show*, p. 214.

157 **"Yeah, I'm happy—and so are him and him and him"** Anthony Cotton, "Don't Blame Me, I Just Want to Have Fun," *Sports Illustrated*, November 30, 1981.

157 **"That's the kind of basketball I like to watch"** Randy Harvey, "Lakers Go Back to Run-and-Shoot; It Works," *Los Angeles Times*, November 21, 1981.

158 **"Dignity, respect, pride"** Kenny Moore, "Not Just a Pretty Face," *Sports Illustrated*, October 28, 1985.

158 **"In twenty-two years he gets a cup of coffee"** Mark Kriegel, "Escape from New York," *Esquire*, December 1995.

158 **"We were always in hotels"** Kenny Moore, "Not Just a Pretty Face," *Sports Illustrated*, October 28, 1985.

159 **"I could sense his disappointment"** Mark Heisler, *The Lives of Riley*, p. 9.

159 **"A guy chased me home with a butcher's knife"** Randy Harvey, "Living the Life of Riley Isn't All That Easy," *Los Angeles Times*, April 26, 1982.

159 **"My dad came down," he said** Mark Heisler, *The Lives of Riley*, pp. 11–12.

160   **"One day he'd go off on attitude"** Kenny Moore, "Not Just a Pretty Face," *Sports Illustrated*, October 28, 1985.

160   **Riley averaged 28 points per game** Mark Heisler, *The Lives of Riley*, pp. 16–17.

160   **"I could throw the hell out of the ball"** Austin Wet, stringer file to *Sports Illustrated*, December 17, 1973.

160   **"I used to have a hard time with coaches"** Kenny Moore, "Not Just a Pretty Face," *Sports Illustrated*, October 28, 1985.

161   **Louie Dampier, a fellow freshman** Mark Heisler, *The Lives of Riley*, p. 17.

161   **"He was [General Norman] Schwartzkopf"** Ibid., p. 18.

161   **Before opening the season against Hardin-Simmons** Jon Scott, "Season Review—1966 Kentucky Wildcats," www.bigbluehistory.net/bb/Statistics/roster1965–66.html.

162   **"You could feel the intensity on the court"** Mark Heisler, *The Lives of Riley*, p. 21.

163   **"[Rockets coach] Jack McMahon drafted me first"** Kenny Moore, "Not Just a Pretty Face," *Sports Illustrated*, October 28, 1985.

163   **"I'll never forget my first day in training camp"** Mark Heisler, *The Lives of Riley*, p. 25.

164   **"I was always afraid of losing my position"** Kenny Moore, "Not Just a Pretty Face," *Sports Illustrated*, October 28, 1985.

164   **As a disposable part on some of the greatest clubs** *West by West*, Jerry West and Jonathan Coleman, p. 129.

164   **In 1971, when Bill Sharman replaced** Kenny Moore, "Not Just a Pretty Face," *Sports Illustrated*, October 28, 1985.

164   **"When I finally realized that I couldn't"** Mark Heisler, *The Lives of Riley*, p. 31.

166   **On the morning of December 2** Randy Harvey, "Lakers Decide Riley Is Coach—With No Strings," *Los Angeles Times*, December 3, 1981.

166 **They were outscoring opponents by an average** Randy Harvey, "Lakers Are Scoring More and Enjoying It More," *Los Angeles Times*, December 11, 1981.

169 **Multiple newspaper headline writers** Randy Harvey, "Nets' Owners Don't Let Lakers Deal for McAdoo," *Los Angeles Times*, December 24, 1981.

CHAPTER 9

171 **During the early years of Showtime** Catherine Cloutier, "Looking Back: Real Estate in Fox Hills," *Culver City Patch*, December 11, 2010.

173 **"I was used to structured ball"** Harvey Araton, "Newest Knick's in Dreamland," *New York Post*, February 1, 1981.

173 **"I put a lot more emphasis on making the club than I should have"** Roy S. Johnson, "Man at Work: Mildest Laker Makes Himself Known," *New York Times*, January 10, 1983.

174 **"One day I looked around and I said"** Ibid.

176 **"Rambis has the least physical ability"** Scott Ostler and Steve Springer, *Winnin' Times*, p. 187.

177 **"That's my job"** Randy Harvey, "Living the Life of Riley Isn't All That Easy," *Los Angeles Times*, April 26, 1982.

178 **"I call him a philosopher"** Ibid.

178 **"Riley's not getting near the credit"** Bruce Newman, "They're Not Just Good, They're Perfect," *Sports Illustrated*, May 24, 1982.

179 **"L.A. can't win with a Kurt Rambis"** Anthony Cotton, "Still Kareem of the Crop," *Sports Illustrated*, April 10, 1982.

179 **"The players really remember"** Randy Harvey, "Lakers Sweep Away Their Nightmare of '81," *Los Angeles Times*, May 3, 1982.

182 **In a scene that could take place only in Los Angeles** Chris Cobbs and Randy Harvey, "Proposal at Pickfair," *Los Angeles Times*, May 14, 1982.

183 **A couple of hours before the Game 3 tip-off, Sampson . . . issued a recorded statement** Chris Cobbs and Randy Harvey, "Sampson Says He'll Stay," *Los Angeles Times,* May 15, 1982.

184 **"He was a picture of health"** John Zant, "Honoring Jamaal Wilkes," *Santa Barbara Independent*, September 12, 2012.

185 **"I was looking forward to the year"** Randy Harvey, "Season of Burdens Finally Turns Right for Lakers' Wilkes," *Sporting News*, May 17, 1982.

185 **"His life was depressing"** Randy Harvey, "Lakers Stood behind Wilkes, Now He's Repaying the Favor," *Los Angeles Times*, May 2, 1982.

186 **"To me," Westhead once said, "his shot is like snow falling softly"** Anthony Cotton, "Like Snow on a Bamboo Leaf," *Sports Illustrated*, February 9, 1981.

186 **"I planned to stay in Ventura for my senior year"** John Zant, "Super Shot," *Santa Barbara Independent*, March 23, 2011.

187 **"A long time ago I saw what winning meant"** Anthony Cotton, "Like Snow on a Bamboo Leaf," *Sports Illustrated*, February 9, 1981.

187 **"He was straightforward"** Jack Tobin, stringer file to *Sports Illustrated*, January 16, 1973.

187 **"There he is!" a girl shouted** Dwight Chapin, "Keith Wilkes: An Authentic Campus Hero," *Los Angeles Times*, 1974.

187 **"If Keith Wilkes could have his way"** Cliff Gewecke, "UCLA's Smooth-as-Silk Wilkes," *Christian Science Monitor*, December 11, 1973.

188 **"Keith was fantastic"** Jack Tobin, stringer file to *Sports Illustrated*, May 30, 1975.

188 **"It's about the worst looking shot"** Sam Goldaper, "Wilkes Wins Rookie Poll in N.B.A.," *New York Times*, April 22, 1975.

188 **Shortly after signing with the Warriors** Drew Cryer, "Wilkes," Associated Press, July 25, 1975.

190 **"Let me just say this"** Alan Greenberg, "Fitch Figures Lakers Got Lucky When Celtics Lost," *Los Angeles Times*, May 24, 1982.

190–91 **"Two years ago he couldn't have made"** Scott Ostler, "A Star Is Born," *Los Angeles Times*, May 25, 1982.

191 **"Wilkes looked as if he needed more than just an oilcan"** Mike Littwin, "Wilkes Wakes Up Lakers," *Los Angeles Times*, May 28, 1982.

191 **"It's something we think about"** Mike Littwin, "Lakers Confess They're Thinking Clean Sweep," *Los Angeles Times*, May 29, 1982.

191 **"In our practices the last few days, we taught ourselves"** Dave Anderson, "The Doctor Soars Again," *New York Times*, May 31, 1982.

CHAPTER 10

201 **Behind the bar, Donna** Mark Lacey, "The Ultimate Sports Bar," *Los Angeles Times*, February 23, 1992.

206 **On December 29, in a game against Golden State** Bruce Newman, "At the Head of His Class," *Sports Illustrated*, February 21, 1983.

206 **"They weren't doing anything different"** Randy Harvey, "Celtics Use Lakers and Television to Get a Point Across," *Los Angeles Times*, January 31, 1983.

207 **What crushed him, however** John Papanek, "A Lot of Hurt," *Sports Illustrated*, October 19, 1987.

207 **"My record collection"** Norman O. Unger, "Veteran Cage Star Starts Life Anew after Fire and Breakup," *Jet* magazine, May 1986.

207 **"The beautiful pieces of glass"** Kareem Abdul-Jabbar with Peter Knobler, *Giant Steps*, p. 319.

208 **Combining pragmatism and paranoia** Scott Ostler and Steve Springer, *Winnin' Times*, pp. 195–197.

212 **During Game 3, a microphone caught Jim Lynam** Randy Harvey, "Riley Fuming over Portland's Tactics," *Los Angeles Times*, May 3, 1983.

213 **In five head-to-head matchups** Randy Harvey, "Lakers Run Out of Time for Healing," *Los Angeles Times*, May 8, 1983.

213 **"We're going to have to reevaluate our plans"** Steve Hershey, "Gilmore Falters in Duel with Kareem," *Sporting News*, May 16, 1983.

213 **"Kareem," Riley said, "has brought"** Mike Littwin, "Gilmore Is Doing Job Spurs Hired Him to Do," *Los Angeles Times*, May 12, 1983.

214 **That feeling dated back to January 31, 1982** Roy S. Johnson, "Malone's Dominance Grows," *New York Times*, February 19, 1982.

214 **In 1974, Malone seamlessly jumped straight from** Steve Hershey, "Malone's Windfall," *Washington Post*, September 29, 1982.

215 **"I goes to the rack"** Randy Harvey, "Kareem of the Crop," *Los Angeles Times*, May 30, 1983.

215 **"If I owned a farm"** Sam McManis, "76ers Are Team with a Mission," *Los Angeles Times*, May 22, 1983.

215 **In what *Sports Illustrated* called** Bruce Newman, "Better by Leaps and Bounds," *Sports Illustrated*, June 6, 1983.

216 **"We toyed with people"** Bruce Newman, "Thou Shalt Rejoice, Said Moses," *Sports Illustrated*, June 13, 1983.

CHAPTER 11

217 **Despite a blood test that showed a 98.95 percent** "Lakers' Nixon Plans Appeal in Paternity Suit," *Los Angeles Times*, June 16, 1983.

218 **"Worthy has enough hardware"** Richard Hoffer, "The Leg Has Some Metal but No Rust," *Los Angeles Times*, October 1, 1983.

218 **West had offered Nixon** Steve Springer and Randy Harvey, "Lakers Trying to Trade Nixon; New Kareem Bid," *Los Angeles Times*, June 23, 1983.

218 **"It's inevitable," he said** Richard Hoffer, "This Nixon Is Proving Very Popular—With Inquiring NBA Teams," *Los Angeles Times*, October 4, 1983.

221–22 **"Who can blame John for going with Walton?"** Jon Trontz, "Swen Nater, out from Walton's shadow, off to fast start in pro basketball," *Christian Science Monitor*, November 16, 1973.

222 **"Comparing the Lakers to the Clippers"** Thomas Bonk, "Scott Seeking 4-Year Contract," *Los Angeles Times*, October 14, 1983.

222 **"I think I've got the ability of a smaller Magic"** Thomas Bonk, "Clippers Get Nixon; Trade Nater, Scott," *Los Angeles Times*, October 11, 1983.

222 **That night, Nixon celebrated his twenty-eighth birthday** Bruce Newman, "No Glitz, but Maybe Glory," *Sports Illustrated*, November 21, 1983.

223 **He had been raised by a single mother** Gordon Edes, "Short Road to Stardom," *Los Angeles Times*, April 29, 1988.

223 **"It was like there was a fraternity"** Bob Ryan, "Great Scott," *Sporting News,* June 3, 1985.

227 **"Larry attacked you from so many different angles"** Rick Reilly, "Larry and Earvin Still Magic," ESPN.com, March 6, 2012.

228 **"My thing was when you compete, you're really not friends"** Interview with David Letterman, *Late Show with David Letterman*, April 11, 2012.

228 **"I don't go out to dinner with him"** Roy S. Johnson, "Two Great Rivalries Resume: Bird-Johnson, Celtics-Lakers," *New York Times*, May 28, 1984.

229 **"They're simply two of the all-time greats"** Ibid.

230 **"I suppose you're going to ask me"** Steve Springer and Alan Greenberg, "Each of the Championship Series So Far Has Turned into Banner Year for Boston," *Los Angeles Times*, May 31, 1984.

230 **"I'm a nostalgia buff"** Thomas Bonk, "Lakers, Celtics Renew Old Rivalry," *Los Angeles Times*, May 27, 1984.

231 **By standing alongside the luggage conveyer belt** Larry Bird and Earvin Johnson, with Jackie MacMullan, *When the Game Was Ours*, pp. 128–131.

231 **"This little old man comes up to me"** Rick Reilly, "Larry and Earvin Still Magic," ESPN.com, March 6, 2012.

232 **"The pain was intense"** Gail Buchalter, "The Lakers' Legend Faces an Unfair Foe—Migraines," *People* magazine, May 2, 1983.

233 **"As I get older, it's assumed"** Thomas Bonk, "At 37, Abdul-Jabbar Is Going Against All Odds," *Los Angeles Times*, May 29, 1984.

233 **"Maybe we were so happy to be here"** Sam Goldaper, "Lakers Halt Celtics in Opener, 115–109," *New York Times*, May 28, 1984.

236 **At the time, NBA shot clocks** Larry Bird and Earvin Johnson, with Jackie MacMullan, *When the Game Was Ours*, p. 132.

236 **"I'll never forget the look on Magic's face"** Ibid.

237 **"We snatched defeat from victory"** Thomas Bonk, "Celtics Steal One from Lakers, 124–121," *Los Angeles Times*, June 1, 1984.

237 **"We tried to get them to run themselves to death"** Thomas Bonk, "Lakers' Fast Break Leaves Celtics Broken Down," *Los Angeles Times*, June 4, 1984.

237 **"This series isn't over"** Scott Ostler, "Lakers Are Gone, Celtics Are Going," *Los Angeles Times*, June 4, 1984.

238 **"You guys have already written us off"** Scott Ostler and Steve Springer, *Winnin' Times*, p. 262.

239 **One day earlier, while talking with Ainge** Larry Bird and Earvin Johnson, with Jackie MacMullan, *When the Game Was Ours*, p. 135.

241 **"What Boston did was the equivalent"** Thomas Bonk, "Angry Riley Says Celtics Creating 'an Ugly Situation,'" *Los Angeles Times*, June 8, 1984.

241 **"Before, the Lakers were just running across"** Anthony Cotton, "Greed and White and Red All Over," *Sports Illustrated*, June 26, 1984.

CHAPTER 12

244 **During his final prep season, there was talk** Roger Jackson, "A Big One Who Thought Small," *Sports Illustrated*, December 1, 1980.

244 **Why, when UCLA coach Larry Brown** Sam Goldaper, "Earl Jones: 'Mystery Man' of Draft," *New York Times*, June 18, 1984.

244 **On the morning after his spectacular debut** Frank Sleeper, stringer file to *Sports Illustrated*, December 14, 1979.

245 **The announcement, big enough to garner coverage** "Jones, Top Basketball Star, to Attend D.C. University," *New York Times*, June 10, 1980.

245 **"We're talking about a number one draft pick here"** Ira Rosenfeld, stringer file to *Sports Illustrated*, February 11, 1984.

245 **"All I want to be is a pro and drive an Eldorado"** Dave Kindred, "UDC's Jones: A Slumber Sleeper," *Sporting News*, January 1, 1984.

246 **He signed his $75,000 contract on August 15** Jerry Crowe, "Earl Jones Is Signed by Lakers," *Los Angeles Times*, August 16, 1984.

249 **"People always ask me if I'm a basketball player"** Thomas Bonk, "Taking a Long Look-See," *Los Angeles Times*, August 22, 1984.

252 **On September 29, 1984, Abdul-Jabbar was driving** Pam King, "Kareem Sues Cyclist over Damage to Auto," *Los Angeles Herald-Examiner*, December 18, 1984.

253 **"It was tough for him last year"** Bruce Newman, "Mr. T Crashes through the Sound Barrier and Beyond," *Sports Illustrated*, June 3, 1985.

253 **"I think he's the best shooter in basketball"** Bob Ryan, "Great Scott," *Sporting News*, June 3, 1985.

254 **"Byron's able to guard the great point"** Scott Howard-Cooper, "Scott Has What It Takes at the Finish," *Los Angeles Times*, May 1, 1991.

254 **"He didn't have to help me at all, but he did"** "Lakers Healthy, Hungry, Better than Ever," *New York Times*, May 27, 1985.

258 **Immediately after the loss to Boston** Paul Attner, "In Search of Redemption," *Sporting News*, May 6, 1985.

258 **"I sat back when it was over"** Bruce Newman, "Magic Faces the Music," *Sports Illustrated*, May 13, 1985.

259 **"Can the Celtics slow down the Lakers"** Sam Goldaper, "Celtics Try for Rarity," *New York Times*, May 27, 1985.

260 **"I don't think there's any doubt"** Roy S. Johnson, "Lakers Healthy, Hungry, Better than Ever," *New York Times*, May 27, 1985.

260 **The 34-point margin of victory** Anthony Cotton, "Celtics' Game 1 Message: 148–114," *Washington Post*, May 28, 1985.

261 **"It's definitely time to back off"** Alexander Wolff, "The 'Movie Stars' Changed Their Act," *Sports Illustrated*, June 10, 1985.

264 **"Rambis is generally viewed in Laker circles"** Thomas Bonk, "Lakers Get Two Chances for Redemption," *Los Angeles Times*, June 8, 1985.

CHAPTER 13

266 **Buss resided in Pickfair, the Beverly Hills mansion** Will Wright, "Famous Houses: Pickfair—A History of Beverly Hills' First Mansion," voices.yahoo.com/famous-houses-pickfair-history -beverly-hills-340021.htm, May 16, 2007.

268 **Though not quite as awe-inspiring as Pickfair** No byline, "Magic Johnson's Mixed Emotions," *New York Times*, June 2, 1987.

268 **"Some were secretaries"** Earvin Johnson with William Novak, *My Life*, pp. 250–251.

273 **"He had to psych himself up to be that tough guy"** Steve Kelley, "Maurice Lucas Was a Tough Guy on the Court, a Sweetheart off It," *Seattle Times*, November 1, 2010.

275 **"Those years with McAdoo, that team was awfully close"** Roland Lazenby, *The Show*, pp. 244–245.

278 **On January 15, McAdoo** Mike Barnes, "Manute Bol May Have Future in the Ring," *United Press International*, January 16, 1986.

279 **"It's time to start driving for the playoffs"** Mark Heisler, "Laker Win Has Riley Fired Up," *Los Angeles Times*, March 4, 1986.

279 **Or, as Blazers guard Clyde Drexler noted** Thomas Bonk, "Lakers Sweep Portland, but 60th Win Brings Yawn," *Los Angeles Times*, April 9, 1986.

281 **"Out dripped victory"** Chris Jenkins, "Lakers Work Their Magic," *San Diego Union-Tribune*, May 11, 1986.

282 **"One time, I think they dropped somebody out of the ceiling on me"** Thomas Bonk, "Rockets Have a Block Party at Forum, 112–102," *Los Angeles Times*, May 14, 1986.

CHAPTER 14

284 **"People in Los Angeles are a lot freer"** Steve Delsohn, *Showtime!*, p. 68.

286 **"Earvin, as the vocal leader of the team"** Jerry West and Jonathan Coleman, *West by West,* p. 138.

288 **"Wilt Chamberlain got traded"** Sam McManis, "Worthy Tries to Deal with the Off-Season Trade Talk," *Los Angeles Times*, October 14, 1986.

291 **During a December practice in Richfield** Gordon Edes, "Lakers' Second-Year Forward Will Start Season on Injured List," *Los Angeles Times*, November 1, 1987.

291 **In April, he forgot** Earl Bloom, "Lakers Going Like 60," *Orange County Register*, April 6, 1987.

294 **On the day before the game** Gordon Edes, "Purple, Green Clash Minus Redhead as . . . the Rivalry Resumes," *Los Angeles Times*, December 12, 1986.

294 **Los Angeles returned from an eight-point fourth-quarter deficit** Dave O'Hara, "Lakers 117, Celtics 110," *Associated Press*, December 13, 1986.

295 **With four minutes, forty-one seconds remaining in the fourth quarter** Gordon Edes, "Blowout Turns into a Blowup," *Los Angeles Times*, January 3, 1987.

295 **"I was actually pretty surprised"** Barry Bloom, "Once-Unsinkable Lakers' Ship Now Appears to Be Filled with Holes," *San Diego Union-Tribune*, February 3, 1987.

296 **It was an icy day, and young Earvin** *Homecoming with Rick Reilly* featuring Magic Johnson, ESPN, December 14, 2010.

297 **"What should I do?"** Gordon Edes, "Magic Johnson, 1986–87: His Greatest Act Yet," *Los Angeles Times*, May 18, 1987.

298 **"I've been talking to my folks every day"** Barry Bloom, "Once-Unsinkable Lakers' Ship Now Appears to Be Filled with Holes," *San Diego Union-Tribune*, February 3, 1987.

299 **The Lakers jumped out to a 29–0 lead** Earl Bloom, "Over at the Quarter: Lakers 40, Kings 4," *Orange County Register*, February 5, 1987.

299 **"We don't have anybody who can contain Mychal Thompson"** Kent Hannon, "Even the Shirt Off His Back," *Sports Illustrated*, March 6, 1978.

300 **In one, he grabbed 61 rebounds** Bruce Newman, "He Puts the Court before the Horse," *Sports Illustrated*, August 23, 1982.

300 **He told the media he was cousins** Gordon Edes, "Bahamas' Main Man," *Los Angeles Times*, Fenruary 22, 1987.

301 **"With them beating us in the Garden"** Earl Bloom, "Lakers Shooting for Sweep of Celtics in Regular Season," *Orange County Register*, February 15, 1987.

302 **"There isn't anybody we know about in the league"** Godon Edes, "Is Celtics' McHale 'Unstoppable'?," *Los Angeles Times*, February 15, 1987.

303 **"For the most part"** Gordon Edes, "West Angrily Denies Telling Newspaper that Adbul-Jabbar Is 'Killing' Lakers," *Los Angeles Times*, February 23, 1987.

304 **"They only want to drink champagne when they win it all"** Chris Baker, "Lakers Clinch Sixth Division Title, Put Champagne on Hold," *Los Angeles Times*, March 27, 1987.

CHAPTER 15

309 **"This is their year," Doug Moe, Denver's coach, said** Hal Brock, "Is It the Lakers' Turn, Again?" Associated Press, May 30, 1987.

309 **They got past the Detroit Pistons** Anthony Cotton, "Celtics Gives Pistons Lesson in Survival," *Washington Post*, May 31, 1987.

310 **"The shamrocks, leprechauns, parquet, mystique and mirrors"** Bob Rubin, "Battered Celtics Brace against a Storm," *Miami Herald*, June 2, 1987.

310 **"We know our turn is coming"** Chris Baker, "For the Ninth Time, Boston Will Meet L.A. for the Title," *Los Angeles Times*, May 31, 1987.

311 **"If this were a championship fight"** Tom Zucco, "L.A. Quickly Puts Boston on Defensive," *St. Petersburg Times*, June 3, 1987.

311 **"This was one of those scrimmages they had in Santa Barbara"** Anthony Cotton, "Lakers Make Quick Work of Celtics," *Washington Post*, June 3, 1987.

311 **This time, Boston actually jumped out to a 19–14 lead midway** Bob Sakamoto, "A Wearing Down of the Green," *Chicago Tribune*, June 5, 1987.

312 **"We've got a bunch of gutsy human beings here"** Ira Berkow, "They Went Whichaway?," *New York Times*, June 4, 1987.

312 **The team stayed at the Boston Sheraton** Pat Riley with Byron Laursen, *Show Time*, p. 226.

312 **"Last week we made a deal"** Ibid., pp. 230–231.

313 **"It definitely gets a team excited if another team takes cheap shots"** Anthony Cotton, "Lakers Rally to Overcome Celtics, 107–106," *Washington Post*, June 10, 1987.

314 **"I had the best view of it"** Ken Denlinger, "A Fly Hook Puts Boston in a Hole," *Washington Post*, June 10, 1987.

315 **"A junior, junior, junior skyhook"** Tom Cushman, "Lakers Find a Four-Leaf Clover in the Garden," *San Diego Union-Tribune*, June 10, 1987.

CHAPTER 16

317 **The caricature of West had often** Jerry West and Jonathan Coleman, *West by West*, p. 17.

317 **"I would go to sleep feeling like I didn't even want to live"** Mitch Lawrence, "NBA Legend Jerry West Details Depression, Abusive Father in New Memoir 'West by West,'" *New York Daily News*, October 16, 2011.

317 **"I think most people would agree on this"** Jerry West and Jonathan Coleman, *West by West*, p. 48.

319 **"He can run and jump with the best"** Earl Bloom, "Lakers Tab Glass after Wait," *Orange County Register*, June 23, 1987.

320 **"Thank God Kareem was my teammate"** Larry Bird and Earvin Johnson, with Jackie MacMullan, *When the Game Was Ours*, p. 209.

321 **"The scrimmages were better when Kareem wasn't playing"** Ibid., pp. 210–211.

321 **"The Boston mystique, the crowds"** Gordon Edes, "Short Road to Stardom," *Los Angeles Times*, April 29, 1988.

322 **Jerry Buss fought a $25 million palimony suit** Roxane Arnold, "$25-Million Palimony Suit Filed against Lakers' Owner Jerry Buss," *Los Angeles Times*, July 9, 1987.

322 **Johnson attended a 4-H rally in Michigan** Gordon Edes, "No Big Vacation," *Los Angeles Times*, July 9, 1987.

322 **"Just when we thought we'd done everything we could do"** Roland Lazen, *The Show*, p. 260.

324 **"My first reaction," McDaniel said** Gordon Edes, "A Sonic Boom Hits the Lakers," *Los Angeles Times*, November 25, 1987.

325 **A durable player, he missed** Bill Barnard, "SuperSonics 112, Knicks 109," Associated Press, December 1, 1987.

326 **"When Isiah Thomas smiles"** William F. Reed, "There's No Doubting Thomas," *Sports Illustrated*, April 6, 1981.

326 **"The way I saw it, we would be like the old Oakland Raiders"** Isiah Thomas with Matt Dobek, *Bad Boys!*, pp. 24–25.

327 **The two first met in 1979** Cameron Stauth, *The Franchise*, p. 315.

327 **Through the years, whenever he visited** Earvin Johnson with William Novak, *My Life*, pp. 234–237.

328 **"Your boy Isiah has done it"** Larry Bird and Earvin Johnson, with Jackie MacMullan, *When the Game Was Ours*, pp. 216–217.

329 **"No team is this good"** Scott Ostler, "Let's Focus on Just How Good Lakers Are," *Los Angeles Times*, February 22, 1988.

329 **Once again the game was bestial** Mark Heisler, "Lakers Enforce Their Will on Isiah, Enforcers," *Los Angeles Times*, February 22, 1988.

330 **"The message has to be out that this stuff about"** Jack McCallum, "The Dread R Word," *Sports Illustrated*, April 18, 1988.

331 **"I didn't touch him"** No byline, "Abdul-Jabbar Gets in Scuffle at Phoenix Mall," *Chicago Tribune*, April 24, 1988.

332 **"We've got a chance of being the greatest team ever"** Bob Sakamoto, "Lakers a Step from Greatness," *Chicago Tribune*, June 5, 1988.

CHAPTER 17

335 **As Jack McCallum noted** Jack McCallum, "Still Up for Grabs," *Sports Illustrated*, June 20, 1988.

336 **"At times I was out of position on defense"** Earl Bloom, "One Lakers Defender Is No Match for Dantley," *Orange County Register*, June 8, 1988.

337 **"I don't wish this on nobody"** Anthony Cotton, "Lakers Shake Off Pistons, 108–96, Tie NBA Finals," *Washington Post*, June 10, 1988.

338 **His father, Earvin Sr., was petrified of flying** Don Greenberg, "Lakers Savor Victory, Feast," *Orange County Register*, June 13, 1988.

338 **"I think the flu was a blessing"** Mark Whicker, "Lighter Magic Tips the Scales toward Lakers," *Orange County Register*, June 13, 1988.

338 **"We kept searching for something out"** Jack McCallum, "Still Up for Grabs," *Sports Illustrated*, June 20, 1988.

338 **"We played like high schoolers"** Earl Bloom, "Pistons Lose Their Composure, Then the Game," *Orange County Register*, June 13, 1988.

339 **"You see what I've been getting!"** Earvin Johnson with William Novak, *My Life*, p. 239.

339 **"[Magic] made the statement that if I came through the lane"** Curtis G. Bunn, "Pistons Hot When Magic Sits," *Newsday*, June 15, 1988.

339 **"I *did* target Isiah"** Larry Bird and Earvin Johnson, with Jackie MacMullan, *When the Game Was Ours*, p. 222.

339 **Because Thomas was so hopped up on painkillers** Isiah Thomas with Matt Dobek, *Bad Boys!*, pp. 48–49.

339 **The boy weighed six pounds, five and a half ounces** Jack McCallum, "Tackling a Tough Task," *Sports Illustrated*, June 27, 1988.

340 **"I'd messed around a little bit with basketball"** David Remnick, "Bullets' Mahorn: Picks and Choices," *Washington Post*, December 29, 1983.

340 **"He can dish it out, but can he take it?"** Jack McCallum, "Tackling a Tough Task," *Sports Illustrated*, June 27, 1988.

341 **"We read in the papers the Lakers were going"** Earl Bloom, "Lakers' Rough Play Backfired, Rodman Says," *Orange County Register*, June 18, 1988.

341 **"Who wanted it more?"** Mike Downey, "In the End, Lakers Found Wanting," *Los Angeles Times*, June 17, 1988.

341 **"It's a little villa in southern Italy"** David Kahn, "Riley Says He's Heading for Italy and, by the Way, Lakers Will Win," *Oregonian*, June 19, 1988.

342 **"He was just red hot"** John Freeman, "Lakers Roll One More 7," *San Diego Union-Tribune*, June 20, 1988.

342 **"I couldn't believe this was happening"** Isiah Thomas with Matt Dobek, *Bad Boys!*, p. 51.

342 **Blood dripped from a wound** Cameron Stauth, *The Franchise*, p. 14.

343 **The Lakers had offered help in the form of a bucket of ice** Isiah Thomas with Matt Dobek, *Bad Boys!*, p. 52.

343 **Trainers placed him in the dreaded "Boot"** Cameron Stauth, *The Franchise*, p. 17.

343 **He arrived on crutches** Cameron Stauth, *The Franchise*, p. 16.

344 **"It was a nightmare to the very end"** Roland Lazenby, *The Show*, pp. 263–266.

CHAPTER 18

348 **"He reported . . . looking creaky"** George Vecsey, "Big Fella Goes Back a Few Years," *New York Times*, June 15, 1989.

348 **When he signed his final contract shortly before the 1987–88 season** Mark Heisler, *The Lives of Riley*, p. 130.

349 **"All the guys who broke in with me are now gone"** Kareem Abdul-Jabbar with Mignon McCarthy, *Kareem*, p. 6.

349 **This year it would be the Shirelles' "Dedicated to the One I Love"** Ibid., p. 69.

350 **"When you think about it"** Doug Cress, "Kareem Tries to Say Goodbye," *Miami Herald*, November 1, 1988.

350 **"Everyone is trying to keep up with the Joneses"** "Kareem's Ransom . . . Another Game, Another Gift for Enigmatic Abdul-Jabbar," *St. Louis Post-Dispatch*, April 16, 1989.

351 **"Cap," Johnson replied, "you just ain't been aggressive"** Mike Downey, "He Has Fared Better Than in Farewell Season," *Los Angeles Times*, January 16, 1989.

352 **"Quit while you're even"** Scott Ostler, "It May Not Be Time to Give Him the Hook," *Los Angeles Times*, January 17, 1989.

354 **Woolridge "earned the reputation as a selfish"** Rich O'Brien, "Odd Man for the Job," *Sports Illustrated*, July 6, 1998.

356 **"I'm frustrated from losing"** Sam McManis, "Suns Keep Heat on Lakers; Magic Ejected in 111–96 Loss," *Los Angeles Times*, December 27, 1988.

356 **"There's an ego factor with Pat"** Sam McManis, "Pat Riley Doesn't Always Take the Fashionable Stand with the Lakers," *Los Angeles Times*, January 3, 1989.

357 **"I have failed miserably in trying"** Sam McManis, "Suns Burn Lakers, Riley Sees Red," *Los Angeles Times*, March 29, 1989.

358 **On the afternoon of April 22** Mike Barnes, "Abdul-Jabbar plays final regular-season game," *United Press International*, April 23, 1989.

359 **"They're not the defensive team they were last year"** Brian Biggane, "Pistons Poised to Win NBA Title, Rothstein Says," *Palm Beach Post*, April 27, 1989.

360 **"You see some teams jumping up and down"** Don Greenberg, "Lakers Sweep Aside Blazers," *Orange County Register*, May 4, 1989.

360 **"We wanted to win one"** Michael Hurd, "Lakers Pushed in Gaining Sweep," *USA Today*, May 15, 1989.

361 **"I have never seen a team play any better than the Lakers"** Mark Zeigler, "Lakers Spectacular as They Sweep Suns," *San Diego Union-Tribune*, May 29, 1989.

361 **"Orlando's body was like a missile"** Clifton Brown, "Lakers Make a Full Sweep into Final," *New York Times*, May 29, 1989.

CHAPTER 19

365 **"Our players," he said, "will wish"** Mark Zeigler, "Lakers Won't Be Relaxing," *San Diego Union-Tribune*, May 29, 1989.

366 **During his final season** Mark Heisler, *The Lives of Riley*, p. 131.

366 **"Riley thinks he's doing the team a favor"** Kareem Abdul-Jabbar with Mignon McCarthy, *Kareem*, p. 216.

367 **"Our goal is to go there and work hard,"** Don Greenberg, "Lakers Await NBA Finals at Training Camp," *Orange County Register*, May 31, 1989.

367 **"Pure hell"** Mark Zeigler, "Postseason Excellence Is Lakers' Trademark," *San Diego Union-Tribune*, May 31, 1989.

367 **"The thing that upset us more than anything"** Roland Lazenby, *The Show*, p. 265.

367 **"[The Pistons] are so committed to the revenge thing"** Sam McManis, "Riley Wants a Piston Rematch Rather than 'Easy Way Out,'" *Los Angeles Times*, June 2, 1989.

369 **"It hurt," Johnson said of Scott's absence** David Aldridge, "Pistons Back Court Leads Game 1 Rout with Scott Sidelines," *Washington Post*, June 7, 1989.

370 **"You've just got to get them"** Anthony Cotton, "Question by Magic: 'Why Me?'" *Washington Post*, June 9, 1989.

372 **With nineteen seconds left in Game 4** David Aldridge, "Pistons Sweep Crippled Lakers from NBA Throne," *Washington Post*, June 13, 1989.

372 **Two months earlier, he had hit a last-second** No byline, "Tulsa Sweeps to CBA Crown," *Chicago Tribune*, April 23, 1989.

CHAPTER 20

374 **In the early morning hours of December 21, 1981** John Schulian, "Dailey Is a Sorry Character in Deed," *Chicago Sun-Times*, July 1, 1982.

374 **During the court proceedings** Fred Mitchell, "Bryant on Dailey: For Anyone Else, It's Jail," *Chicago Tribune*, July 4, 1982.

374 **To celebrate his home debut** Will Urbas, "Dailey's Home Debut Draws Protesters," *New York Post*, November 1, 1982.

374 **"If you really want to know how badly the values"** Robert H. Boyle and Roger Jackson, "Bringing Down the Curtain," *Sports Illustrated*, August 9, 1982.

375 **"It's an honor to play with a team that can win"** Scott Howard-Cooper, "Ex-Clipper Dailey Signs 1-Year Deal with Lakers," *Los Angeles Times*, September 13, 1989.

375 **He entered the gym, shook some hands** Sam McManis, "Lakers' Camp Opens on Sour Note," *Los Angeles Times*, October 7, 1989.

375 **"He just didn't come in mentally or physically"** Sam McManis, "Dailey Misses Laker Practice, Says He Overslept," *Los Angeles Times*, October 13, 1989.

377 **"Laker employees grew used to seeing [Riley]"** Mark Heisler, *The Lives of Riley*, p. 136.

379 **"Riles changed"** Ibid., pp. 136–137.

380 **When West asked his top scouts** Richard Hoffer, "Mister Clutch, Master Builder," *Sports Illustrated*, April 23, 1990.

381 **West arranged for Divac's military** Michele Himmelberg, "Top Pick Divac Signs with Lakers," *Orange County Register*, August 8, 1989.

381 **Divac was presented with a home** Randy Youngman, "Language Barrier Puts Omalev in the Spotlight," *Orange County Register*, August 9, 1989.

382 **Divac dominated a Denver-Sacramento hybrid team** Marc Stein, "Divac Impresses in Debut," *Orange County Register*, August 9, 1989.

384 **"I think Vlade's a good player"** Sam McManis, "Camp Divac," *Los Angeles Times*, October 10, 1989.

385 **"He was really pushing us in practice"** Mark Heisler, *The Lives of Riley*, p. 138.

386 **CBS hired a producer** Pat H. Broeske, "Outtakes: Go, Laker Girls!," *Los Angeles Times*, January 7, 1990.

387 **"I do have faith," Riley said afterward** Sam McManis, "Suns ARE Too Good to Be True," *Los Angeles Times*, May 13, 1990.

388 **"This is a residual award of winning"** Michael Hurd, "Riley Named Top Coach," *USA Today*, May 15, 1990.

388 **"He singled me out the other way"** Mark Heisler, *The Lives of Riley*, p. 143.

CHAPTER 21

390 **"I've been with the Lakers for twenty years"** Don Greenberg, "Riley Unsure about Return with Lakers," *Orange County Register*, May 18, 1990.

391 **"Man's greatest fear is his fear of extinction"** Jeff Hasen, "Riley Resigns; Dunleavy Named Laker Coach," *United Press International*, June 11, 1990.

392 **On December 1, 1984, Dunleavy, at the time** Steve Springer, "Laker Change a Smooth One," *Los Angeles Times*, June 12, 1990.

394 **"I saw a lot at an early age"** Mark Zeigler, "Bullish on Basketball," *San Diego Union-Tribune*, May 20, 1991.

398 **Mychal Thompson, the ex–Portland standout** Kerry Eggers, "Thompson Passed Up on Workout," *Oregonian*, October 13, 1990.

398 **"There wasn't anyone from Maryland State"** Don Greenberg, "Lakers, Blazers Split Exhibitions," *Orange County Register*, October 14, 1990.

399 **According to police reports, James Worthy** Michael Hurd, "Undercover Sex Sting Nets Worthy," *USA Today*, November 16, 1990.

399 **Less than a week after the arrest** No byline, "Worthy's Name Surfaces in Portland Escort Case," *Los Angeles Times*, November 21, 1990.

399 **Stunningly beautiful, with cocoa skin** Angela Wilder, *Powerful Mate Syndrome*, pp. 20–21.

400 **When, on August 15, 1984, James handed Angela** Ibid., p. 160.

400 **She even purchased a license plate** Ibid., p. 74.

400 **"For all intents and purposes my vows"** Ibid., pp. 21–22.

400 **"I no longer love my husband"** Ibid., pp. 97–98.

401 **"After one month I've learned one thing"** Mark Heisler, "They Call Him Coach," *Los Angeles Times*, April 24, 1991.

402 **"Any time you go 27–4 and do it on the road"** Don Greenberg, "Magic Yields Division Race to Blazers," *Orange County Register*, January 3, 1991.

403 **The Rockets won a franchise-record 52 games** Mike Barnes, "Dunleavy Recalls Lifting Rockets Past Lakers 10 Years Ago," *United Press International*, April 24, 1991.

403 **"This maneuver is not permissible in basketball"** Frank Brady, "Scott's Shot Ticks Off Rockets," *San Diego Union-Tribune*, April 26, 1991.

403 **"It doesn't get much stranger than that"** George Shirk, " 'Slowtime' Replaces 'Showtime' for Lakers," *San Francisco Chronicle*, May 7, 1991.

404 **At one point during the regular season** Mark Heisler, "Campbell's Arrival Is Timely," *Los Angeles Times*, May 14, 1991.

404 **Portland had upended Los Angeles** Randy Chase, "Computer Says Blazers Should Dump Lakers," *Oregonian*, May 18, 1991.

404 **"We match up well against Los Angeles"** No byline, "Blazers Feel Good Going into Lakers Series," *United Press International*, May 15, 1991.

404 **The difference was Divac** Paul Buker, "Frustrated Duckworth Will Need to Regroup," *Oregonian*, May 25, 1991.

405 **"A lot of people say that [Showtime is dead]"** Kerry Eggers, "They Were Dancing in the Forum as the Lakers Resurrect 'Showtime,' " *Oregonian*, May 27, 1991.

405 **"The playoffs—that's what it's all about"** Mark Heisler, "For Game 6, Call Him Big Sprain James," *Los Angeles Times*, May 30, 1991.

406 **"I knew they were going to foul me"** Mark Heisler, "Lakers Survive Final Threat," *Los Angeles Times*, May 31, 1991.

407 **"Oh, boy. Oh, boy, oh, boy, oh, boy, oh, boy"** No byline,

"Magic vs. Michael a Dream Matchup for NBA Title Series," *St. Louis Post-Dispatch*, June 2, 1991.

407 **"Michael and Magic, Magic and Michael"** Mark Heisler, "A Rivalry Not to Be Kissed Off," *Los Angeles Times,* June 2, 1991.

407 **"This was the way basketball is supposed to be played"** David Aldridge, "Bulls Just Miss as Lakers Take Game 1, 93–91," *Washington Post*, June 3, 1991.

407 **"We won the first game"** Roland Lazenby, *The Show*, p. 269.

408 **"Tex Winter is a genius"** Jeff Baker, "Tex Winter: Architect and Theorist Behind the Chicago Bulls' Offense," *Oregonian*, June 2, 1991.

409 **"You're dejected. You're frustrated"** David Hutchinson, "Bulls Put Lakers in 'Ditch,'" *Washington Times*, June 10, 1991.

409 **"When I went to congratulate him after the game"** George Shirk, "Jordan, Bulls Win NBA Title," *San Francisco Chronicle*, June 13, 1991.

CHAPTER 22

411 **On August 18, 1991, Magic Johnson visited** Milton Kent, "Life Hasn't Lost Its Magic for Lakers' Johnson," *Toronto Star*, August 23, 1991.

412 **"I felt like God was saying"** Earvin Johnson with William Novak, *My Life*, p. 269.

412 **On September 20, 1991, USA Basketball** Jeff Hasen, "Jordan, Johnson Head U.S. Olympic team," *United Press International*, September 21, 1991.

412 **The man, William Carter** No byline, "Laker Star Asks for Resignation," *New York Times*, September 26, 1991.

412 **During a trip to the Eiffel Tower** Mark Heisler, "Uncommon Marketing," *Los Angeles Times*, October 18, 1991.

413 **"We need to get back"** No byline, "Magic Helps LA Win McDonald's Open," *Oregonian*, October 20, 1991.

413 **"I was actually in the best shape of my NBA career"** Magic Johnson with Roy Johnson, "I'll Deal with It," *Sports Illustrated*, November 18, 1991.

414 **Upon arriving at the physician's office** Earvin Johnson with William Novak, *My Life*, p. 275.

416 **"One o'clock, I want you at the Forum"** Ibid., p. 290.

BIBLIOGRAPHY

Abdul-Aziz, Zaid. *Darkness to Sunlight: The Life-Changing Journey of Zaid Abdul-Aziz ("Don Smith")*. Seattle, Washington: Sunlight Publishing, 2006.

Abdul-Jabbar, Kareem, with Mignon McCarthy. *Kareem*. Warner Books, 1990.

Abdul-Jabbar, Kareem, with Peter Knobler. *Giant Steps: The Autobiography of Kareem Abdul-Jabbar*. New York: Bantam, 1983.

Auerbach, Red, and John Feinstein. *Let Me Tell You a Story: A Lifetime in the Game*. New York: Little Brown, 2004.

Bird, Larry, and Earvin Johnson, with Jackie MacMullan. *When the Game Was Ours*. New York: Houghton Mifflin, 2009.

Buss, Jeanie, with Steve Springer. *Laker Girl*. Chicago: Triumph Books, 2010.

Caughey, John and LaRee Caughey. *Los Angeles: Biography of a City*. Berkeley, California: University of California Press, 1976.

Connelly, Michael. *Crime Beat: A Decade of Covering Cops and Killers*. New York: Little, Brown, 2004.

Cooper, Michael J., with Theodore J. Lynn Jr. *No Slack*. Albuquerque, New Mexico: CompuPress, 1987.

Davis, Seth. *When March Went Mad: The Game That Transformed Basketball.* New York: Times Books, 2009.

Dawkins, Darryl, and Charley Rosen. *Chocolate Thunder: The Uncensored Life and Times of Darryl Dawkins.* Toronto: Sport Media Publishing, 2003.

Delsohn, Steve. *Showtime!: A Celebration of the World Champion Los Angeles Lakers.* Chicago: Contemporary Books, 1985.

Haywood, Spencer, with Scott Ostler. *The Rise, the Fall, the Recovery.* New York: Amistad, 1992.

Hearn, Chick, and Steve Springer. *Chick: His Unpublished Memoirs and the Memories of Those Who Knew Him.* Chicago: Triumph Books, 2004.

Heisler, Mark. *The Lives of Riley.* New York: Macmillan, 1994.

Johnson, Earvin, and Roy S. Johnson. *Magic's Touch.* Reading, Massachusetts: Addison-Wesley, 1989.

Johnson, Earvin, with William Novak. *My Life.* New York: Fawcett, 1992.

Lazenby, Roland. *Jerry West: The Life and Legend of a Basketball Icon.* New York: Ballantine, 2009.

Lazenby, Roland. *The Show: The Inside Story of the Spectacular Los Angeles Lakers in the Words of Those Who Lived It.* New York: McGraw-Hill, 2006.

Mallozzi, Vincent M. *Doc: The Rise and Rise of Julius Erving.* Hoboken, New Jersey: John Wiley, 2010.

McKinney, Jack, with Robert Gordon. *Tales from the Saint Joseph's Hardwood: The Hawk Will Never Die.* Champaign, Illinois: Sports Publishing, 2005.

McKinney de Ortega, Susan. *Flirting in Spanish.* New York: Antaeus Books, 2011.

Ostler, Scott, and Steve Springer. *Winnin' Times: The Magical Journey of the Los Angeles Lakers.* New York: Macmillan, 1986.

Quinn, Eithne. *Nuthin' but a "G" Thang: The Culture and Commerce of Gangsta Rap.* New York: Columbia University Press, 2005.

Ramsay, Jack, and Neal Vahle. *Dr. Jack on Winning Basketball.* Indianapolis, Indiana: Blue River Press, 2011.

Riley, Pat, with Byron Laursen. *Show Time: Inside the Lakers' Breakthrough Season.* New York: Warner Books, 1988.

Rolle, Andrew F. *Los Angeles: From Pueblo to City of the Future.* San Francisco: Boyd & Fraser, 1981.

Rosen, Charles. *God, Man and Basketball Jones: The Thinking Fan's Guide to Professional Basketball.* New York: Holt, Rinehart and Winston, 1979.

Ross, Alan. *Lakers Glory: For the Love of Kobe, Magic, and Mikan.* Nashville, Tennessee: Cumberland House, 2006.

Simmons, Bill. *The Book of Basketball: The NBA According to the Sports Guy Bill Simmons.* New York: ESPN Books, 2009.

Stauth, Cameron. *The Franchise: Building a Winner with the World Champion Detroit Pistons, Basketball's Bad Boys.* New York: William Morrow, 1990.

Streatfeild, Dominic. *Cocaine: An Unauthorized Biography.* New York: Picador, 2001.

Tarkanian, Jerry, with Dan Wetzel. *Runnin' Rebel: Shark Tales of "Extra Benefits," Frank Sinatra, and Winning It All.* Champaign, Illinois: Sports Publishing, 2005.

Thomas, Isiah, with Matt Dobek. *Bad Boys!: An Inside Look at the Detroit Pistons' 1988–89 Championship Season.* Grand Rapids, Michigan: Masters Press, 1989.

West, Jerry, and Jonathan Coleman. *West by West: My Charmed, Tormented Life.* New York: Little, Brown, 2011.

Wilder, Angela. *Powerful Mate Syndrome: Reclaiming Your Strength and Purpose When Your Partner Is the Star of the Relationship.* New York: St. Martin's Press, 2004.

Williams, Pat, and Bill Lyon. *We Owed You One!: The Uphill Struggle of the Philadelphia 76ers.* Wilmington, Delaware: TriMark Publishing, 1983.

World Champion Los Angeles Lakers Are Cookin': Family Cookbook. Dallas: Taylor Publishing, 1985.

Zacchino, Narda, ed. *Los Angeles Lakers: 50 Amazing Years in the City of Angels.* San Leandro, California: Time Capsule Press, 2010.

INDEX

Abdul-Jabbar, Amir, 207, 358
Abdul-Jabbar, Kareem. *See also* Alcindor,
  Ferdinand Lewis, Jr.
  acquisition by the Lakers, 5
  anger and moodiness, 51–53
  Bel Air mansion, 206–207, 212, 251
  Brentwood house, 252–253
  children, 204
  coaching by McKinney, x–xi, 32
  comparison to Chamberlain, 50, 65–66,
    250
  declining performance, 277, 292–293, 295,
    309, 320–321, 331–332, 348–349
  injuries, 95–96, 105, 167
  migraine headaches, 232–233
  money mismanagement, 304, 347
  recollections of Showtime, 422
  relationship with fans/public, 252, 303,
    320, 346–347, 349–351
  relationship with Magic, 66–69, 166, 351
  retirement, 320, 331, 347–350, 352, 358–
    359
  sexual activity, 269–270
  trade to the Knicks, 128–129
Abdul-Khaalis, Hamaas, 62
Abdul, Paula, 179
Adams, Alvin, 180
Adler, Lou, 223
Aguirre, Mark, 125, 285–289, 327
AIDS. *See* Human immunodeficiency virus
Ainge, Danny, 235, 239, 264, 311, 314
Airplane! (movie), 347
Albany Patroons (CBA), 334
Albeck, Stan, 26, 71, 178, 213

Alcindor, Ferdinand Lewis, Jr. ("Lew"; "Al"),
  50, 53–65. *See also* Abdul-Jabbar,
  Kareem
Alcindor, Ferdinand Lewis, Sr. and Cora, 53,
  261, 358
Alexander, Bruce, 403
Allain, Aurorah, 202
Allen, Lucius, 61
American Basketball Association (ABA), 9,
  32, 47, 48, 62–63, 220
American CableVision, 4
Anderson, Dave, 191
Andrews, George, 13, 41
Archibald, Nate, 306–307
Armritraj, Anand and Vijay, 25
Armstrong, B. J., 408
Atlanta Hawks, 206, 289, 329, 353
Attles, Al, 188
Attner, Paul, 257
Auerbach, Red, 230–232, 294
Awtrey, Dennis, 43, 95 & n

Babcock, Pete, 219–222
Bacharach, Burt, 223
Ballard, Greg, 307
Barkley, Charles, 254
Barlow, Kenny, 353
Barnes, Joe, 132–133
Barp, Raymond, 22
Barry, Rick, 101, 188
Bates, Billy Ray, 211
Baumeister, Lou, 107, 415
Bavetta, Dick, 403
Baylor, Elgin, 78

Beard, Dale, 412
Bee, Claire, 192
Benjamin, Benoit, 358
Benson, Kent, 95
Bergen, Barbara, 252–253
Bertka, Bill, 12, 59, 166, 175–176, 192, 233,
    256, 264, 276, 312, 331, 348, 355, 366–
    368, 371, 375, 383, 386, 396
Berwald, Lance, 246
Beshore, Del, 68
Bianchi, Al, 295
Bias, Len, 315
Bickerstaff, Bernie, 323, 360
Bing, Dave, 36
Bird, Larry, 16n, 40, 43, 71, 77, 123, 190,
    206, 227–230, 257–259, 293–296, 302–
    303, 306–310, 325–329, 415
Birdsong, Otis, 215, 299
Blab, Uwe, 318
Blackburn, Tom, 91
Black, John, 287, 291, 328, 376, 386, 390,
    412, 414–415
Black Muslims, 62
Blackwell, Cory, 244
Blackwell, Dave, 143
Blee, Michael (Rev.), 30–31
Bloom, Barry, 296
Bloom, Earl, 319
Boddie, Otis, 246
Boeck, Larry, 162
Boone, Ron, 47
Boston Celtics
    acquisition of Bird, 16n, 77
    championship losses, 257–265, 325
    championship wins, 230, 229–242, 299
    Manguarian as owner, 21
    Pat Riley as player, 158
    trying to play like Showtime, 329
Boxer, Joel E., 59
Brady, Frank (LA Herald-Examiner), 287
Brady, Frank (Philadelphia Inquirer), 93
Brady, Frank (San Diego Union-Tribune), 403
Brando, Tim, 40
Bratz, Mike, 111
The Breaks of the Game (Halberstam), 300
Bresler, David, 232–233
Brewer, Jim, 111, 117–120, 165, 171, 174, 177
Brickowski, Frank, 172, 268, 288–289, 292–
    295, 298–299, 301
Bridgeman, Junior, 65, 307
Brooks, Michael, 254
Brooks, Scott, 334
Brown, Cecil and Jessie Buss, 22
Brown, Freddie, 235–236

Brown, Fred ("Downtown"), 85
Brown, Hubie, 26, 31–32
Brown, Larry, 154, 244
Brown, Mickey, Susan, and Jim, 22
Brown, Rich and Carlee, 172
Brubaker, Bill, 5
Bryant, Joe ("Jellybean"), 168 & n
Bryant, Wallace, 374
Buffalo Braves, 24, 168–169
Burtt, Steve, 244
Bush, George, 358
Buss, Jeanie, 9, 23, 34, 80, 94, 113, 155, 195,
    201, 203, 267, 419–420
Buss, Jerry. See also Showtime
    firing of McKinney, xii
    firing Paul Westhead, 145–146, 149
    followed by the Seven Dwarves, 202
    negotiations for players, 182–184
    palimony suit, 322
    partying at Pickfair mansion, 266–267
    purchase of Lakers, 8–10, 14, 23–25
    relationship with Magic, 113–114, 128–
        129, 139–140, 166–167, 286
    showmanship, 69
    women and, 1, 24, 199–200, 267, 298
Buss, JoAnn Mueller, 23–24, 25
Buss, Lydus and Jessie, 22
Buss, Veronica, 23, 25
Butler, Ardessie, 130–131

California Sports, Inc., 8, 107
Campbell, Eldon, 403–404
Campbell, Tony, 52, 333–335, 337, 341, 344,
    348, 356, 368–371
Candy, John, 201
Cannon, Dyan, 70, 155, 201, 405
Canresecca, Lou, 333
Carlisle, Rick, 334
Carmichael, Scott, 267, 379
Carr, Kenny, 45, 108, 174, 181, 212
Carr, M. L., 231, 239–241, 257, 262, 313, 340
Carroll, Joe Barry, 218, 228n
Carter, Butch, 106, 111, 127, 145, 199
Carter, Donald, 286
Carter, Jimmy, 127
Carter, Ron, 45–46, 83, 109, 113–115, 171,
    174, 195, 198, 201, 204, 210, 222, 224,
    267, 421
Carter, William, 412
Cartwright, Bill, 408
Casey, Don, 374
Chamberlain, Wilt, 5, 50, 65, 114, 140, 248,
    336
Chambers, Tom, 323, 361

Chaney, Don, 403
Chapin, Dwight, 187
Charlotte Hornets, 349, 386
Cheeks, Maurice, 86, 190, 192, 215
Chicago Bulls, 12–13, 68, 110–111, 177, 195, 292, 354, 361, 373–374, 406–409
Chicago White Sox, 9
Chones, Jim, 70–71, 80–81, 84, 89–90, 97–98, 106, 111, 119, 121, 127, 174, 176
Chortkoff, Mitch, 144, 151, 219
Cinicola, John, 108
Clark, Robert N. S., 75
Cleveland Cavaliers, 70–71, 97, 98n, 111, 144, 168, 180–181, 325, 396
Coach of the Year, xii, 30, 357, 387–388
Cocaine. See Drugs
Colangelo, Jerry, 127
Collins, Doug, 306
Collins, Tom, 304, 347
Conley, Larry, 161–162
Conlin, Bill, 351
Connors, Jimmy, 8
Continental Basketball Assoc., 334, 349, 372
Cook, Anthony, 380
Cook, Darwin, 154
Cooke, Jack Kent, 3–7, 11–16
Cooke, Jeannie, 6–7
Cooke, Ralph and Nancy, 4
Cooper, Joe, 211
Cooper, Marshall and Jean, 130
Cooper, Michael, 1
    background and early basketball, 130–133
    beginning career with Lakers, 40–41, 45
    coaching the LA Sparks, 422
    departure from Lakers, 395–396
    drafted by the Lakers, 133–135
    drug use, 196, 209–210
    on Forum Club, 202–205
    injuries, 134, 308, 332, 335, 342
    on Kareem, 51, 66, 95, 167, 212
    on Landsberger, 194–197
    on Lucas blunder, 273–275
    on Magic, 41–42, 44–47, 69, 98–99, 119, 133–134, 255–256, 294, 389
    on Nixon, 110–111, 115, 222–223, 225–226
    playing against Larry Bird, 227–228, 234–235, 294, 306–308, 311
    retirement from Lakers, 395–396
    on Rambis, 172
    on Riley, 357, 367, 377–378, 384–386
    on Scott, 223, 255, 321–322
    sexual activity, 269–270
    Showtime role, 130, 147, 171, 192, 306, 331, 422
        trade rumors, 182–183, 308–310
        on Westhead, 104, 124, 136–146
Cooper, Mickey, 130
Cooper, Wanda Juzang, 83, 135, 199, 203–204, 257, 276–277, 312, 400
Cooper, Wayne, 212
Cornbread, Earl and Me (movie), 188
Cornelius, Ron, 174
Corzine, Dave, 105, 213
Costello, Larry, 32
Costner, Tony, 244
Cotton, Anthony, 157
Cowens, Dave, 95
Crasnick, Richard, 276, 317
Cummings, Pat, 330
Cummings, Terry, 206, 219, 226, 255
Cunningham, Billy, 99, 100, 190, 192, 215–216
Cureton, Earl, 192
Curran, Jack, 45, 81, 134, 141, 196, 233, 308

D'Adamo (Br.), 57
Dailey, Quintin, 373–376
Dallas Cowboys, 163
Daly, Chuck, 325, 329, 333, 337, 342–344, 369
Dampier, Louie, 161
Daniels, Walter, 41, 108
Dantley, Adrian, 47–48, 109, 141, 335–338
Danza, Tony, 201
Dart, Jim, 36
Dave, Darren, 310
Davidson, William, 21, 342
Davis, Al, 329, 343
Davis, Brad, 108–110
Davis, Lance, 200, 267
Davis, Morris, 134
Dawkins, Darryl, 86, 92–95, 100, 190–192, 214, 272
Day, Diane, 204
Daye, Darren, 310
Denver Nuggets, 75, 76–77, 109–110, 278, 304–305
Denver Rockets (ABA), 48, 350
Detroit Pistons, 21, 34, 330–332, 335–345
Divac, Snezana, 381
Divac, Vlade, 380–386, 396, 402–405, 409
Doi, Kenneth, 23
Dolan, Johnny, 175
Donaher, Don, 91
Donohue, Jack, 54–55, 57–58
Donovan, Charlie, 55
Douglas, Michael, 178
Dover, Jim, 22

Downey, Mike, 316, 341, 352
"Dream Team," U.S. Olympics, 411–412
Drew, Larry, 375, 384
Drexler, Clyde, 398
Drugs, 79–84, 87–90, 196, 203, 209–210, 286n
Duckworth, Kevin, 360, 398, 404
Dumars, Joe, 325–326, 335–336, 342–344, 370
Dunlap, Jim, 222
Dunleavy, Mike, 306, 391–402, 409, 414, 416
Durant, Kevin, 421
Dykema, Craig, 180

Eaton, Mark, 212
Ebony (magazine), 414
Edes, Gordon, 304, 324
The Ed Sullivan Show (TV show), 56
Edwards, Harry, 61
Edwards, James, 207, 325, 345
Ehlo, Craig, 396
Ellenberger, Norman, 133
Ellis, Dale, 323, 360
Englebrecht, Roy, 69
English, Alex, 304
Erickson, Keith, 316
Erving, Julius ("Dr. J"), 77, 86, 88, 100–101, 189–192, 215, 254, 349
European basketball, 26–27, 103, 173, 246, 277, 371, 380–384, 395
Everett, Joe, 108
Evert, Chris, 25
Ewing, Patrick, 244
Eyen, Jim, 382

Falls, Joe, 64
Felix, Mark, 133
Ferry, Bob, 126–127, 128, 245
The Fish That Saved Pittsburgh (movie), 114
Fitch, Bill, 190, 249, 280, 282
Fitzgerald, Jim, 21
Fitzsimmons, Cotton, 179
Fonda, Jane, 178
Ford, Don, 45, 67, 80–81, 180
Ford, Phil, 154
Forum Club, 200–205, 420
The Forum, construction and operation, 3–6
Fox, George, 11, 37–38
Fox Hills apartments, 171
Fox, John, 318
Frazier, Walt, 71
Free, Lloyd, 33, 71
Fuller, Elizabeth M., 217

Funaki, Toshio, 202
Furey, Kevin, 31

Gaims, John, 253
Gamba, Allessandro, 27
Garrett, Calvin, 225
Garrett, Walter, 22
Garr, Terry, 329
Gathers, Hank, xii, 413
Gentlemen's Quarterly, 357
Gervin, George, 138, 156, 180, 184
Gewecke, Cliff, 187–188
Giant Steps (Abdul-Jabbar), 95n
Gilliam, Armen, 318, 356
Gilmore, Artis, 68, 177, 211, 213–215, 272, 303
Giminski, Mike, 292
Givens, Jack, 228n
Glass, Willie, 318–320
Gnad, Hansi, 318
Golden State Warriors, 21n, 71–72, 178, 188, 197, 206, 218, 229, 279, 323
Gondrezick, Grant, 295
Goodrich, Gail, 12, 65, 301
Graham, Earnest, 39
Grant, Horace, 408
Green, A. C., 269–277, 293, 302, 305, 310, 318, 330, 349, 352, 355, 384, 396, 399, 402, 405
Greenberg, Alan, 112
Greenbert, Don, 316
Green, Kenny, 318
Green, Ricky, 142, 307
Green, Vanessa, 270
Greenwood, David, 68
Griffin, Paul, 156
Griffith, Darrell, 141–142, 228n
Grinnel, Donna, 201
Gudmundsson, Petur, 277, 280, 282, 299

Habegger, Les, 26
Haenisch, Richard, 246
Halberstam, David, 300
Hall, Arsenio, 415
Hall, Joe B., 40, 228n
Hamilton, Roy, 42
Hano, Arnold, 57
Hardaway, Tim, 403
Hardy, Alan, 105, 107, 126, 171
Hardy, Suzy, 204
Harris, Del, 106, 120, 393
Harshman, Marv, 132
Harvey, Randy, 135, 143, 145, 154, 165, 199, 211, 316

Hawes, Steve, 168
Hayes, Elvin, 136
Haywood, Eunice, 90
Haywood, Iman, 82–83
Haywood, Spencer ("Woody"), ix–x, xi, 48–49, 67, 70–71, 79–84, 87–90, 103, 210
Haywood, Zulekha, 82
Hearn, Chick, 6, 12–14, 78, 107, 137, 163, 165
Heathcote, Jud, 26, 38–39
Hefner, Hugh, 24, 113
Heinsohn, Tommy, 233
Heisler, Mark, 329, 377
Henderson, John, 301
Henry, Conner, 310
Hodges, Craig, 408
Hoffer, Richard, 218
Holland, Brad, 34, 45, 47, 52, 71, 88–90, 97–98, 101, 127, 285, 381
Hollander, Zander, 404
Holland, Wilbur, 13
Holy Cross College, 58
Holzman, Red, 173
Hornacek, Jeff, 387
Houston Rockets, 105–106, 117–121, 135–136, 249, 257, 280–282, 294, 323, 329, 351–352, 356, 360, 386, 399–403
Hrovat, Ron, 180–181
Hubbard, Phil, 38
Hudson, Lou, 109, 134
Hughes, Alfredrick, 318
Hughes, Kim, 119
Human immunodeficiency virus (HIV), 416–417, 421
Hundley, Rod ("Hot Rod"), 6, 67
Hunter, Jo Jo, 39

Indiana Pacers, xii, 102, 140, 168, 175, 358
Inglewood, CA, 5
Isenberg, Barbara, 253n
Islam, 61–65, 185, 281
Issel, Dan, 307

Jackson, Pat, 354
Jackson, Phil, 408
James, LeBron, 421
Jenkins, Chris, 281
Johnson, Arrte, 200
Johnson, Clay, 116, 135, 201
Johnson, Dennis, 77, 180, 227, 313–315
Johnson, Don, 311
Johnson, Earleatha Kelly, 297, 400, 411–414, 417
Johnson, Earvin, Jr. ("Magic")

acquisition by the Lakers, 11–16
beginning career with Lakers, x–xi, 34–35
Bird and, 40, 71, 190, 227–230, 294, 307
charisma and leadership, 14, 70, 98, 107, 112–114, 166, 384–385
criticism by press/players, 259, 288
death of sister, Mary, 296–297
education and early basketball, 35–40
endorsements, 112, 114, 154, 412
injuries, 70, 106–107, 111–112, 226, 278, 306, 332, 335, 369–370
marriage, 297–298, 411–412
no-look passes, 14, 42, 46–47, 105n, 156, 259, 281, 338, 382
origin of nickname, 37
partying at Bel Air mansion, 268–269
relationship with Isiah Thomas, 327–328
relationship with Jerry Buss, 113–114, 128–129, 139–140, 166–167, 224, 286
relationship with Kareem, 66–69, 166, 351
relationship with Riley, 154, 156, 292, 379
relationship with Westhead, 139–146, 149, 153
request to be traded, 142–145
revelation of HIV, 413, 416–417, 420–421
sexual activity, 114–115, 198, 202–203, 258, 268–269, 298
Johnson, Earvin, Sr. and Christine, 15–16, 35, 296–297, 338
Johnson, George, 184
Johnson, Johnny, 86
Johnson, Kevin, 356, 387
Johnson, Larry, Quincy, and Pearl, 36–37
Johnson, Marques, 185
Johnson, Roy, 21, 25
Johnson, Steve, 301
Johnson, Vinnie, 325, 336, 344, 370
Johnson, William Oscar, 8
Jolesch, Bruce, 107, 123, 151
Jones, Bobby, 86, 191, 215
Jones, Caldwell, 88, 99, 207, 214
Jones, Dwight, 207
Jones, Earl, 244–249, 251, 269, 291, 299, 318, 384, 417, 422
Jones, K. C., 229, 233–234, 263, 294, 301, 311
Jones, Major, 106
Jones, Sam, 230
Jones, Will, 245
Jordan, Eddie, 111, 117, 136, 142, 171, 219, 289
Jordan, Juanita, 414
Jordan, Michael, 361, 386, 406–408, 412, 414, 415

Kansas City Kings, xiii, 70–71, 77, 105–107, 128, 175–176, 207, 225, 229

Kaplan, Gabe, 182

Kareem Abdul-Jabear (stuffed animal), 253n

Kean, Thomas, 350

Keaton, Michael, 354

Keith, Larry, 123

Kelley, Rich, 50, 180

Kelser, Greg, 325

Kemmerer, WY, 22

Kenney, Art, 56

Kenney, Charline, 9, 24, 267

Kentucky Colonels (ABA), 32

Kerlan, Robert, 96, 106

Kersey, Jerome, 398

Kiffin, Irv, 41, 43 & n, 45, 51

Kimble, Bo, xii

Kinch, Chad, 181

King, Albert, 218

King, Bernard, 156

King, Victor, 40–41

Kite, Greg, 310, 313

Kornheiser, Tony, 325

Krasnick, Richard, 277

Krause, Jerry, 408

Kupchak, Mitch, 124–130, 135–136, 147, 166–168, 175, 179, 205–207, 226, 246, 249, 276, 282, 289, 301, 334, 380, 393–394

Lacey, Sam, 119

Laimbeer, Bill, 168, 325, 328–330, 335–339, 343

Laker Girls, 69, 155, 178–179, 200, 202–204, 385

Laker Girls (movie), 386

Lamensdorf, Leonard, 188

Lamp, Jeff, 320, 323, 368

Landry, Tom, 163

Landsberger, Mark, 80, 82–83, 97, 114, 119, 136, 144, 171, 174, 194–199, 220, 284, 330

Lanier, Bob, 95

Lapin, Jackie, 52

Lattin, Dave, 162

Layden, Frank, 181, 336

Lee, Butch, 98n, 101, 180

Leonard, Gary, 380

Leshner, Steven, 331

Lester, Ronnie, 177, 254

Letterman, David, 228n, 329

Levasa, Roger, 269

Levin, Rich, 15, 143, 251–252, 310

Liebich, Mary Lou, 98, 107

Lister, Alton, 323

Littwin, Mike, 117–118

The Lives of Riley (Heisler), 377

Lloyd, Lewis, 281

Lombardi, Vince, 279

Lombardo, Steve, 96

Lorch, Howard, 160

Los Angeles Blades, 5

Los Angeles Clippers (formerly San Diego), 24, 278, 299, 301, 310, 358, 371, 373–375, 422

Los Angeles Dodgers, 300

Los Angeles Kings (NHL), 5–7, 9, 267

Los Angeles Lakers. See also National Champions

acquisition of Chamberlain, 5

acquisition of Campbell, 333–335

acquisition of Cooper, 133–135

acquisition of Dailey, 373–376

acquisition of Divac, 380–382

acquisition of Green, 269–272

acquisition of Haywood, 48–49

acquisition of Jones, 245–249

acquisition of Kareem, 5, 65

acquisition of Landsberger, 195

acquisition of Lucas, 272–276

acquisition of Magic, 11–16, 34–35

acquisition of McAdoo, 168–170

acquisition of Nater, 219

acquisition of Nevitt, 249–250

acquisition of Nixon, 15, 108–109

acquisition of Pat Riley, 163–164

acquisition of Rambis, 173–176

acquisition of Scott, 219

acquisition of Wilkes, 15, 189

acquisition of Woolridge, 354–355

acquisition of Worthy, xii, 197–198, 272

coach-player relationship, 357

court altercations, 85, 295, 323–325, 330

drugs, 79–84, 87, 196, 203, 208–210, 374

McKinney as coach, x, 26–27, 33–34, 93–95

player sexual exploits, 113–115, 197–199, 269–270, 277, 399, 421

player's wives, 198–199, 203–204, 276–277, 312–313, 396, 399–400

purchase by Jack Cooke, 4–5

purchase by Jerry Buss, 8–10

pursuit of Tarkanian as coach, 17–21, 26

Sports Illustrated cover shoot, 123–125

training drills, 348, 375

twenty-five year Magic contract, 128, 188

White House tour, 254, 346–347

Los Angeles Memorial Sports Arena, 5, 7

Los Angeles Raiders, 329, 343
Los Angeles Sparks (WNBA), 422
Los Angeles Stars (ABA), 9
Los Angeles Strings, 7–8, 23, 25
Lowe, Rob, 201
Lowe, Sidney, 334
Lubin, Tom, 221
Lucas, Maurice, 210, 272–276, 282, 286, 289
Lupica, Mike, 351
Lyman, Jim, 212

Mack, Ollie, 44, 45, 83
MacLeod, John, 84, 179–180
Macy, Kyle, 228n
Madden Jack, 100, 403
Mahorn, Rick, 325–326, 335, 338–340, 345
Malcom X, 62
Malone, Moses, 24, 106, 117, 119, 128, 136,
    156, 165, 182, 206, 214–215, 233, 254,
    292
Manguarian, Harry T., Jr., 21
Maravich, Pete, 11, 326
Marciulionis, Sarunas, 403
Mariani, Frank, 9, 23, 107
Marshall, Penny, 239
Matthews, Jason, 396
Matthews, Kenny, 39
Matthews, Wes, 202–203, 289–291, 310,
    323–325, 330, 335, 337, 349, 366, 372,
    422
Maxwell, Cedric, 206, 236–238, 240–241,
    258, 261, 313, 340
Maxwell, Vernon, 403
Mazza, Bob, 154
McAdoo, Bob, 147, 168–170, 175–177, 179,
    190, 192, 194, 205, 210–212, 215, 232,
    255, 271, 274, 278, 280, 417, 422
McCallum, 335
McCarthy, Joe, 279
McCloskey, Jack, 26, 325
McCormick, Tim, 126
McCray, Rodney, 280, 281
McDaniels, Jim, 220
McDaniel, Xavier, 323–324, 330, 360
McDonald, Bob, 222
McGee, Mike, 51, 126–128, 130, 177, 197,
    207, 225, 240, 254, 262, 278–279, 289,
    291, 337
McGinnis, George, 33, 80, 168
McGlocklin, Jon, 32, 63–64, 163
McGraw, Ali, 201
McHale, Kevin, 218, 227, 235, 238–241, 259–
    260, 300, 302, 310–311, 313–314
McKay, Larry, 71, 116

McKinney, Claire, x, xi, 30, 73–75, 93
McKinney, Dennis, 32, 94
McKinney-DeOrtega, Susan, 94
McKinney, Jack, ix–xiii, 26–33, 45–46, 72–
    77, 91, 93–95, 102
McKinney, John, xi, 93
McKinney, Paul, 27–28
McLaughlin, Eric, 382
McLaughlin, Joan, 5–6, 44, 178–179, 317, 318
McMahon, Jack, 163
McMillen, Tom, 306
McMillian, Nate, 323
McNamara, Mark, 348, 371, 380, 383, 396
Meisler, Andy, 252
Mellman, Michael (Dr.), 413–414
Mendelson, Barry, 12
Meola, Mike, 159
Mexico City Olympic Games (1968), 61
Meyers, David, 65
Miami Heat, xiii, 349, 386, 421–422
Mieuli, Franklin, 21n, 188–189
Mikan, George, 50, 63
Milwaukee Bucks, 31–32, 62–65, 85, 167,
    184–185, 215, 229, 391–394
Minneapolis Lakers, 4, 230
Minnesota Timberwolves, 371, 386
Mitchell, Mike, 180–181
Mix, Steve, 86, 97, 192, 211
Moe, Doug, 309
Mokeski, Paul, 144
Moncrief, Sidney, 15, 228n
Moore, Johnny, 157, 184
Moore, Ron, 325
Moran, Michael, 111–112
Morgan, J. D., 61
Motta, Dick, 206
Mullin, Chris, 403
Murphy, Calvin, 117, 120
Murphy, Tod, 334
Murray, Jim, 43, 154
Musburger, Brent, 67, 327
My Charmed, Tormented Life (West), 317

Namath, Joe, 178
Nance, Larry, 125
Nastase, Ilie, 25
Nater, Rene, 220–221
Nater, Swen, 67, 168–169, 219–222, 225–226,
    233, 242, 249, 417
National Basketball Association (NBA), 192
    1967 draft, 163
    1970 expansion draft, 163
    1974 draft, 188
    1978 draft, 180, 299–300

1979 draft, 11–16

1980 draft, 173, 180–181, 246, 422

1981 draft, 125, 285, 326, 422

1982 draft, 181–183, 197, 246–249, 374

1984 draft, 182, 243–246, 333

1985 draft, 269, 318–319

1986 draft, 285–286

1987 draft, 316, 318–319, 422–423

1988 expansion draft, 349

1989 draft, 380–381

Coach of the Year, xii, 357, 387–388

expansion teams, 163, 349, 386

handling ejections, 239, 278n, 282, 295, 356

recruitment of foreign players, 382

retirement tours, 349–350

substance abuse, 35, 43, 79–84, 374–375

team ownership, 21–25

televised games, 99n, 386

three-point line, 24, 47, 309

"white guys can't play," 77, 130, 227, 247, 306

white players, role on a team, 173–174

National Champions. *See also other years immediately below*

about Lakers failure to win, 65–66

Los Angeles Sparks (WNBA), 422

White House tours, 127, 254, 346–347

1959 (Lakers-Celtics), 230

1962 (Lakers-Celtics), 230

1969 (Lakers-Celtics), 230

1971 (Bucks-Bullets), 167

1972 (Lakers-Knicks), 164, 317

1977 (Trail Blazers-76ers), ix, 32–33, 272–273

1978 (Sonics-Bullets), 127, 260

1979 (Sonics-Bullets), 77, 84

1981 (Celtics-Rockets), 121, 183, 229, 257, 294

1983 (Lakers-76ers), 213–216

1986 (Celtics-Rockets), 299

1990 (Trail Blazers-Pistons), 398

1994 (Rockets-Knicks), 421

2006 (Heat-Mavericks), 421–422

National Champions-1980 (Lakers-76ers)

advance to the finals, 84–86

championship rings, 105

dismissal of Haywood, 87–88, 89–90

Game 1, 87, 88

Game 2, 88–89

Game 3, 92–93

Game 4, 93

Game 5, 95–96

Game 6, 96–101, 189, 234–235

loss of Kareem to injury, 95–97, 99, 101

National Champions-1982 (Lakers-76ers), 184

advance to the finals, 189–190

Game 1, 190–191

Game 2, 191–192

Game 3-4, 192

Game 5-6, 193

National Champions-1984 (Lakers-Celtics), 257–259

advance to the finals, 229–230

Celtics fans, 230–233

Game 1, 233–234

Game 2, 234–237

Game 3, 237–238

Game 4, 238–240

Game 5-6, 241

Game 7, 241–242

Magic dealing with loss, 328

National Champions-1985 (Lakers-Celtics)

advance to the finals, 259

Game 1, 260–261

Game 2, 261–262

Game 3-4, 263

Game 5, 263–264

Game 6, 264–265

National Champions-1987 (Lakers-Celtics)

advance to the finals, 304–310

Game 1-2, 311

Game 3, 312–313, 321

Game 4, 313–315, 321

Game 5-6, 315, 321

"peripheral distractions," 312–313

victory celebration, 423–424

National Champions-1988 (Lakers-Pistons)

advance to the finals, 330–332, 335

Game 1, 335–337

Game 2, 337–338

Game 3, 338

Game 4, 338–339

Game 5, 339–341

Game 6, 341–343

Game 7, 343–345

National Champions-1989 (Lakers-Pistons)

advance to the finals, 359–361

Game 1, 369

Game 2, 369–370

Game 3, 370–371

Game 4, 371–372

injuries, 368, 369

pre-finals training, 365–368

Riley ego factor, 361, 363

National Champions-1991 (Lakers-Bulls)

advance to the finals, 406–407

Game 1, 407–408

National Champions-1991, (cont.)
  Game 2-3, 408–409
  Game 4-5, 409
National Collegiate Athletic Assoc. (NCAA)
  1966 Kentucky-Texas Western, 162
  1975 Duquesne failure to qualify, 108
  1978 Michigan State-Kentucky, 39
  1979 Michigan State-Indiana State, 11, 38,
    40, 71, 190, 226
  1982 Division II title, 245
  1982 North Carolina-Georgetown
    match-up, 235–236
  Alcindor as Player of the Year, 60
  Coach of the Year, 30
  recruiting violations, 18
National Hockey League (NHL), 5
Nee, Danny, 56
Nelson, Don, 215
Nevitt, Charles Goodrich, 249, 249, 251, 327
Nevitt, Sondra, 339
Newell, Pete, 158, 229
New Jersey Nets, 111, 116, 126, 130, 142,
    154, 168–169, 276, 278, 354, 422
Newman, Bruce, x, 78
Newmark, Dave, 55
New Orleans Jazz, 12, 24. See also Utah Jazz
New York Knicks, 21, 48, 63, 65, 81, 129,
    142, 168, 173, 215, 229, 278, 290, 324–
    325, 330, 356, 360, 421–422
New York Nets (ABA), 62–63
Nicholson, Jack, 155, 201, 223, 229, 405
Nimphius, Kurt, 278
Nissalke, Tom, 48, 141–142
Nixon, Norm, 15, 44, 46, 107–111, 114–119,
    129, 145, 183, 198, 208–10, 212, 215–19,
    222–26, 422
Norman, Jerry, 59
North American Bear Company, 253n
Nucatoloa, John, 60
Núñez, Miguel, 202

Oakes, Billy, 356
Oakland Athletics, 9
O'Brien, Larry, 12, 105
O'Brien, Pat, 12–13, 35, 44, 202
O'Connor Richard, 74–75
O'Koren, Mike, 306
Olberding, Mark, 213
Olson, Lute, 299
Olympic Games, 61, 126, 380–381, 411–412
Omalev, Alex, 381
Orlando Magic, 386
Orozco, Larry, 17
Osborne, Jeffery, 204

Ostler, Scott, 33, 35, 70, 111, 135, 190, 237,
    329

Papanek, John, 113
Parish, Nancy, 263
Parish, Robert, 206, 227, 233–234, 239, 259,
    262–263, 294, 302, 307, 310–311, 313–314
Patterson, Ray, 281
Patterson, Steve, 60
Paul, Alan, 89n
Paul, Chris, 421
Paultz, Billy, 119
Paxson, Jim, 213
Paxson, John, 408
Perdue, Will, 408
Perkins, Sam, 288, 396, 406–407
Perry, Joe, 280–281
Pfund, Randy, 394–397
Philadelphia 76ers, 32–33, 86–87, 101, 213–
    216, 349–350
Philadelphia Phillies, 28, 158
Phipps, Paul, 219–220
Phoenix Suns, 84, 105, 126, 134, 164, 179–
    180, 210, 229, 231, 295, 331, 356–361,
    387–389, 393, 416
Pippen, Scotty, 408–409
Pistono, Cheryl, 99, 204, 252, 347
Polynice, Olden, 323
Pond, Barbara, 252
Porter, Terry, 269, 398, 405–406
Portland Trail Blazers, ix, 26–27, 32–33, 137,
    140, 163–164, 212, 257, 272–273, 277,
    299–301, 359–360, 397–398, 402, 404–
    406
Przybylo, Walt, 160
Pullman, Lorin, 350, 366

Race/race relations
  Dunleavy relating to, 393
  fan attitude toward, 212, 232
  inter-racial sex, 114, 196, 268–269
  Kareem's hatred of whites, 53–58, 61–63
  Magic dealing with, 37–38
  Riley relating to, 160–161
  segregated teams, 40, 162
  sports media and, 57, 64
  "white guys can't play," 60, 77, 130, 227,
    247, 306
Raivio, Rick, 422
Rambis, Becky, 172
Rambis, Kurt, 24, 130, 144, 168, 171–179,
    192–194, 205, 218, 247, 255–256, 270–
    274, 278, 293, 299, 315, 349, 357, 379,
    387, 416, 420, 422

Rambis, Linda Zafrani, 24, 25, 52, 80, 155, 176, 198, 201, 276–277, 419–420
Rambis, Randy, 172
Ramsay, Jack, 29–30, 32–33, 91, 211, 299
Reagan, Ronald, 346–347
Reed, William F., 326
Reed, Willis, 250
Reid, Robert, 44, 120, 214, 281
Restani, Kevin, 144
Richards, Barry ("Dancing Barry"), 155
Richardson, Don, 108
Richardson, Michael Ray, 307
Richmond, Mitch, 403
Rickles, Don, 178
Riley, Chris, 276–277, 400
Riley, Dennis, 159
Riley, Leon Francis ("Lee") and Mary, 158, 261
Riley, Pat
    assistant to Westhead, 78–79
    childhood and early career, 157–160
    coining term "three-peat," 366, 372
    college recruitment, 160–162
    departure from Lakers, 357, 390–394
    drafted by Dallas Cowboys, 163
    drafted by the Rockets, 162–163
    ego, 356, 361–363, 365–367, 376–379
    endorsements, 376, 422
    head coach of Lakers, 150–157, 165–166, 177–178, 190–192, 255–257, 275–276
    head coach of Miami Heat, 421–422
    head coach of NY Knicks, 421
    injuries, 164
    motivational speeches, 212, 275, 279, 341, 356, 387, 421–422
    "peripheral distractions" philosophy, 183, 275, 278, 312–313, 386
    as player, 163–164, 178
    relationship with Magic, 154, 156, 352, 379
    role in Showtime, 178–179
    team dissatisfaction, 365–368, 385–387
    tribute to McKinney, xiii, 275
Rivers, David, 352–355, 368–372
Roberts, Fred, 310
Robertson, Alvin, 301
Robertson, Oscar, 50, 63, 342
Robey, Rick, 228n
Robinson, David, 318
Robinson, Truck, 180
Robisch, Dave, 45, 50, 70–71, 220
Roche, John, 164
Rockford Lightning (CBA), 372
Rockwell, John, 24, 202, 267

Rodman, Dennis, 327, 335–339, 341, 344–345
Rose, Lynden, 281
Rosenfeld, Josh, 52, 192, 195, 207, 212, 219, 222, 232, 243, 247–249, 251, 262–263, 275–276, 290–291, 310, 318–320, 346–347, 350, 376, 379
Rosen, Lon, 47, 155, 195, 211, 219, 230, 248–250, 258, 285, 288, 309, 320, 359, 413–416
Rothenberg, Alan, 5, 7, 9
Rothman, Claire, 3–8, 14, 52, 107, 194, 199, 277
Roundfield, Dan, 325
Rubin, Bob, 310
Rupp, Anthony, 157, 160–162, 279
Russell, Bill, 43, 50, 55, 230, 250
Russell, Cazzie, 65
Ruth, Babe, 27–28

Sacramento Kings, 298–299, 351
Sager, Carole Bayer, 223
Salley, John, 200, 337–338, 369
Sampson, Ralph, 181–183, 197, 219, 245–246, 249, 280–282, 386
Sanders, Jeff, 380
San Diego Clippers (formerly Buffalo Braves), 24, 66–67, 71, 105, 127, 167–168, 181–183, 196, 206, 219, 222, 225–226, 254–255
San Diego Conquistadors (ABA), 9
San Diego Rockets, 157–158, 163
Schayes, Danny, 168, 178, 349
Scheer, Carl, 127
Scholz, Dave, 60
Schulian, John, 374
Scott, Anita, 254, 279, 304, 312, 322, 422
Scott, Byron, 219–227, 253–259, 271–274, 278–279, 293–295, 302–305, 309–313, 321–323, 368, 422
Scott, Dawan, 45
Seattle SuperSonics, 48, 70, 77, 84–87, 127, 260, 305, 323–324, 360
Shackelford, Lynn, 78
Sharman, Bill, 6, 41, 47, 70, 74, 76, 107, 111, 125–127, 140, 149, 158, 164, 166, 168, 180–182
Sheen, Charlie, 201
Short, Bob, 4–5
Showtime, 419–420. See also Buss, Jerry
    about the origins, x, 154–155
    as basketball philosophy, 154–157, 179, 238, 251, 255, 321, 338, 405
    catering to celebrities, 155, 178

Showtime (*cont.*)
  "Dancing Barry," 155
  end of an era, 357–358, 389, 410, 419–421
  Forum Club, 200–205
  the Forum Club, 420
  Laker Girls, 69, 155, 178, 200–204, 385
  Magic Johnson and, 68–72, 417, 421
  The Magnificent Seven, 147, 192
  other team attempts at, 220, 329
  Riley and the return of, 155, 391, 422
  "Slam Duck" (mascot), 155
  Westhead changes to, 102–105
Shue, Gene, 66–67, 340
Sichting, Jerry, 310
Sikma, Jack, 70, 77, 84–85, 292
Silas, Paul, 167
Smith, Elmore, 65
Smith, Larry, 206
Smrek, Mike, 292, 299, 303, 321, 337, 423–424
Sporting News, 33, 64, 68, 71, 80, 220, 257
Sport (magazine), 57, 101
Sports Illustrated, 9, 56, 61, 62n, 78, 123–125,
    179, 215, 285, 332, 335, 354
Spriggs, Larry, 39, 51, 171, 202, 225, 237, 239,
    242, 248, 250, 260, 262, 276, 279, 289,
    337
Springer, Steve, 107, 111, 114, 137, 145, 152–
    153, 195, 251, 308
Stabley, Fred, Jr., 37
Staples Center, 419–420
Starr, Anthony, 20
Steiner, Bob, 34, 69, 74, 376
Sterling, Donald, 127, 181–183, 219–220
Stern, David, 229, 263, 324, 416
Stewart Lane, 123–124
Stipanovich, Steve, 217, 218
Stockton, Dick, 236, 238
Substance abuse. *See* Drugs

Tanter, Lawrence, 156, 370, 372
Tarkanian, Jerry, 17–21, 26
Tarkanian, Lois, 20
Tarkanian, Pamela, 19
Tarpley, Roy, 286 & n
Terzian, George, 131–133
Theokas, Charlie, 169
Therkelsen, Karen, 59
Theus, Reggie, 68, 110–111, 177
Thibault, Mike, 117, 125, 169, 173–177, 195,
    255
Thomas, Irving, 408
Thomas, Isiah, 125, 285, 326–328, 330, 332,
    335–336, 338–339, 342–344, 369–370,
    415

Thomas, Lynn and Joshua Isiah, 339
Thompson, Billy, 289, 291–293, 303, 310,
    334, 349, 405, 422
Thompson, Bob, 186
Thompson, David, 125, 300
Thompson, Mykal, 299–305, 321, 328, 337,
    352–354, 360, 369, 380, 398
Thorn, Rod, 12
Threatt, Sedale, 414
"Three-peat," coining the term, 366
Tolbert, Ray, 126
Tomjanovich, Rudy, 105
Toney, Andrew, 190, 215, 254
Tormohlen, Gene, 244, 246, 269, 380
Toronto Maple Leafs, 4
Traum, Joseph, 57
Travolta, John, 201
Triano, Jay, 422
Trigueiro, Jack, 186–187
Tucker, Charles (Dr.), 13
Tulsa Fast Breakers (CBA), 349, 372
Tyler, Steven, 280–281
Tynum, Tim, 221
Tyson, Mike, 298

University of California Los Angeles
    (UCLA), 5, 8, 23, 58–60, 187, 220–222,
    422
Utah Jazz (formerly New Orleans Jazz), 24,
    47–48, 79, 84, 141, 166, 175, 335, 404,
    413
Utah Stars (ABA), 47

Valente, Renée, 386
Vanderschaaf, Ron, 422–423
Vandross, Luther, 201
Vecsey, George, 348
Vecsey, Peter, 80–81, 303
Vernon, Duane, 39
Vertlieb, Dick, 188
Virginia Squires (ABA), 220
Vitti, Gary, 52, 177, 247, 260–262, 273–274,
    290, 312, 327, 357, 367–370, 383, 386,
    413

Wagner, Milt, 334
Wakefield, Andre, 13, 134
Walker, Foots, 154
Walker, Wally, 85
Walton, Bill, 221–222, 226, 294, 299, 310
Warner, Cornell, 330
Warren, Mike, 59, 61
Washington Bullets, 109, 124, 126–127, 134,
    245, 260, 318, 325, 333–334, 340, 350

Washington Redskins, 4, 6–7, 8
Weiss, Victor, 17–21
Weltman, Harry, 354
Wennington, Bill, 319
West, David, 317
Westhead, Cy and Jane, 91
Westhead, Paul, xi, 45, 72–79, 89–92, 102–
    105, 121–125, 135–146, 149
Westhead, Pete, 91
West, Howard, 317
West, Jerry
    consultant role, 107
    as general manager, 207–208, 243–244
    head coach, x–xi, 16, 78, 109, 149–157
    idiosyncrasies and depression, 316–318
    Kareem and, 50, 349
    Magic Johnson and, 14
    as player, 164, 317
    Ruth's Chris Steak House incident, 378–
      379
    teaching Carter to drink, 201–202
    trade negotiations, 286, 303
    training camps, 131
Whisenant, John, 133
Whitney, "Hawkeye," 106
Wicks, Sidney, 61
Wilder, Dave and Ron, 202
Wilkens, Lenny, 26
Wilkes, Arainni Julise, 184
Wilkes, Jamaal Abul-Lateef (aka Jason Keith),
    15, 20, 27, 35, 65, 77, 102, 105n, 133,
    136, 184–189, 191–194, 206, 212, 218,
    227, 271, 306, 379, 417
Wilkes, Joycelyn, 184, 189
Wilkes, Leander and Thelma, 184, 186, 189
Wilkes, Leonard Bruce, 184
Wilkes, Lucy, 187

Wilkins, Dominique, xii, 255
Wilkins, Gerald, 354
Williams, Buck, 125
Williams, Freeman, 66–67
Williams, Gus, 77, 111
Williams, Herb, 175, 322, 358
Williams, John, 396
Williams, Pat, 127
Willis, Bruce, 311
Willoughby, Bill, 120
Winters, Brian, 65
Winter, Tex, 408
Wohl, Dave, 231, 247, 354–355
Women's National Basketball Association,
    422
Wood, Al, 125
Wooden, John, 26, 59–60, 143, 187, 222
Woolridge, Orlando, 354–355, 358, 361, 372,
    375, 386, 388–389, 396
World Basketball League (WBL), 320
World Invitational Tournament, 39, 40, 228
World Team Tennis, 7–8, 23, 25
Worthy, Angela, 277, 284, 399–400
Worthy, James, 147, 197–198, 205–206, 210,
    218, 228, 239–240, 251, 255–257, 269–
    270, 272–276, 284–288, 293–295, 302,
    305, 309–314, 330, 355–356, 384, 386,
    399–400, 402–405, 420, 422

Yothers, Tina, 386
Youngstown Pride (WBL), 320

Zafrani, Debbie, 25
Zeigler, Mark, 361, 365
Ziegler, Mark, 365
Zoubul, Harold, 200, 203, 204

ALSO BY JEFF PEARLMAN

"The best sports biography of the year."
—*Sports Illustrated*

A NEW YORK TIMES BESTSELLER

SWEETNESS

THE ENIGMATIC LIFE OF
WALTER PAYTON

JEFF PEARLMAN

The *New York Times* bestselling definitive biography of Chicago Bears superstar Walter Payton.

GOTHAM
BOOKS